Franco

Franco

*A Personal and
Political Biography*

Stanley G. Payne
and
Jesús Palacios

THE UNIVERSITY OF WISCONSIN PRESS

The University of Wisconsin Press
1930 Monroe Street, 3rd Floor
Madison, Wisconsin 53711-2059
uwpress.wisc.edu

3 Henrietta Street, Covent Garden
London WC2E 8LU, United Kingdom
eurospanbookstore.com

Printed in the United States of America

Library of Congress Cataloging-in-Publication Data

Payne, Stanley G., author.
Franco: a personal and political biography /
Stanley G. Payne and Jesús Palacios.
pages   cm
Includes bibliographical references and index.
ISBN 978-0-299-30210-8 (cloth: alk. paper)
  1. Franco, Francisco 1892–1975.
  2. Heads of state—Spain—Biography.
  3. Generals—Spain—Biography.
4. Spain—Politics and government—20th century.
  I. Palacios, Jesús, 1952–, author.   II. Title.
DP264.F7P34   2014
946.082092—dc23
[B]
2014007458

ISBN 978-0-299-30214-6 (pbk.: alk. paper)

publication of this history

is supported via a grant from

Figure Foundation

Contents

Contents

Illustrations

Illustrations

Preface

Even in the second decade of the twenty-first century, nearly forty years after his death, Franco and his lengthy dictatorship have not fully been consigned to history but continue to excite considerable passion, at least among a minority of his fellow countrymen. There are many accounts of Franco, but the most extensive biographies are strongly polarized between extreme positive and negative portraits. The chief expression of the latter is the thousand-page work by Paul Preston (1993), while the two principal hagiographies are the equally lengthy treatments by Ricardo de la Cierva (2000) and Luis Suárez Fernández (2005). The brief portrait by Juan Pablo Fusi (1985) is more balanced, but it amounts to only an introductory essay. Other biographical works are either highly uneven in their treatment or very limited in their source material. Though no definitive work on so complex and polarizing a figure is to be expected, we concluded that the time had come for a new effort at description and analysis, one that would also include a somewhat fuller treatment of the personal life of the Spanish dictator.

A number of new sources have become available, ranging from the documentation of the archive of the Fundación Nacional Francisco Franco and the personal observations of his daughter, Carmen Franco Polo, Duquesa de Franco, in the interviews that we conducted in January 2008 to extensive material provided by new secondary studies. Both of the authors have worked in this area for some time. Jesús Palacios pioneered research in the Franco Archive beginning with *Los papeles secretos de Franco* (1996), followed by three other books, while Stanley Payne has authored a number of works on the politics and institutions of Franco's regime. Julia Sherman provided a careful critical reading of the entire text, improving it in both style and content.

The present work represents an attempt to offer a more rounded account of Franco's life, more objective and balanced than either the denunciations or the hagiographies. Our readers can judge if we have added significantly to the understanding of the Franco era in Spanish history.

Franco

1

The Making of
a Spanish Officer

(1892–1913)

M ore ink has been spilled over Francisco Franco than anyone else in Spain's long history. Little of this enormous literature is objective, most of it tending toward one extreme or the other. The real Franco is elusive, all the more so since he left few accessible personal papers, despite the fact that he wrote more than a little—a short novel, a memoir of his early military campaigns in Morocco, quite a few journal and newspaper articles (sometimes under a pseudonym), numerous letters, two brief chapters of an autobiography, and a number of speeches. Yet he has left almost nothing that reveals his more intimate life, and nothing that clarifies the crucial moments of his career or how he reached his most important decisions.

If Franco's supporters have depicted him as a genius, his denigrators have frequently portrayed him as a mediocrity, a historical figure who was remarkably successful due to a combination of low cunning and mere luck. Neither portrait is convincing. One of his leading biographers, Paul Preston, certainly no friend of the Spanish dictator, has accurately observed that the standard anti-Franco literature has failed to take him seriously enough to understand him.

Sources are abundant for some aspects of Franco's life, but scarce to nonexistent on others. He was born on December 4, 1892, in El Ferrol, an important naval base on the green northwestern coast of Spain, in the region of Galicia, which had been the home of the Francos since 1730.[1] He was born into a seafaring family of long standing; six generations of his ancestors had been naval officers, several holding the rank of admiral.[2] The family might be described as upper-middle class, though not affluent; both sides of the family were members of Spain's large hidalgo, or petty aristocratic, stratum, and his mother's side had a connection to the titled Galician aristocracy.

In later years the most insistent rumor about his family background would have to do with supposed Jewish ancestry, though there is no specific evidence to support such an allegation.[3] But it should be kept in mind that the majority of Spain's Jewish population converted to Catholicism over the course of several generations during the fourteenth and fifteenth centuries, with the result that proportionately more Jewish genes were absorbed into Spanish society than in the case of any other modern European country. A genetic study published in 2008 concluded that approximately 20 percent of Spain's population carries Jewish genes.[4] This is so common that if it was the case with Franco, it would be a distinction shared by more than eight million citizens of twentieth-century Spain and would not constitute any sort of unique finding.

Franco's father, Nicolás Franco Salgado Araujo, was an officer in the naval supply system (*intendencia*) who eventually reached the rank of *intendente general* (equivalent to vice admiral) in a purely administrative capacity. He was an unconventional man in a highly conventional profession. In his personal life and views the elder Franco was an eccentric, well-read freethinker, even something of a libertine, none of these things being characteristic of Spanish naval officers. While posted to Manila when he was thirty-three, he seduced and made pregnant Concepción Puey, the fourteen-year-old daughter of an army officer, and his son, Eugenio Franco Puey, was born in December 1889.[5] In the officer corps of some navies, such an outrage might have cost Nicolás Franco his commission at the hands of an honor court, but in the Spanish navy it was hushed up, though he was sent back to the home base in El Ferrol. He was a competent officer who enjoyed respect for the quality of his service on duty, but he was not popular with his peers, who found his personal life too eccentric and deviant.

In El Ferrol he met the twenty-four-year-old María del Pilar Bahamonde y Pardo de Lama-Andrade, the pious and attractive daughter of a senior officer in the naval supply corps, similarly descended from several generations of naval officers. She was distantly related to Emilia Pardo Bazán, Spain's first important woman novelist. They married in May 1890, five months after the birth of Nicolás Franco's illegitimate son. If he revealed the fact that he had an illegitimate child to his new bride, which is doubtful, it remained completely unknown to the rest of the family. During the next eight years, the couple had five children. The oldest son, Nicolás, was born in 1891, more than a year before his brother Francisco. A daughter, Pilar, was born in 1895 and another son, Ramón, before the close of 1896. The last child and second daughter, Paz, born in 1898, lived only five years, though all the other children enjoyed good health.

Franco later portrayed his parents as typical gender opposites of that era: "The men harsh, severe, authoritarian and indifferent to religion, which they considered a women's affair; the women virtuous, faithful and believers, the true angels of the home."[6] The stories of his drinking and gambling were probably exaggerated, but the elder Nicolás Franco was an agnostic who scorned conventional morality and spent much of his free time outside the home, amusing himself as he pleased. Though he indulged his pleasures in town, he was a tyrant at home, a strong-willed, vehement man who paid his children a certain amount of attention but raised them with severity while scorning the Catholic piety and conventional attitudes of his wife more and more with each passing year.

Pilar Bahamonde was totally different in temperament from Nicolás, a loving and self-sacrificing mother, rather typical of her generation, who found incomprehensible the personal and philosophical extravagances of a husband about whom she had probably known little at the time of marriage.[7] She was an obedient and dutiful wife who never spoke ill of her husband and apparently did not even rebuke him, but she suffered a great deal.

After the birth of the fifth and final child, Nicolás Franco moved even farther away from his wife emotionally, finding her tediously dull and conventional. In 1907, when his second son was fourteen and about to enter the infantry academy, he obtained reassignment to the Naval Ministry in Madrid, leaving his family behind. Though a native of El Ferrol, Nicolás Franco found the racier atmosphere of the Spanish capital much more agreeable and lived the rest of his long life in Madrid. At first there was no official rupture. He continued to support the family financially, at least to an extent, and for several years returned to El Ferrol during summer vacations, but eventually the abandonment became complete. At some point, Franco's father made a common-law marriage with a woman named Agustina Aldana, a young provincial schoolteacher who provided unquestioning affection and did not contradict his prejudices. Though Agustina raised a girl in the household as her daughter, the girl was apparently a niece whom she had adopted and not the biological child of Nicolás Franco.[8] Living on a vice admiral's pension after he retired in 1925, he became a celebrated miser who always used public transportation and had a great fear of banks. Nicolás consequently carried large sums of money on his person, and in 1941 a pickpocket on a streetcar relieved him of seventeen thousand pesetas, a considerable amount in those days.

All indications are that of the four surviving children, the one for whom Nicolás had the least regard was his second son, Francisco, known in the family as Paco or Paquito (Frankie). The boy was small and spindly, though hardy enough, introverted and inclined to identify with his doting mother. Nicolás Franco had an unpleasant temper and sometimes cuffed his sons or harshly punished them when they misbehaved or severely displeased him. It is not clear that Paco, however, suffered any great abuse, if for no other reason than that he was obedient, somewhat timid, and well behaved. The father was apparently most severe with his namesake, Nicolás, a bright student whom he frequently punished for laziness or underachievement. Though he attended to Paco's education, his father would later be totally dismissive of his accomplishments. Even after his son became dictator, the father, who was left-liberal in his politics, was sharply critical of him both in public and private, claiming to find his eminence simply incredible. There was thus scant mutual affection between the overbearing Nicolás Franco and the sensitive Paco, the child most affected by his family's drama. Though, unlike his father, he never engaged in any public criticism, Paco never forgave him and completely refused to recognize his father's second household.

Many years later, after Franco's death, the dramatist Jaime Salom wrote a play titled *El corto vuelo del gallo* (*The Cock's Short Flight*), announced as "the history of Franco in terms of the erotic life of his father." On the one hand, like both his brothers, Franco hoped to emulate his forebears in a successful military career, but whereas his father had been a desk officer, Franco became a celebrated combat leader. Otherwise, he absolutely rejected his father's style of life and his religious and political attitudes. His father had been amoral and self-indulgent, while Franco was austere and chaste, a completely devoted husband and family man.

Though in general terms Franco's childhood was conventional and not unhappy, he never overcame his antipathy toward his father. Later, as adults, the other siblings would visit their father from time to time in Madrid, but there is no evidence that Franco ever did. In later years he saw his father only twice, first when both parents had visited him in a military hospital following his only major combat wound in 1916, and then the final time after his mother died in 1934. His father may have been the first figure of importance in his life to become the target of the unforgiving coldness and contempt that Franco, having internalized his father's harshness and authoritarianism, would display toward those whom he scorned. After he became an adult, he seems simply to have removed Nicolás Franco from his life, never speaking badly of him but normally never referring to him at all. He refused the slightest recognition to his father's second spouse, and, when Nicolás finally died at the age of eighty-six in 1942, had his remains buried beside those of Doña Pilar in the Franco family section in the Almudena, Madrid's leading cemetery.

Several years after becoming dictator, Franco wrote (or, perhaps, collaborated in writing) a brief novel, *Raza*, under the pseudonym of Jaime de Andrade, which would serve as the basis for a widely distributed motion picture by a noted Spanish filmmaker in 1941.[9] The protagonist was a naval officer who represented the ideal kind of father Franco would have preferred: a mythic figure of unbendable martial courage and moral rectitude: a devoted family man and a combat leader, not a desk officer.

Much more than either of his brothers, Franco identified with his mother, who always wore a widow's black after she realized that her husband had definitively abandoned the family. From her he learned stoicism, moderation, self-control, a quiet manner, family solidarity, and respect both for Catholicism and traditional values in general.[10] But he never emulated her meekness and resignation, her full measure of religious fervor, her capacity to forgive and work with self-abnegation on behalf of others, or her human warmth and generosity and Christian charity. This uneven inheritance, which a psychologist might term sex-role appropriate, produced an adult of remarkable austerity, self-control, and determination who had a great respect for family, religion, and tradition but who often displayed coldness, harshness, and implacability, who had a limited capacity to respond to the feelings of others, who was capable of generating awe and respect, possessing an attendant ability to impose leadership, but who would restrict human warmth to a very small circle of family and friends.

All three brothers would later show an exceptional drive for achievement, perhaps in order to demonstrate their own worth after being largely abandoned by their father. Even more important, however, may have been the constant counsel of an attentive mother who always urged them to apply themselves and accomplish something important. Each of the three had a very distinct personality, sharing only a common drive to stand out and to rise in the world. Nicolás, the oldest and the tallest (though still on the short side), was astute and intelligent, the best student of all the siblings and also the most conventional of the brothers. He followed family tradition by entering the naval academy, becoming a naval engineering officer. He later transferred to the naval construction corps, which offered faster promotion, and by 1921 he had achieved a rank equivalent to that of a lieutenant colonel in the army at a slightly younger age than his more famous younger brother. Once he reached thirty-five, however, Nicolás resigned his commission to become director of a commercial shipyard in Valencia, at a much higher salary. Something of a sybarite and a dandy in personal affairs, Nicolás also came to enjoy, as he grew older, an extravagant night life that often kept him in clubs and cabarets until very late, all this totally different from the disciplined routine of his younger brother Paco. Nicolás never showed the same thirst for adventure and heroic deeds exhibited by his two younger brothers. In 1933 he returned to naval service to teach in the Naval Engineering School in Madrid. When his first wife died at an early age, he soon married her younger cousin, who became the mother of his only son. An avid conversationalist full of jokes, he led the most normal life of the three brothers.[11]

The most fully conventional of the siblings, however, was their sister, Pilar. She married a civil engineer of conservative Carlist background who was considerably older (as was not uncommon in the Spanish society of that era). Pilar was lively, talkative, opinionated, and extremely prolific. Whereas each of her brothers was the parent of only one child apiece (though both Nicolás and Ramón each had two wives), Pilar bore ten offspring, the last of them after the Civil War, when she was forty-five years old. Four of her six sons maintained the family's military tradition, becoming naval officers, one reaching the rank of counter admiral. Moreover, two of her four daughters married army officers.

By contrast, the youngest of the siblings, Ramón, a shade shorter even than Paco at five foot three, was the most audacious of the children and later, at least for a number of years, a complete rebel politically and socially, even more unconventional than his somewhat dissolute father. Ramón also became an internationally famous aviator, for some time eclipsing the celebrity achieved by his elder brother. Always the most adventuresome of the brothers, he may have been the one with greatest range of talent, but he was the only one to die at an early age, a casualty of the Civil War in 1938.[12]

In his first years Paco was educated within the narrow ambience of the naval society of a provincial port. El Ferrol had only twenty thousand inhabitants at the beginning of the twentieth century, but it featured a magnificent natural bay and was the country's major naval base and was also important in ship construction. In later years Franco would recount the fascination with which he listened to tales he heard in the port district from sailors who had voyaged to distant continents. El Ferrol nonetheless remained a sleepy little city that had no running water until 1923, and conditions for ordinary inhabitants could be harsh and meager. Toward the end of his life Franco would reflect on its "grating social inequalities. I remember the impact on me as a child of seeing the extremely low standard of living of the water women who brought fresh water to homes. After standing in long lines before the fountains in public squares, in every kind of weather, they earned only fifteen céntimos for bearing twenty-five liter jars of water on their heads up to apartments. Or the example of the women in the port who unloaded coal from ships for a peseta a day."[13]

The naval society of El Ferrol had been severely impacted by Spain's disastrous defeat in the Spanish-American War of 1898, which brought the loss of nearly all that was left of the historic Spanish empire. Paco grew up in the shadow of this catastrophe but also lived in a country increasingly dominated by diffuse currents of "regenerationism" that sought to modernize Spain and raise it to the level of the rest of Western Europe.

During the preceding century, Spain had been second only to France in introducing parliamentary liberalism. The very word "liberal" had been a Spanish neologism that passed into other languages. Down to 1923, the country lived for more years under systems of parliamentary liberalism than did France. After undergoing frequent disorders and changes of regime during the "era of *pronunciamientos*" (1815–75), in which the military often played a political role, it enjoyed half a century of stability and very slowly accelerating economic progress. The increasingly influential regenerationists, however, demanded more rapid change and stronger leadership, although they would soon be outflanked to the left by the growth of revolutionary worker movements. There was an authoritarian tinge both to the latter and to certain of the regenerationists, who sometimes despaired of liberalism and talked of the need for an "iron surgeon" to revitalize the nation. Nothing is known of Paco's political attitudes in his early years, but he would later show the influence of the more nationalist and authoritarian forms of early twentieth-century regenerationism.

In El Ferrol the family lived on the two upper floors of a large three-story house owned by Paco's paternal grandfather; the ground floor, at least in the first years, was rented out to a family of more modest means. Paco lived within the social network of an extended family, as was common in that era. Both his parents had numerous relatives in Galicia, and the family circle included many aunts, uncles, and cousins. The immediate family expanded further when his father's youngest uncle, yet another naval officer and a widower, died leaving eleven children, eight of them still minors. Franco's father had been designated guardian, and this set of young people came to form part of his extended household. Doña Pilar was especially fond of and affectionate with children, becoming their surrogate mother. One of these second cousins, two and a half years older than Paco, was Francisco Franco Salgado-Araujo. A tall lad known in the family as Pacón (big Frank), he too would become an army officer and play an important role in his cousin's life, first as military aide and then as head of the personal military staff (*casa militar*) of the chief of state.[14]

Sources on Franco's childhood and adolescence are few and comparatively superficial.[15] The only one of the siblings to produce a memoir, his sister, has left a conventional account that reveals little.[16] His daughter, Carmen, has said that her father, though he liked to narrate parts of his military career, rarely spoke of his childhood. "If you asked him about something, he would answer briefly, but that was not the period of his life that he looked back on with the greatest affection." Paco was a serious child, an adequate student but not at the level of his more accomplished brother Nicolás. He showed a little talent for mathematics but greater dexterity in certain kinds of crafts and drawing. Though it stretched the family's resources, the three brothers received the best private education available at that time in El Ferrol, for Franco's father's main concern seems to have been their education. Before he left the family, he had the habit of taking all the children, and often some of their cousins as well, on long walks through the small city and its port and environs, during which he would discourse to them apparently at some length on history, geography, naval life, and certain aspects of science.

Since the goal for all the boys was to receive a naval officer's commission like their forebears, at the age of twelve Paco was placed in a special private secondary school, like Nicolás before him, whose purpose was to prepare students for acceptance by the military academies. Juan Antonio Suanzes, the son of its director, was only one year older and would become one of Franco's closer friends and later play an important role in his regime. All his classmates were older, and this experience probably helped him to mature, preparing him for the subsequent challenge of being nearly the youngest student in his class at the military academy.

Photos of his childhood and adolescence reveal a small, slight child (leading classmates to occasionally call him "cerillita"—"little match-stick"), timid and uncertain in appearance, with unusually prominent ears. Throughout life his voice would remain distinctive and disconcerting, for it never lost the soft, high-pitched, nasal quality it had when he was a boy. This apparently stemmed from a certain congenital malformation, involving a deviated septum and an unusually narrow palate.[17] It interfered slightly with his breathing and deprived his voice of resonance, a condition that made it difficult to control its tone in his early years and left him with an unusually soft voice for the rest of his life. This added to his air of timidity and reserve, which he later learned to maintain by affecting a coldness and indifference to those around him, though when more relaxed or more motivated, he could be as talkative as anyone else. Throughout his life, he tended to be closed and uncommunicative in personal matters, even though in comfortable surroundings he could quickly turn surprisingly vivacious, at least until he became dictator. Later, he would employ coldness and distance as an instrument of command. But for Franco, as for many, adolescence was not a particularly happy time. During these years, however, he learned to develop ever more self-control, discipline, and determination, to the point of seeming old beyond his years.

Of his fifty nearest paternal ancestors, no fewer than thirty-five had been naval officers, but Nicolás would be the only one of the three brothers to follow in their footsteps, for the Spanish naval command found itself with a surplus of officers and sharply restricted access to the naval academy in El Ferrol. For Paco the logical alternative was the infantry academy in Toledo. Opened in 1893, by 1906 it was increasing the number of new candidates to more than three hundred a year. Moreover, promotion tended to be more rapid in the army, and Paco set his sights on becoming an infantry cadet in 1907. Initially, both parents were opposed, for he would still be well short of his fifteenth birthday, and would be one of the youngest and smallest of the next class. Paco nonetheless exhibited the kind of determination that would become one of his leading characteristics, and his father finally gave in.

In June 1907, on the eve of his transfer to Madrid, Nicolás Franco undertook what may have been his final gesture of paternal guidance, accompanying the fourteen-year-old by train to Toledo for his entrance examination. Paco did not particularly enjoy this long, slow trip, remarking in his truncated memoir, "I have to confess that this first trip with my father, who was rigid and harsh, was not much fun, for he lacked the trust and solicitude that would have made him agreeable."[18] This was the first time in his life Paco had ever traveled beyond his native Galicia in the far northwestern corner of Spain, and he would later reminisce about the shock encountered when he left this verdant region and passed through dry and barren Castile, which gave him a sense of leaving Europe and entering something like Africa. Carmen recalls that her father frequently referred to the impact of this experience, which probably lay at the root of his later policy to reforest Spain.

Though Paco was younger than most, he seems to have had little trouble with the examination and became one of 382 students accepted in the incoming class out of more than 1,000 applicants. His older cousin Pacón, however, was rejected, though he would be successful in the following year. The timing was fortunate, for soon afterward the number of acceptances would be cut by more than half, to 150. Even without knowing that, Paco was pleased and later recalled a feeling of great happiness that he had been accepted. He said that he was particularly impressed by the large statue of Charles V in the patio, bearing the words of his declaration on embarking for the conquest of Tunis in 1535: "I will be slain in Africa or enter Tunis as a conqueror." This deeply moved the teenage cadet, who seems to have internalized the message in the next three years. He readily absorbed the highly patriotic ideals imparted to the academy's students, and one of his biographers has suggested that he came to idealize Spain as his true and greater family, since his own had been partially broken by his father's abandonment. Alone and on his own for the first time, Paco's strong devotion to and protective feelings for his mother may have been transmuted into a new ideal of service to the motherland (*madre patria*).[19]

Of the 382 cadets in his class, only 40 were approximately his own age. Most were between sixteen and eighteen, while another 40 were twenty-one or older. At that time, Paco was only 1.64 meters in height and would only grow a little more, to 1.67 meters (not quite 5 feet 4 inches). It was natural that he would immediately be known as Franquito (little Franco), a nickname that would persist for many years, even after his physique filled out with muscle and he was promoted to a higher rank. It only ended, in fact, after he became generalissimo in September 1936. This was not just because of his height, for in the undernourished Spain of the early twentieth century there were many short officers, some of them distinctly shorter than Franco, but also because of his spindly teenage physique, as well as his high-pitched voice and his customarily quiet and reserved manner. Neither his personality nor his physical appearance was imposing. Respect and deference would only come later and would depend exclusively on a demonstrated toughness, courage and achievement, and the ability to command. Such things lay far in the future. Even then, after he had become master of the destinies of Spain, foreign visitors and diplomats would remark on how disappointing his physical appearance was. The charisma of Franco would derive solely from achievement. The aesthetics were never there.

Almost inevitably, this rather derisible-looking fourteen-year-old adolescent became the butt of the *novatadas* (hazing) of the older cadets; occasionally he was tied up or tossed out of his cot or had his books hidden, to his considerable indignation. His suffering was intense, and in later years Franco would reflect that this had been a "real Calvary," criticizing the absence of internal discipline and the irresponsibility of the academy's directors in mixing together cadets of quite different ages. In 1928, when he was named the first director of a new military academy offering basic training, he would categorically prohibit *novatadas*, assigning a personal mentor from among the older cadets to orient each new candidate. Surviving his first year in Toledo can be considered Franco's initial professional achievement, for it was not easy and called on the toughness, imperviousness, and self-discipline for which he later became proverbial. The fact that he marched in parade drill during his first year with a smaller sawed-off rifle has sometimes been cited as an indication of his puniness, but in fact this was standard practice for first-year cadets, unless they were taller.[20]

Though Franco, like many people, usually preferred to avoid talking about unpleasant things, he never hid the very disagreeable nature of his first year or two in Toledo. His daughter relates that "whenever he referred to his education in Toledo, it seemed to me that he did not much enjoy it, because he was very small. . . . Yes, and short, too, small in both senses. . . . That was what he said. The bigger cadets could march with real rifles, but the small ones were given ones more like a toy." Not least was his resentment of a sort of class system for the housing of cadets, since those with greater means were allowed to live much more comfortably in private quarters in the city. Decades later he continued to express indignation at various privileges enjoyed by such "daddy's boys," which was a typical manifestation of the special interests predominant in the poorly ordered army of his youth.[21] Like many cadets, he was particularly incensed at the prevailing privilege of *redención a metálica* in general army recruitment, which allowed families of greater means to purchase exemptions from service for their sons. In this way, Spain was very different from neighboring France, whose egalitarian standards cultivated a much deeper spirit of patriotism from that of Spain.

Franco was an average student. He later admitted that he was "concerned to pass but not stand out."[22] What he seemed to enjoy most were topographic studies and the technique of military fortification. Instruction in the academy was primarily by rote, and since Franco always had a good memory, he had no great difficulty with it, though his grades were unexceptional. Moreover, the academy also emphasized physical achievement, hardly his strong point. What he most enjoyed among the practical exercises was the opportunity to ride horseback, something that would remain a lifelong passion.[23]

The cadets were predominantly trained using older French and German army manuals, which were no longer state of the art. The world's most recent conflict had been the Russo-Japanese War of 1904–5, which had featured the use of machine guns and new infantry tactics. In Spain, as elsewhere, there was a desire to learn from this, but the Spanish army was very weak in new weaponry and equipment and simply not prepared to function at the level of the best contemporary armies.

Yet there was a lighter side to Franco's life during the Toledo years. Summers were spent in El Ferrol, where he began to show interest in some of the young women in his family's social ambience. This interest was formal and romantic, motivated only by the most honest and "Victorian" of intentions. So far as is known, he had not the slightest taste for the transitory brothel experience so common to young men of his era; he was concerned almost exclusively with seeking a formal relationship that would lead to marrying an attractive young woman of good family. This took more than a little time, partly because he would spend years in military campaigns; he did not end up marrying until the age of thirty. From Toledo he sent romantic verses to several young women in El Ferrol, poetry that he occasionally revealed to his sister, who was not impressed. Franco was not a poet, yet he rather liked to write, and he would continue to do it off and on for the rest of his life, with somewhat greater success in prose. A literary style of courtship, moreover, was typical of that more formal age and was an approach Franco would take on other occasions.

When he graduated in 1910 as *alférez* (second lieutenant), Franco was a slight teenager of seventeen, one of the youngest cadets in his class, ranking 251 out of 312. It was a happy occasion, but also somewhat bittersweet, since he had expected a higher ranking. His placement in the lower part of his class does not seem to have owed so much to his grades as to his age, size, and physical presence. It must have been a matter of grim satisfaction twenty-six years later, when the Civil War began, that none of the cadets with higher rankings had ever gone further than lieutenant-colonel, while Franco was already a major general and would soon become generalissimo.

The newly commissioned second lieutenant had not impressed his instructors very much, but he had a robust constitution, was rarely ill, and was slowly beginning to fill out. He would soon show that he had the physical stamina necessary for active service and, bit by bit, ceased to be *cerillita*, slowly acquiring a mature musculature. He grew a thin moustache, typical of the era, and developed a more confident manner. Prior to World War I, colonial warfare provided the only combat experience available to young European officers and, for Spain, Morocco was the only battlefield, the only place to win fame and glory and rapid promotion through *méritos de guerra* (combat merits). For the moment, however, this was closed, since the army command would not grant newly commissioned officers a combat posting during their first year of service. A little later would Franco have his opportunity in Morocco, where 10 percent of his cadet class died in combat.

In the meantime, Franco asked for assignment to the garrison in El Ferrol, to be near his family. His career officially began on August 22, 1910, when he became the youngest second lieutenant assigned to the Eighth Infantry Regiment in El Ferrol. There for the last time he would experience the regular maternal and spiritual influence of his perpetually black-clad mother. Perhaps as a result, that summer he participated in the novena of the Sacred Heart, joining the devotional society of the Nocturnal Adoration of the Sacred Heart. Franco's biographers are not agreed about the significance of this: whether he was genuinely devoted or simply bowed to the wishes of an adored mother. Very possibly it was a combination of both. Contrary to the personal aura that he exuded, Franco always harbored a strong vein of sentimentality. It was standard for young Spanish officers to give little evidence of religiosity, but Franco always considered himself an orthodox Catholic, even if for years he permitted little public expression of this feeling. The influence of his mother was very important and later would be reinforced by that of a pious wife, a woman whose very piety probably attracted him a good deal.

His senior officers soon learned that though "Franquito" was not physically impressive, he knew his profession and showed an unusual ability to instruct and to command. After the first year, he was named his regiment's special instructor for the training of new corporals, a responsibility that he took very seriously. Then in 1911 he once more asked to be assigned to Morocco, as did his cousin Pacón (now also a second lieutenant) and his school chum from El Ferrol, Camilo Alonso Vega, who had been commissioned in Franco's own class. Franco's father also wrote a letter of recommendation (his last initiative in connection with Franco's life, so far as is known), but the most important support came from the former director of the academy in Toledo, Colonel José Villalba Riquelme, who had just been given command of the 68th Infantry Regiment in the zone of northern Morocco that would soon become officially the Spanish protectorate. He endorsed the three former cadets, who arrived in Melilla in February 1912 as "replacement officers" in their new regiment. They had no specific assignment until they were named to replace some of the fairly numerous casualties among junior officers.

In Morocco Francisco Franco became a mature adult and achieved a special destiny. As he later observed in an interview in 1938, "Without Africa, I would hardly be able to explain me to myself."[24] His daughter relates: "He adored Morocco. Where Papá became a man was in the Moroccan war. . . . His first important assignment was with the indigenous troops of the *regulares*, as they were called . . . , and he got used to them and became very comfortable with them."

The relationship between Spain and Morocco was an intimate one that, because of their geographic proximity, had lasted for millennia. From Morocco had been launched the Muslim conquest that began in 711, and altogether Spain had been the target of four different major invasions from Morocco between the eighth and fourteenth centuries.[25] The Spanish had begun their counteroffensive across the straits in the thirteenth century and initiated the campaign's major phase in 1497, five years after the discovery of America.[26] North Africa and the Mediterranean were the scenes of bitter conflict during the sixteenth century, and for three hundred years Spain was the target of Muslim pirate raids that seized as many as a quarter million captives for slavery and ransom. The Spanish crown had a number of strongholds on the northwest African coast, though these were later reduced to the two main presidios, or fortress cities, of Ceuta and Melilla, on the northern coast of Morocco. The nineteenth century was a rare period of relative peace and stability, with the exception of the brief war of 1859–60, after which Spain imposed a costly peace settlement that was a factor in the internal political breakdown of Morocco and its reduction to protectorate status.

The Spanish-American War of 1898 and the loss of all the remaining Spanish empire, with the exception of a few minor holdings in West and Northwest Africa, had produced a mood of disenchantment in Spain. While other European powers continued to expand in the golden age of European imperialism, most Spanish leaders stressed internal development and modernization. Nationalism was weaker than in any other European country, its only significant support the military.[27] The continued dynamism of French imperialism nonetheless exerted mounting pressure, as Paris concentrated its ambitions on Morocco, which, together with Ethiopia and Liberia, was one of the few independent territories remaining in Africa. The German government sought to intervene on behalf of its own interests, precipitating two diplomatic crises, but French diplomacy proved more astute and obtained international recognition of France's primacy in controlling the affairs of the kingdom of Morocco.

There was little enthusiasm in Spain for being drawn into new imperial expansion, but after 1906 Madrid had less and less choice in the matter.[28] The French were in the process of taking over Morocco, and the prospect of French borders on both the southern and northern frontiers of Spain was too much even for some Spanish moderates. Moreover, Great Britain, though becoming an imperial ally of France, wanted to prevent French domination of northern Morocco, which would allow the French to secure control of the south shore of the Straits of Gibraltar. Spanish expansion in northern Morocco thus became more a defensive than an offensive gesture, an attempt to maintain at least minimal status in the great age of European imperialism.

In March 1912 the sultan of Morocco officially agreed to the establishment of a French protectorate over the entire country, and eight months later, in November, a formal agreement between Paris and Madrid ceded a "zone of influence" to Spain. This amounted to the northernmost 5 percent of Morocco; the lion's share of the country—containing nearly all the major resources—went to France. Spanish administration of this zone was then officially proclaimed in February 1913, one year after Franco's arrival in Africa.[29] Though it would usually be referred to as the Spanish protectorate, in international law it was merely the zone ceded to Spain within the French protectorate of Morocco as a whole. The whole initiative had stemmed from the expansionist policy of France, which sought minor participation by the Spanish to win their support, to placate Britain, and to help hold at bay any possible interference from Germany. One Spanish author has compared the northern strip of Morocco, lightly inhabited and impoverished, to a bone thrown to a dog.

There is said to be a North African proverb to the effect that "the Tunisian is a woman, the Algerian a man, and the Moroccan a lion." The sparse native population of the new protectorate was mainly composed of rural Berber kabyles, illiterate people accustomed to a harsh and meager life but also rebellious and warlike in the extreme. They had often resisted the sultan of Morocco to the south, whose dominion was only tacitly accepted and rarely enforced. In the eastern Riff region, particularly, blood feuds were almost constant and the dominant male ideal was that of the warrior; as a result, most of the native kabyles, or tribes, were divided within themselves, and the killing of other males often became a matter of pride. Modest mineral deposits existed, but the zone's rudimentary agriculture could scarcely sustain the native population, and so the new Spanish enterprise constituted an exercise in what might be called uneconomic imperialism. Moreover, this effort enjoyed little political support at home, and in future years, as military casualties and expenses increased, opposition would grow steadily. The political response in Spain was rather different in tone and quality from what would have been found in most other European countries to imperialistic ventures, with the exception of Switzerland.

The unit that Franco joined in Morocco was poorly armed and supplied, badly organized, and even worse led. Food and provisions were of low quality and medical care deficient (though some of the few physicians were reasonably qualified), and most of the officers were mediocre, while others were corrupt, a number of them appallingly so. A few even sold arms and other materiel to native insurgents, while others pocketed part of the meager allotment of the food for the troops. Franco, never willing to speak badly of his own, would comment very little on such things in later years, but it must have been a shock to a young officer already known as an "ordenancista," that is, someone who insisted on following regulations strictly. Moreover, he soon found that the lessons taught in academy classrooms had little application to irregular warfare in the protectorate, where a new kind of fighting had to be learned the hard way.

He was posted to an advance base at the Kert River west of Melilla, in the eastern part of what was soon to become the Spanish zone, for in this region there had been intermittent hostilities ever since 1908, when one of the local leaders had first declared a jihad (holy war) against the Spanish presence. On March 19 Franco was assigned command of a squad sent out as part of a small reconnaissance column into hostile territory, which momentarily came under a heavy rifle fusilade. No more than a petty skirmish, this was his baptism of fire. Four days later, on March 23, 1912, Franco's regiment formed part of a larger operation composed of six different columns that were to converge on the insurgent *harka* (war band), but some of them ran into ambushes in the broken terrain for which the Spanish had no maps. The army was completely untrained for guerrilla warfare and suffered significant casualties without accomplishing anything. The operation was quickly canceled, and news of the casualties provoked major criticism of Spain's military presence across the straits in the Spanish press, even before the protectorate had been officially established. This abortive operation and the political reaction to it offered a foretaste of what would be repeated, with numerous variations, over the next twelve years. In mid-May the forces west of Melilla tried again, with greater success, killing the insurgent leader in battle and bringing peace to the eastern zone for some time. This was the first significant engagement for the new battalions of *regulares*, native Moroccan volunteers, led by Spanish officers, who henceforth formed part of the Spanish army. They bore the brunt of this successful combat, and Franco was pleased when two of their young lieutenants, Emilio Mola and Manuel Núñez de Prado, both wounded in combat, were immediately promoted to captain.

Soon after, on June 6, 1912, Franco, still only nineteen years old, was given permanent assignment as second lieutenant in his regiment and only a week later received his first promotion, to first lieutenant. This was promotion by seniority, the only time in the next fifteen years that a change in Franco's rank would not be the result of special promotion by *méritos de guerra*. His principal action during the remainder of the year was to help provide protection for the supply convoys that maintained the Spanish outposts. Before the end of 1912, he received his first medal, the Cross of Military Merit, First Class, for having served in the combat zone for more than three months, and in December he enjoyed a fifteen-day leave, which enabled him to spend Christmas in Melilla.

In February 1913 Franco was assigned to a small base near the city, a modest frontier town whose population had swollen due to the presence of the army. It was full of cheap taverns and gambling dens for the troops, as well as a sizable number of brothels of various categories, harboring girls as young as twelve. Venereal diseases were widespread among the military, but no threat to Franco, who shunned the local vices like the plague. He could, however, be sentimental and romantic, as he would soon demonstrate.

There was a formal social life of sorts for the tiny elite and for commissioned officers, which included receptions and dances in the military casino, as well as a local theater and even occasional concerts. The new high commissioner of the protectorate sponsored a reception for two hours every Friday afternoon, which Franco attended. At one of these events he met again a young woman he had first encountered during Christmas leave—Sofía Subirán, the eighteen-year-old daughter of the high commissioner's brother-in-law and military assistant. Franco may have had an introduction from a friend in El Ferrol, but he soon showed that he intended to aim high, however unprepossessing he may have seemed. To someone who had spent most of the preceding year in rough campaign life, Sofía, whatever her real charms (a bit difficult to grasp from her surviving photographs), seemed like a heavenly vision. Franco was dazzled and soon completely in love, apparently for the first time in his life.

Despite the thin moustache that he had been wearing for several years, he was still known as Lieutenant Franquito in his regiment and was bereft of any resources other than his petty salary, which was very low even by the standards of that time. In the military society of the protectorate, he was insignificant, yet he had already shown that in pursuing a goal he could be resolute, even stubborn. For six months he courted Sofía with every intention of becoming her formal fiancé.

Sofía Subirán, who never married, would outlive Franco. In 1978, three years after his death, she described the courtship to a journalist, displaying some of the numerous postcards he had sent her, which she had carefully preserved. On days when he could obtain leave Franco would frequent Melilla's central park, where Sofía was sometimes allowed to stroll with a chaperone, as well as the streets where she might walk during the evening *paseo*. He also attended the Friday receptions whenever possible, despite his limitations when it came to the dancing that Sofía loved. She has described him as very "serious," treating her always with exquisite courtesy, almost as though she were more than human. He was also "very clumsy, poor fellow," and disliked dancing, always preferring to talk. She was flattered by his persistent attentions yet soon found them boring. "Very thin" in appearance, "he was courteous, very refined. Attentive, a perfect gentleman. . . . He showed much character and was very agreeable . . . though overly attentive, to the extent of wearing you out." "Never any witticism, and much less any jokes. . . . I think he was too serious for someone his age. Maybe that was why I didn't much care for him—he was rather boring." She soon found it somewhat uncomfortable to be treated by Franco as "a supernatural being," when (as she put it) she was scarcely more than "an adolescent."

Altogether, this courtship lasted for most of the first half of 1913. During five months Franco sent to her no fewer than two hundred short letters and approximately one hundred illustrated postcards. Sofía's father tried to prohibit them, but she made a secret deal with his adjutant to be allowed to receive them anyway. Sometimes there were as many as three or four missives a day, all in Franco's fine, precise penmanship. They usually bore the picture of a beautiful young woman or sometimes a child on one side and were often embellished with slight additional flourishes and minor decorations by Franco, who always liked to draw. Later, when Franco eventually married, Sofía destroyed all the letters, but she saved the briefly inscribed picture postcards, most of them complaining that the letters often received no reply. Sofía recalled that "I really liked the cards that he sent. They were very pretty. He showed good taste and delicacy. At times he became tedious with his insistence that I answer him, but in general he was refined and well-educated." Sofía called him Paquito, and he always addressed her correctly as Sofía. Every word and phrase was socially and morally very correct. As Sofía commented, "They were postcards that even the pope could read," though, she added discreetly, "He was more intimate in his letters."

At first he began very formally with "My distinguished friend," later changing to "My good friend Sofía," eventually moving to "My dear friend Sofía" and, on at least one occasion, "Very dear friend Sofía." Franco first modestly declared his love on the eighth of March ("from your good friend who loves you"), declaring the next day that "He who waits despairs Sofía but I still wait" (with a customary lack of punctuation), five days later saying that he was awaiting her response "with anxiety."

All in vain. Franco was trying to fly very high, courting the daughter of the brother-in-law and assistant of the high commissioner, while he himself was, as Sofía would put it, a "nobody" ("chiquitito, poquita cosa"), both personally and professionally. His attentions flattered and occasionally entertained her; she found him amiable and fully correct, but he danced poorly, lacked vivacity, and, eventually, simply bored her. Ultimately,

Franco had to face the facts and the last line of his final communication of June 5 began with the words "Adiós, Sofía." He realized that he had lost, but there is little doubt that he had been seriously involved emotionally and, in later years, he would inquire about Sofía from time to time.[30]

Exactly at this point Franco initiated a new relationship of the sort that in Spanish military vernacular would make him one of the "betrothed of death," when he transferred to the elite shock units. It would be easy to conclude that, saddened and embittered in his private life, he volunteered for a place of maximal danger, though potentially of the greatest fame and glory. Many young men, after a personal disappointment or misfortune, have abruptly changed course, seeking a place of adventure or danger in order to conquer or perish. Many have perished, but Franco would be one of the favored few who went on to glory.

Yet such a conclusion is too melodramatic. Franco had already learned that the most rapid path to promotion lay with the shock units, and in fact he had first petitioned for transfer to the native *regulares* months earlier, announcing his new appointment to Sofía in April, when he was still hoping to win her hand. Reassignment was thus not an act of desperation but a logical step in the pursuit of satisfying a professional ambition that was already very strong. Before the end of May he was given the post of lieutenant in a *regulares* regiment, some of whose senior officers would go on to the most prominent posts, including Dámaso Berenguer, José Sanjurjo, and Emilio Mola. At that moment they would undoubtedly have been astonished to learn that the comrade who would become by far the most renowned would be none of these already decorated leaders but the new "Lieutenant Franquito," so insignificant in appearance.

2

The Youngest General in Europe

(1913–1926)

Franco had little time to brood over his failed court- ship, for, less than two weeks after his farewell to Sofía, he was transferred to Ceuta in the western district, which had become the primary scene of hostilities, where he was assigned to a unit of native troops. The first battalions of Moroccan *regulares* had been created at the beginning of 1912, following the model of indigenous troops in the French imperial forces.[1] One difference was that the French had a large empire from which to draw, while Spain did not. Two-thirds of the troops in French Morocco were from various parts of Africa, but in 1913 native volunteers made up only thirteen thousand of the sixty-five thousand Spanish troops in the protectorate. They nonetheless comprised an elite force and were more combative than most of the unenthusiastic, often only semiliterate, Spanish draftees. They were termed "regulares" from the outset, because they were neither militia nor an auxiliary force but regular infantry and cavalry units of the Spanish army. At first most came from Algeria, for it was not clear how many Moroccans could be counted on to fight against insurgents. The *regulares* quickly acquired a reputation for bravery and stamina and were given the most dangerous assignments, though the desertion rate was also fairly high and officers were needed who could maintain discipline and provide firm leadership. In 1914 most *regulares* units would be combined in a new corps, the Indigenous Regular Forces (Grupo de Fuerzas Regulares Indígenas), of four sections, each with three *tabores* (battalions) of troops (two infantry and one cavalry). Volunteers were paid forty-six pesetas a month (about five dollars), plus increments for seniority, unusually high pay designed to attract recruits and discourage desertion.

Franco did not receive his new posting by chance. Only the best young officers were selected to command *regulares*, and in the actions of 1912 he had demonstrated that he knew how to keep his head and lead men under fire. Key characteristics had become evident: physical courage, personal calm, mental clarity under pressure, and the capacity to command. This was not merely a matter of bravery but of nerve, which was more important—the ability not to get rattled in a combat emergency and make the right decisions. It meant having the fiber and judgment to control troops who were tough and seemingly exotic and a bit primitive, carry out orders, and take charge of his subunit's administration. Franco seems to have had little trouble in commanding his Moroccan volunteers, but he later reminisced that the first night had been nerve wracking. He was not yet sure how much he could trust his men and lay awake nearly all night with his pistol ready.[2]

His regiment went into action almost immediately, participating in three sharp skirmishes before the end of June. The combat that took place during the next three months largely succeeded in pacifying the district between Ceuta, on the coast, and the small inland city of Tetuán, which became the capital of the protectorate. To the west a network of *blocaos*, tiny outposts of wood and sandbags, were being set up to extend the range of military control, and a lull soon set in. The following year, as the Great War began in Europe, Morocco was relatively tranquil. Franco participated in only a half-dozen small skirmishes. Despite the reduction in fighting, he attracted more attention, demonstrating that he knew where to concentrate fire in combat and also that, in a campaign where supply of outposts in hostile terrain was crucial, he understood logistics and showed skill in protecting supply units. He received two more minor decorations before the close of 1914.

It was a harsh life under the African sun, but one in which Franco found a peculiar contentment. He had become part of the combat elite and had met the challenge well. His indigenous troops not only respected his physical courage but also his honest implementation of regulations and his sensibleness and effectiveness in leading them. Franco insisted on tight discipline but lived personally by the same code, and his men recognized that though he was very demanding, he was fair and impersonal. He was still "Lieutenant Franquito," but this form of address was now said with a certain respect. The few photos of Franco from this period reveal a smiling, apparently happy young officer who was winning high marks in a hard school, and a new calm and mature confidence could be seen in his expression. He had learned to smile more and had become more handsome.

Nonetheless, Franco generally remained austere and reserved, developing a reputation for being taciturn in an army given to a great deal of talk. He had few personal friends and was socially aloof. The most common diversion for officers was to pass much of the time on long, boring evenings playing cards, but Franco rarely participated, though he enjoyed an occasional game of chess, since it was dominated by analytic logic and less given to chance. He was known as an *ordenancista*, a stickler for the rules. Appointed to a judicial tribunal for the court-martial of a soldier who had murdered his corporal, Franco refused to follow the example of senior officers who urged clemency by informal means. Franco insisted that rules be strictly followed and sent an independent report to the Ministry of War, which responded by temporarily placing the colonel in charge of the tribunal under arrest.[3] This sort of thing did not bring popularity, but it did win him respect, tinged perhaps with an element of fear. Franco seemed a little weird and sometimes incomprehensible and also a bit superhuman.

Military life clearly favored him. He had always enjoyed robust health, and his impressive stamina enabled him to adjust to the rigors of campaign life. Sometimes there was little sleep. Conditions were often uncomfortable, and food was irregular, meager, and poor. It is often said that fatigue, even more than fear, is the soldier's greatest burden, but Franco withstood the physical trials and sometimes even seemed to enjoy them, assisted by his ability to fall asleep rapidly even in difficult circumstances, which maximized opportunities for rest when they were available. Rather than weakening, he appeared to grow stronger in leading a daunting life that frankly was shunned by most young Spanish officers.

In January 1915 his battalion performed particularly well in a hard fight to the south of Tetuán that routed a band of insurgents. Two months later he was promoted to captain by *méritos de guerra*, thanks especially to the personal recommendation of his corps commander, General Dámaso Berenguer. Curiously, this recommendation did not refer to the latest engagement but to his achievements during the first four months of 1914, before the relative lull had set in. This promotion, the first merit promotion in what would soon become a meteoric career, was backdated to February 1, 1914, making him, at the age of twenty-two, the youngest captain in the Spanish army. It helped that, as it was said, he always seemed to have luck in combat. His Muslim soldiers persistently referred to the *baraka*, or good fortune, of Franco, which would later surround him with a kind of superstitious aura. He led from the front but was never touched by enemy fire. At times, after a combat, he would send his mother a laconic telegram: "Yo, a salvo" ("I am safe"). That in itself was somewhat extraordinary, for the officers in *regulares* units suffered the highest casualties of any part of the Spanish army. Of the first forty-two officers assigned to them in 1912, only seven were still alive by the close of 1915. That was certainly an important factor in the prestige he was acquiring among native troops, who did not understand how he could come unscathed through so many tight spots unless he enjoyed a special dispensation from God. "Allah protects him," as they put it, and it was good to fight for such a leader. Such experience probably provided the stimulus for what later became his notorious providentialism—not merely the conviction that everything lay in God's hands but also that he had been chosen by the Deity for a special purpose.

During World War I, the Spanish government's policy was to avert conflict in the protectorate by means of negotiations with local sheikhs. Combat with small groups of insurgents continued intermittently, for most of the territory was not really under military control. The indirect policy was encouraged by France, which sought to avoid significant hostilities in any part of Morocco for the duration of the European conflict. German policy was the exact reverse, as part of a historically unprecedented program to foment sabotage and subversion in the homelands and empires of its enemies. Berlin overtly encouraged jihad among the many millions of Muslims in the British, French, and Russian empires, at the same time that it sought to stimulate violent revolution in Russia, and even within industry inside Spain, which produced for France. The policy's only real success finally occurred when German assistance and money helped the Bolsheviks to seize control of the revolution in Russia in 1917, but meanwhile German agents covertly ran arms through Spanish Morocco for rebels in the French zone, assisted on occasion by pro-German Spanish officers. There is no evidence that Franco, as a junior officer, had anything to do with such matters, but witnessing this activity from afar may have planted a seed that would come to fruition after the beginning of the Civil War.

Spain was also a target. German agents fomented class warfare and terrorism in Barcelona and began to incite rebellion in the Spanish protectorate, not out of any particular enmity against Spain but simply because this was an unpacified area. Fanning the flames of revolt might quickly extend unrest into the French protectorate.[4] Nonetheless, another lull set in during October 1915, and there was virtually no fighting until the following April.

After being promoted to captain, Franco was transferred to the garrison forces in Ceuta for a short period, since there was no vacancy at that rank in the *regulares*. Soon, however, his corps commander, Berenguer, assigned him to train a newly formed unit, which would become the third company of the third *tabor* of the First Regiment of Regulares of Melilla. After just one month, he was named regular commander, and his new unit took part in a series of skirmishes near Larache, in the far western zone. He received a new decoration, a higher category of the Cross of Military Merit, First Class, that he had won earlier. Perhaps more significant was the fact that his new unit's officers chose him as battalion treasurer, putting him in charge of payroll and finances. This was a significant assignment because of the abuses that occurred in some other army units.

The relative calm that had set in during the autumn of 1915 was broken in the spring of the following year by the rebellion of the powerful Anjera tribe in the protectorate's northwest, roughly between Ceuta and Tangier. It was incited and supported by German agents, who hoped the revolt would threaten the international city of Tangier and the area south of the Straits of Gibraltar. If the revolt were successful, it might spread to French Morocco.

The Spanish authorities needed to suppress it as soon as possible, and in June 1916 they launched the most extensive military operation yet seen in Morocco, composed of three converging columns. Franco's *tabor* formed part of the main column, which totaled nearly ten thousand Spanish troops, plus *regulares*. Advancing directly into the heart of rebel territory, it came up against a partially fortified Anjera position on the hill of El Biutz, the "ridge of trenches," as the Spanish attackers called it. The insurgents possessed greater firepower than usual, including several machine guns (possibly obtained from the Germans). Two units that attempted to carry the main ridge of Ain Jir were repelled, incurring heavy losses, particularly among the officers.

At this point Franco's company was ordered to attack, which it did decisively. In spite of intense fire and numerous casualties, it reached the first trench and prevailed in hand-to-hand fighting, provoking the beginning of a rebel withdrawal. Franco, as usual, led by example and was said at one point to have picked up the rifle of one of his fallen soldiers to fire at the enemy. Immediately afterward he was struck in the abdomen by a bullet from a machine gun farther up the hill. Yet even though their captain and two more officers went down, his troops succeeded in occupying the trench line. The price was high: 56 of the 133 men in the unit became casualties. Before the whole operation ended, the main Spanish column would lose nearly 400 men in combat, modest casualties, to be sure, compared with those of the war raging in Europe, but the heaviest thus far in Morocco.

At first it was thought that Franco would be added to their number, because in Morocco most wounds to the abdomen were fatal. Spanish army surgeons were capable, up to a point, but medical resources in the field were limited. In later years Franco would narrate his version of the occasion on which he received his only significant combat wound, describing the protection provided by several of his *regulares* and stressing that he had remained lucid enough to hand over to a remaining officer the twenty-thousand pesetas that, as unit treasurer, he had been carrying for the current pay period. His daughter offers the following account:

> He was extremely lucky, because in those days to have a perforated intestine, as was initially feared, was fatal and you died. He used to tell how he said to his Moroccan aide—no, rather his assistant, because in those days they called an *asistente* the soldier who attended the captain's personal needs—that it did not feel too bad and that he continued to breathe normally. And it was a nice sunny day. When medical personnel reached him, however, they said "No, not this one. He's gut-shot. No point in evacuating him to the medical truck. He'll die shortly." My father then said to his Moroccan assistant that he did not at all feel as though he were dying and had no intention of dying on such a nice day. He told him: "Grab your gun and point it at these chaps until they get me back to the truck." And that's what happened; if he had not been so determined, they would have left him to bleed to death. The physicians later told him he had been very lucky. The

wound occurred when he was inhaling and this raised his organs very slightly so that the bullet just missed. Though it grazed his liver, it didn't hit his intestines. In those days, if you were hit in the intestines, you were a goner. He was very lucky, had a great deal of *baraka*, as they said over there.

Franco was evacuated fast enough that a rudimentary field aid station could staunch the hemorrhaging. As soon as a priest reached him, he made confession, but Franco's luck held again. Of the eleven wounded who were evacuated with him, seven died, but after sixteen days of recovery he was in condition to be moved to the clinic in Ceuta.

The commendation for this action far surpassed anything that went before, the report for his unit stressing "his incomparable valor, energy, and qualities of command." At the end of the month he received a telegram from the War Ministry thanking him in the name of the king, Alfonso XIII, and of both chambers of the legislature, while the new high commissioner, General Francisco Gómez-Jordana Souza, recommended Franco for promotion to major and requested that the evaluation required to award him Spain's top military medal, the Great Laureate Cross of Saint Ferdinand, be conducted.

Franco's mother received word that her son was in grave condition, with the result that she and her estranged husband reunited just long enough to travel together to Ceuta to visit Paco in the military infirmary. They were surprised and delighted to find him out of danger, though he was still weak. Nicolás Franco soon returned to Madrid, but Doña Carmen remained with her son. After five weeks of recuperation, he was granted three months of leave; after four and a half years in Morocco, he embarked for El Ferrol on August 3, 1916, to complete his convalescence. Franco was able to spend three months at home with his mother before returning to his unit at the beginning of November.

Only then did he learn that although the high commissioner had recommended him for promotion and the Great Laureate Cross, the Ministry of War was not inclined to approve either of them, partly because of his youth. Franco immediately sought and won from his senior commander in Morocco, Jordana, the right to petition the commander in chief, Alfonso XIII, to approve the original recommendation. Nearly all Franco's biographers have drawn attention to the audacity of this initiative, which apparently had an effect on the king, who referred the matter to Franco's corps commander,

Berenguer, who also approved it. This marked the beginning of what would later be a special relationship with Spain's sovereign, whose esteem and assistance he would continue to enjoy for years.[5]

Franco remained on reserve in Tetuán for four months, until the king officially ratified the promotion at the close of February 1917. The ministry, however, rejected the award of the Great Laureate Cross. Its evaluation noted with disfavor the extremely high casualties, even though it was his superiors who had given orders for the frontal assault, and also observed that Franco was put out of action fairly early and thus did not direct or participate in the most decisive phase of combat.[6] Instead, he was awarded the Cross of María Cristina, First Class, a less important but nonetheless prestigious decoration.

Barely twenty-four, he was the youngest major in the army, and the promotion brought with it a change in assignment. After more than three years with the *regulares*, he was reassigned to the peninsula, attached to the Third Infantry Regiment in the garrison at Oviedo, not far from his hometown. There, in the capital of Asturias, he would eventually achieve much better fortune in romance than he had in Morocco. His main responsibility was to supervise the training of reserve officers in the garrison, a task he had been assigned because of his reputation for discipline, exacting respect for regulations, and emphasis on fundamentals. It was not a very demanding post and left him with considerable leisure for the first time in his career.

There are few indications about how he used the time. He took up residence at the Hotel París in the center of the small city and, since he had most afternoons free, adopted the habit after lunch of taking a long horseback ride through the quiet streets, a practice that soon made him a familiar figure. At that age he had not yet begun to bald too much, and he cut the figure of the young hero on horseback. In Oviedo he would come to be known as *el comandantín* (the little major), but at that point the diminutive would refer to his youth as much as his stature.

Franco would later claim that this was the first time in his adult life he had much time to read, though there is scant information about what or how much he read. He had evidently begun to read more widely during his convalescence the preceding year, devoting himself to military news and studies about the broader war then raging, which had left Spain the most important European neutral. In military society he discoursed at length about the new weaponry and the campaigns under way, using data and concepts derived from his reading, and also played an occasional game of chess.

Oviedo was a somewhat sleepy provincial capital, and when the writer Clarín had made it the site of his acclaimed novel *La regenta* in 1885, he had given it the name of Vetusta (meaning "ancient" or "decrepit"). Whatever the city's limitations, for the first time Franco had become a figure of some social importance, able to play a role in its elite life, though this did not alter much the rigorous terms of his personal existence. According to his closest military friends, such as Camilo Alonso Vega, the standard sensual vices were unknown to him. The truth seems to be that Franco was not a very sensual person and was probably less tempted to physical indulgence than many, to which was added his lifelong aversion to the bad example set by his father. His only known excess was to continue eating as though he were an active officer in the field, though he drank only a small glass of wine with meals. He began slowly to gain weight. In Oviedo, nonetheless, he was the young hero, vigorous in appearance and no longer spindly. He had become a special personage, and to some an interesting one.

Though a senior officer had more money to spend on women, Franco's only known ambition in this regard continued to be strictly honorable. He sought to make a good marriage of the sort that would complement his career and a stable family. Though not a fortune hunter, he was interested only in a young woman of good family and good social condition—a proper lady (much like his mother). The past four years had been rigorous and austere, but he had not lost the romantic flair he had shown earlier in Melilla, and in Oviedo he was much better placed to succeed.

He now enjoyed the best social contacts, and the reserve officers whom he instructed came exclusively from the middle and upper classes, which helped to open even more doors. In Oviedo he was invited to the receptions and dinners of the two leading local aristocrats, the Marqués de la Rodriga and the Marqués de la Vega de Anzo, joining the Royal Automobile Club and even attending meetings of the chamber of commerce on occasion. He also got to know useful figures in cultural life, such as a very young but noted literature professor at the University of Oviedo, Pedro Sainz Rodríguez (briefly his first minister of education in 1938–39), as well as a university student and aspiring journalist, Joaquín Arrarás, who would later achieve prominence and write the first biography of Franco in 1938.

But by far the most important person whom he met was a very attractive fifteen-year-old, María del Carmen Polo y Martínez-Valdés, the daughter of Felipe Polo, a retired man of leisure and some wealth, one branch of whose family descended from aristocratic lineage in Palencia province.

Like Franco's own father, Polo was a man of progressive ideas, at least to a certain extent, and critical of Spain's enterprise in Morocco. After the death of his wife, the upbringing of his three pretty daughters and only son was carefully supervised by his sister, who had herself made an upper-class marriage and administered Felipe Polo's household. Carmen, the oldest, was a rather tall teenager with dark hair and eyes set off by a fair complexion, and, when the school year began, her father placed her as a resident student (*educanda*) in a local convent school of high quality, her studies there complemented by private lessons in English, French, and piano.[7] She was a very pious girl—a quality that also attracted Franco—but, despite her youth, also revealed a kind of style and elegance that made her stand out.

Franco met Carmen Polo on a *romería* (a country outing) in the summer of 1917 and was quickly smitten. He gained her attention and interest right away, but the initial terms of courtship were difficult because she was so young and protected, and because her father had so low an opinion of members of the Spanish military, he did not want any of them wooing his eldest daughter. In her later years, Carmen Polo loved to go back over their courtship, as her own daughter explains:

> No, my father never talked about it. My mother was the one who did, describing all the details, especially to my own children, her granddaughters. When my father became interested, she was very young, . . . so her father decided to put her in a cloistered convent that admitted *educandas*, who were something like novitiates. My father could only communicate in short letters; the only way to her was when they came every morning for communion, because they all left the convent for the big church, open to the public. There my father could see her every morning at the 7 a.m. Mass. Then he returned home and went back to bed for a little while.

Since she was so young, a lengthy courtship would be necessary before Franco could hope to ask for her hand, but he had always been patient. As in his earlier courtship in Melilla, Franco wrote many letters, but in Oviedo they were normally intercepted by the nuns. Neither Carmen's father nor her aunt found the "comandantín" a satisfactory suitor. Felipe Polo wanted well-established and affluent husbands who could give his daughters a secure family life. An officer like Franco, who gained his promotions by "méritos de guerra," would never have a very great salary, would be likely to abandon his wife for long periods on campaigns, and might well leave her a widow at a tender age. Though Franco was dedicated and persistent, the prospective father-in-law is supposed to have said that taking up with Franco "would be the same as marrying a bullfighter," or words to that effect.

It required all his determination. Carmen Polo was more responsive than Sofía, but while she was in the convent it was even harder to see her. The convent school was strict. Of the twenty-three girls in Carmen's class, her daughter has said that she was one of only three who did not take the veil and that, at one point, even she had thought of doing so. At first there was no way the two could get to know each other very well, and her father long remained adamantly opposed to the courtship. Franco did not hide the fact that he would probably return to active duty in Morocco, and Carmen's father and aunt emphasized over and over again that such a man could never provide her with security. Yet he soon made a kind of public declaration, since he was the only adult male to appear punctually at 7 a.m. Mass every morning in the church when the *educandas* appeared, a practice that is said even to have impressed the nuns, and his persistence very slowly made headway. Eventually, the two apparently found a way to exchange short messages, then to have short encounters at the home of her family physician (one of whose sons was a military comrade of Franco), and even to have brief chaperoned meetings in a public place.

Felipe Polo remained opposed, however, and at times Franco probably steeled himself for another disappointment. When he made his customary summer visit to his mother in El Ferrol in 1919, he attended the annual *juegos florales* (cultural festival) and was attracted by the young woman chosen as queen of the festivities, María Angeles Barcón. She was older—twenty-four—decidedly more mature, with greater freedom of movement than Sofía or Carmen. She was apparently the first relatively mature woman in whom Franco became interested, and she seems to have reciprocated his attention very quickly. According to her subsequent account, "in spite of his military professionalism, he knew how to treat girls. It's true that he was surrounded by a certain aura of mystery. . . . He talked little but to the point. I noticed that he never had warm hands but what I especially liked was his concentrated seriousness, together with his white teeth. I started to become enamored in that impressionable and carefree manner typical of our sentimental era." Whatever the exact nature of this new relationship, it was abruptly truncated by the young woman's father, a wealthy local industrialist who firmly intended for her to marry a member of the social elite. According to Barcón, he was so angry that he slapped her in the face for the first and last time in her life and absolutely prohibited any further contact with Franco.[8]

Carmen Polo remained the object of his affections, and, since she strongly reciprocated, her father finally mellowed, allowing Franco to visit the Polo home and achieve a kind of understanding, though no formal engagement would be announced for another year, since Carmen was still only seventeen. Matters did advance to the point that she was taken on a chaperoned visit to El Ferrol to meet Franco's mother, who is said to have been delighted and charmed by the girl, with her good looks and elegant manners, calling her a "fairy-tale princess." Franco's outspoken, down-to-earth sister was rather less impressed, finding her brother's fiancée a bit pretentious.

Within the military garrison in Oviedo, only a handful of senior officers, veterans of the Cuban campaign, could equal Franco when it came to combat experience, and there he would first display what would become a characteristic of his conversation for the rest of his life: endless anecdotes of military adventures in Morocco. Even Adolf Hitler would later be subjected to a large dose of this, much to his disgust. Franco's conversation did not necessarily make him popular among his fellow officers, but his accomplishments earned their respect. His prestige would always be based on recognition of his personal qualities and achievement, not on any special affection. There were many officers who were better liked, but there was no one like Franco. After a year in Oviedo, he tried to improve his technical preparation and credentials by seeking admission to an advanced course in the army staff college in Madrid, but in this case he was turned down because he was too senior, the course being designed for captains (most of them, needless to say, older than Franco).

During World War I, tension increased within the officer corps as in Spanish society as a whole, for several reasons. One was rapid inflation; low salaries now had even less purchasing power than before, those of junior officers amounting to scarcely more than a pittance. Another was the growth of intense social and political conflict within the broader society, as cleavages became deeper. The spirit of national unity found among the warring nations was nowhere to be seen in Spain. Army officers did not necessarily have any sympathy for worker radicals, but, from a completely different point of view, they agreed with the radicals that the fragmented elite that still dominated government were ignoring the country's vital interests and that Spain needed drastic change.

To advance their own interests, in 1916 officers in the Barcelona garrison organized a military defense council (*junta militar de defensa*), a technically illegal association that functioned rather like a trade union of army officers. During 1917 such councils established themselves in most peninsular garrisons and even, to some extent, in the combat units in Morocco. Franco deemed it advisable to join the local council in Oviedo, though this kind of army politics was not his own priority. Conversely, he was over-joyed when his closest comrades, Camilo Alonso Vega and his cousin Pacón, were both assigned to the Oviedo garrison at the close of 1917, after the end of long tours of service in the protectorate. These and other old friends from the academy and the years in Morocco were always the ones who most drew his affection.

The year 1917 produced a triple crisis in Spain: a political conflict pro-pelled by democratic reformists who convened a rival parliament of their own in Barcelona in July, a growing military crisis as the *juntero* move-ment eroded discipline and even threatened the government, and a social and economic crisis fueled by inflation and then by the general strike called by the Socialist trade union (Unión General de Trabajadores) in August. Labor leaders hoped that the military, as in the preceding century, would support a more radical political breakthrough, but their hopes were in vain: the *junteros* formed a self-styled military elite and closed ranks in the face of a general strike that seemed to threaten social revolution. Martial law was declared in Asturias to control striking miners, and Franco was also mobilized, though at that moment he had no troop command. He was sent with a small column of troops to maintain order in part of the Asturian mining basin during the first phase of the strike, an assignment that was completed peacefully, apparently without a shot being fired. The subsequent myth that Franco first engaged in "brutal repression" of workers in Asturias is completely fallacious. The general strike turned violent in September, but he had no responsibilities in that phase. It was the garrison commander in Oviedo, General Ricardo Burguete, a political liberal, who was famously quoted as saying that revolutionaries would be "hunted down like wild beasts" ("cazados como alimañas"). In Spain as a whole at least eighty people were killed and several thousand arrested. Afterward Franco was named to a military tribunal to judge the cases of workers who had violated the terms of martial law. All this brought him face to face with the growth of revolutionary mobilization in Spain, and he later said that the experience of the general strike opened his eyes to the country's social problems and aroused his sympathy for the harsh conditions of the miners' lives. But he remained a strict disciplinarian, and the tribunal handed down prison terms for some of the miners.

In 1919, with the conclusion of World War I, the Spanish authorities decided to complete the military occupation and pacification of the protec-torate, which had been on hold for nearly five years. The problems this presented stand out more clearly by comparison with the French model. In the French protectorate there was much more emphasis on building civil administration and investing in public works. The inhabitants were less rebellious but also better administered. The French government normally appointed a civilian high commissioner and employed somewhat fewer troops (mainly African volunteers) to control a territory nineteen times larger than the Spanish protectorate.

Spain's administration had achieved little the first six years and faced a daunting challenge in asserting itself. Moreover, service in the rough, grim, and exhausting campaigns of the protectorate was scarcely popular, even for most professional officers, and was dreaded by the poorly trained troops. Thus a small group of army activists proposed to follow the French example of building an elite foreign legion of volunteers. In 1920 the War Ministry approved a proposal by Lieutenant Colonel José Millán Astray to create a *tercio de extranjeros* (a battalion made up of foreign volunteers, named in honor of the elite *tercios*, or battalions, of the sixteenth century). Millán Astray was eccentric, histrionic and verbose, and also very brave, eventually losing both an arm and an eye in combat, which won him the moniker "the glorious amputee" ("el glorioso mutilado").[9] He was not that much of an organizer, however, and decided that Franco, the most celebrated young leader of Moroccan shock troops, known for his ability to train, organize, and discipline, would be the ideal collaborator in creating this elite force and offered him the position of second in command.

By this time Franco had spent more than three years in an agreeable, though occasionally boring, life in Asturias, the highlight being his determined pursuit of Carmen Polo. The military councils had succeeded in imposing an *escala cerrada* (strict seniority promotion) on the army, which eliminated special combat rewards, and Franco hesitated three months before accepting the offer from Millán Astray. His persistence seemed to be paying off, for Carmen Polo had become firmly committed to him. She had worn down her father's opposition, and he finally agreed to a formal *noviazgo* (engagement) in 1920. Yet Franco was being offered a key role in a new kind of elite within the otherwise flaccid and mediocre Spanish army. He decided to accept the opportunity, though it might take him into a life even more dangerous than in the past, and returned to Morocco in October 1920. At that point he seems to have thought that the marriage still would not be too long delayed. His daughter explains: "He was extremely providentialist. He believed deeply in Providence, influenced especially by his time in Morocco. He was a fatalist, that is, he thought that you should do all you can to make things go well, but if something bad should happen, then it could not be avoided." This second tour of service in Morocco, whose length he could not have foreseen, would take up most of the next five and a half years, until early in 1926, and bring him to much greater prominence.

Within a short time the *tercio*, or the "legion," as Franco and Millán Astray preferred to call it, would gain fame as the toughest, most combat-ready unit in the army. Its men received higher pay as special volunteers and got better food and supplies. Though the volunteers, who were initially supervised by Franco as director of basic training, came from many different countries, the great majority were native Spaniards. They were adventure-some and violent men; many came from marginal social sectors, and some had criminal backgrounds. Only strong and experienced officers, capable of demanding the firmest discipline and the most exacting performance, could train and lead the new *banderas*, or battalions, of the *tercio*. Franco, as second in command and head of the First Battalion, proved ideal, for he knew how to control the most hard-nosed recruits.

Whatever their personal background, volunteers in the *tercio* came to be known as "caballeros legionarios," and Millán Astray prepared for them a special honor code, the "credo legionario." This declared that the spirit of legionnaires "is unique and without equal, of fierce, all-out attack." It required each one to swear an oath never to abandon a comrade on the field of battle.

Years later Franco explained to his cousin Pacón that when his battalion first entered service early in 1921, discipline was inadequate. He wrote to Millán Astray for permission to carry out summary executions, if necessary, but the legion's commander replied that this could only be done according to the code of military justice, which required an official court-martial. Franco, however, judged that in a poorly disciplined army the hard cases in the legion could only be converted into first-class soldiers by the strictest measures. Soon afterward, a volunteer who presented one of the gravest disciplinary problems abruptly rejected his rations, throwing his plate on the ground and splattering an officer. Franco calmly had him executed virtually on the spot and then ordered the entire battalion to march past the cadaver. Next he wrote to his superiors, accepting full responsibility, but he heard no more from them. He had made his point.[10]

The legion soon became known for administering the toughest discipline in the army, but meanwhile conflict was deepening among the officer corps as a whole, and by 1921 a split had become apparent between the peninsular bureaucrats, who dominated the *juntas militares*, and the combat officers in Morocco, who had become known as *africanistas*.[11] By the close of 1919 the councils had become institutionalized in the form of officially recognized advisory commissions (*comisiones informativas*) in every garrison or unit of any size. By 1921 *africanista* officers had begun to protest domination by the army bureaucrats and their commissions, and the cleavage within the officer corps came out into the open, particularly at a small meeting held in the western zone of the protectorate early in July. The loudest protest came from the daring Lieutenant José Enrique Varela (known as Varelita, since he was scarcely as large as Franco). Varela had commanded Moroccan volunteers, mainly in *regulares* units, and had been in combat intermittently for six years, without ever being reassigned to the peninsula, but he had only won a seniority promotion to first lieutenant. He would go on to become the only officer to twice win the Great Laureate Cross, the highest decoration of all, and within the next few years he would become one of Franco's closest colleagues.[12] Though theoretically the councils and the commissions represented all officers, the chasm between the two sectors of the officer corps would continue to deepen, and Franco spoke out on several occasions in favor of restoring merit promotions.

The first two *banderas* of the legion went into action as part of a new strategy in 1921 to pacify the western part of the protectorate, but this strategy suddenly had to be reassessed in July, when the entire military structure in the Rif district of the eastern zone collapsed. Within days, the frontier receded all the way back to the city of Melilla, the point from which the tenuous, halting Spanish advance had begun in 1908. Approximately ten thousand troops were killed and perhaps a thousand more soon died in captivity, though another five hundred prisoners, many of them officers, remained in insurgent hands. This was Spain's greatest disaster since 1898, somewhat equivalent to the catastrophic defeat of the Italian army in Ethiopia at Adowa in 1896, which drove Italy to cancel all plans for expansion for nearly a generation.

The collapse, which stunned the nation, stemmed from several factors. One was the absence of political will in Madrid. The government had half-heartedly backed into the Moroccan adventure and then had been unwilling to provide the money and the men needed to put down native insurgency and take control of the territory. This was compounded by rivalry between the high commissioner, General Berenguer, and his subordinate in the eastern zone, General Manuel Fernández Silvestre, which resulted in the former assigning 70 percent of all reinforcements to the western zone, leaving Silvestre shorthanded. Equally, if not more, important was that the army suffered from poor leadership, ineffective training, and lack of equipment. A fourth factor was flawed strategy in the eastern zone by Silvestre, who then lost his head in the final emergency and apparently committed suicide at his advance post, Anwal, after the collapse had begun.[13] A final factor was the negligence of Berenguer in not dispatching reinforcements until ordered to do so by the minister in Madrid.[14]

Military strategy in Morocco posed serious problems. The Spanish generally followed the French policy of trying to construct an interlocking network of *blocaos* (small posts) to control the territory, a tactic that tied down many troops in static defense and required that nearly all the rest be used in endless supply columns to provision the posts, which usually lacked their own water supply. Not many troops were left to make up a strategic reserve. As he advanced into the bellicose and hilly Rif district, Silvestre situated his *blocaos* increasingly in more of a line, which left each one exposed and unsupported. They were badly sited, often on a low hilltop without a source of water. If they were placed at the entrance to a small valley where water was available, however, the position could be dominated by fire from surrounding heights. In the western zone, with more troops under his command, Berenguer operated much more as the French did, consolidating each zone as he advanced. Silvestre's outposts were left suspended in thin air.

The Spanish strategy was predicated on the presumption that the troops would meet comparatively limited resistance from each kabyle as its territory was entered, but at this point insurgents in the Rif found a strong leader, Abd el Krim. He and his father, an important subtribal judge, had had good relations with the Spanish administration in the past, and the well-educated Abd el Krim had held several important positions in Melilla, twice receiving medals from the Spanish authorities. His family had hoped that a Spanish protectorate might be more lenient than rule by France but had also been in touch with German agents (and during World War I may have received funding for an insurrection, which was apparently held in reserve). Abd el Krim was outspokenly anti-French and proposed that the Spanish restrict occupation to the very easternmost sector, leaving the Rif autonomous. Thrown into jail, he broke a leg in a failed escape attempt, which left him permanently lame. After being released, Abd el Krim continued to try to negotiate down to the time he launched the insurgency.[15]

Disastrous weather in part of northern Morocco in 1920 resulted in poor harvests and near-famine conditions, so that resistance to the initially timid Spanish advance into the Rif had been limited. By 1921 conditions had improved, just as it became clear that Spain intended to occupy its zone completely. The heads of the Rifian kabyles looked for a leader, and their chief candidate was Abd el Krim, who invested his funds in contraband arms and began mobilization under the banner of jihad. During the second half of the year, this rallying blazed into the most formidable anti-colonial insurgency to be found in the Afro-Asian world at that time.[16]

The Rifi assaults that began on June 1 were more vigorous than anything the Spanish had previously encountered, and on July 21 their forward positions began to collapse like dominoes, rolling back the entire Spanish frontier more than 150 kilometers, to Melilla itself. For really hard fighting, the Spanish command had relied on the *regulares* and even on the tough native police, but nearly all of those in the eastern zone deserted, sometimes killing their Spanish officers. In some army units discipline vanished as well, leading to a frantic sauve qui peut. There were instances in which officers fled in the only automobiles available, abandoning troops to their fate. A number of others were shot down by their own troops when they tried to halt the stampede. Though there were examples of heroism, military comportment was often shameful.[17] Of the ten thousand or more Spanish dead, few were slain in combat. Most were killed while running away or after they had surrendered.[18]

If the Spanish disaster of 1921 is compared with the defeat of the Italian army in Ethiopia in 1896 or the British defeats in Africa in 1879 and 1883, it becomes clear that the Spanish forces performed much more poorly than their European counterparts. The British and Italian troops were heavily outnumbered, inflicted many more casualties, and in many instances fought to the end. Perhaps most telling of all was the fact that in the disaster only ninety Spanish officers were killed. Many others were either not with their units at all or simply fled, though a considerable number were taken prisoner, since they could be held for ransom.

The war also became more savage. Many Spanish troops who surrendered were slaughtered, while others were tortured and their corpses mutilated. Some of the few Spanish civilians caught in the maelstrom were likewise treated brutally. Decapitation of the fallen, an old Moroccan and Arab custom, was common. (As early as 1913, the high commissioner had admitted that Spanish troops sometimes did the same.) From the start, the Moroccan campaigns had occasionally been accompanied by atrocities against both sides and also against Moroccan civilians, but henceforth the conflict would be more brutal and intense and would sometimes assume aspects of total war against the native population. During the 1840s the French army had resorted to total war to complete the conquest of Algeria; after 1921 that became increasingly the Spanish policy in northern Morocco.

The Spanish government faced its gravest military challenge in a generation, as it became evident that much of the army was poorly prepared and even worse led. At first there was a patriotic response in part of Spanish society, accompanied by a brief surge of volunteering for military service that did not last long. In the immediate emergency, the government's first move was to transfer part of the legion to the critical eastern zone. Franco's own *bandera* had to do a fifty-kilometer forced march back to Tetuán, during which several soldiers perished of exhaustion, and then be rushed by train and ship to Melilla to help prevent the eastern city from being overrun. Once its defense had been made secure, legionnaire units became the spearhead of the limited counteroffensive that followed. Millán Astray, leading his men, suffered yet another severe wound and momentarily transferred command of the legion to Franco. A portion of the territory lost was regained, and this campaign established the legion as the army's new combat elite.

The most detailed portrait of Franco in this phase was penned by the leftist writer Arturo Barea, who served as a soldier in Morocco, in his later autobiographical trilogy *La forja de un rebelde*. He liberally paraphrased the purported remarks of a legionnaire as follows:

> You see, Franco. . . . No, look. The Tercio's rather like being in a prison. The most courageous brute is master of the jail. And something of this sort has happened to that man. He's hated, just as the convicts hate the bravest killer in their jail, and he's obeyed and respected—he imposes himself on all the others—just as the big killer imposes himself on the whole jail. You know how many officers of the Legion have been killed by a shot in the back during an attack. Now, there are many who would wish to shoot Franco in the back, but not one of them has the courage to do it. They're afraid that he might turn his head and see them just when they have taken aim at him.
>
> . . . It wouldn't be difficult to fire at Franco. He takes the lead in an advance, and—well, if somebody's got guts, you just have to admit it. I've seen him walk upright in front of the others, while they hardly dared to lift their heads from the ground, the bullets fell so thick.
>
> . . . Believe me, it's sticky going with Franco. You'll get whatever's due to you, and he knows where he's taking you, but as to the treatment you

get. . . . He simply looks blankly at a fellow, with very big and very serious eyes, and says "Execute him," and walks away, just like that. I've seen murderers go white in the face because Franco looked at them out of the corner of his eye. And he's fussy! God save you if anything's missing from your equipment, or if your rifle isn't clean, or you've been lazy. You know, that man's not quite human and he hasn't got any nerves. And then, he's quite isolated. I believe all the officers detest him because he treats them just like he treats us and isn't friends with any of them. They go on the loose and get drunk—I ask you, what else should a man do after two months on the firing line?—and he stays alone in the tent or in the barracks, just like one of those old clerks who simply must go to the office, even on Sundays. It's difficult to make him out—it's funny, because he's so young.[19]

This portrait is the imaginative reconstruction of a writer thirty years later and should not be accepted as accurate in detail, but it helps to show the kind of impression Franco made on some.

It is doubtful that his troops were as hostile to Franco as the sketch by Barea makes out. He was always a strict disciplinarian but understood the importance of being fair and consistent, and he kept his men better fed and supplied than was the norm. The extensive petty corruption so common in the Spanish army was very rare in the legion. When he was on campaign, Franco knew where he was leading his troops and how to place them in the most advantageous terrain. He had become a master of irregular warfare, unlike most of his fellow officers, avoiding ambushes and sometimes gaining the element of surprise, to the point of ordering unprecedented nighttime assaults.

Before the close of 1922 he wrote a brief memoir in the form of a diary of his battalion's last campaign, *Diario de una bandera* (*Diary of a Battalion*), his first significant publication.[20] At the beginning of 1924 he became one of the founders of a new military journal for the forces in Morocco, *Revista de tropas coloniales*, and, after the first year, head of its editorial board. Over the years he published many articles and short pieces of one kind or another, which eventually numbered more than forty.[21]

General José Sanjurjo, the new commander of the eastern zone, recommended Franco for promotion to lieutenant colonel in recognition of his leadership during the counteroffensive that restored the Spanish position during the summer and autumn of 1921, though at that time he had also reproached Franco for exposing himself to enemy fire unnecessarily while mounted on horseback. Once more the War Ministry ruled that he was too young and instead awarded him another combat decoration.

In the eastern zone Franco was on occasion reunited with his brother Ramón, the bond between the two remaining close, despite their contrasting personalities. Ramón had followed in Paco's footsteps by also entering the military academy at the age of fourteen, but beyond that they were very different. Ramón was highly idiosyncratic and individualistic, rebelling more and more against conventions. In army camps in Morocco he sometimes practiced nudism, walking around in the broiling sun wearing nothing but the broad-brimmed hat that the army wisely provided its troops. On other occasions he would go to the opposite extreme, covering himself with a native *djellaba*. Unlike his brother, Ramón applied himself to Arabic and learned enough to offer rudimentary courses to fellow officers. He soon tired of the infantry, however, which seemed to him prosaic, and applied for entry into the new glamour arm of the military—the small Spanish air force. He was accepted and soon became a skilled pilot of the new hydroplanes, on several occasions flying Paco over enemy positions in order to survey the terrain.

The closing of political ranks produced by the Rif disaster was brief, and by 1922 the conflict generated increasing opposition in Spain, not merely from the left but from moderates as well. Franco seems to have become convinced that Spanish Freemasons were behind the criticism of the army and the determination to prosecute Berenguer and others for dereliction of duty, which he felt generally to be undeserved. From this time may be dated his extreme opposition to the Masons, whom he saw as a supremely sinister and potentially dominating force, especially in Catholic countries. As was customary with conservative Catholics, he became convinced that their goal was to supplant Christianity, though many years later he would come to accept that in countries such as the United States, Britain, and Holland, the Masons were different—"buenos," even "cristianos"—but this recognition would be long in coming.[22]

The legion's commander, Millán Astray, had a reputation as an orator, and, as he recovered from his last major wound, he delivered several outspoken talks on the peninsula praising the work of the army and denouncing some of its critics for want of patriotism. This was judged beyond the pale; in November 1922 he was relieved of command, though that same month the government abolished the divisive advisory commissions of the councils within the army. Since Franco still lacked the rank to replace Millán Astray, Lieutenant Colonel Rafael de Valenzuela was transferred from the *regulares* to command the legion. Franco knew that Millán Astray had urged that he be allowed to take charge, and, since no one had done more than Franco himself to develop and lead the legion, he took the appointment of Valenzuela as an insult and asked to return to a command in the Oviedo garrison. During these last two years he had received several brief leaves to return to visit Carmen Polo. As he passed through Madrid on his way back from Morocco, he was acclaimed by the media for the first time as a major figure and national hero, and at least two banquets were held in his honor. In January 1923 Alfonso XIII awarded him yet another decoration and honored him with the status of *gentilhombre de cámara* (gentleman of the bedchamber), a major distinction enjoyed by very few and received by Franco with great pride.

A great celebration was held in his honor in Oviedo in March, where he was showered with praise. Felipe Polo had consented to the marriage, which was then scheduled for June. Just as the consummation that Franco had sought for so long was finally at hand, another military crisis intervened. Fighting had again become intense and Valenzuela, the legion's new commander, was killed in combat on June 5. In a continuing conflict that the Spanish military could not control, the legion had become more important than ever, and Franco was the logical successor to lead it. Three days after the death of Valenzuela, he was promoted to lieutenant colonel and appointed commander. This meant immediate departure and postponement of the nuptials, leaving Carmen in genuine anguish that her fiancé might suffer the fate of the legion's first two commanders. Franco, however, did not hesitate, and the news that he had postponed his own wedding to return to combat only added to his mystique. In the interviews of those months, he handled the publicity well, responding modestly and saying that he was merely doing his duty.[23]

Before the close of June he was back in the field at the head of the legion. Though he received word the following month that he had received hierarchical approval for the marriage (required for all officers), he devoted four months to reforming the legion and imposing yet higher standards, particularly on the officers. The military situation stabilized temporarily, and, having survived once more, Franco returned to Oviedo, where the wedding finally took place on October 22, with the king himself serving as best man, by proxy, yet another signal honor. In a certain sense he replaced Franco's own father, whom the conquering hero took care to exclude. It was the social event of the year in the small provincial capital, with crowds lining the streets afterward to catch a glimpse of the glamorous couple. The groom, now thirty years of age, and the bride, twenty-one, honeymooned modestly at La Piniella, the country estate of the Polo family outside Oviedo, since Franco could take no more than ten days of leave. En route to their new residence in Melilla, the newlyweds enjoyed the favor of a special audience with the king and queen, Alfonso XIII and Victoria Eugenia. Carmen expressed afterward her gratitude for the queen's graciousness and her wonder at the calm confidence with which her husband could discuss military affairs with the king.

The new couple then took up quarters in Melilla for the next two and a half years. Since Franco spent so much time in the field, his bride often saw little of her spouse and spent her time mainly in the company of other officers' wives. Her reaction to Morocco seems to have been more or less the opposite of her husband's, and in some respects, at least, this may have been for her the most disagreeable period of the long marriage, though not because of any fundamental disharmony between the two.

Franco was not passionate in his personal affections, but he was firm and devoted, and would ever prove a faithful and considerate husband. Though no more than superficial details of the married life of the new couple are known, it would be a happy and successful marriage, essentially the kind he had always sought. At home he called her Carmina, and she called him Paco. There would never be any sign of instability in this relationship, which in most respects was very conventional and fairly typical of the Spanish elite of that era; indeed, it was a constant source of emotional support for Franco all the rest of his life. His daughter remembers: "My father was completely identified with my mother. Yes, they got along very well. And the marriage brought my father a great sense of peace and security. He left in the hands of Mamá everything to do with the household and with my education. . . . Papá was completely identified with her."

The only known anxiety in the early part of the marriage was that two full years passed without Carmen being able to conceive a child. This was troublesome to both of them, and apparently they consulted medical specialists. One concern was that the abdominal wound suffered in 1916 might have interfered somehow with Franco's reproductive functioning, though there was no clear evidence of that. The conclusion by physicians was that this initial sterility would probably be temporary and that the newlyweds must be patient.[24]

Six weeks before the wedding, Lieutenant General Miguel Primo de Rivera had suddenly put an end to parliamentary government in Madrid by leading the last classic *pronunciamiento* in Spanish history. It was the first decisive intervention by the military in half a century and, encountering only weak resistance from the leaders of parliament, was quickly accepted by the king. This bloodless takeover initially even drew praise from key liberal intellectuals, who hailed the appearance of an "iron surgeon" as the best way to cut the Gordian knot of crucial reform, yet the military directorate that Primo de Rivera set up would be the first full military dictatorship in Spanish history. Though the continuing stalemate in Morocco was only one of several factors that led to the *pronunciamiento*—the others being political division and stagnation and revolutionary violence in the industrial centers—the establishment of a military directory indicated how destructive the stalemate had become.

Franco's reaction to the *pronunciamiento* is not known, for in that phase of life he never involved himself in politics. Since even noted liberals like José Ortega y Gasset hoped for decisive change under the new government, Franco may have had the same reaction, but he could not have been pleased with the fact that Primo de Rivera had a reputation as an "abandonista" regarding the protectorate. After the newlyweds' royal audience, Franco had also been invited to dine with the king and the dictator, on which occasion he pressed his conviction that pacifying and preserving the protectorate was vitally important. He admitted the need for momentary military retrenchment, but he maintained that that was necessary only in order to launch a definitive offensive that would occupy the Rif and crush the insurrection. In an article that appeared in the *Revista de tropas coloniales* in April 1924, Franco strongly criticized "passivity" and described the policy that Spain had been following as producing a mere "parody of a Protectorate." The new dictator responded by placing the *Revista* under light censorship, though there was no reprisal against Franco.

Primo de Rivera speculated about the possibility of trading Ceuta to Great Britain in exchange for Gibraltar and then withdrawing from Morocco altogether, but this was a deal that London would not even discuss. Alternately, he explored a political solution, offering a pact to the chief Moroccan strongman in the western zone, El Raisuni, and internal autonomy for Abd el Krim under a formal statute of the Rif, with a personal three-thousand-man army and public works to be subsidized by the Spanish government.[25]

Three years earlier the Rif leader might have accepted such a compromise, but by 1924 his goal was independence. He had declared his own "Republic of the Rif," forming an organized government of sorts, imposed fundamental reforms, and worked hard to overcome tribal disunity. He received strong support from Salafist (neo-orthodox) activists in his territory, as he relied on Islamic revivalism and jihad to motivate and unify his followers. Early in 1924 he began to take over the central zone of the protectorate and then moved farther into the western sector as well.

With the insurrection gaining strength, Primo de Rivera made an inspection tour in July 1924 and on the nineteenth visited Franco's legion base in the eastern zone. It is not clear whether he was aware that Franco and other officers were talking about resigning their commands if Primo ordered a major retreat. At the welcoming banquet the dictator (as he was sometimes called in that more plain-spoken age) encountered a banner on the wall citing the legion's motto of "fierce, all-out attack," and Franco greeted him with a very assertive speech that stressed any withdrawal was unacceptable, while the vehement Varela was even more outspoken. Though greatly provoked, Primo de Rivera remained calm and stressed the overriding need for discipline whether orders were agreeable or not. Franco seems to have offered to resign the leadership of the legion, but the dictator invited him to a conciliatory private meeting, and the resignation, which Primo de Rivera refused to accept, was withdrawn. Though some of the officers in the eastern zone muttered of the need to take action against the dictator, it seems unlikely that Franco was involved in a genuine conspiracy against him, as has been alleged.[26]

Primo de Rivera had to face the fact that the "prompt, sensible and dignified" solution to the Moroccan nightmare he had promised was nowhere to be found and that the growing force of the revolt had created international complications, which only increased the pressure on the Spanish government. He decided to carry out a limited strategic withdrawal, if only to *reculer pour mieux sauter*. Should Abd el Krim continue to refuse to negotiate, Primo de Rivera would have to carry out a major reorganization of the armed forces in order to launch a new initiative to crush him. This meant holding the line of limited occupation in the east while withdrawing from much of the western sector prior to an eventual counteroffensive.

He moved Franco and all the *banderas* of the legion back to the western zone to help cover this operation, which required abandoning some four hundred small positions. Franco played a key role in the operation and directed the rear guard in its most dangerous phase, the retreat from Xauen to the vicinity of Tetuán, a complex operation that lasted nearly a month.[27] It was a sad and bitter experience that he later described in an article for the *Revista*. He temporarily became the director of the review, writing an article a month for the next year or so. Franco's obedience and customary strong performance were rewarded with another decoration and promotion to colonel in February 1925, with a full year of seniority added, while the legion was expanded to eight *banderas*.

Primo de Rivera improved both the discipline and training of an expanded army that was being equipped with somewhat better weapons and supplies, the military budget having been bolstered by the rapid expansion of the economy during these years. The air force grew with the addition of more than 150 planes and began playing a more active role.[28] More sinister was the use of poison gas in Morocco, first tentatively employed on a very limited scale in November 1921, soon after the Anwal disaster, and then with ever greater frequency from mid-1923 on. By 1924 Spain had become the first state to drop mustard gas bombs from the air, something not done during World War I.[29]

All the while France maintained a kind of neutrality in the increasingly ruthless conflict waged in the Spanish zone. It was eventually drawn in nonetheless because the geographical delimitation between the spheres of the two powers had been vague, and there was a tendency for French authority to extend northward. Abd el Krim found his southern flank exposed and, after the French refused to negotiate with him, decided to take control of disputed territory. He gambled that he could strengthen his position by pushing the French back, attacking the northern tier of their outposts in April 1925. This proved a fatal miscalculation, though Abd el Krim's veteran forces, even if small in numbers, at first took the French by surprise. They surged to within thirty-five kilometers of Fez, yet he continued to devote much of his strength to attacking Spanish positions in the north. The situation suddenly became very threatening to Paris, and after Abd el Krim once more rejected a moderate compromise, the two European powers signed a pact of military cooperation to suppress the insurgency completely. A French army of 160,000 troops would move from the south while a Spanish force of 75,000 men would attack from the north. The key operation would be a Spanish amphibious invasion of the Bay of Alhucemas, at the heart of the insurgency in the homeland of Abd el Krim's own kabyle.

Despite the relative backwardness of the Spanish military, this complex amphibious undertaking became the first fully successful joint forces operation (land, sea, and air) of the twentieth century. The Spanish command wisely decided not to land in the bay itself, which would be heavily defended, but around the corner of an adjacent peninsula. Like several other senior officers, Franco had a number of opportunities to scout the scene of operations from the air, in his case in a military hydroplane piloted by his brother Ramón. Despite choppy seas, the operation began about noon on September 8, 1925, and at first faced only light opposition. Franco was in charge of the initial force, whose core consisted of seven battalions of the legion and the *regulares*. Contrary to the preference of the naval commander, he insisted that the operation go ahead, despite very difficult conditions at sea, which capsized some landing boats and dashed others on the rocks. He nonetheless soon established a firm beachhead. There the Spanish units dug in, unable to bring their full strength and all their supplies ashore for a number of days because of the continued rough water. Determined counterattacks were beaten off on the thirteenth and fourteenth, the breakout finally beginning on the twenty-third, with Franco commanding one of the five columns. He was the only senior officer to receive special praise in his brigadier's initial report.[30] The advance made steady progress and soon occupied the heartland of the insurgency, while the French moved forward from the south, catching Abd el Krim between two fires. The campaign continued for more than seven months, until this remarkable leader finally surrendered to the French in May 1926. The insurgency in the protectorate had at last been put down, the final small rebel groups being brought under control in 1927.[31]

The Spanish administration then began to replace its harsh military policy with greater conciliation. It retained virtually all Abd el Krim's key reforms—linguistic Arabization, the building of more schools, imposition of Islamic sharia in place of the customary law of the kabyles, the ending of blood feuds and of clan independence and the development of greater central administration. The Spanish relied on a carrot-and-stick system, controlling local Moroccan leaders through a network of military administrators and special payments that might alternately be called subsidies or bribes.[32] Native leaders came to find the Spanish terms acceptable, at least for the time being. After 1927, the society of northern Morocco enjoyed the benefits of peace for the first time in many years. This, together with improved sanitary and medical conditions, produced an increase in population. Later, in an ironic reversal, Abd el Krim's native kabyle would not welcome Spain's final departure in 1956, when it fell under the central control of the newly independent sultan in Rabat. Two years afterward, it rebelled again and, though the Spanish had eliminated firearms in the Rif, for several months the Rifis resisted with determination, leading to a second invasion of Alhucemas by the new Moroccan army (its initial commander was a native Moroccan who had earlier reached the rank of general in Franco's forces).

The war in Spanish Morocco was the most prominent conflict in the Afro-Asian world between 1921 and 1926, except for the civil war in China, receiving much publicity abroad. Abd el Krim had become an international figure who elicited the mediation of the papacy and the League of

Nations and who, in the English-speaking world, was romanticized in the musical and movie *The Desert Song*. His had been the most powerful anti-colonial insurgency in that era, and in the long struggle the Spanish forces had lost nearly sixty-five thousand men, though less than twenty-five thousand of them were combat fatalities (almost half of these occurring in the collapse of the eastern zone in 1921). Like many colonial and counterinsurgency conflicts, it eventually became a kind of total war, marked by many atrocities on both sides, including the use of poison gas, and some legionnaires and other Spanish troops mutilated the enemy dead, just as the insurgents did.

The Moroccan conflict became the central experience of Franco's life. Though he never showed any particular interest in Moroccan culture and apparently never tried to learn Arabic as did his brother Ramón, he considered the retention of the protectorate absolutely fundamental to Spain's status, which he hoped to see increase further. There is some evidence that over the next few years he hoped to return again in a higher capacity, possibly even as high commissioner.

Flanked by the expanded units of the *regulares*, Franco's legion had established itself as the elite of the Spanish army. It eventually numbered six thousand men, and in six years of fighting it suffered eight thousand total combat casualties, two thousand of them fatal. Its first commander had been gravely wounded, its second slain in battle. The legion's grim motto as "Los novios de la muerte" ("The Betrothed of Death") reflected its special mystique, which attracted attention in France as well. An admiring French feature film, *La bandera*, starring the popular Jean Gabin as a French volunteer in the legion, would appear in 1934.[33]

No field officer had accomplished more than Franco, and in recognition he was promoted to brigadier general on February 3, 1926. At thirty-three years and two months, he was said to be the youngest general in any army of Europe, and he had become the most celebrated single figure in the Spanish military. Franco was made head of the First Brigade of the First Infantry Division in Madrid, the most prestigious such assignment in the army, though he was disappointed that a rival, the capable young brigadier Manuel Goded, had been promoted to major general (*general de división*) and made the new chief of operations in the protectorate, equivalent to second in command. Carmen Polo, however, was delighted to depart bare, hot, dusty Morocco, so different from her native Asturias. The "Moroccan period" of Franco's life came to an end, and he had to watch the final year of campaigning from the Spanish capital. The struggle in Africa had constituted the formative part of his career, an experience that he would ever after recall with nostalgia. For the remainder of his long life, reminiscing about Morocco would be his favorite conversational theme, highlighted by the unprecedentedly successful landing in the Bay of Alhucemas, which he recounted innumerable times.

It was a very specific and also very limited kind of experience, a colonial war waged against irregular forces and not against a modern army, though for an entire century such campaigns had formed a common apprenticeship for younger European officers. Franco had learned very well the art of command, how to maintain the discipline and cohesion of troops under enemy fire, how to deal with crisis situations in combat, how to organize new units and how to administer logistics. He had become a notable specialist in counterinsurgency warfare, and in his memoir he explained that he had learned that the common Franco-Spanish tactic of direct bayonet assault was not necessarily the best approach.[34] He had learned the importance of distributing his forces so as not to present concentrated targets and of the need for mobile reserves to reinforce attacks or deal with emergencies. Firepower and advanced weaponry could be crucial, but so were experienced officers and noncommissioned officers, as well as proper rest, food, and supplies. Yet he had never commanded more than ten thousand troops at a time and had gained no experience in the complexities of larger forces or of combat with sophisticated enemy units supplied with the most advanced weapons. The handful of tanks that had supported his battalions during his last year in Morocco had played little role, and the latest concepts and tactics being developed at that moment in Berlin, Moscow, and elsewhere were unknown in the Spanish army. Franco learned only a little of these innovations through reading and desk study.[35]

Paradoxically, on the very day that his promotion to general was announced, he would suddenly find himself only the second most famous of the Franco brothers. That day the Spanish press was full of headlines about the remarkable feat of Ramón Franco, the pilot in charge of the first Spanish flight across the Atlantic to South America. After a long trajectory that involved seven different stages and landings, totaling nineteen days, his hydroplane reached its final destination in Buenos Aires.[36] This accomplishment was hailed as the twentieth-century technological equivalent of the voyage of Columbus, occurring more than a year before the remarkable solo flight of Charles Lindbergh across the North Atlantic. It earned the enthusiastic plaudits of the Spanish government and those of Latin America, for some time making Ramón Franco the most famous living

Spaniard. One historic flight temporarily eclipsed the celebrity of many years of combat in Morocco, but there was no indication of resentment on the part of Franco. Though the two brothers had grown far apart in personal values and style of life, the bond between them remained close. Soon afterward, Franco would declare that the three happiest days of his life were those of his marriage with Carmen, the successful landing in Alhucemas, and the news of Ramón's safe arrival in South America.

3 | Director of the General Military Academy

(1926–1931)

In Madrid a new life opened for Franco, and during the first weeks he enjoyed considerable acclaim. His old classmates from the infantry academy in Toledo held a special ceremony in honor of the first of them to reach the rank of general, presenting him with a dress sword. During the week of February 7, 1926, a series of celebrations took place in El Ferrol in honor of his mother, Doña Pilar, acclaiming the exploits of both of her famous sons, though neither was present to enjoy the tribute. The mass turnout that took place in Madrid on February 10, however, cheered only Ramón's flight to Buenos Aires, not the achievements of his older brother. Later, during the Corpus Christi procession in the capital, Franco took a place of honor in command of the troops escorting the host, and then in 1927 he was invited to accompany the king and queen on an inspection trip to Morocco.

The most important event of the first year back in Spain, however, took place in Oviedo, where Franco's only child, Carmen, was born on

September 14, 1926, in the Polo family home. Becoming a father may have been the greatest pure joy of his life and, near the end of it, he recalled, "When the baby girl was born I almost went crazy" with delight.[1] Long known to the family as Carmencita to distinguish her from her mother, Doña Carmen, for many years, her parents and other intimates usually called her by the nickname Nenuca.[2] This lively little dark-haired girl would grow into a handsome woman and would ever be the apple of her father's eye, living her entire life near him. The father/daughter bond always remained close, though, being so traditional, Franco left the rearing of his daughter to his wife. He was a proud parent, sometimes even doting, but, as Carmencita was growing up, his increasing responsibilities would leave him less and less time with the family, at least until the end of the Civil War. She recalls: "He was a very good father, but he did not always deal that much with me, since, as a girl, my upbringing was much more in my mother's hands. This was especially the way it was in that era. . . . He, Mamá and I made up the nuclear family . . . , but if he had major professional or patriotic responsibilities, he would tend to us in the background. Then, when he was not so pressed, he devoted more time to his family."

Gossip soon developed about the daughter's birth and would continue in one form or another for many years. This would take many guises, usually related to speculations regarding Franco's sexual vigor (more precisely, his lack of it), often alleging that he was not the real father.[3] It would be claimed that no one had ever seen Doña Carmen pregnant, or that the real father was Ramón Franco, or even that Carmencita was a year or so older than reported and was a Moroccan orphan adopted before the couple left Melilla.[4] All this gossip, however, is baseless, for regarding her birth and parentage there was never anything more than meets the eye. Franco's sex life may be considered prosaic, depending on one's values, but there is no reason to think it abnormal in any way. His wife had returned to Oviedo at the beginning of June 1926, to be with her dying father and, after his rapid demise, decided to remain in the family home to give birth. Her friends there witnessed her in an advanced state of gestation, and the birth was announced in the Oviedo press two days after it occurred. In later life, Franco would sometimes wistfully remark that he and his wife would have liked to have had more children, but that apparently it was not to be.

Franco's assignment in Madrid was relatively prestigious, but not particularly demanding. In typical military style, he delegated considerable responsibility to his staff, so that he had a good deal of free time. In addition to spending more time with his now expanded family, he also did more reading. In one interview he indicated that his favorite contemporary writer was the eccentric modernist Ramón María de Valle-Inclán, though he would later say that his reading was directed more toward history and economics. He began to form a personal library, later destroyed when the family's Madrid apartment was looted by revolutionaries in 1936. He also had the opportunity to become better acquainted with the Prado Museum, one of the world's finest, which attracted him because of his lifelong devotion to drawing and his later passion for painting. His favorite painter was Velázquez.

The two years in the capital were a time of expanded social life, though it was somewhat limited by the fact that even a brigadier's salary was not that large. The Francos enjoyed going out, mainly to movies and the theater, and Doña Carmen liked to shop for antiques. She soon was bequeathed property and other items from her father's estate and would manage her own financial interests throughout the marriage with a separate account that Franco apparently always respected.

He became a member of the elite club, La Gran Peña, on the Gran Vía, and also participated in the circle of the veteran liberal politician Natalio Rivas, who was interested in the celebrated general and drew him into his conversations. Rivas well knew that the present dictatorship could not last long, and he saw Spain's future as uncertain. In February 1926 he had arranged for Franco to meet briefly with José Sánchez Guerra, a progressive conservative and a leader of the opposition to the dictator. In his diary, Rivas recorded that he urged Franco to inform himself as broadly as possible about public affairs but that he was dismayed to find that although Franco seemed at first not to be personally committed to Primo de Rivera per se, he preferred an authoritarian system to a directly elected parliamentary regime.[5] This reflected a significant development in his political thinking, such as it was. He had not become a supporter of the ultra-right, however, if for no other reason than that he remained a professional officer who sought to stay out of politics.

In 1926 he had a very brief stint as an actor, appearing in the silent film *La malcasada* (*The Unhappy Wife*), hardly the kind of theme that he normally dealt with, in the part of an officer who had recently returned from Morocco. Franco did not have a voice for the stage, but that was irrelevant in silent movies. On another occasion, he participated in an early version of a home movie, made in his social circle, revealing a very different young Franco from the later image. In the film, he was talkative and even vivacious. This aspect of his personality, always recessive, would be increasingly repressed after the beginning of the Civil War, though under the right circumstances, it was never entirely absent until his ailing later years, when he suffered from Parkinson's disease.

Nonetheless, although aspects of elite social and cultural life in the capital were enjoyable to him, this was not the ambience in which the Francos could be most comfortable at that stage of their lives. Even in Madrid, his only close companions were old comrades from Morocco, such as Millán Astray, Varela, Luis Orgaz, and Emilio Mola. He also arranged that his second cousin and great friend Pacón be assigned to his staff as his personal military aide, which began a long period in which Pacón would hold that post, one that later grew steadily in importance and rank as Franco assumed ever greater prominence.

Most important was that Franco held the favor of Primo de Rivera, who had come to appreciate him not only because of his leadership in the field but also because he was careful to keep his nose out of politics. This was the more important because the most serious opposition to Primo de Rivera did not come from the politicians whose parties and movements had been suppressed but from mounting dissatisfaction within the army.

Some of the resistance came from elderly generals who supported the constitutional system, but much of it stemmed from professional opposition to the dictator's efforts to reform the army itself. The army's worst problem over the last hundred years had been the hypertrophy of the officer corps, which in 1927 included twenty thousand officers and more than five thousand reserve officers, amounting to one officer for every seven soldiers. Now that the Moroccan campaign was over, Primo de Rivera sought a smaller, less expensive, and more professional army. Another problem that stood in the way was the lingering division between *junteros* and *africanistas* and the opposition among the former to merit promotion. This was particularly strong among the artillery and engineers, two technical corps that stood to gain little or nothing from merit promotions. There were two abortive politico-military conspiracies and revolts, both the work in large measure of dissident officers, the first in 1926 and the second three years later. On each occasion, the dictator dissolved the artillery corps and then reconstructed it. In neither case was Franco involved, but the policies of the dictatorship, military and civil, had divided the officer corps, and this, for the moment, at least, had become Primo de Rivera's most serious single problem.[6]

One conclusion the dictator reached was that these divisions stemmed at least partly from the fact that since 1893 there had been four separate military academies, one for infantry, one for cavalry, one for artillery, and one for engineers. He judged that a more unified esprit de corps could be achieved by reestablishing a military academy to provide basic officer development for all four corps, though members of the technical corps would also have their own advanced instruction.

Franco, he concluded, would be the man to lead it, because he was not merely a skilled combat officer but also a commander of superior mental ability, as well as a proud and strict professional who did not meddle in politics. In the dictator's judgment, Franco could build an academy that would imbue cadets with a patriotic spirit that concentrated on improving discipline and professionalism. Franco, scarcely thirty-five years of age, was thoroughly pleased with the new assignment, which he found both flattering and challenging.

He would have preferred that the academy be located in El Escorial, because of its identity with imperial Spain, but Primo de Rivera insisted on the Aragonese capital of Zaragoza. Franco went to Zaragoza in December 1927 to begin the preparation of the new facilities, and the family moved to the city two months later. The domestic circle also expanded, since at that point two of Doña Carmen's younger siblings, Ramona (always known as Zita) and Felipe Polo (her only brother, named for his father), devoted much time to visits, finding life with the Francos more stimulating than life in Oviedo.[7] This also initiated a lifelong pattern in which Franco's family circle was filled to a large extent by his in-laws—first the siblings of Doña Carmen, then, later, the large family of Carmencita's husband— rather than his own siblings or other close relatives on his own side of the family. It also reflected the extent to which, despite his close relations with his older brother and his sister, he left such things to his wife.

The newly reestablished General Military Academy (Academia General Militar) welcomed its first class in Zaragoza in the autumn of 1928. Franco devoted himself heart and soul to development of the academy, which stipulated that all entering cadets must be between seventeen and twenty-two years of age. He was determined that there be no more fourteen-year-old candidates who would have to suffer what he had endured. The academy stressed the moral and psychological formation of cadets, building a structure that emphasized discipline, patriotism, a spirit of service and sacrifice, extreme physical valor, and also loyalty to established institutions, such as the monarchy. He established a "decalogue" for his cadets, a set of ten commandments rather similar to the Credo legionario, stressing duty, honor and country, and especially courage, sacrifice, and self-denial. These were themes drawn from the director's own life. Technical education was not the primary goal, for candidates for specialized corps would later be sent to advanced training elsewhere. A fundamental problem, however, was that the academy did not have all the facilities to prepare its pupils fully in the rapidly changing military theory and practice of the 1920s.

Its curriculum was primarily drawn up by the man Franco chose as sub-director, Colonel Miguel Campins, a personal friend who had participated in the Alhucemas operation and was one of the army's most studious officers.[8] In appointing instructors, preference was given those who had won promotion by combat merits, as well as by exhibiting special ability in technical areas or in developing their individual units. The academy was therefore dominated by the *africanista* sector of the officer corps and reflected their prizing of physical valor and decisiveness. The academy stressed above all moral values, courage, and determination, and to that extent resembled more the Japanese military culture of the 1920s than it did innovative European military thinking.

Practical training drew more emphasis than the book learning of the old Toledo academy. Franco banned official textbooks, demanding that the instructors draw on experience and stress practical adaptation. Weapons training received attention but, at a time when the most innovative armies in Europe were looking toward tanks and armor, Franco emphasized horsemanship, a drill that he sometimes personally supervised. He would have liked to provide more training in the field, but facilities were limited.

Franco was very fussy about certain matters. Though he emphasized toughness, he also took measures to eliminate hazing. He even interfered in the mess hall, where he arranged to import a special new machine from Germany to slice and chop bread crumbs for soup. Even more than in Africa, Franco achieved a reputation as a martinet, setting traps for cadets who might pass him in the streets, when he was looking in the opposite direction, without saluting. He hoped to inculcate his own personal values. Even though he recognized that he could not eliminate fornication, for example, he was determined to curtail venereal disease and was said to have required that each cadet carry a condom whenever going on leave into the city. However much a stickler in minor matters, the concepts which he sought to impart seem, on the whole, to have been absorbed. When the Civil War began in 1936, approximately 95 percent of the former Zaragoza cadets would line up with Franco, a distinctly higher proportion than in the army as a whole.[9]

Among his peers, Franco does not seem to have been a harsh or even especially rigorous administrator of his academy staff. He personally selected all the instructional officers, then delegated considerable authority, which was normal for an army commander. He allowed subordinates to follow their own specialties, so long as they fit in with the curriculum. There was little turnover during the academy's short life, and Franco did not intervene much to improve, nor did he dismiss, the more laggard instructors, so long as they followed the general guidelines.

Like Spanish military doctrine since the early eighteenth century, the academy was to model French and German military culture, as evidenced by Franco's preparatory visit to the French military academy at St. Cyr in 1928. A year later, while director, he received an official invitation to visit the German infantry academy in Dresden, which he accepted with pleasure. During his brief time there, Franco was deeply impressed by German military culture and traditions. Though this did not result in any new initiative to reorient the academy, the visit to Germany had a lasting effect, and his respect for the German military would only grow in the future.

In each of his temporary homes in Spain, from Oviedo to Madrid to Zaragoza, Franco had leaped a step up the social ladder. In the Aragonese capital, the new academy enjoyed great prestige and the Francos moved in the highest circles of society. These were probably the years of the most active normal social life they would ever know. The general dressed in civilian clothes when off duty and the couple frequently attended movies and the theater. Franco would long maintain certain of his contacts in Zaragoza and continued to use the services of his favorite photographer and his favorite shoe store there for years. It was in Zaragoza, apparently, that Franco began to join the local elite in hunting excursions, and, with the years, hunting eventually became his favorite form of physical recreation. And in Zaragoza the first street to be named after Franco was christened in May 1929.

Doña Carmen, still only twenty-five when they moved to the Aragonese capital, was able to shine in the public eye for the first time. She came into her own as a social leader and hostess, frequently organizing receptions and other events for the wives of the academy instructors.

In May 1929 the magazine *Estampa* published an interview with Doña Carmen as part of a series on the wives of important Spaniards, and the general also took part. She referred discreetly to her husband's determined courtship, while Franco himself revealed that his favorite hobby was painting, though he rarely had much time to pursue it. He had always drawn high marks for drawing as a schoolboy, but this was the first public reference to a hobby that he would later develop at least a modest degree of skill in, in the form of water colors. His wife pointed out helpfully that he did paint rag dolls for Carmencita. When asked to mention several of the more frustrating qualities of her illustrious spouse, she declared that he was "too fond of Africa and reads books that I don't understand." She cited music as her favorite pastime, and when asked to state her greatest antipathy, she declared "the Moors," for she most decidedly did not share Franco's enthusiasm for Morocco. Franco made clear that he was not necessarily satisfied with the high status he had already achieved, when, after being asked for his greatest ambition, he replied that it was to see Spain "become great again," a political goal that he held much more highly and consciously than did other officers.[10]

The most important social contact that he made during the academy years was a man who became a member of his own family. Doña Carmen's younger sister, Zita, considered by some the most attractive of the three Polo girls, won the heart of a young man who stood out as the city's most eligible bachelor. Ramón Serrano Suñer was born in 1901, nine years after Franco, and had gained a brilliant reputation as, reportedly, the top law student in Spain. He soon qualified as an "abogado del Estado," a "state lawyer" in the Spanish system modeled on the French administrative elite. The handsome, blond, and blue-eyed Ramón Serrano was considered so appetizing a catch by the young ladies of Zaragozan society that they nicknamed him "jamón Serrano" (Serrano ham, the most popular kind). The one he fell in love with was Zita Polo, and the two were married in Oviedo in February 1931, in one of the major social events of the year. Franco was one of three "testigos" ("witnesses," or best men), another being Serrano's best friend, José Antonio Primo de Rivera, the talented and attractive eldest son of the dictator. These three would all play major roles in the Spanish drama of the following decade, which would eventually place the country's destinies in the hands of Franco and also, to a much lesser degree for a brief time, in those of Serrano Suñer.

The only part of his family life during these years that proved worrisome was the increasingly scandalous antics of his famous brother Ramón, still at that point the most celebrated of the Francos. Though a shade shorter yet than the general, the green-eyed Ramón was an extrovert, normally jolly and expansive, and also increasingly radical in his personal leanings and political sympathies. He also liked to write, his principal publications being his three brief memoirs of his main adventures, and he was interested in the world of art, inclining in his tastes toward the Bohemian and the avant-garde (in contrast to his brother, who tastes were traditional). Ramón also became a Freemason, while during these same years

Franco developed an extreme abhorrence of Masonry, which would remain his major phobia until the end of his life.

Pilar Franco later spread the story that her brother had married a cabaret singer, but this was not the case. In 1924 Ramón had wed Carmen Díaz, a young woman of solid middle-class background, daughter of an industrial engineer. The only irregularity was that he had just been assigned to service in Morocco and, rather than waiting for the approval required by statute for the wedding of an officer, he and Carmen dashed across the French border to be married in Hendaye.[11] Only a few years later, after he had become a celebrity, Ramón (who may have been clinically bipolar) developed an increasingly manic style of life, spending large amounts of time on the town enjoying himself, developing multiple personal and political contacts, drinking, gambling, and running up debts. Moreover, as a rabid atheist and anticlerical, he even insisted that his wife stop going to church. It eventually became too much for Carmen Díaz, and the two separated, later to be divorced, as Ramón sought greater freedom to pursue his extravagant lifestyle.[12]

He was as brave as Paco, but, rather than being a rigidly disciplined professional, Ramón was much more a freewheeling adventurer, despite (or perhaps owing to) his serious study of aeronautics. In 1927 he was placed under military arrest for five days for disrespect of authority. Ramón then attempted a second Atlantic crossing in 1929, this time to North America, on the first leg of an attempted around-the-world flight, but his aircraft failed and had to make an emergency landing in the Atlantic. The crew floated at sea in their plane for seven days before being picked up. Moreover, it was a new Dornier hydroplane manufactured in Italy, which was more reliable than the same model assembled in Cádiz, with Italian parts. The Spanish authorities, however, had insisted that the flight be carried out in an aircraft "made in Spain," whether or not the assembly process in Cádiz was fully efficient. Ramón was charged with having disobeyed orders and having improperly changed the plane's license, leading to the false rumor that he had been bribed by the Germans. All this created a scandal. Colonel Alfredo Kindelán, commander of the small Spanish air force, removed Ramón from military duty, placing him on the inactive reserve list, a great humiliation for him and for the entire Franco family.[13]

Things got worse. Following expulsion, Ramón became a political subversive and in 1930 joined the Republican military conspiracy against the monarchy, which appalled his siblings. Through it all Franco remained an aggrieved but still affectionate and concerned older brother. Ramón criticized him for running a "reactionary" academy, while prating that he would only obey what he called his "conscience," which seemed capable of following any fad. Franco lectured him through letters and other communications about the errors of his ways and urged him to reform. In October 1930, when he learned from the police that Ramón was in serious trouble, Franco traveled to Madrid, where he talked to Ramón until 3 a.m. in an attempt to convince him to draw back before it was too late. Within a matter of hours his brother was arrested, charged with preparing explosives for subversive activities and engaging in illegal arms trafficking. Six weeks later, in keeping with his larger-than-life persona, Ramón escaped, fleeing abroad to join other Republican conspirators.[14]

Around this time, Franco's elder brother, Nicolás, came to Zaragoza to discuss the situation. The increasingly pudgy Nicolás, putting on weight like all the brothers, had become the prosperous director of the Unión Naval de Levante, a Valencian shipyard owned by Juan March. He made a considerable impression when he arrived at the academy attired in an expensive suit, his personal limousine driven by a black chauffeur in a fancy uniform.

As the director of an important national institution, Franco developed a greater interest in politics. In 1927 Primo de Rivera gave him a guest subscription to the *Bulletin de l'Entente Internationale contre la Troisième Internationale*, an anti-Comintern newsletter edited in Geneva. Thenceforth he added Communism to Masonry as the second major subversive menace threatening Spain and the Western world, thus further crystalizing his political thinking. His early opposition to the dictator had nothing to do with democratic ideals but simply with their differences over the protectorate, and he ended as a firm supporter of Primo de Rivera, who had overlooked his initial abrasiveness and had promoted his career decisively.

At this point, however, Franco was more interested in economics than politics. His new brother-in-law Serrano Suñer later declared that in Zaragoza Franco talked much more about the former than the latter, considering himself "strong" in the field of economics. This was to some extent a matter of self-delusion, since he was a rather superficial autodidact on economics, but his opinions grew ever stronger. By the summer of 1929 he felt capable of giving advice to the government.

Primo de Rivera presided over the most humane dictatorship in twentieth-century Europe, which carried out no executions for purely political offenses and imprisoned very few. It constituted Spain's first experience in direct authoritarianism without any cover of constitutionalism, but it fell apart in 1928–29, when it convened a controlled parliamentary assembly in a vain attempt to achieve legitimacy. Not a Fascist regime, its political organization, the Unión Patriótica, was essentially a kind of claque, a propaganda support group that lacked political structure and could not become the basis of a new regime; Primo de Rivera had failed to institutionalize any new system. When, at the end, he looked toward Italian Fascism as a model, it was too late. He faced widespread military conspiracy, and Alfonso XIII demanded his resignation at the close of January 1930.

Primo de Rivera did not fundamentally change the structure of Spain's economy, which soared to a new level of relative prosperity and accelerated modernization amid the boom of the 1920s, but he instituted statist and corporatist policies, with new regulations and central coordination and restrictions, including a system of bilateral committees (*comités paritarios*) to negotiate urban labor contracts. Under Primo de Rivera, Spain capitalized on all the achievements and investments of the past half century, reaching an economic plateau it would not find again for two decades.

One of its numerous mistakes, however, was to try to maintain an overvalued peseta, which handicapped exports. By the summer of 1929, the peseta was already under attack because of large-scale imports and a poor harvest. On vacation in Gijón on the north coast not far from his home town, Franco encountered Primo de Rivera and his ministers and was invited to have lunch with them. On that occasion, he offered his first known economic advice, advising the able young finance minister José Calvo Sotelo that there was no need to worry about the run on the peseta. The government should spend its money on internal development and not concern itself much about the currency. A sovereign state could ignore currency fluctuations, keeping its internal reserves secret (at that moment rather sizable in Spain) and concentrating instead on its main priorities.[15] In 1929 this was inconsequential advice from an amateur, yet it was also one of the first indications of Franco's own economic concepts, strongly oriented toward voluntarism, statism, internal development, and deficit financing, all of which would later become official policy under his dictatorship.

After forcing the resignation of Primo de Rivera, Alfonso XIII appointed an interim government under General Dámaso Berenguer to prepare the return to constitutional rule. This became known as the "dictablanda" ("soft rule"), as distinct from the "dictadura" ("dictatorship" or "hard rule"). The new government was lenient and sought to appease the opposition, but it still governed by decree and was unable to find civilian politicians to lead a return to constitutionalism. Spain's most able and responsible leader, the Catalan politician Francesc Cambó, might have been willing to undertake the task but he was suddenly afflicted with throat cancer and unable to function for the next year. In one of the most extraordinary failures of leadership in a European era known for such failures, no other experienced civilian figure would accept responsibility to conduct new elections. This was only the first in the sequence of massive failures of political leadership in Spain during the 1930s, revealing a pathology almost without parallel in Europe. Berenguer thus governed for more than a year without proceeding to the next step, losing all credibility while opposition to the monarchy became more intense.

Franco was dismayed by this course of events, which he largely attributed to internal subversion. It began to seem the political equivalent of the military disaster in 1921. At one point Berenguer, seeking to strengthen his weak government, discussed with Franco the possibility of promoting him to major general and naming him undersecretary of war. Berenguer was evidently hoping to solidify the army politically by appointing a strong disciplinarian and hard-liner not likely to be influenced by agitation, but ultimately he abandoned this line of thinking. Appointing a hard-liner would have undercut the general strategy of appeasement, and the decision might have come too late, in any event. Instead, to the disgust of Franco, Berenguer appointed a personal rival of his, General Manuel Goded, who had acted as chief of operations during the final campaign in Morocco but more recently had been one of the leaders of the military conspiracy against the government. This feeble attempt at cooptation did the government little good and, to Franco, represented another failed effort at appeasing subversion.

At the close of October 1930, Franco's academy received an official visit from the French war minister, André Maginot, designer of the famous defense line. He awarded the academy's director the French Legion of Honor for his achievements in Morocco and invited him to participate in a special brief course for senior commanders to be held in the following month at St. Cyr. Franco attended, his third visit to foreign military academies in a little more than three years. He basked in Maginot's praise of the Spanish General Military Academy and may or may not have been surprised to hear it described (with considerable hyperbole) as the most modern of its kind in the world.

The first phase of the long-planned Republican military revolt broke out at Jaca in the Pyreenean foothills, north of Zaragoza, on December 12. Since there were few other troops in the region, Franco acted immediately on his own initiative, arming several companies of cadets with weapons and live ammunition, dispatching them in trucks to block the highway to the north. They were not needed, because another small force blocked the road even sooner. The rebels threatened with summary execution anyone who dared resist, shot down two members of the Civil Guard (Spain's national police constabulary) who refused to join them, killed a general who attempted to negotiate, then abruptly disintegrated in the face of the first firm resistance. These totally unprovoked killings opened the steadily accelerating cycle of leftist violence in Spain that would eventually bring civil war. Within little more than forty-eight hours, the two officers responsible for them were court-martialed and executed. For years they would be hailed as political martyrs by the left, who had no tears for their three innocent victims.

On December 15 the Madrid phase of the revolt took place. With fellow conspirators, Ramón Franco seized control of a small military airstrip outside Madrid, then flew over the royal palace to drop leaflets proclaiming the coming of the republic. He would later claim, perhaps hyperbolically, that his intention had been to bomb the palace but instead only dropped leaflets after seeing children playing nearby.[16] The revolt in the capital collapsed abruptly, but Ramón escaped the fate of the Jaca rebels by flying his plane to Portugal.

Bereft of means in Lisbon, he wrote to his "reactionary" brother to ask assistance. The lenient Spanish government made no effort to embargo this correspondence, and on the twenty-first Franco replied that he was sending two thousand pesetas immediately, all that he could get together on short notice. Once more he implored Ramón to come to his senses, saying that the nineteenth-century scheme of military revolt was hopelessly outmoded and that only orderly, legal reform would bring progress. Franco explained, "The well-reasoned evolution of ideas and of peoples, bringing democracy under law, constitutes the true progress of the Fatherland, while any extremist, violent revolution will drag it into the worst kind of tyranny." This proved an accurate prediction of the future path of Spain, ending in civil war, and also indicated that Franco was not absolutely averse to democratic reform, provided that it was legal and orderly and preferably accomplished under the monarchy. To this sound judgment Ramón could only reply from Paris three weeks later that "your liberal ideas are really more conservative than those of the Conde de Romanones," the Monarchist politician.[17]

On the twenty-seventh Franco dispatched a lengthy letter to his old comrade Varelita (Colonel José Enrique Varela), denouncing recent events and particularly criticizing changes in military policy, above all a new decree curbing merit promotions. Concerning the attempted revolt, he wrote that

> what happened in Jaca was nauseating. The army is full of cuckoos and cowards, so that a crazy extremist can bamboozle his unit in the most contemptible way.
>
> They murdered poor Gen. Las Heras in a cowardly manner, just as they did the captain and soldier of the Civil Guard, firing on him with rifles and a machine gun when he tried to stop them on the road from Jaca. Then in the face of a smaller force that opened fire they threw down their arms and tried to change colors. Fortunately it was demonstrated once more that the ones who behaved well were our old comrades. . . . What a clean-out our army needs![18]

Less than three months later, Franco was appointed a member of the military tribunal that tried sixty-three military personnel arrested in the failed Republican revolt. He was known as a hard-liner and also as someone unusually well-versed in the code of military justice. The tribunal handed down one death sentence and many lesser penalties, though six of the accused were absolved and the death sentence was immediately commuted by a lenient government. Franco found the situation paradoxical in the extreme. For more than a generation the left had stringently criticized military policy and any political influence by the military, yet, as soon as it served their own purposes, they revived the long series of pro-liberal military revolts of the preceding century.

In February 1931 Berenguer resigned and Alfonso XIII appointed an even weaker government led by Admiral Juan Aznar, a long-time opponent of Primo de Rivera. In mid-April it finally proceeded to hold elections but in reverse order, beginning with municipal elections, to be followed two weeks later with elections for provincial chambers and then in May for a new Cortes (national parliament). This scheme overlooked the fact that the left always received its greatest support at the local level. In the municipal elections of April 12 the new Republican-Socialist alliance gained a slight plurality and swept the voting in all the larger cities and nearly all provincial capitals. Since it had been accepted for some time that the cities registered a higher level of political consciousness and more authentic elections, much of public opinion concluded immediately that the alliance had "objectively" won the election, though it failed to gain a majority of all the municipal council seats in Spain.

In this crisis nearly all the Monarchist politicians deserted Alfonso XIII and Franco's former commander, General José Sanjurjo, at this point head of the Civil Guard, made it known that his troops would not engage in civil strife to keep the king on the throne. Though part of the army command (certainly including Franco) might have been willing to take action in his support, the king rejected any prospect of civil war and left the country on April 14. Leaders of the Republican alliance immediately occupied the seat of power and announced the establishment of Spain's Second Republic the same day.[19] The takeover, accompanied by mass demonstrations, had been largely peaceful, the principal exceptions being destructive riots in Madrid and in Tetuán, whose repression, according to varying reports, left seven dead and nearly fifty injured.[20] These fatalities, like those in the Jaca revolt, provided only the slightest foretaste of what was to come.

In Zaragoza, Franco was aghast. He believed that most of the population still supported the crown, even if the larger cities did not. He was even willing to arm his cadets and march to the support of the king, but his old comrade Millán Astray informed him from Madrid that Sanjurjo was saying the situation was hopeless and that the change should not be resisted. Franco judged the Republican takeover to be a usurpation, a kind of "peaceful pronunciamiento," but there was not the slightest organized opposition. The Republican alliance seized power by default, as Monarchists refused to resist.

On the following day, Franco addressed his cadets, announcing to them the proclamation of the Second Republic and stressing the need for discipline and respect for the newly constituted power, though he also indicated his sorrow at this turn of events. He only lowered the Monarchist flag, however, five days later, after he had received a written order from the new captain-general of Zaragoza.

Franco always believed that most of the army had remained loyal to the crown, though there was no way of knowing that.[21] He was extremely critical of Sanjurjo (who had always treated him very well in Morocco), attributing his refusal to fight for the crown alternately to resentment over the dismissal of Primo de Rivera (whom Sanjurjo had strongly supported) or bitterness stemming from the fact that he had not been granted a peerage as reward for having commanded the final campaigns in Morocco.

The monarchy had shown Franco great favor, and he would always speak in very positive terms of Alfonso XIII. As a Monarchist general, he would face an uncertain future in what was being hailed as Spain's first genuinely democratic political regime.

4

From Ostracism
to Chief of Staff

(1931–1936)

Under the Republic, Franco's role changed in line with the three different phases of the nation's politics: the reformist leftist phase of 1931 to 1933; the centrist and rightist counterreform from 1933 to 1935; and the quasi-revolutionary reign of the Popular Front in 1936. At the outset Franco made his attitude clear: he regretted the end of the monarchy and did not welcome the new regime, but he would obey orders and serve the established government, whose legitimacy he never challenged. As he reiterated in conversation years later, Alfonso XIII had made no effort to contest the Republican takeover, so that legitimacy passed to the new regime by default. This same point of view was shared, in varying ways, by a majority of Spaniards, though their individual political preferences differed enormously. In the army, some of the more diehard senior Monarchist commanders chose retirement, but Franco was only thirty-eight and he could not imagine life as a civilian. He observed in private correspondence that Spain's public institutions probably had to change with the times, regrettable from one point of view but also understandable and, if the new regime was fair and honest, acceptable.

The Second Republic revealed considerable ambiguity, for, though originally introduced as a liberal democratic and parliamentary regime, there was soon increasing disagreement within the governing coalition. The centrist or moderate Republicans stood for liberal democracy and the rules of the games, free and fair elections, and only moderate reforms of a legal and democratic nature. Their principal organization, led by Alejandro Lerroux, was the misleadingly named Radical Republican Party.[1] Niceto Alcalá-Zamora, an experienced former Monarchist politician who became the first Republican prime minister, formed a separate small center party and then was made president of the new regime. The Radicals, however, abandoned the ruling coalition after one year, alleging that it had moved too far left and was catering to the Socialists.

During the first biennium of 1931–33 the dominant Republican sector was the cluster of parties known as left Republicans, or the "bourgeois left." Their chief leader was Manuel Azaña, a writer and Ministry of Justice official who became the first minister of war and soon afterward prime minister. The left Republicans pursued an intense anticlerical policy and a series of major reforms, some moderate and some radical, though they generally respected the principle of private property. They held that the Republic must be a completely leftist regime under which no conservative party or coalition could ever be accepted as a legitimate government, even in the remote possibility that one were democratically elected. All Catholic interests, however large the proportion of society that supported them, must be permanently excluded from government. Such an attitude made the development of a genuinely liberal democratic regime almost impossible.

The third leg of the coalition, the Spanish Socialist Workers Party (Partido Socialista Obrero Español), was an orthodox Marxist group from the old pre-Communist Second International that reflected the ambiguity of its sister parties. Unlike the Communists, the Spanish Socialists participated in democratic reformism, though they did not go as far as the German and Scandinavian parties in categorically embracing democratic parliamentarianism. On the other hand, they went farther than their French counterparts by becoming full members of a parliamentary coalition government in 1931. The Spanish Socialists did not clearly define their ultimate goals and strategy, but Francisco Largo Caballero, the new Socialist labor minister, insisted that in Spain there was no room for what he called "radicalism." Their expectation seemed to be that Spain had become so modern and progressive—virtually a "Scandinavian"-type country—that democratic reformism could have no possible outcome other than a prompt transition to a Socialist regime. When it became clear in 1933 that such was not the case, the Socialists began to veer more and more toward revolutionary violence, led by none other than the previously moderate Largo Caballero.

The first parliamentary elections in 1931 were swept by the tripartite governing coalition, partly by default, since at first there was little effectively organized opposition. The extreme left or right posed little threat. The Monarchists were slow to organize and in fact at first were forcibly prevented from doing so by the governing parties, though the completely traditionalist sector of Monarchists, the Carlists, who championed corporative institutions from the ancien regime, experienced a revival.

The main rival of the Socialists was the anarchosyndicalist National Confederation of Labor (Confederación Nacional del Trabajo [CNT]), the only mass movement of "organized anarchism" in Europe, whose support came primarily from labor unions. Since the anarchist creed affirmed apoliticism and direct action, the CNT concentrated on radical labor agitation and soon turned against the new regime. The Spanish Communist Party (Partido Comunista Español) was tiny and inconsequential, though it was more radical yet, reflecting the Comintern's priority of violent revolution. Separate organizations of independent Leninists and Trotskyists were even smaller, though they came together in 1935 to form a separate anti-Soviet Communist organization, the subsequently notorious Worker Party of Marxist Unification (Partido Obrero de Unificación Marxista).

For two years the Republican coalition devoted itself to an extensive reform program, dealing with the military, labor and trade unions, regional autonomy, education, land reform, and restrictions on the Catholic Church. The land reform was confused but generally moderate, and a statute of Catalan autonomy was passed in 1932, leading to a new autonomous government in Barcelona. The most divisive and destructive reform was the anticlerical program, which did not merely separate church and state officially for the first time in Spain's history but moved to crush Catholic education, outlawing all teaching by the clergy and also persecuting Catholics in numerous petty ways that violated freedom of expression and conscience. Azaña acknowledged that such a policy was not "liberal," but the left claimed this was the only way to put the Catholic Church in its place, and it insisted that the large Catholic sector of the population must play no role of any influence whatsoever in government, unless it were willing to abandon its beliefs and values.

At first it was rumored that Franco might have a new role under this regime. On April 18, 1931, four days after the inauguration of the Republic, the Madrid newspaper *ABC* reported that the interior minister, the moderate centrist Miguel Maura, was offering him the post of high commissioner of Spanish Morocco, from Franco's view a real plum appointment that would have pleased him greatly. The rumor was correct insofar as Maura had indeed made such a suggestion within the government. He judged that Franco was more politically astute than, for example, his former commander Sanjurjo, who had been high commissioner right after the fighting ended in the protectorate. The Republican cabinet, however, thought otherwise, judging Franco of dubious loyalty, and so the post went back to Sanjurjo for the time being, a reward for his rejection of any attempt to keep Alfonso XIII in power.

The same day that the rumor appeared in *ABC*, Franco dashed off a reply to the Madrid daily insisting that it was false and that, even if it were not, he could not accept so important a post from the new regime because a sudden appointment would be interpreted as political favoritism, whereas he had served the monarchy faithfully and would simply continue to do his duty, without regard for political fashion. At the same time he made it clear that he recognized the principle of "national sovereignty" and accepted the new order. Thus from the outset of the Republic he staked out a position of disciplined professionalism that acknowledged his previously untrammeled support for the monarchy until its final hour but that accepted the newly established order. This reaffirmed his basically conservative principles, on the one hand, while stressing, on the other, a creed of apolitical professionalism, whatever his personal sentiments. It was a position that he would maintain for some time, not abandoning it completely until just four days before the Civil War began.

The new war minister, Manuel Azaña, immediately began reform of the army, which was led by a bloated, redundant officer corps and, though in slightly better shape than ten years earlier, remained poorly equipped and badly trained. The swollen officer corps had been a curse for more than a century. The army needed to be reorganized and modernized, but Azaña also aimed to democratize and "republicanize" the officer corps, reversing key policies of the dictatorship and encouraging the corps' more liberal sectors. This meant relying on former *junteros* rather than *africanistas*, the majority of whom tended, like Franco, to be more conservative. On April 21, 1931, all officers were required to swear an official oath of loyalty to the Republic, though this meant little, since their earlier oath of loyalty to the monarchy had proven meaningless. Four days later, the new minister announced his key reform, generally referred to as the "Azaña law," which offered all officers immediate retirement at full pension for their rank regardless of age. This was a generous "golden handshake" that cost the state budget a great deal, though the carrot was accompanied by the stick of an announcement that any who did not accept retirement and were found to be redundant in the structure of a reorganized army would be liable to summary dismissal. Altogether, more than seventy-six hundred officers, or nearly 40 percent of the officer corps, chose retirement, reducing the number in service in a single blow from more than twenty thousand to fewer than fourteen thousand. Moreover, about a thousand NCOs opted for retirement.

In private discussions and correspondence, Franco held that it was the responsibility of patriotic officers to continue to serve, maintaining the spirit and values of the army as much as possible. The officer corps harbored a wide variety of political attitudes, and among the numerous retirees might be found both very liberal and very conservative military men. No sample was ever taken that would have it made it possible to determine the most common tendencies, though later it would be alleged that the more liberal officers were more eager to retire, so that a paradoxical effect was not so much to republicanize the army as to give the officer corps a somewhat more conservative cast. However that may be, the law had no immediate political effect, for under the new regime at first only a very few officers were willing to evince any overt political hostility.

Another initiative of the new government was to prosecute all those who held high office under the dictatorship for incurring political "responsibilities," criminalizing their actions, even though they had been obeying what had then been the established government. As a military professional who had never had a political assignment, this did not touch Franco, but, in the procedures about to get under way, General Berenguer, who had been indicted as head of the 1930–31 government, asked Franco to serve as his defense counsel. This acknowledged Franco's professional prestige, his record of apoliticism, and his detailed knowledge of the code of military justice. He was not altogether happy with Berenguer, who had passed over him the year before for promotion to major general in favor of a much more elderly candidate, but Franco thought the prosecutions unfair and agreed to serve as counsel. Azaña, however, quickly ruled him ineligible, since his own appointment was in a separate military district.

Advised by a coterie of liberal-minded officers, Azaña moved rapidly to reform the army, beginning at the top, eliminating the district captaincies general and abolishing the rank of lieutenant general. Thus the top rank under the Republic was *general de división* (major general). On June 3, 1931, Azaña announced a systematic review of all the combat merit promotions from the Moroccan campaigns. This proved slow and was not completed until the end of the following year. About five hundred cases were examined. In a number of instances, officers were demoted one rank, though partial loss of seniority was more common. Ultimately, Franco retained the rank of brigadier, though he was dropped to the bottom of the list.

The unit structure of the army was reformed along French lines, reorganized into a series of eight organic divisions. Both the army and navy were downsized somewhat, though the air force was slightly expanded and organized as a separate branch of the armed forces. The six military academies were reduced to three, though a new one was planned for the air force. Franco's General Military Academy was closed at the end of the 1931 term, on the grounds that it fomented a narrow caste spirit and needed to be replaced by institutions that offered greater technical preparation. One measure to democratize the army was the creation of a new subofficer corps, between the regular officers and the lowest ranks of NCOs and troops. Modest downsizing made it possible to reduce the military budget somewhat, but the cost of paying the permanent full pensions of nearly nine thousand newly retired officers and NCOs, though assigned to a separate budget category, meant that the full costs were scarcely reduced at all. Though the budgets for new equipment and maintenance were slightly increased, there was not enough money to permit any significant modernization.[2]

Though the army had not really been transformed, the ultimate reaction of the officer corps was one of hostility. None of the attempts to reform the Spanish army during the last century had been well received and most had been thwarted altogether. In this case, however, the antipathy stemmed not so much from the reform measures, which varied in their utility and consequences, as from the way in which they were carried out. Azaña was extraordinarily acerbic and supercilious for a parliamentary politician and often began new decrees with contemptuous rhetoric that put down the military and made its members understand they were no longer important. He was widely quoted as saying that his intention was to "pulverize" ("triturar") the army, though in fact he did not apply this term directly to the army itself but to political rightists in general.[3] Not too much should be made, however, of this developing cleavage between the leftist government and the military during the first Republican biennium. The officer corps was divided internally and, though there was growing resentment, very few officers on active duty were interested in getting involved with politics.

Though he had no quarrel with some of Azaña's structural reforms, the closing of his academy was the most severe blow that Franco had suffered in fifteen years, since the abdominal wound in 1916. He delivered a bitter farewell speech to his cadets on July 14, 1931, which emphasized the importance of maintaining discipline, all the more when "thought" and "heart" are in opposition to the orders received from a "higher authority . . . in error." He alluded to the fact that some of the senior military had been rewarded for their disloyalty to the monarchy and also implied that "immorality and injustice" characterized the officers now serving in the Ministry of War, concluding simply with "¡Viva España!" rather than "¡Viva la República!" Later in life he prided himself on never having uttered the latter slogan. Moreover, Franco published the speech as his final order of the day and, according to his cousin Pacón, had tears in his eyes as he prepared to leave his post.[4]

Azaña was irritated in the extreme, writing in his diary that this was a thoroughly anti-Republican speech that would have provided grounds for "immediate dismissal," save that Franco's post had already been abolished and he was being left temporarily without assignment anyway. Therefore he merely entered an official reprimand into Franco's personnel file.[5]

Such a thing had never happened to him before, and he immediately dashed off a letter to the minister of war expressing his "respectful appeal" of what, he said, was an "erroneous interpretation" of the speech. Franco insisted that he always respected the government in power and was a strict professional who never involved himself in politics. In the following month he had an interview with Azaña in which he tried to clear himself. He did convince Azaña that he would not be involved in political machinations against the regime, though in Madrid he was kept under police surveillance. The minister of war recognized Franco's ability and also his astute pragmatism, factors that, combined with his basic conservatism, made him of all the generals "el único temible" ("the only one to be feared"), but he also understood—correctly—that he would not cause any further trouble. Franco was left without assignment for eight months, time he spent in withdrawal at his wife's family home in Asturias. He, in turn, reciprocated the hostile esteem of Azaña, declaring, shortly before his death, that of the leftist politicians, "he was the most intelligent one of all."[6]

For twenty years fortune had smiled on him, but now Franco had been demoted and reprimanded, and the future of his career had been put in doubt. Although he was not involved in political maneuvers against the government, the advent of the Republic marked the beginning of Franco's politicization. Henceforth he would be more cautious and calculating than before and learn to take political factors into consideration in every major decision. Though he would never become highly paranoid in the manner of some dictators, after 1931 he became even more withdrawn, more suspicious and prudent. This would bring a further slow change in aspects of his personality. After his marriage and especially after his return from Morocco, he had become more relaxed, sometimes even appearing jovial. This greater openness began to disappear after 1931, and Franco gradually became more closed and reticent. Though he could still be very talkative on certain occasions, as he moved into middle age his personality gradually assumed the characteristics that would remain dominant for the rest of his life.

By contrast, his brother Ramón was rewarded for his political activism by being named the new regime's first director general of aeronautics, but such recognition failed to abate his radicalism. He had become what one of his biographers calls a "fantastic personage" and a political adventurer.[7] Ramón saw the Republic (accurately enough, as it turned out) as merely the first phase in a more extreme revolution and threw himself into radical politics with continued frenzy, maintaining contact with revolutionary anarchosyndicalists and associating himself with the "Andalusian nationalist" Blas Infante in Seville, standing with him as a candidate in the first Republican parliamentary elections on June 28, 1931. A rumor then circulated that Andalusian radicals and anarchists were planning an insurrection, soon to become known as the "Tablada plot" (after the airport in Seville they purportedly intended to seize), even before the elections could take place. Having caught the bug of violent insurrection, Ramón had difficulty leaving it alone. His new post of director general of aeronautics was summarily abolished by the Republican government, which sent orders for his arrest, but a day later he was elected to parliament on an extremist ticket, giving him immunity.

In the Cortes, Ramón joined forces with the Radical Socialists and the ultra-left, forming part of the coterie known as *jabalíes* (wild boars), which always took the most incendiary position on whatever issue was at hand. In parliament, however, Ramón failed to stand out. He had no knowledge of complicated issues and lacked the oratorical skill that still remained the sine qua non of the successful Spanish parliamentarian. Franco bore all this as best he could, continuing occasionally to urge his brother to come to his senses, always without effect. He also took note of Ramón's failure in parliament, and several years later this probably was a factor in Franco's own decision to withdraw from the opportunity to run for the Cortes in the repeat elections of May 1936.

The black sheep of the family later took advantage of the Republic's new divorce law to shed his wife Carmen Díaz, and then he married a young woman named Engracia Moreno, with whom he had been involved since she gave birth to his daughter, Angeles, in 1928. In the eyes of his siblings, all this constituted further scandal, and neither his second wife nor his daughter would ever be accepted by the extended Franco family.

By 1933, however, Ramón finally began to settle down. The unmitigated failure of all his radical escapades seems to have exerted a stabilizing effect, and the second marriage, combined with fatherhood, may have contributed to reforming him as well. When a more moderate Republican government came to power, it restored Ramón's commission in the air force, judging that he would do less damage on active duty, and, since in Latin America he was one of the most famous living Spaniards, it sent him on a goodwill mission to Mexico to keep him out of the country during the next elections. After showing signs of stability, in 1934 he was appointed air force attaché in Washington, a post he retained through numerous changes of government.[8] There he was much less of a celebrity than in the Spanish-speaking world, and he seems to have devoted himself exclusively to his professional responsibilities, giving studious attention to North American aviation. In Washington he would be startled in July 1936 by the news that his brother Paco, in a sudden reversal of roles, was one of the leaders of a military insurrection against the Republican government, which would present Ramón with the gravest dilemma of his life.

Franco's older brother, Nicolás, still directed a commercial shipyard in Valencia. Like Paco, Nicolás was a capable professional, though always much more jolly and extroverted. Though he made more money in Valencia, he later resigned from the shipyard to return to the navy as a professor in the naval engineering school in Madrid. He and Paco always remained close. Carmen Franco observes that their relations "were always very good, since my father respected his older brother. They spoke frequently and spent time together whenever Nicolás came to Madrid, I think they really got along very well, though their personalities were quite distinct. Nicolás was much more extroverted, a very different kind of person."

The eight months without assignment that Franco spent restlessly, mainly at the Polo home in Asturias, was the longest period of inactivity in his life. There is little information as to how he passed his time, but it provided opportunity for reading and for reflection. He still received the *Bulletin Internationale* and his strong anti-Communist sentiments hardened further. In Spain Communism remained very weak, but, like many conservatives, he tended to view the revolutionary process in general as a functional equivalent. To this was added his growing anti-Masonic fixation, since for some time Masons had been influential in liberal and leftist politics in Spain. Yet they were by no means a single bloc, and during these years Franco never expressed this antipathy publicly, since it was possible he could be favored by some of the more moderate Masons, as indeed proved to be the case. Everything indicated that he accepted the Republican regime as permanent, even legitimate, though he wanted to see it develop in a more conservative direction. As he wrote much later in his mini-memoir: "Our hope should be that the Republic succeed . . . , and if unfortunately it should fail, that it not be because of us."[9] In view of what happened in 1936, this may seem self-serving, yet the evidence would indicate that it described his position fairly accurately until the election of the Popular Front. In 1931 he was determined above all to reestablish his professional life, and that depended on adhering rigidly to the strict posture that he had invoked in his letter and interview with Azaña. Yet how long he would be left in limbo, along with many other conservative senior commanders, there was no way of knowing.

Franco was called to appear on December 17, 1931, before the Responsibilities Commission that was dealing with the abuses of the Primo de Rivera regime and specifically in this instance with the executions of the two officers who had led the initial Republican revolt in the garrison at Jaca on December 12, 1930. Though Franco had had nothing to do with that, he had been a member of the subsequent tribunal in the court-martial of other indicted military personnel, which had imposed lighter sentences. In sworn testimony, Franco did not back down, affirming that the court-martial had properly prosecuted army men guilty of military revolt, according to the official code of military justice, and that in the case of the two Jaca captains the code authorized immediate execution. At the same time he recognized the responsibility of all military personnel to respect national sovereignty and the established government. Thus he both held his ground and repeated his earlier guarantee of strict professionalism.

Whether that did him any good, the months of ostracism suddenly came to an end on February 5, 1932, when he was assigned to La Coruña in his native Galicia as commander of the Fifteenth Infantry Brigade. This had the added advantage of being near El Ferrol, so he was able to visit his mother almost every weekend. Azaña apparently had concluded that the new regime was consolidated and that Franco, despite his conservative views, was a reliable professional who should not be alienated further. And indeed, had a constitutional Republic become fully consolidated, that is undoubtedly the way things would have continued, with the name Francisco Franco later known only to a few specialists in military history.

The assignment in La Coruña was no more onerous than the earlier command in Madrid, and the years 1931–33 were the last ones of a more relaxed life for Franco, not weighed with major responsibilities. His command brought with it a rather grand residence, and, as in recent months in Asturias, Franco could spend more time with his six-year-old daughter. He enjoyed telling her stories, though she would later say that playing games was simply not his style. In La Coruña he made a new friend who would remain one for life, a civilian named Máximo Rodríguez Borrell, or Max Borrell, for short, practically the only nonmilitary close friend that he had. It was apparently Borrell who introduced him to fishing as a serious hobby, which would eventually become a major summer recreation of Franco's. The La Coruña command also provided a pleasant ambience for Doña Carmen, who enjoyed high status in local society. She appeared frequently at the elite Club náutico for *meriendas* (teas), card games, and similar activities with other ladies.

That Azaña had apparently judged him correctly was demonstrated by the fact that Franco carefully avoided any involvement in the *sanjurjada* (Sanjurjo revolt) of August 10, 1932, the only attempt at military rebellion under the Republic prior to the Civil War. The attitude of many officers toward the new regime had been relatively favorable at the beginning, but the mood had significantly soured by the end of its first year, although not to the point of exciting much organized dissidence. A number of clandestine meetings took place among the extreme right, but by far the greatest opposition came from the revolutionary left, which manifested itself first in the burning of more than a hundred Catholic churches in May 1931. There followed an increasing number of violent strikes and riots, mainly fomented by the anarchosyndicalist CNT, which soon adopted a posture of revolutionary defiance of the Republic. Some Socialist workers were also extremely militant, and a group of farmworkers at Castilblanco in Badajoz province turned on a detachment of four Civil Guards and beat them to death on the final day of the year.

This focused the limelight on Franco's former commander, General José Sanjurjo, who had been commander of the Civil Guard for the preceding two years. He had bent over backwards to cooperate with the inauguration of the new regime, which strongly favored him at first, recalling him for a few days from his temporary post in Morocco at the end of June 1931 to put down the planned revolt in Seville in which Ramón Franco had taken part. A few months later, when the prosecution of "responsibilities" for the dictatorship had begun, Sanjurjo offered his resignation, saying that he also was "responsible," but the government assured him that his loyalty to the Republic was well demonstrated. For some time, Monarchists regarded him as a traitor, though soon he would be transformed into the military talisman of the right.

Sanjurjo was in many ways a polar opposite to Franco. They were both physically courageous, cool under fire, capable field commanders, and successful as counterinsurgency leaders in Morocco. In most other respects they were different. Sanjurjo was twenty years older and an inch or so shorter even than Franco and had reached the rank of lieutenant general before retiring to direct the Civil Guard. He often had a twinkle in his eye, was genuinely well liked, and enjoyed having a good time. After he entered middle age, his appearance sometimes caricatured that of the *militar crapuloso* (dissolute officer), and this was not entirely deceiving. After the early death of his first wife, he became a womanizer and a habitué of brothels, contracting syphilis in the process, though this seems to have been successfully treated.[10]

Sanjurjo publicly sprang to the defense of his murdered guards, declaring that their mutilated corpses were even worse than anything he had seen in Morocco. Five days after the Castilblanco killings, a larger detachment of the Civil Guard fired on an angry demonstration of striking workers at Arnedo in the north, killing possibly as many as eleven, including several women and a child. The government viewed this as an act of revenge for Castilblanco, and on February 5, 1932, the very day that Franco was assigned to La Coruña, Sanjurjo was relieved as director of the Civil Guard, but, to indicate that the government did not want to alienate him, it immediately appointed him director of the *carabineros* (border and customs police).

From that point, Sanjurjo began to undergo a political shift, though at first it was perhaps not drastic. As Republican reformism advanced toward autonomy for Catalonia, Monarchist plotting intensified, and even some conservative Republicans contemplated the need for a special "correction" of government policy that would put an end to the more radical initiatives and drive the Socialists from power. By this time no resolute Monarchist generals held senior command, and so potential conspirators looked to Sanjurjo as the leader of a *pronunciamiento* against the government.

He finally succumbed to their blandishments and decided to act before Catalan devolution took place. There was, however, little planning behind his *pronunciamiento*, which was underwritten by Monarchists but also appears to have been tentatively encouraged by conservative Republicans. Sanjurjo would later claim that the goal was not to restore the monarchy but to install a more conservative Republican government whose charge would be to hold a plebiscite on the issue of regime change, something that the Republican leaders had declined to do the preceding year. The conspirators spoke with Franco, who, like nearly all commanders on active duty, refused to become involved, though he is alleged to have said that he would try to avoid having to take up arms against the *pronunciamiento*.[11]

The rebellion, designed to break out in five cities, immediately fizzled in Madrid, where ten people were killed. It succeeded only in Seville, where Sanjurjo quickly took over the garrison and municipal government. Lacking support elsewhere, however, Sanjurjo had to abandon the city and was apprehended early the next morning. Facing court-martial, he asked that Franco come to talk with him and, as Berenguer had done a year earlier, requested that Franco serve as defense counsel. This time Franco refused, understanding that the penalty for violent rebellion was likely to be death. He later claimed that he told Sanjurjo, "I can't do that. You, having failed, have gained for yourself the right to die."[12] He was court-martialed within a fortnight and sentenced to death, which was commuted to life imprisonment.

The new Republican security law made it possible to suspend constitutional guarantees arbitrarily. The government arrested several thousand members of conservative and extreme rightist groups, deporting a hundred or so to Equatorial Guinea without trial and closing 114 newspapers, some for long periods.[13] This extended the policy by which the government had arbitrarily banned or otherwise blocked fifty conservative political meetings in the nine months preceding the attempted insurrection.[14] Autonomy for Catalonia was approved, and for the next six months the political balance tilted even more strongly to the left.

As a reward for Franco's loyalty, in February 1933, after a full year in La Coruña, he was promoted not in rank but in assignment, named military commander of the Balearic Islands, whose post was headquartered in Palma de Mallorca. This assignment would normally have gone to a major general, so it appeared to be a mark of favor from Azaña, though the prime minister noted in his diary that it was preferable to have Franco far from Madrid.[15] The Republican government gave scant attention to foreign affairs, but it was aware that Fascist Italy had shown strategic interest in the Balearics, which needed improved defenses.

Franco threw himself into his new assignment. The Spanish military possessed little sophistication in the art of coastal defense, and so he turned once more to Paris, asking the military attaché in the French capital for technical literature and advice. The military attaché placed the matter in the hands of two comparatively young Spanish officers of his acquaintance currently engaged in advanced study at the French War College (École de Guerre), Antonio Barroso, a lieutenant colonel, and Luis Carrero Blanco, a naval lieutenant, who got together a set of recommendations. Franco was grateful and impressed, and by mid-May had sent to Azaña a detailed proposal for improving the islands' defenses, which was approved by the government, though budgetary limitations prevented significant changes.

Nonetheless, by the middle of 1933, Franco was becoming somewhat discouraged. He had managed to retain his rank and had been restored to active command, but under the Republic military affairs had become completely secondary and prospects were not encouraging. Things had gone rather flat in what had for years been a constantly ascending career. For the first and only time, he may have considered an alternative profession, though he had no very useful technical specialty to offer the private market, as did his brother Nicolás.

On the other hand, despite this uncertainty, the early Republican years were not a time of great tension for Franco. There were frequent leaves in Madrid, where the Francos had bought an apartment, that allowed them to attend the theater and movies and provided ample opportunities to shop (particularly for antiques), and they took extensive summer vacations in Asturias and Galicia. Franco enjoyed driving and rented a car for summer trips, which he drove himself, and these produced the first family memories for his daughter: "I remember my father . . . singing as he drove, because he used to enjoy singing, especially zarzuela /Spanish operetta/ songs. . . . He particularly liked to sing on these trips, which were long and tiresome in that era. . . . But, on the other hand, he hardly ever sang at home, so I think he did so on the trips just to pass the time." There are no references, even by his daughter, to Franco singing after these years.

He apparently read more about politics, economics, and international affairs than he had in all the earlier years put together, though there was never any evidence that he learned much about economics. The menace of revolution and the Comintern concerned him, but the chief idée fixe maturing at this time was that the Western world was being corroded from within by the left-liberal conspiracy of Freemasonry, all the more insidious because the Masons were not proletarian revolutionaries but in most cases prosperous and respectable bourgeois. Indeed, he believed that they were allied with big business and finance capital, entities that knew no morality or political loyalty but simply sought to exploit society and amass wealth at the cost of general social and economic ruin. The early Republican years coincided with the Great Depression, which probably had some effect on his thinking, though proportionately the economic impact in Spain was less than in some other countries. The conviction was crystalizing that the contemporary world was menaced by the "three internationals"—the Comintern, Freemasonry, and international finance capitalism, which sometimes fought one another but in significant ways aided and abetted each other in undermining social solidarity and well-being, and Christian civilization more generally.

By comparison, Franco was not strongly anti-Semitic, as he thought that the greatest danger presented by Jews was simply their contribution to international finance capitalism and to Communism, which he judged was comparatively small. Conversely, he seemed to have formed a relatively favorable opinion of ordinary Spanish-speaking Sephardic Jews in Morocco, the only Jews whom he had met personally. Many of them treasured the opportunity to gain Spanish citizenship and seemed reliable and trustworthy.

The opposition to Freemasonry constituted Franco's principal bête noire. It was extreme and obsessive, but within the Spanish context not totally surprising, insofar as Masons had played a major a role in leftist and liberal movements ever since the early nineteenth century, and many of the left Republican deputies elected in 1931 were Masons.[16] For a century, the Catholic opinion generally had been that Freemasonry was the Church's archenemy.

On the other hand, Franco could not entirely ignore the fact that many Spanish Masons were moderate liberals who were becoming increasingly opposed to the left. This was particularly the case with the Radical Party, many of whose leaders were Masons but who stood for centrist liberal democracy. Franco had been introduced to Alejandro Lerroux, who had founded and still led the party, years earlier and was undoubtedly pleased with Lerroux's firm stand against the Socialists.

Franco had made it clear that he would have nothing to do with the extreme right, under current circumstances doomed to failure, and much preferred a more pragmatic conservative alternative, though at first this was slow to develop. He nonetheless took note of the founding of the Fascist movement, Falange Española, in Madrid in October 1933. The first intellectual to propound Fascist ideas in Spain, the literary avant-gardist Ernesto Giménez Caballero, had already drawn attention to Franco, at least in passing, as the kind of vigorous military leader who could lead and inspire a new Spanish nationalism, but Fascism long remained weak in Spain, and Franco showed no interest in it. The movement's extremism was beyond his ken, though several years later that would change.

In 1933 the political landscape began to shift rapidly. During the spring a strong reaction set in against the leftist government, whose coalition showed signs of strain. In September, by which point it had weakened irremediably, Alcalá-Zamora appointed Lerroux as prime minister, charging him to prepare a broad and more moderate Republican coalition that would exclude the Socialists.

Lerroux quickly summoned Franco to Madrid to offer him the post of minister of war, as reported by *ABC* on September 12. To the Radicals, Franco seemed to be the most outstanding leader in the army, and the most reliable. His military credentials were of the highest esteem, and he was a strict professional who had kept his skirts clean politically. He was a principled moderate conservative who had had nothing to do with the leftist clique of officers connected with Azaña but who at the same time had steered clear of diehard Monarchists and the extreme right. Franco was undoubtedly pleased and flattered by this turn of the political wheel, but he politely rejected the offer. On the one hand, he grasped that Spanish politics was entering a new phase of instability and that the Lerroux government might not last long, so that were he to accept, he might be boarding a sinking ship. On the other hand, the changing situation probably presaged a different military policy that could offer important professional opportunities. Hence it was still advisable to stay out of politics. The wisdom of his refusal was shown when left Republicans voted out the new Lerroux government in a matter of weeks.

Meanwhile the largest sectors of conservative opinion were beginning to coalesce around the new Catholic party, the Spanish Confederation of Autonomous Rightists (Confederación Española de Derechas Autónomas [CEDA]), led by a balding young lawyer, José María Gil Robles. Its opportunity came when, with the leftist coalition undone, general elections were scheduled for November 1933. The CEDA was even more interested in Franco than were the Radicals, for he seemed to fit perfectly their own posture of nationalism, strong Catholicism, firm conservatism, and equally firm commitment to legal procedure. They offered him a safe place on their electoral list for Madrid, but once more, he refused.

The Azaña government had passed a heavily unbalanced electoral law that strongly favored coalitions, so long as they could win even a modest plurality of the vote, based on the calculation that this would guarantee permanent power for the left. In fact, the electoral regulations boomeranged on them, for the Socialists, turning toward revolutionism, rejected further alliance with the "bourgeois" left Republicans, while, in the decisive second round of the voting, the CEDA formed a victorious alliance with the centrist Radicals, who championed the moderate, secularized sectors of the middle classes against the left. The CEDA suddenly emerged as the largest single party, though it had scarcely more than a quarter of the seats in parliament. It was followed by the Radicals as the second largest delegation, while the left Republicans were left with only five deputies. The campaign and the voting were not free from violence. At least twenty-eight people were killed and many more injured, primarily but not exclusively at the hands of the left, but women were allowed to vote for the first time and the votes were fairly and accurately registered in what stood as the only fully democratic election in Spanish history until 1977.[17]

The left Republicans and Socialists then made three different efforts to pressure Alcalá-Zamora, the president of the Republic who was a Catholic liberal, to cancel the results. They did not allege that the balloting had been unfair, but simply rejected a victory by the center-right, holding that the Republic constituted an exclusively leftist project, which only leftists could govern. The fact that a majority of the original founders of the Republic did not accept the results of valid elections, when they did not win, did not augur well for the future of a democratic constitutional regime. The CEDA made it clear that the party rejected conspiracy and violence and would follow the rules of Republican legality. They had not responded in kind to the violence directed against them by the left during the electoral campaign, in which at least six *cedistas* had been killed. But the CEDA did insist on fundamental changes that would create a more conservative and at least partially Catholic regime, something that the left, in the rhetorical excess typical of the era, equated with "Fascism."

Alcalá-Zamora could not accept demands to cancel the electoral results or to enable the left to decree still further electoral changes in order to manufacture an artificial victory in a further round of balloting. On the other hand, to some extent he shared their distrust of the CEDA as crypto-Monarchist and crypto-authoritarian, since it did not run under the banner of the Republic and proposed major constitutional reforms. So Alcalá-Zamora appointed a minority centrist coalition under Lerroux that would govern with the voting support of the CEDA, an arrangement to which Gil Robles agreed for the time being. The CNT meanwhile responded in December with its third revolutionary insurrection within twenty-three months. It soon failed, like the first two, but outright terrorism featured in these revolts and resulted in the deaths of several hundred people.

After his first minister of war resigned in January 1934, Lerroux appointed Diego Hidalgo to the post. Hidalgo was a political crony, a Mason, and a rising young leader who wanted to follow a more vigorous military policy. At the beginning of February he approved Franco's request for a short leave in Madrid, nominally for further treatment of the sequelae of the old abdominal wound. This was probably a pretext by Franco to enable him to spend more time in the capital, where his mother, Doña Pilar, was visiting her daughter en route to fulfilling her lifelong ambition to visit Rome.

In Madrid she was suddenly stricken with severe pneumonia and died on February 28. After his wife and daughter, she was the person Franco loved most, and he later termed her death the greatest grief (*disgusto*) of his life. Ramón was still in Washington, so the other three siblings arranged her funeral, which was not attended by her estranged husband, of whom the death notice made no mention.

It has been said, nonetheless, that months earlier, toward the end of 1933, Franco had had a brief meeting with his father in Madrid, probably the first in seventeen years. According to this account, he proposed reconciliation, but only so long as his father was willing to lead a more respectable life and give up his current spouse. The offer, if made, was spurned. After the death of Doña Pilar, the elder Franco met briefly with the three siblings in Madrid to address problems concerning the family's financial estate, but allegedly he arrived late, refused to remove his hat, and behaved arrogantly. Whatever the accuracy of these anecdotes, the mutual hostility between father and son would remain unabated until the death of Nicolás Franco nearly eight years later.[18]

While in Madrid, Franco was summoned by the new war minister, Hidalgo, who wanted to meet his most celebrated general. Hidalgo seemed more than impressed, indeed so much so that when in March a vacancy appeared in the army at the rank of major general, he thought immediately of Franco. After the Azaña reforms, this was the highest rank, while the revision of merit promotions had dropped Franco to the very last place in seniority among brigadiers. Hidalgo nonetheless jumped the entire list of brigadier generals and promoted Franco to major general, effective immediately. Though Hidalgo was somewhat taken aback by the laconic coldness and brevity with which Franco's message from Palma de Mallorca thanked him, Franco was in fact extremely grateful, for it was clear that under the new government he had been restored to high favor and, at the age of forty-one, had now reached the highest rank, even though he was the most junior among major generals.[19]

In April the center-right parliament voted a general amnesty for all earlier offenses against the Republican order, restoring full rights to a mixed bag of several thousand people, ranging from the luminaries of the Primo de Rivera regime and Sanjurjo and his few associates on the one hand to many anarchosyndicalist revolutionaries on the other. Alcalá-Zamora believed that the measure went too far and, using his broad constitutional powers to discharge as well as to appoint new governments, he accepted Lerroux's resignation, which he had offered as a matter of course in the wake of the dispute over the amnesty measure. Much the same coalition as in the preceding government was then reorganized under Ricardo Samper, a veteran Radical politician from Valencia.

Political tension increased during the spring and summer. The CNT had already launched three abortive revolutionary insurrections, in which several hundred people had been killed, and the several small Communist parties continued to preach immediate revolt, but more menacing was the increasing turn toward revolution by the well-organized Socialist movement, the second largest political force in Spain. At this point, on May 16, Franco for the first time wrote to Geneva to take out his own personal subscription to the newsletter of the Entente Internationale contre la Troisième Internationale, the right-wing anti-Communist group whose publication he had been reading intermittently for six years.[20] Like most of the right, he saw the various revolutionary movements in Spain as functional equivalents of Soviet Communism, whether or not directly inspired by it.

From June 9 to 11, the navy, comparatively the strongest of the three military branches in Spain, held maneuvers off the Balearics. Franco was invited to observe them, together with President Alcalá-Zamora and war minister Hidalgo, from the deck of the battleship *Jaime I*. Once the maneuvers were completed, Franco accompanied Hidalgo on an inspection of the islands' defenses, which he was in the process of upgrading.

Hidalgo could hardly contain his enthusiasm for his new major general. He would soon write in a brief memoir:

> I first met the general in Madrid in February, but only really became acquainted during my four-day visit to the Balearics, when I became even more convinced that he fully merited his reputation. . . . He possesses all the military virtues to the highest degree. . . . His intelligence, his capacity for work, his culture and understanding are always devoted to the service of the army.
>
> His greatest talent is his steady deliberation in examining, researching, analyzing and dealing with problems, but his deliberation does not keep him from being very detailed and exact in his service, precise in observation, firm in discipline, and demanding, though also calm, understanding and decided. He is one of the few men I know who never rambles on. My conversations with him in the islands about military affairs revealed his extraordinary knowledge.
>
> In the silence of his office, Franco has devoted the eight years of his peacetime assignments to study and preparation. This has borne fruit, so that there are scarcely any secrets to him in the art of warfare. . . . He is not the most eloquent talker, but he can analyze problems, passing from theory to practice and concrete cases, . . . ranging from weaponry to all the issues that affect soldiers and their morale.[21]

This was high praise, but Hidalgo was clearly dazzled. One incident that particularly impressed him was Franco's response to his request, customary when the war minister visited a regional command, that a soldier in detention for breaking discipline be released. Franco replied that he would only do so if he received a direct order, since the only person under his command currently under arrest was a captain who was being disciplined for physically striking a soldier, which he considered one of the worst things an officer could do. So impressed was Hidalgo that, when planning to attend field maneuvers involving twenty-three thousand troops (a large number for Spanish military exercises) in León late in September, he disregarded normal protocol to invite the most junior of the major generals to join him as special adviser.

Gil Robles had already announced that when parliament opened on the first of October, the CEDA would insist on entering a new coalition government or else withdraw its support altogether. Since the Radical coalition could not survive without CEDA votes, a broader coalition that included representatives of the largest party in the Cortes was not merely reasonable but inevitable. The left, however, still counted on Alcalá-Zamora to exclude the CEDA from government permanently, however contradictory this would be to the functioning of a parliamentary democracy. Thus when the logic of the situation required him to authorize the broader coalition that took office on October 4, the Socialists used this to justify the outbreak of the revolutionary insurrection that they had been preparing for nine months.[22] The left Republican parties did not join the insurrection directly, but their leaders issued simultaneous statements that they were "breaking all relations" with the Republican regime they had so recently helped to found. Azaña took up temporary residence in Barcelona, which was slated to be one of the centers of insurrection under the leadership of the Esquerra, the left Catalan nationalists, who were not satisfied with broad autonomy but sought total autonomy within a new federalized Republic.

The three anarchist insurrections that had taken place between January 1932 and December 1933 had covered more than a dozen provinces, and the *sanjurjada* had focused on several large cities, but none had seriously threatened political stability. The Socialist insurrection was something else, for it erupted with varying force in fifteen different provinces and was accompanied by the rebellion in Barcelona. In Catalonia the revolt was quickly suffocated by the local garrisons, but in the mining province of Asturias in the northwest the revolutionaries succeeded in taking over most of the region.

Socialist plans had not entirely been a secret, and CEDA leaders, not making the same mistake as the Monarchists had in April 1931, had contacted various generals to guarantee that the army would resist. The leader who made the most direct effort to get in touch with Franco, however, was the Falangist chief José Antonio Primo de Rivera, who sent a letter by his close friend, Franco's brother-in-law Serrano Suñer, who had become active in the CEDA. José Antonio, as he was known, urged Franco to be prepared to defend the unity and security of Spain. The general, however, was not impressed by the machinations of rightist extremists, whether Fascists or Monarchists. (Six months earlier the latter had signed a secret agreement with Mussolini for limited financial and military assistance for a Monarchist takeover in Spain). So far as is known, he did not reply.

The War Ministry had been monitoring the situation for weeks, and during the recent field maneuvers the garrison in Oviedo, the Asturian capital, had remained at its post, to be ready for trouble, but the exact timing of the insurrection and its strength in Asturias nonetheless took the government by surprise. Franco had returned momentarily to Madrid, having obtained a short leave to dispose of some of his wife's family property in Asturias, and Hidalgo immediately reassigned him to the War Ministry as special adviser to coordinate the repression. He knew that Franco, from his earlier years in Oviedo, was well acquainted with Asturias, but, more importantly, he did not trust the relatively liberal-minded senior officers in his own ministry, a number of them holdovers from the Azaña administration. They, in turn, were resentful, criticizing the way in which Hidalgo had once more jumped the chain of command by abruptly assigning what were, in effect, plenary powers to the most junior major general.

Martial law was decreed throughout Spain, and for ten days Franco never left the War Ministry, sleeping on a couch in his office. His main center of operations was the ministry's telegraph room, where he was assisted by his cousin Pacón and by two naval officers whom he particularly trusted. Franco planned and coordinated military action throughout the country and had authorization to use some of the powers of the Ministry of the Interior, as well. Years later, he would say with considerable exaggeration that the insurrection was part of a vast revolutionary conspiracy "prepared by the agents of Moscow," and there is no doubt that he saw himself as part of an international struggle against revolutionary subversion, the latest phase in a European conflict that had begun in 1917.[23]

A key decision was to move some of the elite units in Morocco to Asturias as soon as possible. Ordinary army detachments were composed of short-term conscripts, some of whom were leftists, and had limited capacity for combat. Azaña had twice brought in units from Morocco to quell recent insurrections (one by Sanjurjo, one by the CNT), so this had become a standard procedure, not a new policy of "colonial brutality" suddenly dreamed up by Franco, as has been often charged. Moreover, he swiftly removed from command his first cousin and old boyhood friend Major Ricardo de la Puente Bahamonde, a liberal-minded air force officer in charge of a small air base near León, who displayed sympathy for the insurrection.

Hidalgo wanted to send Franco directly to Asturias to put down the revolution, but Alcalá-Zamora objected that the person in charge should be a liberal officer thoroughly identified with the Republic. Therefore the chief of operations appointed for the region was General Eduardo López de Ochoa, a noted Republican and a Mason. The key component, however, was an expeditionary force of two battalions of the *tercio* and two Moroccan *tabores*, plus other units from the protectorate, sent by ship to Gijón on the Asturian coast. To command these, Franco summoned Lieutenant Colonel Juan Yagüe, his old comrade and friend from the Moroccan campaigns, who was currently without assignment. Yagüe was a capable combat leader, and his units took the lead in forcing the revolutionaries out of Oviedo and then closing in on their base in the mining district. The insurrectionists had murdered between fifty and a hundred civilians in cold blood, including teenage seminary students, and they had destroyed many buildings in Oviedo in their struggle against the local garrison. They had also stolen fifteen million pesetas from provincial banks, most of which was never recovered. The money was used to finance subsequent revolutionary activity. In reconquering the province, the army units also committed atrocities, and there may have been as many as a hundred summary executions, though only one victim was ever identified, despite the vociferous leftist propaganda campaign that followed for months and years.[24] López de Ochoa negotiated a ceasefire by which the revolutionaries laid down their arms in return for a promise that Yagüe's troops would not enter the mining basin.[25] Franco, meanwhile, was ordered by Hidalgo to remain at the ministry to help coordinate the subsequent pacification, and he stayed in Madrid until February 1935.

Spain's "October revolution" polarized political society to an unprecedented extent. From this time forward, there was more and more talk of civil war, and historians from left, right, and center have variously described it as the "prelude" to or the "first battle" of the great conflict that would erupt less than two years later. For the right, it represented bloody revolution on the march, a preamble to the full horrors of Russia; to the left, it constituted a heroic stand against "Fascism," or at least reaction, which was followed by a repression that was made to sound like the one applied to the Paris Commune, though it had little in common with the latter, which was infinitely more severe.

Some of the rightist minority within the officer corps decided that this provided an opportunity to impose a new right-wing Republican regime backed by the army. One of their principal leaders was General Manuel Goded. He had been a vehement liberal who played a major role in the conspiracy against the dictatorship; as a prominent part of the new left-liberal elite in 1931, he had at first been named inspector-general of the army, but within less than a year he became a bitter foe of the government's military policy and its support for radical reform and Catalan "separatism." On October 18, 1934, while the last battles raged in Asturias, he and General Manuel Fanjul suggested to Gil Robles on the one hand and to Franco on the other that the time had come for the right to seize power. Gil Robles indicated that the CEDA would not oppose the military but that it would have to act exclusively on its own initiative.[26] Franco was categorically negative, insisting that any talk of military intervention be terminated immediately.[27] He similarly discouraged a yet more hare-brained scheme to fly Sanjurjo from his home in exile near Lisbon to the Spanish capital, in order to set off a military *pronunciamiento*.[28] Franco would maintain this position, though with diminishing vigor, as we shall see, until the very eve of the Civil War in July 1936.

The chief drama of the following months had to do with the repression of the defeated revolutionaries, at least fifteen thousand of whom had been placed under arrest, doubling Spain's prison population. The right demanded severe punishment, while the left insisted on amnesty for what it tried to pass off as a labor action and a political protest that got out of control. From that time forward, the country was inundated with lurid atrocity stories from both sides. The left stressed brutal treatment of prisoners, whom they claimed were beat savagely and tortured. These allegations were amplified by a major international propaganda campaign, promoted by Willi Münzenberg and the Comintern in particular and the European left in general, reviving the centuries-old legend of "Black Spain," heir to the Inquisition.[29] There was undoubtedly some mistreatment of prisoners in Asturias during the first weeks, where an investigative journalist was shot dead by a Bulgarian officer in the Legion. Before long, however, an international commission was allowed to talk with prisoners, and none of the political organizations involved in the insurrection was ever outlawed, though in certain provinces Socialist centers were closed and elected leftist officials were deposed.

Hundreds of leaders and activists were prosecuted under martial law, and in the first weeks a number of death sentences were decreed, mainly for military deserters who had gone over to the revolutionaries, but ultimately only two people were ever executed for the most extensive European insurrection of the decade, and one of these was clearly guilty of multiple murders. The CEDA took a hard line, but Alcalá-Zamora, pursuing his self-announced goal of "centering the Republic," believed that the left needed to be conciliated rather than punished, and insisted that nearly all the death sentences be commuted. Gil Robles gave in, since the peculiar terms of the Republican constitution gave the president the power to dissolve the existing government whenever he pleased.

Franco, ever an *ordenancista*, was appalled, believing that the president's appeasement policy—so different from the adversarial relationship that Alcalá-Zamora adopted toward the moderate right—would only encourage revolutionism in the long term, with disastrous consequences. When the fighting still raged, he was quoted by the Italian chargé d'affaires as having told the latter that any failure to punish the insurrectionists firmly and fully would merely "encourage an early extremist response."[30] As events would reveal, the apolitical general understood his country's political dynamics much better than the highly political president. Another extremist response was soon to follow.

In the perspective of contemporary European history, the repression of the revolutionary insurrection of October 1934 was comparatively mild. Key leaders were treated with leniency. Socialists were not proscribed unless they had been actively involved in the uprising, and most leftist deputies continued to sit in parliament. Within scarcely more than a year, full civil rights would be restored to all the left except for the imprisoned revolutionaries, and they would enjoy complete freedom to try to win at the ballot box what they had failed to achieve by violence. This formed a total contrast with the bloody repression of leftist insurrection in such countries as France, Germany, or Hungary. A case can be made that, in fact, the repression—far from being the atrocity alleged by the massive leftist propaganda campaign—was too limited and that only severe and successful prosecution of the revolutionaries would have made possible the survival of a parliamentary Republic.

After much criticism of Hidalgo by the right for his alleged weakness, Lerroux, the prime minister, had personally taken charge of the Ministry of War in mid-November. He too sought a prominent role for Franco—hailed by the moderate right as "savior of the Republic"—awarding him the Grand Cross of Military Merit and keeping him on assignment in Madrid as special adviser. Lerroux wanted him to replace the current high commissioner of the Moroccan protectorate, a moderate Republican civilian, but Alcalá-Zamora blocked that, and so on February 15, 1935, the prime minister appointed him commander-in-chief of military forces there. When his train left Madrid on March 5, a large crowd of civilian and military figures was present to wish him well.

Franco was delighted with this assignment, which he thought in some ways the most important in the Spanish army, which was true enough as far as the caliber of the military units under his command was concerned. Doña Carmen, on the other hand, did not like Morocco, and it is not clear exactly how much of the following three months she spent there, but Franco derived great satisfaction from the new command. Unlike his predecessor, he attended Mass every Sunday, leading many of his officers to do so as well, which would cause him years later to comment on the tendency of subordinates to ape the practices of their commander.[31]

He developed a very good relationship with the civilian high commissioner, who relied on him almost as much as had Hidalgo. He tightened up the administration of the combat units and improved his personal relations with their officers, among whom he had great prestige. All this would be very important a little over a year later, when the Civil War began.

The CEDA chafed under the terms of a coalition government that severely underrepresented the party and in May 1935 insisted on a larger role. Gil Robles nonetheless probably made a major tactical mistake in not insisting on the premiership. The only alternative would have been new elections, which, in the aftermath of the insurrection and amid the disarray of the left, the CEDA would have won more decisively than in 1933. As it was, he settled for less, and in the new coalition the number of CEDA ministers increased from three to five, Gil Robles himself entering the government as minister of war. He insisted on this post because of the importance of the military's counterrevolutionary role, and he wanted to place the army under a capable and reliable general who would strengthen it without himself becoming overtly involved in politics. Though Gil Robles had various candidates to choose from, none seemed to fill the bill as well as Franco, who was named chief of staff of the army soon after Gil Robles took office. Franco later claimed he did not welcome this assignment, since he considered that he could accomplish the most by maintaining the army's top units at their highest combat efficiency in Morocco, whereas the chief of staff could do little to remedy the manifold deficiencies of the army as a whole and would always be liable to partisan political criticism. Gil Robles, however, insisted that no one else could do as good a job and that opinion inside the army was "almost unanimous" in favor of Franco, so he accepted the new assignment.[32]

First, however, the CEDA leader had to overcome strong opposition from President Alcalá-Zamora, who feared that the combination of Gil Robles as minister and Franco, the coordinator of the repression in Asturias, as chief of staff would result in military policy that was too rightist for the Republic, however technically apolitical Franco's record may have been.

Gil Robles, however, was vigorously supported by Prime Minister Lerroux, always well disposed toward Franco, whom he saw as the best man for the post and a capable professional who could be trusted. He and Gil Robles put up a united front, even threatening resignation and the collapse of the coalition, so that Alcalá-Zamora had to give in. Moreover, Gil Robles named other conservative or neoconservative officers to top posts. Goded became inspector general of the army once more and head of the air force, while General Joaquín Fanjul was named undersecretary of the War Ministry.

Gil Robles later described Franco's preeminence among his colleagues in the following terms:

> The officers of his generation were impressed by a series of qualities that invested him with undeniable prestige. There was his courage, less theatrical than that of certain other companions in the Moroccan campaigns, but which, after being subjected to the decisive test of fire on numerous occasions, became legendary; foresight and sure instinct that enabled him to measure the strength of an enemy in order to attack coldly when it was weakened; the cult of discipline, which he did not hesitate to sustain with means as harsh as might be necessary, though without failing to watch over the well-being of his troops with extreme care and striving to avoid wasting lives in combat; careful preparation of operations, indispensable in a colonial campaign, where it is more important to avoid dangerous improvisations than to develop grand strategic concepts; exact knowledge of the enemy's weak points in the material and in the moral order; avoidance of any kind of dissipation that might distract him from achieving his goals, maturely conceived and implacably pursued. . . . All this contributed to surrounding Franco with a special aura that was recognized by his friends and enemies and to create a zone of isolation and reserve about him that enhanced his reputation.[33]

Franco had reached the highest post in the army and would devote himself wholeheartedly to its revitalization. He received full cooperation from the war minister, as Franco would always recognize publicly, so that the military policy of the next seven months can be seen as a joint endeavor of the minister of war and the chief of staff. Altogether, the year 1935 was the period under the Republic when Franco spent the least time at home with the family, putting in long hours in the ministry.

The reform of the army was seen as the counterreform of the Azaña policy, even though most of the structural reorganization effected by the latter was maintained. The new administration introduced numerous changes in such areas as leadership and discipline, and it altered the way new appointments were made. It introduced more intensive training and preparation for mobilization, improved coastal fortifications, and accelerated planning for rearmament. The Azaña appointments in senior commands were generally reversed, and more conservative officers were promoted to high posts. Franco's friend Varela, who held even more prestigious combat medals than he did, was finally promoted to brigadier, though this required passing over eight colonels with greater seniority. Emilio Mola, reappointed to the army the year before, was given the Melilla command and then soon was promoted to Franco's preceding post of commander-in-chief in Morocco. Though it was not possible to restore military honor courts, abolished by Azaña's legislation, discipline and the administration of military justice were tightened. Gil Robles also secured approval of a new decree that lowered the age for promotion to brigadier, with the intention of bringing officers who were both combat veterans and more conservative in orientation to higher command. Moreover, the new cadres of "subofficers," the ranks created by Azaña to "democratize" and undercut the regular officer corps, were reduced in size, the senior subofficers promoted instead to second lieutenant. Political conservatism was not an exclusive criterion in every instance, so long as the officers in question were professionally competent and not leftist. Some senior officers known to be Masons, for example, retained their posts or were even promoted to more important commands, if deemed capable and reliable, showing that in 1935 Franco's anti-Masonic phobia had not become absolute.

The air force, whose officers were the most leftist in the military, received special attention. Azaña had removed the air force from the army's chain of command, placing it directly under the Republican presidency, but the Gil Robles–Franco reforms placed the air force under the army once more and changed numerous assignments, limiting the influence of the most leftist officers. This did not affect Franco's brother Ramón, who had been out of the country for two years as air attaché in Washington and had avoided any further political involvement, becoming a more strict professional, to the immense relief of his elder brother.[34]

There was no money to expand the army, though Gil Robles and Franco did raise the number of new volunteers that could be accepted yearly, on the grounds that they were considered to be more effective soldiers than draftees. The budget was reorganized to spend more money on combat readiness and support of the officers, and there was more attention to training, while the garrison in Oviedo, deemed most vulnerable to another revolutionary assault, was reinforced.

The ministry temporarily recalled Mola from Morocco to help prepare a new general mobilization plan in case of emergency. This plan was intended to address the danger of both foreign war and domestic insurrection. Whenever an internal crisis developed, in at least three different situations between 1931 and 1934, the Republican government had quickly moved elite units from Morocco to quell insurrection, and Mola's plan was designed to facilitate such action in the future. On the other hand, a proposal to create a new motorized infantry division for rapid commitment did not become reality, for lack of funds.

Ever since his tour of command in the Balearics, Franco had been sensitive to the problem of coastal defense, which was quite weak. The main achievement in this area was partial refortification of the chief Mediterranean naval base at Cartagena, though there was neither time nor money for other plans concerning the Balearics and the Gibraltar region.

Alcalá-Zamora vigorously fought some of the changes Franco favored, which he considered too conservative in ethos or goal. He believed Franco was a crypto-Monarchist, or at least dangerously conservative, and he was justly skeptical about Franco's insistence on relying on machine guns, rather than rapid-firing antiaircraft artillery (not readily available for Spain) for defense from aerial attack.[35] In fact, Spain at that time possessed almost no antiaircraft defenses whatsoever.

Weaponry and equipment were, as usual, antiquated and completely inadequate. Gil Robles therefore gained approval from the council of ministers in November for a rearmament plan projected to spend 1,100 million pesetas over a three-year period on new weapons, mainly for the army, to which was added another 400 million for the air force, designed to provide four hundred new warplanes over the same time span. The rapid political changes that soon followed would mean, however, that almost none of these plans were carried out.[36]

Franco created within the general staff a new section on counterespionage to keep watch on the revolutionary movements and particularly on subversion within the armed forces. It was found that about 25 percent of new draftees were members of leftist organizations at the time they were called up. During 1934–35, a semisecret officers' association had been created by some of the more conservative officers, called the Spanish Military Union (Unión Militar Española [UME]). It was not originally an organ of political conspiracy but a kind of right-wing variant of the old *juntas militares*, designed to safeguard the professional interests of the officers and strengthen the military. Franco maintained contact with it through one of his staff officers, Lieutenant Colonel Valentín Galarza Morante, a Monarchist with a flair for conspiracy who in some ways was the central figure of the UME. The minority of leftist officers in the army and in the security corps in turn created the opposing and much smaller Republican Antifascist Military Union (Unión Militar Republicana Antifascista [UMRA]), in which Socialists and Communists predominated.

In October Franco was sought out by Salvador de Madariaga, at that time Spain's leading diplomat and de facto head of its delegation in the League of Nations, as well as one of the country's leading intellectuals and writers. Madariaga was alarmed by the political polarization in Spain and the limited support for liberal democracy, whether on the left or right, and had just published a book called *Anarquía o jerarquía* (*Anarchy or Hierarchy* [1935]), which questioned the viability of direct democracy in the present climate, particularly in the Latin nations. He proposed a more indirect system of corporative representation that he termed "organic democracy," an idea that, in a much more authoritarian form, Franco would later make great use of. On one of his brief trips to Madrid, Madariaga arranged to have lunch with the country's leading general, whom he considered important for Spain's future. Franco was equally interested in meeting Madariaga; he had read his recent book and shared a somewhat similar point of view. In his memoirs, Madariaga briefly recounted their three-hour conversation, saying that he was impressed by Franco's "intelligence," which he described as "concrete and precise, more than original or brilliant," as well as by "his natural tendency to think in terms of public interest, without being at all ostentatious about it."[37] On that occasion, Madariaga did not dream that before many years, when Franco had established himself as dictator, Madariaga would become one of the general's most implacable long-term enemies.

The collaboration with Gil Robles came to an abrupt end in mid-December, when the current short-term government was voted down in parliament and Alcalá-Zamora vetoed the only viable replacement, a majority center-right coalition led by the CEDA, which would have reflected the composition of parliament. The president had relatively good intentions, but his were the kind that pave the road to hell. He detested the leaders of both the Radicals and the CEDA, because the former occupied the main space in the Republican center that he always sought, while the latter had organized the Catholic voters that Alcalá-Zamora had once hoped to lead, and had done so in a much more conservative manner. First the president maneuvered to eliminate Lerroux by manipulating a petty corruption issue into a major scandal in parliament, which discredited the weakly rooted Radicals. They were the only sizable liberal democratic force in the country, but Alcalá-Zamora, with astounding arrogance and naiveté, hoped to replace them with a new centrist force whose creation he could manufacture from the seat of government. He had arbitrarily appointed as interim prime minister an independent, Joaquín Chapaprieta, who had no party support whatsoever, a maneuver with which the CEDA once more cooperated, but Chapaprieta, unsurprisingly, lasted only three months. Gil Robles logically believed that the time had come for himself, as leader of the largest party in parliament, to have the opportunity to form a majority coalition, as would be expected in a normal parliamentary regime. Alcalá-Zamora categorically refused, instead appointing as prime minister a personal crony, Manuel Portela Valladares, who did not even have a seat in the Cortes. This was legal as a short-term measure under the constitution, though so artificial an arrangement could not last long and would inevitably have to lead to new elections.

Gil Robles and most of the conservatives were outraged that the reward of the Catholic party for its two years of cooperation and its respect for the constitution, so different from the behavior of the left, was to be permanent exclusion from state leadership.[38] At that juncture, General Joaquín Fanjul, the undersecretary in the War Ministry, urged Gil Robles to ask the military to intervene. Gil Robles responded that he was pledged to follow legal measures, but that he would not oppose action by the army leaders if they were determined to take the initiative themselves.

Fanjul withdrew to consult Franco and other top commanders. The chief of staff was categorical: the military was internally divided politically and would commit a grave error if it sought to intervene. Alcalá-Zamora had been unjust and unscrupulous, but there was no imminent danger of revolutionary subversion. An ordinary political crisis such as this did not warrant military intervention, which would be justified only by a total national crisis that threatened absolute breakdown or imminent takeover by the revolutionaries. For the third time in three years, he refused to support military interference, and his position was decisive in stopping the potential conspirators in their tracks.[39] Similarly, not many days later, he personally quashed a scheme by the Falangist leader, José Antonio Primo de Rivera, to spark an insurrection from the military academy in Toledo, warning one of the academy's senior officers, Lieutenant Colonel José

Monasterio, to have nothing to do with such a hare-brained plan.[40] For the moment, Franco remained as chief of staff and was the principal speaker at an emotional ceremony in the War Ministry that bade farewell to Gil Robles, whom he lauded, with tears in his eyes, for outstanding accomplishment and for having restored "honor and discipline" to the army. Within a month, Alcalá-Zamora announced the dissolution of parliament, and new elections were scheduled for February 16, 1936.

5

The Destruction of Republican Democracy

(1936)

The elections slated for February 16, 1936, would be no ordinary contest. Given the intense polarization and the highly disproportionate electoral law, victory would go either to the left or the right, and each was determined to introduce decisive changes. The left aimed for an exclusively leftist Republic, the right for major constitutional reforms on behalf of their own interests, the major difference being that only a small part of those on the political right harbored extralegal designs, in contrast to the revolutionary sectors of the Popular Front. There was little middle ground, a reality nonetheless not apparent to Alcalá-Zamora. He held that the existing parliament was too conservative and that, by calling elections two years early, he could maneuver the electorate into a more triangulated outcome. Alcalá-Zamora aimed to have Portela Valladares, the personal crony whom he had arbitrarily selected as prime minister, use government influence to create a new center democratic group that, though it would only be a minority, could gain a balance of power between right and left. In this he showed little respect for Republican democracy, since Spanish society was much too civically mobilized for any nineteenth-century-style manipulation to prosper. The real outcome of all Alcalá-Zamora's maneuvers was to mortally weaken the center, which could not possibly recover in the short term. At the close of 1935, the only constructive policy would have been to allow a genuine parliamentary government to function for the next two years, in order to achieve a more stable situation. Rejection of normal parliamentary procedure encouraged the radicalization of Spanish politics, which led to destabilization rather than recentering.

The left had learned the lesson of 1933 and formed a broad alliance that adopted the new Comintern terminology of the Popular Front, though the Spanish Communist Party was one of its least significant components.[1] The right failed to achieve an equivalent national coalition. The CEDA negotiated alliances either with the center or the extreme right in each province, according to local conditions. The CEDA leaders thought it unlikely that they could achieve an absolute majority and apparently planned a right-center coalition led by the CEDA, which would probably leave out the Monarchists. The left, by contrast, planned only a narrowly leftist government, and the outcome of the electoral campaign, the most intense in Spanish history, remained in doubt until the very end.

Political violence declined sharply in 1935, with the left in defeat and licking its wounds. The constitutional "state of exception" that had maintained minor civil restrictions was lifted by the government for the campaign, except for the provinces of Madrid, Barcelona, and Asturias. As in 1933, there was considerable violence during the campaign, the great bulk of it initiated by the left. Through election day, at least thirty-seven people were killed in various incidents.[2]

Rumors about a military coup increased. These speculations often involved the name of Franco, despite his careful avoidance of direct political involvement, since the chief of staff was the most visible figure in the military, and at that moment the one with the greatest potential influence over other commanders. Portela Valladares later wrote that he was sufficiently alarmed by these rumors that he sent the director general of security, Spain's national police chief, to seek assurances from Franco, who guaranteed that he would not be involved in any plot, pledging his "word of honor" so long as there was no "danger of Communism in Spain" and stressing that he was confident the present government would maintain Spain's security.[3] This simply restated his standard position that the military should not intervene unless the country faced an absolute, national, not an ordinary, political crisis. Franco would remain faithful to this position over the next five, increasingly tension-filled, months.

He was briefly absent from Spain toward the end of January, when he served as part of the Spanish delegation to the funeral of Britain's King George V, which took place in London on the twenty-eighth. He looked on the unfolding electoral campaign with growing apprehension, convinced—as were most conservatives—that the Popular Front was serving as the Trojan horse for violent revolution. Franco hoped that the CEDA would repeat, and even improve on, its electoral performance in 1933, but he also maintained contacts with the UME organization within the army, to be prepared for any eventuality.

The balloting on February 16 ended in a virtual draw between left and right, with the center nearly obliterated by the bias of the electoral system in favor of large coalitions. During the course of the afternoon and evening, however, leftist mobs became increasingly active and in six provinces interfered with either the balloting or the registration of votes, augmenting the leftist tally or invalidating rightist pluralities or majorities.[4] By late evening, the returns indicated some sort of victory for the Popular Front, and the crowds became more militant, breaking into a number of prisons to free revolutionaries under detention.

Franco stayed up late that night at the ministry and eventually became alarmed at the reports, finally telephoning General Sebastián Pozas, director of the Civil Guard, to insist that the security forces act with greater energy and that it might be necessary to seek a declaration of martial law. Pozas replied that there was no need for concern, since what was going on were only demonstrations of "Republican merry-making." Franco then awakened the elderly General Nicolás Molero, minister of war, telling him that he must take the initiative in having the government declare martial law. Molero apparently agreed that he would try to convince the council of ministers to do so in the morning, after which Franco went home to bed.[5]

Gil Robles, on the other hand, was up all night, receiving news that demonstrators were getting out of control in some provinces, which would result in distortion of the electoral returns. He woke up Portela Valladares and around 4 a.m. managed to get him to telephone Alcalá-Zamora, who refused Portela's request for a decree of martial law, though he said he would consider it later on.[6] To Gil Robles, this was unacceptable and he arranged to have his former military aide wake up Franco around 7 a.m.[7]

Franco dressed immediately and went back to staff headquarters, where he met with his old acquaintance Natalio Rivas, who was also a friend of Portela. Rivas asked Portela to arrange a meeting between Franco and the prime minister as soon as possible. Franco next sought to accelerate events by speaking with Goded and General Angel Rodríguez del Barrio, inspector general of the army, both of whom had extensive contacts with district commands. He urged the two generals to get on the telephone and convince regional commanders, who had power to declare martial law in their territories on a temporary basis, to do so immediately, saying that within a short time the government would issue a national decree. They made a number of calls but reported back to Franco that district commanders were unwilling to act until a national decree had been issued.[8] It has also been alleged that Franco contacted Galarza, telling him to alert UME groups all over Spain to be ready for an emergency.[9]

When the ministers met in late morning, Molero made the case for martial law, which was agreed to by the council. Portela Valladares had no time to meet personally with Franco, but he did telephone him to report the ministers' decision, and Franco took steps immediately to implement the decree, presumably around noon. Alcalá-Zamora, however, requested that the council reconvene in the presidential palace and, when they assembled, canceled the decree, which apparently was already being put into effect at four divisional headquarters that between them oversaw at least six provinces. The president ordered that all these preparations cease, only agreeing to declare a state of alarm that would be limited to imposing press censorship and controlling the right to assembly, so as to prevent the formation of large mobs.[10] Alcalá-Zamora was, however, sufficiently concerned to give Portela a signed but undated declaration of martial law, which he might later put into effect whenever he judged it necessary. Portela then phoned Franco again in the early afternoon, telling him that all the previous orders must be canceled, though for a number of days local commanders would maintain martial law in at least three provinces (Alicante, Valencia, and Zaragoza).

Franco finally met with Portela Valladares around 7 p.m., when he was received in the prime minister's office, but he could not convince Portela to put the undated decree into effect. This conversation was repeated once more on the following day, with the same result. By that time Portela was thoroughly frightened and did not know which to fear more, another insurrection from the left or the pressure from the military. Before the end of February 18, he sent word to the Popular Front leaders that he was about to leave office. Goded, Fanjul, and Rodríguez del Barrio conferred further with Franco on that day, insisting that the army must act on its own, if necessary. Once more he referred them to regional commanders, to gauge the degree of support, which yet again was found wanting. For the first time under the Republic, Franco was willing to consider intervention by the military, but he found conditions inadequate.[11]

The panic of Portela Valladares increased hourly, as word arrived that in some provinces civil governors were simply throwing up their hands and fleeing. On the morning of the nineteenth, he told the president that he was resigning immediately. Alcalá-Zamora was appalled, for this was technically improper, since the caretaker government in charge of an election had the duty to remain in power long enough to register the results completely and also to administer the second-round runoff, which would take place two weeks later in several provinces where no electoral slate had received the minimum plurality required by law. To bolster Portela, the president dictated a message to the Supreme War Council, composed of Franco, Goded, Rodríguez del Barrio, and General Manuel Núñez del Prado, a liberal, stating categorically that he would not tolerate any interference from the military, which, if it were to attempt a coup, would first have to overthrow the president of the Republic.[12] Portela then met with the council of ministers, but his morale, momentarily bolstered by the president, collapsed once more with word of more rioting by the left and the illegal seizure by the Socialists of two municipal governments on the edge of Madrid. Reporting back to Alcalá-Zamora, he declared the situation hopeless, saying that he must resign without further delay.

The president once more exhorted him to stand firm and to take back the two municipal governments by force, if necessary, and then arranged for the council of ministers to reconvene in the presidential palace at 2 p.m. In that meeting Molero reported that Franco and the other members of the Supreme War Council had promised there would be no subversion by the military, but this made no impression on Portela, now completely terrified of the left. The only minister willing to replace the premier was the minister of the navy, Admiral Antonio Azarola, with the personal support of Molero, but Alcalá-Zamora pointed out that was impossible, since the Republican constitution prohibited a military officer from serving as prime minister.[13] This show of resolution by the president, who had ended by, in effect, agreeing with Franco, came much too late, and the entire cabinet resigned. Franco then made one last effort, waiting that afternoon for the outgoing prime minister at the Ministry of the Interior to make a final plea that he meet his responsibilities and implement the decree of martial law given him by Alcalá-Zamora. This was equally futile. Portela declared that would be to govern as a dictator, and he was simply incapable of that.[14]

Alcalá-Zamora decided that he had no alternative but to appoint a new government under Manuel Azaña, the leader designated by the victorious Popular Front. Such a step was irregular, since the electoral process had not yet been completed and Alcalá-Zamora had received reports that results were being rigged in a number of provinces, but to him the formation of an Azaña government was the only way to pacify the left. To his credit, even Azaña was critical of the timing of the president's initiative, but he moved rapidly to comply with it.

Thus the Popular Front was permitted unilaterally to register its own victory at the polls, contrary to the spirit and practice of Republican elections. This took place in nearly all provinces on February 20, but was carried out by new leftist officials, who ratified the results produced by major irregularities in at least six provinces, handing victory to the Popular Front. There were runoff elections in several provinces on March 1, but in the face of mounting violence the right withdrew, adding more seats to the leftist majority. Late in March, when the new parliamentary electoral commission convened, the leftist majority arbitrarily reassigned thirty-two seats from the right to the left, augmenting that majority further. Elections in the provinces of Cuenca and Granada, which customarily voted for the right and had done so again in February, were declared invalid, and a new contest was scheduled for May 5. When that took place, systematic pressure was applied to make it impossible for the right to campaign, and these new elections in conservative provinces were swept by the Popular Front. In a four-step process, electoral results originally almost evenly divided between left and right were rigged and manipulated over a period of three months until the Popular Front commanded a majority of two-thirds of the seats, which would soon give it the power to amend the constitution as it pleased. In the process, democratic elections ceased to exist.

On its third day in office, the Azaña government made major changes in the military hierarchy, mostly designed to remove conservative commanders from top posts and to send them far from Madrid. Franco was named military commander of the Canary Islands, far out in the Atlantic, near the coast of southern Morocco. General Emilio Mola, one of those on whom he had most relied in the restructuring of defenses, was switched from

Morocco to the Pyrenean province of Navarre, considered something of a backwater, and would be under the aegis of his divisional commander in Burgos, General Emilio Batet, highly disciplined and completely apolitical, who always eschewed any kind of conspiratorial machination.

Franco was deeply chagrined to lose his post as chief of staff and would later say that he considered the new assignment a *destierro* (banishment). To some extent that was correct, since the new government wanted him far away, yet it was a significant command, worthy of the rank of major general. The family remained in Madrid for three weeks before boarding a vessel to the Canaries, and Franco made the usual courtesy calls to take leave of the president and the prime minister. He later recalled that, though Alcalá-Zamora could not receive him personally, he responded to Franco's concerns by writing that he did not share his anxiety about the political future though that sanguine attitude would disappear within just a few weeks. He had a way of ending up agreeing with Franco, but it was characteristic that he always did so too late. Franco met personally with Azaña, suggesting that an appropriate posting in Madrid would permit him to serve the government in keeping things on an even keel, helping restrain any machinations by the military. Though his proposal sounded rather Machiavellian, it probably indicated that he was willing to serve a responsible leftist government, a position that he would maintain for some time, in keeping with his previous practice. Azaña replied with his customary disdain, saying that he wasn't worried about the army at all. Like Alcalá-Zamora, he too would change his mind, but only after several months. It is clear in retrospect that Franco, the professional soldier, judged the situation better than the two professional politicians.[15]

After reaching the pinnacle of the military hierarchy, Franco was depressed by his banishment to a remote archipelago and equally depressed about the political future. Carmen reports that for a brief time "my father considered asking for a period of leave instead" in the hope that by the end of the leave, the political situation would have become clearer. He may have been thinking of going abroad for a while, to escape the demand by the revolutionaries that he be imprisoned. She adds, however, that "my uncle Ramón Serrano Suñer was the one who pressed him" to consider entering politics, something corroborated by Serrano himself, who discouraged Franco from taking leave as a means of getting out of the country. Franco was toying with the idea of sitting out the looming crisis, either avoiding involvement or possibly even playing a role in military intervention from a safe distance.[16] After some days, he decided, however, neither to go on leave nor to try to play a more direct political role but to follow his customary path of accepting the next military assignment. He concluded that continued active service would probably place him in the best position, one way or another, and this turned out to be correct. Had he chosen either of the other alternatives in the late winter of 1936, the ultimate development of Spanish affairs might have been quite different.

Military conspiracy, which had sputtered off and on for several years, recommenced more seriously after the consolidation of the Popular Front victory. In the first days the ringleader was Goded, still by his own lights something of a liberal but deathly opposed to the left. Goded, however, was given a posting analogous to Franco's, dispatched as military commander of the Balearic islands. His place was taken by General Angel Rodríguez del Barrio, inspector general of the army, who brought together a small, informal group of senior commanders, many of them retired, who met periodically in Madrid. The principal networker was the staff officer, Lieutenant Colonel Valentín Galarza, who had conspired intermittently for several years and was the principal coordinator of the UME, the secret society of officers that claimed by that time to have enrolled more than a third of those on duty.

On March 8, before Franco left the capital, he attended a meeting of key conservative military men, some of them retired, held in the home of a CEDA leader. They agreed to form a council of certain senior generals who remained in Madrid, with the goal of "preparing a military movement to prevent the ruin and dismemberment of the Patria," which, however, "would only take action if circumstances made it absolutely necessary." The memorandum drawn up by General Manuel González Carrasco also stated that "following the initiative of Mola, insisted upon by Franco, it is agreed that the movement be exclusively for Spain, without any specific political coloring. After triumphing, it will face such problems as the character of the new regime, etc."[17] The overall leader would be Sanjurjo, currently living near Lisbon. He was in no position to organize a surefire military conspiracy or rebellion, but he was the most senior rebel commander, both because of his initiative in 1932 and because he was the only one who had reached lieutenant general before that rank was abolished.

For the first time—with a possible brief exception in 1925, in opposition to the first dictator—Franco had become a political conspirator. The conspiracy, however, was inchoate, and Franco had apparently succeeded in imposing the criterion he first invoked three months earlier: a political crisis would not be sufficient grounds for rebellion; rather, it would be justifiable only by an immediate threat of revolution or national breakdown. Moreover, there was no question of restoring the monarchy or trying to follow guidelines of any of the rightist parties. The nature of a new regime, if there was one, would have to be faced when the time came. Franco would remain faithful to these criteria during the increasingly critical four months that followed. He and Mola were agreed on an "open" program concerning the political future, though Franco would begin to veer in a more radical direction several weeks after the Civil War began.

The Franco family arrived in the Canaries on March 11, and he took possession of his new headquarters, on the island of Tenerife, second largest in the chain, two days later. In Tenerife, the leftist trade unions had declared a one-day general strike to protest his arrival, so that on disembarking the family was met with a loud, jeering protest by a mass of workers, to which he apparently responded with his usual icy calm, ignoring the demonstrators altogether. During the next few weeks, he ventured down to the port area several times to talk with workers and probe their feelings. The hostility on the island was palpable, however, and Doña Carmen became alarmed, personally asking that an informal guard made up of a number of reliable junior officers and NCOs be supplied for the commander and his family. This guard, which discreetly accompanied the family on almost every occasion, was organized by his aide Pacón and by his chief of staff.

Carmen, then nine years old, recalls:

> I remember the boat trip to the Canaries, which I found exciting. Then, when we arrived, Papá warned us there would not be much to do there. He had little work and began to play golf. And also to study English, using a small grammar book. He spoke French very poorly, though he could understand it.
>
> In the Canaries the one who thought he was in danger was my mother, not him. In Tenerife she always advised reliable junior officers when he left headquarters, even to play golf. Several would follow in a separate car. About the third time this happened, my father said, "Who are these men in the car behind us?" and Mother replied, "Don't worry, I asked them to come myself."

Whether or not Franco was in any physical danger, he was under semi-constant surveillance, his phone tapped and much of his mail opened, so that the only secure way that he could communicate with his comrades on the mainland was by personal courier. His contact with them was thus intermittent. He was seen by the left as potentially one of the most dangerous generals, because of his authority, skill, and influence, should he ever assume a more overt political role. Late in March the Socialist leader Indalecio Prieto referred to him publicly as the kind of general who could be most effective in organizing a revolt, though Prieto covered himself immediately by saying that he did not mean to imply that Franco was actually trying to do so.[18]

The Canaries command was a relatively quiet post, and Franco usually devoted to it no more than the long Spanish morning—up to five hours—but not always all of that. Most afternoons were free, many of them devoted to his new golf hobby. He was tutored in English by Dora Leonard, an Englishwoman who lived on Tenerife. She gave him three hour-long lessons per week, and he also undertook written exercises, learning to read English but never to speak or write it with any competence. Given the increasing number of arbitrary political arrests by the left Republican government, he joked to the family that studying English would give him something to do in jail. Yet at that time English was a language obviously more useful to politics and diplomacy, to the political career urged by Serrano, than to military affairs.

Franco feared the worst but hoped for the best. Political violence, pre-revolutionary activity by leftist militants, and arbitrary acts of government increased, but not in a straight line. So far there was no indication that revolutionaries were taking over the government. The left continued to demand that all those primarily responsible for crushing the revolution of October 1934 be jailed and prosecuted, but only the moderate Republican General López de Ochoa, who had led the army in Asturias, was in fact imprisoned, and he was later released. Though Franco could not be sure he would not be next, no move was made against him. The Azaña government was gambling that by making many concessions to the revolutionaries, things would soon settle down. Though this was rather like trying to douse a fire with kerosene, none of the revolutionary movements proposed immediate seizure of power, and Franco did not consider the situation hopeless. Despite his perpetual suspicion of the machinations of Moscow, Masonry, and international capital (which involved more than a little cognitive dissonance), his paranoia remained partly theoretical, and he made it clear that he did not share the hysteria of the extreme right, forces with which he had never consorted, save in the most superficial way.

The Francos led a normal social life on Tenerife, guided especially by the chief legal officer in his headquarters, Major Lorenzo Martínez Fuset of the army's juridical corps. Fuset had married into one of the archipelago's leading families, and the Francos found both the major and his wife extremely likeable, facilitating their entrée into local society. After some weeks, Franco came to trust Fuset to the point of taking him into his confidence, at least to some extent, on major issues.[19] He continued to play golf and, in his better moods, speculated about using part of his summer vacation to enjoy the golf courses in Scotland. If Franco had known what he would actually be doing by midsummer, even he might have been surprised.

One way to ensure against reprisal was to gain parliamentary immunity. Electoral defeat had cast doubt on the legalist tactics of the CEDA, but as late as April the right had not given up on the electoral process. Since the results in the two provinces of Cuenca and Granada had been nullified by the new parliament, a rightist coalition planned to contest the new elections to be held on May 5 and was looking for stronger candidates. Urged by his brother-in-law Serrano Suñer, Franco wrote to the CEDA leadership on April 20 to request a place on the list of the rightist coalition, though as an "Independent," since he did not want to be identified fully with any specific party. Gil Robles and his colleagues accepted this request, but also offered a candidacy to the imprisoned Falangist leader José Antonio Primo de Rivera. For the first time, Primo de Rivera was gaining in popularity on the right, as what was called "Fascism" seemed to more and more people the surest salvation from the revolutionaries.

José Antonio, however, took offense when he learned that Franco's name would be included. He had developed a strong dislike for Franco, whom he considered devious, calculating, and untrustworthy. He was suspicious of the military in general, since, when the chips were down, it always refused to take action against the left, and he complained that the inclusion of Franco's name made the rightist list look militarist and reactionary. Serrano Suñer was caught in the crossfire, since he was one of the two or three closest friends of the Falangist leader, whom he visited in prison in an attempt to get him to withdraw his veto. José Antonio was adamant, pointing out that Ramón Franco had been completely inept in parliamentary debate in 1931–33 and had made a fool of himself and that his older brother would probably do the same. Serrano flew to the Canaries on April 27 to discuss the matter with Franco, who took the point and prudently withdrew his candidacy.[20] In the long run it made no difference, because the government ruled all new names ineligible, while a combination of street violence and government pressure made it impossible for the rightist candidates to campaign. The elections in Cuenca and Granada were completely controlled by the left, in the fourth and final phase of its elimination of electoral democracy in Spain.[21] That also provided Franco with his cover story whenever the issue came up in later years, since his initial willingness to stand for parliamentary election became an embarrassment after the Civil War began. He then insisted that he had quickly withdrawn because he was convinced that the elections would be fraudulent, though in fact that had not been his prior assumption. Later yet, he even claimed that he had sought a place in Madrid so as to organize a military revolt more effectively, whereas as late as April the very opposite of that was true.[22]

Early in April the Popular Front parliament voted to depose President Alcalá-Zamora. The constitution authorized the Cortes resulting from the second general elections held during a single presidential term the power to review the latest dissolution of parliament and, if it were found to be unjustified, to depose the president who had ordered it. Alcalá-Zamora contended that this did not apply to him, since his initial dissolving of the Constituent Cortes in 1933 had not been the same as the dissolving of a regular constitutionally elected parliament. Moreover, ever since they lost the balloting in that year, the main leftist demand had been the convening of new elections. Once Alcalá-Zamora had done that in 1936, the new leftist majority, which his decision had made possible, voted to depose the president who had gratified their wishes, on the grounds that he should have called new elections even earlier. They refused the request of moderates to refer the matter to the Court of Constitutional Guarantees, since their goal was to establish by hook or crook total leftist domination by elevating Azaña to the presidency of the Republic.[23]

The self-righteous Alcalá-Zamora was outraged, calling it a "parliamentary coup d'état," but, though he himself had manipulated the law outrageously, he had never directly violated it, and he ignored all pleas to resist. The centrist Joaquín Chapaprieta urged him to dismiss the Azaña government, just as he had forced out many Radical-led ministries, but the Radicals had obeyed the law and were never intimidating, whereas Alcalá-Zamora blanched in the face of an increasingly violent left. On April 8, the day he was to be deposed from office, he wrote in his diary:

> Around eleven this morning a general staff colonel came to visit me.[24] He was in full uniform, to ask me on behalf of the army that I respond to the coup d'état, even without legislative support, by signing a decree that deposes the Azaña government, and thus give moral force to the firm and inevitable intervention of the army, which would save the country from anarchy, still under the Republic. With a courtesy that only underlined the firmness of my position, I completely refused. . . . I know that today opinion, and tomorrow perhaps history, will reproach me for not employing the

force, and the means and arguments, that a different president might use against a parliamentary coup d'état. But I did not hesitate. And with that my presidential diary has now ended.[25]

Had he resisted, it is probable that most of the army, including Franco, would have supported him. Azaña took office as president on May 10, though by that time even the left Republican leader had become alarmed by the wave of violence, disorder, and widespread abuses of the law affecting much of the country.

For two months the multiple conspiracies among small groups of officers remained disorganized. By April the handful of mostly retired senior commanders in Madrid, pompously referred to privately as the "generals' council," had revealed itself to be impotent, and the baton had passed to Emilio Mola, military commander in Navarre. The government had purposely relegated him to a provincial backwater in Pamplona without considering that the ultraconservative atmosphere of Carlist Navarre might give him a more supportive background than he would have found almost anywhere else. Mola would become the mastermind of military insurrection.

Mola was an *africanista* and an old comrade of Franco's, though there were no very close personal ties between them. Five years older, Mola had only reached the rank of brigadier, but General Berenguer had made him the last director general of security, or national police chief, under the monarchy. This provided his introduction to political affairs, and the collapse of the monarchy left him highly susceptible to worry about the dangers of revolutionary subversion. The Republic had briefly imprisoned him and expelled him from the army, but he was brought back after the amnesty and had played a key role in the military reorganization carried out by Gil Robles and Franco.[26] For three months he had been military commander of all the forces in the protectorate and had been given responsibility for a plan of emergency mobilization in the event of yet another revolutionary insurrection.

Mola, like more than a few officers, was obsessed by the danger posed by "Communists," as he commonly referred to the revolutionary left. Once the heads of UME cells throughout north-central Spain recognized his leadership in mid-April, he became the overall head of military conspiracy. At the end of May, Sanjurjo sent word from Lisbon that he accepted Mola's role and made him his personal representative in organizing a revolt.[27]

During May and June Mola drew up political guidelines, which largely followed the thinking of Sanjurjo four years earlier. Sanjurjo, who had held the rank of lieutenant general, would be recognized as the eventual acting head of a new military regime. He was widely liked and respected, both on the personal and military level, but the senior commanders were also aware that Sanjurjo lacked both principles and talent in politics, so that his function was to be in large measure symbolic: he would be a sort of military primus inter pares.[28] The revolt would be carried out in the name of the Republic and its stated goal would be to restore law and order, its only slogan being "Viva España!" All the left would be subdued, after which the country would be initially governed by a military directory that would eventually conduct a plebiscite among a politically purged electorate on the issue of republic versus monarchy. Legislation prior to February 1936 would be respected and church and state would remain separate, though all religious persecution would end. Private property would be respected, as would voluntary cooperatives. This was a program for a rightist but not necessarily Monarchist nor completely reactionary regime. It was not what the Monarchist parties or many civilian rightists wanted, but it represented a kind of common denominator of the extreme and moderate right, and to some extent even of the right center. This partially "open" project would be the one invoked by all military commanders who eventually rebelled, including Franco, though he would soon move rapidly to abandon it and embrace radical dictatorship.[29]

Franco was able to communicate with Mola and keep up with the progress of the conspiracy only distantly by means of secret contacts, mostly in the form of brief ciphered messages. In addition, he received personal visits from Galarza, Serrano Suñer, and others. Afterward, Franco would insist that he had formed part of the conspiracy from early March on, but that, like so much that he said in later years, was misleading. The evidence is overwhelming that for weeks he refused to commit himself categorically one way or another, saying that the time had not yet come for drastic and irrevocable action and that the situation in Spain might yet sort itself out. He had no illusion that armed revolt would be anything but the most desperate undertaking: the odds were stacked against its success, and the left would be determined to exact summary justice on its leaders. A premature, inadequately organized revolt would make everything much worse.

The veteran Monarchist General Luis Orgaz, involved in the early phases of the conspiracy, was summarily exiled to the Canaries by the government in mid-April. Talking with Franco, he chided him for his reluctance, insisting that a decisive revolt would quickly triumph, that it would be like eating a "candied pear," an idea Franco found preposterous. The core conspirators on the mainland grew weary with what they called his "coquetry," and, since Spain had recently begun to hold American-style beauty pageants, one wit in Pamplona nicknamed him "Miss Canary Islands of 1936."[30] Sanjurjo still resented the fact that Franco had refused to support him four years earlier and insisted that he was not needed. He was quoted as saying that "no matter what, with Franquito or without Franquito, we will save Spain."[31] Mola and other conspirators, however, could not afford to be nonchalant, for Franco's prestige could be an important factor. In recent years, he had been a crucial reference point in military politics, and if he committed himself, a good many others might follow his example.

As usual, what most concerned Franco was the army. If the strength and discipline of the armed forces were not diluted, the revolutionaries would be unable to overthrow the government and the situation might yet be rectified. On June 23 he took the unprecedented step of writing a personal letter to the prime minister, Santiago Casares Quiroga, to inform him about "the state of anxiety produced in army officers by the government's latest military measures," such as the reassignments in command and the reincorporation into the army and other security forces of officers earlier convicted of mutiny and subversion in October 1934. Recent slanders and attacks on the army, particularly a major incident in Alcalá de Henares, followed by further reassignments, had produced increasing worry and resentment. Franco suggested that the prime minister might have "inadequate information" about this mood, perhaps due to the limitations of his present military advisors. He quickly added that he did not wish to deprecate these advisors, who might simply be uninformed, but wanted to state that the reports that had apparently motivated these recent initiatives were altogether inaccurate. He declared that some of the army's most capable and experienced commanders had either been removed or relegated to lesser posts, replaced by other officers whom 90 percent of the officer corps regarded as inferior. Franco insisted that those who engaged in political "adulation" and "servility" were no more loyal to the present institutions than was anyone else, since they had done the same under the monarchy and the dictatorship. "Those who present the army as currently opposed to the Republic simply fail the truth, and those who simulate imagined conspiracies deceive." The army, he insisted, was loyal, but it wanted fair treatment. "Lack of equanimity and justice" in administration had provoked the emergence of the *juntas militares* in 1917, and a similar kind of problem had led at the present time to the formation of the UME and the UMRA, harbingers of future "civil strife." Concern over military policy and administration merely redoubled anxiety about the "grave problems of the Patria." Though the army remained loyal, the lack of justice was having deplorable effects. Franco concluded that it was "his duty" to point these matters out to Casares Quiroga, who could easily verify them by conferring with the army's leading commanders.[32]

Franco made public the text of this letter some months after the Civil War began. There is no indication of any reply or whether the prime minister even read it. Critics would later say this was a prime example of Franco's duplicity, but such a judgment goes too far. He was pointing out, correctly, that the great bulk of the officer corps was not involved in conspiracy but that there was grave concern about government policy undermining the army and Spanish security more generally. The letter was a reiteration, with variations, of his earlier appeals to Portela Valladares and, in March, to Azaña. The accuracy of Franco's claim about the army's loyalty, as of that date, was born out by a calculation made by Mola about the same time that no more than 12 percent of army officers could be counted on to join a revolt.[33] At one point Mola is said to have drawn up papers to ask for retirement from active duty and to have considered simply fleeing abroad in the event that he was already too seriously compromised.[34]

His fellow conspirators convinced Mola to stay the course, but one of his main problems was Madrid, where military leaders were completely divided and there was little hope that an insurrection could gain control. Mola's planning became increasingly complicated, the rebellion no longer conceived as a *pronunciamiento* or coup d'état, as in the early stages, but as a full military insurrection and mini-civil war of several weeks' duration, with columns of rebel troops from provinces where success was assured converging on the capital in a second phase. By June Mola had concluded that the peninsular garrisons alone were too weak to pull this off and that the insurrection could only succeed if most of the elite units were brought in from Morocco, something that Franco himself had always considered indispensable.

Franco was offered the command of these key forces, and by the last days of June he seems for the first time to have tentatively agreed to participate, though later he would change his mind once more. Since he was hundreds of miles out in the Atlantic, the first question was how to transport him quickly to Spanish Morocco, and a plan was formed to charter a foreign airplane to do so, the arrangements being first set into motion on July 5.[35]

The policy of the left Republican government was based on a hazardous calculation. It relied on the Popular Front alliance with the revolutionaries for the votes that kept a left Republican minority in power, the goal being to transform institutions in such a way as to consolidate a completely leftist, but not violently revolutionary, Republic. It gambled that by indulging the revolutionaries momentarily, they would eventually settle down, making possible an orderly administration. But four revolutionary insurrections had taken place within the previous four years, and, if there should be another, only the army could guarantee its repression. This consideration induced the government to refrain from purging the military command, for fear of, exactly as Franco said, making an adversary of the army unnecessarily. As far as a serious military revolt was concerned, the army itself was seen as something of a paper tiger. Government leaders believed the country had already undergone decisive change, which left the army incapable of playing a major political role. Should there be any revolt, they were convinced it would be another feeble gesture, as in 1932. Thus the government sought to placate the revolutionaries on the one hand and refrained from purging the army on the other, falling between two stools, unable or unwilling to move resolutely in any direction.

The situation in Spain by the late spring of 1936 was unprecedented for a Western country in peacetime. A Popular Front coalition also won a narrow but decisive electoral victory in France at the end of May, yet the consequences there were different. During June France was rocked by a gigantic strike wave larger in both absolute and proportionate terms than the strikes going on in Spain. Yet, though several groups of strikers in France occupied factories, their mood was more pragmatic than revolutionary and produced little violence; at the same time, the new government in Paris acted promptly and resolutely to arbitrate an end to the conflict. The divided and radicalized Spanish labor movements were more chaotic and harder to deal with, and the Spanish government more irresolute, making many concessions but unable to articulate a policy to restore order.

During the late spring commentators in Spain spoke of chaos, anarchy, and preparation for revolution. As early as April the foreign diplomatic corps in Madrid consulted among themselves about how to react if and when revolution broke out. By June an interest in "Fascism" was developing among the threatened. "Gaziel," the respected editor of Barcelona's *La Vanguardia*, wrote on June 10,

How many votes did the fascists have in Spain in the last election? None: a ridiculously small amount. . . . Today, on the other hand, travelers returning from different parts of the country are saying: "There everybody is becoming a fascist." What kind of change is this? What has happened? What has happened is simply that it is no longer possible to live, that there is no government. . . . In such a situation, people instinctively look for a way out. . . . What is the new political form that radically represses all these insufferable excesses? A dictatorship, fascism. And thus almost without wanting to, almost without realizing it, people begin *to feel themselves* fascist. They know nothing about all the inconveniences of a dictatorship, which is natural. They will learn about these later on, when they have to suffer them.

All this prompts the crucial question—how bad was the situation by July 1936? The frequent overt violations of the law, assaults on property, and political violence in Spain were without precedent for a modern European country not undergoing total revolution. These included massive, sometimes violent and destructive strike waves, large-scale illegal seizures of farmland in the south, a wave of arson and destruction of property, arbitrary closure of Catholic schools, seizure of churches and Church property in some areas, widespread censorship, thousands of arbitrary arrests, virtual impunity for criminal action by members of Popular Front parties, manipulation and politicization of justice, arbitrary dissolution of rightist organizations, coercive elections in Cuenca and Granada that excluded all opposition, subversion of the security forces, and a substantial growth in political violence, resulting in more than three hundred deaths.[36] Moreover, because local and provincial governments were forcibly taken over, decreed by the government in much of the country rather than secured via any elections, they tended to have a coercive cast akin to that of local governments overtaken by Italian Fascists in northern Italy during the summer of 1922. Yet as of early July the centrist and rightist opposition in Spain remained divided and impotent. There had been no revolt against conditions so oppressive that they would already have provoked rebellion in other countries.

A number of historians have recognized that a kind of prerevolutionary situation had developed but conclude that it was doubtful that a significant collectivist revolution could ever have been carried out because of the extreme division among the revolutionary groups, something that also worried several of the leftist leaders themselves. Even if the revolutionaries had managed to seize power, the result might have been an intrarevolutionary civil war (in fact, there were two intrarevolutionary outbreaks in the Republican zone during the conflict that ensued). The viability of any revolution is obviously a valid question, but there is no doubt that a prerevolutionary climate of lawlessness, coercion, and increasing violence now reigned that would have been intolerable in any country. Many major rebellions and civil wars have been initiated with less direct provocation. (Americans may refer to the two great American civil wars, those of 1775 and 1861, the first initiated by a tax revolt, the second provoked by a presidential election. In neither case were the lives and property of the rebels directly threatened, as in Spain.)

Franco, however, continued to hesitate. A chartered British plane left London on July 11 en route to the Canaries, with the goal of transporting him to Morocco, but on the following day (July 12), Franco dispatched yet another message to the conspirators, using the code term "geografía poco extensa" ("limited visibility"), indicating that the time still had not come for revolt and that he was still not ready to participate. This message, relayed from Madrid, reached Mola about 11 p.m. on the thirteenth, and created consternation, since word had already been sent to the military in Morocco that they were to begin the revolt on the eighteenth.[37] Mola therefore switched assignments and ordered that, once the insurrection was under way, Sanjurjo be flown from Portugal to Morocco to command the key forces in the protectorate.[38]

Though the revolt was already set to begin, what suddenly and finally changed the mind of Franco, and many other army officers, was the climax of political violence that took place in Madrid on the night of July 12–13. Around 10 p.m. Lieutenant José Castillo, an officer in the Assault Guard, was shot and killed on a side street in Madrid en route to his night-shift duty. Castillo was a Socialist and a militant of the UMRA who had mutinied in 1934 and been imprisoned but then was restored to duty by the Azaña government as part of its policy of packing the police with leftists, even revolutionaries. He helped to train Socialist and Communist militia on Sundays and shortly before had shot an unarmed rightist street demonstrator in the chest at point-blank range, thereby becoming a marked man for Falangist reprisal.

Leftist Assault Guard officers immediately rushed to the Ministry of the Interior, demanding permission to arrest a long list of rightist leaders, including Gil Robles and José Calvo Sotelo, the Monarchist chief in parliament, though as deputies, both enjoyed immunity and arresting them would be illegal. The interior minister nonetheless proceeded yet again to wink at the law, authorizing the arrests. A mixture of Assault Guard personnel, several off-duty policemen, and various Socialist and Communist activists then set out, one squad being illegally led by the Civil Guard captain Fernando Condés, who had also been imprisoned for mutinous and subversive acts in 1934. Condés had still not resumed active duty and was in civilian clothes. Gil Robles was out of town, but Calvo Sotelo was illegally arrested—more exactly, kidnapped—in the middle of the night, shot in the back of the head in an Assault Guard personnel carrier several minutes later, then dumped anonymously in the morgue of the principal cemetery. He was identified by early morning and the government, as usual, sought to censor the news, but word got out almost immediately and within a short time spread all over Spain.[39]

The effect was electric. The liberal army officer Captain Jesús Pérez Salas, who would remain with the left to the end, later explained its impact on much of the military this way:

> The catalyst sought by the right, which would guarantee a military revolt, finally arrived in the middle of July. That catalyst was the assassination of Calvo Sotelo. I do not know whose idea it was to commit such an outrage, but I will say that, even if they had been set up by the rebels themselves, those who did the deed could not have achieved a greater effect. It must have been planned by someone who really wanted to see the army rebel. . . . If the companions or allies of Lieutenant Castillo had applied the law of revenge and had shot down Calvo Sotelo in the street or wherever they found him, it would have been only one more act of terrorism, added to the many others that summer. The impression this would have caused in the army would of course have been deplorable and consequently would have constituted one more step toward a rebellion. Because of the importance of Calvo Sotelo, . . . his death would have been exploited to demonstrate to military officers the complete impotence of the government to prevent such killings. But in no way would it have been the drop of water that made the glass overflow. Such was the initial effect of the news of the assassination, but after the details were revealed and it was learned that the forces of public order had themselves been involved, the reaction was tremendous. . . . It is futile to deny the importance of this fact. If the forces of public order, on whom the rights and security of citizens depend, are capable of carrying out this kind of act, they effectively demonstrate their lack of discipline and obliviousness of their sacred mission. . . . The resulting action of the army

might have been prevented by a rapid and energetic initiative of the Republican government, punishing the guilty vigorously and, above all, expelling from the security corps all contaminated elements, to demonstrate to the country that the government was determined to end terrorism, no matter where it came from.[40]

The government refused to take such measures. Key figures in the assassination went into hiding, and the only initiative was to arrest two hundred more rightists, as though they had been guilty of the killing. Nothing was done to reassure moderates and conservatives. For decades it would be asserted that neither the Republican government nor the left sought a civil war, but such was not exactly the case. Some revolutionary leaders had invoked civil war for months, and the Socialists who followed Largo Caballero had sought to precipitate a military revolt for weeks, because they planned to crush it with a general strike that would permit them to seize power, a plan in which they "believed blindly."[41] The challenge of civil war was officially accepted in their press on July 15, and, for that matter, even the more moderate sector that followed Indalecio Prieto said civil war now was necessary. The Casares Quiroga government had vague information concerning the conspiracy and had expected a military revolt any time from July 10 on. It no longer had any interest in trying to avert it, for the government was confident that a rebellion would be weak, easily suppressed, and therefore redound to the strengthening of the government. Thus in the final days neither the government nor the leftist parties did anything to avoid the conflict, but, in a perverse way, welcomed military revolt, which they mistakenly thought would finally clear the air. Like Mola and the military rebels, they were calculating on a short conflict that would only last for a few days, or, at most, weeks.

Years later, in a speech of 1960, Franco conjectured that the revolt would never have developed adequate support among the military had it not been for the assassination.[42] This decided many of the undecided, including Franco himself. He received the news in his headquarters on Tenerife at some point on July 13 and was jolted by it, suddenly convinced that the final extremity, which he had always posited as the only thing that could justify armed rebellion, had finally arrived. Now it seemed more dangerous not to rebel than to rebel. Less than twenty-four hours after sending word to Mola that he was still not ready to join a rebellion, he immediately communicated his total commitment and urged that the revolt begin as soon as possible. He also instructed Pacón, his aide, to book passage to Le Havre for his wife and daughter on a German steamer that would leave the Canaries in six days, putting them out of harm's way while the fate of the rebellion was being decided.

Though Franco's decision was firm, it was not taken with ease, or even with much confidence, because he knew that he was embarking on a desperate undertaking in which the odds probably favored the other side and that failure would incur the harshest penalty. Dora Leonard, his English teacher, has said that when she met him for his final lesson on the fourteenth, he looked worried and haggard, as though he had slept poorly, seemed distracted, and had difficulty concentrating.[43]

Not the least of Franco's numerous doubts and worries concerned how he was to get from the Canaries to his projected command in Spanish Morocco, since nothing had been seen of the plane chartered to fly him there. On the fourteenth he apparently received word from conspirators in Madrid that the *Dragon Rapide*, the plane chartered in London, was about to arrive, and that same day its English pilot landed it on Gran Canaria, the largest of the islands and the only one at that time with an all-weather airport.[44] The difficult logistics of the era had kept the plane en route for several days, but even given the trouble the pilot had getting the plane there, the evidence suggests that, had it not been for the killing of Calvo Sotelo, Franco would have been prepared either to keep the pilot waiting as long as possible or even to have sent the plane back to London without him. As it was, Major Hugh Pollard, the British volunteer who had accompanied the flight, together with the two young Englishwomen who participated as "cover," then took the ferry to the neighboring island of Tenerife, site of Franco's headquarters, to let him know early on the morning of the fifteenth that the plane was ready, news that he undoubtedly received with an enormous sigh of relief.[45] During the course of that day and the next, final plans were made for the revolt in the Canaries. Franco kept his wife fully informed of his intentions and, according to Pacón, she fully approved, despite the hazards of the undertaking. If anything, the devout Doña Carmen was more opposed to the left than her husband, and she had great confidence in his ability to succeed in this audacious initiative.

The next sticking point was that regulations required that Franco ask official approval to make a brief inspection trip to Gran Canaria, the real goal of which was to take charge of the revolt and there board the plane for Morocco. This, however, was denied from Madrid, leaving Franco with the option of having Cecil Bebb, pilot of the *Dragon Rapide*, fly the plane to Tenerife during hours of good weather or else proceeding against orders by taking the night ferry to Gran Canaria as the first step of the revolt.

This issue was dramatically resolved around midday on the sixteenth, when word suddenly arrived that General Amado Balmes, Franco's subordinate who commanded the garrison on Gran Canaria, had suddenly died of an accident on the target practice range. The government then authorized Franco's departure for the funeral that would take place on the next day, and the Franco family arrived on the large island on the morning of the seventeenth.

The death of Balmes eventually sparked the first of many controversies concerning Franco's role in the Civil War, for it would be alleged that Balmes had been murdered by conspirators in his own garrison to get him out of the way and provide Franco with an excuse for going immediately to Gran Canaria. According to the conspiracy theory, Balmes was a political moderate who did not support the revolt and had to be eliminated both to ensure the success of the revolt on Gran Canaria and to provide Franco with an immediate reason to go there. The explanation given for the accident was that Balmes had the careless habit of resting a pistol against his stomach when reloading it and that in this case it went off accidentally, fatally wounding him and leading to his death in a hospital within two hours.[46] It has been argued that a veteran soldier could never have been so careless, but, of course, history is full of absurd accidents. There is no direct and conclusive evidence to support the conspiracy theory, an issue that must remain moot. If Balmes had tried to oppose the revolt, he might simply have been overwhelmed by his subordinates, as happened to a good many commanders elsewhere who remained loyal to the government but were arrested by their own officers. That Balmes's sudden demise was convenient to Franco and to the success of the revolt in the Canaries goes without saying.

As it was, Franco, Doña Carmen, and Carmencita abruptly left Tenerife on the night boat the evening of Thursday the sixteenth. They were accompanied by Pacón (by that point a lieutenant colonel), Martínez Fuset, and five other trusted officers and arrived in Las Palmas the next morning. Franco attended the funeral of Balmes and then made final arrangements for the revolt, which began at dawn on the eighteenth, the military forces in the Moroccan protectorate having initiated the insurrection shortly before 5 p.m. the preceding day. Troops seized the key points in Las Palmas, eventually crushing opposition by leftist workers, though at first the rebels held only the centers of power. Franco then turned over command of the Canaries to the exiled Monarchist General Orgaz, with whom he had been in close contact for some time. Assisted by rightist volunteers, the military forces in the islands proceeded to establish complete control of the archipelago over the next few days and soon began a bloody repression of the leftist opposition, just as the left was doing in the territory it controlled.

Franco arranged for the safety of his wife and daughter by sending them to military headquarters, escorted by Martínez Fuset, whence they were later transferred to the naval gunboat *Uad Arcilla* for the night, their identity unknown to anyone save its commanders, before they boarded a German steamer on the nineteenth. Franco's aides had made these arrangements with the gunboat's captain, trusting in the known political conservatism of naval officers. This move in fact placed his wife and daughter in the greatest danger they would encounter during the Civil War, for in nearly all the naval vessels off the south and east coast of Spain leftist crewmen overthrew their officers, murdering many of them, as in Russia in 1917, and seizing control of the ships. That very night the commander of the *Uad Arcilla* had to arrest several sailors trying to incite a mutiny, but he was almost the only captain save for those in El Ferrol to manage to maintain control of his vessel. The next day Doña Carmen and Carmencita, still escorted by Martínez Fuset, were safely transferred to the German steamer *Waldi*, which docked in Gran Canaria for only a few hours before leaving for Le Havre. Their ultimate destination was Bayonne, near the Spanish border, where for two months they would be the houseguests of the former French governess of the Polo children, Mme. Claverie.[47]

Since Gran Canaria would not be made entirely secure for a couple of days, after an emotional farewell to his wife and daughter, Franco was taken by tugboat to the nearby airfield, where the *Dragon Rapide* and its English pilot were waiting to fly him to Morocco. Taking off around 2 p.m. on the eighteenth, they stopped for the night in Casablanca, where Franco, wearing civilian clothes, shaved off his moustache to avoid detection. Luis Bolín, the right-wing journalist who had helped to arrange for the plane and then accompanied Franco on this part of the flight, has reported that Franco was in a state of unaccustomed excitement that night at the hotel in Casablanca, keeping him up until the early hours as he discussed his thinking about the changes he believed must take place in Spain.[48] Franco knew that his country had reached a major turning point, and he was determined that it undergo decisive changes to transform it altogether, though the form these changes would take probably remained rather inchoate in his mind. Very early the next morning, Sunday, July 19, the *Dragon Rapide* flew on to Tetuán, capital of the Spanish protectorate.

While Franco was en route, the Casares Quiroga government collapsed. Ever since becoming prime minister in mid-May, Casares was aware of conspiracy among some sectors of the army, but, like President Azaña, he was playing a complicated double game, for the left was internally divided. Should either the anarchists or the *caballerista* Socialists rebel against the government, the army would be needed to put them down, which helps to explain the government's torturous and indecisive policy. Though there is no indication that the prime minister responded to Franco's personal letter of June 23, a few days later Casares Quiroga's minister of the interior did dispatch a circular to provincial governors urging them to develop better relations with army garrisons. The left Republican leaders were convinced that the culture of most of the Spanish military had been permanently changed and that most officers would never rebel. By mid-July, however, Casares seems to have decided that the tension had become too great and there was no point in trying to discourage a revolt among what was perceived as a small ultrarightist minority in the army. The government had identified some of the conspirators, though not "El Director" (Mola) himself, but others were unknown, and prosecution under what remained of Republican constitutionalism would be difficult. Hence the disastrous miscalculation to undertake no changes nor to attempt conciliation after the killing of Calvo Sotelo, on the gamble that a feeble rebellion could only strengthen the government.

Mola's rebellion was poorly organized and confused in the extreme, because it was the very opposite of a modern coup d'état, which is organized from the center. It resembled an old-fashioned *pronunciamiento*, organized uncertainly from the periphery, with all the key figures—Mola, Franco, Sanjurjo, and others—located at the geographic margins. Mola gave up any hope of concerted action and instead sent instructions for rebellion in three successive phases for different regions over a period of three or more days. The Moroccan protectorate fell completely under the control of the rebels on July 17–18, but the government confidently announced that the revolt was being contained and would never gain a foothold on the mainland. By the afternoon of the eighteenth, however, the insurgents had begun to take over Seville, and Casares suddenly realized that his calculation was mistaken, his gamble failing, as the insurgency slowly, but persistently, spread. Around 10 p.m. Casares Quiroga and his government resigned.

On the night of July 18–19, as Franco was flying to Morocco, Manuel Azaña, for more than two months president of the Republic, was faced with a major military insurgency and potential civil war. He had three options, one of which would be to resign power to the rebels, as had been done on a number of occasions in the nineteenth century and as Alfonso XIII had done twice, in 1923 and 1931, on the first occasion handing power to Primo de Rivera and on the second abandoning the throne to the Republicans. In July 1936, however, the situation was quite different, because in these preceding instances few had been willing to fight, while now the leftist parties were much more mobilized, and the government's revolutionary allies were eager to fight, even if it meant civil war, because they had never assumed that they could gain power without some degree of violence. Surrender would not have been an easy option.

The other two alternatives were to try to reach some kind of compromise or else to mobilize the left to fight a full-scale civil war. Azaña's inclination was to attempt compromise, so in the middle of the night he prevailed on Diego Martínez Barrio, leader of the most moderate of the Popular Front parties, to form a new leftist government that could reach a settlement. Martínez Barrio, who had scarcely slept in forty-eight hours, cobbled together a coalition of ministers from the moderate leftist parties, not totally different from its predecessor but nonetheless more moderate in tone. About 4 a.m. on the nineteenth he began to get in touch with district military commanders, most of whom had still not rebelled, to urge them not to break ranks, promising a new administration of conciliation between left and right. The irony was that such a policy, adopted by the government a week earlier, could probably have avoided the rebellion and subsequent civil war, but Azaña had changed course too late. By definition, it is no longer possible to prevent something from happening after it has already begun to happen.

Martínez Barrio's telephone negotiations averted a military revolt in Valencia and Málaga but were of little avail with key rebel commanders. The evidence suggests that he proposed a broad compromise, with crucial ministries such as War and Interior being offered to military leaders, but in Pamplona Mola categorically refused. He replied that it was too late, since the insurgents had taken a solemn oath not to draw back once the revolt began, and that he was about to declare martial law in Pamplona and bring the northern garrisons into the rebellion. This intransigence on Mola's part was one of the decisive steps to civil war. While these conversations took place, Franco was completing a brief, probably troubled, night's sleep in a hotel near the Casablanca airport.

By early morning word had gotten out to the more extreme sectors of the Popular Front that a new government was attempting to reach a compromise with the right. Around 7 a.m. an angry demonstration was being formed by the *caballeristas*, Communists, and even the most radical wing of Azaña's own party. Soon afterward, an exhausted Martínez Barrio resigned. The attempt at compromise, tried too late, had failed.

Government leaders had always calculated that most of the army would remain loyal, making any rebellion easy to suppress. By the nineteenth it was clear that this was not the case, as the insurgency now had extended into garrisons in the north. Whether those sectors of the army that had not joined it would be sufficient in numbers, or in political reliability, to suppress the revolt was quite unknown. Azaña, meanwhile, accepting the logic of the desperate situation into which he had maneuvered himself and the Republican government, appointed a more partisan left Republican administration headed by the physiology professor José Giral. For several days the revolutionary movements had been demanding that the government arm their followers so that they would be able to suppress the right. Both Casares Quiroga and Martínez Barrio had resolutely refused, declaring that armed masses of revolutionaries meant anarchy, civil war, and the end of the constitutional Republic. The new Giral government, however, decided not to rely on loyal army and security units alone and within a few hours announced the "arming of the people," meaning of course not the Spanish people in general but rather the organized revolutionary movements.[49] This would guarantee both full-scale civil war and violent revolution, the twin catastrophes that would plague Spain for the next three years.

The unfolding of these events was unknown to Franco on the early morning of the nineteenth, as he completed the last leg of his flight to Tetuán. The situation remained totally uncertain, for at that point many parts of the army still had not rebelled, and Franco could not be sure that his rebel comrades even held control of the protectorate. When the *Dragon Rapide* neared Tetuán, he first had Bebb make a slow run over the airfield to determine whether the situation on the ground looked secure and was reassured to spot the blond head of Major Eduardo Sáenz de Buruaga, a trusted associate and key conspirator, among those waiting on the edge of the runway to greet him. Franco ordered the pilot to land, exiting his plane to the applause of the subordinates who awaited him, and took over command of the most important part of the Spanish army. He had feared catastrophe for months, and now that it had occurred, he had to find ways of making sure that his side would win.

6 | Franco Becomes Generalissimo

(1936)

As Franco was driven into Tetuán to a cheering crowd on the morning of July 19, the insurrection was spreading through most of the garrisons of northern Spain. Some units did not rebel until the twentieth, or the twenty-first, however, and others did not join the insurgency at all. Like all the leaders on both sides, Franco hoped that the struggle would be brief, but he grasped that he must prepare for a longer conflict than initially planned, though he still did not foresee its full dimensions.[1] Consistent with this calculation, on the morning of the nineteenth he dispatched Luis Bolín, the journalist who had accompanied him from Casablanca, to continue in the *Dragon Rapide* to Marseilles, whence he was to go on to Rome to ask the Mussolini government for planes and other military supplies. Bolín stopped first in Lisbon to obtain written approval for the mission from General Sanjurjo, nominal leader of the insurrection, only a few hours before Sanjurjo attempted to depart for the Nationalist zone.

By the evening of the twentieth, Mola sent out a radio announcement that the revolt was going according to plan and that converging columns would soon take Madrid. This bravado momentarily caused some consternation among Franco and his aides, for, if true, it meant that Mola and other military leaders would soon gain full power, leaving Franco commander on a secondary front without any prominent role in the new regime.[2] Within less than a day, however, it became clear this was mere propaganda and that the insurgency had seized little more than a third of Spain with scant possibility, at least for the moment, of gaining control of the rest.

Rebellion was attempted or took place in forty-four of the fifty-one principal peninsular garrisons, but the insurgents only gained control of about half the forces on the peninsula, though to these were added the elite units in Morocco, for a total of nearly fifty-four thousand troops.[3] It was above all a rebellion of middle- and junior-rank officers. Of the eleven top regional commanders, only three (including Franco) joined the revolt, as did only six of twenty-four major generals on active duty and only one of the seven top commanders of the Civil Guard, though the percentage steadily increased the farther one went down the ranks.[4] More than half of the officers on active duty found themselves in the Republican zone, though many sought to escape to the other side. Ultimately, about half of the officers on duty, numbering around six thousand, served in the insurgent army, and they were joined by nearly eight thousand retired or reserve officers, compared with no more than four thousand regular officers, in what would become the new revolutionary People's Army.[5] In the navy and air force the situation was much worse for the rebels, for the left retained control of about two-thirds of Spain's warships and of most of the military pilots, together with the bulk of the airplanes. Aside from the forces in Morocco, the only advantage held by the insurgents lay in artillery— they controlled slightly more than half the units. On the other hand, the Republican zone contained nearly all the larger cities, industrial production, and financial resources. Only a few days into the revolt, the situation was looking somewhat desperate for the insurgents.

The only possibility of victory seemed to lie with Franco's elite units in Morocco, the only truly combat-ready cadres on either side, though the Legion and *regulares* combined totaled only twenty-one thousand men.[6] Yet Republican control of most of the fleet made it possible after little more than twenty-four hours to blockade and bombard the protectorate's coast. About four hundred troops had been immediately sent to the mainland, even before Franco arrived in Tetuán, but it then became clear that the only way to move troops across the straits was by air, and Franco had only seven small and antiquated planes under his command. With these he initiated arguably the first military airlift in history, though with such limited means he could scarcely move one hundred troops a day.

From the beginning, therefore, the need for greater airpower and other forms of foreign assistance was apparent, and Franco turned immediately to the governments of Italy and Germany as the most militantly antileftist regimes and the ones most likely to support insurgency against the Spanish Popular Front. Three days after sending Bolín on to Rome, he approached the Italian consul in Tangier to request aid from Mussolini and made a similar petition to Berlin by means of the German consul. On the twenty-third, he commandeered the sole Lufthansa passenger plane in his district to take his representatives, accompanied by the local leaders of the Nazi Party in Spanish Morocco, to seek assistance in person from Hitler's government.

Franco was the last major commander to join the conspiracy, but, once he did, he acted with complete resolution and self-confidence. His declaration of martial law in Las Palmas at dawn on July 18 proclaimed that the Republican constitution had suffered "a total eclipse," as demonstrated by the massive abuses occurring, including "attacks on provincial government and electoral records to falsify votes," and that this devolution justified military intervention to restore order and legality. In his first radio address from Tetuán on the nineteenth Franco demanded "blind faith in victory!," his watchword throughout. He also tried to bluff the Giral government into throwing in the towel, sending it a telegram that insisted that "the Spanish restorationist movement will triumph completely in a few days and we will require of you a strict accounting of your deeds. The rigor with which we act will be proportionate to your resistance. We urge you to submit now and prevent the useless shedding of blood."[7]

By the evening of the twentieth, he learned that the nominal leader of the revolt, General José Sanjurjo, had died in an accident near Lisbon when his plane crashed on takeoff.[8] Though Sanjurjo had played little role in the conspiracy and to some extent was a figurehead, he was the only recognized overall commander. Paradoxically, his death may have been a stroke of luck for the Nationalists, opening the way for a younger, healthier, more capable commander in chief two months later. It is altogether doubtful that Sanjurjo possessed the combination of skills needed for victory in a long, ruthless, and highly complex civil war.

From the beginning, Franco acted as a major leader of the new "National movement," as the insurgents called it, not a regional subordinate, dispatching orders to commanders in southern Spain who were reluctant to join the revolt, as well as sending representatives directly to Rome and Berlin. By the twenty-second, one of his subordinates was referring hyperbolically to "General Franco's National Government," and a week later Adolf Langenheim, Nazi Party chief in Tetuán, reported mistakenly that Franco was part of a ruling triumvirate.[9] Franco may have presented himself that way to make certain that the Germans would take his requests seriously. On July 23, Mola filled the gap in the senior command by forming the National Defense Council (Junta de Defensa Nacional), made up of himself and the seven other principal commanders in the main northern Nationalist zone, led by the most senior in rank, General Miguel Cabanellas, though Cabanellas was a Mason, a centrist Republican, and a former deputy of the Radical Party. Franco, in Morocco, was not at first a member, though on July 25 the council recognized his special role by naming him *general jefe del ejército* of Morocco and southern Spain, that is, commander of the largest and most important part of the army. On August 3, when his troops were beginning their advance northward toward Madrid, Franco was named to the council, along with General Gonzalo Queipo de Llano, leader of the insurgency in Andalusia.

The efforts to gain assistance abroad by Franco, and also by Mola, who had sent his own representatives to Rome and Berlin, soon began to yield fruit. Thanks to the help of the Nazi Party leadership in Berlin, Franco's emissaries finally caught up with Hitler at the Wagner festival in Bayreuth late on July 25. The German führer was taken by surprise, since he had no particular interest in Spain and little knowledge of events there, but after nearly two hours of conversation he accepted the claims that the military insurrection's goal was to counter Communist and Soviet ambitions, that it had support among the Spanish, and that its leaders were friends of the Nazi regime. All this appealed to Hitler as a means of outflanking France, defeating the Comintern, and gaining a friendly power on the opposite side of the Pyrenees. He authorized immediate shipment of a limited number of planes and other arms to Franco.[10] Mussolini made a similar decision a day and a half later, influenced more by Mola's representatives (who drew on earlier Monarchist contacts), reports that France would limit its assistance to the Republicans, and personal intervention by the exiled Alfonso XIII, who lived in Italy. He also sent a small number of planes and other arms, dispatching them directly to Franco.[11]

After a week of fighting, Mola's advance on Madrid from the north had stalled; his troops and militia volunteers were outnumbered and very low on ammunition. He was even considering retreat to a defensive position along the Ebro river, but Franco insisted there be no withdrawal, and no yielding of any territory—one of his main principles throughout the conflict—and promised to get supplies to him.[12] Mola managed to hold his position, though he could advance no further.[13]

By the end of the first week in August, Franco had received fifteen Junkers-52 transport/ bombing planes, six obsolescent Henschel fighters, nine Italian S.81 medium bombers, and twelve Fiat CR.32 fighters, as well as other arms and supplies. The diversionary effects of air power helped Franco send a small convoy through the Republican blockade of the Moroccan coast on August 5, carrying two thousand troops and a large amount of military equipment at one stroke. It was very risky and quite unlike Franco, something that he would never attempt again until the blockade had been lifted, but at this point he was desperate to send more men and arms across to begin his own drive on Madrid from the south. German and Italian planes greatly increased his airlift capacity, and more and more of his troops crossed to the peninsula during the remainder of August and throughout the following month. By the time that the blockade was completely broken at the end of September, twenty-one thousand men and more than 350,000 kilos of arms and supplies had been transported by air alone.

With Mola's troops stymied in the north, the whole struggle turned on Franco's elite units advancing from the south. He had become the key rebel commander, the one with the greatest international recognition, recipient of most of the foreign aid, and leader of the decisive combat forces. Mola usually accepted his initiatives, though Franco's relations with Queipo de Llano in the south were somewhat more tense. He provided Queipo with small additional units to help solidify his position in Andalusia but refused him major reinforcements so that he could use most of the limited numbers of legionnaires and *regulares* for his own drive northward. Franco flew back and forth between Tetuán and Seville three times between July 27 and August 3, and his first two assault columns, numbering only two thousand to twenty-five hundred men each, began to move northwest from Seville on the second and third. They were composed primarily of troops from the legion and *regulares*, supplemented with small support units from Queipo's regular army forces. Franco then transferred his headquarters to Seville on August 7.

After achieving direct contact with Mola by taking the city of Mérida on the eleventh, he did not strike directly north but ordered his columns westward to secure the frontier with Portugal, whose government was providing strong logistical support to the insurgents, seizing Badajoz on the fifteenth. This wide indirect approach avoided the easily defensible mountain pass north of Seville and the concentration of Republican forces in that area. Franco has often been criticized for not moving directly north on the shortest route, though he had good political, logistical, and operational reasons for initially skirting the main obstacles by angling first toward the west, uniting the two Nationalist zones, and securing his Portuguese border.

Two days after taking Badajoz, the march toward Madrid was resumed. Franco's columns were heavily outnumbered by the opposing forces, which were composed of a few small army and police units and large detachments of revolutionary militia. The militia lacked leadership, training, and discipline, even if it was adequately armed, and was no match for veteran, disciplined forces. A standard tactic was to fix the militia in place with frontal fire and then to hit it with a flanking maneuver, usually throwing it into headlong retreat that was accompanied by corresponding casualties.

Yet, despite their combat superiority, the limited numbers of Franco's troops, the need to build a logistical system and supply line from scratch, and particularly the need to peel off more and more battalions to shore up secondary fronts in the south, northwest, and northeast all delayed their advance considerably. Altogether, after mid-August two and a half months would be needed to reach the outskirts of Madrid. Many historians and commentators have criticized the slowness of Franco's march.[14] He was never known to do anything in a hurry—it was counter to his temperament—and in the Moroccan campaigns audacious advances like that of Silvestre in 1921 that failed to consolidate the rear, protect flanks, or build firm logistics had led to disaster. It will never be known if a bold, completely concentrated drive on Madrid in September that left the flanks unprotected, brushed aside the matter of feeble logistics, and totally disregarded the desperate conditions on other fronts might have enabled Franco to seize the capital rapidly, perhaps putting a sudden end to the Civil War. Possibly there was a chance this could have happened, though it is not probable. In practice, however, it was quite unlikely that Franco would adopt so audacious a strategy, which went completely against his customs and principles, as well as everything he had learned in Morocco.[15]

From the first day, both sides carried out brutal repression of the opposition in their respective zones. The steady buildup of calls to revolutionary violence by the left, in progress for several years, and the determination of the insurgents to act similarly, led to massive political executions. Such atrocities were typical of all the revolutionary/counterrevolutionary civil wars of twentieth-century Europe, without the slightest exception, for such conflicts, much more than international wars, emphasized the dehumanization of an internal enemy, who was not merely to be defeated militarily but who had to be exterminated because it represented a kind of metaphysical evil. In the case of the revolutionary left, this would produce about fifty-five thousand executions, among which numbered nearly seven thousand clergy.[16]

The repression by the military was somewhat more extensive and, like almost everything else in the Nationalist zone, better organized.[17] Franco was not initially responsible for it, and it would have taken place had he never existed. He himself was cold, stern, and seemingly remorseless, and he was slow to begin to control the repression, not acting decisively until March 1937. He blanched, however, at two of the early executions, the first that of his first cousin Major Ricardo de la Puente Bahamonde, once a close childhood playmate, executed in Morocco for leading resistance at the Tetuán airbase against the insurrection. By the standards of that moment, it was a clear enough case, and Franco decided not to intervene, for fear of appearing to favor a relative. Since it was up to the commanding general to ratify death sentences by military tribunals in his district, on August 1 Franco transferred his command, for one day only, to Orgaz, just arrived from the Canaries, in order not to have to approve the death of his old playmate, for whom he still felt affection.[18]

The second case concerned his former assistant at the Zaragoza academy, General Miguel Campins, executed for his failure as commander of the garrison in Granada to support the revolt during its first day and a half, even though he did end up joining the insurrection belatedly. In this case, Franco apparently did try to intervene with Queipo de Llano, in charge of the Granada sector, and sent him a personal letter requesting clemency. Queipo, however, had been outraged by the resistance of Campins during the first crucial hours of the revolt and is said to have refused to open Franco's envelope.[19] Franco reluctantly decided that he could not interfere with Queipo's military tribunal. The combined total of executions by both sides reached approximately a hundred thousand before the opposing governments finally took action. The Republicans got the process partially under control in their zone in December 1936. Two and a half months later, Franco for his part, expanded and tightened the formal military tribunals in his territory, gaining control of the process and greatly reducing the number of executions during the period of active fighting. Moreover, in the first days there was a certain amount of shooting of military prisoners by both sides, though this sort of thing was brought under control more quickly. Instructions from Franco on August 12 ordered advancing columns to weaken the enemy's resistance by leaving an escape valve through which outflanked militia could flee, thereby also avoiding the problem of dealing with more prisoners.[20]

At the same time, he used the public threat of severe repression to try to weaken enemy morale and resistance. As his forces slowly drew nearer the capital, he issued a proclamation to the population of Madrid declaring that

> if this suicidal resistance continues, if the people of Madrid do not force the government and its Marxist leaders to surrender the capital, unconditionally, we reject any responsibility for the great destruction that we shall be obliged to carry out to overcome this suicidal stubbornness. BE WARNED, CITIZENS OF MADRID, THAT THE GREATER THE RESISTANCE, THE MORE HARSH WILL BE OUR PUNISHMENT.[21]

Looting and pillaging on a massive scale was a fundamental part of the revolution in the Republican zone and was also practiced systematically by the wartime Republican government, many hundreds of millions of dollars of valuables being looted, while churches and sacred art were sacked and burned en masse.[22] Despite orders to his troops to avoid pillaging, Franco's columns also sometimes engaged in it. Pillaging was, at least theoretically, directed toward leftist properties and it was temporarily being accepted as a perquisite of the Moroccan units, at least during the first months.[23] The Nationalist authorities also imposed significant fines on and confiscated property from their political opponents.[24]

The insurrection had been launched under the banner of "saving the Republic" and restoring law and order. District commanders seemed almost unanimous on these terms and also promised that all "valid" social legislation of the Republic (essentially meaning regulations on the books as of February 16, 1936) would be respected, while Mola's original political program promised full respect for the Catholic Church, though it called for maintaining the separation of church and state. Franco's initial proclamation of July 18, however, had not specifically mentioned the Republic but invoked the goal of "making genuine in our Fatherland for the first time, and in this order Fraternity, Liberty, and Equality." Three weeks later, in an interview with a Portuguese journalist published on August 10, Franco was more specific: "Spain is Republican and will continue to be so. Neither the flag nor the regime has changed. The only change is that crime is replaced by order and acts of banditry by honest and progressive work." But he then contradicted himself by declaring there would be fundamental institutional change, adding that "Spain will be governed by a corporative system similar to those installed in Portugal, Italy and Germany."[25] A few days later he was quoted as acknowledging that the first phase of the new regime constituted a military dictatorship but he went on to say that this would be temporary, since he was in favor only of "brief dictatorships." This was confused and confusing, but it did make clear that the outcome would not be continuation of a democratic republic. The reference to Portugal hearkened to the CEDA's goal of a more corporative kind of republic, whereas the references to Italy and Germany implied something more radical, something probably not yet well sorted out in his thinking, almost completely absorbed as he was by military affairs.

The two sides in the Civil War called each other "Reds" and "Fascists," but the left officially termed itself "Republican," as they began constructing a new revolutionary Republican regime in their zone, while the right called themselves "los nacionales," translated by foreign journalists as "Nationalists." As "nacionales," the insurgents affirmed patriotism, tradition, and religion, and quickly generated mass support, particularly among most of the middle classes, as well as the Catholic population generally.

The insurrection had been planned as a preemptive strike to head off the revolutionaries before they could seize control of the Spanish state or, alternatively, produce total chaos. But its partial failure catalyzed the revolution, once the left Republican leaders armed the revolutionaries en masse, giving them de facto power in the Republican zone. Arming the revolution magnified the size of the new militia, but the military achievements were limited, since most revolutionaries devoted themselves to taking over land and economic enterprises, looting on a large scale, destroying churches and religious art, and carrying out mass violence against their political enemies. The revolutionaries claimed, correctly enough, that their revolution was proportionately more extensive and also more nearly spontaneous than what had happened in Russia in 1917. This was accurate, since Spanish society was more consciously and extensively mobilized than Russian society had been.

Yet the extent and ferocity of the revolution soon proved a boon to the Nationalists, for three reasons. First, it consolidated the support of most of the middle classes and of Catholic and conservative society behind the insurgents. Second, it alarmed Western democracies and rightist dictatorships alike. If the Popular Front had maintained a democracy, other democracies might have come to its aid, but they could not readily support a violent revolutionary regime. Third, the revolution's initial reliance on revolutionary militia was ineffective militarily. Though a portion of the regular army had remained under the orders of the leftist government, it did not trust some of these units and only made limited use of them.

The National Defense Council concentrated on military affairs, and, because of the extreme dispersion of forces across very broad and weakly held fronts, local commanders at first enjoyed considerable autonomy. Little attention was given to forming a regular government. Representatives of the monarchy were kept at a distance, and when Don Juan, third son and heir to Alfonso XIII, slipped across the French border to volunteer for the Nationalist army, he was sent back again by Mola without being permitted to see any of the council members. Franco nonetheless made the first breach in the nominally Republican identity of the insurrection, violating a pledge made only five days earlier, when, at a major ceremony for the Feast of the Assumption in Seville on August 15, he acted unilaterally to replace the Republican flag with the traditional red and yellow banner of the monarchy. He hailed it as the authentic flag of Spain for which patriots had given their lives in hundreds of battles, and his example began to be followed throughout the Nationalist zone. What those commanders who had been more closely associated with Republicanism thought of this is not recorded, but increasingly they followed Franco's lead.

Franco and Queipo de Llano had been added as members of the council on August 3, as the forces in the south became the major military variable. By that time Franco stood out above all the other Nationalist commanders, even Mola, while Cabanellas, the council president, was little more than a figurehead. Franco had cemented relations with Rome and Berlin, receiving all the Italian and much of the German supplies directly, before doling out part to the northern units. All three of the friendly governments who supported the insurgents—Italy, Germany, and Portugal—looked to him as the main leader. On August 16 he flew for the first time to Burgos in the far north, seat of the council, to discuss planning and coordination with Mola. The northern general was cooperative, since his principal ambition was simply to win the war, and he did not exhibit any particular resentment about Franco's growing preeminence. The most prickly Nationalist commander was the ex-Republican Queipo de Llano, who held sway in western Andalusia. Franco was careful not to interfere with Queipo's autonomy, and on August 26 moved his own headquarters from Seville to Cáceres, farther northwest, to be nearer his advance columns, taking up residence in the venerable Palacio de los Golfines de Arriba, a refurbished sixteenth-century structure.

By this time Franco had a political staff of sorts. No other insurgent commander had assembled an equivalent group. Two senior generals, Alfredo Kindelán, who was his air force commander, and Luis Orgaz, served in his military entourage, while his chief political consultant was his brother Nicolás, who with his wife had escaped from Madrid at the last minute.[26] The Monarchist diplomat José Sangróniz became something of a foreign affairs adviser, and, equally important, served as his principal contact with the multimillionaire businessman Juan March, who provided indispensable financial assistance during the first phase of the war.[27] Franco's new friend Martínez Fuset, a legal officer, would soon serve as his juridical adviser and subsequently take up the post of supervisor of military justice. The war had quickly turned into a major propaganda contest, both at home and abroad, something for which military insurgents were poorly prepared, but Franco engaged the services of his former commander and patron, the histrionic one-eyed and one-armed General José Millán Astray, founder of the Legion, as a kind of propaganda chief.

The town of Talavera, little more than a hundred kilometers west-southwest of Madrid, fell to Franco's forces on September 3. Growing Nationalist strength was evident in the fact that Mola had regained the initiative in the far north, beginning the successful invasion of the eastern-most Basque province of Guipuzcoa and seizing control of one section of the border with France. By that point the initial optimism of the revolutionaries had given way to alarm, as they lost combat after combat. In consequence, the first unified all-Popular Front government was formed on September 4 under the Socialist Largo Caballero, and two months later it was joined by four representatives of the anarchosyndicalist National Confederation of Labor (Confederación Nacional de Trabajo). This was the first time in history anarchists had officially entered a central government, even a revolutionary one, and they gave the government the possibility of bringing some order out of the chaos in the Republican zone. In mid-September, the Largo Caballero government began to create a new centrally organized and disciplined Republican army. The revolutionary Ejército Popular, or People's Army, was modeled to some extent on the Soviet Red Army, adopting its red-star insignia and system of political commissars, together with the clenched-fist "Red Front" salute introduced by German Communists in 1927. Equally important, in mid-September Stalin and the Soviet Politburo decided to send major military assistance, and the first Soviet arms arrived early the next month. They were accompanied by numerous Soviet military advisers and hundreds of Soviet aviators and tank crewmen, soon to be flanked by the International Brigades, a foreign legion of volunteers that the Comintern began to organize at the end of September, modeled on the hundred thousand or more foreign "Internationalist" volunteers who had fought with the Red Army in the Russian Civil War. Franco, however, would not become fully aware of this and of the magnitude of the Soviet intervention until the latter part of October, when Soviet arms and military specialists began to enter combat in significant numbers.

If September marked a turning point on the Republican side politically and militarily, it was also the time of a decisive turn by the Nationalists, for during these weeks Franco rose to the very top as military commander in chief and also de facto political dictator. The full details of this process will never be known, for no documents survive and the participants have left only two brief accounts, one direct and the other indirect, both written years afterward.[28]

The initiative apparently did not stem as much from Franco and his immediate staff as it did from two key Monarchist generals, Alfredo Kindelán and Luis Orgaz, perhaps with the personal encouragement of the exiled Alfonso XIII. Kindelán was one of the founders of the Spanish air force. He had once been its commander, directed Franco's few squadrons in the drive on Madrid, and would become commander of the Nationalist air force for the remainder of the war. Orgaz had taken over from Franco in the Canaries on July 18, consolidated Nationalist control of the islands, and then assumed a role in the high command on the peninsula.

Their initiative began probably in the first days of September. Its goal was to steer the military regime toward Monarchism, and they also believed that a unified command would be important to achieving final victory. They saw naming Franco commander in chief as a decisive step toward both objectives, necessary to vitiating the non- and anti-Monarchist influence of Cabanellas, Mola, Queipo, and others. Franco told Kindelán that a Monarchist restoration must indeed be the ultimate goal, but this could not be advanced publicly as long as the war continued, since so much of the support for the Nationalists was not Monarchist in sympathy. Kindelán took the point but suggested that Franco might become military commander in chief and temporary head of state as regent. Franco, however, vetoed any idea of a regency so long as the war lasted, saying that it would undermine unity.

During the first two months of fighting, Franco had been very tactful with his military colleagues. Guillermo Cabanellas, son of the council president, later observed that "Francisco Franco was not prone to deals or the show of emotion. Apparently sincere in his external behavior, good-natured in personal relations, he never sought arguments but showed rigid discipline toward his superiors and informality toward subordinates," and he did not want to give the appearance of claiming dominance.[29] Hence his initial demurral over becoming commander in chief, which was prompted by the fact that when the matter first came up he had no idea how his senior military colleagues would respond. If he were to become a candidate for generalissimo and was rejected, this could permanently poison relations with his fellow commanders and might even seriously compromise the whole war effort. Thus he proceeded with great caution.

There is little doubt that he aspired to the highest rank in the army or, alternatively, the post of high commissioner in Morocco or a key role in a new government. He also wanted greater military authority to mobilize and employ Nationalist resources, but under the present circumstances, that would also mean becoming head of a military dictatorship. Given his high opinion of the Primo de Rivera regime and his own authoritarian instincts, he was not necessarily reluctant to assume such a role, but the concrete opportunity had emerged suddenly and he was keenly aware of the prominence of envy and resentment in Spanish affairs.

Franco received a strong push from his closest advisers—Nicolás Franco, Sangróniz, Millán Astray, and others. Once they saw the interest of the Monarchists in promoting his candidacy, they did all they could to urge him to approve the initiative. Moreover, German and Italian officials looked almost exclusively to Franco as the key leader, and their liaison personnel urged the importance of a more unified and dynamic command. At least one German representative may have directly pressed him to step forward.[30]

The issue began to come to a head as Franco's columns slowly drew nearer Madrid. Need for a commander in chief had become clearer, for Franco had not been able to avoid friction with Queipo de Llano in the south, and on the key central front there were altercations between Mola and Lieutenant Colonel Juan Yagüe, head of the advance on Madrid. Kindelán urged Franco to take the initiative in requesting a meeting of all the council to consider the issue of unity of command. His main ally in convincing Franco to press for the *jefatura* was, by his own account, Nicolás Franco, abetted by Orgaz and Millán Astray.

The meeting was scheduled for September 21 in a small wooden building at the improvised airstrip outside Salamanca, most of the members coming in by plane. Kindelán, who attended, has left the only written account:

> During the morning session, which lasted three hours and a half, we dis-cussed various items of importance, but none as important as that of the *mando único*. I pointed this out three times without managing to bring the issue to discussion, despite having been actively supported by General Orgaz. I seemed to notice, with disappointment, that my goals were not shared by the majority of those assembled.
>
> When the afternoon session began at four, I firmly introduced the ques-tion, without the slightest hesitation, encountering a hostile reception from various members. General Cabanellas was clearly and decidedly opposed, declaring that to him the question still seemed premature and that it was not necessary that a unified command be led by a single person, since there were two ways to direct a war, by a Generalissimo or by a Directory or Junta. I agreed, adding: "There are indeed two methods of directing a war: with the first you win, with the second you lose." My proposal was finally put to a vote and was approved with only General Cabanellas dissenting. Then came the vote on the name of the person who should be named Generalissimo. Since it began with the most junior officers and the two colonels excused themselves because of their rank, I decided to reduce tension and break the ice by asking to vote first, and did so in favor of Franco. My vote was immediately supported by those of Mola, Orgaz, Dávila, Queipo de Llano and all the rest, with the exception of Cabanellas, who said that, as an opponent of such a system, it was not up to him to vote for someone for a post he deemed unnecessary.[31]

The council members agreed that the decision would not be mentioned by any of them until the official announcement was made by Cabanellas, but days passed and no announcement was forthcoming.

The *Anuario militar* for 1936 listed Franco as twenty-third in seniority among the major generals, and he was outranked in years of service by Cabanellas, Queipo, and others, yet no one else had his prestige. There were other commanders as brave as Franco, and others with greater technical knowledge, as well as many others who looked more impressive or were more cordial and better liked, but none had his rare combination of discipline, combat experience, political tact and discretion, foreign contacts, and capacity for command. His lieutenants had already achieved an understanding with Moroccan leaders in the protectorate that secured the Nationalists' rear guard, making Spanish Morocco a crucial staging area that provided numerous intrepid Muslim volunteers, eventually totaling seventy thousand.[32] Cabanellas and Queipo, though more senior, had limited appeal because of their earlier identity with Republican liberalism. The only commander with any equivalent prestige was Mola, but he was only a brigadier and expressed no personal ambitions.[33]

The last part of September represented the culminating moment of Franco's life, and his agenda was so crowded that he had only the most limited time to greet with great relief the arrival of his wife and daughter from France on the twenty-third. They had spent two months abroad in absolute seclusion in Bayonne, trying to remain incognito in the home of the former governess and waiting for conditions in the Nationalist zone to become safe enough to return. The reunited family took up residence at Franco's headquarters in Cáceres, though within a fortnight his headquarters would move to Salamanca.

Carmen recalls that

> Mamá was extremely anxious until we finally got back. We crossed the frontier into Navarre and from Pamplona went on to Cáceres, where we lived only a short time. Then we moved into the archiepiscopal palace of Salamanca. It did not faze me to live in such a building, because the residence of a district commander, as my father had been in the Canaries, was usually a large building with a garden. So this seemed to me normal, though I later realized it was extraordinary, not normal at all. Moreover, when I saw my father again, he looked different. Within little more than two months, his appearance had changed. . . . He had shaved off his moustache and now had more gray hair, so that he looked different . . . He had become a different father also in the sense that I now spent very little time with him. . . . But Mamá always said that it seemed to her incredible that he could sleep so well. If he had a serious problem he was able to put it completely out of his mind when he went to sleep. This always amazed my mother. . . . He was not a nervous man. Not at all.

In the aftermath of the momentous meeting of the twenty-first, Franco made one of his most controversial military decisions. For more than two months, a motley force of eighteen hundred Nationalists (almost none of them regular troops) had withstood a siege in the Alcázar de Toledo, the huge building that had housed Franco's old infantry academy in his years as cadet. Though most of the building was blasted to rubble, the Alcázar's defenders continued to resist from its large subterranean area, engaging in an epic struggle that had captured the world's attention. Toledo was southeast of the main route of Franco's advance on Madrid, but on the twenty-fourth he decided to reroute his spearheads to relieve the Alcázar, a mission accomplished on the twenty-seventh, followed by a round of executions of Republicans in the city, a tit for tat of the earlier brutality carried out by the Republicans. Franco gained considerable publicity at home and abroad for having saved the heroes of the Alcázar. The priority he accorded this stemmed to an extent from his memories of the Moroccan disaster in 1921, when sizable units had been left to their fate by a weak command, and even more to his conviction that political and psychological factors were of special importance in a civil war.

Later, however, the whole episode became something of a cause célèbre, as Franco's critics, which included members of his own side, insisted that he had made a major operational error by delaying the advance on Madrid for a week or more to relieve the strategically insignificant Alcázar. At the beginning of October, the capital was still weakly defended and could have been seized much more easily than would prove the case a month later. Moreover, in December, after his first assaults on Madrid had failed, Franco himself confessed to a Portuguese journalist that he had felt impelled by his obligations as commander in chief to rescue the highly publicized defenders of the Alcázar, even at the cost of a more immediate move on Madrid.[34]

There was, however, no question of an immediate assault on Madrid at the end of September, because Franco's forces were still too distant and had not yet concentrated sufficient power. Inability to begin the attack for another month was not due primarily to the relief of the Alcázar, though that was one factor, but mainly to the limited resources of the Nationalists, together with the decision to divert reinforcements to other fronts in danger of collapse. Given the enormous publicity generated at home and abroad by the defense of the Alcázar, it was not surprising that Franco decided to relieve it immediately. Some of his critics have charged that his main motive was a public relations windfall that would cement his claim to the *jefatura única*. This is not impossible, though there is no direct evidence to support it, and in fact the decision of the council for Franco did not depend on the relief of the Alcázar.

One subordinate who did not agree with the priority of the Alcázar was Yagüe, in command of the forces moving on Madrid from the southwest. He insisted, logically, that if the Nationalists pressed the direct advance on Madrid, they would quickly outflank Toledo and force the Republican units besieging the Alcázar to retreat or be cut off. This was obviously correct, but it did not respond to Franco's immediate priorities. Further-more, Franco and his staff were still unaware that significant Soviet arms and personnel would enter combat within a few weeks. Once that happened, the conquest of the capital would be considerably more difficult. At the moment, this was a secondary disagreement between Franco and his top field commander. Yagüe had suffered from minor heart arrhythmia for years and the pressure of commanding the decisive front in the war was producing cardiac distress. This, not the dispute over Toledo, was the reason why Yagüe was relieved of command on the twenty-second, reassigned to Franco's own staff for rest and medical treatment.

While these events were unfolding, the decision made by the council on September 21 was not being implemented, and Franco and his backers grew more dissatisfied by the day, both with the tardiness of Cabanellas in issuing the announcement and the fact that the extent of his powers as generalissimo had not been clarified. Franco said later in life that he would not have accepted a supreme command that did not include full authority over the government, as well, but that was in retrospect.[35] He was still reluctant to press the issue to a showdown, fearing rejection and the un-hinging of the unity of the insurgent command. Kindelán and Nicolás Franco urged Yagüe, whom they knew to be one of his strongest supporters, to take the initiative. Confined for a few days to bed rest, he roused himself and put the matter to Franco very bluntly, claiming afterward that he said that someone would soon become generalissimo, no matter what, but that it would be much better if it were Franco. Whatever the exact sequence and nature of arguments, they had the desired effect, and a second meeting was quickly called for the twenty-eighth to decide the powers of the *mando único*. The only understanding behind the original unanimous vote had been that Franco would be military commander in chief for the duration of the conflict, whereas his backers, and now Franco himself, held that he must have complete political as well as military power. This second meeting was also attended by Yagüe, for, despite his lack of seniority, he had gained considerable prestige as the field commander of the drive on Madrid and also as the head of the legion. Moreover, on the night before the second meeting, when Franco greeted an exultant crowd from the balcony of his residence in Cáceres, Yagüe stood beside him, hailing Franco as the new "chief of state," no less.[36]

At the second meeting, several council members apparently indicated they had only voted for Franco as military commander for the duration. Franco seems to have been careful not to press on his own behalf, but his backers forced the issue. Kindelán presented a draft of a decree, which he and Nicolás Franco had drawn up the day before, naming Franco supreme commander of the armed forces, a status that would include the powers of "chief of state" "for the duration of the war."[37] This was not initially well received, since it did not reflect what most council members had understood themselves as agreeing to originally, and key figures such as Cabanellas, Mola, and Queipo de Llano at first opposed it. Mola's "open" project had provided for a temporary "military directory" under Sanjurjo, but it did not envision even a short-term political dictator. On the other hand, the council members found that their revolt had caught them up in a ruthless civil war against a revolutionary Republican regime, and the vague framework on which many of them had agreed at the beginning of the insurrection no longer seemed entirely relevant.

During the long Spanish lunch break in the afternoon, Kindelán and Yagüe made a vigorous attempt to convince those comrades, originally a majority, who had opposed their proposal. They argued that the officers in charge of the elite units wanted to see Franco totally in charge and that the German and Italian governments expected the same. The situation had become much more critical than anticipated, and the Nationalists required the strongest and most united leadership possible, the kind of leadership that Franco, plausibly, was best prepared to provide. Mola and Queipo, the other two generals with the most important district commands, at some distance from Salamanca, then departed by plane for their respective headquarters. They were apparently willing to leave matters to the others, who for a variety of reasons were not necessarily prepared to resist the proposal very vigorously. Kindelán has claimed that during the afternoon meeting agreement was finally reached that Franco would have political as well as military command, but Cabanellas is said to have reported that the only agreement was that the council leadership in Burgos would give the matter speedy consideration and render an immediate decision. He made this concession with great reluctance and, after returning to his headquarters in Burgos, had evening telephone conversations with both Mola and Queipo. Queipo was ambivalent but had no viable alternative to offer, while Mola concluded that it was best to accept the decision, for it would guarantee unity and would contribute to military victory, his main concern.[38] As matters stood, there was no convincing alternative. Queipo reportedly later said that "we chose Franco because with Mola . . . we would have lost the war, while I . . . was completely discredited" because of his Republican past.[39]

Mola's perspective seems to have been that this proposal was an emergency measure that would be in effect for the duration of the fighting, after which they could return to his original plan for setting in motion a political process resulting in a national plebiscite—albeit in carefully controlled circumstances—that would determine Spain's future regime. At that moment the council members did not think they were creating a permanent one-man political dictatorship, though, as it turned out, that was exactly what they were doing. Kindelán's proposal was ratified, the official announcement to be drawn up by the Monarchist diplomat José Yanguas Messía, who was assisting the council. What happened next is uncertain, but the most convincing explanation is that either Franco or his principal backers talked immediately with Yanguas, saying that limiting the mandate to the duration of the war was accepted by Franco but that it must not appear in the text, for it would weaken the new government's authority while the fighting still raged.

For several days there was confusion about the exact terminology. The decree that Cabanellas published on the thirtieth declared Franco "jefe del gobierno del estado español" (the equivalent of prime minister rather than chief of state), but the clause about limiting this power to the duration of the war had disappeared.[40] In remarks prepared for the investiture ceremony on October 1, Cabanellas referred to Franco as "jefe del estado," but in his improvised opening words he called him "jefe del gobierno," as in the decree.[41] What is clear is that as soon as Franco was invested with full power, his position was always defined simply as "chief of state."

Meanwhile, on the twenty-ninth, Franco staged his official entry into Toledo, acting for the attendant newsreel cameras as though he were at that moment liberating the Alcázar, much as some years later General Douglas Macarthur would carefully stage for the cameras his return to the Philippines. One day later, he received the endorsement of the bishop of Salamanca, Enrique Pla y Deniel, whose pastoral letter of the thirtieth, titled "Las dos ciudades" ("The Two Cities"), distinguished between the heavenly and earthly cities and between the causes of right and left, between Catholic counterrevolutionaries and anticlerical revolutionaries. It also employed the term "crusade," recently coined in Navarre, to characterize the struggle of the Nationalists.

As usual, the forty-three-year-old general did not cut a dashing figure in the ceremony in which he took power in Burgos on October 1. The son of Cabanellas described the scene his own way:

> On the low stand in the throne room, placing him higher than the audience, appears the figure of Francisco Franco, with the prominence of his stomach marked and his thrown-back shoulders accentuating his natural thickness. In such a posture, his figure seems even more diminutive, reduced to a shapeless ball. His face is round, with an incipient double-chin, his hair black, with strong and pronounced brows, the small moustache closely trimmed, the advancing baldness of his head pronounced. His glance, however, is keen and intelligent. On the right hand he wears a gold ring, which seems to cut into his finger now grown thicker. His clothing is poorly tailored, for his sleeves are hidden from sight and the uniform seems too small.[42]

The investiture speech was relatively brief, delivered with the vehemence typical of Spanish public address in that era. Its most striking passage declared that "you are placing Spain in my hands. My grasp will be firm, my pulse will not tremble, and I shall try to raise Spain to the place that corresponds to her history and to her rank in earlier times." That night Franco delivered a longer radio speech, prepared by Nicolás and Martínez Fuset, which he had shortened and simplified. In it, he stated somewhat contradictorily that "Spain will be organized under a broadly totalitarian concept" but that "regions, municipalities, associations and individuals will enjoy the fullest liberty within the supreme interest of the state." It promised that "the state, while not being confessional, will negotiate with the Catholic Church their respective powers, respecting our tradition and the religious feelings of the great majority of the Spanish people."[43]

In this fashion a determined handful took advantage of the need for unity among the Nationalist commanders to promote the most prominent of the rebel generals to the position of generalissimo and chief of state as well. After the meeting on the twenty-eighth Franco had seen the green light and no longer showed the slightest reluctance about assuming complete power. Mola doubtless had some ironic thoughts about the course of events, in view of his considerable difficulty in getting Franco to join the insurgency in the first place. Though originally an army affair, the elevation of Franco was soon widely accepted by the most diverse political sectors of right and center (though not all of the center) as a military necessity. Even the centrist Republican Alejandro Lerroux, who had fled the revolution in Madrid, argued that the only salvation for Spain lay in a Roman-style legal dictatorship, though he would not necessarily have agreed with what Franco had in mind.[44]

Since he was not introspective, never kept a diary, and left few accessible personal papers, it will probably never be possible to exactly chart the changes in Franco's thinking during the first two months of the Civil War. The German military theorist Carl von Clausewitz referred to what he called the *Wechselwirkung* that takes place during conflicts, by which he meant the effects wrought by the reciprocal interaction of events, leading to pronounced changes, sometimes even to mutual radicalization. Something of this sort took place on both sides during the Spanish struggle, and in some key respects Franco's thinking was transformed. The reluctant conspirator quickly morphed into the determined and ruthless military leader of July 18, but one that, at least in theory, still accepted the partially "open" plan on which the insurrection had been based. In the interview, published by a Portuguese journalist on August 13, in which Franco had said that he was in favor of "brief dictatorships" that completed their task rapidly, he had added that "its duration depends exclusively on the resistance" that it might encounter. The new regime would rely on "technicians" rather than politicians, but it must "transform the structure of Spain completely." The radicalization taking place on both sides encouraged more extreme solutions, and only one month into the war Franco indicated that he was thinking in terms of a corporative, nonparliamentary regime. From the start, he had intended to play a major role, yet the way matters developed in September was not the result of any specific plan that he had but stemmed from the desperate nature of the circumstances and the pressure generated by his supporters, which at times may have surprised even him. The generals who had not supported full power for him had no precise alternative plan of their own and ended up giving in.[45] Ever after, Franco and his closest supporters would contend that he had never sought complete power but had it thrust on him, though that was not exactly the case.

His inaugural speech indicated that he was not thinking in terms of any limited mandate, though it would probably be wrong to conclude that he had assumed that he would be dictator for life. That ambition would only emerge during the course of the long Civil War; after that there would be no looking back. Franco was soon convinced that parliamentary, liberal-capitalist regimes had become hopelessly weak, divided, and decadent, and that the future of Europe lay with the new single-party national dictatorships, led by Germany and Italy. The Fascist dictatorships provided the assistance crucial to winning the Civil War, and Franco came to identify more and more with their political orientation, even though he did not plan to imitate any specific foreign model.

The preferred title for him soon became "caudillo," a classic Castilian term for "leader" dating from the Middle Ages, a Spanish equivalent of "duce" or "führer." For a brief period several newspapers in the Nationalist zone referred to him simply as "the dictator," as had initially been common with Primo de Rivera, but this was quickly suppressed, even though the word was nostalgically associated in the minds of more than a few with the prosperous and peaceful time of the 1920s and no longer had such negative connotations. As it was, the caudillo almost immediately became the subject of a public litany of adulation, orchestrated by an increasingly disciplined press. This adulation soon far exceeded anything ever accorded any living figure in all Spanish history. It would continue to mark public discourse for the next quarter century, becoming more restrained only in the last years of Franco's regime.[46]

During October Franco was inevitably distracted by the problems of setting up his new government. The National Defense Council was dissolved, to be replaced by the strictly administrative Government Technical Council (Junta Técnica del Gobierno) that would administer the new state but would have no political or military authority. Its president was General Fidel Dávila, a reliable supporter of Franco and an administrative officer par excellence, who also took over the post of chief of the Nationalist army's general staff. Dávila was the only member of the National Defense Council to have a position in the new government. The Government Technical Council supervised seven commissions charged with the various branches of state administration, each having its own president plus three other senior members. Three of these presidencies went to Monarchists. Setting the first example of what would become a standard practice of kicking upstairs unwanted notables, Franco made Cabanellas inspector general of the army, a largely honorific post that relieved the former council president of active command. He also created the office of General Secretariat of the

Chief of State, which he placed under the command of his brother Nicolás, who continued to serve as chief political adviser, as well as the office of Secretariat for Foreign Relations, which he named Sangróniz to head, and a general government ministry that functioned as the Ministry of the Interior and Security under another general. No single city in the main northern sector was large enough to house the entire government. The Government Technical Council sat in Burgos, the main center of administration, though the internal security apparatus was centered in Valladolid, foreign relations in San Sebastián, and the military headquarters at first in Salamanca. This was an ad hoc administration for fighting a civil war, what Franco's brother-in-law Serrano Suñer later called "a field-camp state," but it sufficed, achieving its basic goals over the next sixteen months, until Franco was able to form his first regular government at the close of January 1938.[47]

Despite the early imposition of martial law and a general militarization of government, the new regime could not have succeeded had it not been accepted by a large minority of the population, and indeed by a majority in the original Nationalist zone in the conservative north. All Spaniards threatened by the revolution of the Popular Front—from aristocratic monarchists to ordinary middle-class people to the modest Catholic smallholders of the northern provinces—rallied to Franco as their leader in a desperate struggle for survival. To many of them, he was indeed the "savior of Spain," as acclaimed by his expanding propaganda apparatus. In the face of sweeping violent revolution by their enemies, the Nationalists mobilized a broad, increasingly right-wing counterrevolution that within a matter of weeks embraced a cultural and spiritual neotraditionalism without precedent in recent European history. This quickly led to the restoration of traditional attitudes and values on a broad scale. Schools and libraries were purged not only of radical but of nearly all liberal influences, and Spanish tradition was upheld as the indispensable guide for a nation that was said to have lost its way by following the principles of the French revolution and liberalism.

Federico de Urrutia summarized the new spirit: "This is our ultimate guideline. To be what we were before rather than the shame of what we have been recently. To kill the dead soul of the nineteenth century, liberal, decadent, Masonic, materialist and Frenchified, and to fill ourselves once more with the spirit of the sixteenth century, imperial, heroic, sober, Castilian, spiritual, legendary and chivalrous."[48] Religious revival lay at its root.

As in the Canaries, Franco believed that he must set an example, and from the assumption of full power he began the practice of attending daily Mass in a chapel in his official residence, an official household chaplain, Father José María Bulart, being appointed on October 4. There had never been any doubt about his Catholicism, though it had received only limited expression when he was a young officer. This had been intensified by his marriage to the pious Doña Carmen, but it was the Civil War that identified him with frequent religious practice. The public was given to understand that he attended Mass each morning. Certainly his wife did, but Franco himself was often too busy, going to Mass mainly on Sundays and on special occasions, according to his daughter.[49] Much later, after his death, his niece Pilar Jaráiz, no great admirer of her uncle, would conclude that "his faith was genuine and no mere accommodation, though his way of understanding the Gospel might leave much to be desired and be highly debatable."[50] Certainly religious faith and Catholic identity became for Franco an important part of the sense of providential destiny that he was developing.

In his inauguration speech, Franco had said that his new regime would not be "confessional," reflecting the separation of church and state that Mola had preserved in his original program and that had been followed by all the military leaders in the early weeks, but this position was short lived. The massive violence against both clergy and Catholics unleashed in the revolutionary zone, the slaughter of tens of thousands, united nearly the entire Catholic population behind Franco, with the exception of the Basque nationalists.[51] He soon grasped that religion, even more than nationalism, must become the principal moral support of the National movement, and decided that he must give Catholicism much more than the "respect" promised in his inaugural speech. His new state must, indeed, be "confessional." Within a matter of months, Catholic faith and Spanish nationalism had become inseparable, and Franco's nascent regime soon fully affirmed the traditional "Spanish ideology," which under the country's classic monarchy for a millennium had emphasized the unique spiritual mission of Spain.[52]

The new regime would soon use the concept of "the Crusade" as semi-official designation for the struggle, even though, according to Carmen Franco, her father did not employ it in private conversation, and in later years he almost invariably referred to it simply as "the war." The left would forever condemn the Nationalists' use of the concept of "Crusade" on the grounds that their conduct of the war was too ruthless and inhumane to merit such a term, but the concept defines itself much as does the term "nation." That is, something is a crusade if most of its practitioners think it to be, and this was the case with a great many of the Nationalists. The cultural and religious counterrevolution helped to generate a spirit of discipline, unity, and sacrifice that was crucial for an all-out struggle. It provided the most important emotional and ideological underpinning for the Nationalists during the long ordeal of civil war.

7 Forging a Dictatorship

(1936–1939)

The military chieftains who had elevated Franco to supreme power may initially have thought of their leader as a sort of primus inter pares, but this notion did not accord with Franco's ideas. Though careful in his treatment of leading subordinates, whom he allowed considerable autonomy, from the beginning he exercised full personal power and firm authority over the military command, so that some of those who had voted for him were taken aback by his sweeping, and often distant and impersonal, use of authority. Referring to this in later years, Franco said that "as soon as he was made Chief of State the first thing he had to do was to 'cinch up' the military."[1]

Normal political life had ceased to exist in the Nationalist zone, all the leftist organizations having been outlawed under terms of martial law. Gil Robles, leader of the largest conservative party, had directed in a letter of October 7, 1936, one week after Franco assumed full command, that all CEDA members and their militia units subordinate themselves completely to the military leadership. Only the Falangists and the Carlists maintained their own autonomous roles, but they also had to respect military authority.[2] When the Carlists attempted to open an independent officer training school in December, Franco closed it immediately and sent the Carlist leader, Manuel Fal Conde, into exile. Though the Falangists were temporarily allowed to operate two military training schools of their own, on December 21 Franco unified all the rightist militia under regular military command.

Mola and some other commanders had not intended the elevation of Franco to cancel the original "open" plan for the country's future government. During December 1936 and January 1937 several of them may have proposed in discussions with Franco the appointment of a "political directory" to administer civil government and prepare for a new regime, but he showed no interest in anything that reduced his prerogatives or freedom of action. On January 29 Mola delivered a talk over the new Radio Nacional on patriotism and its duties, an indication that he enjoyed a special place in the new order. He was the only general, other than those on his immediate staff, with whom Franco regularly consulted in personal meetings. In a second radio address on February 28, Mola declared that Spain's future regime must have a "corporative organization" but also enjoy an independent judiciary and "freedom of instruction." Several commanders are said to have suggested to Mola that an effort must be made to force Franco to adopt a more collegial system of government, but Mola was intent on winning the war first, telling them that for the moment unity must not be compromised. Once victory had been achieved, it would be time to insist on political changes.[3] Rumors persisted that Franco might appoint another general as a sort of political prime minister, but in fact he did not seem to have had the slightest intention of doing this.

The administration of the Government Technical Council was makeshift and arbitrary, but achieved its principal goals in mobilizing the human and economic resources of the Nationalist zone. Ever-increasing state regulation sought to stimulate and channel the existing system of production and succeeded in encouraging greater proportionate economic output than did the chaotic revolution in the Republican zone. Food production was adequate, mineral exports were sustained, and, after the conquest of the northern Republican zone in 1937, coal and steel production was soon restored and even raised to a higher level. The new state effectively mobilized financial resources; the banks remained profitable and the Nationalist peseta stable, suffering little more than 10 percent inflation per year, while in the opposing zone inflation and monetary depreciation eventually spiraled out of control.[4] Nearly 30 percent of the cost of the war was met by taxation during the conflict, a better record than that of any of the major European belligerents in World War I, and increased wages almost kept pace with rising prices. Things went so well during the war, in fact, that Franco was not prepared for the severe deterioration in conditions (some of it brought on by government policies) that took place once it ended.

Propaganda assumed a major role, and Franco's government was initially handicapped by reliance on military personnel who were inadequate to the task. The first propaganda director, General José Millán Astray, had oratorical ability but completely lacked the talent and sophistication for what was shaping up as Europe's propaganda battle of the decade. Relying on military administration gave Franco an edge in combat and using technical experts in economic affairs also proved effective, but his regime was at a disadvantage in public relations and propaganda.

Millán Astray was himself responsible for the most notorious cultural incident of the Civil War at a university event in Salamanca on October 12 in honor of the "Día de la Raza," the Spanish national holiday that commemorated the landing of Columbus in the Bahamas in 1492. The presiding officer was the lifetime rector of the University of Salamanca (Spain's oldest), the writer and philosopher Miguel de Unamuno, one of the country's most prestigious intellectuals. Unamuno, like some of Spain's other top writers, had come out strongly in favor of the Nationalists, appalled by the disorder and violence of the left, and he enjoyed personal entrée to Franco.[5] He even served as head of a university commission that removed a number of leftist professors. Seated with him at the speakers' table were Millán Astray and Carmen Polo de Franco, the generalissimo's wife, though none of the three was scheduled to speak. Hearing the orators of the day denounce the "enemies of Spain" in the form of Basques and Catalans was, however, too much for Unamuno, a Basque and a lifelong liberal and independent thinker. He rose to make extemporaneous remarks that, while supporting the Nationalists, denounced the current extremes of what he termed an "uncivil war," briefly defending patriotic and Christian Basques and Catalans, as well as "critical intelligence," which brought howls of derision from the very right-wing audience. Millán Astray could not resist joining in, shouting "¡Muera la intelectualidad traicionera!" ("Death to treacherous intellectualism"), and turning to several legionnaires in the audience, he cried out their old slogan "¡Viva la muerte!" ("Long live death"). As the audience became more vituperative, Doña Carmen, who had great respect for Unamuno, got up to leave and (at the suggestion of Millán Astray himself) asked Unamuno to take her arm, so that she could get him safely out of the hall, taking him to his home in her own limousine.[6] Doña Carmen herself did not find Unamuno's remarks particularly objectionable and blamed Millán Astray for having created an unnecessary incident.[7]

The university faculty, however, voted to relieve Unamuno of his rectorship. He continued to support Franco, though he became increasingly critical of the Nationalist policy of repression and of political executions, which he apparently tended to blame on Mola's initial policies in the north.[8] On the final day of 1936, Unamuno died an embittered man, deeply saddened by his country's disaster, and soon afterward Franco transferred Millán Astray to leadership of a new service for military amputees.[9]

During the early autumn of 1936 Franco was faced with the problem of the rescue or exchange of José Antonio Primo de Rivera, leader of the Falange, who had been arrested by the Republican government in March and was currently being held in a prison in Alicante on the east coast. Falangists were desperate to regain the liberty of their chief, who might be executed by the Republicans at any time. Though Franco could not be expected to be enthusiastic about the prospect of rescuing Primo de Rivera, who might then become a political rival, neither could he reject the requests of the Falangists. He provided assistance and placed a sizable amount of money at their disposal to bribe Republican jailers. The Falangists enjoyed limited cooperation from the German navy and also mobilized support from several leading figures abroad who sought to intervene with the Republican authorities. All these efforts came to naught, and one thing that Franco did not do was to authorize a major political exchange of prisoners.[10] Primo de Rivera was tried by one of the new revolutionary People's Courts in the Republican zone and executed on November 20, 1936, though his death was not publicly acknowledged by the Nationalists for some time. His absence and death left the swollen Falange, suddenly the largest political party in Spanish history, leaderless, lacking the political direction to take advantage of its increasing status in the Nationalist zone, a situation that suited Franco perfectly well. For a number of years, José Antonio Primo de Rivera became the subject of an extraordinary death cult among Falangists, the cult of "el ausente" ("the absent one"). Franco accepted this adoration of the dead José Antonio with equanimity, since it generated no live candidate to oppose him.

During his first months in power, Franco concentrated on military affairs and diplomatic relations. Politics had been proscribed, with all the rightist forces supporting the new regime, and only the Falange engaged in proselytism, though it was careful not to get in the way of military administration. There was little in the way of political development, however, such matters remaining in the inexperienced hands of Nicolás Franco, head of the General Secretariat of the Chief of State. Nicolás had been a competent naval engineer, but in government he quickly morphed into a self-indulgent bureaucrat, working only in the afternoon or late evening. He had no particular ideas, other than to safeguard his brother's power. There was some talk about the need to organize a "Francoist Party," but this seemed hopelessly artificial and too reminiscent of Primo de Rivera's "Patriotic Union." Franco considered the Primo de Rivera regime his chief precedent, but he kept in mind that the regime had failed for lack of political and institutional development, and he knew that he must avoid such a fate. But how?

By the early weeks of 1937 German and Italian representatives, particularly the latter, were suggesting the need to follow the model of single-party states, with an official political party, presumably designed along Italian or German lines. When, however, the German ambassador General Wilhelm Faupel encouraged the Falangists to take the lead, he was violating Hitler's tacit policy of political noninterference, whereas in Rome Mussolini and his colleagues genuinely hoped that they could persuade Franco to follow the Italian model. This would mean a Fascist-type party in a regime crowned by a monarchy, which then might develop as a satellite of Italy. Early in March 1937 Mussolini dispatched Roberto Farinacci, a top party *gerarca* (leader), on a kind of fact-finding mission to Nationalist Spain, with the goal of encouraging Franco to name a prince of the Italian house of Savoy as the future king. Franco was categorical that this could never be, since monarchy at that point had few supporters in Spain and any such scheme would be hopelessly divisive. Farinacci was further put off when Falangist leaders told him that, aside from being strong nationalists opposed to Marxism, anarchism, and the internationalist left, they advanced a radical program in social and economic affairs. This seemed the more paradoxical to the Italians, given what they perceived as the extremely "reactionary" character of Franco's government.[11]

An important development was the arrival of Doña Carmen's brother-in-law Ramón Serrano Suñer, who entered the Nationalist zone on February 20, 1937. On the eve of the Civil War, Serrano was moving toward the Falange, hoping to bring much of the CEDA's youth with him. Arrested in Madrid, he sat helplessly in prison while his two brothers were executed. A severe ulcer, however, gained his transfer to a hospital, whence, with the help of confederates, he managed to escape dressed in women's clothing, and he subsequently fled to the Republican zone in disguise. The slender, blue-eyed, handsome Serrano was no longer the dapper blond he had been before the war, for his experiences in Madrid had turned his hair prematurely gray. Doña Carmen was extremely fond of her youngest sister, Zita, and of her brother-in-law. Amid the wartime housing shortage, the couple, together with their four children, were immediately invited to move into the small upper floor of the episcopal palace in Salamanca where the Francos lived.

Serrano was politically experienced and astute, much more sophisticated than the naval engineer Nicolás Franco, and he soon replaced him as Franco's chief political advisor. Like most Spaniards of his era, Franco was strongly family oriented, and in the uncertain early months of his dictatorship, he trusted family members more than anyone else. Increasingly, members of the extended Polo family came to the fore in his entourage, as his brother Ramón was far away in Mallorca and Nicolás was increasingly playing a secondary role. Doña Carmen was always careful to be correct in her relations with Franco's siblings, but inevitably she favored her own relatives, and all the more because she harbored a certain resentment against Isabel Pascual de Pobil, the wife of Nicolás. Isabel was from a wealthy family in Valencia and apparently cut a certain swathe in Salamanca as the spouse of the generalissimo's chief political advisor, but, for Doña Carmen, two "Señoras de Franco" in government circles was one too many.

Earlier, Franco had been impressed by the idea of Catholic corporatism and in 1935 had carefully noted the updating of Carlist doctrine in Víctor Pradera's *El estado nuevo*, but he concluded that these approaches were too right wing and lacked broad mass appeal. Something more dynamic and up-to-date was needed. By the time Serrano arrived in Salamanca, he found that Franco "already had the idea of reducing the various parties and ideologies of the movement to a common denominator. He showed me the statutes of the Falange on which he had made copious marginal notations. He had also made comparisons between the speeches of José Antonio and of Pradera."[12]

Unlike Nicolás, Serrano had a plan of his own, which largely, though never entirely, coincided with Franco's own ideas, and he proposed to create what can be most simply described as a sort of institutionalized equivalent of Italian Fascism, though it would be more identified with Catholicism than Fascism, whatever the contradictions such an identification entailed. This would mean building a state political party, based on the Falange. As Serrano later put it, Carlism "suffered from a certain lack of political modernity. On the other hand, much of its doctrine was included in the thought of the Falange, which furthermore had the popular and revolutionary content that could enable Nationalist Spain to absorb Red Spain ideologically, which was our great ambition and our great duty."[13] It is doubtful that either Franco or Serrano had ever read the early nineteenth-century theorist Joseph De Maistre, but they implicitly agreed with his conclusion that the counterrevolution was not the opposite of a revolution, but rather was an opposing revolution. The revolutionary dimension of their counterrevolution would be provided by a kind of Fascism.

The Falange had swollen enormously from no more than ten thousand members to several hundred thousand, growing even more than the Communist Party in the Republican zone, but its principal leaders were dead, slain by the leftist repression. The second rank who stepped to the fore lacked talent, prestige, or clear ideas and were divided among themselves. They realized that all indications were that the country was moving toward some kind of major new political organization, and in February they had negotiated terms of a possible fusion with the Carlists, the only other significant paramilitary and political force in the Nationalist zone. The Carlists, however, were ultratraditionalist Catholics, who were extremely skeptical of Fascism, and a merger could not be achieved.

While Nicolás continued to handle routine administration of political affairs, Franco decided—strongly encouraged by Serrano—to establish a *partido único*, a single, unified state party. Matters were brought to a head by turmoil in the Falangist leadership between April 16 and 18, as two dominant factions literally came to blows, leaving one dead on each side. By April 18, the sometime ship mechanic Manuel Hedilla, acting head of the party, was elected its new *jefe nacional* by a narrow vote. While that was going on, Serrano supervised the drawing up of a decree of political unification, officially announced on April 19.

This established the Spanish Traditionalist Phalanx (Falange Española Tradicionalista [FET]) as the new state party (a state party being standard "in other countries of totalitarian regime," according to the decree), arbitrarily fusing the Falangists and Carlists. The Twenty-Six Points, the Fascistic doctrine of the Falange, became the creed of the new party and hence of the state, but Franco emphasized that this was not a final and fixed program and would be subject to modification and development in the future. "The Movement that we lead is precisely this—a movement—more than a program. It will not be rigid or static, but subject, in every case, to the work of revision and improvement that reality may counsel," a point that Franco stressed further in his radio address that night.[14] The new political structure would not rule out an eventual Monarchist restoration, for Franco specified that "when we have put an end to the great task of spiritual and material reconstruction, should patriotic need and the wishes of the country support it, we do not close the horizon to the possibility of installing in the nation the secular regime that forged its unity and historical greatness," taking care to term it "instauración" of a more authoritarian monarchy, a concept developed by the neo-Monarchist theorists in the pages of the journal *Acción española* in the early 1930s, as distinct from restoration of the parliamentary monarchy.[15] This was not at all a matter of the party taking over the state; rather, the state was taking over the party. A few years later, that would make all the difference concerning the future of Fascism in Spain.

All remaining political organizations were dissolved (one in fact had voluntarily done so already) and their members were expected to join the FET, of which Franco named himself the *jefe nacional*. The organization would have a secretary-general, a political council as executive committee, and a broader national council, all these personnel to be appointed by the national chief. Five days later, the Falange's raised-arm Fascist salute was made the official salute of the regime (to be abandoned only in 1945). The key Falangist insignia and slogans were also taken over: the dark-blue shirt, the greeting of "comrade," the red and black flag (first adopted by the anarchists), the symbol of the yoked arrows (from the Catholic monarchs, Fernando and Isabel, who had unified Spain nearly half a millennium earlier), the anthem "Cara al Sol" ("Face to the Sun"), and the slogan "¡Arriba España!" ("Upward Spain").[16]

Hedilla had been expecting some sort of political unification, but also, naively, thought that he would be the leader of the new party. Instead, he was merely named the head of the Political Council, the central political committee. The unification was not popular with either the Falangist or the Carlist militants, but under the existing conditions of total civil war the immense majority accepted Franco's initiative. Nonetheless, Hedilla and a small minority of activists, while not rebelling overtly, manifested their recalcitrance. Hedilla was immediately arrested and later court-martialed and sentenced to death, though Serrano had Franco commute this to life imprisonment.[17] Over the next weeks and months hundreds of Falangists who showed a degree of defiance would be arrested. A report given Franco at the close of 1937 listed a total of 568, of whom 192 were convicted by military tribunals. There were no executions, but forty-nine individuals were sentenced to life imprisonment, though all would eventually be released.[18] This was the nearest thing to overt political conflict under Franco's long dictatorship and may be contrasted with the constant strife between the leftist groups in the Republican zone, which altogether resulted in the death of more than a thousand people.[19] The FET became a reality, however much cognitive dissonance this generated. Its members devoted themselves primarily to military service, the provision of auxiliary assistance to the war effort, and the expansion of propaganda activities. The war effort remained the priority.

The goal was to develop a *partido único* of a semi-Fascist kind, though not as the mere imitation of the Italian or any other foreign model. In an interview in a pamphlet titled *Ideario del generalísimo*, published soon afterward, Franco declared that "our system will be based on a Portuguese or Italian model, though we shall preserve our historic institutions." Later, in an interview with *ABC* on July 19, 1937, he reiterated that the objective was to achieve "a totalitarian state," though the example he evoked was the institutional structure of the Catholic monarchs in the fifteenth century. This indicated that what Franco had in mind was not a system of absolute control of all institutions, as in the Soviet Union or even the most categorically Fascist regimes, that is, a true totalitarianism, but rather a military and authoritarian state that would dominate the public sphere but otherwise permit a limited traditional semi-pluralism. As he put it rather ambiguously in an interview with the *New York Times Magazine* in December 1937, "Spain has its own tradition, and the majority of the modern formulas that are to be discovered in the totalitarian countries may be found already incorporated within our national past." Two months before the unification, Franco had declared that it was not a matter of the Falange being a "Fascist" movement: "The Falange has not declared itself fascist; its founder declared so himself." Thereafter, the custom within the Nationalist zone, especially among the press in the first months, of calling the Falangists and some other groups "Fascists" was abandoned. All that Franco had been willing to admit before the unification was that the supposedly non-Fascist character of the Falange "does not mean that there are not individual fascists . . . *within it.*"[20] The function of the new FET was, in his words, to incorporate the "great unaffiliated neutral mass" of Spaniards, for whom doctrinal rigidity would not be desirable. Similarly, in the month following the unification, he had to reassure Catholic bishops that the FET would not propagate "Nazi ideas," a particular concern of theirs.[21]

Nonetheless, partly under the influence of Serrano Suñer, Franco's language became somewhat more "Fascist" during 1938 and 1939. In the draft of his speech for July 18, 1938, commemorating the second anniversary of the National Movement, he applied the adjective "Fascist" to his regime and, more extravagantly, to the Catholic monarchs but decided to delete it from the final version. The official statutes of the party, promulgated on August 4, 1937, structured a completely authoritarian and hierarchical system. Franco's role was defined in Articles 47 and 48:

> The Jefe Nacional of F. E. T., supreme Caudillo of the Movement, personifies all its values and honors. As author of the historical era in which Spain acquires the means to carry out its destiny and with that the goals of the Movement, the Jefe, in the plenitude of his powers, assumes the most absolute authority. The Jefe is responsible before God and history.
>
> . . . It is up to the Caudillo to designate his successor, who will receive from him the same authority and obligations.

The leaders of Franco's army were not particularly pleased, for very few of them were Falangists, and they viewed themselves as the true elite of the National Movement, but they were absorbed in the war effort and had little time or energy to devote to political intrigue. For months, Mola was still viewed by some as a potential political alternative, and he seems to have regretted that Franco had been given so much power, but he continued to tell dissatisfied colleagues that any major political adjustment would have to wait until military victory.[22] Mola's role came to an abrupt end on June 3, 1937, when the military plane carrying him to another meeting with Franco suffered engine failure and crashed, killing all on board.[23] Years later, Serrano would insist that Mola was about to deliver a political ultimatum to Franco, asking him to turn over the political powers of prime minister to another general (such as himself), but there is no clear evidence of that.[24]

In July 1937, with all the Basque country occupied and the conquest of the rest of the northern Republican zone at hand, Franco moved his headquarters to Burgos. The family took up residence in the Palacio de la Isla, a large building ceded by a member of the local elite, which had to be quickly modernized for their occupancy. They were joined once more by the Serrano Suñers and by other members of Doña Carmen's family. As Carmen Franco remembered,

> Until the war was over we all lived together. Since my cousins were smaller, I gave them orders and we all got along very well. . . . Since we lived in a large building in Burgos, both of my mother's sisters joined us, though

Aunt Isabel had no children. The second floor was for us, while my father's office was on the ground floor. We knew that children were not allowed in his office, but we could go into the office of his adjutants, who gave us pencils, which were half blue and half red. And since they were rather bored, with little to do until my father gave them orders, they paid attention to us and we had a great time. I remember once when a German general came to see my father. The naval adjutant was very nice and sometimes very funny, so he had put a lid on his head as though it were a helmet, the lid of a soup bowl. He had it on when the general arrived, and when he came into the office my father said, "You must be crazy. What are you doing with that lid on your head?"

For the daughter of the generalissimo, the war seemed glamorous enough: "For a girl it could be entertaining. Whenever another town was taken, there was a celebration and that could be a lot of fun. We could go out in the streets with other children to sing hymns and patriotic songs. Yes, that could be good fun."

Though the Francos and Serrano Suñers seemed to have formed one big happy family during the war years, circumstances were not so fortunate for several other members of the family. Franco's niece Pilar Jaráiz, daughter of his sister, was trapped with her own infant child in the Republican zone. Limited exchanges of prisoners began in the autumn of 1937, and in 1938 they were exchanged and brought to Burgos. Many years afterward Pilar Jaráiz wrote that the reception by Franco and Doña Carmen had been cold and unsympathetic, all the more surprising since their relationship before the war had been close. It was as though they were blamed for not having escaped earlier. They had spent two years in a Republican prison, and Pilar's child had almost died of meningitis. Doña Carmen's unfeeling and hostile question, "Whose side are you on?," typified the extreme suspicion of anyone in any way associated with the other side, even sometimes of those who had been prisoners.[25] In later years, Pilar Jaráiz showed some sympathy for the political left, but whether she ever did during the Civil War is unknown.

Despite his notorious sangfroid, in the home Franco could not always hide the tension generated by difficulties on the warfront or by political and diplomatic stress. According to his daughter, occasionally, at meals, which in Burgos were always taken with the family, "he was rather tense. Sometimes, and it was evident because then he wouldn't say anything at all." But this was rare, for he normally maintained an even temper and even sometimes showed warmth at home, which contrasted with his cold and reserved, though polite, political and military demeanor.

It was left to Serrano Suñer to develop the first steps of the FET and to conciliate and integrate the *camisas viejas* (lit. "old shirts"), the activist veterans of the original Falange, of whom several thousand survived in the Nationalist zone. By this point Serrano had entirely replaced Nicolás Franco as chief political advisor, and he served during the greater part of the Civil War as political coordinator of the new regime, living in intimate association with Franco. Not the least of his services to his brother-in-law was his acting as a kind of lightning rod for critics, who sometimes blamed him for their political frustrations. Soon they would begin to dub him the generalissimo's evil genius, the *cuñadísimo* (most high brother-in-law).

This enabled Franco to sidestep much of the political criticism that inevitably developed. As Eberhard von Stohrer, the second German ambassador, put it:

> Franco has very cleverly succeeded, with the advice of his brother-in-law, . . . in not making enemies of any of the parties represented in the United Party that were previously independent and hostile to one another, but, on the other hand, also in not favoring any one of them that might thus grow too strong. . . . It is therefore comprehensible that, depending on the party allegiance of the person concerned, one is just as apt to hear the opinion . . . that "Franco is entirely a creature of the Falange" as that "Franco has sold himself completely to the reaction" or "Franco is a proven monarchist" or "he is completely under the influence of the Church."[26]

In the new system, the Church was more important than any other institution save the military. Not quite all the ecclesiastical hierarchy had rallied to Franco, nor was the Vatican—having burned its fingers with Mussolini and Hitler—very eager to provide him with formal diplomatic recognition. The first occasion on which the regime referred to itself as a Catholic state occurred in a minor decree of October 30, 1936, which established the *plato único*, the provision that one day a week restaurants serve only a single plate of food rather than a multicourse meal. The role of military chaplains was made official on December 6, 1936, though they had been present in certain units of volunteers, especially those of the Carlists, from the beginning.

On December 29, 1936, Franco and Archbishop Isidro Gomá, primate of the Church in Spain, reached a six-point agreement that guaranteed complete freedom for all Church activities. They agreed to avoid mutual interference in the spheres of church and state but also that in the future Spanish legislation would be adapted to the requirements of Church doctrine. Though the Vatican made several efforts at mediating between the two sides of the Spanish conflict, during 1937 relations between the Spanish Church and Franco's regime were regularized. The old ecclesiastical budget of state subsidies was not yet restored, but many measures were undertaken to reenforce Catholic norms in culture and education and to encourage religious observance. The Marian cult and traditional symbols returned to public schools, Corpus Christi was once more declared a national holiday, and Santiago was restored as patron saint of Spain. Many more such measures would be introduced over the next decade, before an apogee was reached in the mid-1940s.

Despite the Vatican's reluctance to provide official recognition to the leader of an insurgent movement, Franco pressed the Spanish hierarchy to make an official declaration on his behalf that would counteract Republican propaganda abroad. Once all Catholic Basque territory was conquered in June 1937 and approval received from the Vatican, the Spanish hierarchy released its subsequently famous *Carta colectiva* on July 1. All but five of the bishops, minus those who had been murdered in the Republican zone, signed this document, which explained in detail the position of the leaders of the Spanish Church. It affirmed the legitimacy of the Nationalists' struggle, though it stopped short of endorsing the specific form of Franco's regime as the future government of Spain.

Some of the Republican anti-Catholic laws would not be officially derogated until the spring of 1938, when Franco had gained somewhat greater support from the Vatican. In March of that year religious instruction was made obligatory in all public schools, crucifixes were restored in classrooms, and plans were announced for a new curriculum in secondary schools that would reflect Catholic teaching. The only note of a subdued kind of anticlericalism came from the most radical sector of the Falange.[27] Franco developed a system that was fundamentally, though by no means totally, clerical, and still reserved several cards to play in negotiation with the Church, until an official concordat was finally signed many years later, in 1953.[28]

On January 30, 1938, the eighth anniversary of the downfall of Primo de Rivera, Franco took another major step in the institutionalization of his regime, dissolving the Government Technical Council and replacing it with his first regular government of cabinet ministers. The announcement was part of a new administrative law to define the structure of Spanish government. Article 16 stipulated that "the Chief of State possesses the supreme power to dictate juridical norms of a general character," a kind of self-definition and self-legitimization of the personal powers of dictatorship. It also declared the function of president of government, or prime minister, to be "united with that of the Chief of State," permanently reserving such power for Franco. Six months later, the new cabinet took the initiative of promoting Franco to the rank of captain-general of the army and the navy, thereby creating a new supreme military rank that had formerly been reserved exclusively for the kings of Spain. Franco was in the process of accumulating more power in his hands, as the ruler of a new-style twentieth-century dictatorship, than had ever been exercised by any traditional ruler in Spain's long history.

The cabinet that took office on January 31 provided the first clear example of Franco's policy of balancing off the various sectors (later to be termed "political families") of the National Movement, giving a measure of representation to each. Pride of place went to the military, who occupied four ministries. The most important was the able and respected General Francisco Gómez-Jordana Souza, a Monarchist conservative with much administrative experience, who in June 1937 had replaced Dávila as head of the Government Technical Council. He was made vice president of the government and also minister of foreign affairs. Falangists received only two ministries—Agriculture and Syndical Organization, the latter charged with initiating the new state labor union system.

Carmen Franco has said that aside from the military men and the Carlist justice minister, the Conde de Rodezno, Franco knew none of the other new ministers, all of whom were selected by Serrano. She observes: "He greatly esteemed Gen. Jordana, because they were somewhat similar. Jordana was reticent, not at all loquacious, and had a manner that my father liked very much."

The last major task of Nicolás Franco in the government was to lead a special delegation to Rome in the summer of 1937 to seek even greater Italian assistance (though not more combat troops), marking the beginning of his transition to the world of diplomacy. Initially Franco had wanted to use his brother's background as shipyard director to name him minister of industry in the new government, but Serrano convinced Franco that would simply be "too much family," and so Nicolás was named ambassador to Portugal, a post that he would hold for two decades.[29]

The only one of the Franco brothers who became a casualty of the Civil War was Ramón. When the conflict erupted, the new Republican government had maintained him as Republican air attaché in Washington, but

165

his brother's prominent role in the military insurrection placed Ramón under increasing pressure. He was said to have been strongly affected by news of the killing of his old copilot Julio Ruiz de Alda (who had also been a cofounder of the Falange) by revolutionary militia in a slaughter that took place in Madrid's central prison during the second month of the conflict. Immediately upon learning of his brother's first proclamation in Morocco, Ramón had released an ambiguous statement to the press, declaring that the military insurrection did not signal a return to the monarchy but was a struggle over the future of the Republic, a perfectly correct statement at that time. He was charged by the Republican government with purchasing American planes for the Republican war effort, but that effort was stymied by Washington's new neutrality legislation. Ramón remained in regular contact with Nicolás and finally burned his political bridges in mid-September 1936, two weeks before his brother became generalissimo. On September 15, the *Washington Post* published an interview in which he declared his willingness to join his brothers in their cause, once more observing accurately that the Civil War was going to produce a dictatorship of one kind or another, and that Spain needed a "dictatorship of the middle classes," provided by the Nationalists. He did not leave Washington with his wife and daughter until his brother was officially inaugurated on October 1, which extinguished any remaining doubts he might have had.

When Ramón appeared in Salamanca, Franco forgave him completely for his political past. To protect him from the fierce repression against leftists and Masons, Franco ordered a judicial proceeding to absolve him of his Masonic and leftist background and then late in November 1936 promoted him one rank to lieutenant colonel and appointed him head of the Nationalist air base on Mallorca, an important post.[30]

Nearly all Franco's top subordinates reacted negatively, but none as much as General Alfredo Kindelán, the commander of his air force, who on November 26, 1936, sent to him what may have been the strongest letter of protest that Franco ever received from a subordinate. Kindelán informed him that, though Kindelán would maintain complete discipline in the air force, the appointment of his brother had been received with strong and unanimous disapproval, most of all because the revolutionary forces with which Ramón had once conspired had slaughtered several thousand of their military comrades within the Republican zone. Some air force officers contended that Ramón should be shot rather than promoted.[31] An impassive Franco merely confirmed the order, which was carried out.

The Nationalist air force on Mallorca, together with the Italian planes that accompanied them, played an important role in interdicting Republican shipping and also in bombing the docks of east coast ports. Though Ramón was received coldly by his subordinates, he increasingly won their respect by his attention to duty and his professional skill, especially his personal example in leading many missions, actions in which, as base commander, he need not have engaged. During the first ten months of 1938, for example, Ramón logged 159 hours on combat missions, reportedly sometimes criticizing Italian aviators for being too timid. During his two years on Mallorca, he also took at least three brief furloughs in Salamanca, reunited with his siblings for several last times. It has been said that Ramón suffered increasingly from stress and depression during his final months, though this cannot be confirmed.

On October 28, 1938, Ramón led a small routine sortie of a handful of seaplane bombers that targeted the docks of Valencia, but his plane never reached its destination, hitting a sudden rain squall and disappearing into clouds. His body was found floating in the Mediterranean several days later.[32] Franco merely released a statement that it was an honor that his brother had died doing his duty, like so many others, and dispatched Nicolás to attend the funeral ceremony at Palma de Mallorca. It was almost as though he felt it necessary for Ramón to give his life fighting for the Nationalists, in order to purge a sinful past. Subsequently he would have nothing to do with the widow or niece, since Ramón had divorced his first wife in order to marry her, a telling example of Franco's flint-hearted rigidity in such matters, which never changed.[33]

Franco had comparatively few political problems during the last two years of the Civil War. Though he occasionally had to take disciplinary measures, primarily against Falangists, he largely avoided problems by banishing politics for the duration in favor of total concentration on the military effort, and this was accepted by his followers so long as the conflict lasted. Only one of his chief subordinates got slightly out of line in public, and that was his old colleague Yagüe, now commander of an army corps. He was one of the few Falangist generals in an officer corps skeptical of the new state party. Yagüe delivered an address in Burgos on April 19, 1938, anniversary of the political unification, speaking of the need for social justice, recognizing the courage of the Republicans and also urging pardon for Hedilla and other Falangists who might have shown an excess of zeal. Only a longtime comrade of Franco would have dared to give the speech, and the censorship proved tardy, allowing the *Diario de Burgos* to publish the text, which caused something of a sensation. Moreover, the Falangist chief in La Coruña invited Yagüe to deliver another speech the following month. When this address repeated the same themes, Franco expressed his disapproval by relieving Yagüe of command of his corps for a month, putting an end to such speeches.[34]

The only period of tension came during the second half of 1938, which brought the threat of military stalemate along the Ebro and the danger of new international complications, though this proved transitory. By the final months of that year a number of Monarchist militants became more active, generating renewed speculation about papal mediation, in conjunction with Paris and London, for a negotiated solution and restoration of the monarchy, perhaps to rule over a federation of leftist and rightist Spain. This was quashed by none other than the exiled Alfonso XIII, who made it clear that he supported complete victory for Franco.[35]

With his personal authority consolidated and the military balance tilting ever more in his favor, Franco had a tendency to become overweening in a manner quite different from his earlier political comportment. Victorious on almost every front and constantly praised by a bombastic propaganda machine, he had become convinced that his role was providential, far beyond ordinary leadership. As a national hero in the 1920s, he had taken care to be modest in public pronouncements, but by 1938 he was convinced that he was an instrument of divine providence, endowed with special powers. If that were not the case, how could his extraordinary career and triumphs be explained? No pragmatic empirical calculation could be sufficient to account for his phenomenal success. Thus when he presided over meetings of the council of ministers, he talked more and more, pontificating about economic and other technical problems of which he knew little, sometimes to the irritation or amusement of his ministers.

As has been seen, the idea that Franco was purely laconic was always inaccurate. For years he had been quite talkative in the right kind of settings. By 1938 his verbal excesses had reached the point that some of his ministers mocked him in private. According to the unpublished diary of the Carlist minister of justice, the Conde de Rodezno, after an extravagant peroration by Franco about how easy it would be to deal with foreign debt, Andrés Amado, minister of finance, turned to Rodezno and whispered, "This man is on the moon. This is like talk at a café party." Rodezno further observed, "Moreover, he is someone for whom time doesn't matter. He acts like he never used a watch," while Pedro Sainz Rodríguez, the minister of education, privately declared, "This man possesses a broad culture of useless information."[36]

On the other hand, though he held the floor too long, he did not bully his cabinet members in the manner of some dictators. He almost always kept his temper and remained formally polite. One of the few recorded exceptions took place when the more conservative of the ministers moved to reject the draft of a somewhat radical *fuero de trabajo* (labor charter), proposed by Falangist leaders. Franco angrily seconded them, almost shouting that the text was presumptuous and showed a lack of respect for the "caudillo," having adopted what would henceforth become a lifelong habit of referring to himself in the third person. But he seems to have embarrassed himself by such an unusual outburst, quickly calming down and then acting to smooth things over, though categorically rejecting the draft itself.[37]

The only real arguments that he is known to have had were with a few of his top subordinates about the conduct of military operation. Franco was willing to discuss matters with his generals and cabinet ministers and usually permitted them considerable autonomy, but he always gave the final orders without equivocation. His normal calm would occasionally be interrupted by tears of compassion or rage when he learned of a new atrocity or suffering undergone by his sympathizers in the Republican zone, while he could remain glacial in moments of military alarm or when ratifying the death sentences of those condemned by military tribunals.[38] On the rare social occasions in these months, he preferred the usual light conversation and the recounting of old military anecdotes to any serious discussion. The young Falangist leader Dionisio Ridruejo would later write that he was taken aback by his first meeting with the caudillo: "I was surprised to meet a person who seemed timid rather than arrogant."[39] A number of foreign diplomats, such as the first British representative Sir Robert Hodgson, found his modesty of manner with foreign diplomats attractive, but rather more common was the report that the new Spanish dictator did not look like a military hero—he was too short and unimposing, a tad pudgy in middle age, with a high-pitched voice.

Franco's physical appearance thus continued to contradict the military and political reputation. During the Civil War his uniforms often fit poorly, and on one embarrassing occasion, his jacket split under the arm when he raised his right hand in the regime's Fascist salute. The physical image—timid manner, soft, high voice, and a tendency to waddle with increased weight—made for a cartoonist's delight and brought sarcastic remarks even from members of the regime's elite. In supposed reference to his daughter, Carmen, the witty Sainz Rodríguez observed: "This Carmencita resembles her father more and more, in her voice," while Queipo de

Llano, whose sphere of autonomy would be eliminated at the end of the war, sneeringly referred to him in private as "Paca la culona" (roughly, "fat-fannie Francie"). A good two decades would pass before Franco adopted a more high-protein diet and better tailoring. He would cut a better figure in old age as a more trim and reasonably distinguished elderly dictator in expertly tailored business suits than as the victorious early middle-aged caudillo of the Civil War.

Franco was not a hero for some of his first ministers, and he clearly did not have the personal style, manner, or appearance associated with the standard concept of charisma, but it is nonetheless clear that his leadership acquired genuinely charismatic dimensions during the Civil War. The status of "caudillo" was never fully defined in theory but was based on ideas of charismatic legitimacy.[40] There were numerous factors that contributed to this, including the following:

- His personal history and reputation, dating from the Moroccan campaigns, he having almost always emerged victorious, whereas many others had died or been defeated.
- The dramatic circumstances of 1936 that produced a large national movement that had recognized his personal preeminence among military leaders, making it seem as though he had been raised on the shields of the elite, as in Visigothic times.
- The undeniable effects of the Nationalist propaganda machine, inferior though it may have been to that of the Republicans.
- The development of Franco's style of leadership, not brilliant or for many even especially attractive and not eloquent, but firm, displaying self-assuredness, rendering him convincing in command and capable of communicating his basic ideas to his followers.
- Incipient consolidation of the new culture of the Nationalists, informed by an authority based on a new historico-cultural legitimacy and the appeal to national tradition, combined with new principles and techniques forged during the war.
- Continued victorious leadership that suggested he was well organized and that resulted in his never retreating but instead always advancing.
- Culmination in an incipient new state system that claimed to synthesize all the achievements of tradition, together with the most up-to-date techniques and requirements of the twentieth century, supposedly marking the beginning of a new historical era.

Propagandistic exaltation dated from the beginning of the war, but it increased in the autumn of 1936 when Franco became generalissimo, reaching an apogee in 1939–40.[41] The regime's Press and Propaganda Delegation (Delegación de Prensa y Propaganda) was organized in February 1937, even before the new political system had taken form, and though the cult of *caudillaje* was a state strategy, it was embraced by newspapers and by many notables and associations within the Nationalist zone. Toward the middle of 1937 the anniversary of his investiture, October 1, was declared the annual Fiesta Nacional del Caudillo. The invocation "Franco, Franco, Franco" was made a slogan equivalent to the Italian "duce, duce, duce." The style was clearly Fascistic, quite different from the much more moderate and undemonstrative (theoretically constitutional) authoritarianism of neighboring Portugal under Salazar.[42] Conversely, there was more stress on strictly military leadership, when compared with Italy, producing the slogan "The caesars were victorious generals." Key aspects of the effort to achieve legitimacy were thus more praetorian or Bonapartist than Fascist. All this may not have been either logical or consistent, but it proved pragmatic and effective in practice.

Franco thus became, as the slogan went, "the archetype of the Spanish fatherland," the incarnation of national mission and destiny, and even more broadly, in the struggle against Communism, he was projected as a savior of Western civilization.

8 | Winning the Civil War

(1936–1939)

Franco's long rule began with a major military set-back—the failure to take Madrid in the autumn of 1936, his only significant failure in the Civil War. Throughout the first six months, he sought to maintain his qualitative advantage by relying as much as possible on fully trained and organized army units, especially the legion and the *regulares*. Like their adversaries, however, the Nationalists mobilized militia forces, particularly Falangists and Carlists, and on August 5 they called up the recruiting classes for the preceding three years (1933–35) and began new officer training programs. It would nonetheless take time to produce effective new combat units, and in the initial phase Franco believed that he could rely only on his elite forces for major offensive operations. Yet these amounted to little more than twenty thousand men, and all of them could not be transferred from Morocco until after the Republican government made the blunder of temporarily lifting the blockade at the close of September. Moreover, as Franco built his forces for the drive on Madrid, he also felt it necessary to siphon off segments to shore up other fronts, particularly the heavily besieged city of Oviedo in Asturias. By October the Nationalists had committed almost as many men to the protection of Oviedo as to the drive on Madrid, though most of the units in the north were not of the same quality.[1] As he put it in one of his first operational instructions after taking supreme command: "The situation in Oviedo occupies a great number of the enemy's forces, which, if freed, could apply decisive pressure to other sectors of the northern front. The political and moral impact of a total evacuation of Oviedo would be terrible abroad and in Spain, and immensely harmful to our national cause."[2] This established a policy to which he would adhere throughout the conflict: no secondary front would be abandoned. Every sector, even if of limited strategic value, would be defended tenaciously, because in this kind of conflict issues of morale and prestige, and also international opinion, as well as the sheer control of territory, were paramount. No defeat, even a small or temporary one, would be accepted anywhere.

Two other factors contributed to the failure at Madrid: first, during October he had to devote attention to building his new state apparatus, and second, already in September his spearheads were running into greater numbers of militia and more tenacious resistance, so that the advance was slowed down considerably. Fatigue in the key combat units became a problem, together with the need to obtain better weaponry and build supplies. A shortage of ammunition was not overcome until nearly the end of October. As Colonel Carlos Asensio, one of the column leaders who would become a lieutenant general, would write twenty years later, "Due to the lack of quality troops, our advance became slower and slower."[3] During the main part of August, Franco's columns had advanced at a rate of twenty kilometers per day, but in September this slowed to only seven kilometers per day, and during October decreased even more, as forces were painstakingly marshaled for a major assault to seize the capital. The best of the new battalions of recruits were added, as were the best of the Falangist *banderas* (battalions), commanded as much as possible by regular officers. On the other hand, Franco's military intelligence about the other side was never very good, and it is probable that he did not fully grasp that the Republican government had finally begun to move rapidly to organize new infantry brigades of a regular army. He was also ignorant of the fact that large numbers of advanced-model Soviet weapons and military specialists would soon arrive on the Madrid front. Moreover, a more rapid advance on the capital was impossible without stripping one or two other fronts, possibly precipitating their collapse.

The new Soviet armor, manned by Soviet crews, was first committed to a small counterattack against the right flank of Franco's spearhead on October 29, and this was repeated five days later. The nine-ton Soviet T-26 tanks, with their heavier armor and their 45 mm. cannon, completely outclassed the small number of lightly armored vehicles, lacking cannon, that Franco had received from Italy and Germany. Both attacks were nonetheless failures, for Republican forces lacked the training to coordinate infantry assaults and artillery with a rapid tank advance. The experienced Nationalist infantry responded with an improvised device (a bottle filled with gasoline or other flammable liquid) for use against Soviet tanks, the same sort of contraption that three years later Finnish troops, employing the technique against Red Army vehicles invading their country, would dub the "Molotov cocktail," in derision of the Soviet foreign minister. Similarly, though Franco's small air force had gained combat superiority by October, this was eviscerated the following month in the face of larger numbers of more advanced Soviet planes, manned by Soviet air crews.

Franco chose to reject the doctrine of the General Staff's handbook of 1925, which advised that a major frontal assault should be preceded by secondary attacks to weaken the enemy and force him to commit his reserves and should only be carried out when in command of superior numbers.[4] Since his own numbers were clearly inferior, he relied on qualitative superiority, concentrating his slender forces on a coordinated assault to seize Madrid. He also chose the most direct route—uphill from the southwest—though some of his column leaders, such as Yagüe, preferred to maneuver toward the north/northwest, attacking downhill, or from the southeast.

The operation was finally launched on November 6 by three columns at first totaling only thirteen thousand men, though they were later reinforced to more than twenty thousand. Here his elite units lost their great advantage, which lay in superior maneuverability in the open field. In addition, on the second day the Republicans managed to capture a copy of the plan of attack. All the first available mixed brigades (*brigadas mixtas*) of the Republic's new People's Army were committed to the defense of the capital. Franco's assault gained a foothold on the western edge of the city but failed to advance further. Lacking major firepower to support them, Franco did not force his troops into suicidal attacks, but, in his frustration, he ordered several nighttime terror bombings of parts of the city (since the fast Soviet fighters prevented operations during the day).[5] However, the few planes available and very limited bomb loads produced no results other than the deaths of approximately two hundred civilians. After several days, he forwent the use of such tactics for the duration, finding them not only militarily unproductive but also costly in moral and political capital. Conversely, the first major counterattack by the mixed brigades achieved nothing other than revealing that on the offensive the new People's Army would be only slightly more effective than its militia predecessors. By November 23, however, Franco's elite units had been beset by a casualty rate of at least 30 percent and were losing their edge. During December and early January, he nonetheless persisted, summoning reinforcements for further attempts to penetrate Madrid's defenses, maneuvering farther to the northwest, but lacking the strength for a breakthrough.

The defense of Madrid was the first, and virtually the only, triumph of the People's Army, and it meant that the Civil War would become a longer conflict of attrition. The Republican success was due to several factors: (1) the organization of the first units of the new army, which was superior to that of the militia; (2) the advantage of fighting on the defensive from partially fortified positions; (3) the arrival of significant amounts of Soviet arms, giving the defenders temporary superiority in firepower, armor, and planes, the new late-model Soviet planes being generally superior to the more obsolescent Italian and German models assisting Franco; (4) determined leadership (in which the assistance of Soviet military advisers figured), which raised morale; and (5) the limited size of Franco's forces and his initial reliance on frontal assault. As Franco observed ruefully, "The enemy has mass strength and makes good use of weapons—even though lacking in officers and NCOs and morale."[6]

The battle marked a turning point, the complete end of the Nationalists' original hope for a relatively quick victory. It was the greatest disappointment for them during the entire war. In October they had been confident of taking the capital very soon and putting an end to a gruesome conflict. Failure produced a sag in morale: Major Antonio Castejón, wounded after having commanded one of the advance columns, is reported to have blurted gloomily to an American correspondent, "We who made this revolt are beaten."[7]

Yet if the Battle of Madrid constituted Franco's greatest failure, its aftermath showed that his comrades might not have been wrong to elect him commander in chief. His imperturbable calm and self-confidence was communicated to his staff and other subordinates, who reflected his determination to move forward despite all obstacles. Henceforth both sides concentrated on building mass armies for a grueling contest.

For some months the People's Army grew more rapidly, assisted by the forty-one thousand volunteers of the International Brigades, special Communist-led units recruited by the Comintern from all over Europe and the Americas, who had begun to appear in combat in November. The sizable Soviet intervention had changed the terms of the conflict, and Stalin presumably calculated this might be sufficient to enable the left to win.

That it was not was due in part to a decision by Mussolini and Hitler to top the Soviet escalation with an even greater counterescalation of their own. Hitler dispatched an all-German air unit, the Condor Legion, composed of ninety planes and an eventual total of nearly seven thousand men, together with antiaircraft guns and further light armor, while Mussolini decided to do even more. He sent larger numbers of planes and weapons and soon began to dispatch full-size ad hoc infantry units, at first mostly composed of Fascist Party militia (only slightly more effective than the revolutionary militia), which briefly reached a level of nearly forty-five thousand combat troops (plus artillery and air units) early in 1937, before almost half these troops were withdrawn. Franco's forces were further augmented by intensive recruiting in Morocco, which ultimately yielded a total of seventy thousand combat volunteers.

On November 18 Hitler and Mussolini recognized Franco's new regime as the sole government of Spain, and ten days later Franco signed a secret treaty with Mussolini, his most important agreement of the war. Italy pledged to honor "the independence and integrity of Spain," and both parties promised mutual assistance, consultation, and friendship, also pledging not to allow their territories to be used by a third power against the other, the last point being directed against France and the passage of French troops between Africa and Europe. The treaty also pledged both governments to benevolent neutrality should either be at war with a third power and required them to provide supplies and facilities.[8]

This secret treaty marked the beginning of broad expansion of Italian assistance, though Franco had mainly sought weapons and Italian aircrews and was not entirely happy with the arrival of increasing numbers of Italian ground troops of uncertain quality. On December 9 he had asked, rather, for one regular Italian division and one regular German division "as soon as possible," but Hitler had no intention of sending one.[9] Mussolini had decided to make a major commitment, seeing the outcome of the Spanish war as vital to the future of Italian policy in the Mediterranean. Hitler always remained more detached, having no concrete ambitions in the area, which he was willing to leave to Mussolini. By the end of 1936 he made the first of a series of comments that for Germany the most useful thing about the Spanish war was its ability to distract the other powers from German activities in central Europe. Thus it might be desirable for the war to drag on, so long as Franco did not lose in the end.

In January, as the Italian buildup continued, Franco reluctantly had to accept the services of an advisory staff of five Italian and five German officers, but he hoped to rid himself of them as soon as possible. In February 1937 the southern coastal city of Málaga, its defenses in disarray, fell quickly to a combined offensive by Franco's troops and the Italians.

But for another month his attention would be focused on renewed attempts to capture Madrid. The largest operation to date began in mid-February, when he launched an expanded assault through the Jarama river valley to outflank the capital from the south and east. This represented an effort to reopen the war of maneuver, and for the first time larger forces met directly in the open field. Though the Nationalists gained more ground, they could not achieve a breakthrough. The Republican mixed brigades waged one of their most effective battles, assisted by initial Republican air superiority, and casualties on both sides were higher than in the comparatively limited actions at the edge of Madrid.

The last attempt to outflank the capital was the Guadalajara offensive from the north in March, a joint operation in which the main effort was made by the newly constituted Italian Corps of Volunteer Troops (Corpo di Truppe Volontarie [CTV]), but liaison with the Nationalists was poor. Despite an initial breakthrough, the Italian advance was halted by the mixed brigades, assisted by Soviet tanks and control of the air. Though their assault ended with a small net gain in territory, the Italian troops precipitously abandoned their farthest line of advance, resulting in a major propaganda victory for the Republicans. With nearly two hundred Italians taken prisoner, Guadalajara was hailed by Republicans as "the first defeat of Fascism."[10] The outcome was complete stalemate on the central front.

The Italian failure nonetheless produced a certain grim satisfaction in Franco and many other Nationalists, who had resented the sudden influx of an autonomous foreign army corps. Guadalajara made it possible for Franco to escape further tutelage, as the CTV was drastically downsized and reformed, losing its special autonomy and henceforth integrated under Franco's command.[11]

Italian Fascists in Spain were often taken aback by the extreme rightist character of his new regime, and what they saw as its "reactionary" and "clerical" qualities. By contrast, they liked to view Fascism as "modern" and even "progressive," even though they disapproved of the verbal social radicalism of Falangists. There was some interest in encouraging Franco to adopt a variant of the Italian political model, and more than a little advice was given, but the ultimate conclusion was that the Spanish regime was too idiosyncratic, and too national, and that it would be a mistake to lean on it very hard. Hitler was even more categorical that a German model was inappropriate and that the Third Reich would accept any firm new anti-leftist regime Franco might develop, whether purely military, Monarchist or semi-Fascist. When General Wilhelm Faupel, Hitler's first ambassador, overstepped such guidelines, Franco asked that he be replaced, and the experienced, highly discreet professional diplomat, Eberhard von Stohrer, came in his stead.

Large arms shipments were sent to Franco basically on credit, and in August 1937 his ambassador signed an accord in Rome under which a consortium of Italian banks (partly owned by the Italian government) provided a sizable loan to pay for much of the supplies. These terms were more generous than those granted by Hitler (not to speak of the stringent conditions that Stalin imposed on the other side), requiring only minimal repayments while the war lasted.

In March 1937 the mobilization and training program of the Nationalist army was placed under Franco's close supporter General Luis Orgaz. During the course of the war, the office of Mobilization, Instruction and Recovery (Movilización, Instrucción y Recuperación [MIR]) expanded the number of training schools for officers and NCOs to twenty-two, and each one usually had a few German advisers. This office eventually commissioned more than thirty thousand newly trained reserve officers (*alféreces provisionales*), and nearly twenty thousand NCOs, men who were somewhat better prepared than their Republican counterparts and helped the Nationalist army to retain a certain combat superiority. When the MIR began operating, Franco had already drafted 290,000 recruits. That same month he called up all recruitment classes dating back to 1930 in an effort to mobilize all combat-worthy males in the Nationalist zone from twenty-one to twenty-eight years of age. Subsequently, the age limit would be steadily lowered until by August 9, 1938, the first trimester of 1941, made up of eighteen-year-olds, was drafted.[12] This provided at least 450,000 more recruits, and another 100,000 or more were added by the incorporation of selected Republican prisoners, beginning in mid-1937.[13] From start to finish, the Nationalist forces mobilized well over one million men, and by the end of the conflict Franco's infantry units totaled 840,000 men, though Republican recruitment was more extensive yet. The Nationalist army would never become a first-rate twentieth-century military machine—it was very far from that—but it enjoyed certain comparative advantages, particularly in leadership and organization and eventually in weaponry. Or, as General José Solchaga, one of Franco's veteran commanders, observed in his diary, "Lucky for us that the Reds are worse!"[14]

Mussolini personally, as well as the German and Italian commanders in Spain more generally, criticized Franco for the slowness of his operations, but the new caudillo was constitutionally incapable of proceeding otherwise, and in any event, his military organization did not seem to have acquired the efficiency to enable it to move more rapidly. Franco himself explained this to the Italians in terms of the peculiar requirements of a revolutionary civil war, where the opposition consisted not only of an enemy army but also, to a considerable extent, of an enemy population. He insisted that he could not concentrate for a single knockout military blow but had to maintain morale on all fronts and proceed methodically step by step, occupying and consolidating each advance, province by province.[15] He also insisted that his style of operations limited the cost to the civilian population and produced less of what the RAF a few years later would call "collateral damage."[16]

In later years, Franco's critics would claim that this pace was designed to enable him to carry out massive purges in each conquered district, but the facts do not bear this out. As Franco consolidated his institutional power in the autumn and winter of 1936–37, the number of political executions was increasingly curtailed, and comparatively few occurred during the second half of the war, declining very much as did the corresponding number in the Republican zone.

Franco took his most decisive strategic decision of the war right after the Guadalajara stalemate, when he accepted the advice of his chief of staff, General Juan Vigón, several other subordinates, and also the commanders of the Condor Legion, which concluded that the central zone around Madrid, defended by large numbers of Republican troops partly equipped with new Soviet weapons that provided air superiority, was for the time being too tough a nut to crack. By contrast, the conquest of the isolated

Republican northern zone, which contained Spain's principal heavy industry and sources of coal and iron, together with a skilled population and the chief prewar arms industry, would shift the balance of power.

The northern offensive began on March 31, 1937, at first with inferior numbers (no more than forty thousand infantry), but it was able to concentrate on the points of attack, which gave it local superiority, supported by nearly two hundred planes and two hundred pieces of artillery. The core of the assault force was made up once more of superior units, mainly the recently organized Navarrese brigades, formed in considerable measure of enthusiastic volunteers from the traditionalist Carlists of Navarre, minidivisions of six thousand men each. The tactic was to precede each attack with artillery barrages and intense bombing from the air. This marked the first appearance in Europe of World War II–style combined arms (though in this case minus the tanks), with the first relatively systematic air-to-ground support, though such tactics had to some extent been presaged on the Western front in 1917–18. Made possible by German and Italian air support and weapons, this strategy set the terms for Franco's advances.

The combination of heavy spring rain, hilly terrain, and determined resistance slowed movement to a snail's pace during April, but then it gradually accelerated, and by mid-June, all of the Basque province of Vizcaya was occupied, placing the entire Basque Country under Franco's control. The Republican northern zone had been gravely weakened, while conquest of the bastion of Catholic Basque nationalism (the only Catholic sector on the Republican side) simplified the religious issue, encouraging the Spanish episcopate to issue its *Collective Letter* on behalf of Franco on July 1. Moreover, his power over his own military command increased further after Mola's death in the plane crash on June 3. Franco and Mola had been able to work together on military issues with relative harmony, but Mola was the nearest thing to a political rival in the high command, and the new German ambassador reported that Franco felt relieved by his disappearance.[17] The fully loyal and more subordinate General Fidel Dávila took his place in the northern campaign.

In later years commentators would point to the fortuitous deaths that cleared Franco's path of leaders potentially in his way—first Balmes in the Canaries, then Sanjurjo as nominal leader of the insurrection, and finally Mola, the nearest thing to a military rival.[18] His Moroccan *regulares* would presumably have said that all these were further examples of Franco's *baraka*—his good fortune. Mola's subordinates could find no evidence of foul play in their general's fatal accident, though Franco's agents were quick to impound his personal papers.[19]

During the Vizcayan campaign the by far most notorious, though far from the most lethal, military incident of the war took place—the bombing on April 27 of Guernica, a small town of five thousand that was also the site of traditional political ceremonies. Because Franco had desisted from launching further indiscriminate attacks on cities after the several air raids on Madrid the preceding November, concluding that so-called terror bombing could be counterproductive, in January 1937 he had denied commanders of the Condor Legion permission to carry out a retaliatory terror bombing of Bilbao after Basque civilians had beaten to death a downed German flyer. Only direct military or military-support sites could be targeted, though this included towns near the front lines serving as direct support for combat operations. Thus the Vizcayan town of Durango, an important transport junction behind the front, had been bombed at the beginning of the campaign, resulting in more than two hundred civilian deaths.

Guernica was selected as a target by Lieutenant Colonel Wolfram von Richthofen (younger cousin of the "Red Baron" of World War I), chief of staff of the Condor Legion, for several reasons.[20] It housed several battalions of troops and three arms factories, lay near the front lines, and was connected by means of an adjacent bridge to the road flanking the main Basque defensive position, along which the defenders might have to retreat. Richthofen's chief goal was to block a main junction near the front to stymie Basque troop movements and permit Mola to break through, encircling the forces farther north. As it turned out, the whole operation was a wasted effort, for Mola continued his direct advance in the northeast without any attempt at encirclement.

The attack itself was a routine operation, carried out by twenty-two German and three Italian medium bombers, accompanied by fifteen fighter planes. Each bomber made one run aimed at the town, its military facilities, the bridge, and the adjacent roads. Pinpoint bombing was impossible with the existing technology, and the only way to hit the targets was to carpet much of the area. This was a routine operation, similar to the recent raid on Durango, which had attracted comparatively little attention. Guernica, however, contained much wooden construction, and the incendiary bombs (rather similar to those manufactured in one of the town's arms factories) started a major conflagration that consumed about three-quarters of the buildings. Seven air-raid shelters had been prepared. One of these suffered a direct hit and altogether 126 people died in the attack, fewer than at Durango.[21] This was a comparatively high number of deaths for the Spanish Civil War, however, in which there were few concentrated raids on cities.

Within several days the bombing of Guernica was being widely publicized throughout the world as a uniquely planned atrocity of terror bombing, involving a civilian target of no military significance, and the casualty figure was inflated approximately one thousand percent. George L. Steer, the British journalist who dispatched the first major version of the attack, was not particularly proleftist but instead eager to dramatize for a British public the effect of bombing on cities, to spark greater war preparedness. This turned into a major propaganda campaign, for Republican and Comintern propagandists had already found that aerial bombing rather than the enemy's political executions made the most effective propaganda stories abroad. In Western democracies, ordinary people had no fear of political execution but they became much more alarmed over the prospect of being bombed.[22] The name achieved permanent iconic status in Pablo Picasso's great mural *Guernica*, soon to appear in the Paris World Exposition of 1937 and later to become the leading artistic protest symbol of the inhumanity of twentieth-century warfare, the painting itself having been divested of partisan political content.[23]

In the furor that followed, Franco's government handled the issue poorly, refusing to admit the truth. Franco personally had had no prior knowledge of the attack, since daily operational details of the northern campaign did not necessarily come to him, though Mola's headquarters would have known about it. Instead of recognizing the facts of the matter—that this operation was no different from what all other military commands would carry out in the generation that followed—the Nationalist authorities were embarrassed, tried to dodge the issue, denied that the attack even took place, and alleged that the fires that destroyed much of the town had been set by anarchists as part of their retreat (as indeed they had done in the case of Irún on the French border in the preceding September). As in other such instances, the attempted cover-up did more harm than good. The uproar irritated even Hitler, who insisted that Franco's government absolve the Condor Legion from any responsibility, though, ironically, the whole affair may have redounded to his advantage, for it had the effect of heightening concern about the destructiveness of the Luftwaffe, a fear that encouraged appeasement of Germany.[24]

In the aftermath, Franco reiterated his earlier orders, directing that Kindelán send the following message to Richthofen on May 10: "By order of the Generalissimo I inform Your Excellency that no open town, without troops or military industry, may be bombed without a direct order from the Generalissimo or the commanding general of the air force. Tactical objectives close to the battlefield are exempt from this order."[25]

The assault on Santander, the middle section of the Republican northern zone, began on August 24. Franco was able to commit ninety thousand infantry and to reinforce the artillery, while the Republican defenders were in disarray, some of them lacking motivation. In this campaign his forces conducted a pincer operation that produced a rapid decision, assisted by the fact that the Basque units that had retreated into the province were in the process of negotiating a separate surrender with the Italian authorities. Many prisoners were taken and occupation of Santander was completed by September 1.

The assault on Asturias, the remaining northern sector, commenced almost immediately. Resistance was stiffer, for the Republican forces in Asturias, made up of members of the revolutionary worker movements, staunchly defended their mountainous terrain. This final phase took nearly two months and was finally completed on October 24. Even then, not all Republicans surrendered, for a few took to the hills and maintained limited guerrilla operations for years. As was typical of Franco's operations, this had been a long and slow campaign, but it also achieved complete success and kept casualties to a minimum. It was followed by a severe repression, since Asturias had been a key revolutionary center. Though the more rigorous system of military tribunals Franco had instituted earlier in the year reduced the massive number of executions that had followed the conquest of Málaga (possibly nearly four thousand), there were at least two thousand executions in Asturias, many more proportionately than after the conquest of Vizcaya and Santander.[26]

Loss of the northern zone was a strategic disaster for the Republic. Its forces in the north had been politically divided between three different governments, making it easier to conquer them piecemeal. The Republican government had sent a hundred warplanes, mainly Soviet, but in dribs and drabs that were destroyed seriatim by Franco's superior airpower. The Nationalists captured large stocks of weaponry, which could be used to outfit their own expanding army, and took more than one hundred thousand prisoners, half of whom were "turned" into new Nationalist recruits. Altogether, the whole operation amounted to a "swing" of military manpower of nearly 250,000 men. The military historian Jesús Salas Larrazábal has calculated that as of August 1, 1937, the correlation of strength between the two sides stood at 10:9 in favor of the Republicans, while by the end of October, after the complete conquest of the north, that ratio had declined to 86:100, in favor of the Nationalists. In a memorandum that he prepared a few months later, Franco expressed the conviction that he had decisively gained the upper hand.[27]

Once he shifted his attention to the north, the Republican command had its best chance to seize the strategic initiative, for the main strength of the People's Army lay in the central region around Madrid. The Republicans began with a small offensive to seize La Granja, a little to the northwest of the capital, at the end of May. This failed completely against the usual stiff Nationalist defense but indirectly passed into world literature as the background to Ernest Hemingway's novel *For Whom the Bell Tolls*. The dispatch of reinforcements to the central zone delayed operations in Vizcaya for a week or so, but the Republican command was unable to muster forces for a major effort to divert Franco prior to the fall of Bilbao.

The Republicans then launched their first major offensive of the war on July 5, 1937, an operation that became known as the Battle of Brunete. This would be the only major Republican offensive not waged in northeastern Spain. The Brunete operation was designed as a pincer movement to cut off Franco's forces in their positions immediately west and northwest of Madrid, but the southern prong never got started. The main part of the offensive featured eighty thousand troops from the most experienced and best-equipped units, a considerable number of which were Communist or Communist led. They achieved nearly complete surprise against small defensive forces, scoring an initial breakthrough with overwhelming local superiority in all arms.[28]

What happened after the first day of Republican success would prove predictive of much of the rest of the war. Although the People's Army often fought well on the defensive, the Nationalists showed once more they could do even better, as several small units held out desperately at a number of strong points. Republican field commanders revealed uncertainty and lack of initiative, and their officers were unable to sustain momentum. Soviet tanks, even assisted by air control, proved of limited value because the Republican forces lacked training and coordination in combined arms operations.

Brunete provided a brief respite for the northern zone. Franco initially vacillated, for the Republican initiative could be stymied by sending only small reinforcements, but he decided to follow his usual priority of denying the enemy even a very limited success and chose to shift major air and infantry units. This was carried out more rapidly than usual, his planes gaining control of the skies and helping to shatter whatever was left of the Republican offensive, so that nearly all the small amount of ground lost was soon regained. Whereas he had remained at central headquarters during the Vizcayan campaign, Franco moved his command post very close to the front during his brief Brunete counteroffensive. Failure of this operation left the Republicans seriously weakened on the central front for the first time, but Franco, strongly encouraged by his advisers, turned back to complete conquest of the north.

Thenceforth the Republican command shifted the focus of the war to the northeast, and most of the major remaining battles took place in Aragon and Catalonia, as the Republican government and the Communists, who became increasingly influential, sought to dominate the chief anarchist bastions and to recruit more fully the undermobilized resources of Catalonia. The main Communist forces were transferred to the northeast, and the offensive in Aragon known as the Belchite operation began on August 24, in another failed effort to divert Franco from conquering the north.

All the offensives of General Vicente Rojo, the Republican chief of staff, were well designed on paper, and each aimed at a decisive breakthrough against comparatively weak enemy positions. Each followed the same course, achieving tactical surprise and an initial breakthrough, but in every case small Nationalist strong points resisted with determination, so that each Republican offensive bogged down and then was followed by the relatively rapid arrival of Franco's reinforcements and the end of the offensive. Failure at Belchite, where the attackers enjoyed even greater numerical superiority than at Brunete, was a severe disappointment to the Republican command, which thought mistakenly that its younger combat officers were at last becoming adequately trained.

The struggle of attrition continued as both armies expanded further in the final months of 1937. At approximately seven hundred thousand men, however, Franco's army had achieved numerical parity and was better equipped and led. With his increased strength, he planned another major operation to outflank Madrid from the northeast and seize the capital, though nearly two months passed as the new offensive was slowly organized.

The Republican prime minister, Juan Negrín, and Rojo decided to attempt a preemptive strike, their target being the most exposed position in the long Nationalist front, the narrow salient jutting eastward from Teruel in southern Aragon, surrounded by Republican territory on three sides. Like nearly all secondary fronts, the region was weakly defended, and in December 1937 a limited Republican offensive quickly occupied the entire salient except for the city of Teruel itself, which stubbornly held out.

To the annoyance of some of his staff and of the Condor Legion commanders, Franco reacted "like a bull in front of a red cloth," allowing himself to be "turned into a strategic fireman."[29] He postponed and later canceled his own operation in order to relieve the beleaguered city, largely ignoring a telegram from Mussolini on January 2 that urged him to take decisive action to conclude the war. Extremely bitter weather (the coldest of the entire conflict) and mountainous terrain handicapped the counterattack, however, which also lacked vigor and determination,[30] so that the exhausted defenders of Teruel finally had to surrender on January 8, 1938.

Franco nonetheless had no intention of permitting the Republicans to keep possession of the only provincial capital they had managed to seize since the first days of the conflict. He consulted only with a few staff officers since, after becoming generalissimo, he considered himself increasingly an instrument of divine providence.[31] Continuing to transfer major forces to southern Aragon, he launched a powerful counteroffensive on January 17. By February 5 the forces broke through into better terrain, enabling them to initiate a pincer operation that retook the city on the twenty-second. Only two weeks were then needed to regroup for a full offensive in Aragon, which began on March 9. This offensive was supported by some of the most devastating air attacks of the war, particularly against vehicles and rear areas, and it had a decisive effect on Republican morale, already weakened by internecine political conflict. Franco's forces broke the front wide open for the first time, and for a few days advanced almost as fast as they could go. On April 15 they reached the Mediterranean, cutting the Republican zone in two. Within four days all the southern bank of the Ebro River was in their hands, as the Republicans suffered another disaster almost equivalent to the loss of the northern zone. Some units collapsed, and surrender and desertion became a major problem. During the past year, disciplinary executions had become increasingly common in the Republican army, but they could not entirely stem the rout.

Franco's superiority seemed overwhelming, but during the next six months events took the strangest turn in the entire conflict. The collapse of Republican defenses in the northeast left Catalonia virtually undefended, and Yagüe, whose army corps had entered western Catalonia, urged Franco to advance further and occupy all of it.[32] Instead, the generalissimo renounced a seemingly easy triumph and opted instead for a difficult advance southward through mountainous terrain and along the narrow coastal road toward Valencia. There is no conclusive explanation for why Franco decided to take this approach. Then and afterward he spoke of the need to gain more foreign exchange by controlling the large citrus exports of Valencia, an explanation that bewildered his staff officers. (The Valencian region produced a food surplus, whereas Catalonia harbored a dense population, on the verge of starvation, that could be fed only with difficulty.) Conquest of Valencia might, however, unhinge the central zone, making it possible to cut off Madrid.

More important, however, was the issue of French intervention if Franco occupied all of Catalonia immediately, and this may have been the ultimate factor in deciding to turn south. The Republican zone had been cut in two just as the crisis in central Europe was intensifying. Though in mid-March the French government had made a firm decision not to intervene in Spain, Franco could not be sure France would stick to this policy.[33] Hitler also indicated that he did not want Franco to occupy Catalonia, for the German führer preferred to prolong the war, but it is not clear how hard he tried to force such a decision on Franco, other than to stipulate that the Condor Legion not operate within fifty kilometers of the French frontier.[34]

At any rate, Catalonia was spared for the moment, while the Republican resistance regrouped, then stiffened rather impressively on a well-fortified narrow front north of Valencia, its strongest defensive position since the Battle of Madrid. Given the recent Republican collapse in Aragon, Franco and his generals were apparently surprised by the renewed firmness of the defense. On May 26 Kindelán sent Franco a memo to suggest that, in view of the slowness of the advance and the increased casualties, the operation should be abandoned in favor of an early offensive into a more lightly defended Catalonia. There is evidence that Franco considered this, but he refused to admit that the Valencia offensive might have been a mistake and persisted doggedly.[35] The Nationalists gradually drew ever nearer the city but suffered heavier casualties than in preceding campaigns and the war slowed considerably between May and July 1938, giving the People's Army one final opportunity.[36]

There was much criticism by the commanders of the Condor Legion about the slow pace and unimaginative character of Franco's operations, which sometimes caused morale problems among German personnel.

Faupel, the first German ambassador, had opined of Franco that "his knowledge and personal military experience are not adequate to direct operations of the present dimensions," while General Hugo Sperrle, who commanded the Condor Legion, judged that "Franco is evidently not the kind of leader who can deal with such major responsibilities. By German standards, he lacks military experience. Since they made him a very young general in the Rif war, he has never commanded larger units and, therefore, he is no better than a battalion leader."[37] Unlike Mussolini, Hitler, however, brushed aside such concerns, for continuing the Spanish war, which he sought to exploit in large measure as a distraction, served his purposes well.

Franco's relations with the culturally more distant Germans were not as close as those with Mussolini. He had avoided German suggestions about signing a treaty of friendship, only going so far as a secret protocol of March 1937 that had merely promised Spanish neutrality in any broader war. The principal friction lay in economic affairs, as Berlin, unlike Rome, was determined to extract maximal advantage, particularly concerning Spanish minerals. Relations were administered by two trading corporations, HISMA (Hispano-Marroquí de Transportes SL), an only nominally private corporation that channeled arms shipments, and a German state corporation, ROWAK (Rohstoff-Waren-Handels-Gesellschaft AG), in charge of imports from Spain. The German share of Spanish exports, especially iron ore and pyrites, rose steeply. ROWAK created eleven companies of its own in Spain, though Franco's decree of October 1937 nullified new mining rights purchased since the beginning of the war. The German goal was to create a huge holding corporation for mining and other properties to be called MONTANA, but this was jeopardized by Franco's ruling. After much negotiation, he concluded a deal in June 1938 that permitted Germans to own up to 40 percent of the capital in new mining companies, a level that they hoped to exceed by purchasing additional shares through Spanish proxies.

Hitler soon decided, however, that this was inadequate, and for the first time relations between the two dictatorships began to deteriorate. Attrition sharply reduced Franco's stock of arms and supplies, which Hitler was unwilling to replenish without concessions. This finally forced Franco's hand; in November 1938 he grudgingly agreed to larger German shares varying from 60 to 75 percent of the equity in four of the five main MONTANA mining companies. This brought resumption of German supplies for the final campaign. Franco had succeeded in avoiding German economic domination, and, though Hitler's terms were distinctly less generous than those of Mussolini, only about 18 percent of the cost of German military support was repaid either directly or with raw materials down to the end of the war.[38]

Meanwhile, Juan Negrín, the Republican prime minister, had undertaken all-out mobilization under the slogan "¡Resistir es vencer!" ("To resist is to win!"), which might have argued a defensive strategy. Though Negrín no longer thought the left could secure a clear-cut military triumph, he deemed it essential to score some sort of offensive victory, both to raise faltering morale and to try to convince the Western democracies that the revolutionary Republic was worth supporting. The People's Army was expanded once more to eight hundred thousand men, and its command selected as target a weakly defended bend in the Ebro River near the edge of Catalonia at Gandesa, roughly a hundred kilometers upstream from the Mediterranean. An assault southwestward across the river on the night of July 24–25 crumpled the Nationalist division on the other side, which gave up four thousand prisoners. Though it took several days to get tanks and trucks across makeshift bridges, the attack occupied a sizable stretch of territory, approximately twenty by forty kilometers, southwest of the Ebro bend—the largest Republican advance ever—before running out of steam. This saved Valencia for the time being, and the hilly terrain created a new defensive position for the Republicans.

Franco had persistently ignored warnings by Yagüe, who commanded Nationalist forces on the Ebro, of the danger of a major enemy assault, for the generalissimo thought the Republicans incapable of a new offensive in the northeast.[39] When, to his surprise, this occurred, once again he canceled his own operations and responded to the Republican initiative, assembling forces for a massive counteroffensive. The patch of territory seized by his foes was strategically insignificant, while their new position left a large Republican army corps potentially stranded west of the river. Yagüe and several generals, together with the German commanders, argued that, if there were to be counteroffensives in the area, the Nationalists should use their superior mobility and airpower to bypass the Republicans, driving deep into northern Catalonia and cutting off the forces on the Ebro, thereby killing two birds with one stone. Their warplanes could decimate the Republicans as they sought to escape.[40] Once more Franco disagreed with key lieutenants, possibly still reluctant to occupy Catalonia while the central European crisis threatened to spill over into broader war. Instead, he followed his penchant for frontal assault, launching the first phase of the Ebro counteroffensive on August 6. The struggle that ensued was the longest and most costly of the war, consisting of a series of direct attacks by the best Nationalist units on the defenders of hill after hill in the large pocket west of the Ebro bend, in every case preceded by massive artillery and air bombardment.[41]

Franco gave the battle his closest attention, regarding it as potentially the decisive struggle of the war. He moved his headquarters nearer the front, first to Pedrola, outside Zaragoza, then later much closer, to Alcañiz. Since the battle dragged on, Doña Carmen and her daughter visited a field headquarters for the first time, but only in the more secure setting of Pedrola. The stay was protracted, for Carmencita came down with mumps. Since their residence in Burgos was crowded with children from the extended Franco-Polo family, mother and daughter spent a long quarantine period at Pedrola but saw very little of Franco, who spent most of his time at his advanced headquarters in Alcañiz.

During the course of the battle, the international crisis over Czechoslovakia intensified and Admiral François Darlan, head of the French navy, recommended that a peripheral strategy be adopted against Hitler, which would include limited French military intervention in Spain, including occupation of Guipuzcoa and Navarre. This proposal was soon rejected in Paris, but for several months Franco was not sure the French wouldn't change their minds.[42]

He later admitted grave concern that the international crisis might affect the outcome in Spain. This may have been the only time the stress got to him, since he was ill and confined to quarters for several days late in September. During these weeks the Nationalists suffered a kind of boomerang effect from their own propaganda: they kept announcing that each successive major operation was the definitive struggle, yet it seemed that the war still was far from over.

Morale also declined among the Italian CTV, though less than thirty thousand Italian infantry were left in Spain. A noted Italian journalist would later write that it seemed to them as though Franco's strategy was founded on the principle that "the last soldier standing wins the war."[43] General Mario Berti, their commander, recommended, not for the first time, that the CTV be withdrawn, saying that he feared Franco's eventual defeat, which would damage Italian prestige. Mussolini grew increasingly disgusted, complaining that Franco failed to exploit opportunities. While the battle raged along the Ebro, he pontificated to his son-in-law and foreign minister, Galeazzo Ciano, "Write in your book today, August 29, that I foresee the defeat of Franco. This man either does not know how or does not want to wage war. The Reds are fighters; Franco, no," while Ciano opined that "Franco has no vision of synthesis in war. His operations are those of a magnificent battalion commander."[44]

In the face of a threatening international situation, Franco responded quickly to a British suggestion that his government declare neutrality in the larger European conflict, a statement whose abruptness infuriated Hitler, though he realized that Franco could hardly do otherwise. Franco also sent sixteen battalions of infantry to reinforce the Moroccan protectorate, for the first time reversing a flow of troops that normally moved in the opposite direction, and he placed other units along the western Pyrenees. The international crisis was only resolved at the end of September with the concessions made to Hitler by Britain and France at the Munich conference.

Despite his disgust with Franco's leadership, Mussolini believed that the outcome of the war in Spain was too important to give up on, though he did lower Italy's profile slightly by withdrawing ten thousand troops in October as a diplomatic gesture. By this time, many of the troops in the CTV were Spanish recruits, but they were still supported by Italian air squadrons made up of more than a hundred warplanes, a tank group with a hundred or so tankettes, and the CTV artillery corps of several hundred cannon.

The Republican Army of the Ebro fought tenaciously to defend its hilly terrain, only giving up one hill at a time.[45] The struggle lasted even longer than the Valencian operation. There were heavy casualties on both sides, and Franco's units seemed to be losing some of their edge. For the first time in many months, the performance of the People's Army drew favorable coverage abroad, where a perception developed that Franco's triumph was not inevitable. Morale began to slump among the Nationalists, and there was murmuring among some of his commanders, whom he chastised verbally for failing to carry out orders adequately.[46] This led him to an unusual general meeting with all his corps and divisional commanders on October 23, just before the last major phase of the campaign. It was a tense encounter in which Franco berated some of them for insufficient drive and energy, and they in turn protested the character of the operation, with its cost in blood.[47] He remained insistent and imperturbable, exuding his customary determination and confidence in victory.

Franco persisted in recapturing the territory in the Ebro bend hill by hill. Assisted by potent firepower, his forces maintained their cohesion, if not always the same vigor, and they dominated a grinding battle of attrition. The Republican command was unable to replace either its supplies or its casualties, and finally pulled its last units back across the river in mid-November. Franco's forces had suffered more than thirty thousand total casualties (including at least sixty one hundred dead), but Republican casualties were even greater, the Nationalists taking many prisoners. Some of Franco's best units had been weakened, but overall his army had suffered only limited structural damage and his sources of supply remained intact. By contrast, the best units of the People's Army had been ground up and could not be replaced in either quantity or quality, while arms reserves were dangerously low.

The war's last call-up of recruits took place in November 1938. Altogether, Franco had drafted fifteen recruitment classes, ranging from eighteen years of age to thirty-two, while by the end of January 1939 the Republicans had summoned twenty-seven classes, from seventeen years of age to forty-three. The two armies were of approximately equal size, each counting eight hundred thousand or more, but the Nationalists had more prime manpower and were much better armed and led. The Republicans maintained large numbers of troops in the center and south—probably a strategic mistake—and still enjoyed numerical superiority in the Madrid area, but the Nationalists had built overwhelming superiority in the northeast.

International complications temporarily at an end, Franco invaded Catalonia in December 1938 with a series of decisive blows. As his forces neared the French frontier, the Republic's lifeline, he expressed concern over continued rumors about French military intervention. Ciano repeatedly warned the French and British ambassadors in Rome that, should this occur, Italian forces would be sent to wage war with France on Spanish soil (though, in fact, there was little danger of French intervention). Franco's troops reached the French border by mid-February, 1939, driving the Republican government into exile and shrinking its territory to the southeast quarter of Spain. Though the People's Army was still a large force on paper, many of its troops were new draftees, and most were poorly armed. The struggle was essentially over, for there was no longer much will to resist.

In January the Republican command tried to distract Franco by using its numerical superiority in troops in the south to launch an offensive in Extremadura, a strategy that perhaps should have been attempted earlier. This gained a considerable amount of ground at first and caused the Nationalists more than ten thousand total casualties (including nearly two thousand killed) before it was contained, but this did not affect the overall military balance or influence the campaign in Catalonia.

During February Franco's intelligence agents entered into negotiations with some of the key Republican military leaders, who were opposed to Negrín and sought to overthrow Communist influence. They assumed, rather naively, that as professional military men they could negotiate more lenient terms of surrender with Franco. In fact, he was implacable, insisting, as he had throughout, on unconditional surrender, promising only that Republicans not guilty of crimes would not be prosecuted and that the leaders would be allowed to flee abroad. When he finally opened his "Offensive of Victory" on the Madrid front on March 27, 1939, resistance melted away, and on the first of April an ailing generalissimo, suffering from the flu, announced that the long Civil War was finally over.

How much did Franco contribute to the Nationalist victory? The Republicans liked to claim that it had been won by Germans and Italians, this interpretation amounting to the leftist counterpart to the rightist idée fixe that the Civil War stemmed from a Communist conspiracy and had depended mostly on the Soviets. Neither of these convenient myths is altogether accurate. The left came to depend on the Soviets, and the Nationalists could not have won without foreign assistance, but their own troops did nearly all the fighting, and Queipo de Llano's observation that with a different commander in chief the Nationalists would have lost is very likely correct. Franco was neither a strategic nor an operational genius, and his military initiatives were sometimes slow and simplistic, but he was also methodical, organized, and effective. It is said that amateurs do strategy while professionals do logistics, and Franco, a professional, certainly did logistics. Each successive operation was adequately organized and no advance ended in retreat. Franco saw to it that his forces were better prepared in every respect. This was not merely a matter of military command but of maintaining an effective domestic administration and a home front that sustained morale, mobilized the population, and fostered a distinctly higher level of economic production than the other side, whose economy was increasingly hollowed out by the ravages of revolution. Not the least of Franco's achievements was his wartime diplomacy, which helped to guarantee the neutrality of Britain, only a limited support for the Republic by France, and, most of all, relatively uninterrupted support and supply from Italy and Germany.

Though only about one-third of the combat vessels in the Spanish navy joined the Nationalists, Franco's naval officers employed their resources much more effectively than their adversaries, first gaining control of the northern coast during 1937 and then carrying a naval offensive into the Mediterranean during the second half of the war. The revolution in the Republican fleet, which liquidated much of the old officer corps, left the Republican vessels bereft of leadership and condemned them to an increasingly passive defensive strategy under their Soviet advisor.[48] Franco's navy aggressively hunted down Republican shipping and by September 1937 had closed the Soviet pipeline across the Mediterranean.[49]

In the beginning Franco had gained control of an even smaller fraction of the obsolescent Spanish air force—scarcely more than a quarter—but he built his resources rapidly with German and Italian assistance. After the Soviet Union sent a sizable number of aircrews and late-model planes in the autumn of 1936, the Republicans dominated the skies over Madrid for a number of months, but further Italian and German assistance righted the balance. Franco enjoyed general, though not overwhelming, air superiority from the middle of 1937 to the end of the conflict. His forces made use of more than sixteen hundred planes of all types, the Republicans altogether employing a hundred or so less. From 1937 on, some, at least, of his German planes were later models, and the Nationalist aviators (Spanish, Italian, and German) in general were slightly more skilled than the Spaniards and Soviets who flew on the Republican side.[50]

The Nationalist air force was much more effective in bombing operations and particularly in air-to-ground support, at which the Condor Legion became skilled.[51] Despite the notoriety of Guernica and the emphasis of Republican propaganda on the bombing of cities, there were very few terror raids of any significance by either side.[52] Indiscriminate attacks on cities, almost always small in scope, were in fact more commonly conducted by the Republican air force.[53] Strategic bombing of the kind seen in World War II was never attempted by either side, since neither had heavy bombers. The most destructive individual atrocity was not Guernica but the three days in March 1938 when Barcelona was bombed on the personal orders of Mussolini. Italian planes based on Mallorca killed nearly a thousand people, almost all civilians. This was the only time that Mussolini interfered personally in the conduct of operations. Franco was not initially informed and was hardly pleased, for Pope Pius XI directed his protest to the Spanish dictator rather than to his Italian counterpart, but Franco's expression of displeasure was restrained by his dependency on Italian assistance. Generally speaking, with the exception of several raids on Madrid in November 1936, Franco's policy on bombing was restricted to military and supply targets and was more humane than that of either Britain or the United States in World War II.[54]

Altogether, many factors contributed to the victory of Franco and the defeat of the Republicans. The most important were:

1. the reckless policies of the Azaña/Casares Quiroga government in the weeks immediately prior to the conflict, scorning the opposition while ignoring the serious dangers an armed conflict would present and maintaining a policy of harassment and provocation that seemingly dared the opposition to rebel;

2. superior military cohesion among the Nationalists;

3. the leadership of Franco, who displayed great initiative during the difficult early months, then imposed and sustained a unity that eliminated political conflict and concentrated resources on the military effort, as well as his diplomacy, which secured the support of Hitler and Mussolini while maintaining adequate relations with the democracies;

4. greater military assistance to the Nationalists from abroad, at least during the last two years of the war, which was also employed more effectively than was Soviet aid to the Republicans, as well as the Nationalists' ongoing augmentation of their resources with arms and prisoners captured from the Republicans, so that during the last phase at least one-quarter of their arms were weapons seized from the enemy;

5. more efficient social and economic mobilization of the population and resources of the Nationalist zone, used more effectively than those of their counterparts on the Republican side;

6. the disunity of the Republicans, involving numerous internal splits ranging from the disunity of the Socialists to the dissidence of anarchists and of Basque and Catalan nationalists, including also the sometimes sectarian policies of the Communists, which Negrín and other leaders considered their greatest weakness, impeding mobilization and concentration; and

7. the destructive consequences of the violent revolution in the Republican zone (in particular the launching of a war against religion, which crystalized massive and unremitting Catholic support for the Nationalists, probably the greatest single factor in sustaining their morale and commitment) that divided the left, gravely handicapped mobilization, and at first alienated much opinion in the Western democracies, while solidifying the resistance of the Nationalists.

The Spanish conflict was militarily unique among the European civil wars of the first half of the twentieth century.[55] It was proportionately the most extensively mobilized and the most advanced in operations and weaponry, though both sides employed a bewildering variety of different kinds of imported arms. Sooner or later, the Soviets, Germans, and Italians introduced much of their most advanced weaponry, which included Soviet and German planes, Soviet tanks, and German antiaircraft guns. To a certain extent all three intervening powers used the war as a proving ground for arms and tactics, though this was not the primary reason for their intervention. The most important new tactic was the employment of combined arms—the attempted coordination of infantry, artillery, armor, and, above all, air-to-ground support (including German dive-bombing). Such tactics were becoming standard in the Soviet and German forces but could only be applied in Spain on a rudimentary basis. Use of combined arms was developed more effectively by the Nationalists, playing an important role in all of Franco's major operations beginning in the spring of 1937. Spanish pilots flying for Franco even developed innovations of their own, such as strafing enemy positions "en cadena," in which a succession of fighter planes circled back one or more times to repeat the same attack.

The full World War II tactic of combined arms, however, was never developed. Claims that the Germans tested so-called Blitzkrieg are exaggerated, for neither the doctrine nor the weapons had been fully developed until after the Civil War. German tanks sent to Spain were small and poorly armed, no match for the larger, more powerful Soviet vehicles. Moreover, much of the Spanish war was fought in mountainous terrain, completely different from the fields and roads of Poland, France, or the Soviet Union. Tank operations were consequently fairly simple. The Soviets were rarely able to make effective use of their armor, while small German and Italian tanks could only be used in limited ways.[56]

By the end of the war, Franco's best tanks were the eighty captured Soviet vehicles that had been organized into two small units in his own army.[57] This is only one of many examples in which the Nationalist army made extensive use of captured weaponry, an important aspect of its increasing superiority by 1938. The Soviet Polykarpov fighter planes manufactured in the Republican zone and captured or completed under Franco would fly in his air force for nearly fifteen years, while increasingly obsolete Soviet tanks would form part of his small armored corps for almost two decades.

Militarily, the Spanish conflict was typical neither of World War I nor World War II but represented a transition that combined certain characteristics of each. Much weaponry stemmed from World War I, though armor, late-model artillery, and, most importantly, airpower were at times used in a way that anticipated World War II.

Almost from the beginning, Republicans declared that theirs was part of a broader struggle against Fascism and that it would lead to a much greater war. Soon afterward, when Germany and the Soviet Union invaded Poland, they declared that the Spanish conflict had been the "first battle" or "opening round" of the European war, a "prelude" to it. The problem with such a claim is that the contending forces in Spain from 1936 to 1939 and those in Europe from 1939 to 1940 were not the same. The Spanish war was a clear-cut revolutionary/counterrevolutionary contest between left and right, with the Fascist totalitarian powers supporting the right and the Soviet totalitarian power supporting the left. The European war, on the other hand, only began when a pantotalitarian entente was forged by the Nazi-Soviet pact. This was a complete reversal of the terms of the Spanish conflict.

Only later, when Hitler turned on Stalin, did the roster of wartime allies begin to resemble the anti-Fascist alliance in Spain, but even then it was different. The "grand alliance" of 1941–45 against Hitler was not a leftist Popular Front but an extremely broad international coalition that stretched from the extreme left to the extreme right. Its key leader at first was the British Conservative Winston Churchill, who readily admitted that if he had been a citizen of Spain he would have supported Franco.[58]

Yet it must also be recognized that the Spanish war played an important role in the unfolding of European power relationships in the late 1930s. It was one catalyst, though scarcely the only one, for the formation of the Rome-Berlin Axis in October 1936, and its outcome represented, among other things, a victory for Axis foreign policy. The Spanish struggle was not the beginning of World War II but it was the longest in a series of crises from 1935 to 1938 in which the Fascist powers acted aggressively and the democracies passively, though the issues were different in each case. Hitler's policy of using and prolonging the Spanish conflict as a major distraction to deflect attention from his rearmament and expansion in central Europe was generally successful. He calculated correctly that the war would further divide France internally and distract it from focusing on Germany during the period when German rearmament still had not achieved parity. By comparison, Soviet intervention in Spain proved counterproductive, and the Soviet Union was more isolated in April 1939 than in July 1936, though it had succeeded in enhancing its reputation among the international left.

The outbreak of the European war was not a consequence of the Spanish conflict and would have taken place in one form or another even if there had never been a war in Spain. Moreover, had the Civil War dragged on into the autumn of 1939, it is doubtful that this would have deterred German aggression in east-central Europe. It is also less than certain that the French government, so wedded to strictly defensive operations, would ever have come to the assistance of the Republic in any major way. Yet without the complications arising from Spain, the democracies might have taken a stronger stand against Hitler on other issues, and conceivably Mussolini might have delayed or even avoided an entente with him, despite the seeming logic that brought the two dictators together. Without the advantages provided by these distractions Hitler might not have been able to move as rapidly as he did in 1938.

The Civil War was the most destructive experience in modern Spanish history, rivaled only by the Napoleonic invasion of 1808. It resulted in great loss of life, much human suffering, disruption of the society and the economy, distortion and repression in cultural affairs, and retardation of the country's political development. It is not possible to generate precise statistics, but the cost in military deaths alone was not as great proportionately as in the First Carlist War of the 1830s or the American Civil War. It was, in general, a low-intensity war punctuated by a number of high-intensity battles, and military deaths for Spanish citizens on both sides combined amounted to no more than approximately 150,000, and possibly less, to which must be added nearly 25,000 foreign participant fatalities. The combined total for victims of the two political repressions was almost as great, but the exact numbers will probably always remain contested. There were about 55,000 executions by the Republicans and somewhat more than that by the Nationalists. In addition, on both sides combined about 12,000 civilians died from military action (mostly in the Republican zone), to which must be added thousands of deaths beyond the normal rate due to stress, disease, and malnutrition. The total for victims of violence amounted to approximately 1.1 percent of the population. If all civilian fatalities beyond the norm are added, the number of deaths attributable to the Civil War reaches approximately 344,000, or nearly 1.4 percent of the population. Moreover, the long-term consequences of wartime suffering and the extremely harsh social and economic conditions for the first years afterward resulted in at least an additional 200,000 to 300,000 deaths beyond the norm.[59] More than half a million people fled the country, mostly from the Republican zone in the final months, but the majority soon returned, leaving a net permanent emigration of approximately 170,000, the largest single group settled in southern France. It is noteworthy that proportionately fewer Spaniards chose permanent exile after the Spanish Civil War than was the case after the American, French, or Russian revolutions. This may or may not be explained by positing that counterrevolutionary social sectors with greater means were those more likely to emigrate after final defeat.

The overall demographic consequences were less than might be expected. The war only slightly retarded population growth. The census of 1930 had registered 23,564,000 resident citizens, but the next few years brought the return of hundreds of thousands of temporary emigrants (who had left primarily for economic reasons), so that, despite the wartime losses, the new census of 1940 reported a resident population of 25,878,000, a conclusion confirmed by the next census a decade later. The nominal rate of population growth was thus seemingly almost as great as during the 1920s, but these raw figures concealed the fact that many had emigrated during the 1920s, while large numbers returned during the following decade. That there was no massive overall decline in nutrition and well-being, despite the malnutrition in the Republican zone during the second half of the war, is suggested by the fact that on average army recruits were half a centimeter taller in 1940 than in 1935.

9

Franco and the
Nationalist Repression

(1936–1945)

I n earlier times, European civil wars were fought between opposing factions to gain relatively limited objectives, often no more than a change in rulers. In the twentieth century, however, they became revolutionary contests that took on a new and apocalyptic character, each side seeking to create a new society and a new cultural order. A revolutionary civil war was not simply a political contest but a conflict of ultimates about society, religion, and culture, perceived as demanding a total and uncompromising solution.

The only direct precursors were the French revolution, with its mass "terror" that led to the slaughter of many tens of thousands, and the revolt of the Paris Commune in 1871, in whose aftermath between ten and twenty thousand of the defeated were executed. In the first, the slaughter was conducted by the revolutionaries, in the second by the counterrevolutionaries. In the twentieth century, revolutionary civil war began in democratic Finland early in 1918 and was repeated immediately on a much larger scale in Russia and its environs, then on a small scale in Hungary and, more than a decade later, in Spain, followed, during World War II, by the civil wars in Yugoslavia and Greece.[1]

In the Spanish war, executions began almost immediately on both sides, induced by several factors, the first two of a general nature, the third specific to the Spanish case. First, the conflict in Spain was the last revolutionary civil war of the generation that followed World War I, feeding on the propaganda, fears, and hatreds generated by its predecessors. Second, associated with this was the fact that the 1930s were a time of growing tension in which the earlier example of Bolshevism was followed by the rise of Fascism—a deadly combination that evoked increasingly widespread fear and hatred. More specific to Spain was the run-up to the revolution; political violence surged beginning in December 1930, producing approximately twenty-five hundred deaths even before the Civil War began. Even the Russian revolution of 1917 did not have this kind of extended violent prelude, which was without precedent. The revolutionary movements fomented hatred, violence, and talk of, in one of their favorite terms, "extermination." Before the war began in July 1936, there had been a lengthy period of growing tension, multiple preceding attempts at violent revolutionary insurrection, and proliferation of the most virulent forms of mass propaganda, especially by the revolutionaries, who often spoke of the need to liquidate the bourgeoisie, while the rightist discourse even before the war had sometimes also sought to dehumanize the adversary and legitimize extreme measures.

The first killings by the left in Republican territory on July 18, 1936, were simply an intensification of this violence, but it soon became much more widespread and systematic, while executions also began almost immediately in the areas dominated by the Nationalists. These grew rapidly in volume on both sides. The largest number in most districts took place during August and September, and they continued at a high rate throughout the autumn in both zones and well into the winter of 1936–37 in the Nationalist zone.

Controversy quickly developed as to which side was the more savage and culpable, a controversy that has continued to the present. Partisans of the left insist that there was a basic distinction between the repressions in the Republican and Nationalist zones, insofar as the former was allegedly spontaneous and not planned or organized, while the latter was allegedly centralized and systematic. There was indeed a difference in the structure and function of the two repressions, but it cannot be described in terms of such a simplistic dichotomy. Since the revolutionary movements had been fomenting and practicing violence for years, their own violence could scarcely be considered "spontaneous." In the two major centers, Madrid and Barcelona, the Republican government authorized and sometimes even itself organized some of the death squads.[2]

On July 28, 1936, the Burgos National Defense Council declared martial law throughout Nationalist Spain.[3] Even before that, however, *consejos de guerra* (military tribunals) had been set up within twenty-four hours of the beginning of the military revolt. On August 31 and September 8 the council directed all army and navy courts to proceed as swiftly as possible, and it suspended jury trials even for civil cases.[4] Though there was less autonomy than in the Republican zone, local commanders in the first weeks and months were not subject to very much central control, which was developed only after Franco became generalissimo. The two repressions were similar in that neither was centrally coordinated in the first months, and both were breathtakingly savage.

According to the memoir by his secretary, Mola himself was taken aback by the extent of the violence against civilians, even though in his earliest planning he had emphasized that the military movement "must be violent in the extreme," applying "exemplary punishments."[5] Early in the conflict he reportedly ordered that a truckload of captured leftist militia be executed immediately at the side of the road, but then he changed his mind and rescinded the order, provoking a staff colonel to protest, "General, let us not have to regret later on being too soft."[6] In Seville, Queipo de Llano boasted of summary executions, thinly disguised, in his nightly radio broadcasts, apparently to terrify leftist listeners into submission.[7]

The Nationalist military leaders in each district were ultimately in charge of the repression and sometimes employed regular military courts to carry it out. Other areas, however, bore greater similarity to the Republican zone. In these places, police and civilian militias often played major roles, though not to the extent of the revolutionary militias on the opposing side. The most important Nationalist auxiliaries in this regard were the Falangists, even though one or two top Falangist leaders made an effort to limit the executions. In the first weeks, Falangist groups in some areas acted as judge, jury, and executioner, just as their leftist counterparts. In other districts, Falangist squads served simply as police and executioners, at the behest of the local military. Though the ultimate authority was always military, the modus operandi varied.

The targets of the Nationalist repression were leftist leaders and activists in general and anyone suspected of opposing the National Movement in particular. There was randomness on both sides, hundreds of people being killed by mistake or simply as the result of denunciations motivated by personal resentment. The revolutionaries were more embarrassed by their bloodthirstiness and made some effort to conceal their repression, while in several places in the Nationalist zone a number of public executions took place in the first weeks.[8] There were people on both sides who sought to mitigate the killings, though the effort at moderation became stronger among the Republicans. Catholic clergy and laymen were principal targets of the Republican repression, as much or more than rightist political figures, yet one of the scandals of the war was how little effort the Catholic clergy made to reduce the terror by the Nationalists. A number of prelates and priests spoke up, but not many.

It is now generally agreed that the number of executions by the revolutionaries totaled about fifty-five thousand, while those by the Nationalists were more numerous, with estimates ranging from sixty thousand to one hundred thousand or more.[9] The higher figures appear to be a demographic impossibility, so that the low estimate appears more likely. In the long run, the Nationalist repression became more concerted, was the more effective of the two, and claimed the most lives, particularly with the extensive round of executions after the end of the Civil War.

In the first months, Franco had little to do with the repression, which would have taken the form that it did had he never existed. Even in two notorious cases where he had strong personal feelings on the side of clemency, he either did not try or was unable to intervene. As seen in chapter 6, he recused himself in the execution of his first cousin Major Ricardo de la Puente Bahamonde in Morocco to avoid the charge of favoritism on the one hand or to have to approve the death sentence of his old playmate on the other. Several weeks later, his attempt to stay the execution of his former trusted associate General Miguel Campins was categorically rejected by the commanding officer of the district, Queipo de Llano. Prior to becoming generalissimo, for the most part Franco seems simply to have let events take their course, being fully occupied with military affairs and political and diplomatic issues. Even after taking over the Nationalist state, he was, as so often was the case, slow to act. His intervention was most obvious in the propaganda war, as he repeatedly demanded in announcements and fliers that the Republicans terminate their resistance or else face harsher punishment after their defeat. It is difficult to resist the conclusion that these pronouncements ultimately created a kind of policy.

The first important step he took in this regard after becoming commander in chief was to establish, on October 24, 1936, the Supreme Court of Military Justice, a supervisory and appellate court for military tribunals, in conjunction with a new set of military courts to deal with the occupation of Madrid, at that date considered to be imminent. Seizure of the "Red Capital" would presumably constitute the greatest challenge that the repression had yet faced, and Franco wanted a complete structure to be in place. His chief juridical officer, Martínez Fuset, organized the Military Court of the Army of Occupation, which had eight individual military tribunals. Then, as it turned out, Madrid did not fall, and the military juridical personnel had to be reassigned. Only the main part of the northern zone was subjected to any degree of coordination.

One special problem that Franco had to face during his first weeks as chief of state was the complaint of the Church's primate, Cardinal Gomá, concerning the summary court-martial and execution in Guipuzcoa of fourteen captured priests who had been militant Basque nationalists. The Church leadership was much more exercised by the death of a handful of politically activist priests than by the liquidation of thousands of revolutionaries. Franco responded immediately, giving orders that no more Basque nationalist priests be executed.[10] Moreover, as the weeks passed he eventually recognized that the volume of political killing was exceeding the number of deaths on the battlefield in this somewhat desultory war and that the extent of the executions by local authorities was counterproductive.

Franco finally acted to restrain and control the repression in the aftermath of the Hispano-Italian conquest of Málaga on the southern coast early in February 1937, in which the triumphant Nationalists carried out another mass repression, an unusually brutal bloodbath that apparently resulted in between three and four thousand executions in the city and province combined. This horrified the Italian military, for in their country, where there had been no genuine civil war, political violence had declined, not increased, after formation of the Mussolini government, and the Fascists were not prepared for such things.[11] Italian officers became reluctant to turn prisoners over to their Spanish allies. Italian commanders protested; they asserted that the level of indiscriminate violence threatened their own continued participation in the war, arguing that their soldiers would be reluctant to go on with a struggle in which capture might mean death.

Franco responded by expanding and regularizing the role of military courts throughout the Nationalist zone, forbidding executions by other agencies, and creating five new military tribunals for Málaga, all of these constituting measures that he should have taken much earlier. On March 4, 1937, he informed the Italian ambassador that he had given the strictest orders to end all executions of military prisoners in order to encourage desertions, that death sentences by proper tribunals would be restricted to the two categories of leftist leaders and those guilty of violent crimes, and that, even in these cases, half of all sentences were to be commuted.[12] As far as can be determined, this was no propaganda gesture for the benefit of the Italians but outlined the terms that would be followed from this time forward. At the end of March Franco indicated that he had relieved from duty two military judges in Málaga whose procedures had been improper and overly severe, and from then on he is said to have required that all new death sentences by military tribunals receive his ratification before being carried out, though to what extent he personally maintained supervision is unclear. Very rarely he would entertain personal representations from people of note in the Nationalist zone urging clemency for individuals convicted or in process of conviction, but such pleas were not necessarily successful.[13]

From that time on the number of executions dropped considerably, just as they had already declined greatly on the Republican side since December, though executions continued on both sides down to the end of fighting. Each Nationalist advance brought more leftist prisoners into Nationalist camps and jails, though ordinary captured soldiers were not prosecuted unless there was specific evidence of criminal behavior or political responsibility, and in fact during 1937–38 over half were incorporated directly into the Nationalist Army, as explained in chapter 8. On the other hand, the few brief military advances made by the Republican army in 1937–38 were often accompanied by more political executions carried out by Republicans, though these were limited in number because they were unable to occupy much new territory.

The repression remained firmly in the hands of military tribunals for many years, and Spain continued to live under martial law for another decade, until it was finally lifted on April 7, 1948.[14] When Franco organized his first regular government at the close of January 1938, neither the new Ministry of Public Order nor the Ministry of the Interior played the major roles in the repression. The former was responsible for ordinary police patrols, public decency, censorship of movies and plays, and reduction of cheating in the marketplace. At the close of the year, this ministry was incorporated into the Ministry of the Interior, which conducted civil administration. The repression remained the responsibility of military tribunals.

Even though, as discussed at the end of the preceding chapter, the number of violent deaths in Spain, both military and civilian, during the

Civil War has been exaggerated, with the grand total amounting to less than three hundred thousand, or a little more than one percent of the general population, it would be hard to exaggerate the extent of the accompanying trauma the war inflicted on Spanish society as a whole. The complete destruction of the normal polity, the ubiquity of internecine violence, and the enormous privation and suffering left many of its members shell shocked and psychologically adrift.

In the Nationalist zone, the Civil War had been defined as a conflict between the "true Spain" and the "anti-Spain," a crusade of the forces of light against the forces of darkness. Tens of thousands of Catholics and conservatives had been murdered in cold blood by the Popular Front, and many of Franco's adherents had no intention of forgiving anyone connected with these atrocities in particular and leftist politics in general. Christian charity was not a salient feature. Franco's regime continued to divide Spanish life into categories of victors and vanquished for many years, coercing most of his followers into firm support of the postwar system. The tightening of control was manifest in a decree of April 9, 1938, which required all persons of legal age, for the first time in Spanish history, to hold a personal identification card.[15]

As a major step in the regime's process of juridical legitimization, a special commission was appointed on December 21, 1938, to prepare an indictment of the Popular Front government of July 1936. The commission was composed of noted scholars and jurists, including several former ministers of the monarchy and the early Republic. Its lengthy report, impugning the legitimacy of the left Republican administration because of the numerous constitutional abuses it had practiced or condoned, was published by the new Editora Nacional in 1939.[16] This provided theoretical justification for a subsequent study of the issue of military rebellion, which concluded that "defense of the former political order constituted the true rebellion."[17] The state prosecutor's office also initiated a lengthy investigation of the repression in the Republican zone, results of which were published in 1943 as *La dominación roja en España: Causa general instruida por el Ministerio Fiscal.*[18]

Just before the fighting ended, on February 9, 1939, the Law of Political Responsibilities was issued, defining penalties for politically related activities retroactive to October 1, 1934. It covered almost every conceivable form of political subversion or willful assistance to the Republican war effort, even cases of what were termed "grave passivity." The law automatically indicted all members of revolutionary and leftist political parties (though not rank-and-file members of leftist trade unions), as well as anyone who had participated in a "tribunal popular" in the Republican zone. Being a member of the Masonic order was declared equally insidious. Regional courts were established for each part of the country, and a national tribunal was set up in Madrid. Three categories of culpability were defined, with penalties ranging from six months to fifteen years.[19] And, as if this were not enough, it was supplemented by the Law for the Suppression of Masonry and Communism on March 1, 1940, designed to expedite the prosecution of Freemasons.[20]

The law also provided for other penalties, including partial or complete restriction of personal and professional activities and several categories of limited residence, ranging from expulsion from the country to internal exile, banishment to one of the African territories, or house arrest. Wide-ranging economic sanctions were also included.

The final terms that Franco offered for the surrender of the remaining Republican zone on February 8, 1939, promised, however, that "neither mere service in the Red forces, nor having been a simple affiliate of political forces outside the National Movement will be considered a criminal responsibility." Only political leaders (however defined) and those guilty of violent crimes "and other major crimes," also undefined, would be prosecuted by military courts.[21] These categories would in fact be treated with such elasticity that many tens of thousands of prisoners would be liable to prosecution.

Throughout his military career Franco had been known as an *ordenancista*, a disciplinarian and a stickler for the rules. Initially subject to a harsh father, who had himself been the product of a long military tradition, Franco had entered military training at the impressionable age of fourteen, internalizing a strict code. His policies did not stem from paranoia or a sense of personal vendetta but what he conceived as duty and necessity. His harsh and resolute style had early won him respect and deference, and it is not surprising that he maintained the same manner in a desperate revolutionary conflict and in his governance of a fractured polity.

When in command, he had often seemed so firm and impersonal as to be devoid of human emotion, and it has often been assumed that Franco was totally rigid, complacent, and self-righteous, untroubled by second thoughts or remorse, but that may not always have been the case. He kept his own counsel without fail, yet his life was not always so devoid of doubt as he pretended, though when he finally made up his mind, he acted with resolution, without much looking back. Though he had shown the firmest, most unwavering leadership, he may have had second thoughts even with regard to the Civil War itself.

Many years later, in 1973, after Franco had broken down sobbing at the funeral of his chief lieutenant, the assassinated Admiral Carrero Blanco, his oldest grandson quoted Doña Carmen as saying: "Poor Paco, when he was younger I saw him cry on the day that the Civil War ended; he said that if he had known what would come to pass, he would never have joined the insurrection."[22] Unverified secondary anecdotes are a bane of historians, and this one is not easy to credit, given Franco's customary stance of providential self-righteousness, but, if accurate, would have implied, presumably, that he would have done better to have allowed the contradictory revolutionary turmoil of the Popular Front to play itself out, the position that he had more or less consistently held from February 20 to July 13, 1936. Yet, if Franco really ever said or thought such a thing, he would never have acknowledged it publicly, for he always held that the fiery trial of civil war had been a necessary purging of Spain's modernist and leftist sins, a great evil permitted by God to bring about a greater good, the rebirth of Spain under the victorious leadership of the caudillo.

One group momentarily cheered by news of the war's end were the tens of thousands of prisoners in the jails of the Nationalist zone. A hysterical rumor swept the prisons that the end of the fighting would bring an abrupt change of policy, and that Franco would announce an amnesty to bring the people of Spain together again. The two principal Spanish civil wars in the preceding century had ended with the victory of liberal regimes that offered concessions to the defeated. Though scarcely as much as half the population had supported Franco directly, after their defeat a large number of those on the other side were disposed to accept his regime, at least passively, whether because of hunger, exhaustion, disillusionment, or the complete collapse of any alternative. This at least theoretically provided an opportunity to attempt a program of conciliation that might incorporate the opposition, or some major portion of it, in a positive way. Such a thing, however, was not to be. Franco planned not merely to complete construction of a new authoritarian system but also to effect a broad cultural counterrevolution that would make another civil war impossible, and that meant severe repression of the left. That the regime was dictatorial was not surprising, for democracy had been abandoned by both sides in 1936, but the system under construction by Franco was harsh and exclusionary. The repression followed its own logic.

About half a million Republican soldiers surrendered at the end of the war, and seventy thousand or more returned from France. Some of these were simply allowed to go home, though many were processed rapidly in large detention camps before the majority were released. Nonetheless, the occupation of approximately one-third of Spain during the first months of 1939 led to the greatest single wave of detentions in the country's history. The official prison population of the Nationalist zone at the beginning of that year stood at 100,292, a figure that by the close of 1939 had climbed to 270,710, though within another year or so the number began to drop rapidly.[23]

The Francoist repression, despite its severity, was not a Stalinist-Hitlerian type of liquidation applied automatically by abstract criteria equivalent to class or ethnicity. The great majority of ordinary leftist militants were never arrested, nor even questioned. The repression did apply more categorically to certain levels of responsibility in leftist parties and unions. Cases were then dealt with on an individual basis. As one of the most thorough historians of this purge, himself certainly no admirer of Franco, has put it, "The repression was constant, methodic and regular. Its character was not arbitrary, though it often seemed to be. The repression was fearful, but also selective and rational."[24]

There was no death penalty for political crimes as such, but numerous death sentences were levied on those convicted of political crimes involving major violence. Executions continued, at a decreasing rate, into 1945. Though the total was less than often alleged, it was nonetheless considerable. A report later prepared for Franco indicated that altogether nearly fifty-one thousand death sentences had been handed down, of which no fewer than approximately twenty-eight thousand were carried out.[25]

Penal labor, on the other hand, played a much more limited role than under other major dictatorships. During the war, the Nationalist army had formed disciplinary battalions of soldier laborers, composed of ex-Republican soldiers judged to be not yet rehabilitated, as well as of Nationalist troops convicted of serious infractions of discipline. Members of disciplinary battalions were, however, then eligible for reassignment to regular army units, and many were reassigned. By comparison, Republican labor camps in the Civil War imposed a stricter penal servitude.[26] A decree of June 9, 1939, stipulated that those convicted by military tribunals could have their sentences reduced by up to one-third if they volunteered for labor units. Three months later several "militarized penitentiary colonies" were set up to assist in reconstruction, participation being voluntary.

Thus the close of the Civil War brought neither reconciliation nor political disarmament, for the new state was a rigorous and punitive dictatorship. Yet unlike the regimes in Turkey, the Soviet Union, or Nazi

Germany, Franco's dictatorship did not undergo "cumulative radicalization," that is, increasingly severe repression and persecution over time, but rather the opposite. After the first phase, major aspects of repression were slowly reduced and, unlike in these other cases, there was never any significant recrudescence. Once the major actors and criminals of the Spanish revolution had been prosecuted, there was no need to repeat the process. By the end of 1941 most cases had been completed, representing more than 95 percent of the death sentences. During the next thirty months, military prosecutors asked for a total of 939 additional capital penalties, but many of these were not approved by the tribunals, and others were commuted.[27]

The number of prisoners, in fact, quickly became an embarrassment. Franco took the first step to ameliorate the situation on October 1, 1939, the third anniversary of his accession to power, when he pardoned all former members of the Republican armed forces serving sentences of less than six years. On January 24, 1940, special military juridical commissions were created to review all sentences and were given the power either to confirm or to reduce but never to extend them. By the spring of 1940 the enormously overcrowded jails still held more than a quarter of a million prisoners. On May 8 the director of prisons sent a report to Franco pointing out that only 103,000 of them were serving confirmed sentences. Holding thousands on death row was producing riots and other kinds of indiscipline, to which Franco responded by increasing the number of tribunals and juridical personnel, incorporating more junior officers from the Military Juridical Corps.

On June 4, 1940, provisional liberty was granted to political prisoners serving sentences of less than six years. From that time the prison population began to drop rapidly. Forty thousand more were freed on April 1, 1941, second anniversary of the end of the war, when provisional liberty was granted to all serving sentences of up to twelve years. This was extended to those serving fourteen-year terms on October 16, freeing at least twenty thousand more. During the following winter an additional fifty thousand prisoners were released, and an equally large number were freed on December 17, 1943, when provisional liberty was granted to those with sentences up to twenty years.[28] In March 1944 the minister of justice Eduardo Aunós is said to have informed a British journalist that about four hundred thousand internees had passed through the regime's prisons since 1936, which may have been approximately correct.[29] The number incarcerated continued to drop during 1944, sinking to less than 55,000 and then to 43,812 by the end of the following year, of whom about 17,000 might be classified as political prisoners, less than one-tenth of 1 percent of the Spanish population.[30]

Harsh though this was, the repression was similar to that following the other revolutionary civil wars of Europe in that era, whether won by left or right. In view of the many thousands slaughtered in the Republican zone, particularly during the weeks in which the left thought they were winning, there is no reason to think that conditions would have been significantly better had the revolutionaries triumphed; indeed, had they won under the conditions of the Communist quasi hegemony of 1937–38, they might have been worse.

Some comparisons may offer further perspective. Though in the first years conditions in the prisons of his regime were poor, Franco did not leave so many leftist prisoners to die of hunger or disease as did, in proportionate terms, the democratic parliamentary government of Finland in 1918. In Yugoslavia the approximately seventy thousand prisoners slaughtered almost immediately, mostly without trial, by Tito's Communist regime in 1945 represented about four times as many victims relative to the population.[31] The sole example of a more clement resolution of a major revolutionary civil war would be Greece in 1949, but the government emerging from that conflict was incorporated into the framework of postwar democratic and non-Communist Europe. Franco's regime in the early 1940s was a rigorously authoritarian system that struggled to survive amid world war, facing conditions more severe than those of a relatively secure Greece or of the Soviet Union during the peaceful 1920s.

Though repression remained firm and rigorous, by 1945 it had largely ceased to be murderous. Even the large round of postwar executions had not assumed the dimensions found in the very worst dictatorships. Though it claimed tens of thousands of lives, Franco's repression recognized limits and normally respected its own rules. It began with great severity but grew progressively milder with each passing year.

10 From Civil War to World War

(1939–1940)

After his complete victory, Franco was convinced that he could inaugurate a new era in Spanish history, one that would not only transform politics and culture but also achieve economic modernization and, importantly, increase the country's international role and its standing among the powers. He had every intention of carrying out what he had first announced in his investiture speech in October 1936, and that meant not merely internal transformation and development but concurrently a policy of military power and expansion. Any policy of extreme nationalism implies aggrandizement, and during the course of the Civil War, Nationalist doctrine had found the true identity of Spain to lie in "empire," a status that had to be regained in order for Spain to be fully Spanish.[1] One of the first acts of the regular government of January 1938 was to adopt as the arms of the new state the imperial crown and shield of Charles V, together with the legend *plus ultra* (farther beyond). This attitude even found its way into Franco's religious discourse when he associated "empire" with the reign of Christ in Spain in a major ceremony in the church of Santa Bárbara in Madrid in May 1939.

The first months of peace were devoted to moving the scattered government ministries to Madrid and to expanding administration for the large territory incorporated in the final phase of the war. Franco did not change his headquarters from Burgos to Madrid until October 1939, when he temporarily moved the family into the castle of Viñuelas (property of the dukes of Infantado), eighteen kilometers from the city. Serrano Suñer has claimed that Franco first believed that, as all-powerful chief of state, he should move into the Palacio de Oriente, the royal palace itself, but that Serrano convinced his brother-in-law this would seem overweening and alienate his Monarchist supporters. At any rate, the new permanent residence of the chief of state was established in the extensively renovated palace of El Pardo, just northwest of the city, built by the Habsburgs and expanded in the eighteenth century. It also included a small hunting preserve, though the building had been occupied by Communist Party militia and regular troops during the war. It was both set apart from the city and yet not far away. In March 1940, after its renovation was finally completed, the family took up residence. El Pardo, with its large expanses, rich tapestries, and artworks, would remain Franco's home until his death.

He had already been given a country home in 1938, when supporters in his native province of La Coruña bought for him the Pazo de Meirás, a grand estate renovated a generation earlier by his distant relative Emilia Pardo Bazán, Spain's first important woman novelist. The previous owner, Pardo Bazán's son and heir, together with her grandson, had been executed by one of the Republican death squads in Madrid, and the project had been conceived originally by the provincial leaders of the FET as a gift from the people of La Coruña. They arranged for a very small deduction from the wages of the municipal employees of the province and opened a public subscription, but most of the money was provided by the leading local banker and other major businessmen. Situated in the cool and green Galician countryside not far from his birthplace, Pazo de Meirás would become Franco's summer vacation residence for the rest of his days, and, since it was personal property, would be inherited by his daughter.[2] The expense of maintaining these residences was borne by the state, while the salary of its chief was set at seven hundred thousand pesetas (nearly ninety thousand dollars), to which were added various other emoluments. As might be imagined, all the family soon became prosperous, though direct embezzlement or kickbacks were never part of Franco's practice. Despite the lavish routines of chief of state, and the strict protocol of visits and receptions, Franco never lost his reputation for austerity in his personal manners, though, by comparison, the truly austere regime was the one run by Salazar in neighboring Portugal.

Franco devoted considerable time during the spring of 1939 to a series of official visits to different parts of the country. These trips would continue at a diminishing rate for three decades, always in a heavily escorted private limousine, for, after the experiences of Sanjurjo and Mola, Franco more or less abandoned flying, largely, it would seem, at the urging of his wife. The goal of these visits was to accelerate the consolidation of the regime by establishing a form of contact with the public in various parts of the country. Security was tight.[3] In each major city or provincial capital that he visited, Franco would make one or more personal appearances. On these occasions, he would often (but not always) make a brief speech to a large audience, its size typically guaranteed by mobilizing on the part of the local FET or the official labor unions, though there was usually a good deal of popular interest in catching a glimpse of Franco.

In the aftermath of the Civil War, the Fascist style predominated. Crowds ritually intoned "Franco, Franco, Franco," and the caudillo's name was painted on the facades of many public buildings throughout the country and his photo placed in public offices (sometimes accompanied by that of José Antonio Primo de Rivera), while his effigy appeared on certain categories of new stamps and coins. Public festivity was a major part of the new style, and victory celebrations during the first seven weeks of peace were lavish.[4] A month of parades in the major provincial capitals was climaxed by the great *desfile de la victoria* (victory march) of May 19, 1939, in Madrid, the grandest event that the regime would ever sponsor, during which much of the military passed in front of Franco's reviewing stand in a parade that lasted for hours, rivaling in proportionate size and pomp the November celebrations of the Russian revolution in Moscow's Red Square. On this occasion Franco received the highest military decoration, the Gran Cruz Laureada de San Fernando, awarded to him as a victorious generalissimo who "by his genius won the war." This was pinned on his lapel by his old comrade Varela, appropriately enough since Varelita was "bilaureado," the only person to have received the award twice for combat merits.

The leaders of the new Spanish state were firmly convinced that they stood in the vanguard of history, forming part of the new "organic" authoritarian and nationalist regimes that represented the most modern and innovative trends of the day. During the first four years after the Civil War, Franco ran his government almost as though it were an army, by means of decrees and laws resting simply on the prerogatives of the chief of state. These were expanded in a new law promulgated on August 9, 1939, that amplified the powers defined in the earlier decree of January 29, 1938. It declared that the full powers of government were "permanently entrusted" to the incumbent chief of state, who was totally exempt from any need to submit new laws or decrees to his ministers, should "urgent problems" (otherwise undefined) arise. José Larraz, finance minister in the new government that Franco formed at that time, sought respectfully to suggest that, for reasons of "delicacy," he might wish to have the appropriate minister cosign such laws, but the caudillo ignored him.[5]

Revised statutes of the FET, published a few days later, further expanded his personal domination of the state party. Even though the regime did not seek to exert total control over all civic, social, and economic institutions, as in the Soviet model, it was a strictly personal dictatorship whose powers were less restricted both theoretically and practically—at least in a nominal sense—than those of Germany, Italy, or the Soviet Union.[6]

Franco rewarded his military colleagues with promotions and special perquisites, though the salaries of ordinary officers inevitably remained low. The only senior general who seemed troublesome at first was Queipo de Llano, in his satrapy of Seville. Franco received reports in May that Queipo was reviving speculation about the need to form a new military directory to take charge of policy and resolve the question of the future of the regime. Queipo was ordered to report to Burgos in July. He was then replaced as captain-general of Seville, kept under house arrest briefly in a hotel, and then quickly shunted off to Rome as military attaché. He went quietly, and his fellow generals took note. Talk about a military directory quickly died away.[7]

Franco named his first postwar government on August 8, 1939, cleaning house almost completely. The only two ministers he retained were Serrano Suñer and Alfonso Peña Boeuf, the engineer-technocrat who administered public works. Five ministries went to Falangists and neo-Falangists (*camisas nuevas*, or "new shirts," those who joined the party after the official unification). This seemed on the surface an effort to align the Spanish state with the ascendancy of a new Fascist era in Europe, but three of the five Falangists were in fact senior army commanders, and, aside from Serrano, who remained interior minister, the two other civilian Falangist ministers had no assignment but were simply ministers without portfolio.

The able and experienced Gómez-Jordana Souza was dropped, replaced as foreign minister by Colonel Juan Beigbeder, who for most of the Civil War was the adroit high commissioner of Spanish Morocco. Beigbeder, grandson of an Alsatian immigrant, was a linguist who had served as attaché in Paris and Berlin. He had a little Arabic and was a devout believer in Franco and in Spain's imperial mission in northwest Africa. The vice presidency of the government held by Jordana was eliminated, replaced by a new subsecretary of the presidency to coordinate Franco's personal agenda and administration. This was given to Colonel Valentín Galarza, the inveterate conspirator and coordinator of the prewar UME, a Monarchist who looked askance at the FET. Carmen Franco remembers that Galarza "seemed pretty harsh" and was surprised that her father worked so well with him, but Franco had a high opinion of him and even appointed Galarza's son, a very young officer, to a minor post in his personal military staff (*casa militar*).

Franco had toyed with the idea of creating a grand "ministry of the armed forces," but apparently concluded that this would be unwieldy and concentrate too much power in a single pair of hands, something that he always sought to avoid. Instead, he decided to set up three individual ministries, choosing personal favorites to head them in each case. The "very likeable and extroverted" (in Carmen Franco's words) José Enrique Varela was made army minister.[8] Juan Yagüe, another close comrade, became the first minister of the air force, and Franco's fellow *ferrolano* Captain Salvador Moreno, a key naval commander in the Civil War and also a personal favorite, was made minister of the navy, a post that he would hold for a total of twelve years in two different tours as minister.

Though some have called this a "Falangist government," it was not. Even more than the preceding wartime government, it showcased Franco's policy of seeking a balance between the various ideological "families" of the regime. Of these, the military was clearly the most important, though Franco was careful not to grant the military any direct corporate power in government. In these early years, he relied on military appointees more than any others, though each was only an individual official of the state, subject to Franco's own will and command, and none was ever an autonomous corporate representative of the armed forces. During the entire first phase of the regime, down to 1945, military men held 45.9 percent of the ministerial appointments and 36.8 percent of all the top government posts; these positions were concentrated in the military ministries and in interior, which controlled the police. Falangists, by comparison, would hold 37.9 percent of the ministerial appointments and only 30 percent of all the top government posts; these positions, by contrast, were concentrated in FET administration, labor, and agriculture.[9] It was noteworthy that, according to Larraz, the civilian members of this government addressed Franco as "Your Excellency," the required form, while the military ministers still addressed him in the familiar second person. This was particularly the case with old comrades like Varela and Yagüe, though with a little more time and greater consolidation of the regime, even the senior military, if they were not old personal comrades, would have to adopt greater formality.

The new secretary-general of the FET was General Agustín Muñoz Grandes, an old *africanista* and tough-bitten professional who had demonstrated his administrative skills by serving as principal organizer of the Assault Guards under the Republic. His surreptitious return to Madrid in July 1936 to rally the Assault Guards against Casares Quiroga had failed, leaving him trapped, though a People's Court finally absolved him of wrongdoing in April 1937. He had disappointed Republicans, who had hoped to attract him to the People's Army, by slipping away to the other side as soon as possible. In earlier years he had fought in Morocco directly under Franco, surviving nine combat wounds, and during the Civil War was given command of a division. By its end Muñoz Grandes had become politically radicalized, even though he had been comparatively well treated in revolutionary Madrid, and he became one of the few "Falangist generals."[10] He exhibited an unusual combination of austerity, dedication, and ambition, and Franco preferred to assign the state party to the administration of a military officer. Muñoz Grandes was also made commander of the postwar Falangist militia, but this was a stunted organization that could not be compared with the Italian Fascist militia or the Nazi SA. The only other Falangist in the government of any importance was Serrano Suñer himself.

In 1939 the FET numbered approximately 650,000 male members. Affiliation was useful above all as a means of personal advancement, and membership would continue to increase for three more years before reaching a peak of 932,000 in 1948. The FET was responsible for indoctrinating the population and for providing much of the political and administrative infrastructure of the system, though in the latter sphere it had to face increasing competition from the old conservative elites.[11] Nearly all new mayors and provincial governors joined the party, but most members were passive, and active mobilization was comparatively limited. Soon hundreds of disillusioned *camisas viejas*, who saw that the "new Spain" little resembled their own aspirations to a dynamic new national syndicalist revolution, would begin to abandon the state party.

The symbolic apotheosis of Falangism took place in November 1939, around the third anniversary of the execution of José Antonio Primo de

Rivera. His remains were exhumed from the prison graveyard in Alicante, then borne on the shoulders of endless relay teams of Falangists on a three-hundred-kilometer trek to the great church at El Escorial, just north-west of Madrid. This sanctuary, built by Philip II, contained the pantheon of the monarchs of Spain, but the remains of José Antonio were interred directly in front of the high altar. This grandiose ceremony represented the most elaborate death cult found anywhere west of Lenin's mausoleum and also demonstrated the regime's willingness to enshrine "el Ausente" ("the Absent One"), permitting and encouraging the political myth of a dead leader so as to reinforce the living authority of Franco.[12]

A handful of the most discontented *camisas viejas* were so angry with Franco's domination of the party and his "reactionary" policies that by the end of 1939 they formed a conspiracy to assassinate him. When they sought assistance from Hans Thomsen, the *Landesgruppenleiter*, or leader of the small Nazi Party organization in Madrid, they were told (or so they later claimed) that German support could only be granted if they placed them-selves unconditionally at the orders of Adolf Hitler. These vague plans simmered on and off for a year, and were finally abandoned altogether by March 1941, after the conspirators ruefully concluded that, even if they succeeded in killing Franco, they had no one with whom to replace him and that they lacked popular support.[13]

The most important new task that Franco had given Falangists was the development of the state labor unions, the so-called vertical syndicates that were to bring workers and employers together in the same institutions, though the main emphasis lay on labor organization. The syndical leader, Gerardo Salvador Merino, looked not to Italian national syndicalism or corporatism as his model but to Nazi Germany. He intended to make state-organized labor the strongest institution in the new regime, a goal that earned him the intense enmity of the military elite as a "Fascist Red," a sort of Spanish Ernst Roehm, who planned to subvert the social and political hierarchy. He was finally removed in July 1941 and then tried for his earlier association with Freemasonry.[14] This would normally have brought severe punishment, but he was saved by his German contacts, who obtained annulment of his sentence. Like Manuel Hedilla when he was finally freed in 1946, Salvador Merino would retire to private life and become a prosperous businessman. Franco was usually generous with people on his side of the political fence, but he placed the syndical system under more modest and bureaucratic leadership.

He outlined eight of his priorities in a document that he drew up on December 20, 1939, and distributed to his ministers. At the top of the list was establishing public order, followed by improving medical care, especially critical in light of the scourge of tuberculosis, which Franco calculated was taking more than thirty thousand lives per year, and reducing what he called Spain's "very high infant mortality." He further judged that "more than thirty percent of all Spanish dwellings are unhealthy" and needed to be repaired or replaced. Full employment was another goal, as was the transformation of secondary education and the universities. He recognized that the budgets of the armed forces represented "heavy expenses" that caused financial strain, but there could be no question of further reduction while war raged in Europe. Franco concluded by remarking on the very low wages of state employees, whose "thread-bare suits" he had ample opportunity to observe on his travels about the country, such problems being, he averred, merely part of "the great tragedy of Spain and the urgency of the revolution that the timid are still so afraid of."[15]

Postwar economic reconstruction proved harder than imagined. The destruction wrought by the Civil War was considerable, though not necessarily overwhelming. Expenditures by both sides combined had amounted to at least 1.7 times the GDP, to which must be added the loss of most of the sizable gold reserve and $500 million of debt to Italy and Germany. Losses were heaviest in shipping and transportation, with 225,000 tons of merchant shipping—at least one-third of the total—sunk.[16] The eastern ports were heavily damaged, and half the railway locomotives were lost. At least 8 percent of all housing and more than a third of the livestock had been destroyed. The cost of the looting in the Republican zone, partly carried out by the government itself, most of which was shipped abroad, can never be measured, but only a small portion was recovered.[17] Total lost production amounted to 1–1.5 times GDP, to which must be added the extensive disruption of production in the revolutionary zone.[18] In 1939 total industrial production was 31 percent less than in 1935, agricultural production had declined by 21 percent, the labor force had declined by nearly half a million, and per capita income had decreased by approximately 28 percent. To all this was added the effects of the growing economic crisis that accompanied the outbreak of general war in Europe.

There is no evidence that Franco ever proposed to implement the full national syndicalist revolution of which radical Falangists talked, parts of which he did not even understand. In economics, as in other areas, the nascent regime combined cultural and religious ultraconservatism with ambitious renovationist schemes; the goal was not to "syndicalize" the economy fully but to develop it rapidly while transforming its social framework only by degrees and altering its basic financial structure little.

Franco had a reasonably consistent general orientation, having grown up in the regenerationist era of the early twentieth century, and he believed that the government should provide a coordinated solution to economic problems. He approved of the military industrial commissions that had been set up, manned by artillery and engineers officers, during World War I to prepare to coordinate industrial production, should Spain enter the war. Franco was convinced that liberal economics, like parliamentary democracy, had become totally passé and insisted instead on a policy of state voluntarism. He had imbibed a simplistic kind of Keynesianism that became widespread during the depression, and was also impressed by the achievements of statist policies in Italy and Germany. Franco firmly believed that a program of economic nationalism and self-sufficiency was feasible, partly because of Spain's mineral endowment, riches that he mistakenly extended to include raw materials in general. In August 1938 he had declared to a French journalist, "Spain is a privileged country that can become self-sufficient. . . . We do not really need to import anything."[19] A year later, in his New Year's Eve address of December 31, 1939, he declared that "in this connection I am pleased to announce that Spain possesses enormous gold deposits, worth much more than the amount looted by the Reds," which, at least for a brief time, he apparently was convinced existed.[20]

Franco therefore announced on June 5, 1939, that Spain must carry out reconstruction on the basis of economic self-sufficiency or autarchy, which, though foreign models were not invoked, implicitly paralleled the policies current in Italy and Germany. He declared, "Our victory also represents the triumph of certain economic principles opposed to the old liberal doctrines, under whose myths many sovereign states were subjected to colonialism."[21] Thus, shaking off the constraints of the "liberal plutocracies," Franco inaugurated the era of autarchy in Spanish policy, which would continue with diminishing vigor for twenty years.

The basic ideas were outlined in an extensive document he signed on October 8 titled "Bases and Guidelines for a Plan to Reform Our Economy in Harmony with Our National Reconstruction."[22] This laid out a vague ten-year plan to achieve economic modernization and self-sufficiency, proposing simultaneously to increase exports and reduce imports without relying on foreign investment. The policy was based on state direction and control, and, as it transpired, none of the targets could be achieved within the timeframes proposed, while some had to be abandoned altogether.

The most competent administrator in the new government was the minister of finance, José Larraz, earlier connected with the CEDA and the Editorial Católica. Franco invited him to his modest ground-floor headquarters at Burgos on August 6, 1939, to offer the position, subjecting him to a five-hour harangue on the priority of statist economics. In his memoirs, Larraz recalls that at that point Franco had still not found a tailor, encountering a leader "whose appearance was more modest than that of his own aides, dressed in an old, worn uniform, frayed at the elbows, the golden tassels of his sash worse than worn, almost stringy. That office and its inhabitant exuded sparseness and austerity."[23]

The relation that developed over the next year and a half was unusual, for Larraz became the voice of reality and orthodox policy in a government of unprepared visionaries and spendthrifts.[24] On certain occasions when Franco would launch into a description of the grand social, economic, and military projects to be achieved within the next few years, Larraz had the feeling that the chief of state was reading aloud from a novel by Jules Verne, but he kept a straight face, and Franco permitted the ever respectful Larraz to argue with him about technical issues. He never liked to put all his eggs in one basket and seemed to understand that Larraz offered something the government needed.

Between late 1939 and early 1941 Larraz did a good job of unifying the national currency, stabilizing internal credit, restructuring and refinancing the national debt, and developing a somewhat more coherent budget, as well as gaining approval of a modestly progressive tax reform to make the system slightly less regressive and inefficient. He was frustrated, however, in his broader attempts to unify the budget and end special funds and additional appropriations or to control inflation. Major aspects of his tax reform would not go into effect for years. He judged, correctly, that a basic problem of the new government was that it treated the situation of a country emerging from a destructive war as though it were merely recovering from a depression. In a postdepression scenario, with productive capacity intact but depressed and capital available but immobilized, it was important to spend money domestically to stimulate the economy. In a country recovering from a destructive war, however, the situation was quite different: productive capacity was gutted and capital exhausted. Most of Spain's gold and silver reserve had been liquidated by the wartime Republic. Therefore the notion that the country must simply work hard to pull itself up by its bootstraps would condemn it to years of misery, since the only swift remedy was large-scale injection of foreign capital. After the European war began, this could only come from the United States.

Autarchy, however, required self-reliance, and so the government refused to make a major effort to secure foreign loans or investment. Only minor trade agreements were signed with the Western democracies, accompanied by a small loan from London. Relations with Washington were poisoned partly because of the regime's politics but also because of its quarrel over the continued ownership of the Spanish telephone company by the American ITT, which Franco said perpetuated "a colonial situation." The caudillo continued to insist that Spain could achieve its goals by printing large amounts of money for domestic investment—as he put it, "We have to create a lot of money to carry out great projects." Money printed to fund public works and new enterprises would not generate inflation, he contended over and over again, because it fostered production and would come back to the state in the form of tax growth and the repayment of loans. Franco sought to explain this in the New Year's Eve address, believing that in the nineteenth century governments had printed mountains of paper money that had been converted into great economic progress. When it was pointed out that Salazar had always maintained a balanced budget and an orthodox financial policy in Portugal, Franco replied that was why Portugal was so poor.[25]

His nerves shattered by constant intracabinet conflict, a frazzled Larraz finally resigned in May 1941, the first and one of only a very few of Franco's ministers to walk out on him. Since he respected Larraz despite their disagreements, Franco accepted the resignation without recrimination, replacing him with Joaquín Benjumea, a submissive mediocrity. As he once candidly remarked to Larraz, "I prefer the docile to the efficient," which would remain a problem of his regime for some time, until he was able to find more ministers who were both docile and efficient.

Initially much of the responsibility for implementing the policy of autarchy lay with the new minister of commerce and industry, the army colonel Luis Alarcón de la Lastra, who survived in this exacting task for only a year before giving way to the Catalan businessman Demetrio Carceller, a neo-Falangist crony of Serrano Suñer. Carceller, however, had little faith in extreme autarchy, correctly gauging that Spain lacked the resources to implement it fully and that the government straitjacket was hampering the economy.[26]

Franco's government failed to seek vitally needed loans from the Western democracies, but at the same time it still faced war debts with Italy and Germany. Hitler expected full repayment, but Mussolini—always generous with Franco—unilaterally wrote off as much as a third of the Italian debt, reducing it to little more than $250 million. An agreement was then negotiated to begin paying it off in installments over a twenty-five-year period beginning in mid-1942. This was mostly done at increasingly depreciated rates of exchange that became less and less of a burden, the final payment being made on schedule to the postwar Italian Republic on June 30, 1967.

Despite Franco's earlier remarks, his government did not pretend that Spain could become fully self-sufficient. The practical goal was the best compromise that could be reached between domestic self-sufficiency and the international division of labor, which was very difficult to achieve in practice.[27] The industrialization drive was initiated by a decree of October 1939, the Law to Protect and Stimulate National Industry, which provided a wide variety of incentives, tax benefits, and special licensing arrangements for industry. The subsequent Law to Regulate and Defend National Industry of November 24 targeted certain industries for particular assistance and remained in effect for twenty years. These measures would culminate in the establishment in 1941 of the National Institute of Industry (Instituto Nacional de Industria [INI]), a state investment and holding company whose purpose was to stimulate industrialization, partially modeled on the Italian Institute of Industrial Reconstruction (Istituto per la Ricostruzione Industriale). The goal was especially to satisfy Spain's defense needs and to stimulate development of energy, shipbuilding, steel and chemical production, as well as the manufacture of cars, trucks, and airplanes.

The INI's head was the senior naval engineers officer Juan Antonio Suanzes, childhood friend of Franco (and especially of his brother Nicolás) and son of his old school superintendent in El Ferrol. Suanzes had been minister of commerce and industry in Franco's first government. He was honest, personable, and energetic but lacked any training in finance or economics. Nevertheless, he forged ahead and would continue to direct the INI for more than twenty years.[28] Whereas economic policy right after the Civil War had tended to privilege the Falangist unions in tandem with private business initiative, the elimination of Salvador Merino and the growth of military influence encouraged state capitalism. The INI would become a key institution of the regime, absorbing 34 percent of all public investment in 1950 and 42 percent in 1955.[29]

Autarchist policy was full of inconsistencies and loopholes and led to grave distortions. What had worked well, supported by patriotic enthusiasm, in the Nationalist zone during the war was made much more rigid afterward and faced the challenge of incorporating all the economically disarticulated revolutionary zone (a problem somewhat similar to that which Germany faced with the former East Germany in the 1990s). Rigid controls for foreign exchange, imports, and certain domestic products resulted in artificial cost allocations based on the levels of 1935. Arbitrary and unrealistic policies, sometimes quite restrictive but financed by currency expansion, fueled inflation and impeded growth. They also discouraged the government from seeking loans, credits, and investments from abroad, which to some extent might have been possible even in the straitened circumstances of 1939–40.

Franco's policy reflected the overconcentration on industry typical of agrarian countries eager to expand rapidly. Agriculture, the basis of the economy, was neglected. The effects of the Civil War, stiff government and price controls, lack of investment and especially lack of fertilizer, together with bad weather, combined to limit food production, which in the postwar years generally remained nearly 25 percent below the admittedly high levels of 1934–35. Almost as soon as all the Republican zone had been incorporated, severe food shortages developed, partly a continuation of the dearth that existed in it. On May 14, 1939, general rationing of staples was imposed and sustained at varying rates for more than a decade, accompanied by a bureaucratic labyrinth of controls and procedures.

Austerity and self-sacrifice were announced as keynotes of economic policy. Raw materials were rationed or allocated for industry, and the accompanying controls and shortages soon produced a widespread black market, or *estraperlo* (the word came from a government financial scandal in 1935). There was eventually a black market for nearly all items, from consumer goods to major industrial supplies, resulting in extensive manipulation and bribery. Arrests and even a few executions were inadequate to control it, as corruption developed into a system of its own. What the tensions and ideals of wartime had largely avoided in the former Nationalist zone subsequently emerged on a massive scale as a result of the acute shortages and state controls. For ordinary people in the former Nationalist zone, at least, the immediate postwar years were in some respects worse than the Civil War itself. During the five years beginning in 1939, there were at least two hundred thousand deaths from malnutrition and disease over and above the prewar death rate.

These years also produced a number of desperate searches for quick solutions, involving a variety of scams. Even before the Civil War ended, Franco had briefly received an alchemist who promised to manufacture gold from other materials. The most noted charlatan was an Austrian, who used the name Albert Elder von Filek and presented Franco with a scheme early in 1940 for producing synthetic fuel for internal combustion engines. This turned out to be a pure fraud that landed its proponent in jail.[30]

The extremes of autarchy and the black market that accompanied it produced widespread corruption by 1940, and this continued for years. Some were dismayed by the fact that Franco showed little interest in curbing it; indeed, Franco may even have desired the extensive complicity with the new system that it brought about. Muñoz Grandes, the minister secretary-general of the Falange, was an austere military man who wanted to impose discipline and hopefully reduce corruption, but he complained to friends that he could never get through to Franco, who always diverted the conversation to small talk and trivial anecdotes. When he received complaints about the corruption of certain top administrators, on at least one occasion Franco merely replied that he would pass this information on to the personnel involved.[31]

The very conservative fiscal policies of Franco's regime reduced the percentage of national income collected in taxes from 17.83 under the Republic to 15.07 during the first five years after the war. During this period the percentage of the national budget devoted to public works fell from 14.04 to 7.74. Unemployment declined, but that was because of a process of deurbanization in which workers returned to their rural villages, and this only increased the massive agricultural underemployment in the south.

The new economic policies thus did not initially produce the conditions of national solidarity envisioned either by the Falangists or the regime's propaganda. The years between 1940 and 1942 were the time of the most acute shortages and suffering for most of the population, though desperate conditions continued in the southern countryside for several more years, and the overall situation only improved in the latter part of the decade. To Franco, the suffering endured was in large measure a judgment brought on by the political and spiritual apostasy of half the nation. As he put it in a speech in Jaén on March 18, 1940, "The suffering undergone by a nation at a given point in its history is no accident; it is a spiritual punishment imposed by a God on a distorted life, on an unclean history."[32]

Franco's foreign policy was oriented toward Italy and Germany, the two powers who had made his victory possible. They were the prime exemplars of the new national authoritarian state whose strength seemed to be steadily increasing. At the close of March 1939, as the Civil War was ending, he signed a treaty of friendship with Germany requiring mutual consultation in the event of an attack on either and also joined the Anti-Comintern Pact initiated three years earlier by Berlin and Tokyo, though this was a gesture without concrete obligations. On May 8, the Spanish government officially withdrew from the League of Nations.

The goal was to restore Spain as an international power, not to become the satellite of either Axis state. This would require a major military buildup. The first proposals were drawn up by the navy's general staff in June 1938 and April 1939. These projected a gigantic eleven-year construction program (initially approved by the government on September 8, 1939) to build four battleships and two heavy and twelve light cruisers and no fewer than fifty-four destroyers, thirty-six torpedo boats, fifty submarines, and one hundred torpedo launchers within the next decade. Costs were estimated at approximately 5,500 million pesetas, to be paid at the rate of 500 million per year.

In devising this plan, the naval staff assumed that Spain would join the "autarchist group," meaning the Axis, but would maintain full "liberty" and "independence." The hope was that in a new European war the Spanish fleet might, at the right moment, become decisive. It would then "break the equilibrium" between the Axis and its enemies, making Spain "the key to the situation," the "arbiter of the two blocs."[33]

General Juan Yagüe, the air force minister, presented an equally grandiose plan on October 3, 1939, to expand air strength by thirty-two hundred planes. The air force subsequently increased this number to a projected five thousand planes, and in June 1940, no less—such grand schemes assumed technical assistance from the Axis powers, but in June 1940, none would be forthcoming, and in fact they scarcely got off the ground.[34] The existence of these plans did not mean that Franco necessarily intended to pursue an aggressive policy, at least for the time being. He was well aware of Spain's weakness and, when Italian foreign minister Ciano made a state visit in June 1939, Franco emphasized to him that the country needed at least five years of peace to strengthen itself.[35] He was urged to proceed cautiously by his military attaché in Paris, Colonel Antonio Barroso, who pointed out that the superiority of the Nationalist army in the Civil War had been only a relative one and judged that a new European war might produce a deadlock between Germany and France.[36]

As tension increased in Europe during the summer of 1939, Franco used the term "supple prudence" to describe Spain's foreign policy. His regime was seeking to establish closer relations with Latin American countries, the Philippines, and the Arab world to achieve greater international weight. Franco's policy in Europe was discreet, though more friendly to the Axis than to the democracies, and the German ambassador, Eberhard von Stohrer, repeated the advice given by Hitler in an earlier letter to Franco. The German government expected no more than a benevolent neutrality from Spain, urging Franco to be as noncommittal as possible, since it was of "maximal importance" that London and Paris remain uncertain about Spanish policy. Franco agreed and Colonel Juan Beigbeder, the foreign minister, informed Stohrer that "Spain wants to help you as much as it can."[37]

Signing of the Nazi-Soviet pact toward the end of August came as a surprise to Madrid, which assumed that anti-Sovietism was as fundamental to Hitler's policy as it was to Franco's. The possibility of a German-Soviet invasion of Poland was received with consternation, since the Warsaw government was a national Catholic authoritarian state that had much in common with the Spanish regime, even though it was more liberal. Franco and his generals feared that Soviet invasion of Poland would open east-central Europe to the Red Army only six months after its Spanish counterpart had been liquidated. He nonetheless considered Poland guilty of having developed an impasse with Germany by its rejection of any compromise on the Danzig corridor and informed Mussolini that he was prepared to undertake mediation if Mussolini would consider it useful. The Italian dictator replied that he would undertake such an initiative himself, but when the French foreign minister suggested that Spain undertake mediation between Berlin and Warsaw on August 30 (scarcely twenty-four hours before the invasion), Mussolini vetoed the proposal on the grounds that it came too late.

When Britain and France declared war on Germany on September 3, Franco called on all parties to reconsider their position and return to negotiation. His urging that all belligerents undertake "voluntary limitation" of the means of destruction was not intended to be pro-Polish, even though Beigbeder had to inform Berlin that the pending Hispano-German cultural pact could not be completed (vetoed by the adamantly anti-Nazi Spanish bishops). One day later Spain's neutrality was announced, and on the sixth Franco telegraphed his ambassador in Rome to ask Mussolini to press that "the Poles surrender as soon as possible," to avoid a Soviet invasion. When, a little later, he condemned publicly the destruction of Catholic Poland, his main concern was the Soviet advance. Only the most radical Falangists were initially happy with the outbreak of war, for they were sure that it would lead to the establishment of an authoritarian new order on a continental scale.

Nonetheless, Franco wanted to be prepared for military action, even though Spain could not possibly undertake such a thing at the moment. He had already appointed a commission to begin the fortification of the southern coast and to draw up plans for an attack on Gibraltar, though this proposed operation was abandoned after it was concluded that the British base was too heavily defended. On October 31 he convened the first (secret) meeting of his new National Defense Council, comprising the head of the recently created Supreme General Staff (Alto Estado Mayor) and the three ministers of the armed forces. The council quickly agreed to a massive military expansion that could place the armed forces in a position to close the Strait of Gibraltar, seize the British base, occupy all or part of French Morocco, and dominate the waters around the peninsula, closing the sea routes to southern and southwestern France, though it was recognized this last goal could not be attained without the active assistance of the German and Italian fleets.[38] No timetable was drawn up, for Spanish policy would depend on the future course of events. The plan called for mobilizing fifty *divisiones de asalto* totaling 450,000 men, supported by fifty second-line divisions, with another fifty third-line divisions in reserve. How all this was to be paid for was not discussed, and the grand plan never in fact materialized, but over the next year and more the army, initially reduced to less than 300,000 men, was eventually expanded to approximately 450,000 poorly armed troops.[39]

During the first part of the war, the principal means by which the Spanish government demonstrated, however covertly, the pro-German tilt of its neutrality was the permission it gave for the resupply of German submarines in three ports: Cádiz, Vigo, and Las Palmas de Gran Canaria. There was a very limited precedent for this in World War I, though that precedent had technically involved a violation of Spanish neutrality. Franco gave his approval on the eve of hostilities in Europe, then suddenly revoked it on September 4, the day after Britain and France declared war, explaining that it had become too risky. Nonetheless, four days later the caudillo changed his mind, and the arrangements for submarine resupply were reauthorized.

Operations began at night in the bay of Cádiz in January 1940. The Germans used several tanker and supply ships from among the fifty-four German vessels confined in Spanish ports after the outbreak of war, drawing on Spanish stocks and torpedoes sent from Germany. British intelligence soon learned about this, and, after both London and Paris launched official protests, Franco temporarily canceled such activities. They were resumed on June 18, 1940, during the fall of France, and then continued for eighteen months, until one of the resupplied submarines, with its logbook, was captured by the Royal Navy in December 1941. The British embassy protested more energetically, threatening to cut off petroleum and other vital imports. Spanish denials had little effect, leaving Franco with no option but to suspend further resupply, while informing Berlin that he hoped to resume such operations at a more favorable time in the future. Altogether, some twenty German submarines were resupplied in Spanish ports during this period.[40]

The French government attempted to guarantee Spain's neutrality by offering Franco a nonaggression pact, but in the aftermath of the Civil War, resentment against Paris was intense on the part of the victors in Spain, who were aware of, and even exaggerated, the extent of the facilities France had provided the Republicans. Franco refused the offer, pointing out that Paris had still not officially ratified a recently negotiated bilateral trade agreement. The foreign minister, Beigbeder, proposed his own initiative to mobilize cultural and political support in Latin America, concert international pressure on the Gibraltar issue, and strengthen ties with Italy, which had not entered the war. The outbreak of fighting had postponed Franco's planned visit to Rome, but Beigbeder stressed the importance of "establishing a Rome-Madrid axis," which might coordinate the policies of the two countries and would be even more useful after peace had returned. Franco knew that Spain could never replace Germany for Mussolini and was skeptical, writing in the margin of Beigbeder's proposal "An axis without strength?"[41]

When Finland was invaded by the Soviet Union at the beginning of December, Franco and Mussolini both expressed their support for the former. An official statement denounced the invasion as "barbarous"— apparently, it was worse than the German invasion of Poland—and Franco placed a small quantity of Spanish arms at the disposal of the Finns. This attack by Hitler's erstwhile friend and quasi ally slightly diminished German prestige in Madrid, for many remembered that Finland had provided more volunteers relative to its small population for Franco's army than any other European country. For part of Finnish society, the Spanish Civil War had seemed a sort of extension of Finland's own counterrevolutionary civil war of 1918. Meanwhile, the lack of a strong direct response by the Western democracies—compared with their declaration of war when Hitler invaded Poland—confirmed in Franco's mind the notion that Britain and France lacked firm principles.

In March 1940 the generals who made up the army's Supreme War Council endorsed a memorandum by General Alfredo Kindelán (now disillusioned with Franco) that concluded that Spain was in no condition to enter the war, especially because of its economic problems and shortages. They also challenged the role of the FET, the principal backer of war, declaring that the army was "the only reliable institution to guide Spanish policy."[42] This attitude changed dramatically, however, two months later, when Germany successfully invaded France and the Low Countries.

11 | The Great Temptation

(1940–1941)

The dramatic success of Hitler's offensive in the West astounded the world and had a profound impact in Rome and Madrid, where reluctance to consider entry into the war melted. At the end of May, the astute Portuguese ambassador Pedro Teotónio Pereira lamented in a report to Salazar, who was genuinely neutral, that Spanish government ministers "who are cognizant of the dangers of a German hegemony . . . are rarer than a four-leaf clover."[1]

Mussolini had felt humiliated nine months earlier when he had to admit that Italy was too weak to honor its military alliance with Germany, and he had invented for his regime the status of "nonbelligerence," a category that did not exist in international law. This term was coined to define a new Italian policy, aligned in favor of Germany but that precluded participation in the war. Then, on June 10, 1940, convinced that the Allies were on the verge of total defeat, Mussolini took the final step, abandoned this status, and officially entered the war. He knew that Spain was too weak to do likewise but urged Franco to adopt a policy of nonbelligerence. The caudillo agreed, officially announcing Spain's status of nonbelligerence on June 12. That would remain the policy of Franco's government for more than three years, until October 1, 1943—that is, for the greater part of World War II.

José María Doussinague, head of policy planning in the Foreign Ministry, then prepared for Beigbeder a report emphasizing that "Italy's precedent shows that a declaration of nonbelligerence is a state preparatory to entering the conflict and must have a certain intimidating effect on countries that may be threatened by our forces." This could make it possible for Spain to "request boldly" from other powers much more than it might in other circumstances.[2]

During the victorious phase of German military expansion, and quite irrespective of Hitler's own priorities, it was common for his principal allies and sympathizers to plan their own "parallel wars" and empires.[3] The term "parallel war" had been coined by Mussolini to characterize his ambition to wage an Italian war that would build a great empire in the Mediterranean, Africa, and the Middle East. This was the most ambitious goal of any of Hitler's allies, but Hungary hoped to regain much of its former empire, and Rumania planned to grow to the north and east at the expense of the Soviet Union. Before the war, Hitler had dangled an equivalent opportunity before the Polish government, which had rejected it. The greatest parallel war of all was waged by Hitler's ally Stalin, who used the cover of Germany's war to seize half of Poland, all three Baltic states, northeastern Rumania, and southeastern Finland. And that was only the beginning, since the Soviet leader was planning further expansion in the Balkans, Turkey, northern Iran, and western China. It was therefore not surprising that somewhat equivalent ambitions quickly mounted in Madrid. Franco began to conceive a program smaller than that of Stalin but otherwise symmetrical with it, expanding outward into Africa from the opposite end of Europe. Like Stalin, he hoped to do this while avoiding direct warfare with a major power as long as possible and then engaging in such conflict, if necessary, only in the very best circumstances.

At the beginning of the twentieth century Spain had shown less interest in imperialism than any other large European country, as explained in chapter 2, and even less than some small ones, such as Portugal, Belgium, and Holland. But Franco's National Movement generated an intense and aggressive modern nationalism. Even during the Civil War "empire" had been added to its aspirations, though most Spaniards were uncertain as to what that might refer, other than to the small, poverty-stricken protectorate in northern Morocco. The imperialist thrust was combined with the regime's neotraditional religiosity in the grandiose Falangist slogan "Por el imperio hacia Dios" ("Through empire toward God"), which presumably was meant to affirm the renewal of a Spanish "civilizing mission" in the world abroad. The tense and dramatic perspective of Europe in those years, which threatened massive changes and fueled hopes for a new international role for Spain, explains the grandiose, if totally unrealizable, plans for military expansion hatched from 1938 to 1940. These ambitions were expressed above all by Falangists and, somewhat less consistently, by the military. They seemed the more natural in that World War II, or more precisely, the first half of that war, represented the grand climax of modern European imperialism, and many Spaniards longed to participate in the imperial adventure. The experience of colonial war had been the making of Franco, and for two or three years he firmly believed that it was his destiny to build a great new empire for Spain in northwestern and western Africa. In the process, Spain could settle historical accounts with Britain and France for the abuse suffered in the three preceding centuries.

The number one objective was greater Morocco, which was under the control of Vichy France, but as a first preliminary step, on June 14, two days after Franco's announcement of nonbelligerence, he ordered Moroccan units of the Spanish forces to occupy the international zone of Tangier. Though this would be the only measure of territorial expansion that Franco would ever take, at the time it was conceived as merely the beginning, though prudently announced not as a conquest but as an altruistic measure required by altered circumstances. Spain was the only member of the international commission governing the city that was not at war and hence would safeguard the situation for all involved. These terms were accepted by London, Vichy, and Rome for as long as the war lasted.

A much more ambitious scheme was drawn up for the invasion of the French protectorate, which occupied more than 90 percent of all Morocco, and was designed to take place after the fall of France. Sizable military reinforcements were dispatched to the Spanish zone, while agents were sent to stir up resentment against France in Morocco and also in northwestern Algeria, where many descendants of Spanish immigrants numbered among the European population.[4] The plan was to present a Spanish military initiative not as an act of war against France but simply as a response to France's defeat that was needed to maintain order in Morocco. Nonetheless, the Spanish units were not as strong as the remaining French military in northwest Africa, momentarily reinforced by much of the surviving French air force, which flew in from Europe. Meanwhile the German consul in Tetuán, Hans Georg Richter, reported that "one cannot describe the Spanish military organization here in bad enough terms,"[5] and Franco was not in a position to act by the time the campaign in Western Europe ended.

His ambassador in Paris, the clever, slippery, and cynical José Félix de Lequerica, served as mediator of the official armistice between Germany and France that codified the terms of the German victory. Hitler decided not to demand any change in the French colonial empire, allowing France to maintain most of its colonial military establishment as a sop to it as a defeated and now collaborationist country and also as means of introducing an element of international stability that would be useful while he brought England to her knees.

Nonetheless, though both the military balance and Hitler's decision were for the moment discouraging to Madrid, the idea of expansion with German backing remained a Spanish priority. Since the rapid defeat of France had not been anticipated, the new Spanish program for northwest Africa only began to take form after mid-1940, finding full expression in books and pamphlets published from 1941 to 1942, reaching its climax in José María de Areilza and Fernando María Castiella's *Reivindicaciones de España*, which would not come out until the moment of opportunity was already passing.[6]

British policy constituted the other side of the coin, restricting rather than encouraging Spain, and it was represented by a new ambassador, Sir Samuel Hoare, who arrived at the close of May 1940 with the goal of keeping Spain out of the war. While its public leverage lay in London's power to regulate vital Spanish imports by sea, its clandestine stratagem was financial bribery of senior Spanish military commanders on a vast scale. This operation was conceived and administered by Captain Alan Hillgarth, naval attaché, friend of Churchill, and agent of British intelligence. Between 1940 and 1942 Hillgarth expended approximately thirteen million dollars, a great sum for that time, the largest share going to the increasingly liberal-minded General Antonio Aranda, who gave British intelligence endless versions of a "junta of generals" scheming against Franco and who may have personally garnered as much as two million dollars, deposited in personal accounts in New York and Buenos Aires. Approximately thirty senior commanders received smaller sums, though others had nothing to do with the bribery.[7]

How effective was it, and what, if anything, did Franco know about it? There are no data on the Spanish side to answer such questions. Franco knew, of course, that Aranda was in frequent contact with the British and never gave him an important command. Conversely, the monarchist General Luis Orgaz, who apparently also received sizable payments and who had been one of the top sponsors of Franco in 1936, long retained his confidence and held important posts, such as high commissioner of the Moroccan protectorate from 1941 to 1945.

Foreign minister Juan Beigbeder, who evidently also received payments, was a different case. He was a top *africanista* and one of the old comrades who continued to address Franco in the second person. His adulation of the caudillo could be extreme—"you can sculpt Spain as you like," he said to Franco—and apparently even suggested that Franco crown himself king. Like most of the generals, he was momentarily swept by pro-German euphoria in June 1940 and was one of the strongest proponents of Franco's African dream. Nonetheless, he found that he got along very well with Hoare and soon adopted a more even-handed approach in foreign policy, something possibly not unrelated to British money and also to his affair with a young Englishwoman normally referred to as "Miss Fox," supposedly an agent of British intelligence, although that has not been proven.[8] The German ambassador eventually launched an official complaint about his attitude, leading to Beigbeder's dismissal in October.[9]

Bribery, of course, guarantees nothing. Mussolini had several top Greek generals on his payroll, but this seems to have done little to reduce Greek resistance to the Italian invasion in 1940. There is no evidence that any of the generals bribed had any decisive influence on Franco, though one consequence was a considerable improvement in their economic situation, which may have reduced interest in a "Fascist" military intervention but also had the effect of making them more conservative and also more "Francoist," determined to support a regime that would maintain their privileged position without plunging the country into war.

If Franco's victory in the Civil War created a certain charisma for him, it had not settled problems about the future. The loose coalition that had supported him remained seriously divided between the military, Falangists, Monarchists, Carlists, and the Church and major Catholic laymen. There was still a lingering tendency among the senior military to consider him as a first among equals. In addition, there was a continued disposition among some to think that, with victory won, his personal dictatorship should give way to a different form of government.

Franco had always been willing to debate military affairs with his senior commanders, at least to some degree, but he was strict about any sign of political disobedience. On June 27 he abruptly dismissed his old comrade Yagüe, the first air force minister, for talking too much and criticizing the government and its ministers. Strongly pro-Axis, Yagüe had not conspired against Franco but had been far too loose with his tongue and had drawn the enmity of both Serrano and Varela, the minister of the army.[10] His dismissal came only three months after the resignation of Muñoz Grandes as secretary-general of the Falange, a political post for which he had been ill suited. Thus, at the very moment of Hitler's apogee, two of the top Falangist generals had disappeared from Franco's government. Muñoz Grandes, however, had not lost Franco's favor and soon drew a top military command, while Yagüe was sent into internal exile for more than two years. Franco replaced him as minister with General Juan Vigón, the experienced engineers officer who had served as his wartime chief of staff. Vigón was pro-Monarchist but discreetly so, much more circumspect than his predecessor, and that was what the caudillo expected. Moreover, Vigón had been one of the Spanish commanders most esteemed by the Germans during the Civil War.

The hour of temptation for Franco arrived in June 1940, when it seemed to almost everyone that Adolf Hitler had become master of continental Europe. Though he was surprised by the suddenness of the French collapse, it inevitably added to the romantic conception that Franco had formed of Hitler, whom he described to the Portuguese ambassador as an "extraordinary man." The führer seemed to Franco something like an instrument of divine providence, a historical avenger or *justiciero* sent to revolutionize the international order and avenge the wrongs done by France and Britain, restoring the worthy nations of Europe, such as Spain, to the place they merited. To understand this feeling it must be kept in mind that Nazi and Fascist propaganda always emphasized the idea that the Axis powers represented a new order that would overturn the established Western liberal empires, as well as the Marxist system of the Soviet Union. Hitler had already redrawn the map of central and east-central Europe, and he made appeals even farther beyond to the Islamic world, as had imperial Germany in World War I. Japan, his Asian ally, went farther yet. The inferences that Franco drew from this expansion suggested that the concept of the Third Reich commonly held in Madrid during 1940–41 amounted to an unrealistic vision of Hitler's primary intentions.

On June 3 Franco sent a personal letter to the führer declaring that the current French campaign was "the greatest battle in history," one that "my people . . . feels is its own," since "your soldiers shared with ours the war against the same enemies, even though camouflaged." For the first time he identified the Civil War with Hitler's aggression in World War II. Franco further insisted that "I need not assure you how great is our desire not to remain apart from your concerns and how great is my satisfaction to lend you in every moment the assistance that you might find most useful."[11] Hitler's response was evasive and noncommittal. In the moment of victory he had, as usual, little interest in Spain one way or the other. Franco nonetheless continued to express these sentiments vigorously, declaring in a major speech on July 18, the fourth anniversary of the military insurrection, that Spain was building "an empire" and that the Spanish war had been "the first battle of the new European order." He even boasted that Spain "has two million warriors ready to fight in defense of our rights."[12] The next day the press reported that Hitler had awarded Franco the highest medal the German government could give to a foreigner, the Grand Cross of Gold, but his response to the caudillo's overtures was oblique. Beigbeder had already explained in some detail to Stohrer, the German ambassador, the extent of Spanish aspirations in Morocco, but the Germans showed no interest in pressuring Pétain, the leader of Vichy France, and for a while nothing changed.

By the end of July, however, Hitler had come to realize that the Churchill government had no intention of giving in, and for the first time he began to look for a new strategic advantage to pressure Britain further. This might take the form of Spanish cooperation with Germany's seizure of Gibraltar and the closing of the Mediterranean. A German military commission arrived in Spain to survey the task, while Larraz, the minister of finance, prepared a detailed list of all the economic assistance that Spain would need in order to enter the war. On August 15 Franco wrote a personal letter to Mussolini soliciting his assistance in convincing Hitler to grant Spain's claims. He stressed that "from the beginning of the present war it has been our intention to make every effort to intervene to the extent of our possibilities when a favorable moment arises," which was largely correct. He asked Mussolini's aid in helping Spain "occupy its place in the struggle against our common enemies."[13]

Germany's most important friend in the Spanish government was Serrano Suñer, who would have liked to direct Spanish politics as a kind of prime minister under Franco as chief of state.[14] His ambition and arrogance made him "the most hated man in Spain," in the words of his good friend, the German ambassador. Franco continued to rely on him more than anyone else, so that it was Serrano, not the suspect foreign minister, who led a large delegation that left for Berlin on September 16 to negotiate the terms of cooperation between the two countries that could bring Spain into the war.

Serrano seemed very sure of himself and of Spain's policy. Before leaving Madrid, he gave an interview to the *Völkische Beobachter*, the official Nazi Party newspaper, which was published in Berlin on the sixteenth, even before he arrived. Serrano identified his brother-in-law's regime with the Fascist doctrine of "proletarian nationalism," stressing that "we hold the thesis that our war was the first phase of the present war. We fought, at the same time, against the Red revolution and against what we might call the 'old regime' of Europe. . . . The Republic and the Popular Front were the last arms of the enslavement of Spain to the capitalism of the great democracies." He expressed confidence that Spain, Germany, and Italy would be fully compatible and complementary allies, declaring that "the understanding with Germany and her ally will be perfect. Not a single one of their rights conflicts with ours; not a single one of their interests is contrary to our vital interests and to our natural expansion. Seldom have three friendly nations had spheres of expansion more perfect and more definable."

The talks in Berlin continued intermittently until the twenty-fifth, but they remained preliminary. Joachim von Ribbentrop, Hitler's foreign minister, offended Serrano by asking for the cession of one of the Canary Islands to Germany as a naval base. Like nearly all German officials, he was ignorant of Spanish affairs and may have thought that the Canaries were a colonial possession such as Ifni or Equatorial Guinea. Franco maintained contact with Serrano by means of almost daily personal letters, in one of which he affirmed that "there is no doubt as to the alliance." On the twenty-fourth, he specified that "we must make a pact about the future and, though there is no doubt as to our decision, we must consider the details of this agreement and the obligations of both sides."[15] It was finally agreed in Berlin that problems would be resolved in a personal meeting between Hitler and Franco. Two weeks after returning, Serrano replaced Beigbeder as foreign minister.

What Franco could offer Hitler was Spain's entry into the war, which would guarantee the fall of Gibraltar and the expulsion of British forces from the west Mediterranean, together with economic concessions, such as mineral deposits in Morocco and key exports from Spain. In addition, he seems to have been willing to grant limited terms to Germany for establishment of a military base on the coast of Moroccan territory that Spain would acquire, though he did not agree to a base in the Canaries. What Franco asked was the cession to Spain of all French Morocco, northwestern Algeria, and a large swathe of territory from French West Africa below the Sahara. In addition, he insisted on very extensive German military supplies and support as well as large shipments of goods of various kinds to sustain the faltering Spanish economy. Hitler, in turn, was willing to provide some military and economic assistance, though considerably less than what the Spanish government was asking for, but what neither Franco nor Serrano understood was that Hitler had decided he could not offer any French colonial territory, at least at that time. Pétain's Vichy regime had become a satellite of Germany: its sizable modern economy was important to the German war effort, and its overseas empire and colonial forces supplied strategic stability during the struggle with Britain.

Franco's only meeting with Hitler took place at Hendaye, on the Atlantic border with France, on October 23. He hoped for a positive outcome but realized that he had to be prepared for anything. He knew his country's history well enough to remember that in 1808, as erstwhile allies of France, Carlos IV and his crown prince had gone to Bayonne—not far from Hendaye—to negotiate with Napoleon and had been kidnapped, while French troops marched into Spain. Thinking on both sides of things as he often did, he clearly considered that a similar plot could now be afoot.[16] Since he was leaving Spanish territory briefly to enter the German-occupied zone of France, he appointed General Agustín Muñoz Grandes, his new commander of the Gibraltar district, head of a triumvirate that would, if necessary, exercise power in his absence.

The meeting would come to be the most mythified single event in all of Franco's long life, supposedly the sole occasion on which someone had outtalked the loquacious führer. The first element in the myth concerns Franco's tardy arrival by train, supposedly a deliberate gesture to hold Hitler at bay. In fact, the delay was due exclusively to the disastrous state of Spain's railroads since the Civil War and mortified Franco.[17] A more substantive problem stemmed from Hitler's expectation that it would be possible to reach a firm agreement quickly, while Franco was determined to bargain seriously, since, as he stipulated in the notes he had prepared that morning, "Spain cannot enter just for fun [*por gusto*]." Moreover, the

Spanish caudillo could not suppress a small element of uncertainty concerning Spain's possible role in the war, expressed in a further paragraph of the memorandum he had prepared: "Lequio [the Italian ambassador] to Fontanar [a Spanish diplomat]. That Italy has already lost because if Germany wins in the end it will treat her badly because of her weak contribution, which many are convinced of. And if she loses nothing will be left of Italy. Thus if it came to that Spain remaining outside could help to save them."[18]

Whatever internal doubts he may have had, newsreels and photos taken at the meeting showed a smiling and apparently self-confident caudillo. The first part of the meeting lasted three hours. Franco began by thanking Hitler effusively for everything that Germany had done for Spain and proclaimed the sincere desire of the Spanish nation to participate in the war on Germany's side. Hitler then launched into his standard monologue, insisting that Britain was finished, though it continued to be dangerous on the periphery, which meant that should the United States come in to assist Britain, the most problematic spots would be northwest Africa and the key Atlantic islands. Hence the importance of taking Gibraltar. What was needed was a "broad front" of all the continental powers, including Vichy France, against the Anglo-Saxon world. Therefore at present it would be a mistake to discourage the French by imposing on them territorial losses in Africa; such issues would be resolved in Spain's favor in the final settlement.[19]

Perhaps the most unusual feature of the meeting is that Franco apparently talked more than Hitler. In his later years, after he became a victim of Parkinson's disease, the caudillo would appear rigid and increasingly terse and laconic. That would hide the fact that for most of his life Franco had been loquacious whenever circumstances encouraged it. His long discourse to Hitler about Spain's history in Morocco, featuring the numerous personal digressions that normally filled most of his private conversation, bored Hitler to no end. Franco went on about his personal experiences, complementing this with details of military affairs and of the history of Morocco, which would lead to Hitler's subsequently famous remark to Mussolini that he would prefer to have three or four teeth pulled rather than go through that again.[20] Five days later he would complain to the duce that Franco "lacks the stature of a leader or organizer" and that "the Spanish have unrealistic goals," a claim supported by Serrano Suñer's having apparently suggested obtaining a small slice of southwestern France in return for what Louis XIV had taken in 1659.[21]

The caudillo's aim was to negotiate concrete terms of large-scale territorial aggrandizement as well as massive military and economic assistance, but Hitler refused to discuss details at that time. He assured Franco that Spain's vital needs would be satisfied but that no concrete territorial concessions could be made in the middle of the war. Franco ventured that the war seemed far from over and that Churchill might continue to resist from Canada, with American assistance. When he made the observation that seizure of the Suez canal would be particularly important, Hitler replied that Gibraltar was more significant, as gateway to Africa and the Atlantic. No opportunity arose for Franco to present the lengthy position paper that had been drawn up detailing the extensive Spanish demands in French Equatorial West Africa.[22]

A second session between the respective foreign ministers lasted only thirty minutes, devoted to technical negotiation. The position announced by Hitler was completely disappointing to Franco and Serrano, but they were not ready to give up. Ribbentrop presented Serrano with a draft of a secret protocol by which Spain would commit itself to entering the war soon, though not by a specific date, while Germany promised assistance, without going into details. Moreover, the Spanish government was to agree to sign the Tripartite Pact (the new defensive alliance of Germany, Italy, and Japan) as a fourth member and even join the Pact of Steel, the military alliance between Germany and Italy. Such agreements would give Spain a status equivalent to that of the two Axis powers, altogether superior to that of other German associates such as Rumania, Vichy France, or Hungary. According to article 5, Spain was to receive Gibraltar and unspecified French colonial territory, though only if France could be compensated elsewhere, presumably with territory at the expense of Britain.[23] Ribbentrop commented that Franco had not understood the führer correctly, to which Serrano replied that Franco had a "plan" of his own, and all this might be accommodated by exchanging secret letters, so as not to alarm Pétain's government, that recognized Spain's demands. He further indicated that the Spanish side would want to introduce certain changes in the protocol.

A frugal but cordial supper was served in Hitler's restaurant car at 8 p.m., followed two hours later by a final session between the two dictators, at which each reiterated his position without reaching a final conclusion, though they still maintained a friendly tone. This discussion ended shortly after midnight, at which point the Germans accompanied the Spanish delegation back to their train. Franco remained standing on his car's platform in order to salute the führer as he pulled away, but (if Serrano is to be believed) the train's sudden lurch forward almost threw him off onto the pavement. At the end, both sides remained convinced that each would still get its way, though doubt had begun to enter the minds of the Spaniards. An unusual aspect of the negotiations was that Hitler had not attempted to deceive Franco about his terms, as was his wont, and as some of the members of Hitler's entourage suggested he do. His interpreter later reported that immediately after the talks ended, Hitler observed to Ribbentrop that there was no point in making any artificial promises to Franco, because the chattering Latins could not keep secrets and anything promised would soon become known to Vichy.[24]

Back in San Sebastián, Franco and Serrano drew up a new draft of the protocol in the middle of the night, but soon afterward the caudillo was rudely awakened by the arrival of General Eugenio Espinosa de los Monteros, the ambassador to Berlin, who insisted that relations were nearing a crisis because of the nervousness of Ribbentrop and the impatience of Hitler. He insisted that the original draft needed to be signed immediately, which Franco agreed to do, adding the comment that "today we are the anvil, but tomorrow we will be the hammer." The next morning, after sleeping briefly, he instructed that an additional protocol be drawn up that specified Spain's economic requirements and also slipped in a reference to "the French zone in Morocco, which will subsequently belong to Spain," but the Germans would not accept it. The only change they were willing to make in the original document was limited to reiterating a vague promise that Spain would receive territory in Africa, provided that France could be adequately compensated and that the interests of Germany and Italy were not infringed. The final version was not ready until November 4, and it was then signed in triplicate by Serrano Suñer a week later. Franco quickly wrote another letter to Hitler, reiterating Spain's claim to all Morocco and the Oran district in Algeria, which seems to have been ignored by the führer.[25]

The final revised text read:

Hendaye, 23 October 1940
    The Italian, German, and Spanish governments have agreed as follows:

   1. The exchange of views between the Führer of the German Reich
      and the head of the Spanish state, following conversations between
      the Duce and the Führer and among the foreign ministers of the
      three countries in Rome and Berlin, has clarified the present position

of the three countries toward each other as well as the questions implicit in waging the war and affecting general policy.

2. Spain declares its readiness to accede to the Tripartite Pact concluded 27 September 1940 among Italy, Germany, and Japan and for this purpose to sign, on a date to be set by the four powers jointly, an appropriate protocol regarding the accession.

3. By the present protocol Spain declares its accession to the Treaty of Friendship and Alliance between Italy and Germany and the related Secret Supplementary Protocol of 22 May 1939.

4. In fulfillment of its obligations as an ally, Spain will intervene in the present war of the Axis Powers against England after they have provided it with the military support necessary for its preparedness, at a time to be set by the common agreement of the three powers, taking into account military preparations to be decided upon. Germany will grant economic aid to Spain by supplying it with food and raw materials, so as to meet the needs of the Spanish people and the requirements of the war.

5. In addition to the reincorporation of Gibraltar into Spain the Axis Powers state that in principle they are ready to see to it, in accordance with a general settlement that is to be established in Africa and that must be put in effect after the defeat of England, that Spain receives territories in Africa to the same extent as France can be compensated, by assigning to the latter other territories of equal value in Africa, but with German and Italian claims against France remaining unaffected.

6. The present protocol shall be strictly secret, and those present undertake to preserve its strict secrecy, unless by common agreement they decide to publish it.

Prepared in three original texts in the Italian, German, and Spanish languages.[26]

It seemed that Hitler had once more gotten what he wanted and that the Spanish government had pledged to become a full military partner of the Axis and enter what was soon being called the Second World War. The protocol appeared decisive, though in fact it was not, for no date had been set, and everything remained secret.

Franco's government immediately took a number of measures, mostly military, to follow up on the protocol. On November 3 it dissolved the international administration of Tangier, absorbing the city into the Spanish protectorate. The general staff prepared a new mobilization plan that would theoretically expand the army to nine hundred thousand, tripling its present size and restoring it to the dimensions existing at the end of the Civil War. Such an expanded force would have to be supplied by Germany and Italy, and most of the expansion never took place. Ever since the summer of 1939 Franco had eyed the possibility of an attack on Gibraltar, and a Spanish assault plan, "Operación C," was presented to him just before or just after the meeting at Hendaye. It envisaged an attack launched exclusively by Spanish forces, the Germans to serve only as backup in the event of a major British strategic response.[27] The Germans, on the other hand, considered Spanish forces inadequate for this task, and Hitler was already training his own all-German assault contingent.

Another collateral issue was the question of Portugal. Franco, Serrano, and others thought Portugal should be included in any general plan of expansion and be brought under control by diplomatic or military means. When Admiral Canaris, the German military intelligence chief and a veteran of Spanish affairs, asked Franco early in July whether he would permit the passage of troops to attack Portugal in the event of a British landing there, Franco replied that Spain's forces would guarantee the integrity of the peninsula. He only wanted German troops on Spanish soil if and when that should become absolutely necessary.

Earlier, before he became foreign minister, Serrano Suñer had undertaken an initiative to try to place Portugal under Spanish hegemony, informing Pereira, the Portuguese ambassador, that Hitler would not long permit the continued existence of an independent and neutral ally of Britain on the continent. He suggested that Portugal undertake a new arrangement that would allow Spain to protect it. In Lisbon, Salazar, facing "consistent and total peril on every side," adroitly sidestepped this pressure by negotiating personally through Nicolás Franco, the ambassador to Portugal. This resulted in an additional protocol to the friendship treaty that had been signed by Madrid and Lisbon in 1939, now pledging both governments to consult with the other in the face of any threat to their security or independence. Franco was willing to accept this understanding, at least for the moment, to the chagrin of Serrano.[28]

The meeting at Hendaye, however, was followed by Mussolini's invasion of Greece five days later, and, by analogy, raised the question of a direct Spanish takeover of Portugal. By December the general staff had prepared a memorandum titled "Study for Campaign Plan Number One" for the invasion of Portugal. Though Portuguese defenses were slight, this extensive document made it clear that any such operation would tax Spain's slender military resources to the utmost and that, should Britain respond vigorously, Spain would have to rely on German assistance.[29] It was all a moot point; by the time the plan was ready, it had become clear that Mussolini's invasion of Greece was a disaster, and the plan was filed away.

Meanwhile, soon after the signing of the final version of the protocol, Hitler became impatient and summoned Serrano Suñer to Berchtesgaden to set a date for Spain's entry into the war. He reiterated that economic and military needs would be met but said that it was impossible to arrange everything in advance and that German troops would soon be ready to enter Spain in order to seize Gibraltar. In Madrid, however, the extent of economic shortages and production shortfalls became ever more apparent, and Serrano replied politely but firmly that such disastrous conditions must first be remedied before Spain could enter, leaving things at an impasse.[30]

Franco agreed to further refueling of German submarines early in December, but in the meantime he was given further pause by a report on the strategic situation by Captain Luis Carrero Blanco, chief of naval operational planning, which Franco received from the naval minister Moreno on November 11.[31] It reinforced the point that, exactly as Franco had told Hitler, taking Gibraltar alone would not be decisive. The Royal Navy would still control the North Atlantic, permitting Britain to strangle Spain economically. Therefore Madrid dare not enter the war until the Axis had occupied the Suez Canal, turning the Mediterranean into an Axis lake. Even then, Carrero Blanco pointed out, if Spain entered the war, the Canaries would be completely open to the Royal Navy, which, as he put it, could blow the Spanish fleet out of the water, as the Americans had done in 1898.[32]

By December Hitler grew increasingly impatient and wanted the German assault force to enter Spain no later than January 10, 1941. He finally sent Admiral Wilhelm Canaris, principal "Hispanist" among top German officials, to insist on a concrete date from Franco. In the six weeks since Hendaye, the situation inside Spain had only worsened; it was so bad that the occasional individual could be found fainting from hunger on the streets of Madrid. Vital imports of food and fuel depended on passage through the British fleet, whose government could scarcely be challenged in such a situation, for Germany could not replace all these vital supplies. Moreover, it was clear that Hitler intended to send German army units directly into Spain for the Gibraltar assault. After Canaris arrived on the seventh, Franco, probably more at ease with the German admiral than with Hitler, took a firmer line. Under the present circumstances, Spain could not possibly defy Britain and initiate hostilities. Being able to enter the war would depend on building adequate reserves, but he could not say how long that would take. Telegraphed by Hitler to try again to get a firm date, Canaris replied on December 10 that he had done his best but that the real problem was that Franco would not enter the war so long as Britain was in a position to inflict great damage on Spain.[33] Hitler, increasingly preoccupied with other problems, then ordered that preparations for the Gibraltar operation cease for the time being.

Six weeks later, however, Berlin attempted to pressure Franco again. Stohrer met with him on January 20, 1941, and stressed to Franco that in Spain "everything was heading for a catastrophe that only Germany could prevent." He emphasized that if Spain waited until the war was almost over, it would be too late and of no use to Germany and pointed out that the Germans would do all the fighting in the Gibraltar operation, not grasping that this was a major negative for Franco. "Spain would hardly be called on to make any great sacrifices" and would receive major economic assistance.

Franco remained calm, reiterating his confidence in Germany's ultimate victory and his desire to enter the war as soon as circumstances permitted, protesting that "Spanish policy had undeviatingly followed a straight line." (From Franco's own point of view, this was undoubtedly so.) There followed the usual litany of problems and shortages. According to Stohrer, Franco emphasized that "it was not a question at all of whether Spain would enter the war; that had been decided at Hendaye. It was merely a question of when. . . . Supported by the Foreign Minister, Franco then protested sharply against the assumption that he had told Admiral Canaris he would enter the war only when England had already been laid low. Spain intended to participate in the war fully and not obtain anything as a gift." Stohrer retorted that as soon as Berlin knew that Spain was ready to enter, economic assistance would be immediately forthcoming. Franco and Serrano both then stated that this put a new construction on the matter that required further consideration. In a subsequent conversation, Serrano told Stohrer that he completely agreed with the German view, the only question being the exact timing of Spain's entry into the war.[34]

On January 21 Ribbentrop fired off an abrupt six-point communiqué to Stohrer, which he directed be read to Franco verbatim. It began by declaring that Franco could never have won the Civil War without German assistance and insisted that the time had come to act. He concluded, "The Führer

and the Reich government are deeply disturbed by the equivocal and vacil-
lating attitude of Spain," which made no sense, and that the country was
headed for "a catastrophe." If Franco did not enter the war immediately,
"the Reich government" could not but "foresee the end of Nationalist
Spain."[35]

When this was read to Franco, he replied that these communications
were extremely grave and contained untruths. Franco very heatedly asserted
that he had never vacillated and that because he was grateful for the help
rendered during the Civil War and because he was a man of honor, he had
taken care to ensure that his policy always unswervingly aligned with the
Axis. He had never lost sight of entry into the war. This entry would come
when economic weaknesses, which he elaborated on yet once more, had
been overcome. Serrano chimed in that he had made all this clear from the
beginning, so that Germany, by not responding thus far, was "coresponsible
for the fact that Spain was still so little ready for the war."[36]

This brought a curt reply from Ribbentrop on the twenty-fourth,
demanding that Franco immediately set a date, promising one hundred
thousand tons of grain as soon as he did so. Serrano answered a day later,
repeating all the standard arguments, which were in turn reiterated by
Franco when Stohrer next spoke with him on the twenty-seventh. "The
only noteworthy item in this recital was that the Generalissimo did emphasize much more strongly than hitherto that Spain would undoubtedly
enter the war, . . . which, he felt, would still last for many months." Ribbentrop shot back on the twenty-eighth in a tone of outrage, demanding that his
ambassador explain what was going on and why he was permitting Franco
and Serrano to turn the tables by blaming the situation on Germany.[37]

All this was infuriating to Berlin, but Hitler finally accepted the fact
that the date for a Gibraltar operation had slipped and would have to be
postponed indefinitely so as not to interfere with Germany's next military
initiatives in the east. Nonetheless, he decided not to give up altogether,
and on February 6 prepared the longest letter he ever sent to Franco. It
emphasized the ideological dimension of the war and that the future of the
Spanish regime depended on Nazi Germany. "Jewish-international democracy" would never forgive the fact that their systems were based on "national conditions and not on bases obligated to capitalism" (nach völkisch
bedingten und nicht kapitalistisch verpflichteten Grundsätze). He repeated
the offer of a hundred thousand tons of grain and other assistance and
promised that Spain's territorial ambitions would eventually be satisfied
"according to the way in which they are coordinated with, and to some

extent complemented, an acceptable new order of African colonies for Europe and its states." Hitler underlined quite a few phrases and added exclamation points for emphasis.[38]

In response, the caudillo told Stohrer that he was in full agreement with all of Hitler's fundamental ideas, remarking that "I identify myself completely with them," and that it was a misunderstanding to think that he intended to delay entry into the war until the next autumn or winter. Franco promised a complete reply after his upcoming meeting with Mussolini, which would take place in four days, and in the meantime he sent off to Berlin his longest list of needs yet, including, among other things, sixteen thousand boxcars of food and strategic necessities and an additional small navy—two cruisers, thirteen destroyers, and four submarines—to hold off the British.[39]

The only meeting between Franco and Mussolini then took place at Bordighera, on the Italian Riviera, on February 12, 1941. Six weeks earlier Hitler had written to the duce that Franco had "just committed the biggest mistake of his life," and now the führer was relying on the Italian dictator to convince him. Since Franco no longer traveled by air, he journeyed across southern France to Bordighera in an elaborate motorcade. There Mussolini rehearsed the standard arguments, but his entourage was unable to disguise the discouragement that was beginning to take hold of much of the Italian leadership after the debacle in Greece.

Franco gave Mussolini the same assurances he had provided Hitler. One Italian diplomat described his performance as "verbose, disorganized and losing itself in petty details or long digressions about military issues," all of which sounds like a typical Franco conversation. He claimed to be "more convinced" than the duce himself of final Axis victory and assured Mussolini that he did not want to delay Spain's entry until it was "too late." He lamented that shortages of every kind had made it impossible to expand the Spanish army much beyond three hundred thousand indifferently equipped troops, while Serrano observed that domestic conditions were so dire that if Spain were to enter the war at that moment, it would be more a liability than an asset to Germany, an assessment that was surely correct. Franco insisted that he still wanted to seize Gibraltar with Spanish forces (an ambition the Germans thought ridiculous, as indeed it probably was). He seems to have been pleased with the meeting, which put little pressure on him and confirmed his impression that Mussolini was truly a great man.[40] After receiving Mussolini's report, Hitler finally gave up for good, and his representatives made no more direct efforts to pressure Spain to enter into the war. Hitler's relations with Franco were notable primarily for the fact that he made no effort to deceive the caudillo directly, nor did he seriously consider using force against him, first because German arms were already heavily committed elsewhere and second because the Civil War, modest though it was as a military encounter, had given him the impression that the Spanish were hard nosed and difficult to deal with; they were "the only Latins," as he once put it, "willing to fight."

Later the German leaders would become convinced that the "Jesuitical" Serrano and the "Latin charlatan" Franco had deceived them all along, but the evidence supports Javier Tusell's conclusion that the Spanish leaders were basically honest in their dealings, telling Hitler and the German diplomats what they believed to be the truth about their situation. They were not feigning allegiance to the Axis cause but sincerely believed in it, and they were willing to enter the war, if only the proper conditions could be attained. As Juan Peche, Serrano's undersecretary in the Foreign Ministry, incisively put it, "We didn't get into the war not so much because Franco resisted German pressure as because Hitler didn't want it that badly," and, when he attempted to induce Franco, he could not offer enough to make it an attractive proposition.[41] Every indication was, however, that both Franco and Serrano were still hoping that these conditions would change during the course of 1941. They believed sincerely in the need for a "new order" in Europe, though their concept was that of a new kind of general balance in which Spain would become dominant in southwestern Europe, promoting the limited hegemony of a kind of Hispano-Catholic civilization, and Germany would be only the leader, not the total master.[42]

On his way back from Italy, Franco had a brief meeting with Marshal Pétain, the French chief of state, at Montpellier on February 13. He said nothing about Spanish ambitions in French Morocco but reassured Pétain that his policy was to avoid involvement in the war and intervene in Morocco only in the event that future developments there threatened Spain's vital interests. With the passing of weeks, he began to see the importance that a weakened Vichy France could have in a new power balance in the west Mediterranean and northwest Africa, possibly preventing complete German dominance. In April he sent General Francisco de Borbón as a personal emissary to the Vichy ambassador to feel out the French position further, since "greater French-Spanish understanding is desirable for our two countries."[43]

In fact, the Spanish regime was doing almost everything else that it could to be of service to Germany, short of entry into the war. Any Spanish government in power between 1940 and 1942 would have had to collaborate with Germany to some extent, as did democratic Switzerland and social democratic Sweden, but Franco's collaboration exceeded in degree and variety that of any government not engaged in the fighting. This included resupplying German submarines off and on for a year and a half, providing a small amount of Spanish shipping to supply German forces in North Africa (and, in the last part of the war, in western France), active collaboration with diverse aspects of German espionage and intelligence, and cooperation with the Nazi press and propaganda.[44]

What was the significance of such collaboration to the German war effort? With the exceptions of the resupply of submarines, the supply of German forces in the Mediterranean, and sabotage operations against Gibraltar, these activities were marginal. It did make a real contribution to these three areas, however, resulting in the sinking of a number of Allied ships and directly assisting German activity. The most important contribution, of course, was Spain's sending an entire reinforced infantry division, the Blue Division, plus a squadron of fighter pilots, to fight with the Reich against the Soviet Union on the eastern front.

Pressure from London and Washington to terminate such activities steadily increased. Moreover, at no time did Franco give the Germans any sort of blank check. They asked for much that he refused to give, beginning with entry into the war itself, and they would have liked to have greatly expanded the various kinds of collaboration that did take place, but the Spanish authorities always placed a cap on these activities. In some cases, technical collaboration was intended as a kind of compensation for the fact that Spain had not entered the war directly. Though collaboration had been greatly reduced by mid-1944, as a result of severe Allied pressure, collaboration did not end completely until the disappearance of the Reich itself. Economic collaboration was also extensive, though no more than in the cases of Switzerland and Sweden.[45]

The last moment of significant temptation for Franco occurred in April 1941, when Hitler scored another lightning victory in the Balkans, occupying all Yugoslavia and Greece within ten days. This coincided with the first spectacular triumphs of Rommel in Libya. At that point Serrano once more insisted to both Axis ambassadors that only entry into the war could solve Spain's internal problems, particularly its political disunity. The papal nuncio feared that Franco's government was about to take the plunge, and one indication that might be the case was the order given by the Naval Ministry on April 28 to captains of all Spanish merchant ships at sea, accompanied by instructions on their course of action should they suddenly learn that their country was at war. No documentation survives to verify just how close Franco might have been to such a decision, but the moment passed rapidly. During the three weeks that followed, Franco would have to face his first domestic political crisis since the European war began. Its outcome made the importance of immediate entry into the war recede, and the issue never regained the saliency it had previously held, though the general direction of Franco's policy would not change for some time.

Meanwhile, in the political background, the Monarchists were growing increasingly impatient, since Franco made no tangible gesture toward restoration. Alfonso XIII died in Rome in February 1941 and was succeeded by his son Don Juan, whom Franco had never permitted to volunteer for the Nationalist forces during the war, arguing convincingly that his life was too important and that he should not compromise his political future. After his father's death, he also endeavored for many months to play the "German card," looking for Hitler's political assistance in a Monarchist restoration. His representatives negotiated at various times with German diplomats and persistently sought the support of Spanish generals and sometimes even of Falangists.[46] For a while they even advanced the scheme that a restored Spanish monarchy would embrace Falangism and appoint a pro-German general as prime minister to bring Spain into the war.[47] Though that notion had disappeared by 1942, the Monarchist leaders had difficulty grasping that the führer regarded the "monarchist filth," as he privately termed it, with extreme loathing. Only at the end of 1942 did the Monarchists look more directly toward the Allies, when it became clear that they likely represented the winning side.

On April 22, 1941, Ambassador von Stohrer dispatched a long report to Berlin, observing that Spain suffered from disastrous leadership, profound internal division, and near-famine conditions, with Franco increasingly isolated. He judged that the leftist opposition was growing stronger (which was doubtful). "Foreign Minister Serrano saw clearest of all," he commented. "He recommended Spain's immediate entry into war," but Franco would not agree. The military detested the arrogant and overweening Serrano, and so the German ambassador concluded that "a coup d'état in the form of an ultimatum to Franco is possible at any time." Even General Aranda (secretly on the British payroll), "the most politically active of the generals, declared to the [German] Military Attaché that Spain certainly had to take part in the war," while the Monarchists "are endeavoring to win our interest.[48] Don Juan is said to have promised in Berlin to adopt a thoroughly pro-German policy."[49]

The British and American ambassadors' remarks about Spain were equally scathing, though they were slightly more sanguine about the issue of war entry. Despite the reliance of the Spanish economy on overseas imports, relations with London and Washington deteriorated, and Churchill's government developed a contingency plan to occupy the Canaries, if worse came to worst.[50]

Military criticism of internal policy was much more intense during the early 1940s than in any other period of the regime. The generals denounced corruption, the chaos of the burgeoning bureaucracy, the manifold shortages and, most of all, the influence and pretensions of the Falangists, whom they saw as irrational, incompetent, and corrupt, seeking to usurp the role of the military. The personification of this antagonism was the vain and presumptuous Serrano Suñer, the *cuñadísimo*, the generals' enemy number one.

On May 2, 1941, Serrano delivered an unusually aggressive speech that demanded power for the Falange, but Franco was not willing to grant it. He had begun to have second thoughts about his ambitious brother-in-law.[51] Instead of turning toward the Falangists, he appointed the conservative (and very anti-Falangist) Colonel Valentín Galarza to Serrano's former post of minister of the interior (which had been in the hands of its undersecretary the past seven months). This outraged the Falangists and prompted Serrano to remark once more to the Axis ambassadors that only a decision for war would shake things up enough to give power to the FET. On May 5 ten provincial party chiefs resigned in protest. This demonstrated that Serrano and other figures on whom Franco had been depending could not hold the party in line. It created a major internal crisis that he did not fully resolve for two and a half weeks.

The caudillo moved slowly and carefully, as was his wont. He was determined to keep the "Fascist card" in play, but he needed to control it better and so eventually appointed three new Falangists to top posts, each of them a Franco loyalist who could be counted on not to generate dissent. José Luis de Arrese was named secretary-general of the party and would prove a most effective person for that office. He began immediately to build a rival polarity to that of Serrano within the party. Galarza's former post of undersecretary of the presidency, or chief assistant to Franco, was filled by the naval captain Luis Carrero Blanco, who became Franco's right-hand man and would soon begin to have the kind of influence Serrano had. The former Falangist militia leader José Antonio Girón became minister of labor, and the pliable Miguel Primo de Rivera (José Antonio's younger brother), who had just resigned as party boss of Madrid, allowed himself to be kicked upstairs to the post of minister of agriculture, where he would not be causing any trouble, though he would prove of scant benefit to agriculture.[52]

Over the next several years the short, muscular, and astute Arrese would complete the task of domesticating and bureaucratizing the Falange. The most radical leader in the party was the syndical boss, Gerardo Salvador Merino, who, a victim, above all, of the enmity of the military, was arrested, tried, and expelled later that summer for his earlier Masonic affiliation. During this period FET membership reached its peak of nearly a million, but in November Arrese announced the only official purge in the party's history, to eliminate crypto-leftists, ex-Freemasons, and others accused of "immoral activities" or of being "incompatible." Only about six thousand were thrown out in this mild purge, and none of these, so far as is known, was arrested, but it sufficed to get everyone's attention and begin to tighten things up. Henceforth the party's role would be increasingly restricted to cheerleading and organizing public demonstrations on behalf of Franco.[53] This would be ably abetted by Girón as the minister of labor, as he began to develop the first phase of what would later become the Spanish welfare state.

None of the new appointments was more important than that of Carrero Blanco, who would become the caudillo's closest and most devoted collaborator for many years, until his assassination in December 1973. A career officer, the scholarly Carrero had been a professor in the naval war college. Gaining asylum in the Mexican embassy, he escaped the bloody Republican purge of naval officers in the Civil War. This experience only strengthened his strongly right-wing principles. Carrero made his way to the Nationalist zone, subsequently commanding for Franco first a destroyer, then a submarine. He then became chief of operations on the naval general staff, catching Franco's attention with his strategic evaluations of the war. He also found time to publish a general naval history, *España en el mar*, at the beginning of 1941.

In this highly devout, beetle-browed naval officer, Franco found an ideal assistant and a loyal and insightful counselor, a person who was much closer to his own style and values than Serrano and with whom he soon found himself more comfortable. The legend that Carrero had no ideas of his own, which developed in later years, was exaggerated, but he never sought the limelight, and his own ideas aligned more closely with those of Franco than did Serrano's. He was always careful to follow Franco's wishes while discreetly adding his own advice. Though the two never became close personal friends, Carrero understood Franco's thinking better than did anyone else, and their symbiotic relationship was remarkable. Carrero Blanco would eventually become the nearest thing to a political alter ego of Franco. He was only moderately Monarchist and cautiously pro-German, but he was also a devout practicing Catholic who was clear about what he called "Nazi paganism." Though for some time he tended to favor the idea of eventually entering the war, he saw it as a still-distant undertaking that had to be carefully planned.

Most of these matters, however, did not become very clear in the immediate aftermath of the May crisis, so that some, including the spokesmen of the German embassy, at first interpreted the outcome as a victory for Serrano and the Falange. Thus early in June Mussolini sent a letter to Franco urging that he make public his secret adherence to the Tripartite Pact (the defensive alliance of Germany, Italy, and Japan), to which he replied with the usual excuses. Serrano hoped that the new political balance was no worse than a draw, for in the settlement Franco had split off press control and censorship from the Ministry of the Interior to place it under a new Falangist vice secretary of national culture. It was some time before Serrano realized the extent to which his own power had been reduced.

Through all these maneuverings Varela kept the army firmly loyal to the caudillo. As a result, none of the murky scheming of German diplomats, Nazi Party representatives, or SS intelligence operatives with individual commanders during the next two years would come to much.[54] During his first year as army minister Varela had carried out a postwar reorganization that tightened up the officer corps considerably, expelling a number of junior and middle-rank officers of uncertain political background, including some who had fought on the Nationalist side. A paradox of Spanish affairs during World War II was that in some respects the army deteriorated as a military institution. Parts and supplies were not available to maintain all the weaponry, heterogenous in the extreme, that had existed in 1939, and few new sources were available, save for simple equipment. Thus most of the planned expansion remained on paper, and though the permanent incorporation of several thousand *alféreces provisionales* from the Civil War provided junior officers with combat experience, they were also deficient in technical training. They were, however, strongly Francoist, and increased the political reliability of the army. Nonetheless, a common catchphrase of the early attempt at militarization—"la vida es milicia" ("life is military")—could not be translated into practice, and if at any point in World War II the Spanish military had been pitted against any of the powers in the conflict, it would have found itself in dreadful circumstances.[55]

News of Germany's invasion of the Soviet Union on June 22, 1941, was greeted with enormous enthusiasm in Spanish circles, which still saw the country as enemy number one. Conversion of Hitler's conflict into an anti-Communist war, trumpeted as a struggle on behalf of "European civilization," gave it greater meaning and coherence in Spain than at any previous time. When the cabinet met on the following day, Serrano proposed that it organize a contingent of Spanish volunteers to fight beside the Wehrmacht on the Russian front, where hopefully they could soon participate in the final overthrow of Communism.

He was immediately challenged by Varela, who was simultaneously pro-Carlist, anti-Falangist, anti-German, and anti-Nazi, but also one of Franco's better friends in the military hierarchy. He had opposed Serrano's second trip to Germany the preceding November and now opposed sending Spaniards to the eastern front. Varela and Galarza argued that, however desirable the destruction of the Soviet Union, the war had become more complicated and Germany had placed itself in a weaker strategic position, which might have negative implications for Spain.

Franco nonetheless approved the formation of a contingent of volunteers that would symbolize Spain's solidarity in the struggle against the common enemy of the human race, as it was usually put. Varela and his colleagues insisted that all officers be professionals, while the great majority of the volunteers were Falangists—indeed, there were so many at first that not all those who met requirements could be accepted. A total of eighteen thousand were soon organized in the oversized unit that would be called the Blue Division (from the color of the Falangist party shirt), eventually the most celebrated division of any army in all of World War II.[56] Its dispatch marked the zenith of Spanish collaboration with the Third Reich, for no other neutral or nonbelligerent country sent an entire division of troops to fight on a major front. A total of thirty-eight divisions of foreign troops fought in the Waffen SS, but these troops volunteered on their own; they were not dispatched as a division by their home government.[57]

Rafael Ibáñez Hernández has synthesized the principal motivations behind Spain's decision to send a division: (1) German pressure on the regime since mid-summer 1940, (2) the need to repay the blood shed by the Third Reich on behalf of the Nationalists in the Civil War, (3) the desire to mitigate resentment against Spain's delay in entering the war, and (4) the hope that Germany might achieve a quick victory and that Spain might thus share in the spoils.[58] To this might be added the desire to exact vengeance for the Soviet intervention in Spain and help to destroy Communism.

Once more Franco's government had identified its own struggle in the Civil War with Germany's aggressions. Its official communiqué on the twenty-fourth declared that "God has opened the eyes of statesmen in time, and for the past forty-eight hours struggle has been waged against the beast of the apocalypse in the most colossal conflict known to history, to destroy the most savage oppression of all time." It stressed that the first blow in this struggle had been delivered in the Civil War by "the glorious soldiers of Spain, under the command of their glorious and ever-victorious Caudillo, who led the world's first crusade against the Comintern and its diabolical machinations."[59]

The enthusiasm lasted for months, and for some time Franco fully shared it, though eventually he would entertain second thoughts. On the one hand, he saw clearly that present circumstances were too complex and dangerous for Spain to enter the war directly, but there is no doubt that the invasion of the Soviet Union gave him great satisfaction and further stimulated his identification with Hitler's cause. On July 17, fifth anniversary of the insurrection, he delivered the most pro-German speech of the war before the National Council of the FET. It condemned the "eternal enemies" of Spain, clearly alluding to Britain, France, and the United States, who persisted in "intrigues and actions" against her. Franco boasted that "in our fields were waged and won the first battles" of the present conflict, insisting that "not even the American continent can dream of intervening in Europe without exposing itself to a catastrophe. . . . In this situation, to say that the outcome of the war can be modified by the entry of a third power is criminal madness. . . . The issues of the war have been falsely presented and the Allies have lost it." He finished by praising Germany for waging "the battle that Europe and Christianity have long hoped for, and in which the blood of our youth will be united with that of our Axis comrades, as a living expression of solidarity."[60]

Even the Axis ambassadors commented on how imprudent the speech was. Stohrer reported that "it suddenly opened the eyes of the English and the Americans about the position of Spain."[61] In London, the British government took note. The four-month period from mid-April to mid-August 1941 was the second time in the war that it prepared strong potential countermeasures for use against Spain. A British contingency plan to seize the Canaries reached the operational stage, momentarily stimulated by interest in building a defensive position on Spanish territory outside Gibraltar, to defend the straits. Leaders in Madrid were particularly worried about a British landing in the Azores, and Serrano announced that the Spanish government would consider this an act of war. British preparations for the Canaries were only deactivated in mid-August after the embassy in Madrid managed to convince London that at the present time there was little danger that Spain would enter the war.

Internal political dissension continued, and a number of the generals privately criticized the excesses in Franco's speech of July 17. Varela was the top commander most opposed to the Third Reich, though he was evidently not on the list of those being bribed by the British. Stohrer observed to Berlin: "Varela, as reported at various times, is probably the only important Spanish general who is considered to be our enemy; he leans strongly toward England, and holds the opinion that the war will not be won by us. Varela is on the point of marrying into a rich Bilbao family that is strongly Anglophile." He lamented that "Franco thinks a great deal of Varela," which was correct, though he was wrong that Varela was the only general of such views.[62] Moreover, Franco would not tolerate any of his commanders taking the initiative in playing up to the Germans. In December, the captain-general of Burgos, José López Pintos, made the mistake of inviting several Germans across the border to San Sebastián, where they socialized with Spanish officers and shouted "Viva Hitler!" As soon as he learned of this, Franco abruptly cashiered the elderly general, who would die in obscurity of natural causes two months later.

The last months of 1941 were the quietest period for Franco's foreign policy since the beginning of the European war. So long as Hitler's attention remained fixed on the east, there was little pressure for Spain to enter the war, while the country's extreme penury forced Franco to reach better terms with London and Washington. This was a difficult proposition, for Serrano was deeply anti-American. Claiming to have been offended by a discussion in April when U. S. ambassador Alexander Weddell had waved in his face a postcard of Weddell's that had been read and stamped by German intelligence, Serrano had broken off relations with the ambassador and blocked access to Franco. After Franco's outburst of July 17, Serrano had followed up by declaring to the Political Council of the FET, of which he was president, that the United States would soon be finished as a power: "North American intervention in the conflict would bring the ruin of

America and of the world. Once Russia is conquered, Europe will be self-sufficient, and European autarchy will provoke the downfall of the North American economy. That will produce social revolution, whose consequences would have an incalculable effect on the United States, since the democratic system is today on the road to collapse, and that nation, rich and materialistic, lacks the sense of unity and sacrifice that inspires poor countries."[63]

By September, however, Franco and Serrano had found that they had backed themselves into an ever-narrowing corner. American imports had become indispensable, and therefore Juan Francisco de Cárdenas, the regime's competent ambassador in Washington, was called home to help to straighten things out. Before leaving the American capital, he called on Secretary of State Cordell Hull, who gave Spanish undiplomatic behavior a severe dressing-down. As Hull recorded,

> I then proceeded to say that while it was most disagreeable even to recall our experiences in dealing with the Spanish Government, I must state that in all of the relations of this Government with the most backward and ignorant governments in the world, this Government has not experienced such a lack of ordinary courtesy or consideration, which customarily prevails between friendly nations, as it has at the hands of the Spanish Government. Its course has been one of aggravated discourtesy and contempt in the very face of our offers to be of aid. I said, of course, we could not think of embarrassing, not to say humiliating, ourselves by further approaches of this nature, bearing in mind the coarse and extremely offensive methods and conduct of Suñer in particular and in some instances of General Franco. I said that when I thought back about the details of the conduct of the Spanish Government towards this Government what had happened was really inconceivable.[64]

On his return to Madrid, Cárdenas managed to mediate successfully and relations with the United States improved somewhat, increasing the flow of goods. Moreover, with German forces concentrated in the east, all southwest Europe and North Africa was more exposed to the British and perhaps ultimately to the Gaullists and the Americans. Thus by mid-1941 Spanish alignment with the Axis had reached its highest point, which also became a kind of strategic ceiling that slowly, by degrees, would have to be lowered.

During these months Franco devoted more than a little time to writing (more probably, dictating) a sort of brief novel, developed into a script for the new feature film, *Raza*, directed by the well-known filmmaker José Luis Sáenz de Heredia (a cousin of José Antonio Primo de Rivera), which would premiere early in 1942. Franco had a lifelong interest in movies, having himself acted in an amateur film of the late 1920s. He endeavored to stimulate the country's cinematic industry, despite limited resources, and was particularly interested in communicating his fundamental values to the Spanish public through the medium of a historical melodrama. Under the pseudonym Jaime de Andrade (Andrade being the most aristocratic of his family names) and possibly with the help of a ghost writer, he wrote a story that featured a model family with the name of Churruca, fictional descendants of the naval hero of Trafálgar. At the height of the short-lived aspiration to empire, it presented the caudillo's own concept of family devotion and dedication to the struggles of the patria.[65]

In the drama of a naval family in El Ferrol, this story offered an idealized version of what Franco might have wished to have been his own family history. Instead of the upper-middle-class townhouse in which the Francos had lived, the Churrucas seemed to inhabit a virtual castle as though they were a major aristocratic family. The film portrayed a pious and dedicated mother raising three sons and a daughter, as had Franco's own mother, Doña Pilar. The father, however, was entirely different from Franco's own profligate forebear. In the place of the unheroic desk officer was projected the ideal military father Franco would have wished for, who died a martyr to the patria, going down with his ship in heroic battle against superior odds. This was entirely different from the landlocked career of bureaucratic tedium that had filled nearly all the long life of the elder Franco, who was, as it turned out, in his final year as this film was being developed. It is doubtful that he ever saw *Raza*, which came out just two months before his death. Altogether, the Churrucas were projected as a family fully incarnating the values and virtues of the *raza* (lit. "race"), which in Spanish refers not to a biological entity so much as to a cultural and ethnic group of the sort considered by Franco to be true Spaniards. As the text was worked into a script and then prepared as a film in the last part of 1941, Franco probably did not realize that he would never again lead the Spanish in a struggle that would put such heroic virtues to the ultimate test.

The war, meanwhile, reached a crucial inflection point in December 1941, with the German retreat from Moscow, the Japanese attack on Pearl Harbor, and the declarations of war by Hitler and Mussolini on the United States. The conflicts in Asia and Europe had been joined, and the Second World War had finally taken full shape. Hitler quickly drew up a new

Tripartite Pact with Japan and Italy, which this time took the form of a direct military alliance of the three powers against Britain and the United States (though not against the Soviet Union).[66] The old agreement that Franco had secretly been party to had become a dead letter, and hence there would be no question of entering a war against the United States, regarding whom the Spanish leaders had just had to reverse course to avoid economic catastrophe. The bravado and prophecies of Franco and Serrano in the preceding summer were soon to be shattered, and the possibility of Spain's entry into the war receded further.

12 | Surviving World War II

(1941–1945)

A t first there was limited reaction in Madrid to the war's expansion, for most Spanish leaders shared the perception in Berlin and Rome that the entry of the United States would not greatly affect events in Europe. On December 19 the *Boletín Oficial del Estado* announced that the policy of the Spanish government remained unchanged, something that Franco and Serrano Suñer personally reiterated to Axis diplomats.

The most reasoned evaluation was articulated in a memorandum that Carrero Blanco presented to Franco. The war, he concluded, had become a struggle between "the power of evil embodied in the Anglo-Saxon-Soviet coalition directed by the Jews" and a German-Japanese alliance that, though powerful, was certainly not guided by the principles of Catholic Christianity. This created a war of "a duration difficult to determine, but certainly lengthy." To join an alliance dominated by the Jews was totally inappropriate, so that the only option was Germany, however disagreeable its paganism.[1]

Franco nonetheless had second thoughts about the Blue Division, deadlocked on the eastern front in the Soviet winter. He requested that it be withdrawn temporarily for rest and refitting, since it had suffered numerous casualties, but the German government replied that it could not afford to and that reinforcements could be added at the front. Franco had begun to draw back, and he did not attend the big celebration in Madrid's Retiro Park when the first contingent of veterans returned. He also wanted to replace the division's commander, Muñoz Grandes, who had gained the personal esteem of Hitler. Franco thought it prudent to send a non-Falangist replacement, General Emilio Estaban Infantes, but for the time being Hitler would not release Muñoz Grandes.

In April 1942 a new American ambassador, Carlton J. H. Hayes, arrived in Madrid. Hayes was not a career diplomat but a distinguished university professor and the leading American expert on the history of modern European nationalism. The mission of his predecessor had been a failure because of disastrous personal relations, and President Roosevelt himself selected Hayes, a liberal democrat in politics but a Catholic convert, as someone likely to be able to deal successfully with Franco. Indeed this proved to be the case, as the two developed mutual respect. Hayes wrote of his first meeting with the Spanish dictator: "The General, I soon perceived, differed notably from the caricatures of him current in the 'leftist' press in the United States. Physically he was not so short nor so stout and he did not 'strut.' Mentally he impressed me as being not at all a stupid or 'me too' sort of person, but distinctly alert and possessing a good deal of both determination and caution and a rather lively and spontaneous sense of humor. He laughed easily and naturally, which, I imagine, a Hitler couldn't do and a Mussolini wouldn't do except in private."[2] During the next two and a half years, Hayes would be required to impose an increasingly harsh American line, as fortunes in the war favored the Allies more and more, but he did so with tact and discretion and managed to retain the respect of Franco, who had the ambassador's portrait painted by his favorite artist, Ignacio Zuloaga, shortly before Hayes's departure.[3]

As the war expanded and domestic problems became more acute, the Monarchist elites grew more active. During 1940–41 they sought to play the German card on behalf of a restoration, which they continued to do during the first part of 1942 before beginning to turn toward the British.[4] In Spain, their cause depended ultimately on the will of Franco and, secondarily, on that of a group of self-professed Monarchist generals, all of whom, however, remained cautious. Such different figures as Yagüe, still without assignment, and Juan Vigón, his replacement as air force minister, toyed with the idea of a "Falangist monarchy" backed by Hitler as the remedy for the country's political divisions.[5] Franco knew about these murmurings and on June 4 suddenly canceled a trip to Germany by Vigón, though Vigón retained his ministry. As a Falangist, Muñoz Grandes rejected the monarchy, though he told the Germans that Don Juan had been dangling a promise of Spain's entry into the war in return for support for restoration by the military and the Germans. The Monarchists, however, still did not understand that Hitler would have nothing to do with them, and all their maneuverings came to naught.

Franco was momentarily distracted by the death in February in Madrid of his eighty-five-year-old father. After the death of his ex-wife, the elder Franco and his new companion, Agustina Aldana, spent summers at El Ferrol in the old family home, which had remained his personal property. Surprised there by the outbreak of the Civil War, they had passed the entire wartime in Galicia, within the Nationalist zone. The death of Ramón, in some respects his favorite son, depressed Don Nicolás considerably. He and Agustina had returned to their apartment in Madrid at the end of the war. It has been said that Franco made an effort to achieve reconciliation, though on his own terms, which required that the elder Franco abandon his second wife and take up a respectable and decorous position as father of the chief of state. His father refused outright.

He rejected his son's regime, which he called "Fascism," was incensed at the public emphasis on Catholicism, and missed various of his leftist friends who had perished in the repression. Don Nicolás detested Hitler, whom he called a tyrant bent on enslaving and destroying Europe. According to his granddaughter Pilar Jaráiz, he termed his son Paco "un inepto," saying the idea that he was a great leader was simply laughable. He also spoke up for Jews and Masons, declaring that in fact his son knew nothing at all about the latter, many of whom he called "illustrious and honorable men, certainly very superior to him in knowledge and openness of spirit."[6] He claimed that everything would have worked out much better if Paco had shown more interest in women when he was young.

During his last three years, Don Nicolás's health began to fail, as arteriosclerosis advanced. After he lost much of his savings at the hands of a pickpocket, he protested so noisily that Franco heard of it, who ordered that in the future an official car and driver be placed at his father's disposal. Though Franco would never have anything to do with her, on February 23, 1942, Agustina sent word to El Pardo that his father was on his deathbed.

Franco's main concern seems to have been that his father reconcile with the Church and not die in concubinage. He refused to visit his father but called his sister, Pilar, instead, dispatching her, together with a priest, to the apartment. The elder Franco refused to confess or reconcile, however, and died about dawn the following morning. Pilar Franco followed her brother's instructions to have their father's corpse dressed in the uniform of a vice admiral, his final naval rank, after which last rites were performed at the chapel in El Pardo, with only the Francos attending. The remains of Don Nicolás were then buried beside those of his former wife in the Franco family section at La Almudena cemetery. A company of naval infantry was present to honor him at his interment, but none of the family attended. Agustina survived her companion by many years, completely ostracized by the Francos. Henceforth references by the caudillo to his father would be extremely rare, though always expressed in terms of respect. He probably experienced some relief at his father's passing.[7]

A few months later, in July 1942, Franco took another step in the long, slow process of institutional development of his regime by promulgating the second of what would be called the Fundamental Laws of the Realm (Leyes Fundamentales del Reino): the Constitutive Law of the Cortes, a sort of corporative parliament, roughly modeled on Mussolini's Chamber of Fasces and Corporations. The task of drawing up the guidelines was given, significantly, not to Serrano but to the pliant Arrese, and in his speech on the eighteenth of July Franco was much more moderate than the year before, avoiding direct mention of either Germany or Italy.

The regime's second political crisis suddenly erupted in August, when, on the sixteenth, Carlists celebrated a memorial mass in the basilica of Begoña in Bilbao in honor of their fallen in the Civil War.[8] The two highest-ranking Carlists in the government, Varela and Antonio Iturmendi, minister of justice, attended. As they were leaving the ceremony, a small group of Falangists outside tossed two hand grenades, one of which exploded, causing numerous injuries, of which, according to the Carlists, two people later died. Varela was not injured but, spurred on by the anti-Falangist interior minister, Galarza, and other army leaders, he charged that this had constituted a deliberate Falangist attack on the army and on himself, an assassination attempt. He dispatched telegrams to all the district captain-generals and lodged a vigorous protest with Franco, seconded by Galarza. Six Falangists were arrested and tried by military tribunals. Franco was told by Falangists, however, that those arrested had been trying to break up a subversive meeting. He talked with Varela on the twenty-fourth by telephone from his summer home, the Pazo de Meirás. Varela insisted there was nothing subversive about the mass and that the Falangists had been guilty of unprovoked aggression. Since transcripts of the caudillo's personal conversations with his generals and ministers are extremely rare, part of the exchange is worth quoting. Franco began by declaring that he had heard that some of the Carlists had uttered "subversive slogans":

v: Then "Viva España" is subversive.

f: No, "Viva España," no.

v: No, my General, but I say that all by itself, while you have ceased to do so.

f: Because I say "Arriba España," but there is no incompatibility between these two slogans, except that "Arriba" is more dynamic, a slogan envied by foreigners, while "Viva España" is decadent.

v: A slogan for which there have died all those who saved you and Spain and with which this movement was begun.

f: Yes, but a slogan under which many thousands of kilometers were lost for Spain and our empire.

   [. . .]

v: Well, if that is to be prohibited have the courage to issue an order and declare it a crime.

   [. . .]

v: (With great indignation and energy) Look, my General, I see what you're thinking and they have deceived you yet again, like they always do, my General. They've also told you that people shouted "Death to Franco," and that is not true. . . . But I see what you're thinking, my General. . . . I've listened to all your recent speeches and you haven't had a single word of consolation for these poor victims, all of them working-class, and some severely injured and likely to die, among them a mother of twelve children and a soldier who was there to worship the Virgin and who will lose a leg, but no one has said anything on behalf of them nor condemned the criminal assassins, while you on the contrary have abused them by talking of political postures and factions. And this is not just, my General, this is not an adequate response, only to talk in the name of a revolution that you proclaim.

Franco insisted that Basque nationalists disguised themselves as Carlists, but Varela denied that any such people were involved and said that the military trial was going forward. Only an old military comrade could have talked to him with such frankness. Franco, who disliked arguments, finally accepted Varela's interpretation of events and terminated the conversation, simply instructing that "everything be done with the greatest equity possible."[9] The Falangist who had thrown the grenade was condemned to death and executed, despite the fact that on the same day, at the urging of Falangists, Hitler awarded him a medal for his efforts on behalf of Germany and the Blue Division.[10]

The exact background to and motivation for this incident will probably never be clarified. When Varela met with Franco on September 2, he apparently demanded that some sort of political action, as well, be taken with regard to the Falange, and when he found Franco was not forthcoming, he presented his resignation.[11] Varela was the third of his ministers to resign, but Franco never lost his old sense of comradeship and continued to hold him in esteem. Franco also decided that he would have to dismiss Galarza because of the extreme hostility between the interior minister and the Falangists, which had been significantly exacerbated by the denunciations he had sent out on his own initiative.

When he conveyed these personnel changes to Carrero Blanco on the following day, his undersecretary pointed out that the military would be very unhappy to see two army ministers leaving without any equivalent disciplining of the Falangists. Carrero, who apparently had been conspiring with Arrese for several months to get rid of Serrano, pointed out that if Varela and Galarza were no longer a part of the government but Serrano remained, the military and other anti-Falangists would say that Serrano and the Falangists had won a complete victory and that it was Serrano, not the caudillo, who actually ran the government.

Franco needed little prompting, because relations between the brothers-in-law had been deteriorating for some time. Political commentators had been observing for nearly a year that Serrano's star was waning. His pretensions and criticisms had become more grating to Franco, while tension had developed within the family as well that began to drive apart Doña Carmen and her sister Zita, married to Serrano.[12] To make matters worse, Serrano had just fathered an illegitimate child with the aristocratic wife of a cavalry officer, and Doña Carmen criticized Serrano bitterly. For a variety of reasons, Franco was fed up, and in fact the end of this close political association was also accompanied by a growing distance between the two families.

The result was a new realignment of ministers that in some respects went farther than the one sixteen months earlier. Franco decided to replace

Serrano with General Francisco Gómez-Jordana Souza, his former foreign minister and vice president. The new minister of the interior was Blas Pérez González, an army juridical officer and university professor who was a "pure Francoist" and would remain in the government as long as Arrese and Girón. The worst problem was replacing Varela, since nearly all the military hierarchy supported him. Franco finally had to turn to a major general, Carlos Asensio, a likeable person who was normally easy to deal with. In the face of Asensio's reluctance (if Serrano is to be believed), Franco spat out in frustration, "What do you want? For me to be carried out of here one day feet first?"[13] Carrero suggested that Franco simply hand him the assignment as a military order, which Franco did, and Asensio accepted. The result of these changes, however, was to reduce internal conflict in the government and strengthen Franco's authority, giving him the most harmonious set of ministers that he had had. None of the regime's internal factions felt completely satisfied, but in general the army had gained more than the Falangists and, though Franco did not entirely understand it at that time, this would soon be important for the future of his regime.

The most important consequence was the return of Jordana to the Foreign Ministry. At that time, Franco had no intention of changing Spain's policy toward the Axis and he considered several other names, but the diminutive and eminently sensible Jordana, with his combination of honesty, experience, and ability, seemed the best alternative. Jordana was known for his carefulness and discretion, while Asensio, unlike Varela, was pro-German. Franco therefore used the contacts of Arrese and the FET with the German embassy to reassure the Germans that the changes meant no alteration of Spain's foreign policy, though in fact that would not exactly prove to be the case.

Hitler detested the "Jesuitical Serrano," as he called him, but he disapproved of the change, perceiving, correctly, that it would not benefit Germany. He had kept Muñoz Grandes in command of the Blue Division so that the Spanish general could participate in the final assault on Leningrad in September and gain the laurels of victory. The idea was that this would give him such prestige that he could, on returning to Spain, alter the country's foreign policy, but the offensive never took place, since the Soviets seized the initiative in August. Meanwhile, Muñoz Grandes also tried to wring more colonial concessions from Hitler, even if no more than, as he put it somewhat obliquely, "a word."[14]

He insisted to the führer that the dismissal of Serrano was a step forward that probably foreshadowed Franco's entry into the war. That was completely mistaken, but, in accord with this vision, Muñoz Grandes proposed to return to Spain to help prepare public opinion. He assured Hitler that if the führer were to recognize Spain's colonial demands and then ordered German troops into the country for its defense, they would be welcomed as comrades and Franco would have to declare war on the Allies, supported by anti-American opinion in Latin America. Whatever he might have wished, Hitler had no such troops available, and on September 8 he dismissed Muñoz Grandes's ideas as "fantasies," as indeed they were.[15]

Between 1940 and 1943 German diplomats and intelligence agents conducted a lengthy series of conversations tinged by intrigue with leaders of the FET and with high-ranking generals (some of whom were also on the British payroll). This was fairly standard activity for representatives of the Reich and at no time amounted to anything that could concretely be called a conspiracy. Nor did it respond to any specific initiative of Hitler or Ribbentrop, because whenever the German representatives asked Berlin whether they should directly promote a change of government in Madrid, the answer was always the same: Germany did not seek to interfere in Spain's domestic affairs, and relations would be restricted to official channels.

The other foreign representatives active in internal political conversations were the British, primarily with top generals. Their most frequent interlocutor was the elaborately suborned General Antonio Aranda, head of the army war college. The principal political gadfly among the senior military, Aranda talked in 1942 of a shadowy junta of generals, ready to depose Franco. (His conversational imagination knew no bounds, and later, in 1946, he proposed that he take up asylum in the American embassy, from which sanctuary he might lead an anti-Franco opposition government.) There was, however, no junta of generals, for, as Javier Tusell has written, the generals who murmured against Franco "did not conspire, but merely talked about conspiring."[16] Nor were the British very much fooled by them. Finally judging Aranda incorrigible, Franco fired him as director of the war college on November 30, leaving him without assignment and replacing him with Kindelán, who was thereby deprived of command of troops.

The main force for change in Spanish policy was the new minister of foreign affairs, Lieutenant General Francisco Gómez-Jordana Souza. Though a tiny man scarcely five feet tall, at sixty-six, Jordana remained trim and energetic. He had twice been high commissioner of Spanish Morocco under the monarchy, which earned him the title Conde de Jordana. He was notable for good judgment, responsibility, and administrative efficiency. Jordana had observed the foreign policy of his predecessor with increasing apprehension, though without public comment. He had not participated in the fascistization of the regime, yet neither had he overtly opposed it, so that he had no political profile other than that of a conservative Francoist general when he returned to the Foreign Ministry. In private, however, his views were firm and clear. He had written in his personal diary that out-break of war in Europe had stemmed from the "measureless ambition" of Hitler, adding the fervent wish that "God help Spain and protect her from getting into this conflict, which would be a catastrophe for us."[17]

Spanish policy had in fact already become increasingly moderate during 1942, despite the fact that Franco had a contingency plan drawn up to occupy the southwesternmost corner of France, should the Vichy regime be taken over by Hitler, or collapse. There was no indication, nonetheless, that Franco had any particular change in policy in mind when he selected Jordana but instead simply relied on the new minister to be trustworthy and discreet. He had no idea that Jordana wished to end nonbelligerence and return Spain to neutrality. Jordana was not an Anglophile but he had come to the conclusion that the Allies would probably win the war and that Spain's policy must be realigned. He became, after Franco, the second most important person in Spanish government during World War II. Personally loyal, he understood that he could never challenge Franco directly, and at the same time, unlike Serrano, he had too much personal integrity to criticize him in conversation with foreign diplomats. All the while, he was determined to implement a more constructive policy, working with diligence and discretion to influence Franco, several times to the point of offering his resignation.

At the end of September, when Myron Taylor, United States representative to the Vatican, stopped in Madrid, Franco invited him to El Pardo. The caudillo asked him to explain to President Roosevelt his personal theory of "three wars" under way, something that he had already mentioned to several diplomats. The Second World War, according to Franco, was composed of three different conflicts. In the Pacific war between the United States and Japan, Spain was completely neutral. Though his government had agreed to represent Japanese interests in Latin America, it had taken other steps to distance itself from Tokyo. In the West European conflict between the "haves" of Britain and France and the "have-nots" of Germany and Italy, Spain did not formally take sides but did expect to receive the territories due to it in any reassignment of colonial possessions, an idea

that Franco refused to give up. In the struggle between Christian civilization and "barbarous and oriental" Communism, Spain was a belligerent,
though not officially in a state of war. Franco perceived that the period of
American defeats had ended and worried that American participation in
the European war might impact the third conflict and allow Communism
to triumph. He seemed to imply that the Western Allies should sign a
separate peace so that Hitler could destroy the Soviet Union, the outcome
he preferred. Franco even suggested that it was appropriate that Germany's
frontiers extend eastward to the Volga and that it dominate most of Central
Europe, although he did concede that the countries that would come under
its hegemony should retain a certain amount of autonomy.[18]

As the autumn drew on, Jordana became increasingly anxious that the
first major Anglo-American military initiative might take place in North
Africa or the Mediterranean. On November 4 he warned the council of
ministers that the Allied second front might be opened at any time and
would probably affect Spain or its possessions. A strong campaign against
the Franco regime was being waged in the American press, calling for the
rupture of relations and producing rumors that the Allies were preparing
an army of Spanish Republican refugees to invade the peninsula. Therefore on October 30 Ambassador Hayes was authorized to inform Jordana
officially that the United States had no hostile intentions against Spain or
any of its territories, an assurance that had already been provided by Hoare
on behalf of Britain.

Operation Torch, the first Allied campaign against Germany, opened
on November 8, 1942, with the landing of British and American troops in
French Morocco and Algeria, each of which bordered the Spanish protectorate. Only hours before, Franco received personal letters from both Roosevelt and Churchill assuring him that there would be no military incursion
against the protectorate or the islands and that neither had any intention
whatsoever of intervening in Spanish affairs. In meetings of the council
of ministers on November 9 and 10, army minister General Asensio and
the Falangist ministers urged that Spain adopt a more categorically pro-
German policy, though without entering the fighting, at least for the moment. Conversely, Jordana insisted on absolute neutrality. Soon afterward,
a partial mobilization of Spanish reservists was ordered that increased the
number of troops, though the government was helpless to improve the
quality of their weaponry. The war had now entered its most dangerous
phase for Spain. Hitler responded to the Allied initiative by occupying all
the remainder of France and rushing Axis forces into Tunisia, but the crisis

for Germany would only deepen on November 19, when the Red Army launched a powerful counteroffensive to encircle Axis troops at Stalingrad.

Hitler's military occupation of the entire Pyreneean border provoked alarm in both Madrid and Lisbon. While the British and Americans had contingency plans to occupy the Spanish protectorate and enter southern Spain should Germany send troops into the peninsula, the Germans formed a contingency plan to occupy the far north of Spain in the event of the entry of Allied troops. Both plans were defensive in nature and neither contemplated a major invasion of Spain, but Spanish leaders could not be sure they wouldn't invade. After a few days, Berlin notified Madrid that it understood why the Spanish government would have to accept the British and American guarantee for the time being but urged it to make no agreement with the Allies.

The new strategic situation only accentuated domestic political tensions. For perhaps the first time the leftist opposition made open gestures in Spanish cities in support of the Allies, while Basque nationalists increased their efforts to gain Allied support for a partition of the country. Within the regime, however, this only had the effect of uniting the military and the Falangists behind the caudillo, and General Asensio informed the German embassy that the army would permit no new "political experiment" during the crisis.[19]

The best expression of the thinking of Franco and Carrero Blanco during these weeks is found in two confidential memoranda that Carrero prepared for the caudillo, The first, dated November 11, only three days after the initiation of Operation Torch, criticized Hitler's policy in the Mediterranean, concluding that all northwest Africa should already have been under German and Spanish control. Since the führer had failed to act in time, the situation had become much more complicated, but Carrero concluded that Germany still possessed great strength and could still win a complete victory in North Africa. Therefore Spain should retain "the decided will to intervene on the side of the Axis" but in view of the new complications should continue to postpone such an initiative, secretly planning future action with Germany while continuing to "deceive" the Allies.[20]

The second memo, dated December 18, presented quite a different perspective. Germany no longer seemed capable of responding effectively either on the eastern front or in North Africa. The war would be a very long one in which Germany would probably not be able to win clear-cut victory, and it might even lead to a new deal between Hitler and Stalin.

Carrero pointed out such negotiation was entirely possible, given that there was "no fundamental difference of a religious or spiritual type" between Germany and the Soviet Union. To prevent a catastrophe in the east, Spain must strive to convince Britain to change its policy and come to terms with Germany.[21] The strategic situation had become so desperate that there could be no further consideration of Spain entering the conflict directly.

Franco struggled to maintain his basic strategy. He remained convinced that, one way or the other, the war would yet produce major political and territorial changes that his regime could take advantage of. On the first anniversary of the Japanese attack on Pearl Harbor, he addressed the National Council of the FET, remarking that "we are witnessing the end of one era and the beginning of another. The liberal world is going under, a victim of the cancer produced by its own errors, and with it is collapsing commercial imperialism and financial capitalism with its millions of unemployed." After once more praising Fascist Italy and Nazi Germany, he insisted that "the historical destiny of our era will be fulfilled, either by the barbarous formula of a Bolshevist totalitarianism or by the spiritual and patriotic formula that Spain offers, or by any other of the fascist peoples. . . . Therefore those who dream of the establishment of demoliberal systems in Europe deceive themselves."[22] A very few years would reveal this to be another of his failed prophecies. The speech also indicated that he still believed that Nazi Germany would survive the war in a reasonably strong position, which at that moment he still considered necessary for the continuation of his own regime. Consequently he would further declare before the war college on December 18 that "the destiny and future of Spain are closely united with German victory."[23]

Nevertheless, one decisive change was that Franco abandoned the idea that Spain could ever enter the war militarily. On December 3, for the first time he notified Ribbentrop that he had become firmly convinced that such a step was undesirable both for military and for economic reasons, and to that extent thinking in Madrid and Berlin was beginning to converge. A few days later, Hitler finally agreed that Muñoz Grandes could be replaced as commander of the Blue Division. He had a farewell meeting with the Spanish general before his return to Madrid during which he told Muñoz Grandes that he had no interest in any plan to pressure Franco heavily or overthrow him; all he asked was that the departing commander do all he could to oppose the Allies and influence Spanish policy on behalf of the Axis.[24]

Muñoz Grandes returned to a hero's welcome in Madrid on December 17, greeted by a huge crowd. The generalissimo immediately promoted him to lieutenant general, a rank that had the advantage of making him ineligible for any further active divisional command. Franco then invited Asensio and Muñoz Grandes to dinner on New Year's Eve, but, according to the latter, was evasive about any more strongly pro-German policy. For two and a half months, he left Muñoz Grandes without assignment, then on March 3, 1943, named him head of his personal military staff (*casa militar*). This was intended to seem an honor that would please Berlin, but in fact it left the Blue Division's former leader without active troop command and under Franco's thumb, where he could cause the least trouble. He continued to maintain secret contact with Berlin for a while, but military and political events increasingly undercut his pro-German posture, and he was effectively neutralized, soon having no alternative but to become a mainstay of Franco's regime, which he would serve to the end.[25]

Though both sides in the war had attempted to reassure Franco during the early phases of the campaign in Tunisia, it was by no means clear in the first weeks of 1943 that Spain was safe from invasion. The greatest concern was German troop movements in occupied France and the new German position along the Pyrenees, where German officers frankly said to a number of visitors that they expected soon to receive orders to enter Spain, though Hitler seems never to have contemplated such a thing seriously.[26]

The last high-level visit to the führer by a Spanish leader was a journey to Berlin by Arrese, secretary of the FET, in January 1943. He bore a personal letter from Franco, who had carefully briefed him beforehand to carry out a purely pro forma mission whose goals were to obtain a shipment of German arms and expedite commerce between the two countries. There was no concrete political aim, for Jordana supervised foreign policy and, with the looming defeat of the Axis in North Africa, even the Falangists had begun to moderate their position. Under the new one-year commercial agreement worked out by Arrese, Madrid opened a credit of 130 million marks, and Germany would export goods to the value of at least 70 million, permitting a sizable difference in the trade balance in Germany's favor. This would guarantee the first German arms shipment since the Civil War, intended for defense against an Allied invasion. During 1943 and the first weeks of the following year the Reich shipped weaponry to the value of 160 million marks, a quantity that nonetheless was insufficient either to cover the full trade deficit with Spain or to remedy altogether the shortage of quality arms there. The good news was that during the first half of 1943 economic conditions in Spain improved slightly, and shortages saw a modest reduction.

The new feature of Spanish policy at the beginning of 1943 was a persistent effort by Franco's government to mediate the conflict. A "Plan D," conceived largely by José María Doussinague, chief of policy planning in the Foreign Ministry, was based on the calculation that the war would continue for some time, with neither side able to achieve total victory. This would produce the need for "an arrangement" resting on "a policy of just and benevolent reconciliation." Spain's goal should be to "intervene" at the right moment to achieve this, and in the process gain the influence to "make Spain a great power." It was supposedly in an ideal position as "the most important of all the neutral nations" and also "the number one Catholic country," offering Spain the possibility of building a sort of Catholic entente with Portugal, Ireland, Hungary, Croatia, and Slovakia.[27]

This was more fantasy than plan. It dreamed of making Spain the principal mediator without having to change Spain's tilted policy of non-belligerence in favor of the Axis and expected that it could make use of the Vatican, though relations remained prickly with a papacy that did not necessarily see Spain as "the number one Catholic country."[28] The idea that a collection of very minor powers and satellite and puppet states of the Third Reich all possessed the autonomy to pursue a policy designed by Madrid was illusory. Finally, on June 16, Hans Heinrich Dieckhoff, the new German ambassador, asked Franco to end his mediation initiatives and, above all, to cease giving the impression that he was acting on behalf of Germany to palliate its weakness. Franco replied innocently that he was merely trying to create "a psychology of peace that would be useful to Germany" and that while Italy had become a "heavy weight" for Germany, Spain was simply seeking to help her. For the first time he criticized the Nazi persecution of the churches, terming it "totally mistaken," and told Dieckhoff that complete victory over the United States was probably impossible.[29] A further concern was his fear that if the war were not soon resolved, a new Nazi-Soviet pact might be negotiated.[30]

The most agreeable event for Franco that month was a special ceremony in the ruins of the Alcázar on June 5, honoring the caudillo and his fellow cadets of the fourteenth promotion of infantry from the class of 1910. A total of 258 of its original 382 members were dead by that time. Of the former, only sixty-eight had died of natural causes. Another sixty-seven had been killed as infantry officers either in Morocco or the Civil War, thirty-eight had been executed in the Republican zone, and others had died serving in diverse branches of the armed forces. The event also marked the full reconciliation of Franco and Yagüe, who had recently been placed in command of the Tenth Army Corps in Spanish Morocco. Yagüe returned to Toledo to take command of his former comrades for this occasion, delivering a vehement speech on behalf of Franco and his regime, symbolizing the unity of the military behind their caudillo.[31]

Conversely, a massive shock came the next month, when, on July 23, the Grand Council of the Italian Fascist Party, in connivance with the king and the military, overthrew Mussolini on the grounds of his disastrous military leadership. This had a major impact in Madrid; though Franco maintained his customary calm, the Allied invasion of Italy in September closed off strategic space and made his pro-German posture increasingly unviable. During August, Spanish institutions began a slow and limited process of de-Falangization. On the twenty-fourth the FET's university syndicate forbade all comparisons between the Spanish regime and "totalitarian states," and this soon became official policy, as a new program of defascistization proceeded by degrees, gradually accelerating.[32] The press also received instructions to show greater neutrality in reporting and commenting on the war.

Contact with the post-Fascist Italian government was frozen. For six months the Spanish regime had been maneuvering to present itself as peacemaker, but when the first concrete opportunity presented itself Franco refused to take advantage of it, ignoring feelers from the new Italian government about helping to arrange a separate peace, for fear of being tarred with the Fascist connection by the Allies on the one hand and of offending the Germans on the other.

The Monarchists insisted that only a restoration could ensure the future of Spanish government, and a majority of the lieutenant generals, at the top of the military hierarchy, finally agreed with them. Asensio suggested that they put their position in writing and, on September 15, when Franco returned from his long vacation in the Pazo de Meirás, the first visitor on his agenda was Varela, the de facto leader of the senior generals, who burst into the caudillo's office still carrying his general's baton. Franco knew the purpose of the visit, and ordered him to go back out, ask permission to enter, and leave his baton behind.[33] Visibly irritated, Varelita complied, coming back in to present Franco with a letter signed by eight lieutenant generals and apparently endorsed by two more (a majority of the senior command), inquiring in the most polite terms if he did not think that circumstances were right for restoration of the monarchy. The lieutenant generals promised firm obedience and guaranteed that complete discipline would be maintained throughout Spain during the transition. For the first and only time, a majority of Franco's senior commanders had asked him, most respectfully, to resign.[34]

The Monarchists had begun a new initiative three months earlier, in June, when a group of *procuradores* (deputies) in the new corporative Cortes had signed the "Manifesto of the Twenty-Seven," sent on to Franco by the president of the chamber. Written in obsequious terms, it suggested that he step down in favor of the monarchy as the only kind of government that could avoid political extremes and have any chance of surviving the war. Another variation was the idea floated by a few of a transitional military regency under General Luis Orgaz, high commissioner of Spanish Morocco.

Franco dealt with each challenge in turn. Nearly all the dissident *procuradores* were punished, either dismissed or arrested or both. With regard to the petition of the lieutenant generals, Franco called in Orgaz for a personal dressing-down and was assured that he would take no independent initiative, even though he had signed the collective letter. Franco then received each of the other lieutenant generals who were signatories, though never more than one or two at a time, and explained that the present situation was much too complicated and dangerous to hand over to a novice king, who might have little support anyway. None of the signatories was willing to challenge him personally, and none was punished directly. Of the six lieutenant generals who did not sign, four seem to have been opposed to the letter, but Franco decided to change the political texture of the army hierarchy. Since the end of the Civil War, he had engaged in annual rounds of promotions, normally on October 1 (Día del Caudillo), to keep his senior commanders happy, but the new initiative of 1943 was the most extensive, elevating no fewer than twenty-six of his most hard-line supporters to lieutenant general. In strictly military terms, the move was preposterous, for the weak Spanish army, as in the past, would have more chiefs than Indians, but it watered down a high command that henceforth would be thoroughly loyal politically. That Franco was conceding nothing was shown by his proposal to recognize Mussolini's new puppet government under German occupation in northern Italy, though Jordana managed to talk him out of it by threatening to resign. Only a semi-official representative, not an ambassador, was sent to the new puppet regime.[35]

Political definitions in Madrid continued to gradually shift. An announcement on September 23 directed that the FET would no longer be called a party; henceforth, it would be known as the "National Movement," the broader name for Franco's coalition that had no necessary Fascist connotation. Its doctrine would henceforth be moderated more and more toward a Catholic corporatism, the Fascist model progressively abandoned. Jordana also convinced Franco that he must withdraw the Blue Division, a decision taken during the course of two long meetings by the council of ministers from September 24 to September 25. The unit's official dissolution was then announced on October 12.

The policy of nonbelligerence finally came to an end, though it was never officially repudiated. In a speech to the National Council of the movement on the first of October, Franco defined Spain's policy as one of "vigilant neutrality," the first use of the term in more than three years. In a second speech on October 12, the national holiday, he made no reference to the Axis but declared that the dominating impulse of his policy was inspired by the Catholic and humanitarian goals of the historic Spanish empire. The term "neutrality" finally began to figure in the press four months later, in February 1944.

Yet this change was highly nuanced, for in the latter part of 1943 Franco did not intend a policy of full neutrality so much as a return to the "tilted neutrality" of 1939–40. The objective was to maintain the status of special friend of Germany, for he still could not conceive that the Germans would be completely defeated. Franco calculated that Germany would somehow survive as a great power, and, if Spain were its last remaining special friend, Madrid might enjoy significant support from Berlin in the future.

After the Allied invasion of Italy, Allied pressure on Franco increased. For most of the war Portugal and Spain had been Germany's principal source of wolfram, a vital component in strengthening steel and in making certain kinds of explosives. The trade had been very lucrative, as the price of wolfram skyrocketed, but in November 1943 Ambassador Hayes transmitted Washington's demand for a total embargo, which Franco rejected. Even so, certain other aspects of Spanish policy had to change, and on December 3 Dieckhoff had a long meeting with Franco to protest his recent concessions to the Allies. These included withdrawal of the Blue Division, free flow of refugees across the Pyrenees, the internment of several German submarine crews, and the release to the Allies of a number of interned German and Italian ships. Franco replied that such measures had been required by specific circumstances but that it was "inconceivable that Spanish policy would change" its basic orientation.[36]

Throughout the war Washington had sought to take a stronger line with Franco than London, but Spanish authorities were shocked to hear a radio announcement on January 29, 1944, that the United States was suspending all shipments of petroleum, a move that could cripple the economy. Washington was determined to put an end to all of Franco's collaboration with Germany, all the more because American codebreakers had gotten into the secret code of the Supreme General Staff and had learned of Spanish assistance to German and Japanese military intelligence. The embargo, which also included other items in addition to oil, created the greatest economic emergency of the war in Spain and encouraged growing domestic unrest.

A graphic example of the latter was the report of an informer inside the Institute of Political Studies (Instituto de Estudios Políticos), the regime's think tank, which revealed that "in this Center they speak of His Excellency in very pejorative terms" and that some referred to him alternately as "a simplistic optimist," "vain and pretentious," "a hopeless fellow," or "unwitting." There was much speculation about a major change, though others concluded that "nothing will happen. He will fool everybody. . . . They also say that although everyone in the army speaks badly of the Caudillo they are not likely to lift a finger," because the general opinion was that the generals had been bought. There was a sense that corruption pervaded Spanish institutions. "The general attitude is one of frank pessimism and that any part of our territory might be occupied at any moment, with or without a declaration of war, or with the bombing of Madrid in the same ways as Berlin, the difference being that here we have no air raid shelters." If elections were held, the left would likely win, but a general conclusion was that "we can perhaps expect to see in Spain a grand 'Competition' of groveling and abasement to win the favor of England and the United States."[37]

That same day another report concerning the atmosphere within the Falangist hard core observed that "they are in a state of deep pessimism," and believed the only solution might be "that the Caudillo will have to leave and be replaced by General Asensio."[38] This similarly reflected the worry that the next Allied invasion might target Spain and that, if things got too bad, Franco's only hope would be to flee to neutral Portugal.

By February even *Arriba*, the official organ of the movement, began to refer to Spain's policy as "neutral," affirming that it had been so ever. As the screws tightened, Franco accepted the fact that he must make further concessions, and before the end of the month Jordana negotiated a preliminary agreement with Washington, but this was rejected by hard-liners in the government.[39] Nonetheless, Franco explained to Dieckhoff that while Spain would continue to do all it could to help Germany, he could not allow his country to be strangled economically. As reserves were touching rock bottom, a formal agreement was completed with Washington and London on May 2, 1944. The government agreed to eliminate almost all wolfram shipments to Germany and also to retire the Blue Legion, the small successor to the Blue Division on the eastern front, as well as to close the German consulate in Tangier and expel all German spies and saboteurs from Spanish territory (this last measure, however, was never fully carried out).[40]

Though a small amount of clandestine collaboration continued, the new agreement placed Spain in a position of relatively authentic neutrality for the first time in the war. Indeed, the main tilt was now in favor of the Allies, sole providers of the prime goods the country needed to survive. Franco would still not accept the idea of complete German defeat, however, and continued to hope that Spain, rather than Italy, would be Germany's principal postwar associate.[41]

The German response to Franco's shift was angry, and there was even talk of breaking relations, but Hitler intervened, judging that Franco might be doing the best he could and that the best thing for Germany was to salvage what remained of the special relationship. The treaty of friendship signed in May 1939 was up for renewal. Since it specified automatic renewal for another five years unless one of the parties objected, it was automatically renewed.

What finally changed Franco's perspective was the success of the Allied invasion of France in June. Once German forces were in full retreat, he acknowledged that Germany had been completely defeated and accepted that it would be occupied by its enemies, as he admitted in conversation with foreign diplomats. Carrero Blanco prepared his last two strategic analyses in August and September, concluding that there was no hope for the Reich.[42] In October, Spanish Communist forces, based in liberated France, launched an invasion of Spain through the Val d'Aran and Navarre, in the hope of stimulating popular support for revival of the Civil War.[43] Franco ordered in sizable army contingents that completely blocked the effort, though small guerrilla groups, using the French Resistance name of Maquis (or "partisan bands" and "bandits," as they were termed by the regime), alternately composed of either Communists or anarchists, would continue the struggle for years.

Jordana suddenly died after a hunting accident in August 1944 and was replaced as foreign minister for the final phase of the war by José Félix de Lequerica, who had been Franco's representative in Paris for five years. Lequerica had mediated the Franco-German armistice and was so close to

German occupation authorities that in some quarters he had become known as "the ambassador of the Gestapo," due to his frequent lunches with the Gestapo chief Otto Abetz. Lequerica was a cultured man, however, and spoke both French and English. Devious, cynical, and astute, he had an agreeable personality and was an accomplished opportunist.[44] For Franco, he had the advantage of a past that tied him firmly to the regime.[45]

Lequerica understood that his task was to transform foreign policy sufficiently to ensure the survival of Franco's regime, bringing it nearer to the Allies. He emphasized Spain's "Atlantic vocation" and the importance of its connections to the Western hemisphere, making much of the doctrine of "Hispanidad" and of Spain's cultural and spiritual role in the Spanish-speaking world. The new policy stressed the "democracy" of Spanish tradition and above all the strongly Catholic identity of the regime and the Catholic corporatism of its institutional structure. The relationship with Portugal became more important and was used to help project an "Iberian model" that could play a special role in the postwar crisis of culture and values.[46]

At this point Spain's policy regarding the genocide that had been perpetrated by the Nazis and their collaborators became important as a means of establishing the regime's humanitarian bona fides. Though Franco made occasional negative references to Jews, and though a certain amount of anti-Jewish language was inherent in the regime's ultranationalist discourse, the caudillo was not particularly anti-Semitic by the standards of his era in continental Europe.[47] He had had Jewish friends in Morocco and had even intervened publicly on one occasion to quash an outbreak of discrimination against Jews in the protectorate during the Civil War. Though they were not totally free from abuse, Spanish Jews served in his army under the same conditions as anyone else, and there was never any regulation by his government restricting Jews or discriminating against them, as German officials noted with disgust.[48]

Possibly as many as thirty thousand Jews had crossed through Spain to safety during 1939–40, and a trickle did so in the following years of the war. There is no evidence that any Jew, once in Spain, was ever sent back to the Germans.[49] The Spanish government arranged to repatriate from occupied Europe Sephardics who held Spanish citizenship, as well as a small number of other Jews. This process was slow and sometimes grudging, since the regime wanted to limit the number of Jews admitted at any one time and move them on to other countries as soon as possible. There had been no particular effort to save non-Sephardic Jews in occupied Europe, and the rescue of potential victims that took place in Greece, Bulgaria, and Rumania stemmed, at least at first, from the spontaneous humanitarian efforts of Spanish diplomats in those countries.[50] The same might be said of the intervention in Hungary, but in this case Lequerica finally made it a deliberate feature of Spanish policy in October 1944. There the initiative was carried out by Angel Sanz Briz, the Spanish chargé in Budapest, and his courageous Italian ex-Fascist assistant, Giorgio Perlasca, who saved more than three thousand Jews at the height of the SS deportations in Hungary. Meanwhile, Nicolás Franco cooperated assiduously with Jewish humanitarian representatives in Lisbon to expand opportunities for refugees.[51]

The nearest thing to a friend that Franco had among the major Allied leaders was Winston Churchill. Though he had adopted a neutral policy in the Civil War, toward the end tilting slightly in favor of the Republic for geostrategic reasons, Churchill had always said that if he had been a Spaniard he would have supported Franco. On May 24, 1944, he rose in the House of Commons to speak positively of Franco's policy during the world war, which he said had been beneficial, though he may have done so in part to assure a benign posture by Spain during the impending invasion of France. As it was, the Allied ambassadors in Madrid reported that the Spanish government was still not abandoning Germany completely,[52] but on October 18 Franco wrote a personal letter to Churchill for the first time, suggesting that a closer relationship between Britain and Spain was needed to save Europe from the Soviet Union. That was going too far, because even the anti-Communist Churchill thought that Stalin must remain a firm ally until final victory over Hitler. Though privately the prime minister may have thought much the same thing as Franco, he did not reply for three months, and then in guarded terms. The British ambassador emphasized to Lequerica that there could not possibly be good relations with Spain so long as its government remained a dictatorship, to which the Spaniard innocently replied that this surely could not be the case, since Britain was so friendly with the Soviet Union.

The generalissimo made another effort in November, when he gave an interview to the United Press. He declared that his regime had observed "complete neutrality" throughout the conflict and that "it had nothing to do with fascism," because "Spain could never associate with other governments for whom Catholicism was not a fundamental principle." In view of the way that the Popular Front had manipulated democracy in Spain, Franco emphasized that "institutions that produce excellent results in other countries have contrary effects here, due to certain peculiarities of the Spanish temperament."[53] Developing a line of argument that would remain constant for the next three decades, he tried to relate his regime to the postwar world of European democracy by defining it as an "authentic democracy" in the form of "organic democracy," based on religion, the family, local institutions, and syndical organization, as distinct from "inorganic" democracy, which favored direct elections.[54] Simultaneously, government spokesmen drew attention to recent elections of low-level syndical representatives that had taken place on October 21–22, and municipal elections were announced for some unspecified future date.[55] Franco had begun preparations for constructing a new facade for his regime as early as December 1943, when he first instructed the minister of justice to prepare the draft of a human rights law.[56]

Franco had been a partisan of Hitler for much of the war and had committed enormous errors, but his view of postwar relations with the Soviet Union to a large degree coincided with that of Churchill and was more realistic than Roosevelt's. Though Churchill could not endorse Franco, he saw to it that there was no British interference in Spanish affairs and repeated that Franco "had done us much more good than harm during the war," also observing that he personally would rather live in Spain under Franco than in the Soviet Union under Stalin.[57] By contrast, American policy toward Spain was more categorically hostile, despite the relatively good relations between Hayes and Franco.

The only sharp change in Spanish policy during the final phase of the war was the breaking of relations with Tokyo on April 11, 1945, provoked by Japanese atrocities against Spanish civilians during the American reconquest of Manila. Japanese troops fortified themselves in the old Spanish district and surrounding neighborhoods, which were then blasted apart by the potent American artillery. After Warsaw and Stalingrad, Manila became one of the world's most heavily damaged cities. More than fifty thousand civilians died, many of them deliberately slaughtered by the Japanese, including fifty Spanish civilians who were murdered during the wanton destruction of the Spanish consulate.[58]

During the final days of the European war, leaders of the movement distributed an undated "very restricted circular," sent to local groups to quiet the complaints of diehard Germanophiles. It stressed that at no time had the caudillo "betrayed Germany" but that he had instead worked tirelessly to save Spain and to try to save Europe. It posed a rhetorical question to critics: "What do they want? For Spain to commit suicide because Germany is losing the war?"[59] On April 18, 1945, the vice secretary-general of the movement sent instructions to all provincial chiefs that the end of the war be presented exclusively as a victory of the regime and of the movement, which had always sought peace and had kept Spain out of the war. It underlined the conclusion that "celebrating peace is to celebrate the triumph of the Falange and of the Caudillo." Notwithstanding, less than a fortnight later news of the death of Hitler led *Arriba* and *Informaciones* to render homage to the fallen führer.

When the Truman administration took office in Washington that month, after the death of Roosevelt, it seemed yet more hostile to the Spanish regime than its predecessor, while the Soviet government relentlessly called for the overthrow of Franco. At the same time, Clement Attlee was elected prime minister in Britain, replacing Churchill. At Potsdam in July and August, the Allied conference recommended to the new United Nations that relations with Franco's government be broken in favor of "democratic forces." Such forces were not defined and would have been hard to find in any number, but the goal was somehow to permit Spaniards to choose a new political regime of their own.

The government of Mexico, Latin America's most resolute foe of the Franco regime, presented to the founding session of the United Nations in San Francisco a motion whose terms, excluding the Spanish government from membership, were accepted by acclamation.[60] On June 30, the government of Panama broke off relations with Madrid, which braced for other countries to follow suit. The postwar tide of the left in Western Europe, which swept the Labourites into power in London and would soon place a leftist coalition in charge of France, established governments whose leaders had already sworn deep hostility to Franco. The Soviet Union, ever his most unremitting foe, went one step further, launching a diplomatic campaign against the five neutral governments—Spain, Portugal, Sweden, Switzerland, and Argentina—it accused of favoring Germany during the war, urging active measures against them.[61]

Thus began the official ostracism of Franco's regime, which would reach its high point at the end of 1946, when nearly all ambassadors were withdrawn from Madrid. This semi-isolation continued until 1948, by which time the consequences of the Cold War began to change world affairs increasingly to the benefit of Franco and his regime.

13 Franco at Bay

(1945–1953)

The ostracism inflicted on the Spanish government after the close of World War II was without precedent in the modern history of Western Europe, the nearest equivalent being the pariah status held by early Soviet Russia, when it was seen as a revolutionary and subversive state. The hyperbole associated with "Europe's last surviving Fascist dictator" was remarkable. One French intelligence report had it that a hundred thousand Nazis and collaborators were being sheltered in Spain, while Soviet spokesmen at the United Nations, in an accusation incredible even for Soviet propaganda, charged that two hundred thousand Nazis, no less, had escaped to Spain and that atomic bombs were being manufactured at Ocaña, seventy kilometers from Madrid, with plans afoot to invade France in the spring of 1946.[1] Similarly, the puppet Polish foreign minister maintained in April 1946 that Franco was developing an advanced war industry supervised by German scientists, preparing an atomic bomb and maintaining an armored corps of 250,000 men for aggressive purposes.[2]

In fact, at that time most Spanish soldiers had no boots and were wearing sandals instead, while the feeble Spanish army almost completely lacked mobility and was equipped primarily with pre–World War II arms. Its only newer weapons were a small number of German planes and tanks dating from the shipment of 1943. The only element of truth in all this was that well over a thousand Nazis and collaborators, mostly low level, did obtain refuge in Spain. At war's end, nearly all regular German personnel in Madrid had been interned and then returned to Germany, and no major Nazi was sheltered in Spain, though in the postwar months no more than two hundred or so German refugees were further handed over by Franco's government.[3]

The leftist opposition came back to life with the Communist guerrilla insurgency that began in October 1944, seconded by the independent actions of the anarchists, followed by reorganization of all leftist Republican parties abroad in the new National Alliance of Democratic Forces (Alianza Nacional de Fuerzas Democráticas [ANFD]).[4] The Communists, who during the war had followed Soviet policy by trying to organize a broad national union, joined the ANFD in January 1946, restoring the old Republican alliance.[5] The refugee flow into France, mainly of oppositionists, resumed in limited volume, as more than five thousand Spaniards crossed per year between 1946 and 1952.[6] Nonetheless, there is no indication that there was any plan for a foreign armed intervention in Spain; the only concrete demand made of Franco was that he abandon the city of Tangier, which he did on September 3, 1945. The attempt of the insurgency to revive the Civil War drew little response; in fact, it boomeranged insofar as it had the effect of rallying much of the population in favor of the status quo, which was certainly meager but slowly improving.[7]

Though the Ministry of Justice informed the British and American embassies in April 1945 that penalties for crimes during the Civil War were being canceled and that the tribunal that had been prosecuting political responsibilities was being dissolved that same month, the growth in opposition activity was met by new repression.[8] Security had been tightened in the middle of World War II with the promulgation of new laws for the court-martial of political rebels in March 1941 and March 1943. Their terms made any kind of organized political activity liable to prosecution as military rebellion, bringing almost any act of defiance under *sumarísimo* proceedings. That was moderated and made more precise by a new penal code promulgated on December 23, 1944, but military courts continued to hold jurisdiction over opposition activity. The army officer corps itself underwent a limited purge in 1944 to remove any doubtful personnel.[9]

Meanwhile, the Pyreneean fortifications that had been begun in desultory fashion in 1941 were expanded in 1943 and then further augmented two years later.[10]

Though some jailers were said to be showing greater consideration for leftist prisoners in anticipation of drastic political change, the regime's sense of danger produced an increase in executions during 1944. Sporadic information coming directly or indirectly from official sources indicated that several hundred capital sentences were carried out that year and that, on the recommendation of the papal nuncio, a petition for clemency was signed by all the Spanish bishops and submitted to the justice minister, Eduardo Aunós. The spate of new executions, however, only petered out in the spring of 1945 when it became clear that the regime would not have to face a military challenge.[11] The total prison population, however, continued to decline.

Waverers who had begun to abandon their blue shirts in anticipation of regime change rallied to Franco when the upswing in leftist activity seemed to indicate that the alternative was return of the revolutionaries. Radical Falangists responded with direct action of their own, including physical assaults on known or presumed leftists. A new paramilitary formation, the Guardias de Franco, was formed of the most fanatical young Falangists in August 1944. Franco continued to pack the army officer corps with Falangist reservists at the junior level, not merely former *alféreces provisionales* but also even younger reservists from the Falangist student syndicate (Sindicato Español Universitario [SEU]) and the *milicias universitarias*.[12] Between 1939 and 1945, a grand total of at least ten thousand younger officers were incorporated, and they would form the backbone of the future officer corps. These members of the army's "Franco generation" were if anything more staunch than their senior commanders in their loyalty to the caudillo.

The promotions of 1943 guaranteed a loyal cadre of lieutenant generals, but on March 3, 1945, Franco reshuffled the top command, naming as chief of his personal military staff (*casa militar*) the ever faithful José Moscardó (in charge of the defense of the Alcázar in 1936), who as captain-general of Barcelona had recently repelled the Vall d'Aran incursion. As a military technician, he suffered from grave limitations, but his commitment to Franco was total. The new captain-general of Madrid was Muñoz Grandes, who had burned all his bridges and was also fully committed to the regime. Carlist generals were more trustworthy than mainline Monarchists, and thus José Solchaga was named captain-general of Barcelona, and Varela replaced Orgaz as high commissioner of Spanish Morocco. Before Varela departed for Tetuán, the caudillo observed to the new high commissioner that he would have to maintain a tight rein over Spain for another decade, but after that he would be able to ease up a little.

Franco was confident, correctly, that there would be no major response among the general population to the new offensive by the revolutionary left. The bulk of Spanish society was preoccupied by its economic problems, and most of the middle classes had accommodated themselves to the existing situation. The combination of Civil War memories and continued repression meant that the leftist opposition could be well confined. A different but in some ways more serious danger, however, came from the growing activism of the Monarchists.

The nearest thing to a serious alternative to Franco was the pretender to the throne, Don Juan de Borbón (Conde de Barcelona), heir to Alfonso XIII, living in exile in Switzerland. He might draw support from much of the right and perhaps even from the moderate left. On February 10, 1945, the Conde de Barcelona wrote to the most reliable of the Monarchist generals, Alfredo Kindelán: "This dictator and his regime, whether we seek it or not, is inexorably condemned to be overthrown amid grave convulsions, which only benefit the forces of disorder. Therefore it is important to take a position before world opinion by publishing a document or a manifesto, in which, while specifying the fundamental principles of the Monarchy, Franco is urged to hand over power to those who gave it to him, so that the King can receive it from the army unanimously."[13]

On March 19, 1945, six weeks before the fighting in Europe was over, Don Juan released a political manifesto from his residence at Lausanne. It declared that the caudillo's regime, "inspired from the beginning by the systems of the Axis powers," had failed, gravely compromising the future of Spain. Franco was called on to abandon power and give way to the monarchy to avoid leading the country to an irreparable catastrophe. Don Juan offered the alternative of "the traditional monarchy," promising "immediate approval of a political constitution by popular vote; recognition of all the rights inherent in the human person and a guarantee of the corresponding political liberties; establishment of a legislative assembly elected by the nation; recognition of regional diversity; a broad political amnesty; [and] a just distribution of wealth and the removal of unjust social contrasts."[14]

This added a rightist opposition to that of the revolutionary left, at the very moment that Franco faced a wall of denunciation from the victorious Allies. Moreover, he witnessed the example of the Brazilian regime of

Getulio Vargas, which was overthrown soon after the fighting ended, even though it had officially entered the war on the side of the Allies. The neighboring Salazar regime in Portugal faced considerably less pressure than its Spanish counterpart, however, for it had been genuinely neutral and had never adopted the fascistic trappings of Francoism, yet, even so, Salazar thought it necessary to introduce nominal reforms, liberalizing somewhat his highly restrictive electoral system.

Franco would also make adjustments but would concede as little as possible. There was no thought of resigning or withdrawing, and the vigor of the postwar purges in France, Italy, and the Low Countries only strengthened his determination. By this point he viewed the *caudillaje* as a lifetime "obligation," partly out of a stubborn determination not to yield, but also because he was convinced that God had given him a providential mandate, and that he was right, whereas liberal capitalists, moderate Monarchists, and leftist revolutionaries were all wrong. He was firmly convinced that in another twenty years, after postwar crises had played themselves out, West European political systems would be more like that of Spain than vice versa. In the meantime, it was a matter of steady nerve, something never in short supply with Franco. As he said to Kindelán, "I will not be as foolish as Primo de Rivera. I will not resign; from here only to the cemetery."[15]

During its six years of complete power the regime had created a broad and firm network of mutual interest—the opposition called it complicity—with all the elite elements of society and also with most of the middle classes, including the Catholic rural population, who had been saved from the revolution and were able to maintain their way of life, with a glimmer at last of some modest improvement. The Monarchist opposition was poorly organized, and when the pretender ordered prominent Monarchists in Franco's diplomatic service to resign their ambassadorships, the only one to do so was the Duque de Alba in London, and even he was induced by the caudillo to remain at his post for another six months.

Immediately after the Lausanne manifesto was issued, Franco convened the longest meeting of the army's Supreme War Council in the history of the regime, from March 20 to 22. Though there is no record of the proceedings, it may be presumed that Franco restated his position that a properly installed and structured monarchy would be the logical successor to his regime, which he would in due course prepare, but that such a monarchy must not reject the principles for which they had fought and that stability and security could be maintained at this perilous moment only through his continued leadership, which would lead to important reforms. He was apparently assured full support from the military, nearly all of whom respected his leadership and the firmness of his command, as well as his capacity for diplomatic maneuver. Hardly any had interest in abandoning their commander in chief for a new experiment amid mounting international hostility and a leftist offensive abroad. Most civilian Monarchists responded in similar fashion. Antonio Goicoechea, number two leader of the Monarchist opposition under the Republic but governor of the Bank of Spain under Franco, spoke out publicly against Don Juan. Thus reassured, the caudillo presided over the annual victory parade on April 1, 1945, using the occasion to announce nationalization of the telephone system through an arrangement with ITT.

Franco still sought rapprochement with Don Juan through private channels, suggesting that the Conde de Barcelona take up official residence in Spain. He refused, but Franco announced to the National Council on July 17, 1945 (ninth anniversary of the Civil War) that a law would be prepared to transform the Spanish state into a monarchy. Carrero Blanco had already pointed out that although the Conde de Barcelona himself might never make an appropriate successor, it was important to try to cultivate good relations with the royal family, for his seven-year-old son Juan Carlos might be trained and educated as a more appropriate heir.[16] Though no understanding could be reached for the moment, reassurance was provided by Don Juan's announcement in September that he would "incite no one to rebellion," even though he maintained the position that Franco should hand power over to the military in order to form a provisional government that would conduct a referendum on the question of monarchy versus republic and that would then be followed by general elections to write a new constitution.

Franco realized that he faced the turning point in his regime, which had to be altered in some way to survive in the world of postwar social democratic Western Europe. By the spring of 1945 he had a fairly clear design. New "fundamental laws," as his regime called them, would have to be introduced to give his system more objective juridical content and provide some basic civil guarantees. A major effort would be made to attract new Catholic political personnel and intensify the Catholic identity of the regime in order to win the support of the Vatican and reduce the hostility of the Western democracies. The National Movement would be further deemphasized but not abolished, for it was still useful, and no rival political organizations would be tolerated, though censorship might be eased slightly. A municipal government reform would be promulgated, and ultimately a new statute to legitimize the regime as a monarchy under Franco's regency would be submitted to popular plebiscite.[17]

This represented a major effort to introduce the main features of a Catholic and corporative authoritarian monarchy, as had been preached varyingly by Carlists and then by rival neotraditionalists for a hundred years. It also proposed to create a limited Spanish version of the old German ideal of the *Rechtsstaat*, the authoritarian administrative state based on law. This formula, which had impressed right-wing Spanish legal theorists of the preceding generation, had nothing necessarily to do with a directly representative system but would depend on an indirect and corporatist scheme of representation. Eduardo Aunós, the justice minister, who had long been associated with such doctrines, had begun a sketch for a new legal superstructure as early as 1943, when the formal defascistization began, and this was encouraged by Lequerica, who urged Franco to make haste in a memorandum of June 30, 1945.[18] The project of a set of civil guarantees had first been assigned to Arrese but ultimately transferred to the Institute of Political Studies, where Arrese had appointed as director Fernando María Castiella. Castiella had been a neo-Falangist, coauthor of the 1942 *Reivindicaciones de España*, the key book outlining Spain's goals abroad that later had to be quietly forgotten. He was, however, flexible and relatively imaginative. Assisted by several of the institute's intellectuals, he elaborated a new *fuero*, or bill of rights, for Spanish citizens that was strongly opposed by Arrese and some of the core Falangists but accepted by Franco.[19]

The Charter of the Spanish People (Fuero de los Españoles, its title employing the neotraditionalist language that recalled medieval local and regional rights and that was so dear to the regime) was promulgated on July 17, 1945. The third of the Fundamental Laws of the Realm, following the Labor Charter (Fuero del Trabajo) of 1938 and the Constitutive Law of the Cortes of 1942, it was based in part on the constitution of 1876 but pretended to synthesize the historic rights recognized by traditional Spanish law. It guaranteed some of the civil liberties common to the Western world, such as freedom of residence and correspondence and the right not to be detained more than seventy-two hours without a hearing before a judge. Castiella was apparently responsible for adding article 12, which specified freedom of expression of ideas unless the ideas attacked the fundamental principles of the state, and article 16 on freedom of association, but the freedoms pledged were compromised in article 33, which stated that none of the rights stipulated would be permitted to attack "spiritual, national and social unity," as well as in article 25, which allowed them to be "temporarily suspended by the government" in time of emergency.[20]

This was accompanied by a major cabinet change on the following day (July 18). Most notable was the downgrading of the movement and the installation of Alberto Martín Artajo as foreign minister. Artajo was president of Catholic Action in Spain and as such was the country's leading Catholic layman. He became the centerpiece of the endeavor to accentuate the regime's Catholic identity and present a new appearance to the world. (To that end the cabinet changes had been preceded by a new law pertaining to primary education, subordinating all elementary education to Catholic norms.) The faithful Arrese had to go, even though his achievement had been a complete domestication of the Falange that reduced its Fascism.[21] His secretary-generalship of the movement was left vacant, though the Falangist Girón, whose pliant demagogy was quite useful, remained as minister of labor (a post that he would hold for sixteen years, making him Franco's most durable minister after Carrero Blanco). The *camisa vieja* Raimundo Fernández-Cuesta became minister of justice, and another Falangist replaced Miguel Primo de Rivera as minister of agriculture. Blas Pérez stayed on as interior minister and José Ibáñez Martín, a very right-wing Catholic, remained minister of education. Franco's childhood friend Suanzes, head of the state INI, also continued as minister of commerce and industry, having again taken this post in the preceding year. Asensio, who seemed too much an "Axis general," was followed as minister of the army by General Fidel Dávila, a small, colorless man who had held major posts in the Civil War and was an experienced administrator. There was just enough "political Catholicism" in this mix to provide a somewhat new look, but Franco was justifiably confident that none of these ministers would cause him any trouble.

The nominal exception might have been Artajo, who had discussed the wisdom of collaborating with Franco with leading Catholics from the primate on down.[22] Most, though not all, of them urged him to enter the government to encourage major reform. He is alleged to have told associates in Catholic Action that they could expect a basic transformation in four months and to have remarked to American ambassador Norman Armour on August 28 that Franco must now realize that it would soon be necessary to resign.[23] Franco, of course, realized nothing of the sort, and in practice

Martín Artajo's goals proved less than drastic, aiming for the rapid evolution of the system into a corporative, Catholic, and still semiauthoritarian monarchy—perhaps not so different from Salazar's regime in Lisbon.

Meanwhile Don Juan, convinced that Franco's days were numbered, named a new alternative Monarchist "provisional government." General Kindelán presided, with Salvador de Madariaga as foreign minister, Gil Robles in interior, General Antonio Aranda as minister of defense, and General Juan Bautista Sánchez and General Varela as ministers of the army and air force, respectively. Circumstances quickly overtook this initiative, however, which was never announced publicly, for on August 20 Ernest Bevin, the new British foreign minister, proclaimed in the House of Commons that any foreign interference in the internal affairs of Spain might have the counterproductive effect of strengthening Franco, and President Truman agreed. Meanwhile, the convening of a new rump Republican Cortes in Mexico City had no concrete impact. Franco could heave a sigh of relief.

Serrano Suñer, completely cut off from all government affairs since his ouster three years earlier, decided to break his long silence and on September 3 (the anniversary of his dismissal) he sent Franco a long letter that recommended a fundamental political change. He observed that the regime had taken form during the Fascist era and had been aligned with the Axis, but present circumstances left it isolated in a newly democratic Western Europe. This situation required that the Falange-National Movement be honorably retired, its complete dissolution followed by creation of a broad new national front government that would include representatives of "all non-Red Spaniards." Serrano suggested the name of the old Monarchist liberal Francesc Cambó and the intellectual luminaries Ortega y Gasset and Gregorio Marañón. Franco read this missive carefully, underlining portions with a marking pen and adding numerous marginal comments. Beside the names for the suggested new government he simply jotted "Je, je, je" ("Ha, ha, ha").[24] He did, however, receive his brother-in-law for a long and frank discussion, their first in three years, and, according to Serrano, expressed a certain perplexity about how to proceed on some issues.[25]

During cabinet meetings in September and October Franco seemed to support Martín Artajo's point of view against the resistance of Girón. A number of limited changes were discussed, such as a full amnesty for Civil War crimes, electoral reform of the Cortes, relaxation of censorship, and a referendum law. At times Franco sounded almost as though he believed in a system of checks and balances, observing, for example, that Nazi Germany suffered catastrophe through "the will of a single man" and that the same danger existed in monarchies, which ran the risk that the king could go "off the rails by only looking at himself in the mirror."[26]

Yet the changes that emerged were piecemeal, minimal, and in many respects merely cosmetic. The most influential voice counseling Franco to make as few changes as possible was that of Carrero Blanco. In one memorandum, Carrero stressed that the regime must rely on "order, unity and standing firm," and so it did.[27] On October 12 new legislation was sent to the Cortes that would slightly liberalize regulations on meetings and associations and broaden civil guarantees. The first municipal elections were announced for the following March, in which members of city councils would be chosen through indirect procedures (one-third by heads of families, one-third by the syndicates, and the remaining third by those already selected through the first two channels), though the government would continue to appoint all mayors directly. On October 20, 1945, the government declared an amnesty for prisoners still serving sentences for Civil War crimes, and two days later the Law of Referendum was announced, which provided that issues of broad national concern would be submitted to popular referendum at the discretion of the government.[28]

The Falange was downgraded but not eliminated. One week after the change in cabinet the vice secretariat of popular education, which controlled censorship, was removed from the movement and placed under the Ministry of Education, a Catholic fief. The raised-arm Fascist or Roman salute, the regime's *saludo nacional* since April 1937, was officially abolished over the objection of the remaining Falangist ministers on September 11, 1945. The movement bureaucracy was left under the administration of its vice secretary, Rodrigo Vivar Téllez, a former judge. Vivar Téllez was no Fascist, and apparently skeptical that the movement organization was still needed.

Franco, however, was clear in his own mind regarding its value. In an earlier conversation with Martín Artajo, he had observed that the Falange was important in maintaining the spirit and ideals of the original National Movement of 1936 and in educating public opinion. As a mass organization, it organized the popular support that Franco insisted he saw on his travels. It also provided the content of and the administrative cadres for the regime's social policy and served as a "bulwark against subversion," for after 1945 Falangists had no alternative but to back the regime. Finally, the caudillo observed somewhat cynically, it functioned as a kind of lightning rod: "People blame them for the mistakes of the government," relieving pressure on it. He declared that it was simply a sort of administrative "instrument of national unification" rather than a party. Fleeting clandestine activities by a handful of activists who resented their new subordination could largely be ignored. A proposal by José María de Olazábal, vice secretary of the Ministry of Syndical Organization, that the state syndicates be replaced by a system of free associations of workers and professionals that could take the place of political parties was flatly rejected by Franco, who carefully annotated the proposal, as much too liberal.[29]

The construction of a "cosmetic constitutionalism," as the sum effect of these changes has been called, was for the moment completed by publication of a new electoral law for the Cortes on March 12, 1946. It altered very little, maintaining indirect and controlled corporative elections, but did provide for representation from provincial councils and increased syndical participation. None of these reforms amounted to fundamental change, but they began the elaboration of a façade of laws and guarantees that spokesmen could refer to in terms of political representation and civil rights, however stark the contrast with reality.

Thus the new line in 1945–46 was to present the regime as a limited system of government bound by law, which was partly true with regard to routine aspects but fundamentally misleading with respect to political superstructure. On May 14, 1946, Franco would insist that "the first mistake that people commit is to try to present our regime as a system of dictatorship, pretending that our judicial system exercises extraordinary and despotic power, . . . when in fact it is administered by professional magistrates and judges. . . . Never in the life of the nation has a judicial system enjoyed greater independence."[30] Ten months later, he informed a visiting correspondent, "I am not, as people think abroad, master of whatever I do, but, as in governments everywhere, I have to rely on the assistance and agreement of my government," once more defining the regime as a "democracia popular orgánica," repeating the new catch phrase, initiated in 1944, that would be employed with many variations during the next three decades.[31]

Throughout 1945 and 1946 Franco's regime mounted a campaign to try to convince foreign opinion that the Spanish government presided over a system of organic Catholic institutions and had never been committed to or believed in the victory of the Axis. One ploy was to send the Spanish president of the international Catholic student organization Pax romana, Joaquín Ruiz Giménez, on a tour of Britain and the United States to speak with Catholic leaders and lobby on behalf of the regime. For the moment, none of this had much effect. The confiscated archives of the Third Reich yielded considerable evidence of the regime's extensive collaboration, and the American ambassador abandoned Madrid on November 20, 1945, leaving the embassy in the hands of the chargé d'affaires.[32] Sometime earlier, however, he had been informed by either Franco or Lequerica (the attribution varies) that the Spanish government "could not be expected to throw itself out the window."

Within Spain, the international campaign against the regime was energetically depicted as simply anti-Spanish, a foreign left-liberal conspiracy designed to tar the entire country with a new black legend. The role of Soviet and Communist forces, such as the Soviet-dominated World Federation of Trade Unions, was played up to the fullest extent, while with respect to the Western powers Franco himself referred publicly to the machinations of a world "Masonic superstate" that lay behind the animosity.[33]

To rally support, he revived his motor tours to various parts of the country. These were often exhausting trips that lasted from dawn to dusk for one or more days, but they brought him to provinces and regions where he was seen and heard by large crowds, even if the crowds sometimes had to be manufactured by the movement.

There is little doubt that much moderate opinion rallied to the regime during the period of international ostracism. The largest disaffected strata were, as usual, urban workers and agricultural laborers. Nearly all Catholics, who in 1945 accounted for more of Spanish society than a decade earlier, supported the regime. This included most of the northern rural population and a significant portion of the urban middle classes. Franco continued to depend on much the same social strata, groups, and regions on which his military victory had been based. The Civil War was too recent and memories too bitter for much erosion to have occurred. During January 1946 demonstrations were held in cities all over the country in support of Franco, variously orchestrated by the movement.

Meanwhile, the Mexican government, principal enemy of Franco among Spanish-speaking countries, urged an end to all relations with his regime. The new Republican government-in-exile, though scarcely more than a paper creation, was recognized by a number of countries, including Mexico, Panama, Guatemala, Venezuela, Czechoslovakia, Yugoslavia, and Poland. Moreover, six months after Churchill failed to win reelection, on January 23, 1946, the French assembly voted overwhelmingly to dismiss De Gaulle, and the new French government turned sharply to the left, announcing that "Franco is a danger to the world." The border between the two countries was closed on March 1, immediately after the Spanish regime's execution of Cristino García, a top captured Communist guerrilla chief, who happened also to be a French resistance veteran. The Spanish dictator strengthened troop dispositions on the frontier, while his security forces continued to repress vigorously the internal leftist insurgency.[34]

On March 4 the governments of France, Britain, and the United States reiterated their view that Spain should be excluded from the United Nations so long as Franco remained in power. They also repeated that they had no "intention of intervening in the internal affairs of Spain," trusting that "the Spanish people will not be subjected once more to the hatred and horrors of a civil war" and expressing "the hope that patriotic Spaniards of liberal mentality will soon find the means to achieve the peaceful withdrawal of General Franco, the abolition of the Falange and the establishment of an interim caretaker government" under which they could freely elect their leaders "in order to achieve full liberty."[35] On the following day, however, in Fulton, Missouri, Winston Churchill delivered his famous speech denouncing the "Iron Curtain" that the Soviet Union had drawn across Eastern Europe. In Madrid this was taken as a sign that, as long expected, the Western powers were finally beginning to take note of other and graver concerns that were more consistent with Franco's own priorities. Moreover, there were hopeful indications that Spain's commerce with the democracies was expanding.

Meanwhile, both Aranda and Beigbeder remained active in conspiracy against Franco, who was fully informed and gave them plenty of rope. It was at this point that Aranda proposed to take up asylum in the United States Embassy, where he would lead a new Spanish provisional government, but he was informed by the embassy personnel that such a plan was unworkable.

Franco presented this diplomatic boycott as something that had to be endured in order for Spain to survive, declaring to the Cortes in May 1946 that "we would have to renounce our independence and sovereignty or surrender to anarchy if we wanted to quiet these campaigns."[36] As it was, he contended that Spain bore the higher mission of defending Christian civilization and sustaining anti-Communist resistance for all Europe.[37] In Burgos on October 1 (during the Fiesta Nacional del Caudillo), Franco announced that "the objectives of Communism" lay especially in the Mediterranean area and were aimed most directly at "Spain, the last bulwark of spirituality in the world. Once more Spain has a special international role."[38]

The Western world continued to apply pressure during 1946. A special report of the UN Security Council concluded that "the Franco regime is a fascist regime," and on December 12 the General Assembly voted thirty-four to six, with thirteen abstentions, to ask for the withdrawal of diplomatic recognition altogether if a representative government was not soon established in Madrid. This resolution led to the withdrawal of the British ambassador, the last remaining representative of a major country, though no Western state broke relations completely.[39] The Arab countries and South Africa, however, had abstained, while Portugal, Argentina, Switzerland, Ireland, and the Vatican had opposed the measure and maintained their ambassadors in Madrid. All this had the effect, moreover, of rallying much Spanish opinion in support of Franco. In anticipation of the UN vote, on December 9 several hundred thousand people gathered in the Plaza de Oriente, in front of the royal palace, to applaud him. It may have been the largest single gathering in Spanish history to that point, only surpassed thirty-six years later on the occasion of the visit of Pope John Paul II.

Franco had always sought to cultivate closer ties with Latin America, particularly through the doctrine of "Hispanidad," and this became more important than ever during the period of ostracism.[40] The most helpful response came from the Argentine government of Juan Domingo Perón. Leader of a new Argentine "social nationalism" that sought greater independence from the existing international framework, Perón regarded the Spanish system as a kind of distant brother with similar goals and problems. He soon defied the United Nations and named a new ambassador to Madrid. A resulting Franco-Perón protocol promised large Argentine grain shipments to a country where wheat production had declined greatly due to the absence of imported fertilizer and phosphates. At their high point in 1948, imports from Argentina provided at least 25 percent of all goods brought into Spain and for a crucial two years guaranteed vital foodstuffs.[41]

The social high point of this special relationship came in June 1947, with the state visit to Madrid and Barcelona of Argentina's first lady, Evita Perón. This was a grand occasion and a mass spectacle. The Francos received her with great affection, and the leaders of the regime introduced her to huge Spanish crowds, to whom she, the voice of the Argentine "descamisados" ("shirtless ones"), delivered several vibrant speeches. Carmen Franco keenly remembers this visit, which left her

> charmed, delighted, because she stayed at El Pardo. The Moncloa palace was fixed up for special events, but she stayed with us in El Pardo, in the Habsburg chambers, the oldest part, with its lovely ceilings, the part most

distant from our own quarters. She stayed there with all her people, including her hairdresser. . . . With her entire retinue, though in fact some of them had to be up in the Ritz Hotel. She was gracious and likeable, and quite different in style from my mother. I really liked her and followed her about, right at her side. When I observed that she was very blonde, she simply looked at me and commented: "Huy, my hair is darker than yours, but I tint it." And she was always late, though in Madrid my father hurried her along, because he and my mother were very punctual and kept her on schedule. But when we went to Barcelona he did not accompany us. It was my mother and I and Evita Perón, with all her people. The municipal government arranged a garden reception with a musical concert, but when it was time to go she still wasn't ready, because her hairdresser and other attendants weren't finished. Then Mamá said: "For heaven's sake, Eva, they've been waiting for us." And she replied very calmly, "Ha, let them wait. We are not the *presidentas* for nothing."

I also remember that she was going on to visit the Holy Father in Rome. Before she left Madrid she showed my father what she was going to say to him. She gave him several pages for his opinion, and he was scandalized. "This is dreadful!" he told her. "How can you say that to the pope? No, no, something like that, but more gently." And my father began to edit her address to the Holy Father, because Evita had no sensitivity about dealing with the pope. . . . She spoke well, however, she was a person who made a big impact, but she was used to making herself up with great elegance, and liked jewels overmuch. I still have a little brooch that she gave me from her jewel box. At one point Papá said to her, "But how can you talk to the workers dressed like that?" because she was wearing an elaborate plumed hat. "No, no," Papá told her, "dress a little more discreetly." "Oh, well, General, if you insist," Evita replied. . . . But she was very pleased, everybody paid her a great deal of attention, and she was really a likeable woman at the height of her power.

The special relationship with Argentina later deteriorated sharply, however, and the protocol between the two states was broken in 1950. By that time, interests had diverged, and Franco would seek an explanation in terms of the influence of Masonry and the large Jewish community in Argentina. Eventually, after a harsh confrontation with the Church, Perón would be overthrown and seek asylum in Spain, where Franco never forgot a friend who had provided assistance in an hour of need. Afterward he said that he tried to warn Perón that conflict with the Church could be fatal, supposedly admonishing, "Juan Domingo, keep calm and try to reach an agreement. Remember that the Church is eternal while our regimes are transitory."[42]

This was hardly Franco's problem, for in the metamorphosis of his regime that had begun in 1945, the Church was his strongest support. Though the pope, other Vatican leaders, and the hierarchy of the Spanish Church preferred that the Church remain above and apart from political life, they all worked to gain international acceptance for the regime, and over time their efforts were rewarded. Franco took advantage of the situation by adopting the practice, when entering a church, to walk under a special portable canopy (*bajo palio*), a ritual that had been the special prerogative of Spain's monarchs alone. This was a visual symbol of the special relationship.

The 1940s brought marked revival of every aspect of religious life, from the most purely spiritual and devout to the most showy and political, resulting in a pronounced resacralization of Spanish affairs, though it would last scarcely two decades. Critics later termed this a system of "national Catholicism," in a pun derived from the regime's national syndicalism. Not all the Catholic hierarchy, however, was pleased with the role of Catholicism in the regime. The most vocal critic was Pablo Segura, the cardinal archbishop of Seville. One of the most right-wing leaders of a very rightist institution, he detested Franco, whom he considered a political tyrant and opportunist who merely instrumentalized religion. Cardinal Segura rejected all requests for special "Falangist masses" and even delivered a public sermon asserting that in classical literature the term "caudillo" had signified the leader of a band of thieves and that Loyola's *Spiritual Exercises* classified such a figure as a demon. For some years the Vatican, long somewhat unsure about Franco, refused to remove Segura, and the caudillo may have toyed with the idea of expelling him from Spain, as the Second Republic had done, but he finally resigned himself to the idea that Cardinal Segura was a cross to be borne.[43]

Although not all prelates were enthusiastic about Franco, the main Church leaders were firm and outspoken in their support, providing key backing during the years of ostracism. Though Franco refused to carry out certain reforms that Catholic corporatists deemed important, and though Church publications and social initiatives were never completely free from harassment, the balance was satisfactory to Church leaders. Franco told the Cortes on May 14, 1946, that "the perfect state for us is the Catholic state. For a people to be Christian in our view moral precepts alone are not sufficient: laws are necessary to maintain principles and correct abuses."[44] By that time the broadest assortment of religious regulations seen in any twentieth-century Western state had been established, crowned eventually by the 1953 concordat with the Vatican.

This close relationship between the Spanish government and the Church offered many advantages to the Church. It became a dominant voice in primary education and won manifold financial subsidies and tax exemptions. On its behalf, the government rebuilt hundreds of destroyed or heavily damaged church buildings and constructed many new ones, renovated and expanded seminaries, enforced Church norms in many aspects of life, and established a special juridical procedure and protection for clergy accused of violating civil law.

Such a strong embrace of the Church served Franco and his regime in a variety of ways, the most important being that it helped solidify the regime's legitimacy and expand its base of support. The association with the Church provided means through which Catholic organizations and groups might participate in public affairs. It offered a sounding board for certain interests otherwise ill represented (even if this was no more than a chance to blow off steam), it provided new cadres from which top political personnel might be selected, and it contributed to elaborating the subsequent programs and objectives of the regime.[45]

While accentuation of Catholicism was one major strategy the regime used to achieve legitimacy, another was the invocation of a carefully controlled Monarchism. Had Hitler won the war, a perpetual semi-Fascist dictatorship might have been feasible, yet Franco had been sufficiently astute from the beginning to understand that the most viable outcome of his regime would probably be authoritarian monarchy, combining traditional legitimacy with authoritarian features. On July 17, 1945, several months after the publication of Don Juan's Lausanne manifesto, Franco had informed the National Council that "of all the systems universally accepted for the governing of peoples only one presents itself to us as viable" so far as assuring his succession went, namely, "the traditional Spanish one . . . in accordance with the principles of our doctrine," indicating that the Cortes would shortly prepare legislation to this end.[46]

Two months later Carrero Blanco presented a thirteen-page memorandum, defining the two cornerstones of Spanish policy. On the international level the regime need only sit tight, for Britain and the United States would never directly intervene and hand the government of Spain over to a divided, unstable, potentially pro-Communist Republican government in exile (which in fact was never recognized by any of the major powers). Internally, the solution would be the monarchy, but only on Franco's terms. The Monarchist politicians lacked the slightest power to impose their will; Don Juan must be weaned away from them and brought to an understanding with the regime.[47]

While hoping to gain the support of the legitimate pretender, Franco had been careful never in public or private to endorse directly the principle of dynastic legitimacy. He claimed to regard this as especially dubious in the case of the Spanish Bourbons, in view of their family history. Referring to a promiscuous nineteenth-century queen, Franco once observed that the father of the king could not be "the last person who goes to bed with Doña Isabel." Monarchical succession was a complex matter involving both principles and personal capacity and should not be decided by biology alone. One of his typically blunt private comments was to the effect that one must be careful about "whatever comes out of the queen's womb, to see if it is fit."[48]

The generalissimo maintained contact with Don Juan through intermediaries during the autumn and winter of 1945–46 and decided not to oppose the pretender's plan to move his residence to Portugal. Franco apparently believed the move might facilitate an interview that he could use to his advantage, and therefore he indicated his approval to the Portuguese government. On February 2, 1946, Don Juan took up residence in Estoril, a posh suburb of Lisbon, establishing a base as close to Spain as possible but showing no interest in visiting Franco on Franco's terms. The Salazar regime permitted him complete freedom and did not allow Nicolás Franco, the Spanish ambassador, to supervise his activities. Moreover, his arrival in the peninsula sparked rumors of an agreement with Franco that produced a letter of support for the Conde de Barcelona signed by no fewer than 458 members of the Spanish elite, including two former Franco ministers (Galarza and Pedro Gamero del Castillo).[49]

This infuriated Franco, who had Nicolás announce to the pretender on February 15 that, given the extreme differences in their positions, relations were now broken. Soon afterward General Kindelán, whom Franco held most responsible for collecting the signatures, was ordered to undergo a period of internal exile in the Canary Islands.[50] At the beginning of 1947, the caudillo also put an end to the inveterate plotting of Antonio Aranda, packing him off for two months of exile in the Balearics.

As the months passed, Carrero Blanco urged Franco to make use of the current wave of popular support for his government to proceed with setting up a workable Monarchist succession on his own terms.[51] Such a move would seize the initiative from the Monarchist politicians and, making use of the recently promulgated Law of Referendum, both ratify Franco's existing powers and legitimize them by converting the state system into a monarchy. This would provide a much stronger answer to foreign critics. Moreover, Washington's announcement of the Truman Doctrine on March 12, 1947, inaugurating the first official phase of Western resistance to Communist expansion, opened prospects of a polarized international situation that a relegitimized Spanish regime might exploit to end its ostracism.

Franco agreed, and the Law of Succession was ready by March 27, 1947. Its first article stipulated that "Spain, as a political unit, is a Catholic social and representative state which, in keeping with her tradition, declares herself constituted into a kingdom." The second specified that "the Head of State is the Caudillo of Spain and of the Crusade, Generalissimo of the Armed Forces Don Francisco Franco Bahamonde." The Spanish state was thereby declared to be a monarchy, which Franco would govern until his death or "incapacity." He would have the right to name his royal successor for approval by the Cortes. The future king must be male, Catholic, and at least thirty years of age and must swear to uphold the Fundamental Laws of the Realm and of the National Movement. There was to be no mention of any legitimate right of succession in the royal family until after Franco had designated a royal successor, while the law reserved to him the power to cancel the right of succession of any member of the royal family in the event of "notorious departure from the fundamental principles of the state."[52]

Two new institutions, the Regency Council and the Council of the Realm, were also created. The Regency Council would be composed of three members: the president of the Cortes, the most senior general of the armed forces, and the highest-ranking Church prelate who had served as councilor of the realm for the longest period. It was to serve as interim regency during the transition to Franco's successor and, in the event that he were to die without having named one, convene the Council of the Realm and the cabinet jointly to select one.

The Council of the Realm, modeled on Napoleonic precedents, was designed as a special deputy to the executive. It would have precedence over other consultative bodies to "assist the Chief of State in matters of his exclusive competence that are of the highest importance."[53] The president of the Cortes would preside, flanked by the highest Church prelate in the Cortes, the most senior general, the head of the Supreme General Staff, and seven other members. The Council of the Realm would have responsibility for declaring war and for reexamining all laws voted by the Cortes.

This legislation stipulated that the head of state could not be relieved of his powers without the vote of two-thirds of the government ministers and two-thirds of the Council of the Realm, followed by a two-thirds vote of the Cortes. Since all members of these bodies had been appointed either directly or indirectly by Franco, his ever being relieved was an altogether implausible prospect, provided he did not fall into a prolonged coma. Finally, in lieu of a written code or constitution, article 19 recognized as the Fundamental Laws of the Realm, the Charter of the Spanish People, the Labor Charter, the Constitutive Law of the Cortes, "the present Law of Succession," the recently instituted Law of the National Referendum, "and any other which may be promulgated in the future in this category."[54]

Carrero Blanco personally delivered the text of this legislation to the pretender in Estoril on March 31, only hours before Franco announced it to the nation. This aroused rage and consternation in the royal circle, for it made the succession elective and purely dependent on the pleasure of the dictator.[55] On April 7 Don Juan launched a public manifesto that declared Franco's legislation to be "completely opposed to the laws that historically have regulated the succession to the Crown."[56] The Carlist pretender Don Javier de Borbón-Parma also protested in a personal letter to Franco, but both messages were completely suppressed within the country, while the official media immediately launched a harsh press campaign against Don Juan and various members of his council, denounced as enemies of the regime and of Spain.

Franco, now defined as a sort of regent for life, spent the second half of May in Barcelona, his longest visit to any city in five years. Much of the next month was devoted to the gala reception for Evita Perón, who was in Spain from June 8 to 25. Meanwhile the Law of Succession was rubber-stamped by the Cortes on June 6 and became the subject of Franco's first national referendum exactly one month later. In preparation, on June 25 the *Boletín Oficial del Estado* announced that ration cards would be requested for voter identification and would be stamped at the polling place. By that point the failure of both international diplomatic pressure and the internal insurgency was becoming apparent. Whether or not most Spaniards supported the regime in a positive sense, relatively few saw any real alternative to it. The turnout on July 6 was by all reports massive. The government announced that of 17,178,812 qualified adult voters, a total of 15,219,565 cast ballots. Of these, 14,145,163 were reported as voting yes, 722,656 no, with 336,592 votes null or mutilated.[57] Whatever the real figures, this was a major step for Franco, creating at least a certain theoretical or polemical legitimacy as well as a mechanism for the succession, and it had been done without making any concessions. Carrero Blanco defined the new situation in a memo to Franco: "The past ten years have witnessed passage from the most absolute dictatorship (with all rights and authority concentrated in the person of the victor in the Crusade) to the present stable and definitive regime of representative monarchy."[58]

One of Franco's first measures in the use of his newly minted "regential" prerogatives in October 1947 was to create new titles of nobility. Three of the first recipients of dukedoms in 1948 were the heirs of Primo de Rivera, Mola, and Calvo Sotelo. Altogether, he created thirty-six new titles over the years, most of them by 1961. Two-thirds of the surviving members of the original National Defense Council of 1936 were ennobled. Seventeen new titles went to the military, but only three to Falangists. So far as is known, the only recipient who refused to show gratitude was the retired Queipo de Llano, named Marqués de Queipo de Llano in 1950. This was an attempt by Franco to offer recognition to an important general whom he had completely marginalized since 1939. Queipo had never been entirely intimidated but remained as prickly and sarcastic as ever. He may have thought he merited a dukedom, and in a letter of June 18, 1950, he told Franco that the title was of scant value; it was a title that, as he put it, "with the passage of years could be confused with that of any marqués de Casa López."[59]

The guerrilla insurgency of the Communists and anarchists continued but after 1947 weakened steadily. The most troublesome features were the terrorist acts of railway sabotage, which totaled thirty-six in 1946 and reached seventy-three the following year, including fourteen derailments in 1947, before declining. The worst single terrorist incident took place, however, in February 1949 when a band of Communist guerrillas planted a bomb in the small train station of Mora la Nueva (Tarragona province), blowing up part of the Madrid-Barcelona train, killing thirty-three and wounding several hundred. Franco used the army to seal the frontier and cordon off areas, but he knew that frequent employment of the military in police activities could be counterproductive, and he relied primarily on the highly disciplined constabulary of the Civil Guard, but on one occasion, he did call in two battalions of *regulares* from Morocco. During 1949 the number of incidents dropped by half, with a similar decline the following year. None of this received the slightest publicity within Spain. According to the data presented to Franco, the insurgency carried out 8,054 actions (sabotage, assaults, and a few kidnappings) between 1943 and 1950, in which 2,036 were killed and 3,211 taken captive. The Civil Guard lost 243, with 341 wounded, and arrested 17,861 people as accomplices.[60] New strike activity spiked in 1946–47, then quickly declined under firm repression. The leftist opposition, as usual, divided internally, and the attempt by the Socialists to reach an entente with the Monarchists failed.

A decree of April 7, 1948, finally ended the terms of martial law that had been in effect since the end of the Civil War, though all political offenses of any magnitude would continue to be prosecuted by military tribunals. Once he was certain that Spain would not be invaded, Franco also began to reduce the military budget, which had devoured a large part of state income during the early years of his regime. In 1945 the armed forces consumed 43 percent of the budget (more than two-thirds of this going to the army), public order 6.57 percent, and the movement only 1.9 percent. By 1947 the military budget had been reduced by more than 20 percent, to little more than 34 percent of state expenditures.[61] In November 1948 Franco felt secure enough to implement a reform announced three years earlier, holding the first indirect corporative municipal elections. So controlled a process involved no risks, though a note he received from the foreign minister lamented the clumsiness of the official notification of the results, which, as the minister put it, "reveals the limited extent of the voting."[62]

During 1948 the position of Don Juan weakened further. Kindelán advised him firmly that Franco was not going to be overthrown and that the monarchy either would be restored by the generalissimo or not restored at all. Similar advice was received from Julio Danvila, a personal friend of Alfonso XIII, who reflected the opinion of the majority of Monarchists in Spain. He urged that good relations be restored before it was too late, suggesting that Don Juan's elder son, the blond, cherubic Prince Juan Carlos, be educated in Spain, rather than in exile.[63]

Danvila was finally authorized to meet with Franco at El Pardo at the close of July, just before the latter left for his summer vacation at the Pazo de Meirás. The caudillo was at first skeptical, saying that "Estoril is a lost cause," but he agreed that conceivably the education of the prince might constitute a "first step" in better relations.[64] This led to the first personal meeting between Franco and Don Juan, which took place aboard the dictator's yacht *Azor*, off the northern coast, on August 25, 1948. They talked alone for three hours and reached an agreement that the ten-year-old Juan Carlos would begin his education in Spain that fall. Franco assured

Don Juan that the pretender was indeed the "gallo tapado" ("hooded cock") implied by the Law of Succession, which, he explained, would go into effect when the time came, adding that at present there did not exist in Spain political support for either a monarchy or a republic and that the caudillo would have to remain in power at least twenty years more. Soon there might be a world war against Communism in which Spain would be on the front lines. The conversation ended with nostalgic recollections of Alfonso XIII.[65]

The meeting attracted considerable attention in the foreign press. The *New York Times* termed it a victory for Franco, and French newspapers emphasized that this would put an end to negotiations between Don Juan and the Spanish Socialists. The controlled press in Spain barely mentioned the encounter, while the pretender's closest collaborators, who had been kept in the dark, received the news with astonishment and stupefaction.[66] Some were very harsh in their comments: "The monarchy has ended today. . . . We have all been 'Bourbonized'. . . . Don Juan is crazy and has lost his dignity. . . . He is one more traitor to the cause of Spain. . . . I never thought the king would go down on his knees before Franco . . . and then hand over his son as a hostage."[67]

Don Juanito, as the prince was called, arrived in Madrid by train aboard the Lusitania Express on November 8. Looking at the bare countryside, he is said to have inquired of his entourage "Is all of Spain like this?," a reaction very similar to that of Franco himself when he had first journeyed into central Spain four decades earlier. The prince took up residence at an estate seventeen kilometers north of Madrid, where a special elite school had been established for him and seven other children carefully selected from aristocratic families. Two weeks later, on the twenty-fourth, Juan Carlos was received for the first time by Franco and Doña Carmen at El Pardo. He came face to face with the man who had been spoken of in such negative terms by his royal parents (and about whom, as the prince recalls, he had asked a year earlier, "And why does Franco, who has been so good in the war, now cause us trouble?"). The conversation was amiable and ranged widely, though for a time the attention of Juan Carlos became fixed on a mouse scurrying beneath Franco's chair.[68]

Franco seems to have been pleased, and his daughter observes of the prince that "he was a very lively and responsible lad. My father always looked on him favorably, in fact was enchanted with him. . . . If you're born and grow up in exile that becomes very difficult. You don't even have any friends in the country over which you will reign, so Papá was really concerned that he be educated in Spain and become acquainted with the Spanish character, rather than through people who come to interview you, or some such thing."

Franco did not entirely make good on his pledge to eliminate anti-Monarchist propaganda, and on September 19, 1949, the Conde de Barcelona wrote a strong letter to Franco threatening not to allow his son to return for the new school year. The generalissimo took his time, as usual, and did not reply for a full month. José María Gil Robles, at that time the chief adviser of Don Juan, described Franco's letter as follows:

> It is a very long note whose two principal characteristics are overweening pride and poor syntax. The chief ideas of this absurd fabrication, doubtless edited by Franco himself, are the following: 1—that in the interview on the *Azor* he made no promises; 2—that he ought to be thanked for having initiated the possibility of a monarchist regime with the Law of Succession, since it would have been easier to install a different system; 3—that the education of the Prince in Spain is a benefit for him and for the dynasty that has not been adequately appreciated; 4—that he fails to see that the presence of the Prince creates any equivocal situation, though this was clearly made manifest by Franco in his speech before the Cortes in May where he violently attacked the monarchy; 5—that in no way should one think about replacing the present regime; 6—that the King's attitude comes from a little clique of monarchist busybodies and the negative activity of bad counselors; 7—that the King should consider how difficult monarchist restorations are today. All this in a confused and exaggerated tone in which he calls himself Caudillo while addressing the King only as Highness and making repeated references to what is good for the dynasty.[69]

The problems of the Monarchists only increased in December 1949, when Don Jaime de Borbón, the older brother of Don Juan, who had earlier renounced his rights to the throne because he was a deaf-mute, suddenly announced in Paris that his abdication was no longer valid, since he had been cured of his afflictions.[70] This presented a serious challenge for the succession, not so much with regard to Don Jaime himself, since it was altogether unlikely that Franco would ever name a handicapped successor, but rather in the form of his two healthy young sons, Alfonso and Gonzalo.

Without having taken the slightest initiative himself, Franco henceforth held the ace in the hole that would keep Don Juan in line. The number of potential candidates to the throne only lengthened. These included Don Juan, Don Jaime, his elder son Don Alfonso, the Carlist pretender Don Javier of Borbón-Parma, his son Don Carlos Hugo, and even, for a while, Don Carlos of Habsburg-Lorraine ("Carlos VIII"), grandson of the earlier Carlist pretender Carlos VII. Carmen Franco describes her father's attitude toward them:

> My father did not recognize Javier de Borbón Parma but simply deemed him to have no dynastic possibility at all. Not at all, and even less his son Carlos Hugo. For my father, the possibility of the Carlist branch for the throne came to an end with Don Carlos. He always felt sorry for Jaime de Borbón, whose figure inspired pity because he suffered the severe handicap of being a deaf-mute, . . . and the truth is that life had treated him very badly. He always said "I feel sorry for Don Jaime" but of course never considered him in political terms, though he wanted to help him in his personal affairs. Beginning in 1949 he began to try to reclaim his right to the throne. . . . They taught him to talk so that he became convinced that he had overcome his limitations, since he did speak, but since he was still deaf he talked very badly, though he didn't realize it. On the other hand, my father . . . liked his son Alfonso de Borbón Dampierre well enough. But he talked with him very little, very little.

In this unequal contest Franco held all the cards. The final hope of the Monarchists, such as it was, lay in the military, and the last attempt at conspiracy took place in 1949. Antonio Aranda made one more effort in July of that year to gain support among the generals.[71] That was finally too much for Franco. He treated high-ranking military men with tact and even indulgence, but he had had too much of Aranda's years of intriguing and so promulgated special ad hominem legislation to place Aranda on the permanent retirement list, thereby putting an end to the agitation of the army's most persistent political gadfly.[72] Early in 1950, when a Monarchist note was handed to the American chargé in Madrid urging support for the monarchy as an alternative to Franco and bearing several hundred names, the generalissimo felt secure enough to let the entire list be published in the Monarchist *ABC*, for he thought they would appear as a set of traitors to the nation.[73]

All the while Franco maintained his obsession with the subversive machinations of Masonry, even though some of the anti-Communist leaders of the West with whom he had to deal were also Masons. To inform the Spanish public in more detail, he published a series of articles in *Arriba* under the pseudonyms variably of "Hakim Boor," "J. Boor," or "Hispanicus." The first had appeared on December 14, 1946, at the time of the condemnation by the United Nations, when he denounced "the mindless proposal of Trygve Lie, a thirty-third degree Mason, who is also, at the same time, in the service of Moscow." In that article Franco specified the secretary general and also the president of the United States as the Western leaders of the conspiracy against his regime. "The whole secret of these campaigns against Spain can be discovered in two words: Masonry and Communism."[74]

The articles denouncing Masonry continued intermittently for a number of years. Another piece in *Arriba* on February 16, 1949, titled "Those Who Refuse to Pardon," declared that "the Masonic inspiration of all these plots stands out everywhere." It observed that since Spain had held patronage of certain sites in the Holy Land since the sixteenth century, the papacy's effort to gain approval of a statute internationalizing Jerusalem should be supported.[75] Such sentiments added to the tension between his regime and the new state of Israel. Franco successfully cultivated good relations with the Arab world, which largely supported his government, while the Jewish state twice voted in the United Nations against lifting the sanctions on Madrid.[76] When Franco attempted to initiate relations with Tel Aviv, he was rebuffed, which he decried as ingratitude for his regime's efforts to rescue Jews. As it was, normal relations would never be established between the two states during Franco's lifetime.[77]

At the beginning of April 1949 Western countries formed the North Atlantic Treaty Organization (NATO) for mutual defense against Soviet expansion. Portugal was invited to become a charter member, since the Salazar regime, which had never dallied with the Axis, provoked much less hostility abroad than Franco's. Pursuant to the original Iberian pact between Lisbon and Madrid, Salazar championed Spain's entry into NATO, but the opposition from the West European democracies (not necessarily from the United States) was too strong.[78] Franco's response, which he issued to a leading American journalist, that "organizing NATO without Spain is like making an omelet without eggs," resonated internationally, and Churchill declared in the House of Commons that ignoring Spain left an "open breach" in Western defense.[79] From that point Franco would focus primarily on developing a bilateral relationship with Washington.

In the same month that NATO was formed, the United Nations held a vote on continuing the sanctions against Spain in which each proposition failed to carry sufficient votes, in effect nullifying the original decision. Nonetheless, a two-thirds vote was required in the General Assembly to recall ambassadors, and an energetic effort by Spanish diplomats failed to achieve that. Twenty-five countries voted in favor of normalizing relations, fifteen opposed it, and fifteen more abstained. The American representative was one of those abstaining, in large measure not to offend West European allies. Franco was particularly outraged by Abba Eban, the Israeli foreign minister, who, after Israel had voted no, charged that Franco had aided Hitler in persecuting Jews. Later, in January 1950, the American secretary of state, Dean Acheson, dispatched a letter to a Democratic senator that ended up in the *New York Times*, concluding that since there was no viable alternative to Franco it was better to deal with him and hence soon there would be an ambassador in Madrid. One consequence of the continued improvement in the international situation was that in November 1949 Franco decided that it was safe to reappoint Raimundo Fernández-Cuesta to the position of secretary general of the movement, a post that had been vacant for four and a half years.

The steady improvement in the international climate encouraged the Francos to travel abroad in 1950, for the first and only time in their marriage. First, the caudillo enabled Doña Carmen to realize a lifelong ambition to visit the Vatican, sending her to Rome in April aboard the *Azor* so that she could be received by Pope Pius XII and enjoy the special indulgences of the current Holy Year.[80] Then in October she joined Franco on his longest trip ever as chief of state as the couple traveled aboard Spain's most modern warship, the cruiser *Canarias*, to visit the Spanish Sahara. They returned by way of the Canaries, spending a few days in Santa Cruz de Tenerife, where they had undergone months of growing uncertainty in the spring of 1936. They also visited Franco's old friend and former juridical aide Martínez Fuset, at this point a prosperous civilian lawyer and notary.

It has been alleged that Doña Carmen attempted, unsuccessfully, to convince Fuset to take over Carrero Blanco's role as subsecretary of the presidency. The devout, ultraconservative Carrero had momentarily fallen into disfavor because of his separation from his wife, with whom he had several children. Carrero sought a reliable lawyer and counselor, finding one in a priest and law professor at Santiago de Compostela, a member of the Catholic secular institute Opus Dei, who succeeded in negotiating a marital reconciliation. This not merely saved Carrero's position but initiated his relationship with the members of Opus Dei, a number of whom would later become some of the regime's most influential ministers.[81]

A further shift of international affairs in favor of Franco occurred on June 25, 1950, when North Korea launched its invasion of South Korea. The three-year Korean conflict greatly intensified the Cold War, making the stability of Spain and its geostrategic position all the more important to Western powers. The *Times* of London came out in favor of an understanding with Franco. The chargés d'affaires who had been left in charge of the Western embassies negotiated various formulas and agreements that increasingly regularized relations with the Spanish government, while the three key powers—the United States, Britain, and France—were almost ready to put an end to the policy of ostracism.

Franco had placed the vital Washington connection in the hands of his former foreign minister, José Félix de Lequerica, who had been dispatched to the American capital in 1948 with the artificial title of "inspector of embassies." His mission was to take charge of what became known as the "Spanish lobby," which paid a hefty retainer to its American adviser, a well-placed lawyer. Alberto Martín Artajo, the foreign minister, had opposed this special initiative, preferring to emphasize internal reforms and normal negotiations, but Franco thought a major effort to reach agreement with Washington was indispensable. The suave, jovial Lequerica, no longer "ambassador of the Gestapo," did his job well. The lobby won increasing support from conservative and Catholic congressmen, as well as backing in the press and important financial credits for Spanish trade. The American military leadership was the other major source of support, for it had begun to prioritize a strategic defense arrangement with Madrid. Should the massive Red Army overrun Western Europe, General Omar Bradley, head of the Joint Chiefs of Staff, saw the peninsula as "the last foothold in continental Europe" that might be held.[82] President Truman was beginning to give way, strictly for geostrategic reasons.

On November 4, 1950, the General Assembly of the United Nations voted thirty-nine to ten, with twelve abstentions, to lift the sanctions voted four years earlier and resume normal relations with Spain, marking the end of ostracism. Though as late as November 2 President Truman declared that it would be "a long, long time" before there was an American ambassador in Madrid, Washington's policy changed the following month. A new ambassador arrived in January 1951, while Lequerica became regular ambassador to Washington. During the first part of the year ambassadors from the other boycotting countries returned. Problems remained, for one of Franco's top diplomats, Fernando María Castiella, was rejected as ambassador in London because of his personal record as a volunteer in the

Blue Division and coauthor of the expansionist *Reivindicaciones de España* (1941). Amusingly, the British were willing to accept instead the tall, handsome, and mediocre Miguel Primo de Rivera, former minister of agriculture and younger brother of the founder of the Fascist Falange, of which he also had been an important leader. The difference, it was said, lay in Primo de Rivera's aristocratic title (*grande de España*) and his family's origins in Jerez, an area closely connected with England in the sherry trade.

Franco hoped to reestablish with Stanton Griffis, the new American ambassador, the relationship of mutual respect that he had enjoyed with Carlton Hayes. Griffis was welcomed with a lavish reception (exceeding anything given an ambassador of Hitler's), flanked by the colorful uniforms of Franco's Guardia Mora, the mounted Moroccan ceremonial escort of the caudillo. In their initial interview, Griffis went directly to the point, inquiring whether Franco was concerned to join NATO, whether he was willing to send troops outside Spain, and if he had interest in negotiating an agreement to establish American bases in Spain, as well as bringing up the standard sore point of the liberties of Protestants. Franco replied that he had no desire to enter NATO and did not want to be involved in a defensive arrangement with the leftist governments of Britain and France. He preferred a bilateral arrangement with the United States.[83]

This was followed in July by the visit of nine American senators. After meeting with Franco, the Democrat senator Theodore Francis Green, earlier very critical of the generalissimo, observed that he did not at all resemble a "conventional dictator." A few days later, Franco received Admiral Forrest Sherman, chief of naval operations, in El Pardo, amid protests from London and Paris. Franco restated his interest in a bilateral pact and his distaste for NATO, agreeing to meet with an American military commission to begin negotiations on the twentieth, but not before then, since he was replacing his council of ministers on the nineteenth. Discussions then began that in some respects resembled the haggling with Hitler over Spain's entry into World War II, for they proved very complicated, with much attention to detail, and would not be completed for nearly two years.

The new cabinet appointed on July 19, 1951, was Franco's seventh, and reflected an attempt to give a more balanced expression to the connubium between the Catholic Church and the National Movement on which the regime was based. Fernández-Cuesta remained secretary general of the movement, which under the new circumstances no longer needed to be further downgraded, and Muñoz Grandes, Hitlerian Iron Cross and all, became minister of the army and was, in effect, recognized as the top general (Varela was at this point near death from leukemia). A new ministry was created, the Ministry of Information and Tourism, a dual assignment that regulated censorship and was also supposed to develop what might become a major tourist industry. This post was given to the ultra-Catholic Gabriel Arias-Salgado, who had already been administering state censorship as vice secretary of Popular Culture. Education was normally placed in Catholic hands, though Franco had wanted to reassign that ministry to Castiella, who rejected the post. He therefore recalled Joaquín Ruiz Giménez, one of the country's most distinguished Catholic laymen, from his post as ambassador to the Vatican. Ruiz Giménez took over education, while Castiella went to Rome, and Carrero Blanco's position was raised to ministerial rank, because Franco was tired of having to relate the proceedings of cabinet meetings to him verbally.[84]

Appointment of this new government followed the first large public protest in the history of the regime, when several hundred thousand people demonstrated in Barcelona against an increase in streetcar fares. This was of course symptomatic of greater unrest and produced minor disorder. Carrero Blanco published two articles under his pseudonym in *Arriba* assuring readers that, as usual, the Masons were behind it. Franco was upset by the lackadaisical response of the security forces in Barcelona and moved in tougher units to bring the situation under control.

In July 1951 Don Juan wrote to Franco to inform him that in the autumn he would also send his second son, Alfonso, to be educated with Juan Carlos in Spain, henceforth at a palace in San Sebastián. He further declared that the recent protests were a consequence of the economic crisis and "administrative corruption" that were driving the masses to despair. Don Juan invited Franco to make arrangements with him for restoring the monarchy, warning that he did not intend to renounce his rights to the throne.

Franco did not respond for two months and then told the Conde de Barcelona in a lengthy missive that his expectations were preposterous. He had, the caudillo declared, taken over a country in ruins, "an unviable fatherland," and still had much work and reconstruction to complete, warning the pretender that it might become necessary for him to abdicate his rights.[85] This was the last communication between the two for three years, but meanwhile the young princes continued their education in Spain.

Some of the most severe restrictions of economic autarchy had been relaxed after 1945, and other measures of liberalization were taken in 1951, though the national economy remained highly regulated. Excluded from multilateral economic associations, Spain had had to concentrate on bilateral trade since 1945 and had done so successfully, despite the diplomatic ostracism.[86] Foreign credit nonetheless remained limited, and foreign investment, discouraged by autarchy, was almost nil, but at least the stagnation of the World War years was slowly being overcome. Severe drought and international restrictions had worsened conditions in 1946, producing another increase in food shortages, but domestic production began to rise, and by 1951, when the improvement was much more marked, the country finally recovered its per capita income of 1935. Industrial and electrical production expanded considerably, despite intermittent power shortages due to drought, while agricultural output also increased. Elementary education also grew, and the number of students in secondary schools increased nearly 50 percent between 1940 and 1950, the majority in Catholic institutions, while the number of university students doubled. The proportion of female students increased at both levels. In another measure of well-being, the height of army recruits continued to increase by more than a centimeter every five years, a slightly better record than in the prosperous 1920s. Maternal and infant mortality declined noticeably. During the decade of the 1940s wages had fallen disastrously behind inflation but had largely caught up by 1950, while the minister of labor, Girón, expanded the scope of the Instituto Nacional de Previsión (the national insurance institute) to provide broader insurance coverage. The first year of rapid and sustained overall economic growth was 1951, and the gross domestic product subsequently increased about 50 percent between 1950 and 1958.[87]

This improvement, both in international relations and in the economy, gave Franco the leeway to launch a campaign against Britain's continued occupation of Gibraltar, the small fortified strip of territory at the southern tip of Spain seized more than two centuries earlier. In one speech Franco even declared there was no difference between "the socialist imperialism of London and the communist imperialism of Moscow," though he never used that line after the Laborites lost power. The Rock of Gibraltar became a permanent theme of protest in diplomatic exchange, in the press, and even in the streets of Madrid, with numerous protests by young Falangists chanting "¡Gibraltar español!" An annual date was set aside every year in Spain as Gibraltar Day. Franco hoped that the issue might be taken up in the broad schemes of decolonization officially encouraged by the United Nations, and he also looked for American support, pledging that a Gibraltar under Spanish control would firmly safeguard the Straits for the West. London in turn feared that in the ongoing negotiations between Madrid and Washington the latter might recognize Gibraltar as part of the Spanish defense system, though the Americans soon reassured the British this was not the case. The offensive eventually petered out in the face of British resistance and opposition by the residents of Gibraltar, but it would be revived in the following decade.

Relations with the United States had improved greatly, and new American credits and loans were made available to the Spanish economy, but President Truman remained suspicious. In February 1952 he wrote to the caudillo inquiring specifically about the liberties of Protestants. Franco was, as usual, in no hurry to reply and, when he did so a month later, he sent up his standard smoke screen, devoting most of the missive to commonplaces about the importance of relations between the two countries. Only at the end did he add that "our regime does not interfere with the private practice of other cults, protected by the basic laws of our nation in the same way that they have been traditionally respected."[88]

That was exactly what Truman was worried about, however, and he was not reassured by actions by and statements from the right wing of the Church in Spain, particularly the notorious Cardinal Segura in Seville, where on occasion Protestant venues were attacked or torched. The American president therefore replied in a brief and very skeptical letter, expressing the hope that the current negotiations could be successfully concluded but drawing a sharp contrast between Spain and the United States on the issue of religious freedom.[89]

The news from Washington continued to be encouraging. Franco was pleased to receive a report that a new book by a top American diplomat chided Cordell Hull, former secretary of state, for having supported the Republicans in the Civil War, concluding that if they had won Spain would have become Communist.[90] In January 1952 he received a visit from Senator Owen Brewster, to whom he suggested that the slogan of the Republican Party in the forthcoming presidential elections should be "We won the war in the West, we won the war in the Pacific and we have lost the peace in both regions."[91] He made no effort to hide his support for Dwight Eisenhower in the presidential contest, and, after Eisenhower won, he even offered to send a division of Spanish volunteers to fight in the war in Korea, by that point in its third year.

The partial international rehabilitation that Franco had achieved, together with the partial defascistization of the regime, combined with its close association with religion, finally made it possible to begin to negotiate the long-coveted concordat with the Vatican. The old concordat had been signed in 1851, but the only agreement the papacy had heretofore been willing to make with Franco was a very limited one in 1941 concerning the naming of new bishops. On the centenary of the old concordat in 1951, Franco wrote to Pope Pius XII that his government sought to enter negotiations for a new one, and this eventually led to serious discussions.

Both sets of negotiations, with Washington and with the Vatican, were brought to a successful conclusion in 1953. The new concordat was signed on August 27. It was one of the most advantageous agreements signed by the Church in the past generation, for the Vatican obtained almost everything it asked for. The Church would be not only exempt from all taxation but would receive state financial support for each diocese, the clergy would enjoy judicial immunity, only canonical marriage would be legally binding, the state would administer religious instruction at all levels of education, an insult to someone in clerical habit would be treated as equivalent to an insult to someone in military uniform, and the chief of state would continue to have to select new bishops only from the Church's short list of three for each diocese. For Franco, the concordat achieved complete mutual identification of church and state, though he sounded a little defensive when he presented the measure for approval by the Cortes on October 26:

> In Spain the Church will not only enjoy all the freedom needed for its sacred objectives, but also the assistance needed for its fullest development. I am certain that the Church of Spain, its prelates and its clergy, are aware of the great responsibility that we take upon our own shoulders on recognizing its rights, privileges and liberties, on contributing to the economic support of the altar and its ministers and, above all, the seminaries in which the ministers are formed and, finally, on opening the doors of Spanish society to its apostolic labor, especially for what that means for the development of our youth.[92]

A month after completion of the concordat, on September 26, three pacts were signed in Madrid with Washington, bringing to a close nearly two years of at times arduous negotiations. The agreements dealt with "assistance for mutual defense," "economic assistance," and finally common defense arrangements "to face the dangers that threaten the Western world," the latter referring to the opening of American military bases on Spanish soil.

The military assistance agreement would provide more up-to-date weaponry to replace the stock of the Spanish army and air force, scarcely rejuvenated since 1939, together with new training programs for Spanish officers. The old German and Soviet planes and captured Soviet tanks could eventually be retired, replaced by Spain's first jet aircraft and better armored vehicles, though the process would take several years. This modernization of the armed forces would nonetheless be severely limited by lack of interest in spending money on the military, after a disproportionate amount of the budget had been consumed by the latter in the first troubled years after the Civil War.

The economic assistance amounted to $226 million, later supplemented by further grants. The counterpart measures that the United States required were steps to liberalize the heavily regulated economy, and the new ministers appointed in 1951 were already hesitantly moving in that direction. Since Spain had been excluded from the Marshall Plan, this was the first major foreign aid ever received, and it helped to promote the rapid and sustained economic growth that continued through 1958.

In the third pact, the United States gained the right to establish three air bases in Spain in Torrejón (Madrid), Morón (Seville), and Zaragoza, plus a submarine base on the southern coast in Rota (Cádiz). The bases would display the Spanish flag and be under the joint military command of the two states. In addition, the bases pact contained a secret clause that provided that, in the event of "clear Communist aggression," the United States could take action unilaterally so long as "both countries communicate mutually their information and intentions with maximal urgency." This clause would not be eliminated until 1970.[93]

Franco presented the pacts to the Cortes on October 1, declaring that no Spanish territory had been handed over to the United States. He also used the opportunity to condemn Churchill publicly for having refused his offer of alliance in October 1944, observing that it had been the mistake of an imperial power in decline. This was the final step in the international rehabilitation of Franco, though it always remained relative and limited.

It was also the coup de grâce for the Republican opposition, which at this point virtually gave up, though a shadow government in exile, periodically renewed, would continue to exist. Perhaps the most bitterly disappointed were the Basque nationalists, who, more than any other opposition group, had played the "American card" consistently since Pearl Harbor, providing secret intelligence to Washington from Spain and from Latin America.[94] They had looked confidently toward American assistance in the overthrow of Franco and the future partition of Spain. All hopes dashed, they moved their headquarters to Paris, though the clandestine Basque nationalist trade unions always received some support from the AFL-CIO as the only non-Marxist, nonrevolutionary alternative to Franco.

Ferrol 27 9 1910

Niceto Alcalá-Zamora, first president of the Second Republic (1931–36).

Left above: Franco as a seventeen-year-old second lieutenant, in his first assignment in El Ferrol, September 27, 1910. (Photo dedicated to his cousin "Pacón.") (Courtesy FNFF)

Left below: Enthusiasts celebrating the inauguration of the Second Republic in Madrid, April 1931.

Left: Manuel Azaña, leader of the moderate left, prime minister of the Second Republic, and later president of the revolutionary Republic.

Below: Manuel Portela Valladares, prime minister (Dec. 1935–Feb. 1936).

Franco and his daughter, Carmencita, in 1937.

Above: Guernica after
the bombing, 1937.

Left: Franco at field
headquarters during the
Civil War.

Nationalist troops entering the Valencia region at war's end, 1939.

U. S. Ambassador Alexander Weddell and German Ambassador Eberhard von Stohrer leaving a reception in Madrid, December 6, 1940.

Left: General Antonio Aranda.

Below: Franco in Falangist uniform, followed by José Luis de Arrese, entering a meeting of the FET's National Council, December 8, 1942.

Franco and the Papal Nuncio, Monseigneur Ildebrando Antoniutti.

Franco presiding over a cabinet meeting in his summer home, the Pazo de Meirás, probably in August 1951. (Campúa, Courtesy FNFF)

Franco attending American naval maneuvers aboard the aircraft carrier *Coral Sea*, October 1954. (Courtesy FNFF)

Left above: Franco relaxing with his minister of the army, General Carlos Asensio, in the quarters of his Guardia Mora at El Pardo Palace, following the annual Victory Parade in May 1945. Leopoldo Eíjo y Garay, bishop of Madrid, in the foreground. (Courtesy FNFF)

Left below: Eva Perón with Franco and his wife, Doña Carmen, at the Royal Palace in Madrid, June 1947.

Franco entering the cathedral of Toledo "bajo palio" (under a canopy), in the style of the kings of Spain, with the Primate Cardinal Enrique Pla y Deniel. (Courtesy FNFF)

Franco following Mohammed V, sultan of Morocco, greeting the reception line at the time of the sultan's state visit marking the independence of Morocco in April 1956, General Agustín Muñoz Grandes opposite the sultan. (Courtesy FNFF)

Admiral Luis Carrero Blanco addressing the Cortes, 1957.

Franco holding the hand of one of the fifty-three sons of King Saud bin Abdulaziz during the latter's state visit in February 1962. (Courtesy FNFF)

Left above: Franco and his wife with the Primate Cardinal Enrique Pla y Deniel at the Royal Palace in Madrid, 1958.

Left below: President Eisenhower parts from Franco with a Spanish *abrazo*, December 1959.

Franco in full-dress uniform at an official reception.

Above: Franco during a pause in a hunting expedition, his son-in-law Villaverde behind him.

Right: Franco near his firing range, with his faithful physician, Vicente Gil. (Courtesy FNFF)

Franco on another hunting expedition, the head of his personal household, Fernando
Fuertes de Villavicencio, in the background. (Courtesy FNFF)

Left above: Franco adjusting his camera aboard his summer yacht, the *Azor*. (Courtesy
FNFF)

Left below: Franco presiding over a cabinet meeting at his summer home, the Pazo de
Meirás, August 18, 1967. Carrero Blanco is to his right, Lieutenant General Camilo Alonso
Vega to his left.

Franco preparing to record an address to the Spanish people (possibly Christmas Eve, 1969). (Courtesy FNFF)

Franco receives one of his most ardent admirers, the painter Salvador Dalí, who painted the portrait of his oldest granddaughter (ca. 1970). (Courtesy FNFF)

Franco receives a visit from Charles De Gaulle, with foreign minister Gregorio López Bravo in the background, May 5, 1970. (Courtesy FNFF)

Franco laughing with his oldest granddaughter, Carmen Martínez-Bordiú, who would soon marry the grandson of Alfonso XIII. (Courtesy FNFF)

Franco, accompanied by Prince Juan Carlos, waving to a mass of supporters in the Plaza de Oriente, from the balcony of the royal palace, at the time of the Burgos trials in December 1970. (Courtesy FNFF)

Franco receives Ronald Reagan, governor of California, at El Pardo, with foreign minister López Bravo in the background, July 11, 1972. (Courtesy FNFF)

Franco's last cabinet meeting at his summer home, with prime minister Carlos Arias Navarro, August 22, 1975.

The last public demonstration on behalf of Franco in the Plaza de Oriente, October 1975.

Left: Stricken with thrombophlebitis, Franco enters the Clínica Nacional Francisco Franco on July 9, 1974.

14 | Franco at His Zenith

(1953–1959)

After 1953, Franco reached the height of his limited international rehabilitation. The Spanish govern-ment entered the World Health Organization the following year (requiring the closure of legal brothels in Spain), and Spain became a member of the United Nations in 1955. Though the social democratic governments of Western Europe never fully accepted his regime, it achieved relative normal-ization in diplomatic and economic relations.

In accord with his standard procedure of two steps forward, one step back, Franco followed this up by convening the first mass congress of the National Movement since World War II. Addressing nearly one hundred thousand people on October 29, 1953, the twentieth anniversary of the founding of the Falange, he declared that the recent pacts were the "second battle that we have won against Communism." It was no longer necessary to keep the movement in the closet or even to disguise its name, so that Franco felt free to observe that "the Falange is superior to every challenge, flanking and supporting the constituent force of our army."[1]

The Cold War moderated after the death of Stalin, and nearly all the remaining Spanish prisoners in the GULAG, most of them men of the Blue Division, were finally released, following secret negotiations with Moscow. The Spanish ship *Semiramis*, with 286 former prisoners, docked in Barcelona in March 1954, bringing to a close the history of the expeditionary corps of 1941. They were greeted by their former commander, Muñoz Grandes, minister of the army, but Franco was not present and the celebration very muted. Only toward the end of the year were some of the returning veterans feted at the Madrid city hall. Among those in attendance was Léon Degrelle, a much-decorated, seven-times-wounded senior officer of the Waffen SS, one of a number of ex-Nazis who had found refuge in Spain. The photograph at this event of Degrelle, who had been condemned to death for treason in absentia in his native Belgium, drew much negative commentary in Western Europe.

At the beginning of May 1954, Franco was in Salamanca to receive the degree of doctor honoris causa from Spain's oldest university. The rector, Antonio Tovar, a philologist who had been one of the leading Falangist intellectuals, revived the tribute the university had once paid the Catholic monarchs, Fernando and Isabel, five centuries earlier: "The Caudillo for the university and the university for the Caudillo." Franco used the occasion to acclaim José Antonio Primo de Rivera, founder of the Falange, as "the martyr of our struggle and an exemplary university student."

Franco himself would no longer travel farther abroad than Portugal, but his daughter, Carmen, and her new husband, the surgeon Dr. Cristóbal Martínez-Bordiú, traveled a great deal after their marriage in 1950. That year they were received by the pope in Rome, and in 1954 the young couple made a lengthy trip to the United States, accompanied by a second Spanish surgeon and his wife. Ambassador Lequerica served as their host in Washington. Carmen was already acquainted with the veteran diplomat, whom she recalls remarking to her on this occasion that "you must realize, Carmen, that you are in the modern equivalent of the city of Rome under the Roman Empire."

Several months later Franco accepted an invitation from the commander of the U. S. Sixth Fleet to observe maneuvers in the Mediterranean from the deck of its command ship, the carrier *Coral Sea*. On that occasion, he dispatched a friendly telegram to President Eisenhower, ending with "¡Arriba los Estados Unidos!," using the Falangist slogan that he always found preferable to the traditional "¡Viva!"[2]

In October 1954 his cousin Pacón (General Francisco Franco Salgado-Araujo), who had served as his aide in one capacity or another for so many years, began to record by longhand his conversations with Franco. Pacón admired his eminent cousin and, aware that Franco did not keep a diary, felt a responsibility to record his thoughts for posterity. He also set about collecting remarks, recollections, and anecdotes from many of Franco's aides, ministers, and associates. Pacón persisted in this effort until his own health began to fail in 1971. After his death, followed by that of Franco, his widow, Pilar Rocha Nogués, published an edited version in 1976 under the title *Mis conversaciones privadas con Franco*. The book was criticized by members of Franco's family, though none of them made any effort to point out errors or distortions. The book has the merit of presenting a record of sorts of some of Franco's private conversations and opinions, recorded by a person who was absolutely loyal to Franco, who was concerned with accuracy, and who also avoided hagiography.[3]

At the beginning of November, the Vatican finally did the generalissimo the favor of recalling Cardinal Segura, the archbishop of Seville, who for years had intermittently gestured defiantly toward Franco as well as encouraged incitement against Protestants. The testy old prelate did not go willingly, shutting himself up in the archepiscopal palace, and he finally had to be removed by the police, who took him away as though they were carrying out a protester. Franco expressed his relief to Pacón, saying that he had endured the long tenure of Segura "as a cross that God had imposed, bearing it with the maximal patience."[4]

At the end of November 1954, the regime held its second round of municipal elections. Representation was divided into thirds, one-third of municipal councilors being chosen by the official syndicates, one-third by municipal officials, and one-third elected by family voters, the last group consisting of heads of families and of married women. Despite the weakness of the opposition, the elections were not easy to control. The official list in Madrid, the "candidacy of the Movement," was challenged by a list of independents and by another list that Monarchists presented. This last was resented and even feared by the government, which manipulated the vote to the degree necessary and then declared the complete victory of the movement candidates.

With the close of the academic year 1954–55, Prince Juan Carlos would complete his preuniversity studies, raising the question of his further education. Franco and Don Juan initially agreed that he would receive military training at the General Military Academy in Zaragoza, which had been restored by Franco.[5] The majority of royal councilors, however, led by Franco's one-time chief Gil Robles, insisted that that would associate the monarchy too closely with the regime and convinced the Conde de Barcelona to announce that Juan Carlos would pursue higher education at the Catholic University of Louvain in Belgium. Franco was angered, saying that in Estoril Don Juan was being deceived by his "council of rabbis," as he termed them. He and Don Juan had not corresponded directly for three years, but now they resumed contact. Franco dispatched a threatening letter, warning that he might close the only "natural and viable path . . . to the installation of the monarchy," demanding Don Juan's full confidence and cooperation. Otherwise, he said, it would indeed be better for Juan Carlos to be educated abroad, in which case although "one might have lost a prince, one would have gained a private citizen."[6]

Multiple Monarchist candidates continued to present competing claims. Don Javier, the Carlist pretender (though himself a French aristocrat), still asserted his rights, which he suddenly proclaimed at a meeting in Catalonia, while the elder surviving son of Alfonso XIII, Don Jaime, had regained paternal custody of his two sons and presented his own claims to Franco, who agreed that the boys ought to be educated in Spain. All this created a quandary for Don Juan, who referred Franco's demands to his council, even though these involved the danger that the generalissimo might eventually try to jump the line of succession, offering the throne to the young prince, or, for that matter, to someone else. The majority voted to accept, with only six nays, and therefore Franco and Don Juan agreed to meet together again, this time at the country estate of the Conde de Ruiseñada, not far from the Portuguese border. A devoted Monarchist, Ruiseñada was convinced that only Franco, with whom he was on good terms, could restore the monarchy.

The meeting of December 29, 1954, which began with an effusive embrace between the pretender and the caudillo, was only the second time that Don Juan had set foot on Spanish soil since 1931, the first having been when he tried to volunteer for the Nationalist army in 1936 but was rejected by Mola. Franco insisted on the great advantages of having Juan Carlos educated in Spain: "Highness: entrust to us the education of your sons. I promise you that we shall make of them exceptionally well-prepared men who are outstanding patriots." He assured the Conde de Barcelona that Monarchists would be allowed greater freedom in Spain, though certainly not in order to, say, as he put it, "get out so that we can take over, no, not that." Spain would have a king at a future date, for, though there was little popular support for the monarchy now, with time "everybody will end up being monarchist out of necessity," a prophecy that proved more or less accurate. Franco recognized the need for further institutional development. The time would come when the positions of chief of state and chief of government would have to be separated, "due to limitations of my health or my disappearance." He agreed with Don Juan that his son should not be given the title of "Prince of Asturias" (that is, immediate heir to the throne), though he added somewhat ominously that if the father's abdication should ever become necessary, "given the patriotism of Your Highness . . . , you would do so without hesitation."[7]

This meeting made a great impression on the Conde de Barcelona, who now became convinced that Franco indeed planned eventually to restore the monarchy. According to what Ruiseñada later told Pacón, Don Juan felt like someone "who had put aside a fraudulent deception to enter into possession of the truth." Talking afterward with one of his advisers in Estoril, he tapped him on the knee emphatically several times as he said, "I'd like to shoot all the people who have been speaking badly to me of this man for so many years. . . . Now the only thing is give him our confidence and collaborate, collaborate."[8]

There is no reason to doubt that Franco was sincere in 1954 when he indicated that Don Juan would probably become king, though it was typical of him that he hedged his bet when he indicated, at the same time, that, depending on circumstances, an abdication might be necessary. It would all depend on Don Juan's future loyalty to the regime and his willingness to accept a role as Franco's successor rather than his repudiator. Like most people who met with the jovial, informal Conde de Barcelona, Franco, as Carmen says, found him "very pleasant." Ruiseñada observed to the Francos, "When you talk with Don Juan he captivates you, because he is a person who has the special charm of the Bourbons."

Before the end of the year Franco changed ambassadors in Washington, replacing Lequerica with José María de Areilza, one of his top diplomats. Areilza dedicated himself to building a personal relationship between Eisenhower and Franco, encouraging the exchange of greetings, personal and family photos, and small personalized presents. The Eisenhower administration was distinctly more friendly than that of Truman, and visits to Madrid were planned both for Secretary of State John Foster Dulles and Vice President Richard Nixon. Criticism of Franco nonetheless remained strong and active on the part of American liberals, and several years more would pass before Areilza could arrange a visit by Eisenhower to Madrid.

The new relationship offered advanced training facilities for Spanish military officers, and eventually at least five thousand would pass through

American programs. In October 1954 the minister of the army, Muñoz Grandes, visited the United States. He was not at all concerned about wearing the small Blue Division shield on his uniform or, on dress occasions, about exhibiting the Knight's Cross of the Iron Cross with Oak Leaves awarded by Hitler, but American cordiality and hospitality began to win him over. Muñoz Grandes visited a variety of military facilities and was received by President Dwight Eisenhower, while General Matthew Ridgway, the army chief of staff, pinned on his lapel the Legion of Merit, the highest decoration that can be granted to a foreign commander. This highly successful trip somewhat altered the perspective of the hitherto very anti-American general.[9]

The cantankerous Muñoz Grandes was the most prestigious figure in the military after Franco himself, and the caudillo always handled him with care. He was not very attentive or efficient in administering the Spanish army, which had continued to decline prior to receiving American aid. Since the end of the Civil War Franco had devoted himself more and more to politics and affairs of state. After the close of World War II, he steadily lost interest in military institutions themselves, since all the regime's plans for military development had proven illusory. By the 1950s the Spanish army was proportionately in worse shape than in 1939, its old equipment rusting, its facilities totally antiquated, its troops threadbare. The navy and air force did benefit from the American connection and improved their efficiency somewhat, but the gains for the army were marginal. Franco is said to have received more than a few complaints about the growing neglect of Muñoz Grandes's administration, but his primary concern was political loyalty. Muñoz Grandes continued to enjoy considerable autonomy, for he was no Monarchist and would be unable to advance any alternative political project of his own.[10]

Though the regime had weathered all storms, its institutional development remained highly uncertain. The defascistization hesitantly begun in August 1943 came to a dead stop ten years later, as Franco began to reinvigorate the National Movement, which he believed was an indispensable support and mobilization device. By 1955 he was dissatisfied with the youth section, for the student syndicate had become very weak, and in fact in a few more years would disappear altogether.[11] He also thought that the program of partial liberalization being carried out in the universities by the education minister, Joaquín Ruiz Giménez, had gone too far, permitting, among other things, the organization of a center for young writers, which was becoming openly critical of the regime.

Though the movement had steadily lost members, it retained its official position, and the core Falangist sector aligned itself vociferously "against the bourgeois and capitalist monarchy." Anti-Monarchist slogans appeared on walls in the larger cities, with messages such as "We don't want any idiot kings!" Activists circulated a popular ditty with the refrain "We don't want idiot kings who don't know how to govern." And in the movement's youth front (Frente de Juventudes), another song could be heard occasionally, satirizing Franco's long fishing holidays and his frequent inauguration of new dams and hydroelectric sites, sometimes accompanied by the epithet "Paco la rana" ("Frankie the frog"). Though increasingly concerned, he felt no pressure to react immediately. On February 22, 1955, a rare public interview with the caudillo appeared in *Arriba*, in which Franco assured his public that he still felt youthful and vigorous, entrusted with a lifetime mission that he must ensure would be carried on by a successor to, not a substitute for, him.

John Foster Dulles came to Madrid in November 1955, the first time that an American secretary of state had visited Franco. The two main items of discussion were the entry of Spain into the United Nations and the increasingly urgent question of independence for Morocco. Franco had always recognized that the Spanish protectorate was just that, a protectorate, and that someday Morocco would regain its independence, but he had been confident that that time lay many decades in the future.[12] From 1945 to 1951, the period when Varela had been high commissioner, Moroccan nationalism had been repressed in cooperation with the administration of the French protectorate.[13] The policy changed after Varela was replaced by General Rafael García Valiño, who provided sanctuary and multiple facilities for nationalists so long as they directed their actions against French domination of the main part of the country. For several years there seemed little understanding that this spiteful anti-French policy would inevitably weaken the position of Spain. Once alarming signs appeared that France might simply abandon its protectorate altogether, Franco assured Dulles that Spain was willing to do the same, pending satisfactory negotiations with Sultan Mohammed V, though privately he was chagrined, even mortified, by the prospective loss of the centerpiece of Spain's remaining overseas possessions. In the long run, there was little that Spain could do to maintain its status in Morocco, but Franco's policy in the final years of the protectorate was petulant, resentful, and even self-destructive.

The entry of new members into the United Nations had been frozen in the late 1940s by the Cold War, but Dulles assured Franco that enough thawing had occurred to make possible Spain's accession. It was the last of a group of eighteen countries to make application, only doing so that month, once assurances had been received. When the initial vote was taken on December 13, the Soviet Union vetoed Spain's candidacy, only to withdraw the veto without explanation the following day. A total of sixteen countries officially became members on the fifteenth, only Japan and Outer Mongolia being vetoed.

In the months following their meeting at Ruiseñada's estate, Franco and Don Juan had agreed that Juan Carlos would undergo a special preparatory course in order to enter the General Military Academy in December 1955. They had also agreed that the erudite senior artillery commander General Carlos Martínez Campos would take over as head of the prince's staff and chief preceptor. Carmen Franco observes that her father had a high opinion of Martínez Campos, "but he said that he understood that for a teenager he might seem rather harsh, since he was not such an affable or likeable person, though he was very upright."

Franco's attention became ever more fixed on rapidly changing developments in Morocco, where he still maintained a force of sixty-eight thousand troops. In the autumn of 1955 France had restored Mohammed V to his throne, but the high commissioner of the Spanish zone, García Valiño, continued the double game of tolerating activities against the French, hoping that somehow Spain would continue to enjoy a special status. By the end of 1955 he realized, however, that matters had simply gone too far, and he warned Franco that the Spanish government must prepare concrete guarantees of independence. Washington urged Paris to move rapidly, in view of Soviet pressures in the Mediterranean and the Middle East, and the French government suddenly agreed to independence for the main part of Morocco on March 2, 1956.

To his deep chagrin, Franco had no alternative but to follow suit. The sultan landed in Madrid on April 5 and irritated the Spanish authorities with his arrogance and his refusal to recognize the autonomy of the caliph of the northern zone, appointed by Franco. The caudillo was forced to accept facts, signing the treaty of Moroccan independence on April 7. The press announced it as an act of Spanish generosity that Franco had long planned, which was not true. Some army officers reacted with anger, and at the academy in Zaragoza two cadets burned a photo of Franco in protest. Though there was little danger from his well-domesticated army, Franco purchased insurance by decreeing the largest salary increases for officers in years, camouflaged amid general, but proportionately much smaller, increases in general labor contracts that were needed for wages to catch up with inflation. It is doubtful that anyone was more disturbed by the loss of the protectorate than Franco himself, who had once said that "without Africa I could hardly explain me to myself." He saw fifteen years of his life, the years that had first made him a public figure, vanish as distant history. Yet the geopolitical change was total, and all he could do was to reinforce slightly the remaining garrisons farther south in Ifni and the Spanish Sahara, though all the troops in northern Morocco were not pulled out for several years.[14]

While the Moroccan drama unfolded, a political crisis erupted at the University of Madrid, because of tensions between Falangists and opposition students who had begun to voice opinions criticizing Franco and the movement. On February 7, 1956, the university administration announced that it was considering the annulment of recent elections for delegates of the SEU, the official student syndicate, in the Faculty of Law, while Falangist groups talked of occupying the law building to expel "the Reds who are asking for dissolution of the SEU." February 9 was a special Falangist anniversary, the Day of the Fallen Student, to commemorate the death of the first official Falangist martyr, a medical student gunned down by a young Socialist in 1934. Falangist marchers encountered a crowd of opposition students at a street corner near the law building, which led to a free-for-all that went from fists to rocks to a crescendo of, depending on which account one reads, from six to eight gunshots. The main casualty was a nineteen-year-old Frente de Juventudes militant, Miguel Alvarez, shot in the head, whose life was saved by emergency surgery.

The movement press was vociferous in its denunciation, and Carrero Blanco himself quickly published an article under his customary pseudonym, Ginés de Buitrago, which compared the gravity of this incident with the one at Begoña in August 1942. More worrisome was the fact that arms were being distributed among movement activists, which infuriated military leaders. The captain-general of Madrid, Miguel Rodrigo Martínez, was the army's most decorated senior commander, and he warned that the military would not permit any Falangist violence. Once Rodrigo Martínez had secured the support of Muñoz Grandes, Franco ordered the arrest of the troublemakers. It turned out that the near-fatal shot had been fired by a fellow Falangist. Franco did not receive the final report for several months, but this demonstrated conclusively that at least five shots had been fired by Falangists, mostly into the air as a means of intimidation, one of them falling and striking Alvarez in the top of the forehead.[15] Its conclusions were never made public.

Franco acted rather more quickly than in earlier crises, appointing a new government on February 14. He might have moved even earlier, but he was distracted by events in Morocco and now was faced with a kind of crisis of identity for the regime. The Falange movement, despite a superficial bellicosity, was growing ever weaker, while Monarchists became more active, as did Catholic leaders, and even the leftist opposition showed signs of life. In these circumstances, Franco looked toward a reconsolidation of his regime. The most important change he made was to restore his favorite Falangist, José Luis de Arrese, to the post of secretary-general of the movement, giving him a new opportunity to more firmly institutionalize the state party. In addition, a series of younger leaders in the movement were promoted, Jesús Rubio replacing the reformer Ruiz Giménez in education, Torcuato Fernández-Miranda becoming director general of universities, and the bright young Manuel Fraga Iribarne taking over the brain trust, the Institute of Political Studies.

The long-term labor minister, the *camisa vieja* José Antonio Girón, was worried about the future. On April 25, he sent to Franco a twenty-page letter that he wrote by hand so there would be no copies:

> One refrain is dominating . . . the Spanish landscape: "How will things be held together after Franco?" . . . And people ask: "What will happen when we no longer have Franco?" If the monarchy is unpopular and anachronistic to begin with . . . and without institutional and legal support on its behalf, it will not have adequate defenders. . . . The monarchy would be likely to perish. . . . Now even the Movement is juridically defenseless. The existing laws are inadequate. . . . For this reason the defense of the regime must be carried out by the police instead of being done through the law. And instead of tranquility, police action causes alarm.
>
> The very facility with which this idea of insecurity has been propagated to the entire nation . . . has convinced Spaniards that the juridical system on which the Movement rests has weaknesses that will impede its perpetuation. People don't even debate . . . the conclusion that when it comes time to replace the Caudillo everything will come to an end. Spaniards are convinced that by that point there will be nothing more to do.[16]

Holy Week of 1956 was a time of special tragedy for the royal family. The young princes, eighteen-year-old Juan Carlos and fourteen-year-old Alfonsito, returned to Estoril for spring vacation after dutifully saying good-bye to Franco at El Pardo. Juan Carlos, always a gun fancier, had received a pistol as a present at the academy, but, when he reached home, his father prudently placed it in a locked closet. On Good Friday, March 29, after attending religious services, the princes were assigned a period of study in their rooms. Since his father was away, Juan Carlos talked his mother into giving him the key to the closet, saying that he wanted to go out for a little target practice after studying. Retrieving the pistol, he placed it in a drawer of his desk. While he was trying to concentrate, the mischievous Alfonsito came into the room simulating a commando attack on his brother, who drove him out, finally locking the door. Undeterred, Alfonsito came back through a different door, adding sound effects: "Ra-ta-ta; ra-ta-ta; you're dead, coward." Finally, going along with the game, Juan Carlos looked up, pulled the presumably empty gun from the drawer and, aiming it, clicked the trigger: "The one who is dead is you." But the gun was not empty, and the shot hit the adolescent prince right between the eyes. He fell dead instantly.[17]

Franco was informed immediately, and he and Doña Carmen quickly dispatched joint telegrams of condolence to Don Juan and to his wife, Doña María de las Mercedes. Both the Francos were deeply moved. This tragedy would haunt the royal family for years, and Doña María never entirely pardoned the deed as long as she lived. Grave infirmities had removed both of Don Juan's elder brothers from the line of succession, his brilliant younger brother Gonzalo, a hemophiliac, had died after a minor car crash, and now his second son had perished tragically. Though details of the death were hushed up in the controlled Spanish press, rumors quickly abounded, some to the effect that Juan Carlos was so crushed that he would renounce his rights to the throne and retire to a monastery. This was untrue; two days after the funeral, he returned to his studies in Zaragoza.

In the meantime, with the formation of the new government, the issue of the future institutionalization of a regime led by a dictator nearing sixty-five, however good his health, was becoming more pressing. In July Franco urged the National Council of the movement to play a more active role, which Arrese saw correctly as a green light to prepare new legislation on the role of the state party, a project he announced at the annual mass ceremony in honor of Franco, attended by approximately twenty thousand people, on September 29, 1956.

The draft commission led by Arrese could not reach agreement, and eventually three different proposals went forward: that of the secretary-general, a Monarchist draft championed by Ruiseñada, and an intermediate proposal presented by Carrero Blanco and the justice minister, Antonio Iturmendi, much of this last having been written by Laureano López Rodó, a young protégé of these two ministers whose intelligence and energy impressed Carrero. López Rodó stressed the need for a law of administrative procedure to reform government structure and personnel before proceeding to a new political charter.

Ruiseñada had succeeded in convincing most Monarchists that the strategy of cooperating fully with Franco in order to make Don Juan the future king was the correct one, but he feared that the power and independence of a restored monarchy might be seriously compromised if new legislation were to give the movement greater power once Franco died. He continued to maintain close relations with Juan Bautista Sánchez, the captain-general of Barcelona, generally recognized as having become the leader of "juanista" sentiment in the army after Kindelán retired. Ruiseñada therefore proposed that Sánchez sound out the military leadership regarding his own proposal, which was not so dissimilar from one first proposed by Don Juan in 1941. It outlined a process based on full cooperation between Franco and the pretender, under which the generalissimo would remain regent and chief of state but designate a new president of government, possibly Sánchez himself, who would prepare the way for the restoration of the monarchy in the person of Don Juan.

Under Arrese's proposal, however, the National Movement was defined as "the union of all active forces carrying out the political doctrines of Falange Española Tradicionalista y de las JONS, which represents and permanently expresses the political will of the Spanish people." In the future the key political role would be that of the movement's secretary-general, appointed by the National Council, to whom he alone would be responsible, while the council would serve as supreme court or arbiter of all national legislation. On the recommendation of the secretary-general and of the president of the Cortes, the future chief of state would name the president of government for a period of five years, though the president might be removed from office by the National Council. Franco would remain lifetime head of the movement, but the next chief of state would not hold such a position. All this represented a maximal effort to institutionalize a dominant role for the movement in the future of Spain and was guaranteed to meet a firestorm of criticism.

The key opponents were the leaders of the military and of the Church, but strong criticism also came from Monarchists, the so-called political Catholics, Carlists, and even important members of the government. Among the last group, Carrero Blanco was the most discreet, but he did ask López Rodó to draft a counterproposal. To their dismay, Franco reiterated publicly his support for Arrese, who was attempting to complete the institutional structure of his version of "organic democracy." In a speech in Seville, Franco insisted that "we are, in reality, a monarchy without royalty, but still a monarchy, yet the Falange could survive without a monarchy, while the monarchy could not survive without the Falange." He warned that "whoever might oppose the Movement" would face "torrents of blue shirts and red berets [Falangists and Carlists] ready to wash [them] away."[18] Here he may have been rejecting not merely reformists within the system but also reacting to reports he had been receiving of a change in tactics by the Communist Party, the only significant leftist opposition force. Having abandoned their failed insurgency, Communists had reversed their policy, going back to the old World War II concept of national union, proposing Spain's "national reconciliation," while at the same time party members sought to infiltrate the movement and promote new labor conflicts.

The initiative, however, that finally convinced the generalissimo to reverse course was a visit from the three Spanish cardinals, senior leaders of the Church, led by the primate, Cardinal Pla y Deniel, at the beginning of 1957. They gave him a statement supporting the goal of new fundamental laws but declared Arrese's project to be in violation of pontifical doctrine. Its proposal of an all-powerful state party "resembles National Socialism, Fascism or Peronism, all forms rejected by the Church. . . . The two projects, Organic Law of the Movement and of the Government, do not stem from Spanish tradition but from foreign totalitarianism. To assure continuation of the spirit of the National Movement it is necessary to avoid both the liberalism of an inorganic democracy and a single-party dictatorship, while promoting true organic representation."[19]

Franco realized that he could not afford to ignore such a protest, since for more than a decade he had staked the legitimacy of his rule on accordance with the doctrines of the Church. As he noted in one of his rare private memos that have been preserved, "Everybody wants the establishment of laws that define and guarantee government functions, but this cannot be done in a way that satisfies everyone. Could this project be carried forward without fundamental changes to satisfy the people important to us, when it encounters resentment and lack of understanding in such important sectors as the Church, the army and the Cortes?"[20]

Though he may personally have preferred Arrese's project, he called the secretary-general to El Pardo to inform him that it would have to be abandoned.[21] Arrese could only obey, but he prepared a pamphlet for restricted distribution as counterblast to his many critics, declaring that it was ridiculous to think that the Falange was dominating everything, since it had never held more than a small minority of state positions. A devout Catholic, Arrese insisted that the Falange could never be "totalitarian," since totalitarianism was an atheist Communist concept.[22] His conclusion that "if everything else fails, a quiet return home can be agreeable" seemed to indicate acceptance of his defeat.

The failure generated tension among *camisas viejas*, who lamented that Franco had sold out to "capitalism" and talked of resigning en masse, as in 1941. Carrero Blanco saw danger for the regime, which he believed was facing problems similar to those it confronted in its very first phase, and on January 26 he sent Franco a memorandum outlining his views on how to resolve the crisis.[23] His approach would mean downgrading the movement further, bringing in highly qualified new ministers who could deal with complex issues of economic growth and development, figures who soon were being called "technocrats." Falangists would have to be shunted to an even more subordinate role than before. During the final eighteen years of the regime they would criticize it more and more as it deviated farther from their ideals, and to some extent they would become a sort of internal loyal opposition.

Franco, as usual, ended up accepting Carrero's suggestions. These reflected a strategy outlined by López Rodó, who had been appointed technical secretary of Carrero's Ministry-Secretariat of the Presidency, and proposed the formulation of four projects to build a fully developed *estado de derecho* (state of law):

1. Definition of the essential principles of the National Movement.
2. Harmonization of the powers of the future king with those of the government and the senior advisory Council of the Realm.
3. Reorganization of state administration.
4. Definition of the powers and functions of the National Council of the movement.

Franco had become acquainted with López Rodó and was sufficiently impressed to charge him with preparing a new law pertaining to administrative reform, which the inefficient state bureaucracy badly needed. From that time forward López Rodó would become one of the key policy formulators in the new "technocratic," postmovement phase of the regime.

It came as a stroke of good fortune for Franco that the captain-general of Barcelona, Juan Bautista Sánchez, most prominent member of the military hierarchy after Muñoz Grandes and currently the most contro-versial of all the generals, suddenly died of a heart attack on January 29, 1957. Because of his increasingly prominent role with the Monarchists, Franco had been keeping him under surveillance for some time. Wide-spread rumors linked Sánchez with a Monarchist plot to restrict Franco to the role of chief of state, so that a Monarchist general could take over the government. Muñoz Grandes was sent to Barcelona to settle him down, and this had resulted in a violent personal altercation between their respec-tive aides and supporters in which the air force general Joaquín González Gallarza had been injured.[24] The corpulent Sánchez had suffered from heart trouble for some time. Franco was critical of him not merely because of his Monarchist maneuverings but also because of his passive response to a recent strike against public transport in Barcelona. The death of Sánchez from natural causes spared the generalissimo from having to remove him from his post. It was a major loss to the Monarchists, and led to the inevita-ble rumors that the regime had been involved in his death, though there is not the slightest evidence of that.[25] The weakening of the Monarchists then made it all the easier for Franco to subordinate the Falange even further.

On February 25, 1957, he appointed his eighth government, acting on the recent suggestions by Carrero Blanco. This marked the end of major ministerial appointments for old-guard Falangists, for, after sixteen years, he dismissed Girón from the post of minister of labor and downgraded Arrese to the new Ministry of Housing, a post he would hold for only one year. Conversely, Franco did not want to appoint any alternative power group of Monarchists or political Catholics, and so he named a govern-ment in which key ministers were selected for professional competence, not political identity. Some of the most important appointees were mem-bers of Opus Dei, the new Catholic secular institute that had many of the characteristics of a religious order but was dedicated to advancing spiritual values in the workplace. Most of its members took only partial vows, re-maining laymen, and were particularly visible because so many held elite professional positions.

With the definitive downgrading of the Falange/National Movement, however, Franco was also shunting aside the original politico-ideological basis of the regime, which, in the future, would turn more and more into what some political scientists call merely "bureaucratic authoritarianism," without a political and ideological basis and also without any clear future. After having labored to overcome the "Primo de Rivera error," in his later years Franco could not entirely avoid falling into it again.

This also produced the resignation of the abrasive Muñoz Grandes, who supported the Falangists and opposed both the Monarchists and the new technocrats.[26] He had increasingly irritated Franco, who referred to him as "a bull in a china shop," and was not a good administrator, but he remained the most prestigious general and ultimately a loyal one. Muñoz Grandes was replaced by General Antonio Barroso, head of Franco's *casa militar*, a comparatively enlightened modernizer who in the next five years would carry out the most extensive military reform that would ever take place under Franco.[27] The special place of Muñoz Grandes was then recognized by immediate promotion to captain-general, making him the only commander to hold that rank other than Franco himself, and in 1958 he would be named head of the Supreme General Staff.

Girón, the outgoing labor minister, had established the beginning of a Spanish welfare state, which would eventually become fully developed, though only completed after the end of the dictatorship. Franco offered Girón an ambassadorship, but the burly Falangist lacked the sophistication and retired to his home on the Costa del Sol, where he dedicated himself to the development of tourist properties. He was replaced by the Navarrese Fermín Sanz Orrio, previously national delegate of syndicates. Blas Pérez González, for sixteen years an effective minister of the interior, was replaced by General Camilo Alonso Vega, Franco's oldest comrade of all (along with the recently retired Pacón). The new secretary-general of the movement was José Solís Ruiz, a veteran syndical leader, jolly and sycophantic—"the smile of the regime," as he would become known. Though his Falangist orthodoxy was questioned by the old guard, he would be its major representative in the new government. After twelve years, Martín Artajo left foreign affairs to assume direction of Editorial Católica, Spain's leading Catholic publisher.[28] He was replaced by Castiella, who moved up from ambassador to the Vatican. The key new technocratic appointments were Mariano Navarro Rubio in finance and Alberto Ullastres in commerce, two ministers who would be decisive in leading the Spanish economy into full modernization through a policy of greater openness and liberalization.

Both of these key ministers, like López Rodó, were members of Opus Dei, and before long, political circles and the newspapers began to receive reports about the activities of members of the secular institute that accused them of trying to dominate the government. Many of these denunciations came from Falangists, bitterly resentful over being increasingly displaced from positions of power.

With the terminal decline of Falangism, a political vacuum was slowly opening that the Communists, the only active leftist opposition party, hoped to fill, particularly by infiltrating the syndicates. Moreover, some Church leaders began to distance themselves from the regime more and more. The Catholic Action trade union movement, Catholic Action Workers' Fraternities (Hermandades Obreras de Acción Católica [HOAC]), demanded drastic social and economic changes, and in the following decade began to collaborate with the Communists. The councilors of Don Juan encouraged Church leaders to abandon the regime and sent a report to the Vatican secretary of state insisting on "the damage that the Franco dictatorship does to the cause of Catholicism, because it places the Church in opposition to the people." HOAC would employ the term "comunitario" for dissident labor, and its agitation would become an increasing cause of concern, a matter for discussion in the council of ministers.[29]

Before the close of 1957 the Moroccan government delivered an ultimatum demanding that the Spanish enclave of Ifni, on the southwestern coast of Morocco, be handed over as part of Moroccan independence. Franco was still bitter over having been pressured to abandon the protectorate a year and a half earlier but only feebly reinforced the threatened territory, for the Spanish army had little in the way of combat-ready units. The sultan sought American support and a favorable vote in the UN Security Council, while his son and heir, Muley Hassan, commander of the armed forces, prepared a military coup de main by nominally irregular insurgent forces, in fact organized by the Moroccan government. A self-styled Sahara Liberation Army had been carrying out armed raids for two years.

At the end of November, the Moroccan irregulars launched a direct assault on Ifni, which hoped to take the small Spanish garrison by surprise. The Spanish defenders were isolated in Sidi Ifni and a few outposts, but they managed to hold out. Franco dispatched an armed flotilla with reinforcements, though the pact with Washington prohibited the use of arms provided by the United States against any of its allies, of which Morocco was one. He could bring only limited force to bear, and air attacks had to be conducted, at least to some extent, with ancient Junkers 52s and Heinkel 111s, mostly left over from the Civil War but somehow miraculously maintained by Spanish mechanics. France had been seeking cooperation with Spain for some time, and an agreement was quickly made for a joint counteroffensive in both Ifni and the Sahara, employing French air power. By early 1958, all the Moroccans had been expelled. The Spanish army had revealed its weakness as a modern force, but the ordinary troops had fought well, losing nearly three hundred men.[30] In a subsequent agreement,

Franco handed over to Morocco the Tarfaya Strip, a small slice of territory in the Spanish Sahara, but all this marked only the beginning of the next phase of Franco's "Moroccan ulcer," as its government would initiate new activities against Spanish interests down to the time of Franco's death, which would be hastened by his grave preoccupation with the fate of the Spanish Sahara, the last remaining African territory.[31] Africa had made Franco, and Africa finally would help to kill him.

Carrero Blanco recommended that the best solution would be to re-organize Ifni and the Spanish Sahara as an integral province of Spain, just as Portugal had done with its own African possessions.[32] Franco realized that Ifni, as a small coastal enclave on the Moroccan coast, could probably not be retained in the long run, but he approved the plan in order to gain time. He realized that this was merely the first in a series of Moroccan demands; as he said to Pacón, Morocco might not merely try to seize all Spanish territory in northwest Africa but also make a grab for the Canaries, Granada, and all southern Spain.[33] Another consequence of this brief con-flict was that Franco finally had to dissolve his colorful mounted Guardia Mora, which he replaced with a Spanish guards regiment.

On December 17, 1957, John Foster Dulles returned to Madrid. Franco emphasized to the American secretary of state that Moroccan independence meant that international law prior to 1913 applied, and so the treaties signed by the Moroccan government before that date, which had specifically recognized the rights of Spain in all the territories it still occupied, were now in force again. He also pointed out that Spain greatly resented the un-provoked attack that had just been repelled. Franco was able to maintain the status quo for eleven more years, until he signed an agreement in January 1968 that handed over Ifni and the tiny Cabo Juby farther south, in return for which the new Moroccan ruler, Hassan II, recognized ample rights in Moroccan waters for the Spanish fishing fleet, which had become among the largest in Europe. None of this prevented Hassan, in a typical gesture, from unilaterally denouncing the fishing agreement three years later.

In March 1958 the Conde de Ruiseñada suddenly died of a heart attack as he was returning from a trip to Paris to regularize the financial affairs of Don Juan's elder brother, Don Jaime. This was another blow to the Monarchists, for he was the guiding spirit in maintaining good relations between Franco and the pretender. Franco's basic opinion of Don Juan was epitomized in a remark he had made to Pacón in February 1956, when he observed that "Don Juan's defect is his weak character, so he is influenced by the last person to come to peddle him gossip."[34] At some point in 1958, appar-ently, the generalissimo composed a twenty-three-page document that contemplated the publication of an article in the Spanish press concerning the claims of Don Juan to explain how he might gain the trust of the government, since Franco was still awaiting, with some impatience, his complete endorsement of and identification with the regime. As he put it,

> If Don Juan is willing to change his position by agreeing that the cause of the monarchy is what serves the nation and that there is no greater obligation than the supreme interest of the Fatherland, on behalf of which we must all give up our own desires, I would be willing to consider that, but only on the unequivocal basis of his full support of and identification with the regime, without any reservation.
>
> . . . Explaining all that we can, . . . while carrying out an effective publicity about what the monarchy is really to be, getting rid of the idea of a decadent and aristocratic, unpopular monarchy, a mere coterie of the privileged and powerful under the control of nobles and bankers.
>
> . . . With everything good that we could do in that direction, if fate has it that, despite our efforts, Don Juan would not enjoy its fruits, they would be enjoyed by the institution itself and his descendants. The important thing for us is to guarantee the future of the nation and for Don Juan that this happen only through a true monarchy.[35]

This full and final identification of Don Juan with the regime would never, however, take place.

The first institutional initiative of the new government was to promulgate in May 1958 a new law outlining the principles of the National Movement, the much watered-down alternative to the Arrese statute, prepared mainly by Carrero Blanco, López Rodó, and the rising young diplomat Gonzalo Fernández de la Mora. This provided a new statement of the ideological basis of the regime and essentially completed its doctrinal defascistization, though it used a few phrases from José Antonio Primo de Rivera. It was an anodyne document that invoked unity, tradition, religion, and patriotism.

Franco received with sadness the news of the death of Pope Pius XII in October. For the generalissimo, he had been "the pope of the Crusade," and, after much uncertainty, he had eventually established close relations with the regime. He was replaced by John XXIII, about whom Franco was more skeptical. During his brief pontificate, John XXIII made arrangements for convening the general conference known as Vatican II, which would introduce reforms during the following decade that would make Catholic policy incomprehensible to Franco.

On the twentieth anniversary of his victory, April 1, 1959, he inaugurated the great mausoleum of the Valley of the Fallen (Valle de los Caídos) at Cuelgamuros near El Escorial, fifty kilometers northwest of Madrid. It had cost a billion pesetas over two decades, part of which had been covered by private donations, beginning with funds that Gil Robles and the CEDA had donated to the military insurgency of 1936 just before it began. The monument, excavated from granite rock, formed a basilica 262 meters long and 41 meters high. The great cross on the hill behind it, visible for many kilometers, was 150 meters high, with arms extending 46 meters, and weighed 181,000 tons. It featured sculptures of the four apostles and many other figures by the noted sculptor Juan de Avalós, achieving a unique combination of austerity and grandiosity.[36] A large Augustinian monastery was located behind the basilica. The purpose of this monument was to commemorate the fallen on both sides during the Civil War, and the remains of thousands who had been killed, either in battle or by execution, from both sides were interred there. Franco's idea, however, was that only Catholic Republicans would be eligible for burial in this site, though it is not clear what kind of background checks were done on the remains.[37] The day before the inauguration, teams of Falangists had brought the remains of José Antonio Primo de Rivera from its resting place in the church of El Escorial to be buried in front of the high altar in the new basilica. When Franco died, the government decided to bury him there as well, whether or not this had been his original intention.[38] He had been intensely involved in the planning of the monument and its development, since it was basically his idea, and he was responsible for certain of the key features.[39]

This remarkable monument, perhaps the greatest of its kind in the twentieth century, later became the source of intense controversy, when leftist critics of a subsequent generation charged that it simply constituted another of the crimes of Francoism. They pointed to the use of prisoner labor in the construction, claiming that it had been built by slaves. Such accusations are exaggerated. Between 1943 and 1950 a little more than two thousand prisoners convicted by military courts were employed, but they received both modest wages, as well as fringe benefits for their families, and a steep reduction in their prison terms, ranging from two to six days of credit for each day worked. Each was a volunteer for the project, and there were rarely more than three to four hundred at any given time. They worked under the same conditions as the regular laborers, and some of them later returned to join the regular work crew after completing their sentences. More than a few of the prisoners simply ran away, which was easy enough to do, since prison supervision was minimal. The great bulk of the construction was carried out by ordinary paid workers. Over twenty years fourteen workers perished in accidents, the great majority regular salaried laborers.[40]

On the final day of July, the Cortes rubber-stamped the new Law of Public Order, adapted from the Republican legislation of 1933, so that even crimes judged as sabotage or political subversion could be prosecuted in civil courts. Prior to this law, they had remained under the jurisdiction of military tribunals. This was intended as a further moderation of the repression, though it was a limited one, for a special court was created to deal with such actions, which still would not be prosecuted by the ordinary judicial system. The tribunal would have its hands full during the following years, as acts of protest and defiance increased, and the terms of prosecution would remain controversial right down to the end of the regime.

The year closed with another major public event, the first visit of an American president to Franco, when Dwight Eisenhower touched down briefly on December 21. This had not been easy to arrange, since there was much opposition in the American Congress to having a president visit the Spanish dictator, and the British government was also strongly against it. Spanish diplomacy, on the other hand, pressed hard, even hinting that if Franco were snubbed on Eisenhower's European trip Madrid might have to realign its foreign policy fundamentally.

Franco was waiting at Torrejón airbase for Eisenhower's arrival, a bomb attempt on his life having been discovered and aborted the night before.[41] The two rode into Madrid together in an open car, greeted by a throng of more than a million people lining the streets. The president's interpreter, General Vernon A. Walters of the CIA, wrote: "The crowds in Madrid were very large and their welcome extraordinarily enthusiastic. I rode in the car with the President and Franco and I can only report that there were a lot of 'Viva Franco' shouts. The visible popularity of the man regarded by many as a hated dictator was not reflected in the [American] press accounts of the visit. Eisenhower, however, was much impressed by this and the way Franco moved through large crowds."[42] Eisenhower declared that this was the warmest greeting he had received anywhere in the world, to which Franco modestly replied that it constituted an enthusiastic referendum on his own foreign policy. Prior to a gala dinner at the Royal Palace, the two had a lengthy conversation that touched on Morocco, Western security, the evolution of Soviet policy, the development of the Spanish economy and its further international integration, and bilateral relations and military aid. Franco expressed confidence that "it would not be many years before Spain became a prosperous country" like others in Western Europe. When asked for his view of Soviet policy, "Franco, speaking calmly, gave a most detached and unemotional appraisal of what they were trying to do," saying that the Soviets would seek to avoid major war but would continue to press their interests as hard as possible, trying to exploit any opening and to subvert the will to resist.[43]

Eisenhower finally raised the question that perpetually vexed Americans—the limited freedom of Spanish Protestants. That produced a change in the tone of the conversation. Franco replied defensively that there were very few Protestants in Spain, "not even one out of a thousand," and that it was "a local matter" that would be resolved. Eisenhower was not satisfied, saying that his American Catholic friends were also concerned, since they were a minority in the United States. Franco replied forcefully that this was really a problem of Church leadership, and the Americans, therefore, should take up the matter with Rome. Castiella, the foreign minister, then intervened to smooth things over, and when he went to Washington three months later he bore a special message saying that the problem was being resolved, which was not exactly the case.[44]

In general, the meeting went well.[45] Franco exhibited the modesty he customarily did in the presence of anyone remotely his equal, and was friendly and for the most part straightforward, while Eisenhower was his normally winsome self. Later, in his memoirs, the president would observe that "I was impressed by the fact that there was no discernible mannerism or characteristic that would lead an unknowing visitor to conclude that he was in the presence of a dictator."[46]

Breakfast together the next morning was "so good-humored and relaxed" that Eisenhower asked Walters to tell Franco one of his favorite jokes about generals. Walters recalled: "There was much laughter from all present— some of whom were generals. Franco joined in and commented slyly to Eisenhower, 'Did you notice how much harder those who are not generals laughed?' I had not suspected Franco of this kind of humor. Then he said, "'The reason why generals are as bad as they are is because they are chosen from among the best colonels.' At this the generals present really laughed."[47] Franco then accompanied the Americans back to the airbase by helicopter. He observed that he had never ridden in one before, but "one would never have guessed it from his composure."[48] On parting, he and Eisenhower said good-bye with a very cordial embrace, captured by a photographer in what was perhaps the single greatest photo opportunity of Franco's long life. It marked the high point in the international relations of his regime.

15 | Franco at Home

By the 1950s Franco, actively courted by the Americans, was secure. The West's oldest and most successful anti-Communist was seemingly transformed from "fascist beast" into "sentinel of the Occident," as the title of his latest semiofficial biography had it.[1] From all this derived a mounting sense of complacency and self-satisfaction that was reinforced by the shameless rhetoric of the official organs.[2] On the Day of the Caudillo, October 1, 1949, *Arriba* hailed him as

> beyond all simple, spare, narrative description. It would be a mistake merely to place him at the level of Alexander the Great, Julius Caesar, Gonzalo de Córdoba, or Ambrosio de Spínola. Francisco Franco, the greatest sword of them all, belongs to the vanguard of providential destiny. He is the man of God, the one who always appears at the critical moment and defeats his enemies proclaiming himself champion of the forces of heaven and earth. If

we heed Niccolò Machiavelli, he holds the titles of Caudillo, Monarch, Prince and Lord of the Armies. Caudillo by his own military achievement; Monarch by his well proven nobility; Prince by his keen political talent and Lord of the Armies by his courage, skill and knowledge of tactics, strategy and other complex problems of war.

. . . On this day, let us devote a moment to meditation in honor of the figure of Francisco Franco. Let us renew our promise of loyalty to his person and in the name of Christ pardon those who do not understand him. On this day we see ourselves petty, dwarfish and ridiculous by comparison.

Or, as the Falangist organ put it on October 21, 1950, "Franco is the Caudillo and star of the entire world." Bathed in this sea of extravagant rhetoric by his own press, he maintained absolute indifference to the harsh criticisms that still came from abroad.[3]

Franco once indicated that he did not find the government of Spain a particularly heavy burden, and, given the way he ran it, that was doubtless the case. In an interview with an American history professor, Philip Powell, he declared that his role had been analogous to that of the sheriff in the typical American western, a film genre that he enjoyed. When he came to town, the bad guys were collared. Franco went on to observe with considerable mirth that the Spanish, rather than being difficult and rebellious as they were often portrayed, were generally patient and long suffering. "And the proof of this," he said suddenly breaking into a loud cackle, "is that they have put up with my regime for so long."[4]

His most demanding trials came during the first eleven years of the regime when he was still in his prime and had abundant stamina and emotional resilience. The final quarter century, as he aged and lost his acuteness, was mostly a period of routine administration conducted according to a schedule that was regular and attuned to his personal rhythm of life; he was up by 8 a.m. each morning and then went to bed comparatively early each night.

Cabinet ministers and principal subordinates were almost always given latitude in running their departments, so long, of course, as what they did followed the guidelines of the regime. Thus Lequerica would opine that being a cabinet minister "was the only serious role one could have in Spain, for a minister of Franco was like a little king who could do what he wanted without the interference of the Caudillo."[5]

His willingness to let his ministers run their departments did not stem from any intrinsic confidence in his collaborators. Franco's suspiciousness was notorious, even though its extent has been exaggerated. As he once remarked to Pacón, "I have to tell you that I don't really trust anyone."[6] Yet this did not lead to the morbid paranoia that possessed some other dictators, for Franco was a shrewd judge of character and was adept at assessing when and to what extent he could rely on his appointees. Moreover, like other dictators, he would not tolerate anyone who had the capacity to create divergent policies or political followings of their own. As Pacón put it, "Surely His Excellency does not want to have ministers with their own political personalities who might create difficulties."[7]

The relative autonomy given ministers was accompanied by a blind eye to malfeasance and corruption, at least in the early years of the regime. From 1940 on it was a common complaint that Franco simply refused to listen to charges of personal corruption, to the frustration of such close associates as Martínez Fuset and Muñoz Grandes. He followed his standard tack of changing the conversation, which he normally did whenever it strayed to a theme he found troublesome. Occasionally, as Muñoz Grandes complained, he would reply to a critic who denounced the malfeasance within a given minister's domain by saying, "I will let him know that you have informed me about that."[8] He may have regarded corruption as a necessary lubricant for the system that had the advantage of compromising many and binding them to the regime.

Franco was normally polite and correct in manner but rarely cordial, except on informal social occasions. When the mood struck him, he could still be talkative in private, but the occasional vivacity of his younger years had largely disappeared, except on certain convivial family occasions or hunting excursions. He never, however, lost a certain sly capacity to joke. From the viewpoint of his daughter, Franco's personality began to change as soon as he became generalissimo:

> I think my father changed a good deal when he became Chief of State. . . . My Aunt Isabel, my mother's sister, who had no children and spent a lot of time with us, especially in the summer . . . , used to say that once Papá had been a talkative person, "like his brother Nicolás," she said, because really Nicolás seemed very different from my father, but no, she said, earlier "he talked a good deal and told jokes but then he turned very serious and got to be extremely boring." . . . I think it was the weight of responsibility, and then because people repeat what you say and may twist it a certain amount. And he didn't like that.
>
> Many times he simply didn't want to say anything. . . . He didn't like disagreeable scenes and so if he would have said something that would have

been disagreeable, he kept quiet. It was a matter of discretion. . . . My father did not enjoy speaking ill of people and was scrupulous in that. He thought that to give an opinion about someone or something, you have to know that person or thing really well. So he was careful not to speak lightly. Yes, he was really very discreet. . . . And he was not a passionate person, certainly. He was rather cold and reflective, and his manner showed that, but he enjoyed listening. That gave the impression that he was colder in temperament than he really was, but I don't think it was a tactic, for my father did not dissimulate. He was quite sincere and didn't simply try to give the appearance of being cold, no. What happened was that he was cordial with some people but with others he drew back into his shell.

One of his favorite maxims was "One is a slave of what one says and a master of what one does not say,"[9] and, though he would continue to be modest and unassuming in private with his most important visitors, a public demeanor of hauteur and severity was accentuated with the passage of time, and his flashes of humor became less frequent. Words of praise were few, even to those whom he trusted and appreciated. When Franco replaced cabinet ministers, they often received no more than a curt notice by motorcycle courier. When a longtime household staff member sought to tell him what a privilege it had been to serve him for many years, the attendant received the brusque response that he had not served a person but rather the cause of Spain, like any other soldier. Some of his key ministers would complain that they never knew exactly where they stood with him, which was doubtless by design. José Antonio Girón, for sixteen years one of his favorite ministers, lamented that Franco exhibited "a coldness that at times freezes the soul."[10] A stern demeanor, forged decades earlier in the army, had been typical of Franco's manner on serious occasions, and it solidified more and more into a routine. This had the advantage of permitting him to discuss the most stressful and troublesome matters without altering the expression on his face or the tone of his quiet, high-pitched voice. The most arresting aspect of his facial expression had always been the keen, penetrating glance of his large brown eyes, and the effect of that gaze never disappeared altogether, even in the final years of his life. He never became excited, and overt displays of anger were extremely rare. The fits of rage shown by some dictators were unknown. A positive aspect of his laconic style was that he scarcely ever spoke badly of anyone, though what he thought might have been quite a different matter.

His emotional tone during public ceremonies could, however, vary considerably. At appearances in commemoration of the Civil War or on other occasions when he was strongly applauded by hard-core followers, the caudillo might reveal considerable sentiment and grow misty eyed, particularly as he aged. During routine public occasions, however, he rarely emerged from his shell. By the 1950s public ceremonies had mostly lost whatever animation they had earlier possessed and were often cold, formal, stiff, and rather tense. Those meeting Franco for the first time were often taken aback by the manner of his handshake, for he held his hand fixedly by the side of his waist, almost as if it were attached to his belt, instead of extending it in the normal manner. This required much taller men to lean over and partially bow in order to grasp it, which is no doubt why Franco adopted this approach.

Cabinet meetings became legendary for their marathon length and Spartan style. During the 1940s Franco often dominated conversations, speaking at length, launching into harangues, or wandering from subject to subject. As he grew older he became more reticent and eventually went to the opposite extreme, speaking little. In later decades cabinet meetings were held every Friday during the greater part of the year, though after 1956 they sometimes met biweekly.

Manuel Fraga Iribarne, a major figure of the 1960s, wrote:

> Cabinet meetings with Franco were long and in general interesting. They began at ten in the morning, though ministers might ask to see him earlier, if they had new and important business. . . . Meetings in the summer were held in the dining room of El Pazo de Meirás. When the morning was over [around 2 p.m. in the Spanish schedule], everyone left for lunch and returned at five in the afternoon. We then worked until we had finished, into the small hours. During my period, our longest meeting lasted until four in the morning, but people recalled that the record for the longest cabinet meeting was held by one from earlier times, which ended at 8 a.m.
>
> Franco not only did not restrict or cut off discussion, as did De Gaulle, or prevent debates, like Salazar (who only accepted reports from his ministers) but sought confrontation among his ministers and administrators in order to clarify matters.[11]

On busy occasions, the midday meal might be taken on the premises and restricted to one hour. The lengthy sessions were often a trial, since Franco did not believe in rest breaks and did not permit smoking in his presence. Even water was sometimes absent. His own bladder control was legendary, and he is not known to have left a cabinet meeting to relieve himself until

December 6, 1968, after his seventy-sixth birthday.[12] Ministers had to catch his eye to be excused or go out for a smoke. Only in his last years did cabinet meetings grow shorter, sometimes limited to a single morning session.

Franco's interest in and knowledge of government was uneven. In later years "his attention at cabinet meetings varied considerably. Problems of ordinary administration did not interest him at all and in general he took little part in the discussions, which could sometimes be quite lively. Nonetheless, some matters visibly awakened his interest and he followed them with attention. Among these were foreign policy, relations with the Church, public order, and problems having to do with the communications media and with labor."[13] When disagreement arose, "he rarely took positions pro or con. When he thought the matter had been sufficiently discussed, and there were no fundamental objections, he terminated the discussion and the proposal was accepted with appropriate modifications. On the other hand, when no agreement emerged, instead of imposing a solution he directed the ministers involved to study the matter further and seek a common solution to present at the next meeting."[14]

One of Franco's more attractive qualities was his optimism. He rarely communicated a sense of worry, and this self-confidence had always been an important factor in his leadership. He expressed great pride in the fact that he had improved the mores of the Spanish people and that the crime index was lower in the 1950s than in the 1930s. He believed, to some extent correctly, that he had instilled a greater respect for authority and for religion, and he confided, with satisfaction, that "blasphemy is not heard anywhere, according to what they tell me"—a pious exaggeration if ever there was one.[15]

Though the slogan "organic democracy" was a concession to the democratic climate of postwar Western Europe, Franco was serious about not considering himself a dictator (as for that matter was Hitler). He claimed to derive great satisfaction from the fact he did not personally interfere in the regular judicial system, and he insisted at least for the record that there should always be free discussion in the Cortes.[16] He was undoubtedly sincere in his conviction that the regime was working for the progress and development of the country, and in private he was critical of the financial elite, as were many members of the military. Franco was convinced that Spain rested on the shoulders of the *macizo de la raza*, the ordinary middle classes, and the fact that the Monarchist opposition was centered in the upper classes only encouraged this conviction. He believed that in modern

Spain major accomplishment came from those in the middle and even lower classes who had risen to the top, and he looked toward a society with fewer rich and fewer poor. When in 1961 he happened to be driven through a benighted slum in Seville, a route that was not on his original itinerary, he expressed genuine shock, but, as was typical for him, he thought that the matter would be corrected by orders given to local authorities.[17]

Franco continued to write, briefly and sporadically. In the first years, he wrote much of the text of his speeches and often prepared outlines and memoranda to analyze major problems or prepare for important interviews.[18] The pseudonymous articles denouncing Masonry continued to appear under his various pen names during the early 1950s but then petered out. A crack in the anti-Masonic fixation developed after the establishment of amicable relations with the United States, when even Franco came to admit that, at least for the most part, American Masons were all right, even "good," and so, as a concession to Washington, he began to drop Masonry from speeches in his catalog of evils, confining the latter more and more to Communism.[19]

Franco's religiosity continued to be a crucial factor in his governing. The cynical military in Morocco used to refer to his *baraka*—"Franco's luck"—but after 1936, if not before, the caudillo saw it as divine guidance and blessing. It was said that he attended Mass daily at his private chapel in El Pardo (and even that during some of the major crises of the regime he spent part of the night there), but, as already indicated, this seems to be an exaggeration. Carmen reminisces that he never sought to explain the source of his religious faith:

> No, it seemed to him natural. He never analyzed his reasons for faith. We attended Mass in the palace of El Pardo. My mother heard Mass, I think about 9:30 in the morning, every single day, but my father did not because that was the time he always went into his office. He attended on Sundays and special occasions, and then every day during Lent, so at that time of year Mass was held a little earlier. . . . One thing that particularly concerned him was how much a good Christian should give to the poor. . . . I remember he put that question to several priests and one had told him that a certain saint, I think San Francisco de Sales, had said that you should divide all your income among your wife, your children and yourself, and that the poor are one child more. That was what was just. He always thought that you should give a tithe, as they used to say, one-tenth of all you had, though he preferred more the recommendation of San Francisco de Sales.

Franco's religiosity was distinctly of the traditional Spanish kind—formalistic, given to liturgy and ritual, but not overly informed by personal meditation, religious study, or too much practical application of doctrine. He made confession regularly in his later years, not to his household chaplain, José María Bulart, as often reported, but to a friar specially brought to El Pardo periodically for that purpose. Eventually El Pardo would include no fewer than ten different chapels, oratories, and altars.[20]

Franco believed devoutly in the efficacy of relics, his personal favorite being the remains of a petrified hand of Santa Teresa de Avila, the most prominent woman in the history of the Spanish Church, founder of the Discalced Carmelites. Preserved for more than three centuries in a Carmelite convent in Portugal, the hand had been transferred to a convent in Ronda in 1925. During the looting of the convent by revolutionaries in 1936, the relic had been seized, only to turn up during the Nationalist conquest of Málaga in February 1937, discovered in a suitcase full of cash and jewels. It was immediately awarded to the caudillo, and after a solemn ceremony of purification in Salamanca, he retained possession of it for the duration of the conflict. Franco gained permission from the Church in 1939 to keep it for his lifetime; he maintained it in a special reliquary in his bedroom (but not on his nightstand, as the sensationalist version long had it). Santa Teresa was hailed as the "santa de la raza"—saint of the nation—and this woman from a family of Jewish origin became Franco's personal patron saint, his favorite Spanish religious figure.[21] Nevertheless, despite the ultra-Catholicism of his regime, Franco did not like to have his personal devotions overpublicized, sensitive as he was to criticism of excessive church influence in state affairs.[22]

Anonymous personal threats arrived in the mail regularly down to the final days of his life. Franco rarely saw these, and there is no indication that they much bothered him. The anarchist opposition, true to its violent history, having assassinated no fewer than three parliamentary prime ministers, conceived nearly all the assassination plots, which were most frequent between 1945 and 1950. Particularly elaborate preparations were set in motion on the occasion of his visits to Barcelona in 1947 and to San Sebastián the following year. At another point a scheme was briefly hatched to tunnel into El Pardo. Franco's security apparatus was sufficient to foil each of the forty or more assassination plots concocted by anarchists down to 1964, when these efforts petered out. Very rarely a few Falangists or Monarchists dawdled with such ideas, without going very far. There was also a rumor concerning a false monk who managed to enter the monastery adjacent to

El Pardo and was discovered with firearms in his possession, but this story was never confirmed. Not a single one of these schemes ever reached the point of violent action.

Franco's personal tours to various parts of the country continued at a diminishing rate through the 1960s, and the crowds rarely failed to present themselves, whether spontaneously or not. On these and other occasions he still delivered his regular ceremonial speeches, in addition to two or three major addresses every year. Much of his terminology was rather simple, but it succeeded in getting across his main concepts. His later speeches had a less grandiloquent air than the earlier ones. Franco seems to have been the one who established in Spanish rhetoric the custom of saying "many thanks" at the end of a speech; before his time the style of public orators was to end more commonly with the peremptory and slightly arrogant "he dicho" ("I have spoken") or "he terminado" ("I have finished").

Yet his travels did not really keep him well informed, for he talked only with a limited set of people, who normally told him what he wanted to hear. Even within the military he restricted his personal contacts more and more, and his only personal associates, beyond the ever present but obsequiously formal Carrero Blanco, were family relatives and a very few old friends of his childhood and youth, such as Admiral Pedro Nieto Antúnez and General Camilo Alonso Vega, the minister of the interior.

His preferred conversation topic would always remain the personal memories of Morocco and his early military career. He liked to reminisce about the days, as he put it in later years, "cuando yo era persona" ("when I was an ordinary person"). Franco also enjoyed discoursing a good deal about hunting. He naturally did not expect to be contradicted or, as Carmen puts it, "Papá, when he said something, wanted everyone else to say amen." On the other hand, he was always willing to accept a degree of challenge and argument from his closest associates and advisers.

Franco's austere personal habits never varied. Smoking never attracted him, and he never drank more than a single glass of wine with meals. If he took coffee, it was decaffeinated. Artificial stimulants were thus almost completely rejected. He was normally up at 8 a.m. He breakfasted on fruit juice, tea, and dry toast, and, in later years, apple compote. Prayers or occasionally morning Mass would follow, and he was ordinarily in his office before ten. Tuesday morning was reserved for personal audiences with the military and Wednesday for civilians. In addition to receiving individuals of importance — the total number of audiences of both military and civilians eventually amounting to 9,169 — he also received a large number of visiting commissions of all sorts, either on Wednesdays or special occasions.[23] Foreign diplomats got their turn on Thursday morning, and the rest of Thursday was normally dedicated to meeting with Carrero Blanco. Cabinet meetings took place, as indicated, on Fridays. Until his last years Franco devoted four full afternoons a week, from Monday to Thursday, to personal consultation with his ministers, each of whom enjoyed about an hour per week with him.

Mealtime was not a major event at El Pardo. For many years the chief cook was a former sergeant in the Civil Guard of unquestioned loyalty but limited culinary talent. Franco was not a gourmand, and in later years he was known to observe sardonically to luncheon guests that he understood it was said that one did not dine well at El Pardo. As his daughter observes, "It mattered little to him whether he ate well or not."

> Eating was not very important to my father, though he could enjoy special occasions. When we had the Guardia Mora, sometimes there were receptions with kebabs, with long pieces of lamb kebabs grilled and very well seasoned, and he loved those. . . . In time, his physician, Vicente Gil, put him on a diet. For main courses he was very fond of paella, both fish and shellfish paella. And then he liked fish very much. When we were on vacation in Galicia or San Sebastián, he ate a lot of fish rather than meat. A dessert that he really hated was rice pudding. . . . He never touched it. Rice pudding was never served at El Pardo, but he liked other desserts well enough.

Franco's idea of an after-dinner drink was either a small glass of manzanilla (sherry) or a cup of decaffeinated coffee. In later years he always took a brief siesta after the midday meal. If it was not a work day, then after the siesta Franco often played a late afternoon round of golf on his personal course or fired at pigeons in the hunting preserve at El Pardo. Most evenings were quiet and domestic. Periodically, there were private movie screenings, though about once a month these screenings were turned into larger social occasions. In the 1960s Franco became addicted to television and was especially fond of soccer matches, bullfights, and boxing.

Before that, late evening was often for reading. Franco did not read as much as Stalin or some other dictators, but he read a fair amount. During the day he read all manner of government materials and sometimes looked at the *New York Times*, which he considered the semiofficial voice of Masonry, to practice his limited English reading skills.[24] Books were mainly for the evening, and, according to his grandson, Franco's personal library eventually amounted to nearly eight thousand volumes.[25]

In the later years he and Doña Carmen usually retired to their private chapel around 10:30 p.m. for evening devotions, saying the Lord's Prayer and various Ave Marias together.[26] Though Franco had sometimes continued to read late at night, the habit was generally discontinued in the later part of his life. During his early years on campaign he had learned, like many soldiers, to seize any respite for taking a nap. He had had a facility throughout his life for relaxing and going to sleep easily and then sleeping soundly. Doña Carmen learned early in their marriage that, once he started to turn over to go to sleep, if she had anything to say or a question to ask, she had to do so very quickly, for soon he would be sound asleep.[27]

After 1945 he was seen less and less in uniform, and by the 1950s, he dressed normally in well-tailored business suits, much more deftly cut than the clumsy uniforms of Civil War days. The diet that Franco's physician Vicente Gil put him on in the 1950s left him slimmer than in the two preceding decades.

As dictator Franco had to forego the private *tertulias* (conversation parties or after-dinner groups) that he had enjoyed when younger, but during the first twenty years or so of the regime he and Doña Carmen attended a certain number of Madrid's top social and entertainment functions, including operas, bullfights, and soccer matches. Such appearances naturally became rarer in the later years. Daytime social and charity events were the province of Doña Carmen, who developed her own set of activities as first lady, though her individual social circle was limited.

Franco sometimes worked long hours, but there was little danger of overwork, given the absence of stress and tension that he normally showed and the length of the vacations that he permitted himself. He enjoyed fresh air and being out of doors, and, prompted by his physician, he made an effort to avoid the sedentary life. He was fond of horseback riding as long as his physical condition permitted and played a little tennis from time to time. Franco had first taken up golf in 1932 and later had a golf course set up at El Pardo, of which he made frequent use. Some days he only practiced on the driving range, but when he had more time, he would play a longer game, involving several kilometers of walking.

Franco's greatest diversion, amounting almost to a mania, was hunting, which he had first taken up seriously during his years in Zaragoza. As in the case of golf, this was pursued in various ways. If he was pressed for time, he might just blast away at pigeons for a half hour, but when he had more time, he would go on major hunting expeditions lasting three or four days. Franco had a small hunting domain at El Pardo and at the summer palace of Aranjuez, as well as at a new estate, Valdefuentes, southwest of Madrid, but he also was the central figure in major hunting parties arranged on the finest private estates and public lands in different parts of the country.[28] These could be strenuous outings during which Franco would do considerable walking and climbing and would fire off great numbers of cartridges either in the open range or in specially prepared shooting zones. In time he became a good shot.[29] This absorption in hunting eventually led to a steady stream of invitations from the wealthy and those seeking help. He was often attended by what some called *cazadores aduladores* (flatterer hunters) looking for jobs or influence and by *cazadores comerciantes* (business hunters) interested in government backing for business deals. Pacón, head of Franco's *casa militar* during much of the 1950s, when the hunting mania was at its height, was critical of Franco's devotion to it, noting that during November 1955 seventeen days were spent on hunting, leaving at most thirteen for state business, which, in his view, gave "an impression of frivolity."[30] The lobbyists, however, gained only collateral advantage from participating in these *cacerías*, for Franco categorically refused to permit anyone to importune him directly about economic matters on such occasions. There is no question that Franco derived great satisfaction from these carefully contrived slaughters, boasting in October 1959 that he had set a personal record by shooting nearly five thousand quail on his last outing.[31] Moreover, when she became old enough, Carmencita, who loved to ride horseback, would sometimes accompany her father on hunting expeditions, firing a slightly smaller shotgun.[32]

Franco's blunt, devoted physician from Asturias, Vicente Gil, believed that he exerted himself too much on such occasions, observing in November 1954 that "His Excellency extends himself too much in these hunting expeditions, which provide no rest, since he sleeps little. Yesterday, . . . he shot off six thousand cartridges, and that is terrible for a man of sixty-two. He might burst his aorta when you least expect it."[33] His summer fishing trips in Asturias would similarly find him standing for long periods in hip boots in the icy waters of mountain streams, but Franco evidently registered no ill effects from these exertions. He suffered from no chronic health complaints until he was advanced in years, and even in his sixties displayed impressive stamina on long days in the open. During his first three decades in power he experienced only three illnesses that required him to stay in bed for a day or more: two cases of flu and one bout of food poisoning.

For thirty-seven years Franco and his family mainly spent their summers at the Galician estate of Pazo de Meirás presented to him before the end of the Civil War, though Franco also spent time aboard the *Azor*, the former minesweeper converted into his personal yacht, a slow but comfortable vessel that was docked in San Sebastián. Franco's primary summer sport was fishing, both in trout streams and at sea on the *Azor*.[34] As late as 1966 the press carried stories of his prowess, on one occasion reporting that he had bagged thirty-six small whales with a harpoon gun. He sometimes invited his old fishing partner from La Coruña, Max Borrell, as well as a few other friends, on these brief cruises on the *Azor*. Muñoz Grandes also appeared once or twice, but could not stand it for long, being prone to sea sickness. During the summers Franco also played golf and cards, read, and practiced his painting.

He had always enjoyed sketching and in later years turned to painting, primarily water colors, as a hobby. He took up painting partly as a more physical kind of activity that he could practice informally, since Gil was always after him to spend more time on his feet moving about on days otherwise mostly devoted to sedentary affairs. Franco could turn to painting for short periods after lunch without having to mobilize his escort and spend the extra time required for an outdoor activity.[35] Most of his painting was thus done at El Pardo, and he became a competent amateur painter. Since these works, mostly still lifes of landscapes and of hunting and fishing trophies, would have looked completely out of place in the grandeur of his official residence, he took to hanging his best products on the walls of the Pazo de Meirás, a much more suitable setting.[36]

Franco also showed an interest in photography. As this became more broadly known, he received all manner of cameras as personal presents. In the final years, Franco learned to use a video camera to photograph dancing and other events at extended family get-togethers and displayed his home videos on an impromptu screen at the Pazo de Meirás in the summer.

Another distraction of Franco's later years, as he became absorbed in football matches on television, was betting on *quinielas* (football pools). He signed his betting lists using the name Francisco Cofrán, Vicente Gil serving as a middle man, depositing them in the pool office for him. Franco placed bets almost every week during the football season and got to be rather good at it. In May 1967 he won a pool worth nearly a million pesetas (around ten thousand dollars).[37]

Franco's health only began to decline at the end of his seventh decade from the inevitable ravages of age and especially from the effects of Parkinson's disease (in his case possibly a sequel of the infection he had

suffered during the great influenza epidemic of 1918). This was first diagnosed around 1960, shortly before he turned 70. It was not the most severe
and accelerated form of the disease, and to a certain degree it was controlled by new medications, but over the next decade it began to take its toll.
Though it never affected the clarity of his mind, he slowed down more and
more, talked less and less, and in his last years one of his hands trembled
considerably. The largely silent Franco known in later years suffered from
a combination of advancing age and the effects of this illness.

The family circle was Franco's ultimate refuge, and the only persons to
whom he was ever close in emotional terms were Carmina, his wife, and,
in a different way, Carmencita, his daughter. Doña Carmen was probably
the only person who ever really influenced him in the later years, with the
partial exception of Carrero Blanco. She was rarely concerned with affairs
of state and did not presume to be a political advisor (except perhaps in his
final declining years), but she had complete control of the household and
family affairs, in the traditional manner. It was Doña Carmen, not Franco,
who always attended Mass each morning without fail, and she fully adjusted
herself to his rather austere routine, while maintaining a schedule of her
own affairs.

Doña Carmen was refined, elegant, and demanding. Like her husband,
she lacked human warmth, so her manners and bearing made her increasingly imperious. This only added to the formality and relative coldness of
life at El Pardo. From the time that the Francos moved in to their permanent residence, she insisted on being known as "la Señora." She was patient,
however, with photographers, just as Franco was, and sought to accommo-
date such publicity.

Life at El Pardo was nonetheless less ostentatious during the 1940s,
as Doña Carmen devoted herself to the role of wife and mother and also
dedicated at least a portion of her time to charitable activities. After Carmencita's marriage in 1950, the style of Doña Carmen became more expansive,
as she was free to play a grander role. She became used to even greater
deference and also, as Spain grew more prosperous, to greater and greater
luxury. Doña Carmen was inordinately fond of jewelry, amassing a huge
collection. After her husband became generalissimo, she adopted her signa-
ture style of a three-string necklace of large high-quality pearls, which over
the years would lead critics to dub her privately "la señora de los collares"
("the necklace lady"), or simply "la collares."

In addition to all the other perquisites, the ruling couple received an
endless array of costly gifts, though most of them could not be put to use.
These were greatly augmented by the increasingly frequent shopping trips

of Doña Carmen, not only in Madrid but sometimes in other cities, as well, usually accompanied by someone from her small circle of lady friends. These even extended into Portugal, where she was said to be particularly fond of the Gomes jewelry shop in Povoa de Varzim. Antiques were a life-long interest, and Doña Carmen amassed an extraordinary collection of jewels, furnishings, artworks, and other fine items.

Her numerous purchases inevitably became the subject of gossip. One of the most common rumors had it that she demanded so many free gifts that the jewelers of Madrid created an informal insurance syndicate that spread the costs more evenly among them. This is probably malicious gossip, for the available evidence suggests that Doña Carmen paid for what-ever was not initially offered as a gift, although she was not above haggling to reduce the price or seeking free exchanges of items to her own advantage.[38]

She had few intimates (much like her husband), though a small number of close friends. Her principal companion during the 1950s was Pura, the Marquesa de Huétor de Santillán, wife of the head of Franco's household chief of staff. Another close friend was Ramona, the wife of Franco's de-voted chum and interior minister, Camilo Alonso Vega. Since they were both Asturians, the two ladies would travel together back to their native region once or twice a year to visit relatives. Like most husbands, Franco waited for a phone call to know that they had arrived safely.

Within the regime, Doña Carmen came to be increasingly resented, not least by the minister of the army. Muñoz Grandes was quoted as remarking that "to me it seems a mistake that the Caudillo's wife wears so many jewels. It does not make a good impression on any one and among the military is mentioned with disgust, since we insist on austerity in every-thing and all the more in the life of a head of government who is always in the public eye. Too much luxury, too much luxury and ostentation! And that is damaging him a great deal!"[39]

Doña Carmen also played more of a role on public occasions as the couple aged, and she tended to be increasingly controlling of Franco's per-sonal schedule as his health and energy began to decline. She accompanied him on most hunting trips, though she never hunted (unlike her daughter), and she became increasingly vocal about political matters, especially in her criticism of aristocratic Monarchism, whose supporters she would have preferred to be more closely restricted. She sought increasingly to screen her husband from any who might raise unpleasant questions and instructed guests in later years not to introduce disagreeable topics. Despite Franco's proverbial steadiness of nerve and serenity of mind, as he grew older a very troublesome problem was sometimes capable of disturbing his sleep. Similarly, though he had never given the slightest indication of having a roving eye, Doña Carmen preferred as much as possible to keep pretty young women away from his social receptions, simply to be on the safe side.

She maintained close relations with her sister Isabel, a childless widow who dined weekly at El Pardo. Isabel had always spent a good deal of time with the Francos and enjoyed summer vacations with them even before her own husband's death. By comparison, Doña Carmen suffered from the continuing partial estrangement from her younger sister, Zita, with whom she had once been very close. The rupture stemmed from the break between Zita's husband Serrano Suñer and Franco. Doña Carmen had become quite fond of the six Serrano Suñer children, for during the Civil War they had all lived together as one big happy family, but after 1942 she saw comparatively little of them. There had been a possibility of reconciliation between Franco and Serrano in 1952, after Serrano published several articles in *ABC* that were well received and then made a trip to Paris that received positive coverage in the Spanish press. There was talk of naming him ambassador to France, but nothing came of this.

Franco's own sister, Pilar, was a less frequent visitor, busy raising ten children and then dealing with her grandchildren and her business interests. Pilar was always talkative and outspoken, however, and she was the only person known occasionally to berate Franco, demanding that he do something about various matters that concerned her, such as rising prices or the rapid growth of traffic congestion in the 1960s. His custom was to respond mildly, saying that he would see what could be done.[40] Though Doña Carmen was always careful to maintain correct relations with her husband's siblings, it was not surprising that Pilar found her rather pretentious. Pilar recognized that Doña Carmen was the "perfect wife" for her brother, as she later said, but she resented the way that her sister-in-law took over the complete redecoration of the old Franco home in El Ferrol, expunging its original style and furnishings, and also was critical of her small and close clique of friends, "the witches of El Pardo," as she later termed them.[41]

Franco's other close family relationship was with his brother Nicolás, who had been the ambassador in Lisbon for twenty years. Though Paco and Colás always remained on the most affectionate terms, the playboy style that his brother developed was totally foreign to Franco. Nicolás was noted for his extravagant hours, sometimes spending all night in nightclubs, rarely rising before noon—quite a different life from that during his young years as a naval officer. Stories about his womanizing may have been exaggerated, but they were stimulated particularly by an incident in 1950. While Nicolás was still ambassador, he vacationed in Cannes, and the British tabloid *Sunday Pictures* portrayed him as the leading lothario of the local beach, printing a photo of the portly, middle-aged diplomat in swim trunks beside a pretty young English model in a bikini. There are three different versions of Franco's reaction. One had him quipping, "Nicolás is getting a bit fat; he should lose weight." It is doubtful, however, that the caudillo was amused. Another version has Nicolás trying to convince his brother that the photo was fraudulent, a mere montage. Franco rarely argued very long with anyone, and the second version has him replying, "Agreed that it's a montage. But, Nicolás, were you there or not?" In the third, most believable, version, he is said to have told Nicolás, "From now on, bathe at home, alone, and with the door closed."[42]

The great love of Nicolás in his later life was a young woman less than half his age, Cristina Albéniz (granddaughter of the composer Isaac Albéniz). As brother of the caudillo, Nicolás enjoyed dispensation from certain rules binding the rest of the diplomatic corps and was able to make frequent trips back to Madrid to visit her. Whatever the exact nature of their relationship, Nicolás became completely obsessed with Cristina. Soon, however, she died tragically in a highway accident while driving with a young American woman friend. Nicolás was disconsolate and visited her gravesite for a number of years.[43]

In 1958 Nicolás retired from his twenty-year post as ambassador to Portugal. He had retained his commission in the corps of naval engineers, where he had been promoted to senior rank in 1942. After he left Lisbon, Franco named him inspector general of the corps, though he had to retire on reaching the age of seventy, three years later. In the last years of life he devoted himself to privileged business deals, some of dubious propriety.

Though Franco maintained good relations with the ten children of Pilar, he shunned other relatives whom he considered illegitimate, having nothing to do with Ramón's widow or his surviving daughter or with his father's second companion, who survived for many years after his father's death.[44] He must have been taken aback in April 1950 when he found that, even from the grave, his father was having the last word, for that month he received a letter from a young veteran of his army informing him that his father-in-law, Eugenio Franco Puey, was the natural son of Nicolás Franco Sr., born in Cavite in 1889 of an adolescent Spanish girl whom the elder Franco had seduced in the Philippines. Franco Puey had been adopted by his mother's subsequent husband, an artillery officer, though he retained his original name and eventually made a career as a topographer in Madrid. According to the letter, he had been legally recognized by his natural father, as well, who had extended to him the paternal blessing at the time of his marriage in 1918.[45]

The continuing rigidity of the caudillo's standards about marriage was illustrated by his treatment of his old friend and comrade Millán Astray. Earlier in life the founder of the Spanish Legion had married a young woman who informed him on their wedding night that she had taken a vow to the Virgin of perpetual chastity. Though Millán Astray was entitled to a Catholic annulment, he decided to maintain a "companionate" marriage. Later, after the Civil War, he became a good friend of Rita Gasset, niece of the philosopher Ortega y Gasset and one of the few noted feminists in Spain. She confided to the aging general that, though she would never consider getting married, she would like to have a child. Since the possibility of artificial insemination did not then exist in Spain, Millán Astray offered to volunteer his services, and his wife-companion assented. Once she became pregnant, however, Rita changed her mind and said that she wanted to marry the father of her prospective child. Since his marriage had never been consummated, Millán Astray still had the right to an annulment, which would leave him free to marry. Knowing Franco's views, however, Millán Astray decided that he should obtain the caudillo's approval, and Franco categorically refused. No general of his would ever be allowed to obtain an annulment or a divorce, under any circumstances.[46]

Most cherished of all by Franco was his daughter, Carmencita, the apple of the caudillo's eye. She led a secluded life, educated by private tutors, with classes in English and French, living to a large extent in a world of adults. Her upbringing was not so rigorous as that of her mother's in the convent school, but it was conventionally conservative and Catholic, training her primarily to become a wife and mother, even though she failed to become as formally pious as her mother. She was an attractive dark-haired girl, a competent but not outstanding student, physically vigorous, emotionally stable, and relatively outgoing, but she grew up in a sheltered environment that exposed her to very little of the world. Her *puesta de largo* (coming-out party), held on December 22, 1944, when she reached eighteen years of age, was a gala event, the social happening of the year in Madrid, but she continued to lead a rather secluded life at El Pardo. When she went out into the city alone, she was chaperoned by a nun, even when she was past twenty. As she said much later in a published interview, "I had to live through the era of energy shortages and couldn't go out without being driven even on Saturdays and Sundays. So we spent weekends at El Pardo, and I only got to see girlfriends who lived near by or came to spend the weekend with us."[47]

She enjoyed brief social outings with girlfriends in some of the better *cafeterías*, and on one of these occasions in 1948, when she was scarcely twenty-one, she met a young medical intern, Cristóbal Martínez-Bordiú, training to become a surgeon, who was introduced by one of the girl-friends.[48] Cristóbal came from a good family. His Andalusian father was a mining engineer without any great wealth but with aristocratic lineage on the side of his Aragonese mother. He was tall, athletic, somewhat hand-some, extroverted, histrionic, and subsequently also a competent surgeon. Cristóbal set his cap for the caudillo's daughter, and in the formal court-ship that followed, in which the two were never left alone until their wedding night, he was careful to make a good impression on her mother. Franco's personal reaction is unrecorded, and it would be typical of the dynamics of his small family that the opinion of Doña Carmen in such matters would prevail. Eventual announcement of the engagement came as something of a surprise to Madrid society, which had supposed that Carmencita's leading suitor was a son of Franco's boyhood friend and key minister, Juan Antonio Suanzes.[49]

The wedding took place on April 10, 1950, in a lavish ceremony at El Pardo attended by eight hundred. The primate of the Spanish Church, Cardinal Enrique Pla y Deniel, officiated, uttering a somewhat blasphemous comparison when he intoned to the young couple that "you have a most exemplary model in the family of Nazareth and a more recent one in the exemplary Christian home of the Chief of State."[50] Many items from the vast array of presents were distributed to charities.

The newlyweds enjoyed an elaborate honeymoon abroad, being received by the pope at the Vatican and traveling extensively, which pleased Carmen, who had never had opportunity to travel. For a brief time, Cristóbal was made "medical inspector of embassies," enabling the young couple to visit a number of countries and even to play a minor role representing the re-gime. Once the two got a taste of foreign travel, they never gave it up. This became something of a passion that Carmen would continue to indulge even at an advanced age. They lived a busy life, combining travel with major responsibilities at home, for Cristóbal practiced surgery, with a specialty in heart and lungs, for nearly three decades, while attending medical conferences abroad. A year after the marriage, his mother legally rehabilitated her family titles, so that henceforth the young couple would be formally known as the Marqués and Marquesa de Villaverde.

Having been carefully trained for the role of wife and mother, Carmencita performed it well, though her children would in large measure be raised by their nanny and tutors. Eventually there would be seven Martínez-Bordiú children, three boys and four girls, born between 1951 and 1964, for Carmencita proved almost as prolific as her aunt Pilar. All seven children would be born at El Pardo, and they visited their grandparents frequently, often spending entire weekends with them, enjoying special screenings of films.[51] The grandchildren would be the principal delight of Franco's later years. Their preferred nickname for him was "Abu," short for "abuelo" ("grandfather"), and, on occasion, they might also visit him briefly around nine in the morning before beginning the day's activities, a diversion that he much appreciated.

The grandchildren were under the tutelage of their British nanny, Beryl Hibbs, whom they would come to refer to as Nani and La Nanísima. Though a strict disciplinarian, she lavished the children with affection as well and in later life at least two of them recalled, that, by comparison with their frequently absent parents, she was the person who did the most for them and loved them the most, a sentiment they deeply reciprocated. The formidable Miss Hibbs is the only person known to have successfully contradicted the caudillo, at least when it came to the supervision of the grandchildren.[52] She is also said to have tried to impress on them that their life was likely to change a great deal once their grandfather died, for their privileged status would vanish.[53]

Since Franco had no male heir, when the first grandson, named Francisco for obvious reasons, was born in December 1954, Cristóbal's father, a *procurador en Cortes* (deputy), petitioned that the Cortes officially legalize the reversal of his names. This was done, so that the boy would be Francisco Franco Martínez-Bordiú (rather than Francisco Martínez-Bordiú Franco in the normal order). Thus he was in a position to perpetuate the Franco family name. Later, after a falling out with his own father, Francisco (or "Francis," as he was known) came back to live with his grandparents at El Pardo during his university years, and of all the grandchildren he was the one who got to know Franco best, since they both loved to hunt.[54]

In a memoir Francisco admits that, for Franco, his father Villaverde "was not exactly the ideal son-in-law," a considerable understatement.[55] Villaverde was a huge disappointment. He was energetic and part of the time hard working, often putting in long hours as a surgeon and sometimes receiving no more in payment than the modest social security fee. He became head of the heart section of a major hospital and carried out the first heart-transplant operation in Spain in 1968, though the patient died after eighteen hours. The down side was that, though he often worked hard, he also devoted a good deal of time to playing hard, becoming increasingly presumptuous and exhibiting a swagger that would gain for him the most negative reputation of any member of Franco's family. Though a competent professional, Villaverde never led the life of a normal surgeon, for he always had something of the adventurer about him. He became increasingly self-indulgent, devoting considerable time to society life, amusements, and insider business deals, and he became a serial womanizer. There were frequent spats in the marriage, after which the Marquesa sometimes returned briefly to her parents at El Pardo, though reconciliation seems almost always to have been relatively rapid.

On the other hand, Carmen Franco earned a different reputation as discreet, responsible, and comparatively unassuming; no hint of scandal or wrongdoing attached to her. Even her father's political foes could find little to criticize, and few would disagree with the assessment by one of Franco's physicians that "Carmen, during her father's lifetime, was always considered a sensible, prudent, and intelligent woman, qualities difficult to sustain when you are the daughter of someone placed like her father and, moreover, have been surrounded ever since childhood with every kind of calculated flatterer."[56]

For the Francos, the behavior of their son-in-law was disgusting, and even humiliating in the way that it violated their own values. Franco eventually came to feel a certain contempt for his son-in-law, though, given his rigid ideas of marriage, there was nothing to be done about it. He remained reticent, as usual, saying almost nothing, and this was also the case when he came to feel that the grandchildren were not being properly reared. Muñoz Grandes spoke for many when he observed to Pacón that the Francos "had not been fortunate" in the marriage of their only daughter. Though the elderly couple found the grandchildren a special delight, Doña Carmen is said sometimes to have referred to Villaverde pejoratively when speaking to her daughter as "that man you married," while on at least one occasion, according to one of her sons-in-law, the Marquesa referred to her husband as "mentally unbalanced."[57]

Franco and Villaverde were never comfortable with each other, having such extremely different personalities, and Francisco reports that his father normally tried to avoid being left alone with the generalissimo, who would sometimes ignore questions or attempts at conversation by his son-in-law. Villaverde always addressed his father-in-law formally as "my General" or "Excellency," though he was on somewhat more familiar terms with Doña Carmen.[58]

A few years before Franco died, Villaverde got into an altercation in a Costa del Sol nightclub with a Dutch tourist, who punched him in the nose, breaking it. The tourist was heavily fined and expelled from the country. Carmen reported the incident to her father, demanding that strong measures be taken. But the caudillo, who was having lunch at the time, was unimpressed, and refused to be distracted from his soup. According to one of the staff present:

> The Caudillo sipped spoonful after spoonful, as though listening to the rain.
>
> The Marquesa began to get worked up, trying to get a reaction from Franco by using the argument of defending the prestige of Spain. This had no effect at all. . . . The Generalissimo . . . seemed to be thinking: "Take that! It serves you right for being a bully and a blowhard."[59]

During a hunting expedition in his later years, Franco was in the front seat of an all-terrain vehicle, while the Villaverdes and a second couple were seated in the rear. His son-in-law, who detested Opus Dei, went on and on about the sinister role of members of the institute, who, according to him, were supposedly conspiring to overthrow Franco and restore the monarchy. When he blabbed that the Spanish were fed up with such people, "Franco would not let him finish. Pounding his fist on the dashboard he said: 'The one fed up is me, listening to you tell falsehoods about something you don't know the least thing about.'"[60] But that was about as far as he went.

For fifteen years, from 1927 to 1942, Franco had been surrounded domestically by members of the extended Polo family, a pattern only terminated by the breakup with the Serrano Suñers. During his final quarter century, however, the numerous members of the Martínez-Bordiú family, including Villaverde's three brothers and other relatives, came to the fore, dominating the family circle more and more, becoming known to critics as "the clan of El Pardo." With his usual passivity in domestic life, Franco largely accepted this state of affairs, though he permitted little intimacy and always had to be addressed as "Excellency." To his annual round of activities was added a lengthy New Year's vacation at Arroyovil, the Martínez-Bordiú family estate in Jaén province, which had its own hunting reserve, where, in his final period, Franco would most frequently unlimber his video camera. Taking place normally between December 27 and January 5, this was the largest get-together of the year, to which many people from the highest social strata were invited. Franco seems to have enjoyed it well enough. The Martínez-Bordiús could be highly agreeable and outdid themselves in hospitality. On these trips, Franco might stay up on New Year's Eve till 1 a.m., considerably past his normal bedtime.[61]

All the family became wealthy, as might be expected. Franco did not embezzle, nor did he take kickbacks on state contracts, so the Francos did not have hundreds of millions of dollars in Swiss accounts, as did Third World dictators, but the amounts that they made and deposited were large enough. His relatives, however, made money the way that politicians in all systems make money—through special favors, special deals, insider information, and insider trading. Both Nicolás and Pilar, a widow with ten children to raise and educate, had been into such things for some time, and the widening of the family circle in 1950, coinciding with the flourishing of the Spanish economy, meant that there were more people in his family engaging in such activities.

Throughout his life Franco, nonetheless, was very scrupulous in his personal finances. His accounts were supervised by his personal lawyer, his brother-in-law Felipe Polo. His disposable income was not especially large because his salary as chief of state was hardly exorbitant. It was raised to 250,000 pesetas per month, but its real value dropped to the point where this amounted to only around $40,000 per year, though in his last years it was more than doubled to 600,000 pesetas per month. Franco was also entitled to the salary of a senior general, but he assigned that to a military charity. Sums of money that he received from time to time from wealthy supporters were sometimes earmarked for charity and, whatever the intention of the donor, were routinely assigned to various Catholic causes.

His estate nonetheless increased because he only spent part of his regular income, writing checks only for such things as the expenses of his annual birthday party and to pay for gifts to and occasional requests for assistance from his nieces and nephews, primarily the ten children of his sister.[62] Franco did not engage in financial speculation but remained faithful to his public policies by investing almost exclusively in public enterprises, such as the Canal de Isabel II, CAMPSA (the state oil monopoly), RENFE (the national railroad system), the Instituto Nacional de Colonización (providing land to small farmers), certificates of the Banco de Crédito Local, and state bonds. About half his financial estate was held in liquid form in checking and savings accounts in the Banco de España, Banco de Bilbao, Banco Hispano Americano, Banco Español de Crédito, and similar institutions. He wrote numerous checks to charities, several of his accounts designed primarily for this purpose. During the third quarter (trimester) of 1956 his checks to charity totaled 370,000 pesetas, for example, but dropped to 200,000 for the last half of 1961.[63] During the years 1950 to 1961, for which records are most complete, Franco's total financial holdings ranged between twenty-one and twenty-four million pesetas. This amounted to no more than four hundred thousand dollars, a paltry sum for a dictator in power for a quarter century, divided about equally between cash savings and investments.[64] If he ever opened a secret Swiss bank account, no evidence of it has come to light.

As he aged and prices increased, Franco eventually lost all sense of the real purchasing power of money, since, though he paid for certain expenses, he never had to buy anything personally. Not long before his death, when he found that his grandson was going out to dinner, he reached into his pocket to give him something to spend and handed over the stray ten-peseta bill that he found, evidently not realizing that it would scarcely be sufficient to buy a soft drink.[65]

Franco made only one direct investment in landed property, when in 1951 he purchased on easy terms an extensive agricultural estate, Valdefuentes, comprising nearly ten thousand square meters in the Arroyomolinos district twenty-one kilometers southwest of Madrid. It became a significant food producer and was converted into a joint-stock company owned by the caudillo. Valdefuentes was also attractive because it contained an extensive woodland and open space that was ideal for Franco's favorite sport, hunting.[66] It was managed by the principal wheeler and dealer in the Villaverde clan, known as Tío Pepe (Uncle Joe). This was José María Sanchiz Sancho, Cristóbal's uncle by marriage. When, however, Tío Pepe, whom Vicente Gil called "a big blowhard," suggested that Franco could make a great deal of money by speculating in prime real estate for tourists in Marbella, Franco stopped him short.[67] The caudillo's goal was to exercise power, and making more money held no interest for him, even seeming a betrayal of duty.

Things were different with his family members, however, and one way or another the family made quite a bit of money, though there was little evidence of major accounts abroad until the end of Franco's life. This was not a matter of direct theft or embezzlement, but corners were cut and de facto legal immunity existed. In the final, most liberal, year of the regime, a banker had the temerity to bring suit against Nicolás Franco for defaulting on a four-million- peseta loan (about sixty thousand dollars). The banker was arrested on charges of corruption (which may or may not have been valid) and quickly abandoned his suit, returning the loan document to Nicolás Franco.[68]

Throughout her marriage, Doña Carmen maintained her own personal estate, based originally on property inherited from her father. She later invested in properties in Madrid, often in partnership with her close friend Pura (Marquesa de Huétor de Santillán), purchasing apartments and buildings and renting them out. The long-term home of her daughter, son-in-law, and grandchildren was a large apartment in a building that she had bought on the Calle de los Hermanos Bécquer, not far from the center of Madrid. Later, as they matured, she gave apartments as presents to her grandchildren.[69]

Very many things of all kinds were given to the Francos by individuals, corporate entities, and local governments. There were no laws against gifts to public officials. Nearly all of this was simply stored up, most in a large warehouse at El Pardo, the rest at the other residences—the two possessions near Madrid, the Pazo de Meirás, and the elegant house that had been given to Doña Carmen in La Coruña. Dealing with all this stuff, in fact, became something of a problem after Franco died.

Some of Franco's old comrades did not like what they saw. As early as 1956, Muñoz Grandes lamented, "I don't know what is going on, for they used to be completely austere and that was one of the best things about them. Now that has disappeared to an alarming extent." Pacón further observed that "unfortunately that is also the opinion of many generals who talk to me. . . . My only consolation is that I will soon be leaving the Casa Militar and won't have to see and put up with so many things of which I disapprove and which sadden me. But Franco doesn't like to have you talk about corruption or have people come forward with complaints."[70]

By Franco's last years the staff at El Pardo had become quite extensive. His military staff consisted of four infantry companies who were based in nearby barracks, plus a dozen specialized units and a detachment of the Civil Guard. His civil staff was smaller but included 264 attendants, from protocol officials to cleaning maids and gardeners. The atmosphere at El Pardo had long been rigid and, if anything, grew more somber as its residents aged. In the last years Franco was still awakened at his usual time, 8 a.m., and was bathed, shaved, and dressed by two attendants, supervised by his chief valet and factotum, Juanito (Juan Muñoz), who had joined his service as a soldier in the Civil War and served the caudillo almost until the end of Franco's life. The main course at breakfast in the final period was an apple compote. The caudillo then maintained his customary morning schedule, though in his last two years, there were a few limitations in what he could do.

Meals with the Francos always seem to have been deadly dull and only got worse. Even during the 1950s, however, Pacón had complained that "lunches [at El Pardo] are usually excruciatingly boring, since no one strikes up a theme of conversation. If he is worried about something, he scarcely utters a word but devotes himself to chewing on toothpicks that he leaves on the table. He has a sad expression without fixing on anything. An angel and the whole heavenly host might pass by. Silence is absolute, leaving one uncomfortable but unable to say anything. If you try to introduce some subject, you fail miserably."[71] On these dreary daily occasions, the possibility of conversation depended entirely on Doña Carmen. Franco only spoke when asked a direct question, which he would normally try to dispose of in two or three words. On the other hand, when Doña Carmen got going, she could be imperious, so that invited guests entered the conversation only at their peril. The national news broadcast at 3 p.m. was usually seen on television in the dining room, but Franco rarely commented on the news, mostly watching it silently out of the corner of his eye. This funereal scene was only livened when Carmencita, who had a meal with her parents at least once a week, was present.[72]

In these last years the only person outside the intimate family who could speak to Franco in sharply critical terms was his longtime physician, the old-guard Falangist Vicente Gil. Like Muñoz Grandes, Gil was a radical populist disgusted with the new modern, glitzy, and materialist Spain of the 1960s. As late as 1970, he normally entered the generalissimo's presence by clicking his heels together loudly and giving the Falangist salute. The servants would always have coffee ready for him while he waited for his regular appointments, and they were accustomed to hear a string of obscenities from the veteran physician as he read the morning paper with its news of the government ministers. To his patient, Gil regularly denounced many of the latter as worthless and highly corrupt. Franco had no doubt of his loyalty and trusted Gil fully and in fact often found him amusing, so that his only response was an occasional sly smile and a mild rebuke such as "Don't be so crude, Vicente."[73]

A favorite diversion of the Francos was the screening of movies in the late afternoon or evenings, and over the years a total of nearly two thousand different films were shown at least once at El Pardo.[74] In the later years the Francos occasionally turned these into social occasions on Saturday afternoons, inviting a select number of guests to their small theater. The entertainment began with a presentation of the current official newsreel, after which the lights were turned back on, and light refreshments were served for half an hour, following which the main film would be shown. Nothing in the least risqué or sensationalist appeared on the screen at El Pardo, the chief censor being not so much the caudillo but Doña Carmen.

On one occasion Don Gonzalo de Borbón, whose older brother would soon marry Franco's oldest granddaughter, was invited. He was scarcely acquainted with the caudillo and made the mistake of telling an off-color story within his hearing. Franco's tolerance of such things in no way increased with the years. As Don Gonzalo was beginning to guffaw, he saw Franco fixing him with a cold, hostile stare. No one dared laugh. Don Gonzalo quickly changed the subject and then moved farther away.[75]

The atmosphere at El Pardo was normally imperious, and Franco would only gruffly offer a word of condolence if he was informed that someone on the large staff had suffered the death of a relative. The counterpoint to the caudillo's ever-increasing silence and unresponsiveness was that, as is often the case with old people, he could shed tears quite readily if something touched a deeper personal sentiment. The most moving public occasion in his final years came when a group of children, cited for various accomplishments, were invited to El Pardo to meet the caudillo. As he greeted them, Franco suddenly encountered a little boy, both of whose arms had been amputated. Onlookers saw the crusty old dictator's eyes glisten with tears as he bent over to give the lad a special kiss on the cheek.[76]

16 | Development Dictator

(1959–1964)

The year 1959 marked a turning point in the history of Franco's regime, for it brought decisive liberalization of economic policy, resulting in an accelerated expansion that transformed society and modernized Spain. As has been seen, Franco was a "regenerationist" who sought to economically develop his country while restoring and maintaining a conservative cultural framework, contradictory though these objectives were. Though few would have guessed it at that time, the 1950s were the last decade of the traditional culture and society, which would soon be transformed by the massive changes of the years following.[1]

Since 1945 the government had been slowly liberalizing its highly statist policies, but some of the new ministers appointed in 1957 wanted to go faster. The country had become increasingly integrated into the international network, first joining the Food and Agricultural Organization and then, in 1952, UNESCO. In January 1958 an initial agreement was signed with the Organization for European Economic Cooperation (OEEC), embryo of the European Union, and two months later Spain was invited to join the International Monetary Fund (IMF).

Though the economy had grown steadily from 1950 to 1958, it had been hampered by continued state control and restrictions, limited credit and investment, slow growth in exports, reliance on deficit state expenditure that produced high inflation, and a rigidly overvalued peseta. The budget of 1958 therefore added modest export incentives and timidly began to open the door to greater foreign investment. By the end of that year the major West European countries made their currencies completely convertible, increasing pressure on Spain to do the same, even though an artificially pegged peseta had always been a hallmark of Franco's policy. The extent of the problem this created was revealed in December 1958, when two Swiss bank agents were arrested as they tried to smuggle out a large bundle of pesetas. They were found to be carrying a list of 1,363 wealthy Spaniards—among them some leading figures in the regime—who maintained secret Swiss bank accounts.

The situation became critical several months into 1959, after four successive years of high inflation and severe deficits in the balance of payments. In May the OEEC issued a report detailing the need for drastic reform in Madrid, as the Instituto Español de Moneda Extranjera, which controlled currency exchange, slid ever nearer suspension of payments. The stock market went into sharp decline after restrictive measures were taken to deal with these problems. The Spanish government was almost bankrupt.

Mariano Navarro Rubio, the minister of finance, insisted that the only way forward was to liberalize drastically, eliminating many regulations and restrictions, devaluating the peseta by nearly 50 percent to its true market rate, and encouraging large-scale foreign investment and rapid export growth. This flew in the face of Francoist economics, and the caudillo was at first loathe to change course. During the Civil War he had rejected the opinion that the Nationalist peseta was overvalued and had been largely successful in maintaining its rate. His belief in state voluntarism was undiminished. Since the economy had grown impressively for most of the preceding decade, his recent speeches had used the term "crisis of growth" to explain current difficulties. Franco was willing to allow a degree of reform, but he resisted abandoning basic principles of autarchy. His innate opposition to liberalism still extended to economic liberalism, as well, as he underlined in an undated memorandum that he drew up in these weeks:

The interest of the nation, the common good and the will of the Spanish people urgently require a transformation of the capitalist system, an acceleration of economic growth, a more just distribution of wealth, social justice, transformation and modernization of credit, and the modernization of many means of production.

When the state nationalizes certain industries and services this is labeled socialism, even though that is accepted in many self-styled liberal states who adopt it from socialism as licit and desirable.[2]

If anything, Carrero Blanco was yet more rigid, suggesting that all they needed to do was to tighten up the old policy. Even the commerce minister, Alberto Ullastres, like Navarro Rubio a member of Opus Dei, thought his fellow minister might be going too far too fast.

Franco was nothing if not stubborn, but neither did he ignore facts once they finally became absolutely pressing. When the finance minister presented his plan, Franco "basically showed not the least confidence in it."[3] Moreover, he had always believed that greater economic liberalism would bring in its wake greater political and cultural liberalism and that a major opening to international trade and investment would open the door to subversive influence from abroad. On the other hand, to reject the plan would probably also mean having to carry out another change of government, the third in three years. He personally trusted Navarro Rubio, a multidecorated thrice-wounded former *alférez provisional* who had ended the Civil War a captain of *regulares* and was also an officer in the army's juridical corps. The finance minister bombarded Franco with data and technical arguments, at the same time appealing to his patriotism and national pride, presenting the new course as the only way to save Spain from bankruptcy.[4] Despite holding firm with respect to certain ideas, in the final analysis Franco also showed pragmatism on key issues. Eventually, as on foreign policy in 1943–44, the generalissimo decided to reverse course a bit, becoming convinced by the data that he had little practical choice. However skeptical he remained, he finally decided to bite the bullet, and it was one of the most productive decisions he ever made.[5]

On July 22, 1959, Franco issued a decree-law announcing a new stabilization plan for the Spanish economy, discussed in greater detail in the following chapter. There was a brief recessionary readjustment, but within a year the economy was growing rapidly once more, and in the following decade it registered the highest rate of sustained expansion in Europe, a "Spanish miracle" that would enable the generalissimo, before he died, to preside over the definitive social and economic modernization of Spain. This was the only part of his governing program that would ever be permanently fulfilled, and even this did not take the form originally prescribed. Moreover, as Franco discovered ruefully in the last years before his death, economic liberalization would have disastrously counterproductive social and cultural consequences.

The 1960s was one of the two decades of most rapid change that Spanish society and economic structure had ever seen, but change in Franco's other policies came more slowly.[6] Of the leftist opposition, only the Communists remained very active and they had considerably moderated their tactics, having abandoned any idea of overthrowing the Spanish dictator directly. The only political sector that really concerned Franco to any extent were the Monarchists.

A new crossroads in relations with the royal family loomed at the close of 1959, as Juan Carlos finished his education in the military academy. Don Juan, as usual, was pulled in different directions by his advisers; some, like Pedro Sainz Rodríguez, sought independence from Franco and others, such as new advisers from the ranks of Opus Dei, showed greater flexibility. The Conde de Barcelona proposed a special advanced education program for his son in San Sebastián, but Franco vetoed that. Instead the generalissimo accepted Don Juan's proposal that the Duque de Frías, a scholarly aristocrat, take over as preceptor, but he insisted that Federico Suárez Verdaguer become his new spiritual director and also that the prince take up residence in a small palace in El Escorial. Father Suárez was a well-published right-wing historian and a leading figure in Opus Dei. The issue was the subject of lengthy correspondence between Franco and Don Juan, the dictator charging the latter with proposing an "eclectic monarchy," which would be totally unacceptable.[7] He had his own ideas about the prince's education and threatened to turn the matter over to the Council of the Realm, the senior advisory body of the Spanish state, all the members of which had of course been personally designated by Franco.[8] Don Juan drew back, brought in a new adviser closer to the caudillo, and insisted to Franco that he did indeed accept the Principles of the National Movement and that the monarchy would function as continuation of the regime.

This pleased the generalissimo; he proposed a new meeting between the two, lecturing Don Juan that the monarchy must support the movement totally and that he had to understand that liberal capitalist regimes in Western Europe would not be able to survive too much longer. Their third meeting ever took place on March 29, 1960, at the estate of Ruiseñada west of Madrid, its owner having died in the interim, and was hosted by Ruiseñada's two sons. Two lengthy conversations ensued that ratified the new plan for completion of the prince's education. Franco insisted that Don Juan must get rid of Sainz Rodríguez, whom he wrongly accused of being a Freemason. This upset the pretender, who knew that was not true. He himself had been accused of being a Mason in a book published in Madrid the preceding year by an ultra-rightist zealot (Mauricio Carlavilla's *Anti-España 1959*) and had hired Serrano Suñer to bring suit for libel. The lunch was more relaxed, however, and Franco turned garrulous, going through his lengthy repertoire of army stories.[9] The Conde de Barcelona, meanwhile, was delighted to hear Franco say that he had no intention of going outside the royal family to name his successor. Don Juan left what would be his final meeting with the caudillo in a state of euphoria, since he assumed that the member chosen from the royal family would be its legitimate heir, that is, himself. All the evidence, nonetheless, indicates that Franco remained suspicious of the pretender and was skeptical that he could become an adequate successor.

Toward the end of October Franco received in audience for the first time the two sons of Don Juan's older brother, Don Alfonso, who was trying vainly to reassert his own dynastic rights. The elder of these young *infantes*, or princes, the handsome Don Alfonso, told Franco that he had no personal ambition to inherit the throne, and Franco said to Pacón afterward that he found the young man "intelligent and cultured."[10]

The only public incident of opposition that year occurred on November 20, at the anniversary of the death of José Antonio Primo de Rivera, which had been restored as a major observance of the regime and was now celebrated at the newly inaugurated Valle de los Caídos.[11] As the caudillo presided, a young Falangist shouted in a loud voice that could be heard throughout the basilica, "Franco is a traitor to the Falange!" The generalissimo never changed expression, and the protester was immediately arrested, prosecuted, and sentenced to several years in jail.[12]

After Nikita Khrushchev launched into a tirade against the Spanish regime at the United Nations on October 1, 1960, Franco canceled a European Cup match between the Soviet and Spanish teams that was to have been held in Spain, though this prompted a fine against the Spanish soccer federation. Franco explained privately that he feared incidents, pro and con, and that he had decided to refuse the Soviet government the propaganda advantage of flying its flag and having its anthem played in Spain, since there were still no formal relations between Madrid and Moscow.[13]

Though Castiella as foreign minister vigorously attempted to develop a more independent foreign policy that would reduce Spain's reliance on Washington, he had only limited success.[14] This was partially counterbalanced by closer economic and cultural association with Western Europe, which was facilitated by Spain's accelerating economic development. Franco always opposed the idea of a united Europe and publicly attacked "Europeanism" as late as 1961, but, as the Common Market grew and gained new members, he began to see the handwriting on the wall and authorized Spain's application to join, as well. The OEEC members persistently dragged their feet, largely for political reasons, and Franco was in no hurry, realizing entry would require major structural adjustments in Spain. He accurately pointed out that more than mere political antagonism was involved.[15] Ullastres was eventually dispatched as ambassador to the OEEC in 1965, but not until April 1967 did the Common Market leadership deign slowly to begin negotiations.[16]

One of Franco's greatest concerns was still the tense relations with Morocco, whose sultan, Mohammed V, failed to fulfill his economic agreements with Spain. The final contingent of troops left the territory of the old protectorate on August 31, 1961, but then the Moroccan government began putting more pressure on the Spanish government to give up the cities of Ceuta and Melilla and the remaining possessions of Ifni and the Spanish Sahara. On July 30, 1962, the Moroccan government extended its claims to territorial waters to a distance of twelve miles off the coast, in order to thwart Spanish fishing operations. Madrid refused to recognize such an unusual claim and declared that it would protect the rights of fishermen, a problem that would continue to fester for years. Franco was willing to negotiate the cession of the Ifni enclave on the southwest Atlantic coast of Morocco in return for a favorable agreement on Spanish fishing rights but had no intention of yielding at all on the two Spanish cities of Ceuta and Melilla or on the Spanish Sahara. The cities he, of course, considered inherently Spanish, as their populations were predominantly Spanish, while the Sahara had never been part of Morocco.

The new American administration of John F. Kennedy, which took office in Washington in January 1961, initially adopted a rather hostile attitude toward the regime in Madrid. It seemed to want to limit the relationship between the two and perhaps even to negotiate a new agreement that would drastically reduce American aid. This momentarily encouraged signs of life among the otherwise dormant Socialists, in their émigré headquarters in Toulouse, though these were short lived. Carrero Blanco reiterated to

Franco his standard advice to hang tough, recommending in a memo of February 23, 1961, that the regime maintain "the most absolute intransigence."[17] There was little to worry about, for Kennedy's first year in office proved to be something of a diplomatic disaster for Washington. Revising the relationship with Spain disappeared from view, and in October Secretary of State Dean Rusk announced that he would soon pay a visit to Franco. By the time that he arrived in Madrid in December, the American administration was much more concerned about other problems, and the Spanish relationship seemed considerably more important. Franco used the opportunity to say that when the Pact of Madrid came up for renegotiation in a year and a half, his regime would ask for fundamentally improved terms.[18]

Privately, he described the Americans as "infantile" and observed that he would have preferred the British to lead the Western alliance. He criticized the Kennedy administration for botching the Bay of Pigs invasion in Cuba, declaring that it should have been possible "to have Fidel Castro with all four feet in the air within twenty-four hours," and he harbored the notion that Washington had erred in not "unleashing" Chiang Kai-shek in a guerrilla war against the Chinese Communists. He also cited Alonso Vega to the effect that the greatest favor done by the American military was to "clean out the 'B-girls' from the bars and the cabarets of Madrid, since nearly all of them have married sergeants or soldiers."[19]

The plateau Franco's regime achieved during the 1950s extended well through the following decade. It had developed a system of essentially bureaucratic, politically almost unmobilized authoritarian rule, and the success of its new economic policy along with the impotence of the opposition seemed to indicate that it had little to fear until the demise or incapacity of Franco. During the course of the 1960s, however, a better educated and increasingly affluent society began to stir, though at first motivated more by economic than by political aspirations.

In mid-1961 the old guard of the movement made a kind of last-gasp effort, sending to Franco its final grand proposal for political change. This strongly criticized the goal of a Monarchist succession and called for a return to a much more statist economic model, as well as a diplomatic opening to the Communist world. It also attempted to revive one feature of the old Arrese plan, calling for the creation of a *cámara alta* within the movement, a kind of senate, to advise on state policy and to review and veto legislation. This proposal was signed by most of the leading figures of the Falange, including the two-time party secretary Raimundo Fernández-Cuesta and Pilar and Miguel Primo de Rivera, the latter personally bearing the proposal to Franco. That issue, however, had already been decided and Franco seems to have ignored the proposal, writing in the margin "notion is very bad, as are those who inspired it."[20]

Much greater concern was aroused by the prospect that the new encyclical Pope John XXIII was preparing on social and other issues, *Mater et magistra*, might issue a blanket condemnation of regimes that did not permit free and independent trade unions. Spanish diplomacy lobbied the Vatican intensively, placing the best possible construction on the regime's "vertical syndicalism," which combined workers' and employers' sections in the same syndicates and largely provided job security, though no right to strike. The response was reassuring, John XXIII indicating that he valued the peace and prosperity brought by the regime and its support of the Church and that there would be no statements in condemnation of Spanish policy.

On July 18, 1961, the twenty-fifth anniversary of the Nationalist insurrection, fifty thousand army veterans paraded in Burgos before Franco, who seemed more in command than ever.[21] Later, on the annual Day of the Caudillo (October 1), an elaborate ceremony took place, also in Burgos, to celebrate the twenty-fifth anniversary of his accession to power. Franco used the occasion to reaffirm the doctrinal basis of his state:

> The great weakness of modern states lies in their lack of doctrinal content, in having renounced a firm concept of man, life, and history. The major error of liberalism is its negation of any permanent category of truth—its absolute and radical relativism—an error that, in a different form, was apparent in those other European currents that made "action" their only demand and the supreme norm of their conduct. . . . When the juridical order does not proceed from a system of principles, ideas, and values recognized as superior and prior to the state, it ends in an omnipotent juridical voluntarism, whether its primary organ be the so-called majority, purely numerical and inorganically expressed, or the supreme organs of power.[22]

Don Juan, under the influence of new, more conservative advisers, tried to draw closer. In a personal letter of congratulations to Franco, dated July 10, he avowed, "I must proclaim the union of the monarchy with the rising of the 18th of July 1936." He added that "the political system of an open constitution that currently rules, and that will be inherited by a future regime, enables me to affirm, without doing violence to my own thought, my adherence to the Principles and Fundamental Laws of the Movement, which, in addition to being implicit in Spanish traditional doctrine, also contain in advance the necessary flexibility to face all the needs of evolution and of life."[23] This completed the Conde de Barcelona's second 180-degree turn within the past two decades. Needless to say, it pleased Franco immensely, and he was quicker than usual to dispatch an appreciative response.[24]

A reminder of the Caudillo's mortality suddenly struck on Christmas Eve, 1961, when he was injured while firing at pigeons, accompanied only by his aide Juanito, in the hunting reserve at El Pardo. His shotgun suddenly blew up, damaging his left hand, which held the stock. Franco was taken to an emergency first-aid station set up in Carmencita's old bedroom, where Vicente Gil decided that he would need surgical intervention at the Hospital General del Aire, the air force clinic, which was the nearest hospital to El Pardo. Before leaving, Franco had a brief phone conversation with Muñoz Grandes, informing the head of the Supreme General Staff that, as the most senior active general, he should be prepared, if necessary, to "take charge of the situation." Muñoz Grandes had been confidentially designated as the regent and chief of state to succeed Franco in the event that Franco should die or be incapacitated before naming a successor.[25]

The surgery was successful, and the ensuing investigation revealed that the accident resulted from a simple error by the faithful Juanito, who had reloaded the shotgun while its chamber already contained a smaller cartridge, jamming it and creating a backfire.[26] Sabotage was ruled out, though Alonso Vega seemed certain that an assassination attempt had been involved.[27] Full recuperation was slow, however, and after a month the injured hand and arm would be subjected to intense therapy sessions that continued on into the spring, by which time Franco regained almost complete use of the hand.[28]

On December 30, as Franco was convalescing, the Greek monarchy announced the formal engagement of the Greek princess Sofía to Juan Carlos, the wedding to take place four and a half months later in Athens. This was a dynastic match by the two royal families, and the Spanish government was not involved. The only complication was that the Greek Orthodox Church insisted that the wedding first be carried out in the Greek Church, followed by a Catholic ceremony. Since it was agreed that the princess would subsequently announce her conversion to Catholicism, the Vatican finally consented, with the understanding that the Orthodox ceremony would be pro forma, held prior to the formal Catholic wedding that would follow, putting an end to the murmurings among Spanish Monarchists.

Don Juan had first informed Franco of the impending engagement three months earlier, in a letter that also declared that, on the twenty-fifth anniversary of Franco's elevation to power, he was bestowing on the generalissimo the Order of the Golden Fleece, the monarchy's highest decoration. The Conde de Barcelona termed this more a personal than a political gesture, simply recognizing Franco's great service to Spain and to the monarchy. Franco approved of the marriage but politely declined the award, pointing out that it could only properly be granted by a ruling king. Having put Don Juan in his place once more, four months later Franco invited Juan Carlos to a personal meeting at El Pardo on March 1, 1962, and told the prince that he was awarding to Juan Carlos the newly created Order of Carlos III, as well as the Gran Cruz for his prospective bride. This impressed on the prince that Franco, having rejected the Golden Fleece, was himself de jure regent who had the authority to exercise a reigning monarch's right to bestow aristocratic titles, even on an eventual heir to the throne. He also wanted particularly to stress how important it was that Juan Carlos and his bride take up permanent residence in Madrid, because, as he is said to have told him on this occasion, the prince had "much more possibility" than his father of eventually being named king. As a loyal son, Juan Carlos is said, in turn, to have mildly protested, but this was a very clear hint to which the prince had every intention of responding positively.[29]

Franco gave the young couple his blessing, but no one in his immediate family attended the wedding. His daughter and her husband might have gone had she not been well advanced in one of her numerous pregnancies. Instead, Franco dispatched Admiral Felipe Abárzuza, aboard the cruiser *Canarias*, flagship of the Spanish fleet, as his personal representative at the wedding, which took place, amid much pomp, in Athens on May 14, 1962. Time would show that Juan Carlos was extremely fortunate to have this tall, intelligent, discreet, and attentive woman as his future queen.[30]

When the royal couple returned to Madrid on June 5 after the honeymoon, they were met at the capital's military airport of Getafe by Carmen, who had recently given birth, and also by Villaverde, who invited them to dine on the following day with the entire Franco family at El Pardo. The old dictator was charmed by Princess Sofía, and particularly pleased to see that she was making rapid progress in learning Spanish.[31] Sofía was surprised by "the extensive security measures: everything enclosed, sentinels up on their posts, guards all over."[32] Though Greece had been through a vicious revolutionary civil war even more recently than Spain, the Greek royal family was not accustomed to such a level of protection, but then it was not under such constant threat of assassination.

She found the caudillo, however, quite different from what she had imagined: "He was a Franco quite different from the idea that I had gotten from the press and the opinions I heard: a Caudillo, a proud Generalissimo, an imposing dictator. . . . I had imagined him to be harsh and unpleasant. But I found a simple man, wishing to please, and very timid."[33] Later, as she became better acquainted with him, she could see that he appeared to be genuinely fond of Juan Carlos, and she commented to her husband that "Franco's eyes light up when he sees you. . . . He likes to have you near, to explain things to you, to feel that he is your Pygmalion."[34] This perception was substantially accurate. Franco had no son of his own and was disappointed in his son-in-law. Juan Carlos slowly became a kind of surrogate, though Franco, typically, always maintained his emotional distance.

Franco faced an unprecedented act of political defiance in the spring of 1962. On June 5, the assembly of the European Movement met in Munich, and representatives of seven different Spanish political groups, from both inside and outside Spain, ranging from the left to the right-center, attended. This was the first formal meeting of groups opposed to the Franco regime from both left and right, Christian democrats among them. They jointly signed a declaration demanding the return of political parties and representative and democratic elections in Spain.

The regime had already asked for the opening of negotiations concerning Spain's membership in the European Union, though the European Parliament had earlier voted to recommend that no country lacking democratic institutions be allowed to join. The joint opposition statement thus came as a particular embarrassment.[35] The controlled press roused a great storm, *Arriba* denouncing the meeting as the "conspiracy of treason." In its own response, the government suspended article 14 of the Charter of the Spanish People and indicated to signatories resident in Spain that they could choose between voluntary exile or imprisonment on their return. Nearly all of them chose exile.

The publicity this incident generated constituted a setback for the image that the Spanish government had been seeking to create of a reformist and developmental regime that, though not a democracy, was becoming more liberal and representative. Franco's diplomats in the major Western capitals had to work hard to put the best face on it and to assure leaders that Spain was headed in the right direction. To a degree, they succeeded. Neither Kennedy in Washington nor Pierre Couve de Murville, De Gaulle's premier in Paris, wished to criticize the Spanish regime at that time, and the French prime minister even declared his willingness to assist in negotiations for Spain's entrance into the Common Market.[36]

The greatest damage done by the Munich declaration, as it turned out, was to Don Juan's relations with Franco. The signatures of two leading Monarchists convinced Franco that the pretender would always play a double game, and this recognition on Franco's part essentially burned the remaining bridges between them. Franco would not accept Don Juan's explanation that he had nothing to do with the affair, nor was he mollified by the fact that his old minister of war, Gil Robles, one of the signatories, was then dropped from Don Juan's personal council. To top it off, the secretary-general of the movement later sent to Franco a report that the whole business had been agreed on at the wedding in Athens, though in fact at that time the Conde de Barcelona had only been told, rather vaguely, that Monarchists would meet with other Spanish political figures in Paris.[37] Franco's final judgment was that Don Juan was telling him the truth but that the advisors of the pretender had been involved in the Munich affair and afterward sought to cover themselves.[38] From that point, Franco never again seriously considered the possibility of naming Don Juan his successor. The only question was when and if he would recognize Juan Carlos.

A new front had opened, however, with the emergence of a Catholic leftist opposition, something that had never before existed under any regime in Spanish history. The reforming and liberalizing currents of Vatican II were already being felt, and a number of bishops had become critical of the regime. The focal points were the Catholic trade union groups (HOAC) and the Catholic Worker Youth (Juventud Obrera Católica [JOC]), who had become the targets of Communist infiltration, though with what degree of success, it is hard to say. They participated in illegal strike activity and were defended by Church leaders, even if the primate, the elderly Pla y Deniel, was taken aback to see the Catholic worker groups calling for revolution, which was part of the new (primarily rhetorical) climate of the 1960s. All this was more than Franco could understand.[39] The pace of change in nearly all aspects of Spanish life was accelerating, and, as it turned out, 1962 was the biggest year for labor unrest in some time. Though there were arrests, the government's response was unusually moderate, and in August it introduced a significant hike in the minimum wage.

On July 10, 1962, Franco appointed a new government, making several changes designed to cope more effectively with emerging problems, with an accent on sustaining rapid development. The most notable change, however, was naming Muñoz Grandes as vice president of government, a concession to the caudillo's age, concern about which had increased since the shotgun accident. For the first time, there was officially a second in command, though one only four years younger than Franco.[40] The three military ministers were once more replaced with yet another set of old guard loyalists, the new minister of the navy being Franco's fellow *ferrolano*, Admiral Pedro Nieto Antúnez. Two of the most hard-line civilian ministers, however, were replaced by more flexible appointees, and the leaders of the stabilization plan, Navarro Rubio and Ullastres, kept their places, while another technocrat from Opus Dei, the handsome young naval engineer Gregorio López Bravo, who had made a very favorable impression on Franco, became minister of industry. In addition, López Rodó had been made *comisario* of the new development plan that was being prepared, a position very close to cabinet status.[41] The caudillo seemed quite satisfied with this economic team, which was achieving impressive results. He was also content to see more members of Opus Dei in the government. Franco had a high regard for the secular institute and had become personally acquainted with its founder, though he privately expressed a few qualms about the way its members tended to favor and promote each other.[42]

In some ways the most prominent new minister was Manuel Fraga Iribarne, a former academic whiz kid and an energetic administrator who had directed the Institute of Political Studies, the regime's think tank, and now became minister of information and tourism. He had dual responsibilities, first to prepare a more liberal press and censorship law in accord with the present tone of the regime and second to stimulate the booming tourist industry, whose potential was enormous.

Appointing a new government did little to relieve Franco's increasing worries about the succession. In an undated memorandum, "Thoughts," apparently prepared after formation of the new government, Franco debated the issues with himself. Should there be a referendum on his successor? Should the Council of the Realm present a list of candidates? Would it be better to name a regent first and then let him proceed with due deliberation to crowning a new king? What should be the timing? If there were a new regent, how long should his regency last? Ten years? Might such a term be extended? If Franco planned to choose a royal successor directly, the identity of the candidate remained totally up in the air.[43]

He still was uncertain about Juan Carlos, though Sofía had made an outstanding first impression. The summer passed and the royal couple continued to travel abroad on the second very long phase of their honeymoon, and Franco thought that Don Juan might still be trying to control his son. Franco mused in his memo that the only satisfactory solution might be to "require that Don Juan abdicate in favor of his son Juan Carlos" and to demand that Juan Carlos "complete[ly] identif[y] with the regime and the Movement." Meanwhile, since the elder son of Don Jaime, the infante Don Alfonso, had for the first time begun to express a possible interest in the succession, "he should be put to the test."[44] Franco observed to his cousin Pacón that "there are other princes, such as Alfonso de Borbón Dampierre, who is cultured and patriotic, and might be the solution if Don Juan Carlos doesn't work out."[45] Franco did not doubt Juan Carlos himself, Carmen recalls, so much as he feared the continuing influence of the prince's father.

Franco's suspicions were correct. Don Juan refused to give permission for the new couple to live regularly in Madrid, and so, without a fixed residence, for several months they went back and forth between Estoril and Athens. Meanwhile, the new government in Madrid was divided between *juancarlistas* and "regentialists," the latter based on the movement and the military, led by the new vice president, Muñoz Grandes, strongly anti-Monarchist. Certain opponents of Juan Carlos were also, for the first time, directly advancing the potential candidacy of his cousin, Don Alfonso, as hopefully more reliably Francoist. Matters became so serious by February 1963 that the main promoter in the government of the candidacy of Juan Carlos, the technocrat López Rodó, sent a special emissary to the prince in Greece, telling him that his cause might be lost if he did not take up residence in Spain immediately. Sofía's mother called the former queen Victoria Eugenia (mother of Don Juan) by telephone at her home in Lausanne, and she intervened forcefully with her son, who accepted his mother's advice, and gave permission for Juan Carlos to live in Spain.[46] By the end of February the young couple had taken up residence in the small palace reserved for them by Franco, La Zarzuela, also to the northwest of Madrid, which was in the process of being fully renovated.

Franco had great respect for the one-time British princess Victoria Eugenia ("Ena," as she was known to intimates), who prior to 1931 had been his queen for nearly three decades, and in the spring of 1963 twice had her sounded out on the option of the renunciation of rights by her son in favor of Juan Carlos.[47] The former queen replied that she would regret it if

Don Juan could not reign but that the most important thing was for Franco to restore the throne. If that meant passing the succession to her grandson, so be it.[48]

A new cause célèbre developed in April 1963 after a military tribunal passed sentence of death on the top Communist underground leader Julián Grimau, who after nearly two decades abroad had been sent back to Spain. Grimau was a former Republican police officer who had been in charge of a notorious "checa," or prison, in Barcelona in 1937–38, placing him high on the list of those who had committed "blood crimes." He attempted suicide by throwing himself out a jail window in circumstances never clarified, but he survived. Someone with Grimau's record would earlier have been a marked man in the justice system, save that the statute of limitations had expired. An old code of 1894 had to be dusted off, despite the dubious legality of the maneuver, since it allowed thirty years for prosecution. Franco observed privately that he hoped that Grimau would receive the maximum sentence.[49] The Communist leader was painted in the international media, however, as an innocent oppositionist, a peaceful organizer, about to be executed exclusively for being a political opponent. A massive clemency campaign got under way, which was led by the prime minister of England and the mayor of West Berlin and which also prompted a personal letter from Nikita Khrushchev to Franco, his first ever from a Soviet leader. The Spanish embassy in Paris was firebombed.

Execution of Grimau, war criminal or not, would give the regime a black eye at the time that it was seeking to negotiate entrance into the Common Market, but Franco was implacable on what he considered an open-and-shut case. International pressure only made him more obdurate, determined to demonstrate complete sovereignty. More and more exiled Republicans not charged with personal crimes were returning to Spain, but, as Carmen puts it,

> the truth is that concerning blood crimes my father was almost "an eye for an eye and a tooth for a tooth," not quite, but almost. It was very hard for him to pardon someone who had done what Grimau did. And aside from that, he said there was no reason for him to have come back. If he remained abroad, he would never have been prosecuted, but returning to Spain. . . . My father came to believe that Grimau had relied on people who told him, "Franco is now a feeble little old man, and he won't do something that would have such a negative effect on foreign opinion," who didn't care about Grimau but relied on foreign opinion.[50]

One unique feature of the case was that, after Grimau's conviction, the commander of the Civil Guard refused to assign a squad to carry out the execution, saying that it did not bear responsibility for such things. This was technically correct, but that had not kept it from carrying out numerous executions in the early years of the regime. Some army commanders also murmured critically about military courts having to take responsibility. Grimau was executed on April 20, 1963, by a squad of military volunteers, but the affair set in motion a reform to transfer these cases to civilian courts. More importantly, the outcome was a major setback for the regime, since it had the effect of canceling forward motion on entry into the OEEC.

Meanwhile, the ten-year agreement with the United States would soon expire and, though it could be prorogued for five years more, this was not automatic. The Pentagon pressed for renewal, because the tension between Washington and Lisbon over the latter's military action against the multiple insurgencies it faced in Africa might lead to the loss of the American base in the Azores. Liberals in the American Senate, however, remained opposed to renewal, and so Franco's ambassador, Antonio Garrigues, maneuvered for leverage, telling the Americans that Communism was only one of Madrid's enemies, since it had so many critics in the West, and there was no reason why it should not seek to improve relations with the Soviet Union. He argued that Spain should receive much more support from the United States.[51]

Franco had a variety of issues to address. One was the concern that had mounted in Spain over the years about having a major strategic air command (SAC) base, armed with atomic weapons, so near Madrid, a concern that had intensified at the time of the Cuban missile crisis the preceding October. Moreover, Washington had never acknowledged any responsibility for the security of Spain itself, and there was growing resentment over the fact that the military aid mostly consisted of somewhat antiquated weaponry, even though it was better than any Spain could manufacture. Franco insisted that the expansion of the Soviet strategic arsenal made the bases a much greater security threat for Spain. A final point was American backing in the Cold War for the Moroccan government, which still pressed for the territory held by Spain in Ifni and the Sahara. Franco even suggested in one of his memos that Spain could offer the United States a major base in one of the Moroccan territories in exchange for a different U.S. policy vis-à-vis Morocco.[52] Moreover, the Spanish leadership was hoping for more favorable terms from Washington in view of the fact that Communist Yugoslavia had begun to receive aid at the same time as Spain without offering any concrete quid pro quo equivalent to that from Spain (and, as it turned out, over a period of twenty years, it would nonetheless receive more total aid from the United States).

Castiella's display of greater independence in foreign policy was thus calculated to exact a higher price. NATO overflights across Spain to Portugal were restricted and an effort was made to build a special relationship with France. Madrid generally enjoyed more favorable relations with De Gaulle's Fifth Republic than with its predecessor, despite occasional incidents such as the sanctuary provided by Falangist ultras to the French rebel general Raoul Salan for six months during 1960–61. Closer cooperation with France was, however, momentarily brought to a halt by the execution of Grimau.

Franco prepared carefully for a special recorded interview with CBS television, which would be broadcast widely in the United States, but he pointedly rejected any criticism of Spain's political system. He asserted that democracy might currently work in the United States, where there were only two complementary parties, but it had not worked in countries such as Spain under the Republic, with its fragmented multiparty system. Moreover, he insisted that this was a question of historical experience, for Spain was an older country that had already gone through the democratic phase, which he still prophesied would not be a permanent one of the Western world. "Even you Americans, who are so confident, will have to change. . . . We Latins have already gone through this, having begun democracy earlier and having finished with it sooner, and we have had to move to other forms that are more sincere and genuine."[53]

All this had little effect. Washington resisted most of the arguments from Madrid but pledged strong backing for the Spanish government in international financial organs, vital for continued rapid growth, as well as giving new guarantees concerning the use of American atomic weaponry. When the ten-year pact expired, the agreement was prorogued by the two parties for five years more, essentially on American terms, but it did call for modest additional financial assistance, as well as more military support. Washington also assisted Madrid in gaining more support from the World Bank, the International Monetary Fund, and other agencies.

Meanwhile, Franco lost the collaboration of one of his oldest and closest administrators. His boyhood friend Admiral Juan Antonio Suanzes, who had presented his resignation from the leadership of the National Institute of Industry on several occasions because of disagreements over economic policy, finally resigned unequivocally. The root cause was the abandonment

of an ultrastatist economic policy, but the immediate cause was government approval of López Rodó's first development plan, for the years 1964
to 1967, about which Suanzes had not been consulted. Franco insisted to
Suanzes that the INI and state capitalism remained an important part of
economic policy and that the new government was not his enemy, but he
finally gave in, writing to his old friend that "you have not convinced me,
but you have conquered me, and I accept your resignation."[54]

At the close of 1963 the Conde de Barcelona appeared very briefly in
Madrid to attend the christening of the first child of Juan Carlos and Sofía,
his first trip to the Spanish capital in thirty-three years. He and Franco
encountered each other at the event and exchanged polite greetings, but
there was no formal conversation because the caudillo would never again
have anything to say to the pretender. When the Conde de Barcelona sent
Franco a personal memorandum urging him to implement the Law of
Succession by recognizing himself, the legitimate heir, as his successor,
Franco categorically refused, and from that time relations between the two
became increasingly hostile once more.[55] As Franco wrote in one of his
memoranda during these months, he was convinced that "the worst thing
that could happen would be for the nation to fall into the hands of a liberal
prince, the gateway to Communism."[56] He hoped for more from Juan
Carlos, however, and in the spring of 1963 had given orders to Alonso
Vega, the interior minister, that the occasional public denunciations of the
prince by Falangist ultras must be more rigorously controlled.

A rival to Juan Carlos had emerged in the person of the Carlist heir,
whose order of names was reversed from Hugo Carlos to Carlos Hugo.
Though one sector of Carlists—by that point a rapidly declining group—
that was associated with the movement sought to promote his candidacy,
Franco was not impressed. He had a high opinion of traditionalist doctrine
on politics and culture but not of Carlism as a dynastic movement.[57] Don
Javier, the father of Carlos Hugo, was only a nephew of the last Carlist
regent and his dynastic claim was tenuous in the extreme. Don Javier was a
French aristocrat and a hero of the French Resistance, and Franco considered the whole family merely a set of Frenchmen, which in fact they were.
When Carlos Hugo entered Spain to participate in the annual Carlist celebration at Montejurra, Franco had him expelled as a foreigner. In January
1964, however, he deigned to receive the Carlist prince in audience at El
Pardo, but only because his chief of protocol became confused and did not
understand who was being scheduled. The meeting lasted only for the few

minutes required for Carlos Hugo to ask for Spanish citizenship. Franco replied that there was a formal procedure and the prince should make application. Don Javier then wrote a letter to the caudillo asking for citizenship for the entire family, which Franco referred to the justice minister, Antonio Iturmendi. He responded that the request looked dubious to him, and it was denied.[58]

The regime's slogan for the year 1964 was "Twenty-Five Years of Peace," and this became the theme of a year-long publicity festival. One feature was the preparation of a full-length documentary on the generalissimo's life, *Franco, ese hombre*, directed by José Luis Sáenz de Heredia, who two decades before had been in charge of *Raza*. It was viewed by large audiences and became the principal personal panegyric of Franco's long reign. He was strongly applauded in his major public appearances that year. The most important development, however, was the decision by the European Economic Community at the end of March to open negotiations with Spain, both France and West Germany voting in favor. This opportunity was important for the country's future, and, despite his personal feelings of ambiguity, Franco was pleased to have it go forward.[59] It was potentially another major step in international economic integration, and it reinforced the policy of liberalization and rapid growth, which was significantly altering the domestic context of the regime.

Altogether, the decade of the 1960s was the calmest period in foreign relations for Franco in the history of the regime, though it also registered important new developments. In the summer of 1965 the American government informed Franco that the United States would increase its resistance to the Communist takeover of South Vietnam by sending its own troops, and it asked for collateral participation by Spain in the form of items such as medical and sanitary assistance. The West's senior anti-Communist, as the regime liked to style the caudillo, refused to bite.[60] In two letters to President Lyndon Johnson, Franco declared that the United States was making a fundamental mistake in committing its troops to a highly complicated situation on the Asian mainland, where Ho Chi Minh, however Stalinist, would be viewed by many compatriots, and others as well, as a patriotic independence leader. Just as he had correctly foreseen that Roosevelt would fail in his effort to appease the Soviet Union, in 1965 Franco saw clearly enough that the United States would not be likely to succeed in fighting a land war against Communist nationalism in Vietnam. The aging leader of the insurrection against the revolutionary left in Spain recommended that in the complex and polarized world of the 1960s a broader and more flexible policy should be followed. His critique bore some similarity to that of George F. Kennan.[61]

Relations were temporarily strained by a new incident in January 1966, when two SAC planes collided near Palomares, off the southern coast of Spain. One was a B-52 carrying four unactivated atom bombs, the last of which was not recovered for two and a half months. The reassurances that followed featured numerous widely publicized photos of the American ambassador and Fraga Iribarne, minister of information and tourism, entering the water in their swim trunks at Palomares beach to demonstrate that the area was safe for tourists. The positive consequence for Spain was an American pledge that planes on routine missions over the country would never again carry atomic weapons.

The incident also briefly reopened a question that had hitherto been a completely moot point—the question of a Spanish atomic bomb. When anti-Franco propagandists abroad had sought to create a scare about a "Spanish atomic bomb" built by Nazi scientists in 1945–46, their claim had been based on frenzied hysteria alone. Carrero Blanco and General Juan Vigón subsequently became the champions of a Spanish nuclear project, which was directed by the physicist José María Otero de Navascués, who first began nuclear research in Spain in 1947 and later headed the Nuclear Energy Council (Junta de Energía Nuclear), to develop atomic power for peaceful purposes. Collaboration subsequently developed with France for a small Spanish reactor that would help to produce plutonium for the French atomic bomb, and after some time with modest American assistance, Franco inaugurated the first regular research reactor at the Juan Vigón Nuclear Energy Center in Madrid, where scientists would begin to work on atomic power for peaceful purposes.[62]

In 1965 the first study was completed concerning the possibility of developing a plutonium bomb, to be named Proyecto I (for Islero, the famous Miura bull that had killed the bullfighter Manolete), in Spain. This program was directed by Guillermo Velarde Pinacho, an American-trained aeronautical engineer and nuclear physicist who was expert in nuclear fusion and quantum mechanics, and was enthusiastically supported by Muñoz Grandes, vice president and head of the Supreme General Staff.[63]

After the Palomares incident, the general and Otero de Navascués dispatched Velarde to Palomares to obtain samples of the American bombs. Velarde's subsequent report detailed the nature of the American weapons and explained that the Spanish atomic bomb proposed in his report was of a different kind and that its production was feasible, though it would require several years to develop. Muñoz Grandes remained enthusiastic, arguing that atomic weapons would make Spain independent of the United States and of NATO. Spain has the second largest deposits of uranium in Europe and had the prospect of further technological assistance from France.[64] It was already preparing its own nuclear reactor to generate electrical power, which was expected to be functioning no later than 1972. Yet, though the proposal for a Spanish nuclear bomb was also supported more discreetly by Carrero Blanco, Franco flatly rejected it. This would be very expensive and, even more important, would challenge Washington, whose support was more important to Spain than having its own atomic bomb or drawing nearer to France. Muñoz Grandes is reported to have replied that the American government need not know of the project, but Franco made quick work of this naïve idea, saying that Washington inevitably would learn quickly enough. The discussion with the head of the Supreme General Staff was a tense and angry one, ending with Franco's order that no such military project be undertaken.[65] The work on nuclear energy for peaceful purposes, however, went forward and within a few years it led to the opening of several centers for the generation of electrical power.

The most serious foreign policy concerns had to do with the remaining possessions in northwest Africa and Britain's continued occupation of Gibraltar, which were mirror-image problems. Relations with Morocco since the latter's military attack on Ifni in 1957 had still not completely normalized. For that matter, the most annoying single aspect of American policy in the region was its support for Hassan II, the king of Morocco. When a visit by Hassan to Washington was followed by a significant American arms sale, the Spanish government protested, and Franco sent a personal letter to President Lyndon Johnson saying that he found the sale "unfriendly" to Spain.[66]

Nevertheless, there was less and less prospect of maintaining sovereignty over the Spanish territories south of Morocco. When the Salazar regime in Portugal began to face widespread colonial rebellion in its African territories, much larger and more important than those of Spain, in 1961, the response in Madrid was muted. Franco might have been willing to intervene militarily had the internal conspiracy against Salazar at home in Portugal gotten out of hand, for the domestic security of the neighboring regime was important to him, but he refused to identify Spain with Portugal's policy of diehard resistance in Africa.[67]

In return for a favorable agreement on fishing rights, Ifni was finally handed over to Morocco in 1968, the same year Franco suddenly granted independence to Equatorial Guinea. Spain's retreat proved a disaster for the Guineans, as it had for many other Africans in other countries following European decolonization. They soon fell under the rule of a genocidal dictator, who killed tens of thousands in this small country, virtually en-slaving many more.[68]

The remaining bone of contention with Morocco was the lightly in-habited desert territory to its south, the Spanish Sahara. This had never been part of Morocco and its inhabitants were stoutly opposed to being taken over by their more powerful neighbor to the north. The Spanish govern-ment recognized the right of self-determination for the Sahara in 1968 and made gestures toward providing the Saharans with a limited degree of representation, though no more than that enjoyed by citizens of Spain.

Franco recognized the obvious, that the Sahara held little value in and of itself, and saw its worth only as part of a larger strategy, namely, to protect other areas that had long been part of Spain itself and were inhabited mainly or exclusively by Spaniards—the Canary Islands, not far off the coast, and the two Spanish enclave cities of Ceuta and Melilla, on the northern coast of Morocco. His thinking was clearly summarized in a memorandum that he drew up: "Seen in isolation and considering the eco-nomic, political, and cultural aspects, it has scant value. It has no ports and the potential for mining is problematic. But strategically it has enormous importance. It is the counterpart to the security of the Canaries. When we retire from the Sahara we will begin to compromise the Canaries. . . . When we let go of the Sahara they will talk about Melilla and Ceuta and next the Canaries." Subsequently, however, he would qualify this strategy: "Our strategy requires us to remain in the Sahara if we do not want to run the risk of having to face serious problems elsewhere, especially in the Canaries, related to the 'integrity of the lands of Africa.' However, if this idea of iron unity does not reflect the spirit of the entire people but rather the desire to coin an attractive expression to impress superficially, none of the aforesaid has much value. Applause from the rest of the world would definitely be worth a certain number of square kilometers."[69] And, as he lay dying in 1975, that was the way it would work out.

The greatest frustration, however, would always be Gibraltar. Continued British occupation of part of the Spanish mainland remained a deep affront to Spanish patriots, and the fact that the great majority of its inhabitants, of an ethnically varied background, preferred it that way, was no consolation whatsoever. Soon after the Civil War, Franco had begun plans for a military occupation to seize the Rock but, as has been seen, the right opportunity never appeared. The regime did not achieve enough international standing to address the issue until more than two decades after the Civil War, when it was finally presented to the United Nations in 1963. Bilateral negotiations that began three years later went nowhere and a plebiscite administered by London in 1967 registered near unanimity among the inhabitants for maintaining the status quo. After two United Nations resolutions on behalf of the Spanish claim in 1967–68 produced no change, the Spanish government closed the border with Gibraltar in 1969, which would remain closed for the remainder of the caudillo's life. Nonetheless, he rejected all suggestions within his government for more extreme measures, knowing that Spain was in no position to force the issue to a conclusion. It could be settled only by British withdrawal and not by Spanish seizure, a withdrawal that Franco recognized would not be likely until after his own death.[70]

17 Facing the Future

(1964–1969)

With the economy producing spectacular results, the crucial issue during the 1960s was the future of the regime and the successor to Franco. The government of 1962, as well as its successor three years later, was roughly divided into two antagonistic sectors: ministers of the National Movement and their allies, on the one hand, and the technocrats, on the other. The movement ministers, whose most important figure was Muñoz Grandes, the vice president, argued for the political development of the regime and remained hostile to the Monarchist succession. The technocrats, focused on the economy, were less concerned about political issues per se but strongly oriented toward solving the problem of the succession in the person of Juan Carlos, and on this issue they received the support of Carrero Blanco.[1]

Amid the celebrations attending "twenty-five years of peace," Franco declared publicly on April 1964 that "we are planning to prepare laws that complete and define the powers of the Chief of State and of the Chief of Government, together with the means of their designation. . . . The monarchist system is where our doctrine is best accommodated and our principles assured."[2] This reform was supposed to put the finishing touches on the structure and leadership of the regime to enable it to outlive Franco. It had been under discussion within the government since 1959, but, as in the case of almost everything concerning the generalissimo, movement toward it was very slow.[3]

During 1964 the affable and oily José Solís Ruiz, minister of the movement, made increasing use of the term "political development," and altogether the ministers promoted at least three different proposals, though it was not clear that any had Franco's blessing. One notion was to permit limited representation by authorizing diverse "political associations," strictly within the framework of the movement.

The caudillo remained skeptical, fearing innovations that might restrict the government's authority or open a Pandora's box. Even though the draft of the proposed law of associations within the movement carefully avoided any appearance of introducing real political parties, to Franco it smacked of that danger, and he ordered it withdrawn. He still attracted large crowds, however artfully assembled, and loud applause on his visits to provincial centers. As Fraga noted, "Franco continued to receive public enthusiasm and thunderous ovations wherever he went. That was his main argument whenever we spoke to him about changes. And that fervor in the summer of 1964 made him resist accepting certain reforms or enacting political changes."[4] He finally began to yield on two points, however, and in his annual end-of-the-year address he referred to the preparation of a new law pertaining to the organicism of the state and the prospect of greater religious toleration.

The tug-of-war within the government continued during 1965. On January 15 Franco's closest associate in the cabinet, his old chum General Camilo Alonso Vega, minister of the interior, told him that Spaniards were worried about the future, that the top priority should be to complete the institutionalization of and succession to the regime, and that a younger president of government should be put in place of the aging caudillo.[5] The reformist ministers nonetheless encountered steady resistance from him. The most heated debate took place on April 2, with Fraga Iribarne speaking vehemently on the need for new legislation. López Rodó has written that this session included "moments of great tension. At one point Franco said, 'Do you think that I don't understand, that I am a circus clown?' The debate lasted an hour and a half. Most of the time, nonetheless, Franco listened to the opinion of his ministers with a smile on his face."[6] Only the day before had he received word that the cancer from which Muñoz Grandes suffered had probably become irreversible, and the prospect of losing his second in command stimulated concern for the future. Franco was also growing somewhat worried about signs of increasing opposition, especially within the universities, which he believed he could not ignore because he thought that agitation in the universities in 1929–30 had played a role in the downfall of Primo de Rivera.

All this resulted in a cabinet reorganization in July 1965, designed to play off against each other the main tendencies within the government while also facilitating movement toward enacting the reforms under discussion. As it turned out, this would be the last of the typical balancing acts of Franco. The new council of ministers was not designed to introduce major change but to reinforce existing policies. Navarro Rubio and Ullastres departed after nine years, but the former became second-ranking administrator (and later president) of the Bank of Spain, the latter ambassador to the Common Market. Their replacements followed equivalent policies. López Bravo, a favorite of Franco's, remained as minister of industry and López Rodó, director of the development plan, was elevated to cabinet rank, without portfolio.

Some months later, in December 1965, the Church council of Vatican II concluded its labors.[7] Catholic policy would henceforth become increasingly tolerant and even progressive. The more it insisted on the full independence of the Church and on its *aggiornamento*, or updating, the more the Vatican sought to recover the full right of presentation of bishops. The concordat of 1953 had granted that right to the Spanish state. The Vatican did not seek to annul the concordat but hoped that Franco, in a cooperative manner, would give up that privilege, something that he had no intention of doing.[8]

The Church was also sometimes critical of members of Opus Dei, who were reminded of the importance of obeying their bishop and living up to their vows of poverty, but Franco remained unconcerned.[9] He was quite impressed with the secular institute and with the work of his ministers. Franco considered any admonitions of Opus Dei to stem from clerical envy and jealousy. His daughter recalls that "my father considered them to be in the government as individuals, not as representatives of their institute." He thought that "quite the contrary," "they were a guarantee of honesty." As far as the constant tension between the Falangists and technocrats was concerned, "his heart tended to support the Falangists, but his head inclined more to the technocrats," and that would seem to be accurate.

Fraga scored the first victory of the new government, gaining approval of his new press law over the objections of Carrero Blanco and Alonso Vega. Franco noted in a memo the items that he believed still had to be restricted:

> In the same press bill should be established regulations about grave mistakes and laws concerning apologies for crimes, the spreading of news or items that damage the Catholic faith, ministers of the government, the principles of the National Movement or public authorities. Or supporting Communist, Marxist or anarchosyndicalist politics. Campaigns that incite civil conflict or divide Spaniards. Systematic defense of foreign interests opposed to those of the Fatherland. Attacks or scornful judgments about countries or chiefs of state with whom Spain is friendly. Spreading news that may produce discontent or unease or that create alarm among Spaniards. Whatever incites or stimulates part of society to secession, civil disobedience, or actions prohibited by law.

This was quite a list, but, if all these matters could still be controlled, "that would permit the elimination of prior censorship, making it voluntary for those who want advice or are uncertain and want to avoid trouble, leaving them the opportunity to consult the censorship office."[10] He was still skeptical, but, according to Fraga, Franco conceded reluctantly that, while he didn't "believe in so much freedom," this press law was "a measure required for many important reasons. Moreover, I think that if those weak governments at the beginning of the century could govern with a free press amid all that anarchy, we can, too."[11]

After further polishing, the measure was eventually approved by the Cortes on March 15, 1966. Two weeks later prior censorship ended. The rationale was that Spain had become much more literate, cultured, and politically united and that Serrano Suñer's old statute was unnecessary. Censorship would henceforth be "voluntary," with no official guidelines imposed (though many informal new ones would be laid down). Publishing enterprises would be free to name their own directors without official approval, though a variety of sanctions, such as stiff fines, confiscation, suspension, or even arrest could still be imposed. Any editor in doubt was still invited to submit preliminary material for consultation.

This did not establish freedom of the press, but it considerably eased restrictions, opening the way for greater liberalization. Newspaper circulation increased from less than 500,000 copies daily in 1945 to 2.5 million in 1967, and the 420 publishing firms of 1940 had grown to 915 by 1971. In

417

1970 Spain published 19,717 titles, the fifth highest total in the world, amounting to more than 170 million books.[12]

In fact, no more than six months passed before Franco began to register alarm, though he realized there was no going back to the old system. Therefore in October 1966 he sent a note to Fraga saying that his ministry should be more proactive in presenting the regime's message. Franco was upset by the first semicritical and objective comments on the Civil War to appear in the press, telling his minister that "since they are now publishing adverse commentary about our Civil War, but making it seem convincing, we must abandon our policy of silence and support work that deserves it and can receive documentation from us."[13]

Routine political infighting continued within the cabinet, as was Franco's wish. The primary duel was between his two principal surrogates, Carrero Blanco as minister subsecretary of the presidency and Muñoz Grandes, in his final days as vice president of government. It was an unequal contest, given Muñoz Grandes's severely declining health and his incapacity for intrigue. On January 20, 1966, during one of his regular daily sessions with Franco, Carrero tried to convince the caudillo that Muñoz Grandes must be relieved of his post as head of the Supreme General Staff as soon as he reached the mandatory age to pass to reserve status, which was coming up very soon. His primary concern was that an avowed anti-Monarchist might be in a position to thwart the installation of the monarchy after Franco's death. The caudillo replied dryly that Muñoz Grandes "is ill and will not last" and thus there was nothing to worry about.[14]

During the mid-1960s, political protest on the part of dissident workers, university students, and also dissident priests slowly but steadily increased, though in November 1965 the new justice minister Antonio María Oriol had been able to declare on television that Spain had the second lowest prison population in the world, proportionate to population. This was technically correct because of the remarkably low rate of common crime (well below that of most democracies or of Communist regimes), but as political penalties were lessened, dissidence grew. An effort was made to counter unrest by organizing a major visit of Franco to Catalonia in June 1966. This was one of his last grand triumphal tours, for his energy had markedly declined as he neared seventy-five, but the customary crowds were turned out, and by official standards the visit came off well.

The other major event of 1966 was presentation of the new Organic Law of the State, so long in gestation.[15] It incorporated proposals discussed in the cabinet as early as 1958 and was designed not to be a new fundamental law in the sense of introducing major institutional features but rather to serve as a codification, clarification, and partial reform of existing practices. This was intended to complete the process of institutionalization and round out the "open constitution" of the regime, giving mature definition to "organic democracy." It reflected primarily the position of Carrero Blanco and López Rodó and to a secondary extent that of Franco himself. He flatly rejected the final pleas by Muñoz Grandes and Solís that he adopt a permanent presidentialist form of government rather than prepare to restore the monarchy.

The organic law reconciled various inconsistencies among the six Fundamental Laws of the Realm (the Labor Charter, the Constitutive Law of the Cortes, the Charter of the Spanish People, the Law of Referendum, the Law of Succession, and the Fundamental Principles of the National Movement) and eliminated or altered lingering vestiges of Fascist terminology. It separated the functions of the president of government (prime minister) from those of the chief of state, giving the latter very extensive powers, including the right to name and to dismiss the former, convene the Cortes (and also prorogue it, if he so desired), call meetings of the council of ministers and even preside over them if he wished, and submit proposals for national referendums. It also modified secondary details of the Law of Succession while mildly accentuating the institution of monarchy. Membership of the National Council of the movement was expanded to 108 (40 appointed by the caudillo, 50 elected by the provincial sections of the movement, 12 elected by the Cortes, and 6 appointed by its president). The appeal of *contrafuero* (meaning, approximately, "unconstitutionality") was established, specifying that either the National Council or the standing committee of the Cortes might lodge an appeal against any new legislation or government measure held to contradict the Fundamental Principles of the National Movement. Membership of the Cortes was expanded to 565, of whom the great majority would be chosen by indirect corporate representation, as usual, though in a timid gesture toward very restricted direct representation, 108 were to be chosen directly for the first time by votes of "family representatives," who would include married women, as well.[16] Rather than being the real opening sought by some reformists, the organic law represented the final limited readjustment of the system during the phase of Franco's life when he was rapidly losing physical and political energy. No basic changes were introduced.

When he presented the organic law to be rubber-stamped by the Cortes on November 22, Franco labeled it "a broad democratization of the political process." He went on to remark that democracy, which, properly understood, is the most precious civilizing legacy of Western culture, appears in each era tied to specific circumstances . . . There is no democracy without well-being. . . . There is no authentic representation without true citizenship. . . . Political parties are not an essential and permanent element without which democracy cannot be expressed. . . . From the moment in which parties are converted into platforms for class struggle and the disintegration of national unity, . . . they no longer provide a constructive or tolerant solution. . . . But the exclusion of political parties does not at all imply exclusion of the legitimate expression of opinion or the critical analysis of government policies. . . . We do not close the door to further changes and improvements, but these must be carried out through the established channels to avoid dangerous improvisations.

He ended with one of his typical reminders: "Spaniards need to remember that each nation is attended by its own familiar spirits [*demonios familiares*], which are different in each case: those of Spain are the spirit of anarchy, negative criticism, lack of solidarity among citizens, extremism and mutual enmity."[17]

This was accompanied by yet another partial amnesty for political crimes, followed by a massive propaganda campaign for a national referendum on the organic law to be held on December 14. Franco appeared on television the night before to urge full participation and support. The government subsequently announced that 80 percent of the eligible voters participated; of these 95.9 were declared to have voted yes and only 1.8 percent no. Whatever the exact figures, the operation resulted in a temporary propaganda success.

All this amounted to much less than the "new constitution" promised in the subtitle of a booklet released by the Ministry of Information, but the organic law and lesser related measures completed the legal structure of the state and would be described, together with the Fundamental Laws of the Realm, as comprising the "Spanish constitution."[18] Critics suggested that the regime had lost perhaps its last major opportunity to secure popular support for a serious liberalization. This is doubtful, since Franco made it abundantly clear that he had no intention of ever permitting basic alteration of what he termed in 1967 "a modern state with authority."[19]

The coup of the Greek colonels, which took place in April 1967 while the final reform measures were being discussed in Spain, served to reinforce Franco's long-standing prejudices and relieve his sense of isolation in Europe. Within two days he reaffirmed the regime's unyielding opposition to the return of political parties, and for the last time felt a slight swing of historical change in his direction.

Franco presided over a system in the late 1960s that was beyond all doubt more open, moderate, and responsive than that of twenty or even ten years earlier. Though the Cortes never became a genuine parliament and never gained the right to initiate legislation, its members became slightly less timid and occasionally criticized aspects of legislation proposed by the government and even enacted a few minor changes.[20] Membership remained oligarchic in the extreme, about half the *procuradores* (deputies) always being state functionaries who held other positions as well. After 1967, some of the newly elected "family representatives" made brief gestures of independence. Unable to get an adequate hearing in the chamber, they temporarily formed a rump *Cortes viajeras* or *transhumantes* ("traveling Cortes") until their informal meetings were prohibited by the minister of the interior in September 1968.

The state administrative system also remained relatively elitist. Proportionately, those who played the leading roles came from a higher social background than their counterparts in most other Western countries, with the partial exception of France. Technical competence increased significantly in certain areas during the 1960s, but personal influence and clientelism remained powerful factors, though as the regime wound down, they would become less pervasive. Thanks in part to the reforms introduced by López Rodó, by the time that Franco died Spain had a rather more efficient bureaucracy than did democratic Italy (though some might argue that is a low standard of comparison).

Franco's only significant decision of 1967 had to do with the vice presidency. On July 22 he dismissed Muñoz Grandes, though the announcement was not made until several days later. The official explanation was that under the new legislation a member of the advisory Council of the Realm, such as Muñoz Grandes, could not serve as vice president. The real reasons, however, had to do with his age, poor health (advanced cancer), and decided opposition to the present trend of policy.

Since no replacement was named at first, critics said that it showed that Franco was determined to hold on to as much power as possible, but that was not exactly the case. He knew full well that, given his own age, he could not do without a second in command and had decided on Carrero Blanco. Indeed, he may have been ready to hand over the acting presidency, but Carrero replied that it was better to move one step at a time. On September 21 the admiral's appointment to the vice presidency was announced.

For the next six years, down to the time of Carrero's assassination, an elderly caudillo would lean on him more and more.[21]

An insoluble problem was that of defining more effectively the role of the movement. On ceremonial occasions the caudillo reiterated to movement members that he was with them and that their organization was still essential, insisting that "the Movement is a system with a place within it for everyone."[22] In 1967 he even declared that "if the Movement did not exist, our most important task would be to invent it."[23] He was fully aware that *camisas viejas* had criticized him for years because they firmly believed that he had never desired a strong party, but he insisted privately that he had always wished to strengthen it. Franco laid the blame for its weakness on the intransigence of the *camisas viejas* themselves, on their desire to maintain the original radical doctrines and the predominance of the old leaders and their failure to adjust their postulates to attract a broader and more diverse membership.[24] The movement press was so critical of the liberalized economic policies of the technocrats that Franco had complained in 1966 that "the only newspapers who don't say the things their owners want them to are those of the Movement."[25] It was nonetheless typical of him that he did not try to bring the movement press fully to heel, for its hostility to the technocrats put pressure on them, preserving the counterbalance that he always sought within the system.

During the initial discussion of the organic law, the vice secretary-general of the movement presented the draft of a proposal to redefine the function of the movement by authorizing the formation of various "political associations" of heads of families and married women within its ranks. This met a firestorm of criticism from other sectors of the regime and had to be withdrawn, while a second project to expand the role of the movement was vetoed by Franco, and there was no mention of the state party itself in the organic law, though its National Council figured prominently.

To recover some of the ground lost, Alejandro Rodríguez Valcárcel, newly appointed vice secretary-general, proposed a new organic law pertaining specifically to the National Movement and its National Council that was officially approved on June 28, 1967. It ratified the post of minister secretary-general of the movement and again defined the functioning of its local and provincial councils, safeguarding its organizational structure. When López Rodó protested to Franco that this contradicted terms of the general organic law so recently approved, the caudillo dismissed the matter on the grounds that the new Organic Law of the Movement was mere ordinary legislation that could be changed at any time, while the Organic Law of the State was a fundamental law that would always take precedence and could only be modified by national referendum.[26] This indicated that Franco, who never worried about contradictions that served his purpose, was not ready to dispense with the movement, whose functions he still thought important. On the other hand, when Rodríguez Valcárcel presented a new proposal late in 1968 for a large expansion of the movement's budget and renewed control over propaganda and ordinary state jobs, it was quickly vetoed.

Henceforth the main effort within the movement would be to revive its membership and increase its role by fostering new "political associations" within its broader framework. Ultras asked aloud, "What is the difference between a political association and a political party?" but the first proposals were couched in restrictive terms, and, even so, there was no sign of any disposition to approve such a new initiative on the part either of the government or of Franco himself.

On November 23, 1969, a middle-aged *camisa vieja*, Francisco Herranz, shot himself in front of the large church in Madrid's Plaza Santa Bárbara to protest the marginalization of the party. It was to no avail. A subsequent law of April 3, 1970, ratified the definitive abolition of the name Falange Española Tradicionalista y de las JONS, in favor of National Movement; the earlier decree of 1945 had been inadequately worded and had failed to achieve complete derogation of the original nomenclature. Henceforth the name Falange would belong only to various tiny dissident neo-Fascist groups organized semiclandestinely in opposition to the regime.[27]

The late 1960s were a time of mounting opposition and disorder within the universities and the industrial north. The opposition shadow trade unions, the worker commissions (*comisiones obreras*), were strong enough in several districts that they did not feel they needed to conceal themselves, while the two largest and most politicized universities, in Madrid and Barcelona, entered a state of constant uproar that would continue with only momentary remission until Franco's death. Despite intermittent crackdowns, the degree of repression by the police was generally restrained. This in turn provoked strong criticism from the ultraright, while leftists took it as a sign of the weakness and senility of the regime. Franco observed on March 23, 1968, that "many leftists say that we are now entering the same phase as in the fall of Primo de Rivera or of Berenguer. But they are completely wrong, confusing 'serenity' with 'weakness.'"[28] Franco, always bearing in mind the parallel experience of Primo de Rivera, may not have wished to repeat the policy that had united the universities against Primo de Rivera's regime. At any rate, he was on record as having directed the police to go easy, though the minister of education, Manuel Lora Tamayo, resigned in April 1968 because of conflict with the minister of the interior, Alonso Vega, who directed the repression. It remains a moot point whether Franco's relative restraint was due at least in part to the benumbing effects of Parkinson's disease and the medication taken to control it. He had always responded to threats and challenges without excitement, but in the past he had calmly adopted rigorous measures. Here, however, the moderation of the repression was fully consonant with the evolution of his policy over the past decade and more. The new education minister, José Luis Villar Palasí, initiated a broad expansion and upgrading of educational facilities, made possible by a productive economy. Continued rapid growth in the number of university students, however, only compounded the regime's political problems.

The rebelliousness of Spanish students stemmed from broad changes in society and culture during the 1960s and was part of a worldwide phenomenon. The secularization that had suddenly become so marked had its ideological counterpart, for, even though the regime's own ideologists followed Daniel Bell in announcing the "twilight of ideologies" and urged Spaniards to concentrate on economic advancement, students and the younger intelligentsia, now in much closer contact with Western Europe than a decade earlier, discovered a new materialistic ideology in the neo-Marxist ideas they imported, en masse and uncritically, from France and Italy.[29] This new *marxismo cañí* ("gypsy Marxism") amounted to a mere transcription of ideas from abroad with no more empirical content or analytic depth than the tales of Washington Irving, but it provided a mental framework congenial to the new intelligentsia growing up in a suddenly materialistic and semiaffluent society still subject to political repression. Spain, which had never had a real Marxist intelligentsia during the revolutionary generation of the 1930s, began to acquire a secondhand one in the late 1960s.

For Carrero Blanco, this scandalous state of affairs was due to the liberal character of the 1966 press law and Fraga's indulgent direction of the Ministry of Information. Strong pressure forced Fraga to propose new legislation that restricted certain kinds of information, but its terms were so stringent that the bill had to be modified so as not to undo the earlier reform. Franco was also suspicious of Fraga, but unlike the ultras he had less illusion that it would be possible to go back to an earlier order of things.

The government responded much more sharply to mounting labor unrest and to nationalist agitation in the Basque provinces. The new Basque revolutionary organization, Basque Land and Liberty (Euskadi ta Azkatasuna [ETA]), turned to violence in August 1968 with the assassination of the head of the political police (*brigada social*) in Guipuzcoa. This brought a severe crackdown and a new decree that once more broadened the jurisdiction of military courts over political offenses (which had been limited five years earlier). Continued disorder in the universities and unrest in the Basque provinces led to declaration of a state of exception for two months, from January 24 to March 22, 1969. It was followed a few days later, however, on April 1, the thirtieth anniversary of the end of the Civil War, by a final and conclusive amnesty for those few still under legal sanction or liable to prosecution for their activities during the Civil War, though this measure still did not bring military pensions for disabled Republican veterans nor rehabilitation of teachers and civil servants fired in 1939.

None of this dissidence greatly threatened the stability of the regime, and few Spaniards expected its collapse or overthrow before the death of Franco. Most opinion tended to accept Franco's own conclusion that he had prepared the institutions to succeed himself; even as hostile an observer as the American historian Gabriel Jackson predicted that "a Franquist type of dictatorship may continue for decades in Spain and by so doing may provide a 'model' for other nations that achieve a minimum of economic prosperity in the absence of political liberty."[30]

Some of Franco's closest collaborators, led by Carrero Blanco and López Rodó, nonetheless felt that unless Franco took decisive action to give the system greater legitimacy and continuity by recognizing as successor a legitimate heir, more precisely, Prince Juan Carlos, the future of the system he had established would not be assured. Even the caudillo's older brother, Nicolás, became concerned, supposedly drawing this typically sly retort from the elderly dictator: "Don't worry, Nicolás. We Francos, remember, are a long-lived family and, besides, we die in numerical order. You are the oldest."[31]

A proposal introduced by one of his more extravagant sycophants in the Cortes in 1966 would have declared Franco king of Spain, with his powers transmitted through his daughter to his oldest grandson. Franco had better sense than that. He had long since ruled out Don Juan and was generally pleased with Juan Carlos but, as usual, had difficulty making up his mind and had indicated that Alfonso de Borbón y Dampierre, the elder son of Don Jaime, was not to be completely excluded from consideration. The nominal Carlist candidate Carlos Hugo was not so fortunate. After he participated in a Carlist rally in December 1968, the government expelled him from the country for the second time.

In May 1965 Juan Carlos had first taken the place of honor beside Franco at a major military parade, and both López Rodó and Fraga Iribarne, from different political perspectives, publicly promoted the prince's candidacy to the extent permitted by the system. Supporters of Juan Carlos within the government worked to distance the prince from his father politically and to separate him as much as possible from his father's direct supporters. Individually and in succession they beseeched him (in what López Rodó called successive "Stuka dives") to beware of those who sought to create conflict between himself and Franco. Partly as a consequence, Juan Carlos informed Franco that he would not be among those attending a major Monarchist assembly in Estoril to honor his father on March 5, 1966.

Juan Carlos was painfully aware of the narrow line that he must walk. He would later refer to it privately as many "years playing the fool in this country," for he realized that he must avoid controversy to the point of appearing insipid and that he could only reach the throne through the succession created by Franco.[32] Thus on a private trip to the United States in January 1967 he assured journalists that he supported the movement and its principles, stressing that the monarchy would be restored "as continuation" of the present regime, a position that he reiterated at a working breakfast with four provincial movement leaders on July 2.[33]

Franco continued to be generally pleased with the prince, gratified by the relative simplicity of his style of life (maintained on a slender budget) and his attentive manner. He made little attempt to personally indoctrinate Juan Carlos and was even willing to accept the possibility that the prince might make limited changes in the regime after his own death. After all, Franco himself had constantly made limited changes. Thus he showed little alarm on receiving an intelligence report about a special dinner meeting of Juan Carlos with twelve carefully selected moderate liberals on May 27, 1966, in which the prince had expressed a guarded preference for a two-party electoral system under a restored monarchy.[34] The caudillo observed approvingly near the end of 1966 that "I am certain that little by little the entire country will develop affection for the Princes Don Juan Carlos and Doña Sofía, whose conduct is irreproachable, a model in everything, as they lead a life of absolute simplicity and austerity, always trying to be in touch with the needs of the Spanish people. The princes do this absolutely on their own initiative, without my having to be involved, for I think they ought to have freedom of action."[35]

A son and heir, Felipe, was born to the royal couple on January 30, 1968. The infant's baptism became the occasion for bringing together the entire royal family, his elderly great-grandmother, the former Queen Victoria Eugenia, flying in from Lausanne. Franco refused this opportunity to have a conversation with Don Juan, because there was nothing further that he ever wished to say to the pretender. Victoria Eugenia, however, was a different story: she was the queen whom Franco had served loyally to the end and whom he would always hold in the highest respect. When he greeted her for what they both knew was likely to be the last time, there were tears in his eyes.[36] Four months earlier she had sent him a personal message that he must directly choose a successor from the dynasty before he died, and she repeated this once more. He apparently promised to do so.[37]

Not grasping the hopelessness of their enterprise, the *juanistas*—supporters of Don Juan—did not give up. Rafael Calvo Serer, who was a leading intellectual of the alternative right and member of Opus Dei and who backed the pretender, published an article on May 30, 1968, that nominally addressed the current "May crisis" in France threatening the De Gaulle government. This piece, titled "Retiring in Time: 'No' to General De Gaulle," appeared in *Madrid*, the daily newspaper that he directed (owned by a group of friends, some of whom were also members of Opus Dei). Fraga Iribarne assumed that Franco would not take kindly to the suggestion that old generals retire as heads of state and temporarily suspended the newspaper. Calvo Serer appealed directly to Franco in a letter of June 17 that insisted he had not been referring to the generalissimo, but tensions persisted, and three years later the paper was shut down altogether, in a cause célèbre that would not be fully resolved legally for more than fifteen years.[38]

In June 1968 Juan Carlos reached thirty years of age, the minimum required by the Law of Succession to accede to the throne. That summer he was even quoted in the international press as having let the diplomatic corps know that he was willing to accept power directly from Franco and bypass his father in the line of succession.[39] The Conde de Barcelona himself doubted that Franco would ever name a successor, however, and later in the fall wrote to his son insisting that he hold firm to dynastic principles and the proper line of succession, stressing that a direct heir to Franco who lacked full dynastic legitimacy would be hopelessly stigmatized.[40] Franco all the while was leaning heavily toward the prince but continued to avoid making the final decision, telling Juan Carlos in mid-1968 that he would need to wait until the following year to judge the composition of the next

Cortes, since whoever was presented as a successor should receive a unanimous vote.[41] This might seem an artificial excuse, but the Cortes represented the movement, though it did not represent the people, and there was still opposition in movement ranks to the idea of a Monarchist succession.

As each further month passed, mindful of the total physical collapse of Salazar in Lisbon that year, Carrero Blanco, López Rodó and the prince's other chief supporters in the government pressed the generalissimo more vigorously than ever to name a successor before infirmity struck. These conversations were normally injected with strong doses of flattery, assurances that no other historic personality would ever hold his authority and legitimacy and that therefore only he and he alone could guarantee the continuation of his regime by personally investing his choice as successor with his own legitimacy at the present moment, when his prestige and authority were undiminished.

The decisive initiative was undertaken by Carrero Blanco, who prepared another of his lengthy memoranda, this one a fifteen-page document summarizing all the arguments in favor of naming Juan Carlos and also recommending the naming process be completed rapidly, "by surprise," as he put it. This document was accompanied by a thirty-three-page curriculum vitae of the prince, detailing his education and personal experience, prepared by his two top aides.[42] On October 21, 1968, Franco listened silently to Carrero's lengthy presentation, looked at him intently for several moments, and then declared simply, with his customary laconicism, "In agreement with everything."[43] This was the first signal that he had finally made his decision, though he still gave no hint as to the timing of the official announcement.

In an interview with the official news agency EFE on January 7, 1969, Juan Carlos declared himself ready to make "sacrifices" and "to respect the laws and institutions of my country"—meaning Franco's fundamental laws—"most especially." These remarks were carried in all the media and, when the ministers met three days later, Franco expressed his great satisfaction with this public pledge of loyalty.[44] When he next met with Juan Carlos on January 15, the increasingly decrepit caudillo gave him to understand that he intended to name him successor before the end of the year. According to one version, Franco urged him, "Stay perfectly calm, Highness. Do not allow yourself to be swayed by anything. Everything is taken care of." The prince is said to have responded, "Don't worry, my General. I've already learned a great deal of your *galleguismo* ['Galicianism']," after which both laughed and Franco added, "Your Highness does it very well."[45]

The prince was overjoyed but also a bit apprehensive. He consulted with his few trusted advisors and especially with his highly esteemed former tutor in political institutions, the movement professor and politician Torcuato Fernández-Miranda. Juan Carlos was sufficiently astute to understand that he could not govern as dictator in Franco's style, and Miranda assured him that, just as Franco had added or dropped new features to his system, the next chief of state would have the right to introduce further changes, as well, so long as this was done strictly through the means that existed in present law.[46]

General Camilo Alonso Vega, still the caudillo's closest friend in government, was three years older than the general, and on May 29, 1969, Alonso Vega's eightieth birthday, he visited his old chum to request retirement as minister of the interior. He found the caudillo by that point in a somewhat more advanced state of Parkinson's, pale, shrunken, with trembling hands, and Alonso Vega urged him to name his successor very soon. Yet even with his old friend, Franco remained cryptic, refusing to say that he had made his decision, observing only that the former queen seemed to favor her grandson Juan Carlos.[47]

Carrero Blanco redoubled his efforts, and finally, on June 26, the caudillo informed him that the decision was made and that the official announcement would take place within the month, though, typically, Franco would not inform the prince until the very last minute.[48] He transmitted the news to Juan Carlos in El Pardo at about 4 p.m. on July 12, four days before his ambassador to Portugal delivered Franco's personal letter of announcement to Don Juan at his residence in Estoril, the timing designed to minimize any last-minute obstructionism by Monarchist legitimists.[49]

The Conde de Barcelona was devastated, because for years he had been living in denial and never believed that such a day would come. His advisers hastily prepared a long statement completely dissociating him from the impending announcement. This was made public in Lisbon but completely suppressed in Spain. In a state of consternation, Don Juan dissolved his entire council and retired to his yacht. His wife, Doña María de las Mercedes, had seen the handwriting on the wall more clearly and had worked to prevent an open breach between father and son, though completely normal relations would not be fully restored for some years.[50] Despite his great chagrin, the Conde de Barcelona had no intention of abdicating; instead, he would continue to hold in reserve his own candidacy to the throne. Thenceforth he reverted to his overt anti-Francoist position of 1943–47, in his third reversal of political postures, and engaged in further, increasingly futile, machinations all the way down to the death of Franco, by which point the once pro-Fascist pretender had become allied with the Communists, no less.[51]

On July 21, 1969, Franco finally presented the designation of Juan Carlos to his cabinet of ministers and one day later to the Cortes at a meeting that had been already scheduled. After his speech, Franco remained in the chamber for the voting but did not obtain the unanimity that he had claimed he wanted. The Cortes registered approval by a vote of 491 to 19, with 9 abstentions and 13 absences, as a small number of die-hard Falangists and hard-core "regentialists," as well as one or two Monarchist legitimists, held out to the end. At 11 a.m. on the twenty-third in a ceremony at his residence, the Palacio de la Zarzuela, Juan Carlos signed the official document of acceptance, and in the afternoon he and Franco rode together in the same limousine for the swearing-in at the Cortes. The prince became so nervous en route that he even asked the generalissimo for permission to smoke and, though he normally never permitted smoking in his presence, Franco gave his assent. In the formal session, Juan Carlos took an oath swearing "loyalty to His Excellency the Chief of State and fidelity to the Principles of the Movement and the other Fundamental Laws of the realm."[52] He had already made such a declaration during the morning ceremony and repeated it yet again in his public address in the Cortes. All the dignitaries present appeared jubilant, and during the small reception that followed in the government chambers Franco shed tears of emotion. It seemed that the long struggle for the installation of a corporative and authoritarian monarchy, begun by *Acción Española* and the monarchist right in 1932 and then officially embraced by Franco fifteen years later, was about to reach fruition.[53]

18 | Franco and the Modernization of Spain

From the time he took power, Franco pledged to develop his country and achieve prosperity, but at first this proved entirely beyond his grasp. Only after World War II did Spain begin to experience significant economic growth; once it started, however, it continued with little interruption, accelerating during the 1950s and even more during the 1960s. The last twenty-five years of the Franco regime, from 1950 to 1975, was the time of the greatest sustained economic development and general improvement in living standards in all Spanish history. In one sense this was not so remarkable, because it coincided with the greatest period of sustained growth in European, and indeed all world, history as well. Nonetheless, the proportionate rise in productivity and well-being in Spain was greater than under other right-authoritarian regimes such as that of Portugal or those in the Middle East, Africa, and Latin America, and it was also greater than in the totalitarian socialist regimes in eastern Europe, Asia, or Cuba.

If Franco were to be resurrected and questioned, he would doubtless reply that such had been his plan all along. Certainly from the very beginning Franco emphasized his determination to develop Spain's economy, yet the policies under which this was finally achieved were quite different from those that the regime originally adopted after the Civil War. Moreover, in the process the cultural and religious counterrevolution carried out during the 1940s was undermined by the law of unintended consequences. Modernization resulted in a profound social, cultural, and economic transformation that tended to subvert the basic institutions and values of Franco and his regime.

Some of Franco's critics have recognized that Spain's economic modernization took place under the general but insist that it took place "in spite of Franco" and against his wishes and that in fact he would have preferred that it had not taken place at all. Such a contention, however, is not merely ingenuous but downright mistaken. It confuses Franco's undeniable dissatisfaction, not to say profound unhappiness, with major policy outcomes for dissatisfaction with the policies themselves. A more sophisticated approach has been offered by the German Hispanist Walther Bernecker, who has suggested that the great changes that took place in Spanish society under Franco can be divided into three categories:

1. Changes and improvements explicitly planned and supported by Franco and his government.
2. Changes not directly sought but that emerged as a byproduct of state policies and then were accepted by Franco.
3. Changes that were neither sought nor accepted but that took place either as an indirect result of, or in conjunction with, other programs of change and development and that, though not desired and even opposed by the government, could not be reversed.[1]

This is the accurate assessment that makes the most sense.

Franco had always sought modernization of the economy, though one oriented toward heavy industry and national security rather than toward consumer products and exports and certainly not toward market capitalism. He understood that the development and well-being of a country required a literate population and a more advanced educational system, though he wished this to take place under the guidance of a neotraditional Catholic culture. He sought social development, but in terms of basic well-being and patriotic national mobilization, not in terms of individualism and materialism.

It has often been said that Franco had little understanding of economics. That was absolutely the case, but he had very definite ideas, nonetheless.[2] Franco was convinced that liberal market economics had been responsible for Spain's comparatively slow growth during the nineteenth century and that the new autarchist statism introduced by contemporary dictatorships was destined to replace that model in economic theory and practice. Like many military men, he thought of economics in terms of discipline and command and was at first perplexed after the Civil War when the system did not respond. He was also willing to make adjustments and had sufficient grasp of reality to continue to hold in high regard someone such as José Larraz, his first postwar finance minister, even though Larraz's more orthodox policies contradicted Franco's own approach.

His initial economic policy was statist, authoritarian, nationalist, and autarchic, very different from the orientation of Western Europe after World War II and also from that of the later phases of his own regime. It should nonetheless be kept in mind that autarchist economics was the main trend of the 1930s, particularly in the major dictatorships, whether Fascist, rightist, or Communist. The economic policy of his government during the Civil War had been very successful, especially when compared with the resounding failure of its Republican counterpart. Franco had left this in the hands of his administrators, initially of the Government Technical Council and then of his first regular government. The goal had been to maximize the output of the existing system, which would be subject to firm and constant state regulations that channeled and stimulated production.

Once the war had been won, an autarchy was imposed on the entire economy that employed the same techniques but in a broader and more restrictive manner. Franco thought to combine this with a certain militarization of the economy whereby a significant part of an expanded industrial output would be channeled into weapons production. That was reflected in the ambitious arms plans generated between 1938 and 1940, but by 1941 it was already clear that amid the severe shortages of World War II this militarization would be impossible to achieve, which in turn further dissuaded Franco from entering the European struggle. Internal conflict within the regime, meanwhile, discouraged the full development of a national syndicalist system, and before the close of 1941 the Falangist project had been downgraded.

World War II resulted in state programs of rigid controls, restrictions, and stimuli of special kinds all over the world, and to that extent Spanish autarchy was not unusual. Nonetheless, compared with the results in other European neutrals, such as Sweden, Switzerland, Portugal, or Turkey, the proportionate achievement of the Spanish economy was poor. The costs and consequences of the Civil War accounted for only part of such meager results. Equally or more important was the clumsiness and rigidity of Spanish state policy, its foreign trade oriented disproportionately toward Nazi Germany. Thus the economy failed altogether to replicate the growth it had sustained during World War I.[3]

State policy prioritized new industry, particularly heavy industry, and in 1946 industrial production exceeded the level of 1935 by 2 percent. The textile industry, in contrast, declined, even in 1948 functioning at only 60 percent of its prewar level, for autarchy severely handicapped the importation of cotton.[4] The chemical industry did not regain the output of 1935 until 1950, though coal did much better, already exceeding prewar production in 1940 and producing 60 percent more by 1945. The most spectacular improvement was in electricity, which by 1948 had nearly doubled the prewar level, though the severe droughts of those years frequently resulted in temporary restrictions of power. General investment increased from 1948 on, as postwar conditions improved in Europe more broadly, and from that time industrial expansion grew overall, while in 1949 the first transport plane manufactured in Spain went into service.

Agriculture, still the largest sector, remained—together with textiles—the most depressed, a considerable drag on the economy as a whole, total production remaining below the 1935 figure. As seen in chapter 13, the main factors restraining production were the lack of fertilizer and decline in the number of draught animals, though climatic conditions were often unfavorable during the 1940s as well. Autarchist policy and rigidly artificial price controls, assigned the chief responsibility by earlier analyses, seem to have been secondary factors.[5] Low prices benefited the urban population, but the main consequence was that over half the production of wheat was diverted to the black market. The government gave little attention to agriculture, and prior to 1946 production did not exceed 79 percent of the level of 1929.[6]

A weak fiscal policy limited the state investment that Franco sought. Direct taxes had always been low in Spain and there was great resistance to changing this, apparently on the part of Franco as well, since more progressive taxation was redolent of socialism. Similarly, there was little interest in redistributing income directly, so that in 1948 the state only collected 14.76 percent of national income, compared with 21 percent, approximately, in France and Italy, and 33 percent in Great Britain.

The principal achievements of the 1940s lay in medical care and sanitation. A country at Spain's level of development could not provide advanced facilities for all its population, but the government managed to improve natal care and certain aspects of child care. Infant mortality fell from 109 per thousand in 1935 to 88 ten years later, and by 1955 it had been reduced to 55. Death in childbirth likewise fell from 2,196 for every hundred thousand live births to 1,183 by 1945 and to 465 a decade later. The regime pursued a pronatalist policy, reinforced by neotraditional cultural and religious doctrines, and so Spain recovered and maintained a comparatively high birth rate for several decades.

A system of social security began to develop only slowly. The first program for especially needy families was announced on July 18, 1938, and by 1942 approximately 10 percent of the population was receiving some form of auxiliary assistance. The system of old-age insurance initiated on September 1, 1939, was another first step, only extended to agricultural workers in 1942. It was followed by obligatory sickness insurance in December 1942. Though the regime annulled almost all the property transfers carried out in the Republican zone, it adapted much of the Republic's social legislation of 1931–35 and also expanded certain key aspects of it. Subsidized housing construction was taken over by the Ministry of Housing when it was established in 1957. From 1940 to 1944 only thirteen thousand units were created per year; by 1948, this had increased to forty-two thousand. All this was inadequate to meeting needs, but it was the start of what eventually became a sort of Francoist welfare state, a system that never persuaded Spanish workers politically but that expanded significantly by the last years of the regime.

In the limited number of speeches that he gave to workers, Franco sometimes assured them, as in his address to SEAT auto workers in Barcelona in 1949, that his regime rejected capitalism as much as Marxism. But what he meant when he said he rejected capitalism was that he rejected free-market economics in favor of state regulation and the arbitrage of the Ministry of Syndical Organization. The structure of national syndicalism expanded during the 1940s, though many workers were still not included, especially in the countryside and small towns.

Though the policy of autarchy continued until 1959, it was modified in two successive phases. The first limited change was made in 1945, when it became necessary to liberalize certain procedures to achieve greater stability and take advantage of new international opportunities. This led to important policy revisions in 1948 that reduced inflation for the time being and encouraged the spurt in growth that took place three years later. A second modification was undertaken by the government of 1951. The new relationship with the United States that began two years later accelerated interaction with the world economy, though it had only limited effect on the fixed ideas of Franco and his chief subordinates. The external world, Western as well as Communist, was deemed hostile to the regime and to true Spanish culture, so that being as independent as possible remained a major goal. Like most twentieth-century dictators, Franco continued to believe that politics took precedence over economics and that the state should bend the economy to its will.

The objective of stimulating the economy through investment equal to 15 percent or more of the state budget was largely achieved during the 1950s. This policy offered major tax advantages and even guaranteed profit margins for selected industries, requiring in return the fullest possible consumption of national products, regardless of price. The state continued to control foreign exchange, restrict imports, and regulate international trade, Franco insisting on an artificially high rate of exchange for the peseta, which had the effect of handicapping exports. The INI obtained credit from the Bank of Spain at only 0.75 percent interest, and savings institutions were required to devote half of their investment to the purchase of INI shares. This form of import substitution industrialization worked well for most of the 1950s, as the GDP rose at a rate of 7.8 percent annually from 1951 to 1958, one of the highest rates of increase in the world. Since industrial production doubled while agriculture grew more slowly, the latter's share of gross domestic product declined from 40 percent in 1951 to 25 percent in 1957.

This was irregular growth from a low and unbalanced base. It grappled with major obstacles, including poor transport and a deficient road network. Though electrical output grew rapidly, demand rose more steeply yet. Consumption remained low due to limited productivity and poor salaries. Moreover, the quality of many products turned out under state protection was inferior, while much of the industrial plant and its technology was obsolete, requiring expensive imports.

Manuel Arburúa, minister of commerce from 1951 to 1957, considered by some the reference point for the corruption associated with strong state regulation, was in fact a reformer in certain respects. He broadened international commerce, decreasing the number of special exchange rates from thirty-four to six, and secured greater coherence by closing the separate accounts of some state agencies while reducing those of others. Rationing finally ended in 1952, and at the same time tourism increased. Imports grew rapidly, particularly in foodstuffs and consumer goods needed to raise the standard of living. Conversely, not much was done to increase exports, which had risen in the late 1940s but flattened out in the following decade.

American aid provided a boost for several years after 1953, but new problems soon emerged. Continuing inflation was due, above all, to the public deficit, which remained high from 1954 on, consequence of the level of public investment needed to achieve greater self-sufficiency. The deficit rose even more rapidly in 1956. Salary increases engineered by Girón, the labor minister, increased consumption and thereby stimulated domestic production but also fueled inflation. The government printed more and more money, yet it gave inadequate attention to agriculture and needed ever-growing food imports for an expanding population. Rising imports helped improve the standard of living; nevertheless, exports were far from keeping pace, resulting in a trade imbalance so severe that it threatened further growth. New investment and more advanced technology had become indispensable; these, however, could only come from abroad and could only be obtained and financed through a policy change that encouraged foreign investment and greater production for the international market.

The ministers in the new government of 1957 were determined to face these problems, but they lacked a coherent theoretical model or an integrated general policy. As explained in chapter 16, neither Franco nor Carrero Blanco had any intention of making a fundamental change in economic policy and they expected to do no more than adjust the existing program. At the close of 1957 Carrero circulated a coordinated plan for increasing national production, which proposed to intensify autarchy, spurning the powerful trend in Western Europe toward international cooperation. The new economics ministers and their assistants, however, were much more impressed by the opportunities of the international market, and, after initial resistance, Navarro Rubio convinced Franco to accept a new approach that would right the balance of the Spanish economy and enable it to prosper in the future.

Under the 1959 stabilization plan the peseta was devalued from forty-two to sixty to the dollar (its actual rate on the free market), and by the end of the year eighteen different state agencies had been eliminated, together with many regulations and restrictions. Import licensing for 180 key items, which accounted for half of all imports, was abolished, though restrictions on less essential items were kept in place to protect foreign exchange. Investment procedures became freer and simpler, foreign investment being permitted for up to 50 percent of the capital of any enterprise. This did not establish a completely free market, for more than a few barriers remained, but much of the system of autarchy was eliminated at a single stroke.

Though the reform at first produced a jolt for many ordinary citizens, as, for about a year, unemployment increased and real income declined, it began to achieve its goals rapidly, and by the close of 1959 the government had accumulated a reserve balance of one hundred million dollars. Foreign investment jumped from $12 million in 1958 to $82.6 million in 1960, while in the same two-year period the number of foreign tourists doubled from three to six million a year and grew steadily thereafter, becoming a major source of income. The technocrat ministers also introduced a new style of governing that abandoned the baroque rhetoric and ideological dogmatism of their predecessors. Instead, they discussed problems using direct and practical language that reflected the character of their policies. In 1960 they introduced a new tariff, and two years later the government nationalized the Bank of Spain. A modest tax reform in 1964 simplified the system and made it slightly more progressive. Spain's first development plan went into effect that same year.

The greatest economic expansion in all the long history of Spain took place during the years 1950–75, the final quarter century of Franco's life. Living standards for all sectors of society steadily improved, though some prospered more than others. Only Japan achieved greater proportionate growth in this era. By the 1960s Franco's regime had invented, or, if one prefers, anticipated, what twenty years later would become the "Chinese model" of state capitalism combined with free-enterprise economics and integration into the international economy, governed by an authoritarian political system. The two main differences are that there was greater freedom in Spain during the 1960s than there was in China and that the proportion of state capitalism in Spain was much less. With the exception of the newly nationalized Bank of Spain, the banking system and savings and loan associations remained in private hands.

The years 1961 to 1964 were the time of most rapid growth. The GDP expanded by 8.7 percent a year, while inflation remained below 5 percent annually. Many aspects of economic policy had been opened to public discussion and hence a degree of criticism, in contrast to the first two decades of the regime, during which censorship prevailed. Foreign investment and export growth were cornerstones, while Spain's tourist industry became one of the largest and most efficient in the world, attracting twenty-one million visitors a year by the end of the decade, with no end to growth in sight.

Direct foreign investment came second, from 1960 to 1974, amounting to $7.6 billion. Of this total, nearly five billion was invested in property (much of that for the tourist trade), more than two billion directly in commercial and industrial enterprises, and the remainder in the Spanish stock market. Various kinds of credits and loans made available about one billion dollars more from abroad. Foreign investment was directed primarily to the expansion of the automotive, electronic, and chemical industries. By the time that Franco died, 12.4 percent of the new capital in Spain's five hundred largest industrial firms came from abroad.

The new policy limited state investment in the INI but did not eliminate it, so that the INI still grew, maintaining a dominant position in several key industries. As a state holding corporation, it was poorly coordinated and eventually became a support structure for older and less efficient enterprises. In the later years of the regime it took over mining and ship construction even more, trying to cope with mounting debt. The INI was administered by approximately four thousand executives throughout Spain, and half of these positions were little more than political sinecures. Its lack of internal rationalization became more evident with each passing year, together with the relative stagnation of key enterprises, as the number functioning at a loss grew. After 1970 a greater effort was made to achieve reorganization and reform.

Spain still maintained a high tariff policy, two and a half times that of advanced industrial nations and nearly twice as high as in Japan. New procedures introduced in 1967 made certain policies more restrictive once more and further adjustments were needed, somewhat harder to achieve as Franco's health declined and his support for changes became less clear. Further liberalization, nonetheless, took place in 1970–71. From 1966 to 1971 the growth rate declined to 5.5 percent annually, but from a much higher base, and then increased in each of the next three years. Altogether, the average annual rate of growth from 1960 to 1974 was 7.2 percent. In 1969 the country occupied twelfth place in the world in industrial output and then rose higher, to eleventh. In 1971 Spain briefly held the rank of fourth largest shipbuilder in the world.[7]

Agriculture was still neglected. For some time, Spain continued to suffer from its traditional dual problem of hundreds of thousands of landless laborers, mainly in the south, and an almost equally large number of unproductive *minifundios*, or dwarf farms, mainly in the north. Over a period of years, the National Institute of Colonization (Instituto Nacional de Colonización) provided ninety thousand laborers with land of their own (with Franco himself investing a small personal sum in the enterprise), but that only scratched the surface. Concentration of small farms into more productive units was an equally pressing need. The National Service for Land Consolidation (Servicio Nacional de Concentración Parcelaria), founded in 1952, concentrated some four million hectares of *minifundia* land, about 10 percent of the cultivable surface of Spain. That was nonetheless not enough to solve the problem, and a study of 1965 revealed that 48 percent of landowners enjoyed less income than did farm laborers, whose wages had increased dramatically.

Franco's record in the history of Spanish ecology is mixed. Though his regime always pursued the goal of economic development, during the Civil War and immediately after, it advanced a rhetoric exalting rural life and the provinces, particularly Castile, as the soul of Spain and its culture. Yet the countryside itself was neglected, and the budget for ecological protection and the park system, never strong in Spain, declined further. Two environmental goals that Franco strongly pursued, however, were reforestation and dam construction. By the 1970s he had succeeded in transforming a portion of the barren landscape that had so shocked him when he first traveled into central Spain in 1907. Extensive reforestation eventually amounted in proportionate terms to one of the largest such projects in the world, while the country's hydraulic capacity increased tenfold, water capacity in the rapidly growing number of dams rising from approximately four thousand cubic hectometers to more than forty thousand by the time of Franco's death.[8] Irrigation also eventually expanded considerably, sometimes in conjunction with the numerous hydroelectric projects, though more at first to the benefit of larger landowners, with the construction of dams and then a greater number of deep wells. As Spain grew prosperous, the budget for national parks and for several environmental protection measures finally increased, as well. Conversely, the construction boom of the 1960s often ran roughshod over environmental concerns.

Agriculture finally began to receive more attention in the 1950s. Labor emigration greatly increased the wages of hired labor, while the number of *minifundia* declined rapidly from 1962 on. During the following decade about half a million dwarf holdings disappeared and the average size of production units grew from fifteen to eighteen hectares. Despite growth in productivity, the share of agriculture in GDP declined, as in other industrializing countries, dropping from 24 to 13 percent during the decade of the 1970s, a lower percentage than in Italy, as the active agrarian population declined from 4.9 million to 3.7 million by 1970, representing only 22 percent of the labor force. One of the traditionally poorest agrarian provinces, Almería, underwent dramatic transformation as it learned to specialize in winter fruits and vegetables, producing a great increase in per capita income. Problems of agricultural underdevelopment nonetheless persisted in some parts of the west and south.

Thus the real Spanish revolution was not the collectivist convulsion of 1936 to 1939 but the transformation of society and culture wrought by the economic modernization of the quarter century from 1950 to 1975. By the time that Franco died in 1975, 40 percent of the labor force was employed in the service sector (partly reflecting the great growth in tourism), 38 percent in industry, and only 22 percent in agriculture. These sweeping changes transformed social and cultural psychology, replicating in Spain the common materialist mindset and mass consumer culture of the contemporary Western world, though this had never been the sort of thing that the somewhat bewildered caudillo had had in mind.

Income was not merely enormously increased but also in considerable measure redistributed. In the 1950s, personal income in Spain was more unequally distributed than in northwestern Europe, though much more equally than in Latin America. Estimates of the increase in the share of national income devoted to wages and salaries vary somewhat, but even the most parsimonious conclude that it rose by about 20 percent. By 1975, it had reached approximately the same proportionate share as in other Western countries at an equivalent level of development, and it increased slightly more in the years immediately following. The rise in living standards was without precedent, while the average work week declined from forty-eight hours in 1964 to forty-four in 1975. Franco's goal of greater social justice was to that extent achieved, though in large measure not by the policies he had originally employed.

The system of social security began weakly during the 1940s but eventually accelerated, finally including farmworkers in 1964, while the range of services expanded. Small shop owners and independent workers were finally included in 1971, and the system became universal in the following year. By that time there were a growing number of complaints about fraud in disability claims and the granting of early retirement, the kinds of problems found almost everywhere in the developed world. Though full employment still depended on the departure of several hundred thousand emigrant workers employed in other West European countries, the labor laws strictly protected workers from arbitrary dismissal, virtually guaranteeing employment so long as the employer remained in operation.

Educational expansion accelerated. Though as late as 1966, the share of GDP devoted to education was low by West European standards, it subsequently rose rapidly, as the share of the state budget nearly doubled between 1960 and 1970. By the latter year the Spanish state devoted a higher percentage of its expenditures to education than to the armed forces for the first time in history. By 1974 primary schools included nearly all children, even in remote mountain areas, again for the first time in history, and the number of universities had doubled, to twenty-two. The quality was irregular but in some respects proportionately greater when Franco died than after the "democratization" of education carried out by the Socialists in the following decade, which lowered standards. The publishing industry flourished. The number of book titles published worldwide doubled between 1955 and 1970, but in Spain the number increased nearly fourfold, growing from 4,812 to 17,727 per year, the publishing business benefiting from the liberalization of censorship in 1966.

All this produced a drastic transformation of the social structure. In 1950 scarcely a third of the population would have been considered middle class or lower-middle class, and then only if the large number of small landowners in the north were included. By contrast, the 1970 FOESSA (Fomento de Estudios Sociales y Sociología Aplicada) survey, Spain's most thorough inquiry, revealed that 6 percent of the population defined itself as upper- or upper-middle class, 49 percent as middle or lower-middle class, and about 45 percent as lower class. Approximately 40 percent of skilled workers classified themselves as lower-middle class, while some sociologists calculated that the broader middle classes amounted to 54 percent of the population. The subsequent 1975 FOESSA study classified heads of families by social strata and occupational groups as 5 percent upper- and upper-middle class, 35 percent middle class, 20.3 percent lower-middle class, 33.6 percent working class, and the remaining 6.1 percent as "the poor." Though some analysts did not fully agree with these classifications, there was no doubt that a sea change had taken place, the broader middle classes nearly doubling in proportion and the lower class reduced by at least a third.

During the last fifteen years of his life Spain was transformed into a semiaffluent modern industrial society. Long-standing problems of nearly four centuries were being resolved, and this was infinitely more important than building another empire, Franco's other great ambition in 1939. By the close of 1973, per capita income had broken the barrier of two thousand dollars that López Rodó had once said would be necessary for the successful introduction of democracy. In real dollars this amounted to the same per capita income reached by Japan only four years earlier. Spain was slightly ahead of Ireland and far ahead of Greece ($1,589) and Portugal ($1,158).

Notwithstanding, the regime's economic policy faced an unprecedented avalanche of criticism from the mid-1960s on, facilitated by the censorship reform. Critics maintained that Spain was failing to overcome fundamental structural defects, despite the rise in production and income, and that everything depended on foreign capital and the international trade boom. Part of this was a veiled form of political criticism, direct expression of which was still prohibited. It targeted state economic policy, the role and influence of the large banks, the failure to overcome major regional disequilibria despite state planning, the housing shortage for those of modest means, the lack of services in rapidly expanding cities, the inability of the economy to achieve full employment without the need to resort to labor emigration, and the lesser income of the bottom third of society.[9]

Some of these criticisms pointed to serious shortcomings, though others simply dwelt on the normal problems of rapidly changing and developing societies. Large-scale capital transfers are typical of the modern capitalist economy; the United States, for example, had depended on such transfers for an entire century. The large banks played an influential role, but no more than in Belgium and perhaps only slightly more than in France and Germany. The three development plans all sought to equalize income between social sectors and regions, but here progress was limited, as in many other economies. The third plan, in 1973, placed more emphasis on the less developed regions, though again with meager results. As in other countries, capital flowed naturally to the most productive areas with the highest returns, and neither of the differing models of socialist development in either the Soviet Union or Yugoslavia did any better on that score.

Significant problems remained. The system was never completely liberalized or fully opened to the international market, for many state controls and regulations remained. Corruption, at its highest level under autarchy during the 1940s, had declined but had not been eradicated. In most industrial sectors the optimal size of enterprises had still not been reached, full rationalization and cost reductions had not been fully achieved, and the country still lacked the most advanced technology. Despite the broad transformation of agriculture and the prosperity of certain export sectors, domestic food production remained inadequate. Though inflation declined, it never disappeared, and large-scale state credit and the cost of imports subsequently exacerbated it.

The Ministry of Syndical Organization both restricted and protected workers, and its regulations made rationalization of the labor force difficult in many enterprises, limiting productivity. The growth of industry and services was impressive, but in combination with the rapid improvements in agriculture that released hundreds of thousands of redundant laborers, it proved inadequate for full domestic employment. When the first oil crisis provoked the return of many emigrant workers in 1973–74, unemployment increased dramatically. Major efforts to complete the social security system in the final years of the regime raised costs and helped to fuel inflation. Investment and industrial expansion were partly dependent on the international market, which began to flag by Franco's last years, while some of the key industries, such as Basque metallurgy, were aging and in need of new investment. The INI had become a bloated white elephant, requiring constant subsidies, and the efforts to restructure it during the early 1970s largely failed to achieve major results. That much the same was occurring with state industries elsewhere was scant consolation.

Franco's regime disposed of a smaller proportion of the country's resources than did the contemporary West European social democratic governments. Tax reforms in 1957 and 1964 did not greatly alter a highly regressive fiscal system plagued with loopholes. Even including social security and other welfare payments, the state budget in 1973 only amounted to 21 percent of GDP. Direct taxes were only equivalent to 13.5 percent of GDP, compared with 15.6 in Japan and 22.5 in France, the other two industrial countries with the lowest rates at that time. Indirect taxes accounted for 44 percent of the Spanish total, a figure at that time only exceeded by France with 45 percent. Limited funding due to low taxation slowed development of public services, particularly in transportation and highways, municipal services, and low-cost housing.

Spain's economy was initially protected from the effects of the first oil crisis in 1973, because state policy temporarily held prices below cost. The chief goal was to maintain the growth rate, which reached 5.4 percent in 1974, a little lower than planned but acceptable under the circumstances. Increased oil prices nonetheless drained currency reserves and were the main factor in boosting inflation to 18 percent, the highest level in a decade.

When Franco died in 1975 the economy had to cope with international recession, a sharp decline in foreign investment, and drastic reduction in the growth rate that was accompanied by rapidly rising unemployment. Despite the country's transformation, major imbalances remained between advanced and underdeveloped regions. Though income was better distributed than before, 1.23 percent of the population enjoyed a greater share of national income (22.39 percent) than did 52.2 percent of the population at the opposite end of the scale (21.62 percent). At that point, the top 10 percent were proportionately two and a half times wealthier, relative to total national income, than the top 10 percent in the United Kingdom.[10]

These problems notwithstanding, the economy had undergone fundamental modernization, and Spanish society had been transformed. Most of the problems of post-Franco Spain were similar to those of other industrialized countries, albeit more pressing than those of the most advanced ones. They were not the classic dilemmas of the old underdeveloped agrarian society. Spain achieved greater progress than any other country in the world at its level of development between 1950 and 1975. It acquired the resources and structures that would enable it to cope with new problems under the parliamentary monarchy that followed, when it lost most emigrant remittances and had to face high unemployment, making the adjustments needed to continue to grow in the future. Spain would, however, lose a little proportionate ground in later years, and in the long run would not be able to maintain the same convergence or ratio of national income compared to the West European average that it enjoyed in 1975.

Much of this economic success corresponded with Franco's plans, but he was powerless to resist the great cultural and social changes that came with it. The law of unintended consequences accompanied the creation of the first mass consumer society in Spanish history, which embraced a materialism and hedonism completely unthinkable for any earlier generation. The small-town and rural society of the north, the backbone of Franco's movement in the Civil War, was slowly but surely uprooted. Despite the continuation of a liberalized censorship, foreign influences entered Spain on an unprecedented scale via mass tourism, large-scale labor emigration, and increasing economic and cultural contact.[11] Society was exposed to styles and conduct diametrically opposed to traditional culture, and the former proved more seductive. When to this was added the effect of the media, advertising, and entertainments, it is easy to understand the unparalleled cultural transformation that took place.

The first major casualty was not the political system, which remained in place, but its principal cultural base, traditional religiosity. An urban, materialistic, and increasingly sophisticated society, nominally well educated and certainly hedonistic, inclined ever more toward the secular, consumer-oriented life of Western Europe. Though it remained Catholic in name, it ceased to be culturally and socially Catholic in the traditional sense. The

Church itself was changing. Its Spanish branch was proportionately one of those most affected by the reforms of Vatican II and the accompanying generational rebellion of the clergy. During the course of the 1960s, an increasingly dumbfounded and irritated Franco found that he could no longer count on the Church in the same way, for by the end of the decade the clergy had been converted into the principal mouthpiece of opposition. Though the authority of Franco would not be seriously questioned or threatened so long as he lived, after he died Spain's new leaders found that the society and culture on which his rule had originally been based had largely ceased to exist, making it impossible for the regime to reproduce itself. The great changes that had taken place under Franco—some sought by him, others accepted by him, and still others received by him with increasing horror—deprived his regime of its reason for being.

19 Twilight Years

(1969–1974)

The designation of Juan Carlos in July 1969 resolved the question "After Franco, who?" but did not answer the dilemma "After Franco, what?" The general assumption was that despite the increase in dissent and the decline in the internal coherence and determination of the regime, Franco had managed to institutionalize a system that would sustain its main features for at least a certain period after his death. The cautious, smiling, somewhat diffident young prince was given little credit for political insight or ability, and the general opinion was that if he really expected to reign he could do so only by living up to his oath and affirming the laws and institutions of the regime in order to gain the support of the military and the leaders of other state institutions. Though there was little confidence that the system could continue for very long after Franco's death, neither was any viable alternative within view. Informed interest therefore focused much more on further changes and reforms within the system than on its overthrow or replacement. This only sharpened the rivalry between the two main factions in government, the movement officials on the one hand and the technocrats on the other, each seeking to play the major role in any transition.

Franco appointed a new cabinet on October 29, 1969. It was different from any of its predecessors, and it is not clear that he had had any such alteration in mind as recently as three months earlier, when the prince's oath had been sworn. The change was precipitated rather suddenly by the greatest financial scandal in the history of the regime and indeed of all Spanish government to that time—the MATESA affair, which first became news on August 13. This acronym stood for the first multinational corporation in Spanish industry, Maquinaria textil, S.A., which manufactured textile machinery in Pamplona and had outlets and subsidiaries in the process of being formed in Latin America. MATESA had obtained substantial export credits to which it was not entitled, a fraud denounced in December 1968 by the old-guard Falangist who was director general of Spanish customs.[1] It was seized on by movement leaders to discredit the Opus Dei economics ministers, exposure of this affair reflecting the change in the climate of the regime, since other irregularities had been covered up in the past. The case moved slowly, but Juan Vilá Reyes, the chief shareholder and director of MATESA, was arrested at the end of July 1969, and Fraga Iribarne brought the matter up at the cabinet meeting of August 14, held at the Pazo de Meirás, provoking heated discussion. As minister of information and tourism, he also saw to it that the affair received maximal public coverage, though Franco ordered this discontinued.

Carrero Blanco was outraged, believing, not incorrectly, that movement leaders were using the whole affair as a whipping boy against their main rivals, the technocrats. He prevailed on Franco to accelerate a change of ministers, which, in his view, would settle the matter and at the same time provide a way to cope more effectively with other problems, as well.[2] The caudillo agreed but no longer had the energy or will to engage in his standard balancing act. He even suggested to Carrero that the time might have come for him to take over directly the presidency of the government (prime minister), though to this Carrero demurred, insisting that as long as Franco retained sufficient vigor he should not step aside. Such dogged loyalty was what had gained Franco's trust, and the new cabinet of October 1969 represented a complete victory for Carrero Blanco. The broadest change in twelve years, it became known as the *gobierno monocolor*—"monocolor" because virtually all key members were either members of Opus Dei or the National Catholic Association of Activists (Asociación Católica Nacional de Propagandistas), the principal lay association for propagation of the faith, or else their known sympathizers, even though the new cabinet was presented as representing considerable diversity. Key movement ministers such as Fraga, Solís, and Castiella were dropped, as were the technocrats in finance and commerce, tainted in the affair.[3] López Rodó and López Bravo, however, remained, while the joint portfolio of the movement and the Ministry of Syndical Organization was divided. The former was occupied by the former tutor of Juan Carlos, Torcuato Fernández-Miranda, who was expected to advance the continued reform of the movement. Franco saw the new government as a reliable administration of staunch loyalists, though Juan Carlos was also pleased because it was more Monarchist than its predecessor. Franco said nothing at all about the MATESA affair in his annual message to the nation at the close of 1969, in which he declared that "whoever has doubts about the continuity of our Movement" should be aware that "everything has been tied and securely tied," a subsequently much-quoted phrase.[4]

At this point it was Carrero Blanco, not Juan Carlos, who had come to represent the continuation of the regime.[5] Franco saw him as his natural successor as president of government, the surviving prime minister who would guarantee that the transition to Juan Carlos would take place under the laws and institutions of the regime. Carrero Blanco's influence was due not merely to loyalty but also to his lack of personal ambition. He was an introverted and retiring man of fixed ideas, convinced that the world was dominated by the "three internationals," as he termed them, of communism, socialism, and Masonry. Father of five children and grandfather of fifteen, he spent a large part of his time reading and writing, had published several books and many short pieces, and continued to prepare lengthy memos for the caudillo.[6] He was largely immobilist with regard to domestic institutions and viewed foreign affairs in similarly intransigent terms, holding that it would be better for all his descendants to die in an atomic war than survive as slaves of the Soviet Union. Even within the regime he had no great coterie, and a foreign journalist described him as "a shy man, standing alone at social functions, somberly dressed and rarely smiling. With his dark, bushy eyebrows, he bears some resemblance to Leonid Brezhnev, the Soviet leader."[7]

Franco had allowed himself to be convinced by Carrero in the selection of the new cabinet, but, despite his declining faculties, he was doubtful whether an essentially immobilist new government that was not even representative of the regime would be effective. He lacked the energy or stamina to lead a more diverse and representative group of ministers, but he voiced his concern as to the durability of the new arrangement when Fraga Iribarne called on him to take his leave from government.

Meanwhile the MATESA affair ground on. In 1970 the Supreme Court indicted both of the outgoing ministers who were implicated, as well as the former finance minister Navarro Rubio and six other top administrators. Vilá Reyes was himself convicted of wrongdoing and ordered to pay a huge fine and sentenced to a lengthy term in prison. While awaiting an appeal, on May 5, 1971, he directed a blunt letter to Carrero Blanco, warning that if the government did not release him he would make public extensive documentation concerning widespread smuggling of funds abroad between 1964 and 1969. His letter included a "documentary appendix" listing various materials that he could present about such activities involving 453 leading individuals and firms, many of them closely connected with the regime.[8] Though Vilá Reyes would remain in prison a year more, his blackmailing may have achieved results. Carrero convinced Franco that if the whole business were not finished up it might even do irreparable damage. Months later, on October 1, 1971, Franco granted an official pardon to all the principals involved, though this was partially hidden within a general pardon to more than three thousand others, many of whom were still suffering the penalties of political convictions from earlier years.[9] Attended by major publicity under the relaxed censorship laws and occurring at a time of slowly growing mobilization of public opinion, the whole scandal may have brought more discredit to the regime than any other single incident in its long history.[10]

Meanwhile, the final effort to revive the movement hinged increasingly on the possibility of legalizing internal "political associations" representing different points of view. Some saw this as the only way to achieve greater representation, while others denounced it as a way of letting political parties in through the back door. In his speech to the opening of the Cortes on November 18, 1971, Franco declared abstractly that "in our system associations certainly fit," but that there would never be any opportunity for political parties.[11] Despite much talk and maneuvering, the project remained stalled.

Franco became concerned that the downgrading of the movement had gone too far, depriving it of an effective role. On his personal authority as originally defined in 1938–39, he dictated a new decree-law that suddenly appeared in the *Boletín Oficial del Estado* on April 3, 1970, concerning "the normative faculties of the organs of the Movement." It stipulated that certain decisions of the National Council of the movement could have the force of laws or decrees and that its secretariat could issue ministerial orders, in effect placing the movement on the level of the Cortes or of the council of ministers. This abrupt decree seems to have resulted from a personal decision by the caudillo to redefine and enlarge the power of the movement in order to protect the regime from erosion. It had never been discussed by the ministers, and it created confusion, since it contradicted the reforms of 1966 to 1968. Perhaps because of that, the new powers given the National Council were never exercised and instead stood as an example of the disarray attending the further institutional evolution of the regime.

Unrest among workers and other signs of opposition mounted, with the number of strikes in 1970 reaching a new high—817. This brought the resignation in April of Federico Silva Muñoz, the minister of public works, though he had been successful in large-scale expansion and improvement of the transportation system. He was replaced by the rightist diplomat and intellectual Gonzalo Fernández de la Mora, an able loyalist who opposed major political changes, insisting that the regime was fully legitimized by its many positive achievements.[12] A strike by Madrid subway workers in July created an unprecedented crisis that led Franco to call an emergency cabinet meeting in El Pardo, resulting in a decision to militarize the subway workers. The hard line was, however, accompanied by major wage concessions.

The most direct challenge to the status quo did not come from Spanish workers, who were primarily interested in further improving their economic conditions, but from the Basque nationalist revolutionary movement ETA. This group sought the independence of the Basque Country as well as a Marxist-Leninist social revolution. It turned to targeted killing of police (and later military officers), a form of violence that had not been seen in Spain for nearly two decades. This would lead to a program of outright terrorism extending far into the democratic era after Franco's death. Under the dictatorship, however, leaders of other opposition groups rationalized such deeds by declaring that ETA "fights for liberty," even though its aims rejected any democratic alternative. The most spectacular act of defiance ever committed in the presence of Franco occurred on August 18, 1970, when a vacationing caudillo attended a jai-alai game in the Basque city of San Sebastián. An old *gudari* (veteran of the Basque army in the Civil War) set himself afire and threw himself from the upper level of the *frontón* directly in front of the customarily imperturbable generalissimo.

Some months later, in December 1970, six captive members of ETA, responsible for killing security officers and other major crimes, were condemned to death by a military tribunal in Burgos. The case became an international cause célèbre: voices abroad protested against "inquisitorial Spain," and Franco received messages from foreign dignitaries, including Pope Paul VI, urging clemency. Hard-liners in the military command, however, insisted on severe measures, and four district captain-generals met with Franco in mid-December, though not every commander agreed.[13] Franco had already convened a special cabinet meeting that decided to declare a state of exception, suspending once more the civil guarantees provided in article 18 of the Charter of the Spanish People. A similar suspension the preceding year had lasted two months, but this one would continue until mid-1971, during which time at least two thousand strikers and oppositionists would be arrested.

Although international opinion favored the opposition, a sizeable portion of public opinion in Spain still preferred the status quo, and a large demonstration of support on behalf of the hard line was organized in the Plaza de Oriente. On this occasion, Franco was apparently taken by surprise, but, informed at the last minute, he, Doña Carmen, and his ministers greeted the crowd from the balcony of the royal palace. Vicente Gil, his gruff, outspoken physician, was in the background, as usual disgusted by any sign of weakness. He blamed the information minister, Alfredo Sánchez Bella, for failing to uphold a tough policy in the media. Following the demonstration, the pugnacious Gil, an amateur boxer and sometime head of the boxing federation, grabbed Sánchez Bella by the lapels, shaking and insulting him and calling him "un gallo capao" ("a gelded rooster"). Franco was normally indulgent of extreme statements by the ever-loyal Gil, but this was a bit much. When Gil appeared at El Pardo the following day to provide a routine massage, Franco abruptly dismissed him for that session, saying that he was tired of having his hard-line physician insult his ministers.[14]

Franco gave in on the death sentences, however, after the majority of his ministers voted on behalf of commutation. First he permitted the tension to build, waiting almost till the last minute, but then he reduced the penalties for all six of the condemned to thirty years' imprisonment.

This led to mixed feelings among the military. Many older commanders opposed the relative leniency shown the opposition, but others, usually younger, resented the continued use of military tribunals to prosecute political actions, whether violent or not. Change finally came in a reform of November 1971 that considerably limited the jurisdiction of military courts, passing most political cases to the regular tribunals. The military, whose senior generals at this point were men who had been young officers during the Civil War, would remain overwhelmingly loyal to their commander. The armed forces were still being slowly professionalized and modernized, but Franco had long since abandoned any interest in spending much money on them. Though he always insisted that the goal of the military was to serve and that it was to have no corporate role in government whatsoever, it was equally clear that its major function was to maintain domestic security. In terms of equipment, training, and leadership, the Spanish armed forces remained third rate.[15] By 1970 the only European country that spent less money per soldier was Portugal, and the only countries that kept fewer men under arms proportionate to the population were the North European democracies.[16] Early in 1971 Franco reshuffled the top commands, as usual promoting key supporters, though eight ultra-rightist lieutenant generals were designated for retirement before the end of the year.

If 1970 was a trying time in domestic affairs, it was a good year for foreign relations. On June 30 the Spanish government signed a preferential trade agreement with the European Common Market, opening the Common Market partway to Spanish exports without greatly disturbing the Spanish protective tariff. The agreement offered Spain the best of both worlds, providing a new outlet for Spanish goods without subjecting the economy to greatly increased competition. Indeed, an argument might be made that it was the best commercial arrangement that the country ever enjoyed.[17]

During the course of the year the Spanish government signed an agreement for expanded military collaboration with France, relations between Paris and Madrid having become more cordial. In June De Gaulle made his one and only personal visit to Madrid, being freer to visit the ogre of the Occident now that he had resigned as president of France. Though De Gaulle and his wife devoted several days to tourism in Spain, the conversation between the two generals lasted less than an hour. De Gaulle was two years older than Franco but in decidedly better condition. He found Franco "lucid" and "intelligent," able to pay close attention, but also aged and feeble.[18]

The Spanish government had opened several consulates in Communist Eastern Europe and had also begun negotiations with Moscow concerning diplomatic relations, which before long were established, followed by a commercial treaty in 1972. One year later Franco finally recognized the government of Communist China, establishing normal relations. The Foreign Ministry made occasional references to Spain's "neutrality" in foreign affairs, since it was not a member of NATO. This reflected basic Francoist doctrine, which rejected both Communism and liberal capitalism, but the main purpose of the claim to neutrality was simply to create room for maneuver.

Franco remained clear that the connection with Washington was the cornerstone of his foreign policy. He valued the American relationship because of the prestige, political reinforcement, international security, and economic advantages it afforded. Franco finally dropped his long-standing demand that the United States pay a higher price to continue using its military bases, and at the beginning of August 1970 the foreign minister, Gregorio López Bravo, signed a new agreement with Washington, for the first time fully updating the original pacts of 1953. This renewed the arrangement for the American military bases in Spain but at long last suppressed the secret clause in the earlier agreement that authorized American authorities to take direct military action against the Soviet Union, should an emergency arise, without consulting the Spanish government. Washington still refused any direct security guarantee for Spain, but for the first time the American bases were designated simply "Spanish military installations." The new agreement provided for $188 million in various categories of economic assistance.

The renewed pact was crowned by Franco's second visit from an American president, when Richard Nixon briefly appeared in Madrid on his European swing on October 2. "He genuinely liked Spain and Spaniards and had been deeply impressed by the warm welcome" that he received.[19] The crowd that turned out numbered around three hundred thousand, one-third of that for the Eisenhower visit. In this short encounter, Franco's physical decline was painfully evident. His lips and left hand trembled and during one stretch in which Nixon and López Bravo spoke directly to each other in English, the caudillo simply dozed off.[20]

In return Juan Carlos and Sofía visited Washington at the end of January 1971. The intelligent and discreet English-speaking royal couple impressed American officialdom favorably and set policy makers to thinking about the importance of a transition to a reformist Monarchy in Madrid before the irremediable decay of the regime and Franco's death dangerously destabilized the country.

In the following month Nixon sent General Vernon A. Walters, the multilingual deputy chief of the CIA, to Madrid for a talk with Franco. Walters was American military attaché in Paris but not accredited in Spain.

He made use of a prior acquaintance with Carrero to arrange an interview, but the admiral told him that Franco no longer received anyone all by himself. Walters asked him to try, and on his third day in Madrid Franco received the American emissary. The only third party present was López Bravo. When Franco reached out for the personal letter from Nixon that Walters was delivering, "his hand trembled violently and he motioned for the Foreign Minister to take it." As they chatted about international affairs, Franco observed that whatever the Soviets would sign "they would not respect. It was very difficult to get the better of them." Walters "commented with a smile that he had. For an instant, a smile lit the old man's face and he nodded at the compliment." In general, Walters found the generalissimo looking "old and weak. His left hand trembled so violently on occasion that in an effort to conceal it, he would cover it with his other hand. At times he appeared far away and at others he came right to the point." Franco soon volunteered "that what he felt the President was most interested in was what would happen in Spain after his own demise," stressing that the transition would be "orderly" and that "there was no alternative to the Prince." He acknowledged that "Spain would move some distance along the road we favored but not all the way, as Spain was neither America nor England nor France. . . . He . . . expressed confidence in the Prince's ability to handle the situation after his death. . . . He smiled and said that many people doubted that these institutions would work. They were wrong; the transition would be peaceful. . . . He had faith in God and the Spanish people." He was completely matter-of-fact in referring in the third person to "the death of General Franco." "I expressed to him my amazement," Walters reports, "about the calm and unemotional way in which Franco had discussed the subject. Few men could."[21]

Attention focused more and more on Juan Carlos. During long years of waiting, he had been careful never to say anything of great substance. The country had been conditioned to expect hauteur, arrogance, and high-sounding rhetoric from its leaders, qualities alien to this friendly, discreet, somewhat shy but nonetheless highly calculating young man. His reputation had stemmed rather more from his well-cultivated avocations, making him "best known for being a yachtsman, judo expert and radio ham."[22] Once named official successor, however, hundreds of aspiring young bureaucrats and politicians began to beat a path to his door. As the political contacts of Juan Carlos burgeoned, he gained more and more information about the state of public opinion and the opposition.

In some respects, Franco gave him a remarkable degree of freedom. He had never tried to indoctrinate him directly or in detail, and he failed to respond with any precision to the prince's questions about future political issues. According to Juan Carlos, on one occasion the caudillo replied, "Why do you want me to tell you anything? You can't possibly govern the way I have!"[23] One of the household attendants recalled that on another occasion, when Juan Carlos tried to ask a question, Franco shut the conversation down by replying, "Highness, I don't know, I haven't the slightest idea."[24]

In fact the Prince, analyzing his conversations with Franco on political themes, reached the conclusion that he had left him complete liberty, not wanting to mortgage his future, and that it was very possible that Franco honestly did not seek to condition the man who would have to face a future that Franco could not determine.

Or perhaps he thought that the Prince, in his silence, in his observer's stance, was thoroughly imbued with Francoist spirit and that that would lead him to maneuver effectively without ever moving his feet from the regime of the Eighteenth of July. It is very hard, not to say impossible, to know exactly what Franco thought. It is nonetheless easy to learn how he acted. And with Juan Carlos he acted without imposition, almost without pressure, but with vague indications and paternal counsel that were merely general orientations concerning given themes. But he never indoctrinated him explicitly. He never told him what he must do.[25]

In the summer of 1969, soon after Juan Carlos had been officially designated successor, the Francos for the first time invited the royal couple to spend some time with them at their summer residence, the Pazo de Meirás. Princess Sofía assumed that this would provide an opportunity to get to know Franco more intimately and to learn more of his personal opinions, but, as she found out,

"it turned out that, at lunch as at supper, Franco remained silent. His grandchildren, his daughter, his son-in-law, his wife and we ourselves all talked. . . . He listened, observed, ate, and did not say a single word. 'He will later on, when we all have coffee,' my husband and I thought. But no! They sat us down in front of the television set. And we all sat there, watching the announcer and listening in silence. Then he would go off to work, or take a nap, or get some exercise, and we didn't see him again."

. . . It was not easy dealing with Franco. Later on, the experience seemed to Sofía like reading hieroglyphics. And not because he was arrogant, distant, or imposing. Just the contrary! At home, informally and up close, he was a very small little old man of scant bulk, a simple man who even seemed shy. What was incredible was that in his domestic environment Franco did not talk at all. He seemed drawn apart, a listener. Very reserved, very silent: a closed man. But not enigmatic, for there was also something obvious about him. When he did finally open his mouth what he said was basic and obvious. Anyone might have said it. . . . But, since he rarely opened his mouth, if he said "ah . . . ," everyone stopped talking and tried to interpret what he meant and made a big fuss.[26]

Juan Carlos and Sofía were also invited to spend a few days each summer on Franco's yacht, the *Azor*, a visit characterized by the same banal interactions. The most annoying part was probably the peremptory bonhomie and domineering manners of Villaverde, Franco's son-in-law.

The caudillo preferred that Juan Carlos make as few political statements as possible, both to avoid complications for the current regime and to allow him a freer hand of his own in the future. The prince was known for his discretion, yet he occasionally felt the need to seek a broader opinion. Early in 1970 he received a prepublication summary of a survey by the FOESSA Foundation, which revealed that 49.4 percent of the Spanish population preferred a republic after Franco, 29.8 percent preferred a continuation of the present regime, and only 20.8 percent favored a monarchy. This was not encouraging. At that point he granted an interview to Richard Eder of the *New York Times* and told him that in the future Spain would need a different kind of government than that which had emerged at the time of the Civil War and that as king he would become the political heir of all Spain. This was published by the *Times* on February 4, 1970, under the headline "Juan Carlos Promises a Democratic Regime."

Since for a quarter century the regime had relied on official doubletalk about its "profoundly democratic," "organically democratic" character, Franco could not take great umbrage at verbal gestures to American correspondents. He was nonetheless reported to be annoyed by remarks made by Juan Carlos during his visit to the American capital in 1971, as reported by the *Chicago Tribune* and the *Washington Post*.[27] The prince called on Franco immediately after his return to Madrid to gauge his reaction, but the generalissimo merely observed sardonically, "There are things that you can and ought to say when you're outside Spain and things you ought not to say inside Spain. What is said outside may not be convenient to repeat here. And, at times, what is said here it would be better not to have repeated outside."[28]

The activities of Don Juan and his promoters remained a minor complication. Official recognition of his son meant that the pretender had little or no chance of ever achieving his own goals, and relations between father and son remained strained. The Conde de Barcelona's chief representative, the former movement diplomat José María de Areilza, had become a leading adversary of the regime. In February 1970 Juan Carlos reported to Franco on a recent luncheon with Areilza, but the very idea of such a meeting annoyed the caudillo, who responded tersely, "You know how it is, Highness, either be Prince or a private citizen."[29] Franco was further put out by reports that the foreign minister, López Bravo, who had been one of his favorites, was asking the help of European Community leaders, during conversations in Brussels, to steer Spain toward a reformist democratic regime.

Personal relations between caudillo and prince did not follow an altogether easy rhythm. Sometimes long periods would pass without a meeting, and then there would be a rather peremptory summons from Franco. Juan Carlos urged during several conversations in 1970 that he be permitted to attend cabinet meetings or even that Franco appoint his own prime minister so that it would not be up to him to name the first president of government to follow Franco. However, he was told that the first would do him no good—since everything would be different after the caudillo died—and that the second would take place in its own good time. Franco did suggest that the prince come to El Pardo once a week to participate in some of his conversations with cabinet ministers, but Juan Carlos politely declined, not wishing to be involved to that degree in Franco's day-to-day administration.[30]

The generalissimo was displeased by the apparent eagerness of certain ministers to make spontaneous gestures to the prince or to involve him in special visits or study tours. Franco preferred that Juan Carlos only participate in specially approved public activities, and he tried to see that his appearances were restricted to major ceremonies, though in practice so narrow a schedule could not be enforced. Juan Carlos relied especially on López Rodó and Fernández-Miranda, who drew up memoranda for his irregular conversations with Franco. Despite certain differences, which never reached the point of causing tension, Juan Carlos managed to continue to be discreet and convincing, generally maintaining the respect and even the modest affection of Franco along with the strong support of Carrero Blanco.

Though the government of 1969 had pledged publicly to continue the "development" and "evolution" of the system, its apparent monocolor tone was deceptive, for the cabinet tended to divide between hard-liners and advocates of greater opening. The former gained the upper hand, killing a proposal to permit slightly greater political representation and initiative at the local level. Nonetheless, on January 14, 1971, Carrero Blanco handed Franco a detailed memorandum urging him to name a president of government so that he could preserve his own strength and energy and maintain undiminished the prestige of chief of state. Carrero outlined a ten-point program for the next prime minister that had to do mostly with technical reforms and reinforcement of authority. The only proposal relating to political development was the suggestion that political associations be established within the movement.[31] Though Franco made no positive response, he agreed to a proposal by Carrero and López Rodó to clarify the terms of succession, publishing a decree on July 15, 1971, that conferred on Juan Carlos the powers that properly pertained to the officially designated heir to the throne as stipulated in article 11 of the organic law. These included the right to take over the interim functions of chief of state should Franco become physically incapacitated. Meanwhile, a special effort was made by Carrero Blanco and Fernando Liñán, the director general of the Ministry of the Interior, to elect new *procuradores* to the Cortes who clearly supported the succession of Juan Carlos. As a consequence, the final Cortes of the regime, which convened in November 1971, contained proportionately fewer old-guard movement loyalists or die-hard members of the "búnker" than its predecessors.[32]

In general, 1971 and 1972 were the last relatively quiet years of Franco's life. A protest culture continued to spread in the universities, and a new phenomenon emerged in the form of firebombings of left-leaning bookstores by ultrarightist squads (sometimes indirectly subsidized by the government) to protest the expansion of leftist propaganda. There were no new press restrictions, and with each passing year the limited freedom of the press was used more widely, creating an alternative "parliament of paper" to the controlled assembly of the Cortes. More clandestine or semiclandestine opposition groups took shape, but outside the universities most young people did not want to become involved, and nearly all those who did were careful to abide by the unwritten rules of shadow opposition politics that had begun to evolve.[33] Discreetly, the antecedents of a new civil society were being formed, even though the great majority of Spanish youth were relatively apathetic about politics.[34] Among young people the common popular culture of the contemporary Western world, with its overt hedonism and sexuality, had become predominant. Some of the more thoughtful wondered, "Does Franco really know about all this?" The answer seemed to be that he both did and didn't. That is, he was aware that society and culture had changed considerably, which he could see even on the state television that he frequently watched, but he was scarcely in touch with its more extreme aspects.

The caudillo had reached his eightieth year. The slow but steady decline in his vitality left him tired and nonfunctional for a significant part of every day, and he rarely had much to say in cabinet meetings, sometimes dozing off altogether. Though his mind remained clear when he had the energy to talk to visitors and attend meetings, his stamina had become so uncertain that diplomatic audiences were a hazard and an increasing worry to his aides. At the annual victory parade in May 1972 Franco had to use a portable golf seat to maintain the illusion of standing upright through the entire review. He was also undergoing extensive oral surgery for severe fungus infections in the mouth, a condition aggravated by obstructed respiration and his habit of oral breathing. In May, he began to suffer severe pains in one leg, inaccurately reported as a bout of phlebitis. This proved to be a side effect of the oral infection and ended after the oral surgery was completed.[35]

Hope that the cabinet would take the lead in further *apertura* had faded. It was sorely divided and received little leadership from Franco, who seemed content with immobilism. Moderates therefore looked more and more to Juan Carlos as the only hope for a breakthrough, and a new political tendency, *juancarlismo*, emerged as the focus of those who sought new personal opportunities as well as peaceful reform. The regime's own media encouraged this by the constant publicity given "the generation of the prince," basically the affluent, relatively well-educated young middle- and upper-middle-class Spaniards between twenty and forty years of age who had grown up under the regime and were urged to regard Franco's heir as their symbolic personification. Some of the more politically minded had by this time come to do so.[36]

In 1972 prospects for a smooth and potentially reformist legitimist succession were temporarily clouded by the marriage of Franco's eldest granddaughter, María del Carmen Martínez Bordiú-Franco, to Alfonso de Borbón-Dampierre, the elder son of Don Jaime (the handicapped elder son of Alfonso XIII), who had attempted a decade earlier to retract his official renunciation of his place in the line of succession. Don Alfonso, tall, dark, and handsome, had completed his education in Spain and built a career in the diplomatic service, becoming ambassador to Sweden in 1970. The pretty, graceful young granddaughter with dyed blonde hair had been introduced to the prince while visiting Stockholm with her father and an engagement followed within months. It was announced in December 1971, and a lavish wedding took place on March 8, 1972.[37]

With the serious deterioration in her husband's health, for the first time in their long marriage Doña Carmen showed initiative not merely in Franco's personal relations but even to a very limited degree in political affairs, something that would have been unthinkable in earlier years. She was inordinately pleased with her granddaughter's marriage into the royal family and encouraged a campaign to have Don Alfonso recognized as "His Royal Highness" and a full prince in his own right. Though she was careful not to make a fool of herself in public, in smaller, restricted social situations she even did obeisance to her granddaughter as a princess, with the ultimate goal, it was thought, of changing the line of succession and placing her on the throne of Spain. The notion was also encouraged by some on the ultraright, who calculated that an Alfonso married to a Franco promised a more secure future than the possibly dangerously liberal Juan Carlos. Yet, though Franco had seemed to express unusual pleasure at the wedding, there is no indication that he seriously considered changing the line of succession.

At first Don Alfonso remained ambassador to Sweden and the new couple took up no permanent residence. When in Madrid they lived at El Pardo. Encouraged by the attitude of his grandmother-in-law, Don Alfonso presented a series of requests to have his personal status formally upgraded. These included such items as the official recognition of his own father, Don Jaime (rather than the younger Don Juan), as head of the House of Borbón, his placement second in the line of succession after Juan Carlos (rather than Juan Carlos's small son, Felipe), the removal of Juan Carlos from the line of succession should he ever fail in fidelity to the principles of the movement, bestowal of the official title of Príncipe de Borbón (Juan Carlos was Príncipe de España), and budgetary support for his own princely household. Doña Carmen talked her husband into initially supporting the title of Príncipe de Borbón, but when the elderly dictator took it up with his Ministry of Justice, the expert opinion rendered was that the claim of Don Alfonso was ambiguous, at best.[38]

These pretensions inevitably produced a reaction on the part of Juan Carlos. Earlier, when he had learned that both the generalissimo and Don Alfonso planned to wear the Toisón de Oro (Golden Fleece) at the wedding ceremony, medals granted to them by Don Jaime, he protested to Franco that it would be inappropriate, since only the king had the right to grant such an honor. Since he himself had taken the same position years earlier, the caudillo had to accept such logic and set aside the medal.[39] Nonetheless, the pressure by Don Alfonso and his coterie of supporters had an effect on Franco, who ordered the minister of public works to limit the practice of inviting the prince to participate in ribbon-cutting ceremonies. Since such ceremonies were often tedious enough, this did not upset Juan Carlos, but more serious was the fact that, as the months passed, invitations to visit Franco at El Pardo became less frequent.

Ever since the opening of the Valley of the Fallen in 1959, the regime had held a major ceremony there annually on the anniversary of the death of José Antonio Primo de Rivera, founder of the Falange. On November 20, 1972, Juan Carlos and Franco attended the ceremony, the caudillo dressed in full Falangist uniform, as in the old days. The prince took advantage of the situation to ride back to El Pardo with Franco in his limousine, and for the first time, he expressed fully his resentment of the maneuvers to advance his cousin and frustrate the succession arranged by Franco. The caudillo remained silent, as usual, looking at the road, but, according to Juan Carlos, he did change expression, frowning and slightly clenching his teeth. When they arrived, Juan Carlos handed him a memorandum outlining the problem in detail, and when they said their good-byes, Franco looked at him intensely with an expression of pain in his eyes.[40] Carrero Blanco had suggested that the prince himself should propose a proper title for his cousin Alfonso, and it was in this way that he received the currently vacant title of Duque de Cádiz, putting an end to the matter.

María del Carmen gave birth to Franco's first great-grandchild in December, but meanwhile Carrero Blanco, always a supporter of Juan Carlos, was arranging to put an end to the maneuvers on behalf of Alfonso de Borbón. Carrero noticed that Don Alfonso often went out in the evening with his father-in-law, Villaverde, the kind of man Carrero naturally distrusted. Carrero ordered the intelligence agency that he controlled, SECED, to find out what was going on. Its report, submitted to Carrero in January 1973, revealed that the two were engaged in political maneuvers with certain sectors of the opposition, including, it was claimed, members of the Masonic order.[41] Once Franco received this report, he is said to have put a stop to any further machinations on behalf of the candidacy of Don Alfonso that he got wind of.

In his Christmas speech of 1972, Franco seemed to refer to the desirability of further opening, declaring that "we have to reject closed or exclusivist attitudes. Different kinds of ideas and tendencies are not only legitimate but necessary."[42] For a moment, proponents of reform within the system thought that a new signal was being given, forgetting that this was language he had used ever since 1937. Division within the cabinet had grown pronounced, and Franco had difficulty managing it. Violence by ETA increased, flanked in 1973 by the emergence of a small new Marxist-Leninist terrorist organization that went by the acronym FRAP.[43] The government ordered selective crackdowns but no longer possessed the full authority, much less the ruthlessness, of earlier times. Moreover, the Spanish judiciary was increasingly influenced by the liberalization of society and institutions and tended to be much more solicitous of the civil rights of citizens than in past years.

As Raymond Carr and Juan Pablo Fusi put it,

> Something deeper than a mere ministerial malaise was afflicting the Francoist state: a crisis of the regime which had begun with the debates over political associations in 1967–69, a crisis of contradictions. Spain was officially a Catholic state, yet the Church was at odds with the regime. Strikes were illegal but there were hundreds of them every year. Spain was an anti-liberal state yet desperately searching for some form of democratic legitimacy. . . . "In Spain," the ultra right-winger Blas Piñar said in October 1972, "we are suffering a crisis of authority of our own state."[44]

Of the various forms of increasing opposition, probably the only one that concerned Franco gravely was that of the clergy, since the regime had depended so much on the Church. The Church's attitude was incomprehensible to him. In September 1971 an unprecedented joint assembly of bishops and clergy had publicly asked pardon for the shortcomings of the Church during the Civil War: "We must humbly recognize this and ask pardon for the fact that we did not act at the opportune moment as true 'ministers of reconciliation' amid our people, divided by a war between brothers."[45] The Vatican was no longer accepting nominations for new bishops from Franco but rather, when vacancies occurred, simply naming interim "auxiliary bishops" on its own, as was permitted under the concordat. So many younger priests engaged in illegal political activities that it became necessary to set up a special jail, called the "cárcel concordataria" ("concordat jail"), since they were entitled to special treatment under the agreement with the Vatican.

In one of the last memos that he ever wrote for himself, Franco privately expressed his bitterness: "The policy maintained by Rome in the service of the enemies of the Fatherland is scandalous. . . . Not to accept the auxiliaries = not to recognize them. Something must be done. Not to recognize their authority. . . . Separatist intrigues by certain sectors of the clergy. . . . The bitterness of disappointment for all the services to the Church. Playing politics at the expense of the nation. . . . What a stab in the back."[46] In November 1972 Franco dispatched to Pope Paul VI a letter composed by Carrero Blanco and López Bravo. It complained of the

> concern of some . . . to convert the Church into an instrument of political action. This tendency is often exaggerated by the fascination with violence . . . which leads them to participate in subversive activities or publicly take the side of those who violate public order.
>
> The words of His Holiness about the advance at the present time in the process of separation of Church and state is faithfully reflected in my own thought. . . . Therefore the interference of certain ecclesiastical sectors in Spanish political and civil affairs, with serious negative consequences, appears in my eyes a grave contradiction.

This situation "has not prevented the Church from making strict and systematic use of its civil, economic, fiscal, and Concordat rights, as demonstrated by the one hundred sixty-five refusals of authorization for the prosecution of clergy in recent years, though many of them were involved in very grave matters that included true complicity with separatist movements."[47] The assembly of the Spanish Episcopal Conference responded with a new statement the following month, later published under the title *La Iglesia y la comunidad política*, which was relatively conciliatory and stressed the need to observe the law.

Doña Carmen is said to have complained directly to Carrero Blanco in February 1973 about the "disloyalty" of cabinet ministers such as the interior minister Tomás Garicano Goñi and also López Bravo, whom she accused of siding at home and abroad with the opposition and speaking pejoratively of Franco.[48] Garicano tendered his resignation on May 7, following a May Day incident in which a policeman was trapped in an alley by FRAP militants and literally hacked to death. He stated flatly that the movement no longer had any following and concluded in his letter of resignation that he thought "an authentic opening is necessary."[49]

Franco at long last accepted the fact that he was no longer in condition to run the government himself, and for the first time set in motion the mechanism by which a new president would be appointed. This required the Council of the Realm to present a list of three names from which the chief of state would choose. Franco apparently indicated that he wanted Carrero Blanco on the list, and the council added Fraga Iribarne and the old-guard Falangist Fernández-Cuesta. On June 8 the caudillo officially appointed Carrero Blanco, the first time in the regime's history that anyone other than Franco held the position of president of government.

The new cabinet was almost exclusively of Carrero's election. The only member imposed by Franco was Carlos Arias Navarro, military prosecutor during the Málaga repression of 1937, director general of security under Alonso Vega from 1957 to 1965, and more recently mayor of Madrid, who replaced Garicano in interior. Arias had a reputation as a *duro* and had long cultivated the Franco family. Carrero's chief lieutenant was not López Rodó or any other Opus Dei technocrat but the enigmatic, seemingly pedantic Torcuato Fernández-Miranda, former political tutor of Juan Carlos, who remained minister secretary-general of the movement and now received the post of vice president.

The autumn of 1973 witnessed probably the last truly festive public occasion of Franco's life, the celebration of his golden wedding anniversary on October 22. This began with a solemn Te Deum mass in the El Pardo chapel, attended by the entire council of ministers and all the Council of the Realm, together with many members of the extended Franco family, and was followed by a reception for all the guests.

The appointment of Carrero Blanco as president of government was seen by most of the now extensive opposition as little more than an expression of immobilism, designed to provide for the continuation of Francoism after Franco. In fact, the new government was composed of proven loyalists who were not necessarily diehard ultras and who represented a modest degree of change, timidly proposing a few reforms.[50] The hope of Juan Carlos that Franco might retire at this point was quickly dashed, yet the feebleness of his health guaranteed that the end could not be long delayed. Carrero Blanco recognized the need to generate a least a little further opening. He created a mixed commission representing the cabinet and the National Council of the movement in the autumn to study the issue of political associations. Fernández-Miranda presented a proposal for a general law on associations that was discussed at several cabinet meetings and was scheduled to be taken up again on December 20, when the government abruptly came to an end.[51]

Carrero Blanco was assassinated on a side street not far from the center of Madrid about 9:30 a.m. on the morning of December 20, 1973. This spectacular killing was directed not merely against the existing government but against the future of the regime; its purpose, in the words of the assassins, was to "break the rhythm of the evolution of the Spanish state, forcing a sharp turn to the right."[52] Personal security for Carrero Blanco was lax, as tended to be the custom in Spain except in the case of Franco himself. Carrero was a creature of habit, attending Mass every morning in the same church near the American embassy. The ETA squad that executed the assassination, with the key assistance of elements of the Communist Party, rented a small basement apartment on the one-way street along which his official car—a Spanish-built Dodge Dart—drove each morning after Mass en route to the nearby office of the presidency of the government at Castellana, 3. The assassins devoted ten days to burrowing a tunnel with a jackhammer under the center of the street directly beneath the spot where his car would pass. The operation generated considerable noise and debris, but the *etarra* squad did what they could to soundproof the apartment and passed themselves off as sculptors creating large new art works using mechanical techniques. The manager of the building was himself a part-time police employee and became suspicious, reporting the apartment to authorities. A late-evening raid was scheduled by the Civil Guard but canceled at the last minute by leadership, which judged that another raid on inconsequential activity would simply be counterproductive.[53] This easy-going approach was fairly typical of security at that time in Spain, ruled by an authoritarian regime that exercised less and less authority. Elaborate electrical wiring enabled the assassins to set off an enormous blast precisely underneath Carrero's vehicle as it drove slowly down the street on the morning of the twentieth, creating a huge hole in the pavement and lifting the president's car high into the air, finally depositing it right side up on top of the fourth-floor landing of the church and Jesuit monastery across the street, passenger and police escort still in one piece but quite dead.[54]

This created the most serious government crisis in the history of Franco's regime. The date of December 20 had been chosen by the assassins because the trial of the main group of leaders of the primarily Communist worker commissions was to begin that day, and as many as a hundred illegal demonstrations were scheduled to erupt in towns all over Spain. As news of the magnicide spread, it was accompanied by a general sense of foreboding. All but three of the demonstrations were abruptly canceled, and the leaders of the Communist Party quickly moved to dissociate their organization from the assassination. Whether they knew that individual Communists were major accomplices is not clear. In Madrid some shops closed early, and traffic fell off as many citizens remained in their homes. However, the only confusion that arose resulted from an intemperate order by the new head of the Civil Guard, Lieutenant General Carlos Iniesta Cano, directing local commanders to open fire, if necessary, to control any disorder. This ran counter, however, to Franco's instructions not to alarm the country but to maintain the greatest possible tranquility.[55] Fernández-Miranda, acting president of government, moved quickly to cancel the order and was supported by the interior minister Arias Navarro and the navy minister Admiral Gabriel Pita da Veiga (who according to regulations took over the functions of the minister of the army in the absence of the latter).[56] Military units were placed on alert, but there was no shooting and no disorders.[57]

Franco at first accepted the news with his customary stoicism but soon gave way to emotional despair. Though the two had never been genuinely intimate, Franco had relied on Carrero enormously. Privately, he expressed complete dismay, saying that his last link with public life was broken. He retired for the remainder of the day and refused to eat. Though feverish and ill with the flu, the next morning he insisted on presiding at the usual weekly meeting of the council of ministers. At the beginning he broke into tears, the first time that his ministers had ever seen him cry.[58] That same day he was represented at the funeral mass (*corpore insepulto*) and burial by Juan Carlos; as Carrero Blanco was laid to rest in the cemetery at El Pardo, Franco, in tears, watched the entire proceedings on television. At this ceremony groups of ultras shouted "ejército al poder" ("the army to power") and greeted the reformist president of the Church's Episcopal Conference, Cardinal Vicente Enrique y Tarancón, with cries of "Tarancón al paredón" ("Tarancón to the firing squad"). The memorial service (*funeral de estado*) took place on the twenty-second, and when, at its conclusion, the cardinal archbishop moved to embrace Franco, the aged and emotionally exhausted caudillo broke down completely, sobbing inconsolably over the loss of his closest and most trusted collaborator. The same emotion was expressed a few moments later, as Franco sought to comfort the widow. Captured on national television, this was the first time the Spanish public had ever seen the generalissimo cry.[59]

No one could take the place of Carrero Blanco in Franco's thinking. For the moment, the owlish and enigmatic vice president, Fernández-Miranda, was in charge, and he fully expected that Franco would name him the next president of government. Though he looked eventually to at least a partial transformation under Juan Carlos, Miranda was a Franco loyalist who would sustain the regime as long as the caudillo lived. He had made it clear that fall that he did not support associations as political parties; rather he was in favor of there being diverse groups under the umbrella of the movement, which he sought to broaden by incorporating new sectors. He never wore the Falangist blue shirt and hoped to make a diversified movement a main support of the monarchy.

All this was too subtle for Franco, who had never fully trusted Miranda, whom he considered too much of an intellectual and *aperturista* (advocate of "opening"). The regime's old guard were unanimous in their rejection of Miranda, while the more moderate found him cold, esoteric, and lacking in popular appeal.[60] Even Juan Carlos, who depended on him for advice, was never fully at ease with him, since Miranda rarely smiled.

Choosing a successor would be one of Franco's last major decisions, and it was one of the most difficult. As Carrero himself had observed to Miranda two days before his own death, "Franco is no longer the man he was. And the people around him, even in his own family, are not the best, not what he needs. I get the impression that they continually weigh him down. Only his daughter Carmen really helps him. No, he's not the man he used to be."[61] Immediately on arising the day after the assassination, a red-eyed Franco in his bathrobe called his naval aide, Captain Alfonso Urcelay, and said that he had been unable to sleep all night.[62] He showed no interest in discussing a successor to Carrero, and later that day Doña Carmen encouraged Urcelay to take the matter up with Franco. At first he seemed unable to deal with the question, but he did ponder the issue in the evening, before, as usual, he dozed off in front of the television set.

Formal consideration began when Alejandro Rodríguez Valcárcel, president of the Council of the Realm and of the Cortes, came to discuss the alternatives with Franco at 7 p.m. on the twenty-second. The generalissimo first made clear that the candidacy of Fernández-Miranda was unacceptable, saying that some of the generals were vehemently opposed.[63] The regime's hard core was led by his former minister José Antonio Girón, who would easily have gained support as president, but Franco did not want to "burn" one of his most important supporters as president. Doña Carmen tended to favor Arias, the minister of the interior, since his wife, Luz, had become one of her close friends, but Franco was hesitant about him, because, as head of security, Arias had failed to prevent the assassination and seemed a weak candidate. Instead, he favored Valcárcel, but he, in turn, was reluctant. Valcárcel suffered from a serious heart condition (though much younger, he lived only a year longer than Franco) and his constitutional role made him ineligible. Technically, he could resign his posts as head of the Council of the Realm and the Cortes, but he knew that would seem opportunistic. The caudillo expressed considerable perplexity and asked Valcárcel to return within forty-eight hours with a complete list of all the names worth considering. The president of the Cortes returned on the twenty-fourth with a list of twenty candidates, none of whom succeeded in resolving Franco's uncertainty.

The discussion was adjourned for two days because of Christmas and then resumed on the twenty-seventh. By that point time was critical. Franco could no longer delay, as in the past, because the terms of the organic law required that the Council of the Realm meet eight days after a vacancy occurred, which in this case would be December 28, to prepare its official three-name *terna*, or list of candidates. He told Valcárcel that he had made up his mind: the list must include his old friend and sometime minister of the navy, Admiral Pedro Nieto Antúnez, a person on whom he felt he could rely completely. Valcárcel called an initial meeting of the council later that night and faced a virtual rebellion, since Nieto was seventy-five years old, increasingly deaf, and had no political experience or talent, not to mention a checkered record.

On the following morning, Franco told the domestic circle in El Pardo about his choice, and both Urcelay, the naval aide, and Vicente Gil were categorically critical. Their resistance apparently shook the old dictator, who recognized the force of their arguments, which also referred to the involvement of Nieto, or of close members of his family, in a recent real estate scandal on the Costa del Sol, the *Sofico* affair. Four years after the MATESA case, this may have given Franco pause. A rapid decision was required and, as an alternative, they recommended Arias, who would also be supported by Doña Carmen. It was a weak choice, but Franco was stumped and could delay no longer, so later that day Valcárcel directed the council to include the name of Arias in the official list.[64]

Arias was a proven loyalist and a strict Catholic, with a reputation as a good administrator, despite recent events, and he also had lengthy experience in government. He was comparatively well read, had a large library, and at least some sense of the media. It helped also that his wife was a friend both of Doña Carmen and of the caudillo's sister. He had been the only civilian minister in the government of Carrero Blanco who had been named by Franco rather than by the admiral himself. Franco decided not to hold the breakdown in security against him, for the perception was that the diminutive Arias could be relied on to keep things under control while enabling the regime to "evolve" safely.[65]

Nonetheless, this was not an impressive choice; he was chosen through a process of elimination rather than on the grounds of the inherent strength of his candidacy. Rumors soon swirled that it showed the decrepit caudillo was no longer in control. Shortly after Arias became president, a widely publicized photo of the new premier and Doña Carmen laughing together at an official reception reinforced the idea that a so-called *camarilla de El Pardo* (clan of El Pardo), Franco's domestic circle, had manipulated the appointment. This term referred collectively to such personalities as Doña Carmen, Villaverde, Gil, General José Ramón Gavilán (head of Franco's *casa militar*), the naval aide Urcelay, and even Franco's brother-in-law Felipe Polo, his personal lawyer. Yet these formed no unified group, and indeed, several of them harbored their own mutual differences. The only ones who seem to have played any role were Doña Carmen and Urcelay, and that was secondary, though Gil was vehemently opposed to Nieto. Doña Carmen had been apparently willing to support Nieto, though she also looked favorably on Arias. The decision was made by Franco in large measure because he had no other viable options.[66]

Franco delivered his customary end-of-the-year speech to the nation on December 30, for the first time seated rather than standing. He emphasized "serenity" and "peace as the cardinal objective" and praised Prince Juan Carlos. What drew attention was his claim that "it is the responsibility of a political leader to convert the bad into good. Not in vain is the popular saying that there is no bad thing which is not turned into good. Hence the need to reform our political structures and express the sentiments of so many worthy Spaniards who constitute the backbone of our Movement."[67] Though the Carrero Blanco family was said to be offended by the suggestion that the assassination might bring some good, it is doubtful that Franco sought to imply anything other than a routine invocation of providence.

The Arias Navarro government that was announced on January 3, 1974, would be the last to serve under Franco and represented an extensive turnover, fewer than half of Carrero Blanco's ministers retaining their portfolios. It was largely composed of remnants of the inner core of the regime, with Arias relying especially on top personnel from his own Ministry of the Interior, the largest of Spain's ministries and by far the one that he knew best. Franco himself named the three military ministers, otherwise insisting only that the able Antonio Barrera de Irimo be retained in the Ministry of

Finance and that the very loyal José Utrera Molina become minister of the movement. Not one but three vice presidents were named.

It was the first cabinet in the history of the regime that was almost wholly made up of civilians. Arias eliminated members of Opus Dei and their closest associates, even though Franco would have preferred to retain López Rodó. This put a sudden end to the years of hysteria about the Opus domination, though the new government had little appearance of *aperturismo*.

Yet that was somewhat deceiving, for its members were in large measure bureaucratic pragmatists and included only one genuine doctrinaire, Utrera Molina, who served as minister secretary-general of the movement. Arias Navarro's advisors and closest associates soon convinced him that further opening should be encouraged, that a system of political associations within the movement could and should be introduced, and that the government must move toward greater cultural pluralism.

Thus the first major public of address by Arias, on February 12, came as a surprise. It pledged a new local government law that would permit direct election of mayors and presidents of provincial assemblies, a new law regulating conflicts of interest among Cortes deputies, acceleration of a new labor law to permit more "autonomous" activity by workers, and a new statute on associations. In the torturous language of the regime, this would "promote the orderly expression of attitudes," possibly meaning political opinions.[68] This was generally well received, giving rise to the new phrase "spirit of the twelfth of February" and generating hope and expectation.

It sounded somewhat alarming to Franco, though he took care not to overreact. Some days later Utrera Molina made his first visit to El Pardo as minister secretary-general. Though comparatively young at forty-seven years of age, Utrera was a life-long Falangist and the minister whom Franco trusted most. The caudillo expressed his skepticism about the new "spirit," saying that one must not forget the "spirit of the eighteenth of July." He observed that the speech was possibly being misinterpreted but declared with an unaccustomed vehemence that it must not end up in a "death wish."[69]

The new minister who had the greatest impact was Pío Cabanillas, in information and tourism, who promoted the image of reform while reducing further the waning censorship, except with regard to criticism of Franco or, in direct terms, of the government. Censorship increasingly was left to whatever sense of restraint still existed among authors and publishers or to state prosecutors in the criminal justice system, who mostly lacked the personnel to deal with such matters. Though a few individual publishers were still fined or prosecuted, in general 1974 became the year of the great *destape*—the "uncovering"—as the eruption of nudity in common publications exceeded the increase in political discussion.

The initial cause célèbre under the new government was the Añoveros affair: on February 24, Antonio Añoveros, the bishop of Bilbao, delivered a sermon that called for cultural freedom for the Basques and a change in government policy regarding regional rights. Though this was stated in vague, general, and almost Aesopian terms, it was read aloud in more than 90 percent of the parishes in the diocese and quickly led to the bishop's house arrest. Arias was determined to show his authority, enraged at what he considered the political opportunism of the Church hierarchy. Steps were taken to prosecute Añoveros for high treason, the government announcing that a plane was waiting to fly him into exile whenever he chose. The bishop in turn indicated that he had no intention of going anywhere and that his arrest would lead to a crisis. Cardinal Tarancón, in fact, was said to have prepared a letter excommunicating the president should that occur.

The crisis was defused by Franco's personal intervention. Despite his feebleness, he still met weekly with the cabinet and, following a visit by Cardinal Manuel González Martín, primate of the Church in Spain, dismissed the charges against Añoveros. Franco was still mindful of the advice that he had given Perón nearly twenty years earlier. Church leaders arranged for Añoveros to come briefly to Madrid and then take a long vacation abroad.[70]

Arias did not accept Franco's correction with very good grace and remained belligerent in his attitude toward opposition in the Church. Later, in November, three workers sought by police were given refuge in the residence of the papal nuncio, whom Arias then proposed to expel. Franco, of course, also vetoed that.[71]

In the meantime, following the speech of February 12, weeks passed with little movement toward the promised reforms. The government busied itself with numerous personnel changes in senior administration. Within three months it replaced no fewer than 158 *altos cargos* (high officials) who had been appointed during the long tenure of Carrero Blanco and the technocrats. Before long a general perception was formed that little could be expected from the Arias government.

The Portuguese revolution suddenly erupted on April 24, 1974, dramatically, though almost bloodlessly, overthrowing the longest-lived authoritarian regime in the Western world. Its downfall had been provoked by protracted colonial war in Portuguese Africa, a conflict from which Franco, who had peacefully decolonized all of Spain's possessions except the Spanish Sahara, had carefully dissociated his own regime. Nonetheless, the Portuguese Estado Novo had always protected his western flank and had added to his regime's stability. The main difference between the situation in the two neighboring states was that the morale of the Spanish military had not been undermined by a long, stalemated colonial conflict. The revolution encouraged greater rigidity in Spanish military policy, particularly with regard to appointments and promotions, and the state intelligence agencies increased monitoring of opinion and activities within the officer corps.

After Carrero's assassination, rumors began to fly in Spain of military intervention that would take over the reins of government from an obviously enfeebled Franco before it became too late. Political conversations among the top military commanders were, not surprisingly, frequent, yet no concrete conspiracy or plan ever developed. There was no truly dominant figure among them, nor was there ever the slightest agreement on any alternative, though apprehension among many of the generals would continue to mount.

Franco's policy toward Lisbon generally followed the moderate tack taken by the United States, but the course of events in Portugal, in which a socialist revolution was promoted by part of the officer corps, was bewildering to him. He is reported to have said, "What can you expect from an army that is led by its supply corps?," referring to the fact that the Portuguese Armed Forces Movement (Movimento das Forças Armadas) was made up of officers in home garrisons and supply and training cadres. Even worse was the flood of favorable comment in the Spanish press on the revolution, which, Franco commented, amounted to "a press campaign in reverse."[72]

Later, at the time of the abortive Tancos revolt in March 1975 that helped to provoke the most radical phase of the revolution, the defeated Portuguese general Ambrosio Spínola asked for Spanish intervention under the mutual defense terms of the old Iberian Pact. Franco refused, declaring that earlier the Portuguese government had effectively voided the pact. Nor were conservatives granted asylum in the Spanish embassy, for if it had been attacked by radical mobs, Franco said he would have had no choice but to send in paratroopers, virtually involving the two countries in war.[73] As it was, six months later the lovely old Palacio de Palhavã, housing the embassy, was burned to the ground by a leftist mob, as were the Spanish consular offices in both Lisbon and Porto, but major casualties were avoided.

The Portuguese revolution confirmed the worst fears of Spanish ultras. It further slowed the pace of *aperturismo* in Madrid and stimulated a campaign by the *búnker*, led by José Antonio Girón, directed especially against the information minister, Cabanillas, and the relaxation of censorship.[74] Girón accused Cabanillas of permitting ridicule of the caudillo.

Arias's cabinet became severely divided, though the president himself was intimidated by the reaction from the extreme right. In order to placate the ultras, he offered to fire Lieutenant General Manuel Díez Alegría, chief of the Supreme General Staff and a strict professional who stood out as the leading nonrightist general in the military hierarchy. Nicolae Ceausescu, the dictator of Rumania, had invited Díez Alegría to Bucharest as a sounding board concerning the future of Spain. The general seems not to have fully understood the reason for the invitation, but his trip was personally authorized by Arias. Soon, however, it became common knowledge and provoked a strong reaction among the ultraright. The military hierarchy was already upset with Díez Alegría because of a major military reform plan that he had developed. They pressed Franco for action, and he summoned Arias to El Pardo to report in the presence of the three military ministers. Feeling trapped, Arias perjured himself, denying ever having authorized the trip to Bucharest. Díez Alegría was dismissed from his post on June 8.[75] One month later, Franco's health collapsed.

20 The Death of Franco

(1974–1975)

$\mathbf{E}$arly in July 1974, Franco was felled by an attack of thrombophlebitis, and after a few days Gil decided that it would require hospitalization. Aside from the brief surgery for the hunting accident in 1961, this would be Franco's first hospital stay since 1916, over half a century earlier. Amid elaborate security precautions, the eighty-one-year-old generalissimo entered the Ciudad Sanitaria Provincial Francisco Franco, where he and his retinue occupied the entire sixth floor. He refused a wheelchair but was quoted as muttering, "this is the beginning of the end."[1]

Arias was already convinced that the caudillo was becoming too feeble to continue governing and had developed the ambition of being the prime minister of the transition. Rumors had even circulated in weeks before Franco's hospitalization that the government would itself take the initiative in declaring Franco incapacitated, though it is entirely unlikely that it would have done so on its own unless he were to sink into a prolonged coma. Before leaving El Pardo on the ninth, the generalissimo himself, as it turned out, ordered Arias and Valcárcel to prepare the documents for a decree to transfer powers, though he did not indicate that it should go into effect yet.

Carmen observes of the illness: "We lived through it all with him there in the hospital, which now is called Gregorio Marañón but then was called Francisco Franco. How long were we there? An entire week? And increasingly worried, because that was when he began to bleed from the intestines. . . . There were complications, and we could already see . . . though he lasted an entire year more. His spirit was serene. I think that he understood that he was entering the final phase. And he accepted that."

But he showed no real inclination to hand over power. "My mother and I insisted to him that it might be good to hand over everything to the prince when the first transfer of power took place. We talked to him about it but he did not reply either yes or no."

Juan Carlos rather indelicately suggested to Arias that he accelerate the pace of government business so that Franco could clearly see that he could not keep up with it at the same time that he assured the generalissimo that he was as sharp as ever and that he himself had not the slightest wish to take over until Franco decided the time had come. The prince was also wary of receiving only temporary powers for a brief interim, which would compromise him on the one hand while limiting his authority on the other.[2]

For the first time Franco was unable to participate in ceremonies of the eighteenth of July, but the festivities served to undermine his health further. State television presented the sentimental patriotic film *Cartas a un niño* (*Letters to a Child*), which had a major emotional impact on the caudillo, who broke down in tears and then suffered a hemorrhage.[3] On the following morning Arias reported to the cabinet ministers that Franco had entered a critical state: "I see him in very bad condition. I have glimpsed death in his eyes, which are becoming glassy." They agreed to arrange for the transfer of powers.[4]

The person who reacted most strongly to the transfer was Villaverde, who had rushed back from Manila, his latest destination abroad, as soon as he received word of Franco's illness. He resented intensely the role and influence of Vicente Gil, Franco's physician, who in turn detested Villaverde as a pretentious playboy. Their first altercation after Villaverde's return stemmed from the latter's attempt to take photos of Franco in his hospital room, allegedly to show the citizenry that the caudillo was surviving, but Gil had categorically forbidden anyone to take pictures.[5]

A major blowup took place on the nineteenth, when Franco signed the transfer of powers. One of his personal attendants has described the scene when Arias arrived in the hospital room to give Franco the papers. Villaverde was incensed and tried to bar the way, but Vicentón simply pushed him aside.[6] The enraged Villaverde allegedly shouted at him, "What wretched service you give His Excellency! You're just setting things up for this silly kid [*niñaco*] Juanito!" Gil, as vehement as ever, responded with the choice array of expletives of which he was a master.[7] According to the physician, Franco's only response on this occasion was a laconic "Carry out the law, president" to Arias.[8] Two days later, Gil and Villaverde pushed each other again and virtually came to blows.[9] Gil felt himself being marginalized, and on the twenty-second he had a complete falling out with Arias as well, whom he denounced twice to his face as "a shit."[10] Gil lacked the temperament to deal with the situation, and these incidents put an end to nearly four decades of faithful service.

Villaverde demanded satisfaction, insisting to his wife and mother-in-law that Franco's care be supervised by a more expert physician, and Doña Carmen felt that she had to take his side, because, as she reportedly said, "there are many physicians but only one son-in-law." Her opinion of her son-in-law had not always been terribly high, but she felt the need of a family ally in this crisis.[11] During the past two years marital relations between the Villaverdes were said to have improved considerably, partly because of their common focus on the future of their eldest daughter, even though by the summer of 1974 thoughts of altering the line of succession had disappeared. At any rate, mother, daughter, and son-in-law were more united than previously. Gil was replaced as Franco's personal physician by Vicente Pozuelo Escudero, head of the Department of Endocrinology of Social Security. Pozuelo had made a very good impression on the Villaverdes as the personal physician of their children's English governess. Gil was rewarded for nearly a half century of dedication with the gift of a television set.[12]

Pozuelo reduced the use of the anticoagulants that had provoked the hemorrhage and introduced a therapy routine. To the surprise of many, Franco began to recover rapidly. He left the hospital on July 30 and soon was well enough to return to the Pazo de Meirás for his summer vacation. Such trips were now made by air, since the long drives by limousine had become too tiring. At that time there was no level entry into planes at the Madrid airport, and Franco was concerned to look fit walking up the steps, practicing carefully ahead of time with an Iberia stairway transported to El Pardo for his use.[13]

In the meantime, Juan Carlos had assumed the duties of chief of state on July 20. With Franco also in attendance, the prince presided over a cabinet meeting with Arias and other ministers in El Pardo early on August 9, and then, on the thirtieth, directed a second government meeting at the Pazo de Meirás.

August was a month of intense speculation amid all manner of political conversations, some of them verging on conspiracy. The boldest was the position advanced by the information minister Cabanillas (and supported to some extent by Arias's right-hand man, Antonio Carro Martínez, his minister subsecretary of the presidency, and by Barrera de Irimo, the finance minister). It proposed that the logic of the situation and of the succession laws must no longer be resisted, the only responsible course being to proceed directly to the coronation of Juan Carlos with full powers. Arias was torn by doubt, for other ministers disagreed. All the while Villaverde sought to take over as head of the Franco family and to become a sort of surrogate for his father-in-law. He traveled to Málaga to consult with Girón about the best means of thwarting the present course of government and encouraged Franco, who continued to recover fairly rapidly, to resume his powers as soon as possible.

Arias Navarro could not bring himself to take a resolute stand one way or the other, while Villaverde redoubled pressure on his father-in-law. Franco himself had been unsure whether he should resume his powers or simply proceed to the coronation of Juan Carlos. By the close of the month, however, he had firmly decided to return, apparently above all thanks to a report he received from his most loyal minister, Utrera Molina. Utrera paid Franco a special visit on the twenty-eighth to tell him that plans were under way to dissolve the movement, to reinstate political parties (including the Communist Party), and even to have Franco himself declared physically and mentally incompetent.[14] This exaggerated account, together with other things he had heard concerning telephone conversations between Juan Carlos and his father, as well as the prince's indirect contacts with the political opposition, dispelled any remaining doubts in Franco's mind about the need to resume power.[15] Prior to the cabinet meeting on the thirtieth, José García Hernández, the minister of the interior, suggested to Franco in a personal conversation that he had sacrificed enough for Spain and deserved to spend his final days in tranquility, to which the caudillo responded, "You know that is not possible."[16]

On September 1 Franco's physicians declared that his health had returned to normal, whereupon he abruptly called Arias to declare that he was "cured" and would be returning to power right away, an act that took place officially on September 3. Juan Carlos, by that time vacationing on Mallorca, was barely informed of the fact before it hit the newspapers. To intimates, Franco justified his precipitous return on the grounds that a diplomatic crisis was developing with Morocco over the Spanish Sahara.[17]

In some respects this first severe illness of Franco's old age brought out the better side of his character, for he generally showed patience, discipline, and relative good humor throughout the ordeal and the recuperation that followed. His remaining teeth, which had caused trouble intermittently for years, required further attention. The last three had to be extracted, and Franco was fitted with full dentures. Not surprisingly, he had become depressed in the middle of the illness and for some time had seemed to lose the will to act. He had to undergo considerable therapy, learning to walk normally again. Pozuelo used recordings of old army marches to raise his spirits and get Franco exercising. The new physician finally discovered the source of the thrombophlebitis in October, when he found a dried-up abscess under a callous on a toe. Apparently the stiff, army-issue black leather shoes that Franco had worn for decades pinched his feet, causing an abscess to develop underneath a callous. Pozuelo insisted that he must give the shoes up. The generalissimo at first responded that he had worn such shoes all his life and they still seemed comfortable, but ultimately he allowed them to be replaced with softer, slightly larger footwear. Considerable practice was required to improve his voice and speech articulation, though, for some reason, his speech therapist was so cruel as to require him to say over and over the word "Gibraltar"—hardly his favorite. His voice, which had been fading for a number of years, became somewhat stronger.[18]

Pozuelo proved an attentive physician, competent and sensible, polite and astute in his relations with the family and staff. During these weeks he convinced the caudillo that he should prepare his personal memoirs, which Franco began by using a dictaphone. The recorded material was then transcribed by Pozuelo's wife. His brief account only continued through 1921, after which Franco abandoned the project, for reasons unknown. Pozuelo also introduced the practice of issuing precise medical bulletins, though it was disconcerting to some to learn the number of maladies from which the caudillo suffered. When he complimented the generalissimo on his courage and devotion to duty, Franco's reply showed that his sense of being an instrument of divine providence had in no way diminished: "What I do has no merit whatsoever, because I simply fulfill a providential mission with the help of God. I meditate before Him, and generally find my problems resolved." As he had made abundantly clear over the years, he had not the slightest illusion concerning the limits to his mortality but declared that "when He considers that my task is completed, He will call me away. And I have often asked Him that, if possible, this be done with a certain rapidity," a prayer that, as it turned out, would not be granted.[19]

By mid-autumn he had made an impressive recovery, sometimes conducting more than a dozen brief personal audiences in a single long morning. On November 24 he resumed limited hunting, firing off a hundred or so cartridges from fixed positions. A more ambitious expedition on January 4-5, 1975, however, proved too much, stressing Franco's system by exposing him to near-freezing cold for several hours. He had to spend the following morning in bed and canceled the remainder of the hunt.[20]

During the autumn, the conflict with Morocco hung like a menace in the background, but the more immediate problem was the continued growth of the political opposition. The year 1974 was already well on its way as a record year for strikes. Most of this was now being reported in the largely uncontrolled press. The most forceful repression took place in the Basque provinces, where direct opposition to the regime, as distinct from strikes, was the most overt. During the years 1973–75 more than sixty-three hundred Basques were arrested, though the majority were soon released.

The sensation of the late summer, while Franco was recuperating, was a major terrorist act on September 13, the bombing of a coffee shop just across the street from national police headquarters, and right off Madrid's Puerta del Sol. Twelve people died, and eighty were injured. None of those killed was a policeman, though some of the victims were clerks in the police office. Thirteen policemen were among the injured. The deadliest terrorist act so far, its results were so embarrassing that ETA declined official responsibility, while the leaders of the Communist Party were displeased that individual Communists had been key accomplices, as in the Carrero Blanco assassination.

Franco's own perspective was that such deeds were decisively encouraged by the liberalized legal system. He declared privately that "we have a serious problem with the judges and lawyers, because they consider such savage acts to be political, when in fact they are only criminal murders. They talk and talk of human rights, but ignore the human rights of innocent victims who are treacherously murdered. Why should they respect the rights of these killers, cruel assassins who have violated those of their victims? These people who try to disintegrate society should be treated with the maximum energy. Either we finish them off, or they finish us off."[21] They put the caudillo in Civil War mode, reminding him of the Red Terror, and he proposed to deal with them in the same way he had in 1939, as he would demonstrate once more in the very final weeks of his public life.

Arias had been offended that Franco had ignored him in planning his return to power and, petulantly, presented his resignation. Franco refused to accept it, offering kind words, though inwardly annoyed because he could find no one more effective or reliable to run the government. Arias then called a press conference on September 11 and candidly admitted that his government had been divided over the summer, but he declared that it would, as he put it, "continue the democratization of the country from its own constitutional basis with a view to widening social participation and giving deeper root to the monarchy."[22] This may have been a fair statement of his intentions, but how to carry them out proved difficult in the extreme.

For the ultras, on the other hand, it sounded like a declaration of war. If they could not eliminate Arias, they were determined to force the expulsion of Cabanillas and several other ministers. At some point in October, Franco received on his desk a dossier they had prepared that featured not so much subversive political publications but graphic examples of the public pornography produced by the *destape*. The caudillo found such material disgusting but not necessarily subversive of the state. He was said to be more concerned by some of the programs he saw on television, frequent watcher that he was, and particularly by frank and critical discussion of political associations in the press, as well as recent declarations by Socialists.[23] On October 24 Franco abruptly ordered Arias to dismiss Cabanillas. One of the most able of the current ministers, the reformist Antonio Barrera de Irimo in finance, then resigned in sympathy with Cabanillas, as did a number of other top officials.[24]

Arias Navarro found himself trapped in mid-stream, unable to advance or to retreat. He tried to salvage part of his program by moving ahead with a proposal for political associations. When this was transmitted to Franco on November 14, the caudillo gutted the proposal by placing everything completely under the movement. That was the essence of an alternative proposal by José Utrera Molina, minister secretary-general of the movement, the last Falangist true believer to serve as a cabinet minister. Utrera's plan to permit associations strictly under the umbrella of the movement was approved by its National Council on December 16. Franco promulgated this by decree five days later, and it was approved by the Cortes in January 1975.

On December 19 Utrera Molina met again with Franco, who told him, "I know . . . that when I die everything will be different, but there remain oaths that bind and principles that must remain." Utrera claims that he told the caudillo it was not likely that such oaths and principles would survive and that the country would no doubt return to liberal parliamentary monarchy with political parties, since that was what Juan Carlos wanted. Franco then lapsed into complete silence, as he was wont to do, but eventually said, "The institutions will fulfill their functions. Spain cannot return to fragmentation and discord."[25]

Requirements to form a legal political association were strict and complicated; such groups had to have a membership of at least twenty-five thousand people spread over fifteen provinces as well as meet other qualifications. The whole scheme was widely criticized as too restrictive and artificial, the sociologist Salustiano del Campo characterizing it as "a typical Spanish invention," while the *búnker* denounced it as treacherously opening the door to political parties. A series of cautious opinion polls between 1969 and 1975 made it convincingly clear that a majority of Spaniards favored a democratic parliamentary system.[26]

Franco stalled any further *apertura*, convinced that greater freedom would completely unravel the system. He thought that the only hope of a successful Monarchist restoration lay in strict maintenance of the institutions of the regime, observing privately in December 1974 that if a plebiscite were held, the monarchy on its own would gain only 10 percent of the vote.[27]

He wanted to get rid of Arias but remained stymied by the question of who in all of Spain could be a reliable government leader in the present situation. Franco apparently leaned once more in the direction of his old friend Nieto Altúnez, elderly though he was. Nieto was not eager and in the meantime made the mistake of agreeing to a request by the former minister, Fraga Iribarne, who had taken a clear position on behalf of regime transformation, that he pass on to Franco his proposal for a new kind of constitution. After seeing this, Franco is supposed to have responded, with a sly feigned ingenuousness, words to the effect of "And for what country is this?" This may have had the effect of souring him on Nieto, and he apparently began revisiting the idea of appointing Valcárcel, despite his poor health and the minor legal complication involved.[28]

These musings, however, were overtaken by events, when a cabinet crisis erupted on February 24, 1975, as the labor minister resigned in protest against the blockage of his attempt to introduce a more liberal labor relations law.

Arias took advantage of this incident to reinforce his personal authority and reshuffle his ministers in a more reformist direction. Knowing that Franco was uncertain and seemed to lack alternatives, he threatened to resign unless he were allowed to dismiss both of the movement leaders in the cabinet, Utrera Molina and Francisco Ruiz Jarabo in justice, replacing them with more moderate figures. Franco opposed this because he thought more highly of Utrera than of any other minister, but Arias insisted, making it a matter of confidence. For the first time in the annals of the regime, Franco felt as though his back were against the wall, and it was a sign of his weakening authority that he gave in. This led to Utrera's farewell at El Pardo, a scene of great pathos in which the feeble caudillo collapsed sobbing into the arms of the man who had been his last fully faithful minister.[29] The new labor relations law that eventually went into effect nearly three months later considerably liberalized restrictions on labor.

When the new cabinet was announced on March 5, the big change was the appointment of Fernando Herrero Tejedor to replace Utrera. Tejedor was an avowed *aperturista*, the only major figure in the movement who was also a member of Opus Dei, and one of the two most trusted political contacts of Juan Carlos within the regime. He also brought in as vice secretary-general his ambitious young protégé Adolfo Suárez, a sometime favorite of Carrero's who was also markedly oriented toward the prince. Franco accepted Tejedor because he was impressed with the new minister's honesty, ability, and discretion, and especially by the official report that Tejedor had prepared as state prosecutor on the assassination of Carrero Blanco, presented to the government the preceding September.[30] Moreover, the caudillo knew that Herrero Tejedor, who was always careful to underline his loyalty, was not a crony of Arias and to that extent would help balance the new government. On the other hand, he was suspicious of Suárez, believing him to be a young opportunist, but he did not challenge the appointment.[31]

As minister secretary-general, Tejedor presided over the Permanent Commission of the National Council, which held the power to approve political associations under the new law. He apparently was convinced that a set of associations would provide the vehicle for transition to a reformed system under the monarchy, and his centerpiece was a new center-rightist association called the Union of the Spanish People (Unión del Pueblo Español [UDPE]). By late spring seven *proyectos asociativos* had been presented, ranging from the moderate left-center to the extreme right. Yet the whole ploy seemed doomed, for the bulk of the opposition and even many moderate reformists, such as Fraga, refused to participate. By September 1975 a total of only eight associations had been registered, and of these only the UDPE, led by Adolfo Suárez, relying on the movement, had gained the requisite twenty-five thousand members. Six of the eight also emanated from various sectors of the movement, and at best only three or four stood for notable reform.[32]

A general scramble had begun among those previously or currently associated with the regime to define new political identities for themselves. The Communists, who had always been the most active opponents, formed a coalition in Paris on July 30, 1974, that called itself the Democratic Council (Junta Democrática). Aside from two minor neo-Marxist parties, the main bedfellow was the transformed Carlist Party, which under its current leader, Carlos Hugo (as he renamed himself), had evolved from the extreme right to the left, embracing "self-managing socialism." The final grotesque touch was added in Lisbon, where Don Juan joined it, having become "the king of the Reds." The Socialists and other left and liberal parties then organized a separate coalition in June 1975, the Platform for Democratic Convergence (Plataforma de Convergencia Democrática). Yet neither coalition harbored any hope of overthrowing the regime, even in the first phase after the death of Franco. The Communist Democratic Council demonstrated its desperation when it arranged a public hearing in a congressional room in Washington on June 10, 1975, to encourage the American government to exert direct pressure on Madrid once Franco was dead, a singular example of a Communist party urging American intervention in its national affairs.[33]

Aside from the conflict with Morocco over the Sahara, the other major foreign policy issue in Franco's final months concerned negotiations with Washington for a new agreement about the military bases, discussions that had been ongoing since the end of 1973. Franco insisted on an official treaty that included a mutual defense guarantee, giving Spain equality with NATO members, and that upgraded terms of military assistance. The Spanish bases still held a fairly high priority for the American government, but it doubted that a regular treaty would ever pass the U.S. Senate, while NATO would probably object to a full-scale mutual defense agreement. To push these matters along, Gerald Ford stopped in Madrid while on a European swing at the end of May 1975, becoming the third American president to visit Franco. The old dictator, who had scarcely set foot abroad, knew how to provide a lavish reception, and he was sufficiently stimulated to remain awake through all the activities, which lasted the better part of a full day.

Such occasions were nonetheless an ordeal. The diplomat Antonio Oyarzábal, who served as Franco's interpreter, would later recall: "It was really hard, because his teeth—he had dentures—made a noise and he was hard to understand. Ford said to him, 'It's a nice day,' to which he made no reply at all. 'What a lot of smiling people,' Ford commented, and Franco replied, 'Young people are always smiling . . . unless they are being poisoned by other people.' And then not a word more!" Oyarzábal reported that to "Betty Ford, the president's wife, Franco reeled off an interminable list of the different kinds of fish consumed in Spain, while he tried futilely to control the quiverings of his hand as he brought to his mouth spoonfuls of the creamed-pea soup that served as first course."[34] On the other hand, Ford, who had represented the American government at the funeral of Carrero Blanco, also noted that Franco focused clearly enough on the key issues and said afterward to State Department officials that he found the caudillo more alert than in December 1973, when he had been grief-stricken and suffering from the flu.[35]

The visit coincided with the most radical phase of the Portuguese revolution, which was provoking grave concern in Washington. Ford suggested to Franco that the simplest way to control the threat of Communism in Portugal would be by Spanish, not American, military intervention. Franco flatly rejected the idea, stating that it would violate the terms of the Hispano-Portuguese relationship and that it probably would not be necessary because the Portuguese would solve the problem themselves. If Spain were to take such action, it would do more harm than good.[36] Only a few months would be needed to prove the cautious, still calculating old dictator correct.

The reformist plans of the government, such as they were, suffered a major blow when Herrero Tejedor was killed in a highway accident on June 12, removing the main force for new initiatives. Consequently the last six months of Franco's life were largely devoid of further change. Arias himself was bereft of ideas. The new secretary-general of the movement was the veteran loyalist José Solís Ruiz, who also dismissed Suárez, though the latter remained head of the proposed UDPE.

Sixty of the more ultra *procuradores en Cortes* (deputies) petitioned the chief of state to hold over the present parliament, elected in 1971 and due for renewal in a few months. This scheme was not necessarily favored by the cabinet but was devised by Franco himself and the Cortes president, Rodríguez Valcárcel, both of whom feared that new elections could not be sufficiently managed and might produce significant changes, even the ousting of Valcárcel. It was important to keep this ultra as president, because his post carried with it presidency of the National Council, which nominated new presidents of government. On July 31 came the official announcement that Franco prorogued the current Cortes until March 15, 1976, on the grounds that it had much uncompleted work still to do.[37]

Arias was irate, since he had counted on being able to manipulate new elections that would produce a new Cortes largely under his control. That was exactly what Franco feared. He became all the more concerned to replace the premier after having received a recording from the intelligence services, which had bugged the premier's limousine, in which Arias declared that "Franco is an old man and the only balls around here are mine."[38] Valcárcel might be the alternative, but appointing him would require action by the Council of the Realm, where Franco calculated that no more than nine of seventeen members were fully reliable.[39] Nonetheless Dr. Pozuelo observed an unusually good-humored and talkative Franco at the extended family luncheon that took place on the regime's national holiday of the eighteenth of July.[40] Later, he would tell intimates at the Pazo de Meirás that Arias would be replaced before the end of the year, though there was no sign of any new initiative to do so.[41]

In 1975 his meetings with Juan Carlos became more frequent and a sense developed among other government figures that he was finally trying to brief the prince more directly about the role he would soon assume.[42] On their principal visit to the Pazo de Meirás that summer, Juan Carlos and Sofía brought all their children to see the Francos and the generalissimo showed genuine delight in the three handsome royal children, in whom he thought he beheld the future of Spain.[43]

By the spring of 1975, if not before, members of the Franco family, having given up all hope that Franco would alter the line of succession in favor of his granddaughter's husband, Don Alfonso de Borbón-Dampierre, the Duque de Cádiz, had begun to think seriously about the future. The caudillo would soon die and Juan Carlos would become king. This seemed inevitable, making their own future uncertain. The new king might reform the system, or it might simply collapse altogether, and at what cost to themselves could not be known.

Villaverde and his son-in-law, the Duque de Cádiz, began conversations with Juan Carlos concerning their future finances and legal or political liability. The extended Franco family was wealthy enough, but that wealth lay mainly in real estate in Spain (and very secondarily in the two warehouses full of expensive gifts received over the years, which might be hard to convert into much cash). They were particularly concerned about the sale of properties, the transfer of funds abroad, and a guarantee from the crown of immunity concerning whatever might have taken place under the dictatorship. These conversations continued intermittently over a period of several months in 1975, and both the Villaverdes and Don Alfonso and his wife received special diplomatic passports, freeing them from customs inspections and other limitations, but the conversations eventually broke down.[44] In October, as the caudillo lay dying, Juan Carlos and Villaverde came across each other at a one-day hunting party outside Madrid. Villaverde told the prince that he would take his immediate family abroad after Franco died, and there he would write a book about Franco from the inside that would generate considerable income.[45] In fact, the voluntary exile never took place (not being politically necessary) and the book never appeared, though Villaverde would make an abortive effort to get something published in English much later, around 1993.[46]

As far as the danger of political reprisal was concerned, Juan Carlos was categorical that his reign would begin without victors or vanquished. There would be no return to the kind of "historical justice" that the leaders of the Second Republic had sought so arbitrarily to apply to the fallen monarchy in 1931–32 or that Franco had imposed after the Civil War ended. He was grateful for the support he had received from Franco and firm that there must be no reprisals against his family.

Altogether, the prince made three different trips to the Pazo de Meirás during Franco's summer vacation of 1975. His third visit, in mid-August, had as its aim to protest being spied on by Spanish state intelligence, which brought Franco reports on his activities and his contacts with the opposition. Juan Carlos affirmed his loyalty and insisted that the future head of state should not be under surveillance in his own country. Franco's reply is unknown, but it seems to have been a mild one. At any rate, they spent the rest of the morning together at the local golf course.[47] Franco remained firm in his decision for Juan Carlos, but he was much less happy about the current political situation and the reports about the range of the prince's contacts with the opposition. If he had in fact had any plans to accelerate the coronation, these were now postponed sine die. Franco was convinced that he must stay at the helm for some time more to straighten things out, though in fact with each passing month matters seemed to become more complicated.

During the last year or two of his life Franco sometimes sat with his eyes closed, even when others were present. It seemed as though he were asleep, but often he was simply conserving strength and energy, and on occasion he would say a few words that indicated he was fully awake. He also could be brought out of his protracted silences by a statement or event that might touch his personal feelings and arouse strong emotion, even to the point of tears. During his final summer in the Pazo de Meirás, he received a visit from the Brotherhood of Provisional Lieutenants, veteran volunteer officers from the Civil War who once more affirmed its absolute loyalty. This was too much for the generalissimo, who broke down emotionally. His military aide described the scene: "It was hot and Franco collapsed, beginning to sob like a child. I handed him dark glasses and ordered the lieutenants to withdraw. Franco continued to weep on my shoulder, while exclaiming 'They want to destroy Spain!' It was a terrible scene."[48] He seemed almost in a state of collapse, though he recovered fairly quickly.

The final months of his life were complicated by the accelerating conflict over the Spanish Sahara, the westernmost part of the great desert that stretched to the Atlantic coast and bordered southern Morocco. Spain had obtained dominion over this territory early in the century but only occupied it in 1934. Its large phosphate deposits were finally being mined by 1973, and two years later nearly three million tons were exported. Otherwise the region was bereft of significant resources; its population consisted of no more than eighty thousand indigenous inhabitants, mainly bedouin. The Sahara became a nominal Spanish province in 1959, and in 1967 the government created a provincial assembly, which it stocked with one hundred indigenous notables, a few of them also *procuradores* in the Cortes in Madrid.

Though this region had never been under Moroccan sovereignty, King Hassan's government in Rabat long coveted the Sahara, and it had become a major issue. Since 1956, Franco had adhered to the principle that Spain would retire from African territories when circumstances absolutely required it. The protectorate in northern Morocco, the enclave of Ifni, and Equatorial Guinea had all been given up, one by one. There was no point in resisting the tide of history and thus, despite the community of interest between the regimes of Franco and Salazar, Franco had refused to support Portugal in the colonial wars in which it had been involved from 1961 on. Since the Saharans made it almost unanimously clear that they did not want to be taken over by the alien dynasty in Rabat, Madrid obligated itself in 1973 to guarantee the territorial integrity of the region, promising its inhabitants a statute of autonomy that would recognize the right to self-determination. An electoral census of the native population was carried out the following year and a referendum, in accordance with the recommendations of the United Nations, was scheduled for early in 1975.

Hassan became enraged, since the Saharans were bent on independence and would never vote to be taken over by Morocco. Moreover, the new Saharan independence movement, the Frente Polisario, as the Spanish called it, had found an ally in the Algerian government, a bitter foe of Hassan. Conversely, the United States and France backed Morocco, since at that time Algeria was a fairly close associate of the Soviet Union, and they were convinced that an independent Sahara would fall under Soviet influence. Hassan petitioned the International Tribunal in The Hague to recognize the Moroccan claim, and the United Nations suspended the referendum pending the court's decision. To increase pressure on Madrid and score political points at home, Hassan also asserted Morocco's right to Ceuta and Melilla, the Spanish cities on the North African coast. He created his own Sahara Liberation Front to engage in guerrilla activities inside the region, but on May 23, 1975, the Spanish government announced that it would transfer power to the indigenous population as soon as possible, pending the tribunal's declaration and the holding of the referendum.

In negotiation with Spanish representatives, Hassan made it clear that he did not want a war, but that one way or another Morocco must have the Spanish Sahara. He knew that Madrid was in a weak position and specified that he was not seeking an immediate and total withdrawal, for he wanted to prepare administrative cadres and colonizers to implant in the territory. Therefore he urged that Spain begin a carefully phased withdrawal, allowing Morocco to take over the Sahara district by district. Hassan could not win agreement, however, because of Franco's earlier pledge of self-determination. Nonetheless, the Arias government was having second thoughts and, without any public pronouncement, was becoming more amenable to the Moroccan position. War in the Sahara was unthinkable, and during the summer of 1975 the army command drew up plans for Operation Swallow (Operación Golondrina), according to which, when the time came, its forces would evacuate the Sahara zone by zone.

Meanwhile, on August 22, the government approved a new measure to tighten prosecution of alleged acts of terrorism, transferring jurisdiction once more to military tribunals. Four days later a new antiterrorism law established the death penalty for killing a policeman or any other state employee. A selective wave of arrests followed that virtually shut down the FRAP terrorist network. Altogether, 1975 was shaping up as the most violent year in Spain since the armed insurgency of the 1940s, with eight policemen killed during the first eight months of the year. Subsequently the new law was applied retroactively to the cases of eleven revolutionaries from ETA and FRAP who had been convicted for the deaths of three policemen.[49]

These sentences occasioned the biggest international campaign against the regime ever waged by the European left, some of whom exhibited greater indignation over the punishment of these killers than they had, for example, over the Soviet invasion of Czechoslovakia or would, subsequently, over the Communist genocide in Cambodia. Pope Paul VI twice urged commutation, though Franco apparently would not receive his calls. Both Don Juan and Prince Juan Carlos made the same request, as did the generalissimo's elderly and ailing brother Nicolás, oldest living representative of the Franco family.[50] After the Burgos trial five years earlier, Franco had commuted the maximum penalty, apparently at the behest of his cabinet. In this case two-thirds of the government ministers voted to uphold the death sentences, and the somewhat unstable Arias was shrill in his insistence to Franco that the government's authority must be sustained, just as he had been the preceding year in the Añoveros affair.[51] Applying his customary rule of thumb in such matters, the caudillo commuted the sentences of six of the condemned, but five were executed on September 27. This touched off massive and emotional demonstrations against the regime in many European cities, at least two of which were led by prime ministers.[52] Spanish tourist offices, banks, and consulates were assaulted, and the venerable embassy in Lisbon, the Palacio da Palhavã, totally gutted. Fifteen governments withdrew their ambassadors for consultation.

Arguably the only beneficiary of the crackdown on the opposition was Washington. On September 22, as the crisis was building, Franco had instructed his foreign minister, Pedro Cortina Mauri, to go ahead and sign the new agreement on military bases substantially on American terms. Spain relinquished the insistence on a full treaty or a mutual security guarantee. Franco understood well enough that another crisis of international ostracism was developing, and he wanted to be sure of solid relations with Washington. The new agreement, which provided for increased military aid, was announced on October 4, though full ratification would take some time.

Franco professed to be unmoved and untroubled, for he was used to withstanding criticism and pressure from abroad. The tension of September, however, most notably the two attempts by the pope to dissuade him, was different and took its toll.[53] He became increasingly agitated and had trouble sleeping, quite unusual for him. This strain was a factor in the onset of his fatal illness soon afterward. He may also have blamed Arias for having

stacked the deck on him and is said to have reiterated his earlier pronouncement that the prime minister would not survive the end of the year.[54]

The usual crowd assembled in front of the royal palace in the Plaza de
Oriente on October 1, 1975, to hail him on the thirty-ninth anniversary of
his elevation to power, the last that he would celebrate. Though he stood
on a footstool, many could barely see the shrunken caudillo over the side
of the balcony from which he spoke. Franco declared that "everything that
has been gotten up in Spain and Europe results from a Masonic-leftist
conspiracy of the political elites, in conjunction with Communist-terrorist
subversion in society, which honors us nonetheless but degrades them,"
concluding that "evidently to be Spanish is once again something serious
in the world. ¡Arriba España!"[55] Though the words repeated standard
ideas, gone was the icy aplomb of earlier times, for Franco's voice was
feeble and his expression sad and teary eyed. For an instant he even turned
to fall sobbing into the arms of Juan Carlos (who stood behind him), as he
had become wont to do when overcome with emotion. That same day,
four policemen were slain in different parts of Madrid by a new terrorist
organization with the acronym GRAPO, and several more policemen died
four days later.

Franco's last public appearance took place on October 12, when he
appeared at a ceremony in the Institute of Hispanic Culture (Instituto de
Cultura Hispánica), whose president was Alfonso de Borbón. At one point
television implacably revealed an enfeebled dictator making three successive failed attempts to rise to his feet unassisted. The weather had suddenly
become unusually cold for mid-October, and the heat in the building had
not yet been turned on. Franco became chilled and was somewhat feverish
by the time he got back to El Pardo. Diagnosed with a cold or, at worst,
the flu, he seemed to be recovering, but on the fifteenth he suffered a minor
heart attack, having ignored instructions from his physicians to suspend all
activities. Though his vital signs were good and he claimed to feel all right,
henceforth he was surrounded with elaborate medical care around the
clock. Since Franco had indicated that, after his experience the preceding
year, he never wanted to return to a hospital again, his quarters at El Pardo
were converted into an ad hoc clinic, staffed by medical personnel that
eventually totaled thirty-eight specialists, nurses, and assistants. Several of
the attending physicians slept there, though night service was not easy,
since the notoriously austere caudillo insisted that it was important to save
energy and turn off all the lights. The medical personnel sometimes had
difficulty finding their way through the darkened palace.[56]

Franco's last concern was with Morocco, where his career had begun sixty-three years earlier. On October 16 the International Tribunal ruled that Morocco had no claim to the Sahara, sovereignty over which lay with the Saharan people. This accorded with Spain's position, but Hassan refused to accept it, knowing that he would have American backing to seize the Sahara, since Washington wanted to safeguard it from the influence of pro-Soviet Algeria. Hassan announced the imminence of the "Green March," a mass movement into the Spanish Sahara by several hundred thousand Moroccan civilians (with armed military units infiltrated among them). The notion was that they would begin "peaceful occupation" of the Sahara, daring Spanish troops to fire on unarmed civilians. Franco was surprised and distressed, since to that point he had seemed convinced that Hassan was bluffing.[57]

This precipitated a crisis for the Spanish government, which met at El Pardo on the morning of the seventeenth. When his physicians told him that he was too weak to preside and might collapse, Franco replied that he had an ineluctable responsibility to do so, declaring, "All right, if I die, what difference does it make?"[58] He directed his final cabinet meeting connected by sensors to indicators in an adjoining room on which the medical personnel monitored his vital signs. The session consisted of only brief reports by three ministers and lasted scarcely more than twenty minutes, but at one point the caudillo's pulse shot upward. He had scarcely spoken during the brief meeting and, once it was over, he returned to bed and to the ministrations of his physicians. He would never really direct the government again, and it was clear to him that this time he was not likely to recover.[59]

Prince Juan Carlos visited him daily, sometimes only for a brief greeting, though, depending on Franco's energy, they might chat for a while. Franco's last words to him, according to Juan Carlos, emphasized the unity of Spain. He recalled, "More than the words, what surprised me was the strength with which he clasped my hands within his, and the intensity of his look as he told me that the only thing he asked was that I preserve the unity of Spain. . . . I will never forget that last look."[60]

The last time that he entered his private office was probably on the eighteenth, the date that remained on the desk calendar, whose pages were turned only by Franco. On Sunday the nineteenth his bedroom was converted into a chapel where the family chaplain, Padre Bulart, said Mass and administered extreme unction. Mass was said daily for the next two weeks. Franco got out of bed one more time on the twentieth to receive a visit from Valcárcel, president of the Cortes, too official an occasion for him to hold in the bedroom. It may have been on the morning of the twenty-first that Franco called in his daughter, Carmen, to bring him a short text from his study that he had probably prepared weeks before, a public statement that would be his final message to the Spanish people. She found the document and read over the text with him to clarify several items, after which he asked her to prepare a clean copy on a typewriter. Franco ordered Carmen to guard it in the strictest secrecy until after his death, since at that moment he was still not ready to give up.[61]

Soon afterward, when Arias arrived at El Pardo, the physicians told him that Franco's condition was so parlous that he could hardly continue. If he insisted on still exercising power, he would soon collapse and die. Exclusive devotion to recovery would be the only way to preserve his life a little longer. Villaverde himself accepted that the time had come to transfer power, and Arias left to speak with Juan Carlos. When he returned to El Pardo at about 7 p.m. to meet with Franco, the physicians tried to prevent a lengthy political discussion, but the caudillo insisted on going ahead, and once more his vital signs were monitored throughout. Arias reported on the state of negotiations with Morocco, and Franco inquired about the depth of the minefield protecting the frontier, repeating his conviction that Hassan was bluffing. When the president quoted the physicians' verdict that he must abandon all activity, the old dictator feigned surprise, saying that he was feeling surprisingly well, which indicated that he would only willingly transfer power if he found himself in a state of absolute collapse. It may have been that he was hoping to survive at least until November 26, when he could renew the mandate of Valcárcel as head of the Council of the Realm. Franco had not been able to find a replacement for Arias but could only hope that Valcárcel, in his leadership role, would manage to come up with a list of reliable candidates for the next head of government.[62]

Two days later his condition worsened considerably, leading Arias and Valcárcel to make a joint visit to Juan Carlos to propose that he take over the duties of chief of state on an interim basis, as in the summer of 1973. This time the prince flatly refused. He would not act as chief of state in a temporary capacity, only to have the rug pulled out from under him again. Franco should remain in direct control as long as he was able to do so, after which his successor should have full powers. Juan Carlos even went to El Pardo to explain his position, apparently drawing no response from the caudillo, who still thought he would be able to hold on a little longer.[63] The prince was desperate enough to ask Welles Stabler, the American ambassador, to inquire whether Washington would be willing to indicate formally to Franco that the American government believed that the time had come for him to transfer powers, but Henry Kissinger refused to interfere.[64]

By October 26, Franco's condition had deteriorated to the point that the Madrid newspapers published special editions featuring the headline "Franco Is Dying." Father Bulart once more administered extreme unction. Franco's emotional distress, in addition to his physical afflictions, was such that he began to suffer from "stress ulcers" of increasingly large dimensions. When Carmen read to him a telegram from Pope Paul praying for "divine aid" and giving his "apostolic blessing," Franco burst into tears and said "it was about time."[65] Arias decided he could no longer delay ordering the initial phase of Operation Morning Star (Operación Lucero), the measures designed by the intelligence services to assure there would be no disorder or lapse in security attending Franco's death. This operation entailed increased surveillance of all kinds and a series of preventive arrests of opposition figures.

On the thirtieth Franco suffered another mild heart attack and was diagnosed with acute peritonitis, as well as other maladies. When he received this news, the caudillo finally threw in the towel, indicating that the time had come to put into effect article 11 of the succession law, transferring power to Juan Carlos. Assured by physicians that Franco's condition had become irreversible, the prince then accepted the transmission of authority. Though Franco would live for three more weeks, a personal dictatorship of nearly four decades had in fact come to an end.[66]

The most immediate problem facing the government was the Green March and the fate of the Sahara. Arias and his ministers had already decided on October 17 that they would have to abandon the promise of self-determination, and on the following day the army command dispatched instructions to be ready to begin Operation Swallow, the phased withdrawal. Solís Ruiz, minister of the movement, who supervised the Moroccan ruler's investments in Spain, had been dispatched to Rabat to negotiate with Hassan, who agreed to postpone the Green March briefly to give the Spanish time to begin withdrawal. This was an ignominious denouement for the government in Madrid, which reneged completely on earlier guarantees to the Saharans. It is not clear that Franco ever learned of this change of policy by his last government.

As acting chief of state, Juan Carlos immediately called a cabinet meeting, which was all the more necessary because Arias, despite his own personal differences with Franco, was undergoing severe emotional stress. Juan Carlos then flew to El Aaiún, the capital of the Spanish Sahara, on November 2 to bolster the morale of the troops, saying that they would neither fire on civilians nor merely abandon their positions; instead, an orderly withdrawal would be negotiated.

Meanwhile, in his bed at El Pardo, the severely stricken caudillo exclaimed to his personal physician, "How hard this is!" when he had to undergo extraction of a lump of coagulated blood from his pharynx. During these final days of consciousness, the old soldier was variously quoted as lamenting to his family and physicians "My God! What a struggle it is to die!" or "I didn't realize dying was so hard!," as his daughter has confirmed. Her mother, Doña Carmen, had herself suffered from heart trouble in recent years, and was also under great stress and in danger of becoming a patient, as well.

After the end of October, the plan of the family and physicians was to allow Franco to die quietly at home in El Pardo, without any further major intervention. On November 3, however, he suffered a massive, at first uncontrollable, gastric hemorrhage, provoked by an expanding ulcer. The attending physicians thought they heard a barely conscious Franco say something like "Please leave me. It's hard to die," though they could not be sure.[67] He was on the verge of death, and Carmen, on behalf of the family, told the medical staff to do whatever they thought best. The specialists decided that he could not be allowed to drown in his own blood. They established an emergency surgical post in the medical room of his palace guard, where, after several hours of surgery, his life was saved, but just barely, with seven liters of blood transfused. From this point on he was increasingly sedated.

The Moroccan foreign minister had meanwhile traveled to Madrid, and an arrangement was made that recognized the partition of the Spanish Sahara between Morocco to the north and Mauritania to the south, the former gaining the lion's share. The Spanish forces had already begun their phased withdrawal, and the Green March would be allowed to advance ten kilometers into the Sahara to register a propaganda victory. This commenced on the sixth, but the tens of thousands of marchers stopped after only three kilometers for fear of running into a Spanish minefield. Final negotiations for the hasty abandonment were concluded among representatives of the three governments between the twelfth and the fourteenth, when it was agreed that Spanish forces would complete withdrawal by February 28, 1976. Under such pressure, Franco's earlier pledge of self-determination could not be honored, and the United Nations mandate for a plebiscite for the population was ignored. To avoid conflict, the Saharans were abandoned to their fate—years of harsh exploitation by Morocco accompanied by numerous atrocities, another of the disasters in the history of what is usually called "decolonization."[68] This episode has been called by some the most ignominious act in the history of Spain's international relations, but amid the crisis of transition the new leaders of the Spanish state felt incapable of facing a major challenge abroad.

During the next weeks the agony of Franco would constitute an unprecedented spectacle of prolonged and public death, as daily medical bulletins, guarded in expression yet increasingly dire, were flashed around the world. The *New York Times* alone maintained three full-time correspondents in Madrid for the deathwatch. Though Franco had earlier said privately that he hoped his death would be a "rapid" one ("con cierta rapidez"), this was denied him, as he became one of the millions of the hopelessly ill and moribund kept alive artificially by the ingenious ministrations of their physicians.[69] Symptoms of thrombophlebitis and partial kidney failure appeared. Franco's daughter and other family members began to express uncertainty as to whether it was just to permit him to suffer further. His sister, Pilar, was adamant that he be allowed simply to die in peace.

Though Franco had made it known that he did not want to return to a hospital, the medical team concluded that there was no alternative, and Villaverde directed that he be transferred to the nearby Hospital de la Paz, where Villaverde was director of heart surgery, though he did not participate in the procedure. A second complex surgery was carried out, resectioning Franco's stomach in a gastrectomy that required transfusing six more liters of blood, all of which once more barely sufficed to sustain life. Potential donors in considerable numbers lined up outside the hospital to offer their blood. Organ donors also stepped forward. Franco's kidneys had ceased to function, so that he was placed on permanent dialysis. After this, however, the patient rallied for two or three days, to the astonishment of the physicians, one of whom termed Franco "an extraterrestrial." The respiratory tube was briefly withdrawn, but the rally was short, and in a day or so it had to be reattached. At one point Doña Carmen entered the room and implored him to open his eyes. He refused, although he did so after the visitors left, and then his attendants saw that his eyes were full of tears. Juanito, his faithful valet, who had retired from duty not long before, had returned for the final crisis and pointed out that "they don't realize that he doesn't want for anyone to see him this way."[70] On the twelfth, Franco was raised to a sitting position for one hour to carry out vital respiratory physiotherapy. Two days later, on the fourteenth, one of the sutures burst, producing more massive hemorrhaging that was accompanied by acute peritonitis, requiring a third major surgery. From that time Franco was completely sedated and never regained consciousness. Eventually his body was "hibernated" at a temperature of 33 degrees (about 85 degrees Fahrenheit).[71]

Rumors spread, as the agony continued without end, that the family and political associates were determined to sustain life artificially in order to prolong Valcárcel's presidency of the Cortes when it came to an end on November 26, so as to avoid any immediate political change.[72] That may have been Franco's intention in October, but there is no evidence that his family members harbored any such ambition, for this had become impossible after powers had been transferred to Juan Carlos at the end of the month. Carmen Franco vehemently denies it, and she is supported by the physicians, who took responsibility themselves for continuing the procedures.[73] The indications are that the family had given up any hope months earlier that the existing political structure would be preserved. Carmen says that the prolongation of her father's life was due above all to the professional insistence of the medical specialists:

> Yes, physicians are a little manic about that. . . . But when you have reached the end there's no point to it. . . . Yes, it was a series of circumstances. It was very hard, very hard, because it went on so long and I feel a bit responsible for having let him be taken to La Paz, where he died. The truth is that no more could be done, because when the organs begin to fail, it's better not to insist, but the doctors are determined to carry on the struggle to the end. It was more a decision by them than by the family. In the family we were all wiped out. There was a series of heart specialists, because that was the original problem, and then the intestinal surgeons, because of the hemorrhages. And these were the ones who decided to go on. And we could not deny them. That goes without saying. . . . Above all . . . when you see a person bleeding like that.

After the third surgery, Villaverde took a dozen or so photos of the moribund Franco in his elaborate medical support system, for the historical record, he said.[74]

Carmen Franco kissed her father's forehead for the last time as she left the hospital on the evening of November 19. A little later, the acting cardiologist informed Villaverde, who was sleeping in the next room, that Franco was being kept alive only by manual heart message, at which point Villaverde gave orders to cease further efforts and is said to have disconnected the life-support tubes himself. His wife recounts: "My husband did it. Cristóbal was with all the doctors and knew there was nothing more to do. At that point I spent more time with my mother, since my father was unconscious. . . . I was worried more about her, since she also had heart trouble, really more concerned about her, because my father was no longer aware of who was with him. That was the end."

Religious gestures of all sorts were made throughout Spain. Sacred relics were dispatched from the provinces to join the petrified hand of Santa Teresa, which Franco always kept near his bed. Meanwhile, according to reports, champagne supplies were several times exhausted at the headquarters of émigré opposition parties in Paris, where the successive notices of Franco's deteriorating condition provoked several premature celebrations. At the end the little old man weighed only forty kilos (eighty-eight pounds), having received enough blood to completely transfuse him ten times over. His heart stopped beating in the early hours of November 20, and this time it was agreed there was no point in trying to revive him. The official announcement stipulated death at 3:20 a.m.[75] He was fourteen days short of his eighty-third birthday. The official report on the cause of death read like a medical dictionary: "Parkinson's disease. Cardiopathy . . . Acute recurrent digestive ulcers with repeated massive hemorrhages. Bacterial peritonitis. Acute kidney failure . . . Thrombophlebitis . . . Bronchial pneumonia. . . . Endotoxic shock. Cardiac arrest."[76]

On the morning of November 20 a weeping Arias Navarro read Franco's final message on national television. It began:

> Spaniards: When the hour comes for me to surrender my life before the Most High and appear before His implacable judgment, I pray that God may receive me graciously into His presence, for I sought always to live and die as a Catholic. In the name of Christ I glory, and my constant will has been to be a faithful son of the Church, in whose bosom I am going to die. I ask pardon of all, as with all my heart I forgive those who declared themselves my enemies, though I might not have held them to be such. I desire and believe to have had none other than those who were enemies of Spain, which I love until the final moment and which I promised to serve until my last breath, which I know to be near.

He thanked all who had supported him and charged them to serve equally well his successor, King Juan Carlos. They must beware of "the enemies of

Spain and of Christian civilization," while striving for "social justice" and the unity of Spain. "I should like, in my final moment, to join the names of God and of Spain and to embrace you all to cry together, for the last time, at the moment of my death, Arriba España! Viva España!" It was the testament of a devout Catholic, and it may have provided the first example in modern history of a dictator asking for pardon from his foes (even if "enemies of Spain"), although this took place posthumously.

The first corpore insepulto funeral mass was held that day in the chapel at El Pardo, attended only by some of the immediate family, as well as Juan Carlos and Sofía. Cardinal Tarancón presided, with two other priests. He had had his political differences with the caudillo, but his words were both generous and fair minded:

> I think that no one with me here will fail to recognize the complete dedication, even the daily obsession, with which Francisco Franco devoted himself to work for Spain, for the spiritual and material growth of our country. To the point even of forgetting his own life.
>
> This service to the Fatherland—as I have said on other occasions—is also a religious virtue. There is no incompatibility between true love of the Patria and Christian faith.
>
> He who struggled so long and hard in self-sacrifice for our Fatherland will surrender today into the hands of God this effort, which will have been his way of loving, with its human limitations. Like those of everyone, but generous and earnest, always. I am certain that God will pardon his failings, will reward his best efforts, and will recognize his striving. With our prayers today, we join with him in seeking that this pardon and this recognition be complete.[77]

Twenty days of official mourning were decreed, and all public entertainments were to remain closed until the twenty-third. Hundreds of thousands filed past his bier in Madrid as he lay in state in the Royal Palace on November 21 and 22. The longest vigil was maintained by a red-eyed Vicente Gil, who stood near the coffin for many hours. "I want to be beside the Chief until the final moment," he said.[78] According to an opinion survey, 80 percent of Spaniards polled qualified his death as a loss, but 90 percent declared their positive opinion of the succession of Juan Carlos (in one sense validating Franco's judgment).[79]

Nonetheless, the forty-eight hours following Franco's death were a time of great tension for the prince. The law of succession stipulated that power now passed momentarily to a triumvirate headed by the president of the

Cortes, which had to be convened in order to proceed to the coronation of Juan Carlos. Until that took place, anything might happen. The military ministers had already pledged their loyalty to Juan Carlos, so that the principal danger would stem from the state leaders, Valcárcel and Arias Navarro, and the ultras within the regime. Franco's testament was, however, a strong public re-endorsement, and soon after her father's death Carmen delivered to the prince Franco's handwritten original text, asking of him only that he retain Arias as president.[80] Valcárcel convened the Cortes on the twenty-second to receive the official oath of Juan Carlos as king of Spain. The coronation speech was very discreet, containing almost nothing that would offend diehards, though Juan Carlos also promised that "The king wants to be so of everyone, and of each one in his own culture, history and tradition." He promised the "improvements" ("perfeccionamientos") that the Spanish people sought but took care not to define them. The immediate transition was thus consummated without incident. Later that day, the king paid a brief visit to El Pardo, assuring the ailing and grieving Doña Carmen that she and her family would have nothing to fear so long as he was king. A special mass of celebration for the coronation of the king, attended by many heads of state and foreign dignitaries, was held five days later.

Franco's public funeral took place at an improvised altar in front of the Palacio de Oriente on the twenty-third, with the cardinal primate Marcelo González Martín officiating, Tarancón having denied an earlier request by Franco that it take the form of a "conciliar mass" with all the bishops of Spain participating. Later that day the last great avatar of the traditional Spanish national-Catholic ideology was laid to rest in front of the high altar in the great basilica of the Valley of the Fallen.[81] With him was buried a millenary tradition whose roots lay thirteen centuries in the past.

Conclusion

Franco in the Perspective of History

Franco stamped his name on an entire epoch in the history of his country, and even some of his enemies recognized that he had become the most dominant figure in Spain since the time of Philip II. No traditional king held the powers and capacity for penetration, as political scientists term it, of this strong twentieth-century dictator. In addition, whatever his intentions, he presided over a transformation of the country's society, culture, and economic structure.

After his death, many figures in his regime commented on their former leader, and one of the most telling evaluations was made by José Larraz, an early finance minister:

> General Franco had intuition for simple things and was naturally astute but lacked great talent for complex matters. He lacked all cordiality and also was never afflicted by nerves yet possessed great tenacity and was able to ride out the worst storms. He acted as if he were a Galician trained among

Moors, who might also have read *The Prince*. His personal culture was rather mediocre. Franco's private life had no blemish, while in public affairs no one could make him take a bribe. His aspirations for Spain were undeniably good, and his goals for the working classes excellent. In my time, he worked on public affairs without ceasing, albeit in a disordered way. He lacked proper training as a statesman and always needed a civilian adviser. He had good instinct for navigating through the sea of international affairs. He perceived, if crudely, the great transformation under way in contemporary society, though he lacked political delicacy and suffered from one presumption that bordered on the ridiculous: the pretense that he could understand and deal with economic affairs. Though modest in appearance, he had an overly high opinion of himself, which was evident in his calligraphy, even the way he signed his name. With what satisfaction did he sit, for the first time, on the throne of the kings of Spain in the Palacio de Oriente in Madrid to receive the credentials of a foreign ambassador! This grand idea of himself at times led him to laughable declarations. One day he told me that he would restore Cuba and Puerto Rico to Spanish sovereignty. . . . Moreover, his high opinion of himself and zeal to dominate made him prefer mediocre ministers. "I prefer the docile to the competent," he once told me in impulsive but sincere words.[1]

He belonged to the age of European dictators, of Mussolini, Stalin, and Hitler. Franco was no more than the fourth most important of this group, but, in some ways, he was arguably the most normal person among them and perhaps for this reason the most successful dictator. Mussolini suffered from emotional bipolarity, while Franco was as level as could be. Hitler and Stalin revealed profound psycho-emotional aberrations that had no counterpart in Franco. There was no element of sadism in his makeup and only limited paranoia. Franco never had a former ally executed, as did Hitler and Stalin. He was never known to fall into a rage or throw the kind of fit common to Hitler and to a lesser degree to the other two. In fact, he hardly ever spoke very badly of anyone, except in the abstract. Compared with the other three dictators, he suffered from no sexual aberrations or excesses. He was the only one to be a completely loyal and devoted husband and father. And he was the only Christian of the lot, however limited his charity and spirituality.

In some respects he was also the most successful, in one sense even more than the seemingly all-victorious Stalin. Franco failed altogether in his goal of making Spain a significant military power, yet he left behind a happier, more successful, more prosperous, and more modern society than the one over which he initially took control, and that was more than could be said of Stalin, who created a great military power but destroyed part of his society in the process and reduced much of it to misery, further retarding its historical development. Conversely, while part of the success achieved by and under Franco was due to his leadership, other aspects depended on the very limitations of that power and on the era in which his dictatorship found itself.

Franco's capacity to command was first demonstrated in Morocco, though the lengthy counterinsurgency campaigns in which he gained experience were not at all similar to the twentieth-century world wars. In Morocco he never commanded anything larger than a brigade, though he played an elite role, first as an officer of *regulares* and then as co-organizer and subsequently commander of the legion. The army in which he served was small and second rate, yet it produced no senior officer generally more capable than Franco. It produced officers who were more intelligent and many who were jollier and more likeable and certainly more personally popular, as well as a certain number with greater technical knowledge, but there were none better endowed with a combination of self-control, astuteness, firm judgment, professional ability, political discretion, and the singular capacity to command.

Franco became the greatest political general in Spanish history, yet, prior to 1936 he had been a strict professional, not a political general at all. That had been an important part of his initial prestige. He did not engage in conspiracy, though he maintained contacts with those who did. Circumstances moved him to the center of the political stage, though that could not have taken place had he not been motivated, at the same time, by considerable ambition. Strong ambition was present from the start of his career, though it did not take a directly political form until the last months before the Civil War.

Franco's critics accuse him of pure opportunism and lust for power, of being a leader who lacked political principles or ideology. It is certain that he himself never formulated a specific new ideology of his own; like most major political actors, he used the ideas of others. He nonetheless held firmly to certain core values, which changed little over the course of his long life. His attitudes stemmed from his military and Catholic background and only crystallized fully during the ten-year period from 1926 to 1936, when he held a series of increasingly important commands. His values were grounded in a profound dedication to his concept of a semitraditional

Spain, its unity and its mission, an outlook commonly categorized as "Spanish nationalism," even though it was broader than such a term might imply. He was a firm believer in a new imperial role for Spain, growing up, as he did, in the heyday of European imperialism. He never directly opposed the democratic Republic, whose legitimacy he long accepted, but Franco personally favored a strong and authoritarian government, as did many European military leaders of his generation. His principles were fundamentally Monarchist, as he believed monarchy was the most legitimate form of government, though he did not favor it in every circumstance. Franco was a staunch, eventually devout, Catholic of the traditional sort. Unlike his colleague Mola, he preferred close association of church and state, even though he had accepted separation under certain circumstances. He hoped for and promoted the revival of a more Catholic and traditional culture, and his policies, combined with the consequences of the civil war, helped temporarily to bring this culture about. Franco also believed in the vital need to develop a stronger, more modern and productive economy that could transform living standards and achieve what he called "social justice." Of Franco's initial principles, only imperialism and some features of a nationalist economic policy were abandoned in the years after World War II, as he became one of the most nonmilitarist of military dictators. Nonetheless, in practice individual aspects of his core policies were altered very greatly over the years and were expressed in quite a different way at the end of his regime than at the beginning. Eventually, of all the dictators of the twentieth century, he became the one who transformed his program the most.

The coming of the Second Republic was not at all to his liking, but since the majority of Spaniards accepted its legitimacy, so did he, as long as the Republic respected the law. He remained a military professional until its final phase, eschewing overt politicization, though he had established a clear conservative identity by 1935. He did not endorse plans for insurrection, even as the situation deteriorated rapidly in the spring of 1936. Since he left neither memoirs nor many papers that are accessible, his thinking cannot be fully reconstructed, but the option that he favored was the CEDA, the moderate right that stressed obedience to the law and rejection of violence, striving to reform the Constitution and promote Catholic interests. So far as one can see, that was approximately Franco's position from 1933 to 1936. His only political initiative was an attempt to trigger the imposition of the decree of martial law signed by the president of the Republic on February 17, 1936, but never put into effect. There is no evidence that this was an effort to overturn the elections, as has frequently been charged. Rather, it was an effort to control violent disorder and see to it that the law and the electoral results were respected. Franco entered politics directly for the first time when he accepted a place on the new rightist list for the repeat elections in Cuenca in May 1936. This seems to have had two goals: to give him a chance to return to the center of affairs in Madrid and also to protect himself from the numerous arbitrary arrests being carried out under the left Republican government. Even then, he thought better of it, withdrawing under pressure from José Antonio Primo de Rivera.

As conditions steadily deteriorated, Franco sympathized more and more with the military conspirators but still would not join them fully. He understood that armed revolt would be a desperate undertaking more likely to fail than to succeed. Prior to July 15, 1936, or thereabouts, this calculation was undoubtedly correct, and most of his fellow officers thought the same. There is no reason to believe that his letter of June 23 to Casares Quiroga, protesting the army's respect for the law, was a deception, for it was consistent with the position he had always taken. So long as there was any reasonable chance that the existing situation could be rectified, military revolt lacked both justification and much prospect of success. Only after the situation had decayed to a breaking point, with both the Socialists and, to some extent, the government as well encouraging such a rebellion in order to crush it and place even more complete power in the hands of the left, did his position change. Franco only agreed to rebel when he thought it more dangerous not to.

He has frequently been denounced as the general who led a Fascist coup d'état against a democratic republic, but this allegation is incorrect in every detail. The only accurate part of this claim is that he was a general. First, the democratic Republic had been hollowed out from within, the practice of democracy and of constitutional government having generally been abandoned by the left Republican administration. Democracy and free elections had already died at the hands of the Popular Front, and that ultimately was the reason for the insurrection (even though many of the rebels were not democrats). Second, Franco was not its leader, since the organizer was Mola and the nominal chief Sanjurjo. Third, the insurrection was not Fascist, since the Falange played a subordinate role throughout. The revolt sought to install a more conservative and authoritarian kind of Republican government that left the door open to the possibility of subsequently holding referendum on the issue of monarchy. Finally, the action was not designed as a coup d'état, since it had become clear that an initial seizure of power in Madrid would be impossible. Instead, it was a general military insurrection that planned to take the capital only in its final phase.

Had democracy survived, there would have been no general insurrection from the right, just as there had been none during the first five years of the Republic. The disappearance of respect for law or property was the issue. The question at the beginning of the Civil War was not whether Spanish government was to become authoritarian—since it already was, to a degree—but what kind of arbitrary action would rectify the situation, as was accurately pointed out by Ramón Franco in Washington, as he debated with himself on whether or not to join his brother.

Spain had become the most conflictive and divided country in Europe, and Franco had little or nothing to do with creating that situation, which would have transpired had he never existed. The insurrection and Civil War was deliberately provoked by the left, who would have done so whether Franco participated in it or not. To that extent the left was as much or more responsible for the emergence of the political Franco than was the right. He became, however, the one who ended up taking responsibility, for better or worse, for resolving this situation.

The turning point was the first three months of the Civil War. There was nothing inevitable about his election as generalissimo, though that was a logical outcome of the circumstances that had developed. He was the commander of the insurgents' only effective operational force, the only one capable of defeating the Republicans, and he had generated vital foreign assistance, which he channeled and distributed to his comrades. No one else had equivalent prestige, though many held greater seniority.

There is no evidence that Franco conspired to become generalissimo, though, as soon as the insurrection began, he played a bold and assertive role. Desperate circumstances called for no less, and clear ambition had developed by September, though Franco maintained careful discretion with his fellow generals. His candidacy was vigorously promoted by a handful of supporters, and his precise role in its development will probably always remain shrouded in mystery. Most of his colleagues felt that they had little alternative but to vote for him, though with how much enthusiasm is unclear.

Once elected generalissimo, Franco showed no hesitation and never looked back. He insisted on full political power and obtained it, eliminating any time limit and transforming his leadership into one of unfettered dictatorship, though that was not quite what his military colleagues had intended. Some of them were unhappy with this outcome but accepted it.

Even a biting personal critic such as Queipo de Llano grudgingly admitted that, had they not done so, they probably would not have won the war.

The limited evidence indicates that at first he agreed with the "open" political project of Mola. Within little more than two months, however, he had moved to a different and more radical position. In the face of the violent and massive revolution in the Republican zone, he seems implicitly to have accepted the dictum of Joseph de Maistre (whom he probably had never read) that the counterrevolution was not "the opposite of a revolution" but rather "an opposing revolution."

It is beside the point to insist, as many critics of Franco reiterate, that a well-functioning democracy would have been better. This goes without saying, but it substitutes an abstract value judgment for the historically existing alternatives. No such democratic utopia was available to the Spain of 1936, hence the Civil War. The best of the available alternatives would probably have been Miguel Maura's proposal for a limited-term, semi-constitutional "national republican dictatorship," but that too had been rejected by the left. Franco did not create the crisis, but he did resolve it, whether for good or for ill.

If the Nationalists had lost the Civil War, the result scarcely would have been political democracy. The third or wartime Republic was dominated by powerful revolutionary forces dedicated to the political elimination of all antagonists, amounting to half or more of Spain. Mass executions by the Popular Front were almost as numerous as those in the Nationalist zone and, had the left won, there is no reason to believe that the final reckoning would have been more moderate, since new executions took place whenever a small piece of territory was briefly seized by the People's Army in 1937–38. The long-term strength of Franco's dictatorship stemmed not merely from its power of repression, great though that was, but also from the awareness in a large part of the population that the leftist alternative would not have been so different.[2]

The eclecticism of the National Movement stemmed naturally from its heterogeneous composition, which was adroitly manipulated by its caudillo. Moreover, Franco shared, at least to a limited degree, some of the ideas of each political "family" of his regime while rejecting the ideology in toto of any of them. He accepted the principle of Monarchist rule but in a form to be determined and manipulated by himself. He shared the nationalism and imperialism of the Falangists, as he did their concept of an authoritarian regime (to the degree that theirs could be called a coherent concept) and at least a portion of their social and economic doctrine. But he rejected a full

Conclusion

"national syndicalist revolution" or "national syndicalist state" as too sweeping, infringing other values and institutions, among them his own personal power. Franco praised aspects of Carlist traditionalism, such as its ultra-Catholicism, traditional culture, and championing of a nonliberal monarchy but completely rejected what was left of the Carlist dynasty or the idea of a Carlist regime. He believed above all in the military sense of patriotism, national security, and national service, together with the elite role of the senior military, but he rejected any notion of an independent corporate role for the armed forces or a purely military dictatorship. Probably the nearest thing to a prior outline of his regime could be found in the right-radical Monarchist program of José Calvo Sotelo, which had proposed an authoritarian monarchy and an authoritarian parliament, supported by expanded armed forces, and had promoted a modern, strongly statist development program. Yet Franco had at no time supported Calvo Sotelo under the Republic, and he rejected the absolute dynastic legitimacy advocated by some of Calvo Sotelo's collaborators.

The only alternative to parliamentary government with which Franco was personally acquainted was the Primo de Rivera dictatorship, which he had initially opposed (though not out of political principle) but eventually strongly supported. When he grasped the opportunity to become generalissimo and dictator, he saw himself in some fashion as continuing that earlier enterprise, but, having watched its collapse, he understood that he must govern more effectively in order to survive. Only a matter of weeks seems to have been necessary for him to abandon Mola's original "open" project, which had never been fully codified or given official form, though it had been more or less accepted by most senior officers. He believed that the left's exploitation of parliamentary democracy to promote revolution had permanently discredited the concept of a parliamentary regime and that something more radical, dynamic, and modern was needed in order to mobilize and incorporate a Spanish society that in large part had been convulsed by revolution.[3]

The new principle in European politics in the 1930s was the one-party nationalist authoritarian state that sought to combine drastic modernization with certain aspects of national tradition and mission, thereby creating a completely alternative society and culture that was mobilized and militant—in a word, Fascism. There is no evidence, however, that Franco ever completely understood the Fascist revolutionary project or that he ever proposed to implement it fully. Rather, he proposed to use part of the Fascist scheme as a point of departure for building his own eclectic system,

508

emphasizing, when he set up the FET in April 1937, that Falangist doctrine marked only the beginning of something to be developed further. At no time did he propose that the party hold direct power or, as in Germany, a kind of parallel power but only that it fill the specific roles that he gave it. Ismael Saz calls the resulting regime "fascistized," though not fully Fascist, which seems accurate enough.[4]

The final outcome depended not merely on Franco's preferences but also on the broader currents of history, though his regime first took a turn away from the FET in mid-1941, when Hitler was at the height of his power. That turn might have been reversed had Nazi Germany gone on to victory, but, once Mussolini fell in the summer of 1943, Franco's regime moved more directly toward defascistization. This process was progressive but never fully completed.[5]

Franco was not a typical charismatic Fascist leader like Hitler or Mussolini, but the sheer trauma of the Civil War, combined with Franco's complete victory, gave him a degree of de facto legitimacy and even a certain charisma of achievement, as well as an element of traditionalist charisma as the savior of religion and traditional culture. His power was somewhat akin to that of an elective but absolute monarch, stemming first from his election by the National Defense Council. A kind of historic prototype for Franco might be Napoleon Bonaparte, who transformed the government of France. Franco would use certain Bonapartist procedures, such as the referendum (however authentic) and institutional diarchy, relying on a royal council to guarantee legitimacy, continuity, and authority (though that did not work out as he had planned). There is also a slight parallel with the reign of Enrique de Trastámara, winner of the great Castilian civil war of the 1360s. Enrique did not possess dynastic legitimacy, which lay with his defeated opponent, but he presented himself as champion of religion, law, and tradition, opposed to the imputed heterodoxy and arbitrary despotism of his predecessor, Pedro the Cruel. Foreign assistance also played a role in his victory, though the reign of Enrique did not mark so abrupt a rupture as the rule of Franco.

Despite the numerous caudillos and military dictatorships in the history of Spanish America, there is no evidence that Franco was ever influenced by such examples. Rather, several Spanish American regimes were influenced by Franco. He considered his own system to have developed within the context of the new nationalist and authoritarian regimes in Europe. With the principal exception of Argentina between 1945 and 1950, the Spanish media more often than not reflected a degree of ambiguity with regard to authoritarian regimes in the Western hemisphere. Censorship forbade applying the term "caudillo" to any Spanish American dictator, for fear of tarnishing the originality, such as it was, of the term.

The course that Franco carved out, accompanied by the prospect of victory in the Civil War, generated ambition for imperial expansion by 1938. This ambition was new and reflected the *Wechselwirkung*, or mutual radicalization, of the two sides in the war. Franco wished to restore Spain's prestige abroad and then build an empire in northwest Africa, similar to the way Portugal had developed its own modern African empire after losing Brazil. The great difference was that Portugal had done this in a timely fashion in the second half of the nineteenth century and also using only minimal resources, whereas in the twentieth century Spain could achieve such a goal only at the expense of France and would need much greater force or suasion. Hence the concept of a sort of "parallel war" of expansion in conjunction with Germany, a common temptation for European dictators, whether of right or left.

In this regard, Javier Tusell has pointed out that Franco's policy in some ways resembled Stalin's more than Mussolini's:

> It remains quite a paradox that Franco's policy may also be compared with that of Stalin. When Poland was crushed, the USSR intervened in the final phase but obtained territorial gains equal to those of Germany, while suffering military casualties less than a twentieth of the latter's. Then, taking advantage of the German victories in Western Europe, the USSR occupied the Baltic states without the slightest cost. That was the point at which Franco offered to enter the war, and undoubtedly he wished to do with French Morocco something like what Stalin had done in those eastern territories.[6]

Despite extensive collaboration with the Axis, Franco was also cautious, for within a year of the end of the Civil War he realized that recovery was going to be slow and Spain's weakness profound, at least in the short term. Hence his insistence on large-scale assistance and guarantees, which Hitler refused to provide. Even so, from 1941 to 1944 Franco agreed with Hitler that the future of his regime depended on the survival of Germany as some sort of European power. When he finally saw in the summer of 1944 that Hitler was probably not going to survive at all, he proceeded slowly to make adjustments. In the longer run, as the irony of history would have it, Franco's key contributions to foreign policy were both negative, first in never taking the final plunge to enter World War II and, second, when the time came, accepting the peaceful abandonment of all remaining overseas possessions, the very opposite of his original goal. For Spain, this had the happy result of making it the only continental country except Sweden and Switzerland never to have been involved in world war or a war of decolonization after 1939.[7] All Spaniards could be grateful for that, even the Falangists who condemned the timidity of his policies, for Franco's capacity for survival guaranteed their own.

The experience of Spain and its dictatorship from 1945 to 1948 was unique in the annals of contemporary Western states. Franco remained firm and imperturbable, qualities necessary to his political survival, and had the backing of nearly all those sectors that had supported him in the Civil War (the exceptions of Don Juan and a small subset of Monarchists proved inconsequential). No one will ever know what exact percentage of the population truly supported Franco, but what was abundantly clear was that the great majority did not want to undergo another convulsion. Hence the lack of popular support for the insurgency of the Communist and anarchist Maquis, which sought to revive the Civil War and sometimes turned to outright terrorism. A fundamental problem was that the "Spanish democratic forces" invoked by the United Nations as the alternative to Franco had largely ceased to exist after the spring of 1936, repressed by both sides during the war and not represented within the Popular Front. Julián Marías later observed with complete accuracy that most Spaniards "waited without haste" for the evolution of Franco's regime, realizing that they could not have expected much better had the other side won. The only active opposition came not so much from any "democratic forces," practically nonexistent, but from Communists and anarchists, who were not much different from the revolutionaries who had provoked the Civil War in the first place.

The most novel aspect of Franco's rule was not the political radicalism of its semi-Fascism, but its effort to restore cultural and religious traditionalism, a goal that no other European country, not even Portugal, had. The concept of a neotraditional community, basic to Franco's social and cultural thinking, stemmed from Carlism and right-wing Catholic thought. Though the creation of community was important for many modern nationalist movements and regimes, none in Europe placed such emphasis on neotraditionalism. The cognitive dissonance between this worldview and the semi-Fascist political project was managed by limiting, controlling, and then downgrading the role of Falangism.

With regard to individual policies, or aspects thereof, Franco was always a pragmatist, willing—if absolutely necessary—to make fundamental adjustments. Sometimes he could be very stubborn about it, as in his foreign policy in 1943–44, but, if adjustment was necessary, he always made it sooner or later. Consequently many critics have contended that his only fundamental principle was to hang on to power as long as he could, no matter what. In the final instance, of course, that is correct, because almost from the very beginning of his regime he took the position that he would leave power only for the cemetery, as he put it on one or two occasions. He was deeply influenced by the fate of Primo de Rivera in 1930 and of Mussolini between 1943 and 1945. Franco believed that he had mounted a tiger, which could never be safely dismounted.

After Franco's death, one of his regime's early theorists observed that "it turns out to be difficult to understand Francoism because its very development relied on ambiguity and changes of direction. The political forms that Franco established did not undergo direct continuous development, but underwent pauses and superpositions . . . I have sometimes thought that his preoccupation with the forces of chance led him to play with two decks when he spread his cards on the table, so as to have available the greatest number of combinations."[8] He never wanted to gamble everything on one bold throw or one fixed position, though that should not blind the analyst to the fact that most of his basic principles were never compromised: authoritarianism, Monarchism, cultural and religious traditionalism, a developmental national economic policy, social welfare, and national unity.

Friedrich Nietzsche observed that whatever has a history cannot be defined. The definition or simple description of Franco's regime is complicated by its two metamorphoses, which divide it into three periods:

1. The semi-Fascist and potentially imperialistic phase, 1936–45.
2. The period of national Catholic corporatism, 1945–59.
3. The period of so-called technocratic developmentalism, moving toward bureaucratic authoritarianism, 1959–75.

During its first six years, his regime declared itself "totalitarian," but that language was dropped as early as 1942, the ambiguous but semicontinuous process of defascistization beginning in the following year. By 1957, even an analyst as critical as Herbert Mathews was categorizing it not as Fascist but as "fascistoid."[9] In the 1960s, even that seemed excessive, and analysts used terms such as "authoritarian regime," "corporatism," "conservative-authoritarian," and even "limited unitarian pluralism." By Franco's last years, several specialists in Latin American politics were arguing that corporatism was the "natural" politico-economic system of the Luso-Hispanic world.

To the end of his days, however, Franco believed that the FET-National Movement still had an important, if subordinate, role to play in the mobilization of his regime. The later phases of the movement did not constitute a fully "bureaucratic authoritarianism" in Latin American style but sought, with ever-diminishing success, to institutionalize and mobilize the regime, which the government of Primo de Rivera had been unable to do. In 1964, in a classic formulation, Juan Linz termed this a non-Fascist but institutionalized "authoritarian regime."[10]

Franco was well aware that for the greater part of his rule he held the position of chief "ogre," or "last remaining Fascist dictator," among heads of state in the Western world. In this respect, it is interesting to compare attitudes toward Franco with those concerning Tito (Josip Broz) after 1948. Like Franco, Tito came to power through a revolutionary civil war (which in his case the revolutionaries won), in which, despite all the propaganda to the contrary, he dedicated more energy to combating counterrevolutionaries than to fighting the Italians and Germans. He also relied on foreign military assistance (in this case the Red Army) to take over the country. The repressive bloodbath that took place in Yugoslavia in 1945 and 1946 was both proportionately and in absolute numbers even more extensive than the one that took place in Spain between 1939 and 1942, and Tito was much more brutal than Franco and carried out many more large-scale mass executions than Franco did. In its first phase, the new dictatorship in Yugoslavia was even more extreme, inflexible, and repressive, modeled directly on the Soviet Union. However, international circumstances prompted change and moderation in Yugoslavia, as in Spain; the transformation just happened a few years later in Yugoslavia than it did in Spain. Tito's regime eventually became a nontotalitarian dictatorship of limited semipluralism, a major heresy in terms of orthodox Marxism-Leninism. It stood in sharp contrast to other Communist regimes, just as Franco's did by comparison with the Axis powers. Nonetheless, even in its final years it remained more authoritarian and repressive than did Franco's (despite the Yugoslav regime's semifederalism and very limited self-management in factories) and failed to achieve an equivalent level of cultural, social, and economic progress. Tito's death was not followed by democratization but first by a form of collegial authoritarianism and then by separatism and genocidal civil war. Yet Tito was frequently hailed in the Western press as a great reformer and innovator and soon received considerably more foreign aid from Western countries than Franco ever did.

The blackest marks on Franco's record are, first, the repression after the end of the Civil War, second, his pro-Axis policy during World War II, and third, the long repression of his country as dictator. All three charges are obviously valid ones. That Franco's repression was, in terms of the number of lives lost, no worse than that of other victors in revolutionary civil wars and in fact was less harsh than that of some, places the matter in perspective but does not mitigate the facts. The same might be said with regard to the undeniable difficulties that any government of Spain would have faced after the Civil War. To believe that the chaotic, severely divided, and mutually violent "Third Republic" would somehow have done better requires a considerable stretch of the imagination. It must be kept in mind that the Popular Front, not Franco, created conditions of civil war and arbitrary use of power in Spain in 1936, and that for a long time afterward a return to the democracy of 1931 to 1936 was unlikely, as some leftists, such as Gerald Brenan, reluctantly admitted.

Franco's most severe critics make wild charges, such as that he was the worst and most sanguinary of Western dictators, in one sense worse than Hitler because more executions took place in the first six years of the Franco regime than in the peacetime Third Reich of 1933 to 1939. Obviously a peacetime dictatorship and a revolutionary civil war do not constitute what social scientists call a comparison set. By the same anachronistic reasoning it might be alleged that the democratic Republic from April 1931 to February 1936 was also worse than the peacetime Third Reich, since it registered more political killings and instances of mini-civil war.

The hyperbole of denunciation has been racheted up to a new level in the twentieth century with the "historical memory" movement, which imputes to Franco every evil committed by a dictatorship anywhere in the world in the twentieth century. If Hitler carried out a Holocaust against the Jews, then Franco was guilty of a "holocaust" of the left in Spain; if the Turks and others have been responsible for enormous genocides, then Franco too must have committed "genocide"; if leftist victims "disappeared" under South American dictatorships, then Franco was responsible for "disappearances."

Franco perpetuated a personal dictatorship for nearly four decades and saw to it that there would be no direct political representation of the Spanish people. During its first years his rule was repressive in the extreme, approximately thirty thousand people having been executed (some of them for "political crimes"), and for decades his regime maintained a society divided between victors and vanquished. With the exceptions of Alava and Navarre, regional *fueros*, rights, languages, and cultures were repressed, though increasing leniency was shown to language and culture, which permitted a major reflowering by the last years of the regime. In economic terms the Basque provinces enjoyed a privileged position throughout. Even in the final moderate phase, however, when censorship had been greatly curtailed, the full civil rights common to contemporary Western societies did not obtain. Political authoritarianism was accompanied by favoritism and economic monopolies and often by considerable corruption, which was tied to the peculiar functioning of the regime. Franco and Carrero Blanco nonetheless did not embezzle, and the honesty and efficiency of the state bureaucracy increased notably in the later years of the regime. After the 1940s there was nothing equivalent to the massive direct corruption of the Spanish Socialist governments of 1982–96.

Evaluations differ not merely according to the evaluator but according to the kinds of questions asked. Judgments of Franco became less negative as the rigors of his rule eased, the modernization of the country accelerated, and the levels of income and education rose. One of the most widely read books about a modern dictator, Alan Bullock's *Hitler: A Study in Tyranny*, concludes with a description of Germany in ruins and cites the Roman aphorism "If you seek his monument, look around." Viewing Franco in light of this aphorism, the observer finds a country raised to the highest level of prosperity in its long history, converted into the ninth industrial power in the world, with the "organic solidarity" of the great majority of its population considerably expanded, and a society surprisingly well prepared for peaceful coexistence and a new project in decentralized democracy. Franco's policies exercised harsh judgment on the left, but they encouraged family formation and a high birthrate and resulted in improved neonatal care from the beginning, which stimulated substantial population growth. By such standards, Franco could be seen not merely as the most dominant individual ruler in all Spain's history but also as the country's definitive modernizer, leader of the most successful of all would-be "development dictatorships" of the twentieth century.

Thus a decade after Franco's death, an article in a leading upper-brow American publication would declare that "what he actually accomplished was the proto-modernization of Spain. . . . Franco left Spain with institutions of technocratic economic management and a modern managerial class which have enabled what was once a poverty-stricken agricultural country at the time of its civil war to acquire productive resources and a standard of living approximating those of its southern European neighbors. Can this be what its civil war was about?"[11] The answer to this last question is no, but the broader point is well taken.

Franco's legion of critics decry the superficiality of any such positive conclusion about his rule, insisting that the great advances made during his time were simply a product of that era and had nothing to do with him, coming about despite his rule or at least not encouraged by it. In some respects, that observation is correct, though it is normally applied too categorically. As suggested in chapter 18, one of the best approaches is that of the German Hispanist Walther L. Bernecker, who has divided the major accomplishments and changes in Spain under Franco's rule into three categories: those planned and developed by the regime, those not directly planned but nonetheless encouraged or at least accepted once they were under way, and those never foreseen and completely counterproductive for the regime but that it proved increasingly powerless to arrest.

Even many of Franco's critics find some merit in his policy during World War II, though, as has been seen, that probably deserves less praise than it has received. Only in mid-1943 did Franco's diplomacy begin to develop more fully the characteristics often imputed to it. Though he kept Spain out of the war, he failed to design and execute a policy of optimal neutrality, so that whatever merit such a policy had falls more into the second than the first of Bernecker's categories.

Similarly, though economic modernization was a primary goal, the evaluation of Franco's economic policy is equally complicated. It is frequently observed that the greatest growth took place after 1959, once the extreme statism and autarchy of the earlier period was abandoned. That observation is also correct, but it tends to overlook the considerable growth already achieved during the period between 1949 and 1958, without which the later successes would not have been possible. The liberal and international market economics of the 1960s was certainly not Franco's preferred policy, so that the initial period of expansion would fit into Bernecker's first category, while the major achievement of the liberalized phase of the 1960s would fit more into the second, a change not originally desired but one that Franco accepted. As observed earlier, many authoritarian regimes, whether of left or right, were not willing to make such adjustments.

What took Franco two decades took the Chinese Communist regime nearly twice as long, in a later and more advanced phase of the world economy, though admittedly for the Chinese regime it was a yet more drastic change. Deng Xiaoping, who transformed the Chinese dictatorship in the 1970s and 1980s, introduced three basic changes, each of them anticipated by Franco, two decades earlier: replacing a statist economic policy with growing market liberalization, replacing dogmatic ideological politics with increasing technocracy, and realigning foreign policy by embracing the United States.[12] Franco's principal emulators in combining political authoritarianism and rapid market-oriented development have been found in East Asia, though several Spanish American regimes also sought to adopt aspects of his policies. The military dictatorship of General Park Chung-hee, that ruled South Korea from 1961 to 1974, may be the non-European regime that in some respects bore the greatest similarity to that of Franco, but variants of the "Franco model" may be found in a number of countries in the twenty-first century. Franco rather expected this, though he also expected a reversion toward his policies in Western Europe, as well.

Some of Franco's alterations simply represented adjustments to the triumph of democracy in Western Europe after the Anglo-American military victory of 1945, not any prior design of his own. His personal convictions had been oriented toward Monarchism, though he had considered the monarchy a lost cause after 1931, and his relationship to Monarchism during the first decade of his dictatorship was equivocal. The eventual restoration of monarchy—in its technical design, a special kind of new "installation" (*instauración*)—was nonetheless the best possible choice for the succession to his regime, and Prince Juan Carlos was also the best candidate. Yet both choices, of monarchy and of potential monarch, were the product of creative adjustments, not necessarily of Franco's original design, though it must also be granted that he was correct that an attempt to hand power to the monarchy during or immediately after the Civil War would probably have ended in another Spanish political disaster.

By a combination of strict, sometimes harsh, policies and broad-based national development, Franco succeeded in achieving one of his major goals, an increased sense of cooperation and social solidarity. This was based on national corporatism, economic growth, and eventual redistribution of national income through structural change rather than high taxation or revolution, and also on proscription of partisan politics. To a certain extent, it was consciously programmed from the start, and its accomplishment was reflected in the conclusion of a prominent American anthropologist in 1975: "It is clear that the organic solidarity of Spain as a whole has increased."[13]

Conclusion

Franco's responsibility for the enormous improvement in the educational level of the Spanish population is more equivocal. Since nearly all students were educated in state or state-subsidized schools, it might seem that this too was a conscious part of his program, but rapid educational growth emerged as a top priority only in the later years, and then because it seemed an ineluctable feature of accelerated development. Even after a general education law was decreed in 1970, proportionate education expenditure still did not compare favorably to other industrial societies. Thus educational modernization would fall into the second category, though it might also be recognized that the quality of primary and secondary education by the 1970s had achieved a respectable level, and that the post-Franco "democratization" of education in some respects lowered its quality.

Paradoxically, another feature of institutional modernization achieved by Franco was the relative depoliticizing of the military, even though his regime began as a military government and even though Franco was always explicit in his reliance on the military to avoid destabilization. He maintained a special relationship with his generals while also holding them at a certain distance, manipulating them, switching and rotating top posts, and avoiding any concentration of power. The fact that military men held so many cabinet positions and other top administrative posts, particularly during the first half of the regime, obscured the fact that Franco prevented military interference in government and eliminated any possibility of an independent corporate or institutional role for the military outside its own professional sphere. Officers who held civil positions did so as individual administrators in state institutions, not as autonomous corporate representatives of the armed forces. Relative demilitarization of the political process was accompanied by increasing demilitarization of the state budget, due not so much to Franco's respect for education as to his disinclination to spend money on a modernization of the armed forces that might alter their internal balance.

From his own point of view, Franco's greatest failure lay in the inability to sustain the neotraditionalist cultural and religious revival that originally underlay his regime. This was not for lack of effort; it was simply the almost inevitable counterpart of social and economic transformation on a massive scale, compounded by the momentous liberalization within the Roman Catholic Church as a whole in the 1960s. Franco was aware of the contradictions that might result, which was at least partly why he was reluctant to alter his autarchic economic policy and lower national barriers in 1959. Continuation of the regime was made impossible not so much by the mere death of Franco—for the passing of Salazar had not brought the Portuguese regime to an end—as by the disappearance of the framework of society and culture on which it had originally been based. Francoist society and culture had largely been eroded even before the caudillo physically expired. Moreover, the absence of clear ideology after 1957 made it difficult for any consensus in support of a Francoist orthodoxy to develop among the regime's elites in his final years.

The aftermath of Franco's regime was in some ways more remarkable than the long history of the regime itself, for the democratization brought about by King Juan Carlos and his collaborators between 1976 and 1978 was unique in the history of regime transitions to that time. After his resignation as director general of popular culture in October 1974, Ricardo de la Cierva was asked at a press conference in Barcelona for a historical example of an institutionalized authoritarian regime that had transformed itself into a democracy without formal rupture or overthrow, as the more advanced *aperturistas* proposed to do in Spain. He replied that he was studying that very question at the moment, but the answer was of course that no such example existed.[14] Never before had the institutional mechanisms of an authoritarian system in Europe been employed peacefully but systematically to transform the whole system from the inside out.

This new "Spanish model" of democratization then served as a kind of reference for the subsequent democratization of a sizable number of authoritarian systems in places from South America to East Asia. It was part of the "third wave" of world democratization of the twentieth century, but Spain held the place of honor in initiating the process.[15] And unlike the first two waves of democratization, following 1918 and 1945, the third wave was generated in large measure by domestic processes rather than by the convulsion of world war. Its major limitation was that it did not extend to key Communist and post-Communist regimes.

The question has frequently been asked to what extent Franco foresaw or intuited such a development, but, in the absence of any primary evidence, it cannot be answered with precision. As late as the 1960s, he expressed conviction that the flourishing of liberal democratic capitalism in the West was only a temporary phase that would have to give way to systems of greater central state authority. Adolfo Suárez, the prime minister who later led the democratization, has testified that, when he reported to Franco about the progress of the UDPE, the movement's pet "political association," only weeks before the caudillo's death, Franco asked if the movement could in some guise be perpetuated. When Suárez replied that he did not think so, Franco asked if that meant that the future of Spain would be inevitably "democratic," and after Suárez responded in the affirmative, turned on his heel and said no more. The problem with this anecdote is that Suárez has recounted several different versions of it.

What is better established is Franco's insistence to Prince Juan Carlos that a new king would not be able to rule in the same way that he had. He knew that Juan Carlos would make some changes, presumably in a more liberal direction. After all, Franco himself had done the same thing, more than once. Yet Juan Carlos had sworn loyalty to the Fundamental Laws of the Realm and Franco expected, at least hoped, that he would retain much of the substance, if not the entire form, of the regime. In his final months, he probably understood that such was not likely to be the case, but by that time he was too feeble to do anything except to remain in control until his health finally collapsed and then pass on the reins of power. No matter what, he would have been skeptical that a stable democracy per se would be possible, for he remained skeptical that Spaniards had learned to cooperate effectively.[16]

The subsequent "Spanish model" of democratization was able to function as well as it did in part because of eight fundamental changes that Franco had introduced. His key institutional reform was restoration of the monarchy. In the interim, his own jealous monopoly of power prevented the identification of the monarchy with the excesses of the Civil War and its aftermath, including the long dictatorship, so that the monarchy could begin with relatively clean hands, promoting national reconciliation as the symbolic representative of all Spaniards, a moderating power above all factional conflict. Moreover, Franco chose the best candidate. To have restored Alfonso XIII in 1939 would have resulted in disaster, and succession by his heir, Don Juan, intermittently identified with liberalism and the left, would arguably have ended in a coup by the military and the extreme right. Juan Carlos, on the other hand, was able to combine continuity and legitimacy both in terms of Franco's own institutions and in those of the traditional monarchy. He then exhibited the tact and judgment required to put into motion a peaceful process of democratization.

Third, Franco had made possible the profound modernization of the social and economic structure that was a fundamental prerequisite for a functioning democracy. A prosperous, urban, and more sophisticated society, to a large extent middle-class in structure, emerged that found itself increasingly in harmony with the customs of social democratic Western Europe.

Fourth, because of the length of dictatorship, most of the partisan conflicts of the Civil War had been overcome, erased by time and transformation, making it possible to start over again with a clean slate. Though political demobilization left Spanish society without experience or knowledge of democracy, the reorganization of the opposition during 1974–75 and the new system of parties that was developed showed concern, at least for the first decades, for avoiding the mistakes of the 1930s.

Fifth, the peculiar institutional structure of Franco's regime created orderly mechanisms that, in the proper circumstances, could be exploited for fundamental reform. These procedures, limited though they were, had been variously altered at times by Franco himself, accustoming Spaniards to reforms that avoided disruptive radicalism.

Sixth, a democratic system became possible, in part, because of the great expansion of education, as well as the cultural liberalization that took place after 1966. A limited climate of political discussion had already developed in the last years of Franco's life.

Seventh, social solidarity had increased considerably, overcoming the older tendency toward class conflict, which had been a frequent tendency of European societies entering the intermediate phase of industrialization. Greater solidarity was achieved, at least to a degree, not so much because of the tutelage of the dictatorship per se but as a result of basic social and economic development and the expansion of education.

Finally, Franco disciplined and depoliticized the military, depriving it progressively of any corporate voice in government, which had the effect of reducing, at least to some extent, the danger of military revolt after his death.[17]

It will nevertheless not do to suggest, as have a few, that Franco can be given credit for the tolerant and democratic Spain of the 1980s. A dictatorship is not a school for democracy, and Franco was not responsible for the democratization of Spain, though, paradoxically, under his rule the Spanish people were able to develop most of the prerequisites for democracy. While permitting varying degrees of liberalization, he fought any basic alteration to the last and, apparently, with his dying breath hoped that Juan Carlos would not change things too much. Nevertheless, some of his policies and achievements did bring about certain necessary preconditions for a democratization without rupture or violence. Corporative solidarity, despite the numerous frauds committed by Franco's regime in its name, also seems to have made a contribution, but only after authoritarian corporatism was transformed into a kind of consensual corporatism by Adolfo Suárez and his successors.[18] The profound changes that occurred during Franco's long rule, which eventually made possible rapid transformation into a democratic system, were due primarily to the broad secondary effects of his government's policies, and above all to the need to adjust to some of the norms of Western Europe and the international market economy.

As time passed, there was a tendency for opinion surveys to register a more negative evaluation of Franco than those in the first years after his death. The older generation, perhaps not surprisingly, tended to be more positive than the younger. Opinion polls in the twenty-first century, for example, reported more than twice as many viewing the Franco era in negative terms compared with those who saw it positively, though the plurality, usually somewhere in the range of 40 percent, saw his rule as a combination of the good and the bad, not an unreasonable judgment about a complex history.[19]

Franco and his regime represented the climax and conclusion of a long era of conflict between tradition and modernization, spanning two centuries, from the reign of Carlos III down to 1975. In some respects, Franco may be seen as the last great figure of Spanish traditionalism. Seen from this perspective, Franco, with his policies and values, stood for an end rather than a beginning. He succeeded in achieving key aspects of modernization and liquidated certain problems of the past, though resolution of other problems was simply postponed until after his death. Given his own values and political inclinations, he could not construct the new Spain of the future, either in the form that he himself planned or, much less, in the form that it would assume after his departure.

Despite the apparent simplicity of some of his key ideas and statements, Franco was a complex historical personality who dealt with an unusual range of contradictions. He began as a weak, seemingly fragile and insignificant teenage officer only to become the youngest, most laureled general in the army. A Monarchist by conviction, he grudgingly accepted the legitimacy of a democratic republic. In some ways, he defended Spain's liberal constitutional order more consistently than did a number of prominent Republican leaders, but he ended by suddenly playing a key role in the military insurrection, once national order had largely disappeared. A self-proclaimed partisan of "short dictatorships," he vigorously sustained his own for nearly four decades, to the very end of his life. A conservative traditionalist, at first he engaged in a self-styled totalitarian revolution based on the ideology of the Falange. An aspirant to empire in collusion with Adolf Hitler, he ended up holding the latter at bay and eventually liquidated all Spain's African possessions virtually without violence. Initially a firm antagonist of Western liberal democracies, he negotiated major pacts with the United States for defense and assistance yet was always on guard because of his conviction that the Western world was being undermined by Masonry, his bête noire. He firmly resisted German requests for a naval base in the Canaries yet agreed to major American bases on the Spanish mainland, though he subsequently sought persistently to limit the use of them. He initiated a rigorous program of economic autarchy only later to give way to a more liberalized capitalism, inventing the "Chinese model" avant la lettre. A visceral anti-Communist, he spoke appreciatively of Ho Chi Minh as leader of Vietnamese nationalism and counseled Lyndon Johnson not to pursue war against him. He stoutly resisted the Monarchists who supported Juan de Borbón yet restored the monarchy in the person of the latter's son as his own successor. Tenaciously antiliberal and antidemocratic throughout his dictatorship, in his last years he accepted the fact that his successor would liberalize further (though perhaps he did not fully realize how much). A devoted Catholic and son of the Church who promoted the re-Catholicization of Spain, in his later years he was abandoned, even opposed, by the Vatican, which he said had stabbed him in the back.

The importance of Franco for the history of Spain lies, first, in the great length of his rule, in having determined the political destiny of the country from 1936 to 1975, and, secondly, in the profound changes the country underwent during that time, some of them designed directly by his government, others occurring as an accepted by-product of his policies, and still others directly in contradiction to his own purposes. The regime and era of Franco marked the conclusion of a long and convulsive period in Spain's history and opened the way, however contradictorily, to a more promising one, but Franco, like Moses, had to remain on the far shore of its history, never entering it. He was impeded from doing so by his basic character, personality, and values; he was the military caudillo of a conservative society that in large measure had already ceased to exist even before his own death.

Notes

Chapter 1. The Making of a Spanish Officer

1. His full baptismal name was Francisco Paulino Hermenegildo Teódulo Franco Bahamonde Salgado-Araujo y Pardo de Lama. (Pardo de Lama, from his maternal grandmother, had been originally Pardo de Lama-Andrade; she was related to the Andrades of the Galician aristocracy.)

2. L. A. Vidal y de Barnola, *Genealogía de la familia Franco* (Madrid, 1975).

3. The American writer Harry S. May devoted an entire book, *Francisco Franco: The Jewish Connection* (Washington, DC, 1978), to this speculation, without presenting any solid evidence. In the eighteenth century one of Franco's direct male ancestors obtained a certificate of "purity of blood," a common elite practice in traditional Spanish society and something more or less expected in the naval officer corps, which became more socially exclusive than the army. Later, during World War II, when his regime was a pro-German "nonbelligerent," rumors about Franco's possible Jewish ancestry reached Berlin, prompting Heinrich Himmler (chief Nazi watchdog of racial issues) to order an SS inquiry into the matter. This turned up no supporting evidence.

The notion sometimes advanced that in the Middle Ages Franco was a specifically Jewish name has no basis in fact, even though the name was borne by a number of Spanish Jews. It referred not to a Jewish origin but to identity with a *calle* or *villa franca* (a free street or town) or a "free" office or profession and thus originally denoted a sort of middle-class origin, which explains why a number of Jewish families also adopted the name.

4. S. M. Ball et al., "The Genetic Legacy of Religious Diversity and Intolerance: Paternal Lineages of Christians, Jews, and Muslims in the Iberian Peninsula," *American Journal of Human Genetics* 83, no. 6 (2008): 725–36.

5. Despite her teenage indiscretion, Concepción is said to have later married an army officer, Bernardino Aguado, who eventually reached the rank of brigadier general of artillery. The Aguados had several children of their own, and Eugenio grew up with them as a regular member of the family, though retaining the name of Franco. He became a topographer and had a long career at the Topographical Institute in Madrid, and Nicolás Franco later formally recognized his paternity. Eugenio's son-in-law, a young library administrator named

Hipólito Escolar Sobrino, wrote a very respectful letter on behalf of Eugenio's family to Franco in April 1950. According to one version, Franco only learned of the existence of his illegitimate half brother around 1940, just before his father's death. A specialist in the history of the book in Spain, after Franco's death Escolar Sobrino became director of the National Library for nine years and later published an autobiography, *Gente del libro* (Madrid, 1999). The first public revelation of certain aspects of all this appeared in *Opinión*, Feb. 26, 1977, more than a year after Franco's death. See J. M. Zavala, *Franco, el republicano: La vida secreta de Ramón Franco, el hermano maldito del Caudillo* (Barcelona, 2009), 93–97.

6. Franco made this remark in the autobiographical sketch that he began in 1974. V. Pozuelo Escudero, *Los últimos 476 días de Franco* (Barcelona, 1980), 86.

7. Franco's daughter, who as a little girl became fairly well acquainted with her grandmother, describes her as "deeply religious. . . . She was an old-fashioned lady, of the kind who have their name on a prayer-bench in church. Every day she went to mass at least twice, and then to another ceremony in the afternoon, as well." (All quotations from Carmen Franco in this book are taken from the lengthy set of interviews that the authors conducted with her in Madrid in January 2008. For the full original Spanish texts of these interviews, see J. Palacios and S. G. Payne, *Franco, mi padre* [Madrid, 2008].)

8. It has been said, but cannot be verified, that Nicolás later regularized the relationship in a civil ceremony under the Second Republic. In 1938, however, his son would invalidate all civil marriages.

9. This novella was published as J. de Andrade, *Raza: Anecdotario para el guión de una película* (Madrid, 1942). In Spanish the term lacks the notion of biological race that tends to characterize its English equivalent and refers more broadly to an ethnic group and its cultural inheritance. The title was thus intended to refer to the Spanish patriotic heritage.

10. In comparing the early lives of leading European dictators, it might be noted that Adolf Hitler suffered at the hands of a brutal father and lavished his affection on a kindly mother. But by contrast, while Hitler identified with his father's brutality, it cannot be said that his thinking was influenced by his mother. Doña Pilar, on the other hand, had a distinct moral and spiritual profile of the traditional sort, and Franco would ever remain unswervingly loyal to the values and beliefs of his mother.

11. R. Garriga, *Nicolás Franco, el hermano brujo* (Barcelona, 1980).

12. Zavala, *Franco, el republicano*, is superior to R. Garriga, *Ramón Franco, el hermano maldito* (Barcelona, 1978).

13. Pozuelo Escudero, *Los últimos*, 88.

14. After Franco's death, the widow of Franco Salgado-Araujo published his memoir, *Mi vida junto a Franco* (Barcelona, 1976), though it is not entirely clear whether he was fully responsible for the final text.

15. The only serious study of his early years is B. Bennassar, *Franco: Enfance et adolescence* (Paris, 1999).

16. Pilar Franco Bahamonde, *Nosotros, los Franco* (Barcelona, 1981).

17. J. González Iglesias, *Los dientes de Franco* (Madrid, 1996).

18. Pozuelo Escudero, *Los últimos*, 90.

19. Compare the remarks of the psychiatrist Enrique González Duro; see his *Franco: Una biografía psicológica* (Madrid, 1992), 69–70.

20. He did not carry a wooden rifle, as has often been erroneously reported.

21. Pozuelo Escudero, *Los últimos*, 96.

22. Ibid., 99.

23. For what it is worth, there is a very formalistic account of Franco and of the academy during these years in L. Moreno Nieto, *Franco y Toledo* (Toledo, 1972), 11–88.

24. F. Franco, *Palabras del Caudillo, 19 abril 1937–7 diciembre 1942* (Madrid, 1943), 508.

25. The relationship with the Islamic world was of course a major formative factor in Spanish history. A brief survey is provided by R. Damián Cano, *Al-Andalus: El Islam y los pueblos ibéricos* (Madrid, 2004), while the long conflict is narrated in C. Vidal Manzanares, *España frente al Islam: De Mahoma a Ben Laden* (Madrid, 2004). A. de la Serna, *Al sur de Tarifa: Marruecos-España, un malentendido histórico* (Madrid, 2001), presents a useful brief introduction to relations with Morocco. For a broader recent account, see A. M. Carrasco González, *El reino olvidado: Cinco siglos de historia de España en Marruecos* (Madrid, 2012).

26. Four hundred years of military conflict are detailed in A. Torrecillas Velasco, *Dos civilizaciones en conflicto: España en el África musulmana; Historia de una guerra de 400 años (1497–1927)* (Valladolid, 2006).

27. The reasons for this weakness were various but fundamental and deep seated: the absence of a foreign threat, lack of participation in European power rivalries, the close connection between Spanish identity and Catholicism (which discouraged nationalism, associated with liberalism or radicalism), the slow pace of economic development and of a national school system, and the growth of internal divisions.

28. The weak minority current of *africanismo* from the second half of the nineteenth century is treated in L. Sáez de Govantes, *El africanismo español* (Madrid, 1971), R. Mesa Garrido, *La idea colonial en España* (Valencia, 1976), and A. Pedraz Marcos, *Quimeras de África: La sociedad española de africanistas y colonistas* (Madrid, 2005).

29. The literature on Spain and its small Moroccan protectorate has expanded greatly during the past generation. The most recent general account is M. R. de Madariaga, *Marruecos, ese gran desconocido: Breve historia del protectorado español* (Madrid, 2013). R. Salas Larrazábal, *El protectorado de España en Marruecos* (Madrid, 1992), presents a brief overview. J. L. Villanova, *El Protectorado de España en Marruecos: Organización política y territorial* (Barcelona, 2004), explains the institutional structure. The military campaigns are treated in Estado Mayor Central del Ejército, *Historia de las campañas de Marruecos (1859–1927)*, 3 vols. (Madrid, 1947–81), J. L. Mesa et al., *Las campañas de Marruecos 1909–1927* (Madrid, 2001), F. Villalobos, *El sueño colonial: Las guerras de España en Marruecos* (Barcelona, 2004), and M. R. de Madariaga, *En el Barranco del Lobo: Las guerras de Marruecos* (Madrid, 2005). The policy toward culture and religion is examined in J. L. Mateo Dieste, *La "hermandad" hispano-marroquí: Política y religión bajo el Protectorado español en Marruecos (1912–1956)* (Barcelona, 2003).

30. All quotations are drawn from V. Gracia, *Las cartas de amor de Franco* (Barcelona, 1978).

Chapter 2. The Youngest General in Europe

1. The first regular unit of North African Muslim volunteers in a modern European army had been organized by the Spanish at Oran in 1734. This Algerian city had been a Spanish possession for two centuries, and a small portion of the surrounding population accepted Spanish sovereignty. When Oran was temporarily lost in 1708, a number of the

local Muslims asked to be evacuated to Andalusia, and some of their descendants remained there, becoming assimilated into the Spanish population. Others returned when the Spanish crown regained Oran in 1734, and at that time a regular company of Mogataces (Muslim volunteers) was organized. The term "mogataz" was derived from a local Arabic pejorative for "renegade," but apparently was adopted by the unit as a badge of honor.

2. L. Suárez, *Franco* (Barcelona, 2005), 8.

3. According to the way that Franco told the story near the end of his life. R. Soriano, *La mano izquierda de Franco* (Barcelona, 1978), 81.

4. On the German role, see P. La Porte, *La atracción del imán: El desastre de Annual y sus repercusiones en la política europea (1921–1923)* (Madrid, 2001), 135–76, and, more broadly, H. L. Müller, *Islam, gihad ("Heiliger Krieg") und Deutsches Reich: Ein Nachspiel zur wilhelmischen Weltpolitik im Maghreb, 1912–1918* (New York, 1991), and E. Burke, "Moroccan Resistance, Pan-Islam and German War Strategy, 1914-1918," *Francia: Forschungen zur Westeuropäische Gechichte* 3 (1975): 434–64.

5. His daughter has observed that "he received a lot of support from Alfonso XIII. We still have a letter from the king accompanying a medal of the Virgin sent to protect him. Papá always thought that the monarchy was important to Spain as a moderating force." She concludes, however, that her father was "more a Monarchist because of history than because of theory."

6. E. Carvallo de Cora, ed., *Hoja de servicios del Caudillo de España* (Madrid, 1967), 46–57.

7. There have been several biographies of her. By far the best is C. Enríquez, *Carmen Polo, señora de El Pardo* (Madrid, 2012). Though Carmen Polo and Sofía Subirán, the earlier object of his attentions in Melilla, looked considerably different in their old age, when they were young they bore a slight resemblance, although Carmen Polo was by far the prettier.

8. Interview with María Angeles Barcón in *Interviú*, July 22, 1978.

9. L. E. Togores, *Millán Astray legionario* (Madrid, 2003), is a detailed and admiring biography.

10. Franco's version is given in F. Franco Salgado-Araujo, *Mis conversaciones privadas con Franco* (Barcelona, 1976), 184–85.

11. A. Mas Chao, *La formación de la conciencia africanista en el ejército español (1909–1926)* (Madrid, 1988).

12. Varela, in fact, was prosecuted before a military honor court, but by that time he had just received a major wound in combat, and hence the court refused to proceed against him. F. Martínez Roda, *Varela: El general antifascista de Franco* (Madrid, 2012), 43–44.

13. Anwal is the more phonetic transliteration, though it is commonly rendered in Spanish as Annual.

14. Franco, who had always been well treated by Berenguer, did not agree with the extensive criticism of the high commissioner but tended to defend him. He said that the commissioner had promised reinforcements to the eastern zone as soon as the situation in the west was fully under control. Soriano, *La mano izquierda*, 140. He was correct to the extent that Berenguer was not responsible for the foolhardy strategy of Silvestre.

15. The literature on Abd el Krim is extensive, and the best Spanish biography is M. R. de Madariaga, *Abd el-Krim el Jatabi: Lucha por la independencia* (Madrid, 2009), while

R. Furneaux, *Abdel Krim: Emir of the Rif* (London, 1967), though colorfully written, is literally fantastic, based on interviews with his family. The best analytic summaries, however, will be found in D. M. Hart, *The Aith Waryagar of the Moroccan Rif: An Ethnography and History* (Tucson, 1976), 369–403, and La Porte, *La atracción del imán*, 89–134. See also M. Tata, *Entre pragmatisme, réformisme et modernisme: Le role politico-religieux des Khattabi dans le Rif (Maroc) jusqu'à 1926* (Leuven, 2000), and J. M. Campos, *Abd el Krim y el protectorado* (Málaga, 2000).

16. On the immediate background and origins of the Rif war, see M. R. de Madariaga, *España y el Rif* (Melilla, 1999), and G. Ayache, *Les origines de la guerre du Rif* (Paris, 1981). The best narratives of the war as a whole are D. Woolman, *Rebels in the Rif: Abd el Krim and the Rif Rebellion* (Stanford, CA, 1968), and C. R. Pennell, *A Country with a Government and a Flag: The Rif War in Morocco, 1921–1926* (Wisbech, UK, 1986).

17. A major exception was the cavalry regiment of Alcántara, led by Colonel Fernando Primo de Rivera, which was ordered to cover the precipitous retreat and suffered more than 90 percent casualties, said to be the all-time record for any European cavalry regiment in a single action.

18. The best account of the disaster is J. Pando, *Historia secreta de Annual* (Madrid, 1999).

19. A. Barea, *The Forging of a Rebel* (New York, 1946), 365–66.

20. His most important writings from this period are collected in F. Franco Bahamonde, *Papeles de la guerra de Marruecos* (Madrid, 1986).

21. Some of the most important have been collected in *Francisco Franco, escritor militar*, special issue of *Revista de Historia Militar* 20, no. 40 (1976).

22. Soriano, *La mano izquierda*, 125–26.

23. The publicity that Franco received during the first major phase of his career is treated in L. Zenobi, *La construcción del mito de Franco* (Madrid, 2011), 25–58.

24. As distinct from their father and mother, Franco's sister, and Franco's daughter, all of whom produced multiple children, none of the Franco brothers, as has been noted, proved capable of generating more than one child apiece, despite the fact that Nicolás and Ramón were both married twice.

25. S. E. Fleming, *Primo de Rivera and Abd-el-Krim: The Struggle in Spanish Morocco, 1923–1927* (New York, 1991), 108–71.

26. Brigadier General Gonzalo Queipo de Llano later wrote that on September 21, Franco met with him to tell him that he and other leaders of key units had agreed to arrest and depose the dictator but that they needed a man with the rank of general to lead them. Gonzalo Queipo de Llano, *El general Queipo de Llano perseguido por la Dictadura* (Madrid, 1930), 47–48. Yet there is no corroboration, and the only thing that can be known for sure is that Queipo was involved in some kind of activity against Primo de Rivera, who relieved him of command and for a time confined him to a military prison.

27. The fullest account is in R. de la Cierva, *Franco: La historia* (Madrid, 2000), 136–43.

28. A. Flores and J. M. Cicuéndez, *Guerra aérea sobre el Marruecos español (1913–1927)* (Madrid, 1990).

29. R. Kunz and R.-D. Müller, *Giftgas gegen Abd-el-Krim: Deutschland, Spanien und der Gaskrieg in Spanisch Marokko, 1922–1927* (Freiburg im Breisgau, 1990), S. Balfour,

Abrazo mortal: De la guerra colonial a la Guerra Civil en España y Marruecos (1909–1939) (Barcelona, 2002), 241–300, and the summary by M. R. de Madariaga and C. L. Avila, "Guerra química en el Rif (1921–1927)," *Historia 16* 26, no. 324 (2003): 50–85.

30. Franco's role in this key operation was exceptional, though not quite to the extent claimed by certain hagiographers. See P. Pascual, "Así fue el desembarco de Alhucemas," *Historia 16* 23, no. 282 (1999): 64–77.

31. France would complete the full occupation of its own much larger protectorate, where relatively speaking it had to do much less fighting, in 1934.

32. J. L. Villanova, *Los interventores: La piedra angular del protectorado español en Marruecos* (Barcelona, 2006).

33. *La Legión española*, 2 vols. (Madrid, 1973), is the fullest account, and J. Scurr, *The Spanish Foreign Legion* (London, 1985), provides a briefer summary of the legion's history, as does J. H. Galey, "Bridegrooms of Death: A Profile Study of the Spanish Foreign Legion," *Journal of Contemporary History* 4, no. 2 (1969): 47–63. Its role in the Moroccan campaigns is treated in J. E. Alvarez, *The Betrothed of Death: The Spanish Foreign Legion during the Rif Rebellion, 1920–1927* (Westport, CT, 2001), and F. Ramas Izquierdo, *La Legión: Historial de guerra (1 septiembre 1920 al 12 octubre 1927)* (Ceuta, 1933). Total combat deaths of the legion throughout its history reached approximately ten thousand, most occurring in the Civil War of 1936–39. There is an extensive further bibliography in Spanish.

34. There is a good brief discussion of his mastery of counterinsurgency warfare in G. Jensen, *Franco: Soldier, Commander, Dictator* (Washington, DC, 2005), 22–56.

35. In recent years controversy has developed about Franco's skill in military leadership, though it has much more to do with the Spanish Civil War than with the campaigns in Morocco. The best general analysis is J. Blázquez Miguel, *Franco auténtico: Trayectoria militar, 1907–1939* (Madrid, 2009). Other commentaries, pro and con, include C. Blanco Escolá, *La incompetencia militar de Franco* (Madrid, 2000), R. Casas de la Vega, *Franco militar* (Madrid, 1996), and J. Semprún, *El genio militar de Franco* (Madrid, 2000).

36. Together with his copilot Julio Ruiz de Alda, Ramón got a brief memoir of this exploit into press within a matter of weeks, under the title *De Palos al Plata* (Madrid, 1926). This would be the first of three instant memoirs of his successive adventures that he would publish in the next five years.

Chapter 3. Director of the General Military Academy

1. Soriano, *La mano izquierda*, 74.

2. Her full name was María del Carmen Ramona Felipa María de la Cruz Franco Polo. Henceforth she will be referred to in this study as Carmen or Carmencita and her mother as Doña Carmen.

3. For example, during 1962–63 Stanley Payne made the acquaintance in Madrid of José Pardo de Andrade, a relative of Franco's from Galicia, who detested his illustrious distant cousin, then dictator of Spain. A favorite refrain of Pardo de Andrade emphasized that, as he liked to put it, "Franco es un débil sexual" ("Franco is a sexual weakling"), incapable of engendering a child of his own. His version was that Carmencita was an illegitimate daughter of Ramón's who had been adopted by Paco and Carmen when they saw they were likely to have no children of their own. Pardo de Andrade somewhat disingenuously

insisted that she resembled Ramón in appearance, in response to which it was pointed out that since Paco and Ramón also resembled each other, that could hardly prove anything.

4. This stemmed perhaps from the fact that as a young woman the attractive Carmen-cita tended to have what the Spanish call a Moorish (*moruna*) appearance.

5. J. Tusell, cited in González Duro, *Franco*, 129, 410.

6. See C. Navajas Zubeldia, *Ejército, estado, y sociedad en España (1923–1930)* (Logroño, 1991).

7. Doña Carmen's third sister, Isabel, had married but had no children and later would spend more than a little time with the Francos.

8. In 1928, Franco would have undoubtedly been incredulous if told that within eight years he would be unable to prevent the summary execution of Campins by a military tribunal.

9. Or, as Michael Alpert puts it, "of the seven hundred officers who had graduated from the General Military Academy . . . , only 37 were dismissed after the Civil War, presumably for having served the Republic, while 84 had been shot in the Republican zone. The overwhelming majority had been imprisoned in the Government zone or had served in the Insurgent army." Michael Alpert, *The Republican Army in the Spanish Civil War 1936–1939* (Cambridge, 2013), 90.

10. *Estampa*, May 29, 1928, quoted in P. Preston, *Franco: A Biography* (New York, 1993), 57–58.

11. Officers were required to seek approval to marry largely because they were so poorly paid; the government wanted to be sure the officer would be able to support his new wife.

12. Carmen Díaz's eventual memoir, *Mi vida con Ramón Franco* (Barcelona, 1981), published, inevitably, only after the death of her sometime brother-in-law, is fairly convincing. Carmen Díaz later had a much happier second marriage with a more normal husband.

13. To defend himself, Ramón quickly brought out his second memoir, *Aguilas y garras* (Madrid, 1929).

14. Garriga, *Ramón Franco*, 149–67.

15. Franco recounts this himself in his brief *"Apuntes personales" sobre la República y la Guerra Civil* (Madrid, 1987), 6.

16. Ramón Franco soon published a lurid memoir of this absurd adventure, *Madrid bajo las bombas* (Madrid, 1931), his third volume of memoirs in five years.

17. Garriga, *Ramón Franco*, 210–11.

18. Archivo Varela, legajo 148, published by Javier Tusell in *Cambio 16*, Nov. 30, 1992.

19. The background is presented in S. Ben-Ami, *The Origins of the Second Republic in Spain* (Oxford, 1978). The best Republican memoir of these events is M. Maura, *Así cayó Alfonso XIII: De una dictadura a otra* (Madrid, 2007). J. A. Navarro Gisbert, *Así cayó la monarquía: Cinco días que conmovieron a España* (Barcelona, 2008), provides a broad narrative.

20. The only serious riot in Madrid took place on the early hours of the fourteenth, during which the protesters toppled various statues of historic kings and sacked the headquarters of the small Spanish Nationalist Party. The huge demonstrations of the following day were peaceful.

21. Toward the end of his life, Franco gave his own, very one-sided, version of the collapse of the monarchy in his very brief and never completed *"Apuntes" personales*, 7–9.

Chapter 4. From Ostracism to Chief of Staff

1. When Lerroux had founded the party very early in the century, it had indeed been radical and incendiary, but over the years it moved toward the center.

2. The best studies of the military reform are M. Alpert, *La reforma militar de Azaña (1931–1933)* (Madrid, 1982), and C. Boyd, "Las reformas militares," in L. Suárez Fernández, ed., *Historia general de España y América*, 25 vols. (Madrid, 1986), 17:141–73, while the most detailed account of the military under the Republic is M. Aguilar Olivencia, *El ejército español durante la Segunda República* (Madrid, 1986).

3. Colonel Segismundo Casado, last commander of Republican Madrid in the Civil War, lamented years later that "if Señor Azaña had held the army in due esteem, not merely for its patriotic mission but for its loyal obedience to the Republic, it is undeniable that the reforms would have won the support of the majority of officers. But unfortunately Señor Azaña was not well balanced, suffering from a civilian inferiority complex that was reflected in the scorn and hatred that he felt for military men. This complex was fully demonstrated throughout his political career." *Pueblo* (Madrid), Oct. 7, 1986, quoted in Aguilar Olivencia, *El ejército*, 235.

4. Franco Salgado-Araujo, *Mis conversaciones privadas*, 425, and *Mi vida junto*, 11, 104, 122.

5. M. Azaña, *Obras completas* (Mexico City, 1966–68), 4:33, 39.

6. As he informed Ricardo de la Cierva in 1973. De la Cierva, *Franco*, 210.

7. Zavala, *Franco, el republicano*, 278.

8. In the summer of 1935 Ramón and Engracia returned to Spain, following the finalization of his divorce in the preceding year, to be formally married. The legality of this marriage would be among the many that were annulled by a decree of Franco's government in 1938 that voided the Republican divorce law altogether, though Franco did extend a widow's pension to Engracia after Ramón was killed in action several months later.

9. Franco, *"Apuntes" personales*, 16.

10. The nearest thing to a biography of Sanjurjo is the book by his relative, E. Sacanell Ruiz de Apodaca, *El general Sanjurjo: Héroe y víctima* (Madrid, 2004), not a critical study but the usual Spanish hagiography.

11. According to Pedro Sainz Rodríguez, who claims to have been present at the principal meeting between Franco and Sanjurjo. Pedro Sainz Rodríguez, *Testimonio y recuerdos* (Barcelona, 1978), 376–78.

12. So he told his biographer Ricardo de la Cierva. De la Cierva, *Franco*, 228.

13. On the widespread censorship and banning of newspapers under the Republic, see J. Sinova, *La prensa en la Segunda República española: Historia de una libertad frustrada* (Madrid, 2007).

14. Each of these is listed in M. Alvarez Tardío and R. Villa García, *El precio de la exclusion: La política durante la Segunda República* (Madrid, 2010), 195–202.

15. M. Azaña, *Memorias íntimas de Azaña* (Barcelona, 1939), 310.

16. On the various roles of Masons under the Republic, see M. D. Gómez Molleda, *La Masonería en la crisis española del siglo XX* (Madrid, 1986).

17. R. Villa García, *La República en las urnas: El despertar de la democracia en España* (Madrid, 2011), is a thorough and definitive account of the national elections of 1933.

18. The main source is Franco's boyhood friend, Admiral Pedro Nieto Antúnez, who

always remained relatively close to him. R. Baón, *La cara humana del Caudillo* (Madrid, 1975), 36–37.

19. Franco would have opportunity to show his gratitude after the Civil War. Hidalgo had fled abroad to escape the Red Terror, in which many of his political colleagues were killed, but, as a Mason, if he returned to Spain he would be subject to prosecution under the anti-Masonic legislation of Franco's dictatorship. Hidalgo wrote to ask for amnesty for his past Masonic activities, which Franco immediately granted.

20. Fundación Nacional Francisco Franco (henceforth cited as FNFF), *Documentos inéditos para la historia del Generalísimo Franco*, 5 vols. (Madrid, 1992), 1:11–12.

21. D. Hidalgo, *Por qué fui lanzado del Ministerio de la Guerra* (Madrid, 1934), 78–79.

22. Just a few months earlier, the Socialists in Estonia had followed an opposite tack, supporting a moderate authoritarian takeover by the liberal premier Konstantin Päts in order to thwart the greater danger of a more extreme rightist (or "Fascist") threat than existed in Spain. J. Valge, "Foreign Involvement and Loss of Democracy," *Journal of Contemporary History* 46, no. 4 (2011): 788–808.

23. Franco, *"Apuntes" personales*, 11. The broader European issues are treated in S. G. Payne, *Civil War in Europe, 1905–1949* (New York, 2011).

24. Within only a few months leftist spokesmen were permitted to present charges of atrocities before a military tribunal. The resulting inquiry produced concrete evidence of only one killing, though probably there were more. The most extensive study on this point is F. Suárez Verdaguer, "Presión y represión en Asturias (1934)," *Aportes* 21, no. 3 (2006): 26–93.

There is a large literature on the insurrection. The most detailed account is P. I. Taibo II, *Asturias 1934*, 2 vols. (Gijón, 1984), which is very favorable to the revolutionaries. See also F. Aguado Sánchez, *La revolución de octubre de 1934* (Madrid, 1972), B. Díaz Nosty, *La comuna asturiana* (Madrid, 1974), J. S. Vidarte, *El bienio negro y la insurrección de Asturias* (Barcelona, 1978), A. del Rosal, *El movimiento revolucionario de octubre* (Madrid, 1983), A. Palomino, *1934: La Guerra Civil empezó en Asturias* (Barcelona, 1998), and P. Moa, *1934: Comienza la Guerra Civil* (Barcelona, 2004).

25. López de Ochoa is said himself to have had nineteen recently captured prisoners shot while the fighting raged, but Yagüe accused him of being soft on the revolutionaries and of insulting the elite units. López de Ochoa subsequently had Yagüe briefly arrested on charges of slander. L. E. Togores, *Yagüe: El general falangista de Franco* (Madrid, 2010), 97–145.

26. Gil Robles later gave his version in his memoir, *No fue posible la paz* (Madrid, 1968), 141–48.

27. De la Cierva, *Franco*, 246.

28. See the account of the aviator Juan Antonio Ansaldo, who was to have piloted the plane, in his memoir *¿Para qué . . . ? (de Alfonso XIII a Juan III)* (Buenos Aires, 1951), 91–92.

29. On the mythic use of the insurrection, pro and con, see B. D. Bunk, *Ghosts of Passion: Martyrdom, Gender, and the Origins of the Spanish Civil War* (Durham, NC, 2007).

30. Preston, *Franco*, 106.

31. Franco Salgado-Araujo, *Mis conversaciones privadas*, 474.

32. Gil Robles, *No fue posible*, 235; Franco, *"Apuntes" personales*, 24–25.

33. Gil Robles, *No fue posible*, 777.

34. Franco's older brother, Nicolás, spent a brief term in state administration during these months. During one short-lived government, he served from October to December 1935 as director general of shipping and fisheries, then returned to his post in the naval engineering school.

35. N. Alcalá-Zamora, *Memorias* (Barcelona, 1977), 320–21.

36. For a fuller account of the Gil Robles–Franco reforms, see Aguilar Olivencia, *El ejército*, 443–67.

37. S. de Madariaga, *Memorias* (Madrid, 1974), 531.

38. For a critical evaluation of the leadership of Gil Robles, see M. A. Ardid Pellón and J. Castro-Villacañas, *José María Gil Robles* (Barcelona, 2004).

39. The principal version of all this is given by Gil Robles in *No fue posible*, 364–66. It was later publicly substantiated by Franco himself.

40. Franco had earlier had negative dealings with José Antonio when the Francos decided to evict the Falange from an apartment that it used as its headquarters in Oviedo, which belonged to Doña Carmen. They sought to avoid any political complications and used the good offices of José Antonio's close friend, their brother-in-law Serrano Suñer, to persuade the Falangist leader to have the apartment vacated. R. Serrano Suñer, *Política de España, 1936–1975* (Madrid, 1995), 34.

At some point José Antonio himself had a meeting about military insurrection with Franco, who fended him off with his typical patter of professional small talk, consisting mainly of military anecdotes. The Falangist leader was irritated and concluded that Franco was not to be counted on for any daring political enterprise, a conclusion that, generally speaking, was correct. This meeting, variously dated by commentators as taking place in either February or March 1936, more likely occurred in the early winter. The only witness to it was Ramón Serrano Suñer, as recounted in his principal memoir, *Entre el silencio y la propaganda, la historia como fue: Memorias* (Barcelona, 1977), 56. See also the reconstruction of events suggested by J. Gil Pecharromán, *José Antonio Primo de Rivera: Retrato de un visionario* (Madrid, 1996), 410–11.

Chapter 5. The Destruction of Republican Democracy

1. From 1928 to 1935 the Comintern implemented a strategy for what it called the third period of world revolutionary activity, according to which Communist parties attempted to foment immediate revolution, rejecting any alliance that did not directly support such tactics. This was a complete failure, and in Germany, which harbored the largest Communist party outside the Soviet Union, it boomeranged, playing a major role in permitting the Nazis to seize power. In August 1935, Stalin directed the Comintern to change course by abandoning immediate revolutionary extremism and adopting the kind of alliance tactics that had carried Mussolini and Hitler to power. Communist parties were directed to form broad electoral alliances with any other leftist group, however moderate, and to emphasize legal tactics in the short term. Victorious popular fronts were formed in Spain, France, and, later, Chile. The way this functioned in Spain is examined in S. G. Payne, *The Spanish Civil War, the Soviet Union, and Communism* (New Haven, CT, 2004), 1–82.

2. M. Alvarez Tardío, "The Impact of Political Violence during the Spanish General Elections of 1936," *Journal of Contemporary History* 48, no. 3 (2013): 463–85.

3. M. Portela Valladares, *Memorias: Dentro del drama español* (Madrid, 1988), 168–69.

4. These data are drawn from new research by Manuel Alvarez Tardío and Roberto Villa García for their forthcoming book on the elections of 1936.

5. Franco's own version of this, written more than three decades later, relies exclusively on distant memory and is apparently not entirely reliable. Franco, *"Apuntes" personales*, 39–42.

6. N. Alcalá-Zamora, *Asalto a la República, enero–abril de 1936* (Madrid, 2011), 163–64.

7. Gil Robles, *No fue posible*, 492–93. There is some discrepancy regarding details and the sequence of events between the recollections of Franco and Gil Robles, though they agree on essentials.

8. Franco, *"Apuntes" personales*, 42–43.

9. Preston, *Franco*, 116.

10. Alcalá-Zamora, *Asalto*, 167–68.

11. Franco's version of this was first presented in J. Arrarás, ed., *Historia de la Cruzada española*, 8 vols. (Madrid, 1939–43), 4:57.

12. Alcalá-Zamora, *Asalto*, 181–83.

13. Ibid., 180–87.

14. Alcalá-Zamora, *Memorias*, 191–92; Portela Valladares, *Memorias*, 186–96.

15. The only source for these conversations is Franco's own reminiscences, but the attitudes he attributed to the two political leaders certainly reflected their position at that moment. Arrarás, *Historia de la Cruzada española*, 3:58, and Franco Salgado-Araujo, *Mi vida junto*, 131.

16. Serrano Suñer, *Entre el silencio*, 53.

17. Quoted in R. de la Cierva, *Historia de la Guerra Civil española* (Madrid, 1969), 764.

18. *El Liberal* (Bilbao), Mar. 26, 1936. Prieto repeated the reference in a speech on May 1.

19. Martínez Fuset is treated in R. Garriga, *Los validos de Franco* (Barcelona, 1981), but the data provided are limited.

20. The principal sources are Gil Robles, *No fue posible*, 563–67, and Serrano Suñer, *Entre el silencio*, 56–58.

21. R. Villa García, "The Failure of Electoral Modernization: The Elections of May 1936 in Granada," *Journal of Contemporary History* 44, no. 3 (2009): 401–29.

22. The version of his candidacy that he penned in his final years is full of distortions. Franco, *"Apuntes" personales*, 34–35.

23. The most authoritative discussion of this issue is J. T. Villarroya, *La destitución de Alcalá-Zamora* (Valencia, 1988).

24. This was very likely Lieutenant Colonel Valentín Galarza, coordinator of the UME.

25. Alcalá-Zamora, *Asalto*, 410–11.

26. While out of the army, Mola wrote three volumes of memoirs to generate income. These were published immediately, then later collected in his *Obras completas* (Valladolid, 1940) and much later republished as *Memorias* (Barcelona, 1977). In addition, a brief manual on chess that he turned out sold very well and provided welcome income. There are a number of books about Mola, none of much value.

27. There are many accounts of the conspiracy. The fullest are de la Cierva, *Historia de la Guerra Civil*, 735–816, and F. Alía Miranda, *Julio de 1936: Conspiración y alzamiento*

contra la Segunda República (Barcelona, 2011), though the latter is misleading in its presentation of the insurrection as thoroughly and meticulously organized. For a shorter account in English, see S. G. Payne, *Politics and the Military in Modern Spain* (Stanford, CA, 1967), 314–40.

28. Many years later, Franco claimed that he had been behind the selection of Sanjurjo as leader and had ulterior motives: "In that way I could pull all the strings myself, because Sanjurjo, though a brave man, lacked the brainpower for so much responsibility." Soriano, *La mano izquierda*, 138. Franco was right, for Sanjurjo would have been completely incapable of running any kind of government by himself, but Franco exaggerated in claiming any particular role in the selection of Sanjurjo, whom almost everyone saw as the obvious choice for figurehead.

29. Mola's guidelines have been published in various formats, originally in Arrarás, *Historia de la Cruzada española*, 3:449. Limited data may be found in the books by his sometime personal secretary, J. M. Iribarren, *Con el general Mola: Escenas y aspectos de la Guerra Civil* (Zaragoza, 1937) and *Mola: Datos para una biografía y para la historia del Alzamiento* (Zaragoza, 1938), and in A. Lizarza, *Memorias de la conspiración, 1931–1936* (Pamplona, 1954), and J. del Castillo and S. Alvarez, *Barcelona: Objetivo cubierto* (Barcelona, 1958).

30. According to Mola's secretary, José María Iribarren, in an interview with Stanley Payne in Pamplona, Dec. 15, 1958.

31. According to the Monarchist conspirator Juan Antonio Ansaldo, in his memoir *¿Para qué . . . ?*, 125.

32. The letter has been reprinted many times. The full text is in de la Cierva, *Franco*, 280–82.

33. According to his biographer B. F. Maíz, *Mola, aquel hombre* (Barcelona, 1976), 219–20.

34. J. Vigón, *General Mola (el conspirador)* (Barcelona, 1957), 100; E. Esteban-Infantes, *General Sanjurjo* (Barcelona, 1957), 254–55.

35. This was paid for by funds from Juan March, probably Spain's wealthiest businessman, earlier prosecuted by the Republic for his dealings under Primo de Rivera. The full extent of his financial support is a matter of speculation, though he later provided large sums to assist Franco early in the Civil War. Cf. J. A. Sánchez Asiaín, *La financiación de la Guerra Civil española: Una aproximación histórica* (Barcelona, 2012), 167–225, and P. Ferrer, *Juan March: El hombre más misterioso del mundo* (Barcelona, 2008), 354–55.

36. This is the most common estimate, but a total of 444 is reported by J. Blázquez Miguel, *España turbulenta: Alteraciones, violencia y sangre durante la II República* (Madrid, 2009), 624–704. The two principal analyses of political violence in this period are F. del Rey Reguillo, "Reflexiones sobre la violencia política en la II República española," in M. Gutiérrez Sánchez and D. Palacios Cerezales, eds., *Conflicto político, democracia y dictadura: Portugal y España en la década de 1930* (Madrid, 2007), 19–97, and G. Ranzato, "El peso de la violencia en los orígenes de la Guerra Civil de 1936–1939," *Espacio, tiempo y forma*, ser. 5, Historia contemporánea, vol. 20 (2008): 159–82.

37. The timing and content of this message have been confirmed by key participants, but the primary source is the unpublished "Memorias" of Elena Medina, linotypist at the newspaper *El Debate*, who served as a key courier for Mola and carried the message. Cf. N. Salas, *Quién fue Gonzalo Queipo de Llano y Sierra (1875–1951)* (Seville, 2012), 184–85.

38. Serrano Suñer, *Entre el silencio*, 120–21; A. Kindelán, *La verdad de mis relaciones con Franco* (Barcelona, 1981), 173–74.

39. The principal accounts are I. Gibson, *La noche en que mataron a Calvo Sotelo* (Madrid, 1982), L. Romero, *Cómo y por qué mataron a Calvo Sotelo* (Barcelona, 1982), and A. Bullón de Mendoza, *José Calvo Sotelo* (Barcelona, 2004), 677–705.

40. J. Pérez Salas, *Guerra en España (1936–1939)* (Mexico City, 1947), 82–83.

41. S. Juliá, quoted in N. Townson, ed., *Historia virtual de España (1870–2004): ¿Qué hubiera pasado si . . . ?* (Madrid, 2004), 186. Cf. J. Zugazagoitia, *Historia de la guerra de España* (Buenos Aires, 1940), 5.

42. *ABC*, July 14, 1960, quoted in Bullón de Mendoza, *José Calvo Sotelo*, 703.

43. *The Morning Post* (London), July 20, 1937, in Preston, *Franco*, 137.

44. Douglas Jerrold, the British conservative who helped arrange this operation, has provided his version in the memoir *Georgian Adventure* (London, 1937).

45. The most careful and detailed reconstruction of the flight of the *Dragon Rapide* will be found in A. Viñas, *La conspiración del general Franco y otras revelaciones acerca de una Guerra Civil desfigurada* (Barcelona, 2011), 1–108. Some further details from the British side are provided in Peter Day's luridly titled *Franco's Friends: How British Intelligence Helped Bring Franco to Power in Spain* (London, 2011), 7–89. "British intelligence" did not exactly "help bring Franco to power," but there was some knowledge in London of what was afoot.

46. The most thorough presentation of the conspiracy theory is in Viñas, *La conspiración del general Franco*, 48–115. See also F. Bravo Morata, *Franco y los muertos providenciales* (Madrid, 1979), 17–47. In fact, Balmes did not die immediately and could easily have denounced his murderers, had they existed, while the officer who certified the accident officially was not a conspirator but remained loyal to the Republic. Key facts are laid out in A. Monroy, "Chismes en torno a la muerte del general Balmes," *Razón española* 170 (Nov.–Dec. 2011): 341–47.

47. Enríquez, *Carmen Polo*, 65–67; Garriga, *Los validos*, 28–30. Mola did much the same, sending his wife and daughter across the border to France until the situation in Spain was made secure.

Carmen recalls that on the seventeenth "we went to a hotel in Las Palmas, which delighted me because I had never been in a hotel before. . . . Early the next day a car came to take my mother and myself to military headquarters, which was not far from the port. . . . I was reluctant, saying 'Why do we have to leave the hotel?' We spent all that day at military headquarters. I could see a lot of excitement in the streets, but soon we were not allowed to go to the windows because people were being armed. You could see both soldiers and people in street clothes, all of which seemed very strange to me. Then an official from the juridical corps who was very close to my father [Lieutenant Colonel Martínez Fuset] took us to spend the night on a Spanish coast guard boat. On the following day it took us directly to a German ship rather than having us pass through the port, because the Reds were still in the port. We had spent all night on the coast guard boat and were very lucky, because the radio operator received an order from Madrid to overthrow the officers, even to kill them. . . . Mamá was worried, really worried."

48. L. Bolín, *España: Los años vitales* (Madrid, 1967), 47–48.

49. For the argument that relying on loyal army and security units would have been the wiser course, see the memoirs of the Republican officer Pérez Salas, *Guerra en España*, 105–15.

Chapter 6. Franco Becomes Generalissimo

1. In later years, Franco would say that he had always foreseen a long civil war, but this is apparently ex post facto rationalization.
2. According to his aide Pacón. See Franco Salgado-Araujo, *Mi vida junto*, 173.
3. Since this is a matter of learned guesswork, historians have come up with quite varying calculations. Cadres were seriously undermanned in mid-July, as many troops, amounting to half or more, were on summer furlough, and no one knows how many were in the barracks on July 18. The best calculation is that scarcely fifty thousand troops were present in the peninsular garrisons, about half of whom were brought into the insurrection, though there were also about thirty thousand troops on duty in the protectorate. Almost equally important were the roughly fifty-five thousand men in the armed security forces, less than half of whom were brought into the revolt. The most recent study of the division in the armed forces is F. Puell de la Villa, "Julio de 1936: ¿Un ejército dividido?," in J. Martínez Reverte, ed., *Los militares españoles en la Segunda República* (Madrid, 2012), 77–98.
4. The exception occurred at the most senior rank—lieutenant general—which was being phased out by the Republican reforms. None of the three remaining lieutenant generals held active assignments. All supported the revolt but were trapped in the Republican zone. Two were executed and the third, Alberto Castro Girona, finally escaped in 1937 to the Nationalist zone, but he never held a significant command.
5. Altogether, the revolutionaries executed a total of 1,729 commissioned army officers and half or more of all naval officers for complicity in the revolt, while the rebels would execute 258 officers in their zone for having opposed, or occasionally for having failed to support, the revolt. Those officers who stayed with the leftist regime played either senior or only secondary military roles, so that only 130 regular commissioned officers were killed in the People's Army, whereas 1,280 were combat fatalities in Franco's forces. These data are from the detailed study of the conspiracy and revolt by Alía Miranda, *Julio de 1936*, 128–29, 164–65. See also R. Salas Larrazábal, *Los datos exactos de la Guerra Civil* (Madrid, 1980).
6. As can best be determined, there were about thirty thousand troops in the protectorate: forty-two hundred were in the legion, seventeen thousand were in the *regulares* and other Moroccan units, and the remaining ten thousand were ordinary Spanish recruits.
7. Published in *El Telegrama del Rif* (Melilla), July 19, 1936, quoted in Historia 16, *La Guerra Civil*, vol. 5, *La guerra de las columnas*, ed. G. Cardona et al. (Madrid, 1986), 72.
8. Much controversy has surrounded this accident, the chief published accounts of which are incomplete and confused, as in Bravo Morata, *Franco y los muertos providenciales*, 49–96, and Sacanell Ruiz de Apodaca, *El general Sanjurjo*, 227–38. Sanjurjo was sixty-four years of age and physically ailing, suffering from disorders of the kidney, liver, and aorta, as well as a syphilitic infection, though the infection had been brought under control. What seems to have happened was that a good-quality French plane and an experienced pilot were chartered for him in southwestern France, in a manner analogous to the arrangement made for Franco in England. The French plane was intercepted at a refueling stop in northern Spain, en route to Portugal, and its sole passenger, Antonio Lizarza Iribarren (head of the Carlist militia in Navarre), arrested. The plane was allowed to continue on to Lisbon, but, since it had been identified by the Spanish authorities, the Portuguese government denied authorization for its pilot to fly Sanjurjo back to Spain, because it did not want to incite a diplomatic protest from Madrid. At that moment the Monarchist aviator

and activist Juan Antonio Ansaldo showed up in Lisbon in his small, underpowered, two-seat, open-cockpit airplane and offered to fly Sanjurjo to the Nationalist zone, but the two main airports were under surveillance by Republicans, so Portuguese authorities required that Ansaldo use a short, makeshift runway near the coast for a surreptitious takeoff, and his small plane never made it fully into the air, crashing and burning (according to Ansaldo, its propeller having hit a natural obstacle). Though Portuguese anarchists later claimed credit, there is no evidence that it was anything more than an accident due to hastily improvised circumstances. See Ansaldo, *¿Para qué . . . ?*, 140–43.

9. Quoted in N. Cerdá, "Political Ascent and Military Commander: General Franco in the Early Months of the Spanish Civil War, July–October 1936," *Journal of Military History* 75, no. 4 (2011): 1125–57. This is the best brief account of the first phase of Franco's rise to power.

10. The key studies are A. Viñas and C. Collado Seidel, "Franco's Request to the Third Reich for Military Assistance," *Contemporary European History* 11, no. 2 (2002): 191–210, and, more extensively, A. Viñas, *Franco, Hitler y el estallido de la Guerra Civil* (Madrid, 2001), 335–97.

11. J. F. Coverdale, *Italian Intervention in the Spanish Civil War* (Princeton, NJ, 1975), 3–84; M. Heiberg, *Emperadores del Mediterráneo: Franco, Mussolini y la Guerra Civil española* (Barcelona, 2003), 31–66; P. Preston, "Mussolini's Spanish Adventure: From Limited Risk to War," in P. Preston and A. Mackenzie, eds., *The Republic Besieged* (Edinburgh, 1996), 21–51.

12. Franco refers to this in notes for his memoirs that he prepared late in life but never turned into a book: "Proposal by Mola to withdraw to the Ebro, vigorous rejection. . . . Inferiority of arms. Acquiring weapons at the rate of an eyedropper. Germany. . . . Chief concern was arming and organizing our army, its objectives and weapons. Miracles in armaments. But we lacked ammunition." Quoted in L. Suárez, *El general de la monarquía, la República y la Guerra Civil (desde 1892 hasta 1939)* (Madrid, 1996), 358.

13. J. Vigón, *General Mola*, 176–99.

14. Two of the most pointed examples are Blanco Escolá, *La incompetencia militar*, and J. A. Vaca de Osma, *La larga guerra de Francisco Franco* (Madrid, 1991).

15. Franco has been defended by Semprún, *El genio militar*, and others, but the most balanced analysis is to be found in Blázquez Miguel, *Franco auténtico*.

16. An enormous literature in Spanish describes the repression during and immediately after the Civil War, some of it seriously researched and reliable, much larger parts merely polemical. The two best general accounts are S. Juliá, ed., *Víctimas de la Guerra Civil* (Madrid, 1999), and A. D. Martín Rubio, *Los mitos de la represión en la Guerra Civil* (Madrid, 2005). For an evaluation, see J. Ruiz, "Seventy Years On: Historians and Repression During and After the Spanish Civil War," *Journal of Contemporary History* 44, no 3 (2009): 449–72.

17. The most famous atrocity popularized by Republican propaganda—the execution of hundreds of prisoners in the bullring at Badajoz on August 16—was nonetheless an exaggeration (though not a fabrication), as on that day at least three hundred leftists (and possibly more) were executed in Badajoz. F. Pilo, *La represión en Badajoz* (Badajoz, 2001), F. Pilo, M. Domínguez, and F. de la Iglesia, *La matanza de Badajoz ante los muros de la propaganda* (Madrid, 2010), and L. E. Togores, *Yagüe*, 241–312. The repression in Badajoz province continued for some time and was one of the most severe in the Nationalist zone, eventually claiming approximately four thousand victims.

18. According to Franco Salgado-Araujo, *Mi vida junto*, 167. Franco, however, had no illusions about the political leanings of La Puente Bahamonde, whom he had peremptorily removed from command of an air base at the time of the revolutionary insurrection of October 1934, as explained in chapter 4. Members of La Puente's family do not seem to have held his execution against Franco, since a brother of his later served on Franco's personal staff.

19. The letter was personally delivered by Franco's aide Pacón, who preserved the unopened envelope and later published the text of the letter in *Mi vida junto*, 348–53. Campins was executed on August 16.

20. Quoted in Pilo et al., *La matanza de Badajoz*, 305.

21. Quoted in J. M. Martínez Bande, *Frente de Madrid* (Barcelona, 1976), 209–10.

22. This fundamental aspect of the Spanish war has been little studied. See the summary in J. A. Sánchez Asiaín, "Recursos económicos y organización territorial en la República de la Guerra Civil," *Anales de la Real Academia de Ciencias Morales y Políticas* 85 (2008): 516–21, and also F. Olaya Morales, *El expolio de la República* (Barcelona, 2004), M. Mir, *Diario de un pistolero anarquista* (Barcelona, 2006), and A. Herrerín, *El dinero del exilio: Indalecio Prieto y las pugnas de posguerra (1939–1947)* (Madrid, 2007).

23. Particularly in a general order of August 12, quoted in Pilo et al., *La matanza de Badajoz*, 294.

24. For the best discussion and summary of the economic reprisals by both sides, see Sánchez Asiaín, *La financiación*, 749–806.

25. *Times* (London), Aug. 11, 1936.

26. Nicolás Franco taught his last class in the naval engineering school on the morning of July 18, where he is said to have been informed by a friend that his name was on a list of people to be arrested. With the typical Franco sangfroid, he returned the following morning to conduct a final examination and then, having no car at his disposal, he and his wife fled the capital later in the afternoon by public bus, literally at the last minute. In a provincial town they were eventually able to hire a taxi to take them to Avila, once more by the skin of their teeth, but there they would be safely within the Nationalist zone. Garriga, *Nicolás Franco*, 48.

27. Sánchez Asiaín, *La financiación*, 167–225.

28. See Kindelán, *La verdad*, which supplements and corrects his earlier *Mis cuadernos de guerra* (Madrid, 1945), and G. Cabanellas, *Cuatro generales*, 2 vols. (Barcelona, 1977), a part of which is based on what the author learned from his father, General Miguel Cabanellas.

29. Cabanellas, *Cuatro generales*, 2:327.

30. *Documents on German Foreign Policy* (hereafter *DGFP*) (Washington, DC, 1951), D:3, 85–89; Ramón Garriga to Paul Preston, April 30, 1991, in Preston, *Franco*, 176–77, 818.

31. Kindelán, *La verdad*, 29. See also R. de la Cierva, *Francisco Franco*, 2 vols. (Madrid, 1972–73), 1:506–9, who had access to the unpublished diary of Mola's aide Major Emiliano Fernández Cordón.

32. S. E. Fleming, "Spanish Morocco and the *Alzamiento Nacional*, 1936-1939: The Military, Economic and Political Mobilization of a Protectorate," *Journal of Contemporary History* 18, no. 1 (1983): 27–42. There is now a substantial literature in Spanish on Morocco and the Spanish Civil War. Various Republican political sectors came up with several different plans to foment revolt in the protectorate, but none was implemented, and one of them was vetoed by Stalin himself, for fear of alienating Paris and London.

33. Which is not to say that he had none. This is a controversial issue. Mola's civilian assistant, the Pamplona businessman Félix Maíz, who later turned against Franco, left a memoir that only after many years appeared as *Mola frente a Franco: Guerra y muerte del General Mola* (Pamplona, 2007). Maíz claimed that soon after the meeting he had opportunity to read the official minutes, prepared by a general staff colonel who was one of the two secretaries. This is said to have revealed that the initial vote ended in a tie between Franco and Mola, since at least half the council members did not fully trust Franco, seeing him as too cold, calculating, and ambitious, and that Franco, who did not find it expeditious to promote his own candidacy, supported that of Mola. Maíz agrees that Mola lacked political ambition and says that Mola, who favored the *mando único*, quickly had his own name withdrawn and asked that the election of Franco be made unanimous, which was done, with the abstention of Cabanellas.

34. A. Boaventura, *Madrid-Moscovo: Da ditadura à República e a Guerra Civil de Espanha* (Lisbon, 1937), 212.

35. Franco Salgado-Araujo, *Mis conversaciones privadas*, 55.

36. There is controversy over Yagüe's role, as well as his physical condition, which cannot be fully resolved. The best account is in L. E. Togores, *Yagüe*, 326–40.

37. Kindelán, *La verdad*, 108.

38. Cabanellas, *Cuatro generales*, 2:336–38, and G. Cabanellas, *La guerra de los mil días*, 2 vols. (Buenos Aires, 1973), 1:624–25.

39. Quoted in Semprún, *El genio militar*, 68.

40. *Boletín Oficial de la Junta de Defensa Nacional de España*, Sept. 30, 1936.

41. The differing terminology has been most carefully detailed in A. Ruedo, *Vengo a salvar a España: Biografía de un Franco desconocido* (Madrid, 2005), 201–10.

42. Cabanellas, *Cuatro generales*, 2:351. This may be compared with another hostile impression from about that time, by the left-wing American journalist John Whitaker, who interviewed Franco: "Personally I found Franco shrewd but disconcertingly unimpressive. I talked with him first when he was still slender, and later after he had gone to fat. A small man, he is muscular, but his hand is soft as a woman's, and in both instances I found it damp with perspiration. Excessively shy as he fences to understand a caller, his voice is shrill and pitched on a high note, which is slightly disturbing since he speaks quietly, almost in a whisper. Although effusively flattering, he gave no frank answer to any question I put to him. I could see that he understood the implication of even the most subtle query. A less straightforward man I never met." J. Whitaker, *We Cannot Escape History* (New York, 1943), 105.

43. In L. Suárez Fernández, *Francisco Franco y su tiempo*, 8 vols. (hereafter *FF*) (Madrid, 1984), 2:111–13.

44. Letter to Vicente Serra, Sept. 11, 1936, in Boaventura, *Madrid-Moscovo*, 245–47.

45. According to Mola's personal secretary José María Iribarren, in an interview with Stanley Payne in Pamplona, Dec. 15, 1958.

46. The best accounts of the early construction of the myth of the caudillo are F. Sevillano, *Franco, Caudillo de España por la gracia de Dios, 1936–1947* (Madrid, 2010), and Zenobi, *La construcción del mito*. See also A. Reig Tapia, *Franco "Caudillo": Mito y realidad* (Madrid, 1995).

47. Initial legislation of the National Defense Council and the Government Technical Council is collected in J. P. San Román Colino, ed., *Legislación del gobierno nacional* (Avila, 1937).

48. Quoted in R. Abella, *La vida cotidiana durante la Guerra Civil: La España nacional* (Barcelona, 1973), 109.

49. Such a pattern is confirmed by a member of his household staff in his last years. See J. Cobos Arévalo, *La vida privada de Franco* (Barcelona, 2011), 30.

50. P. Jaráiz Franco, *Historia de una disidencia* (Barcelona, 1981), 191.

51. Sixteen priests who had been active on behalf of Basque nationalism were executed in Guipuzcoa, the Basque province that was occupied by Mola's forces in September. The Vatican presented Franco with a formal protest, and he promised that this sort of thing would not happen again.

52. By contrast, during the nineteenth century Church leaders had at first rejected the notion of a modern Spanish nationalism, which they believed to be too tainted with liberalism.

Chapter 7. Forging a Dictatorship

1. Soriano, *La mano izquierda*, 155.

2. F. J. Fresán, "Navarra: ejemplo y problema: El proyecto estatal de carlistas y falangistas (1936–1939)," and F. J. Caspistegui, "La construcción de un proyecto cultural tradicionalista-carlista en los inicios del franquismo," in A. Ferrary and A. Cañellas, eds., *El régimen de Franco: Unas perspectivas de análisis* (Pamplona, 2012), 65–92, 93–148.

3. The publications devoted to Mola generally lack substance and objectivity. The only one that refers in detail to these political strains is Maíz, *Mola frente a Franco*, but it is missing concrete data and documentation.

4. The key study of finance in the Civil War is the massive work by Sánchez Asiaín, *La financiación*. Equally important is the only broad study of the mobilization of resources within the Nationalist zone, Michael Seidman's *The Victorious Counterrevolution: The Nationalist Effort in the Spanish Civil War* (Madison, WI, 2011).

5. It is often alleged that the world of culture strongly supported the Spanish left, as was generally the case outside Spain. Within Spain, plastic artists and poets tended to support the left, but the country's leading intellectuals often backed Franco. All three leaders of the Group at the Service of the Republic (Agrupación al Servicio de la República) of 1931— Spain's top philosopher José Ortega y Gasset, the major novelist Ramón Pérez de Ayala, and the noted physician and writer Gregorio Marañón—fled the Republican zone, preferring to live abroad. Ortega's two sons volunteered for Franco's army, and Marañón's son joined the Falange. Spain's leading novelist, the liberal Pío Baroja, vehemently denounced the revolutionary Republic, and other examples might be cited. Salvador de Madariaga at first came out for the Nationalists but after six months switched to a neutral position. Nationalist propaganda endeavored as best it could to exploit the statements and publications of leading liberal politicians and intellectuals—Alcalá-Zamora, Lerroux, Marañón, Unamuno, and Baroja—though Alcalá-Zamora, unlike the others, never supported Franco. Spanish Relief Committee, *Spanish Liberals Speak on the Counter-Revolution in Spain* (San Francisco, 1937).

6. There are many accounts of this incident, normally not by eyewitnesses. The best reconstruction is that of Togores, *Millán Astray*, 327–47. See E. Vegas Latapie, *Memorias políticas*, 2 vols. (Madrid, 1987), 2:111–12, perhaps the best eyewitness account.

7. Carmen Franco reports that "Mamá said that Millán made a big incident out of a trifle, exaggerating things," which she blamed on his histrionic tendencies.

8. See Unamuno's letter to Quintín de Torre, Dec. 1, 1936, quoted in C. Blanco Escolá, *General Mola: El ególatra que provocó la Guerra Civil* (Madrid, 2002), 294–95.

9. Unamuno would subsequently be denounced by some of the more extreme pundits in Nationalist Spain. See A. Martín Puerta, *Ortega y Unamuno en la España de Franco* (Madrid, 2009).

10. Falangists generally recognized that Franco had cooperated with requests for assistance in the rescue attempts. Personal exchanges between the two zones did take place, but usually not at the highest level. The best summary of the various attempts to rescue José Antonio can be found in J. M. Zavala, *La pasión de José Antonio* (Barcelona, 2011), 137–207.

11. R. Cantalupo, *Fu la Spagna: Ambasciata presso Franco, febbraio–aprile 1937* (Milan, 1948), 148–57. For a general account, somewhat exaggerated, of Italian political machinations, see Heiberg, *Emperadores del Mediterráneo.*

12. R. Serrano Suñer, *Entre Hendaya y Gibraltar* (Mexico City, 1947), 31.

13. Ibid., 32–33.

14. Franco, *Palabras del Caudillo*, 9–17.

15. *Boletín Oficial del Estado*, April 21, 1937.

16. For a detailed account of these events and of the history of the Falange in the early months of the Civil War, see S. G. Payne, *Fascism in Spain, 1923–1977* (Madison, WI, 1999), 239–79.

17. For some time held in solitary confinement in the Canaries, Hedilla would later be moved to internal exile on Mallorca in 1944, at which time both he and his wife received pensions. He was finally released in 1946, after which he was able to develop a career as a prosperous businessman. Carmen Franco insists that there had been nothing personal about it, that it was simply a matter of wartime insistence on complete discipline: "My father . . . was a great believer in discipline and this person broke discipline, but he never had any personal animus against him and always said that Hedilla had made a mistake but did not have bad intentions."

18. FNFF, *Documentos inéditos*, 1:97–103.

19. More than half of these died in the two mini-civil wars within the Civil War of May 1937 and March 1939. For exact data, see M. Aguilera, *Compañeros y camaradas: Las luchas entre antifascistas en la Guerra Civil española* (Madrid, 2012).

20. Franco, *Palabras del Caudillo*, 167.

21. S, Martínez Sánchez, "Los obispos españoles ante el nazismo durante la Guerra Civil," in Ferrary and Cañellas, *El régimen*, 23–64.

22. According to José Ignacio Escobar, who spoke with him around the beginning of April 1937, in Escobar's *Así empezó* (Madrid, 1974), 160–61.

23. According to newspaper reports in the Nationalist zone, summarized in Escolá, *General Mola*, 337–40, and confirmed by Mola's secretary José María Iribarren, in an interview with Stanley Payne in Pamplona, Dec. 15, 1958.

24. Serrano Suñer, *Entre el silencio*, 212–13. After both Sanjurjo and Mola died in plane crashes, Franco, who had traveled by air frequently in the first months of the Civil War, would rarely use an airplane again.

25. Jaráiz Franco, *Historia de una disidencia*, 97–98.

26. Report of May 19, 1938, *DGFP*, D:3, 657–63.

27. On the tensions between the Church and the party, see A. Lazo, *La Iglesia, la Falange y el fascismo* (Seville, 1995), and J. Andrés-Gallego, *¿Fascismo o estado católico? Ideología, religión y censura en la España de Franco, 1937–1941* (Madrid, 1997).

28. There is an enormous literature on relations between Franco's regime and the Church, and on Catholicism generally under Franco. The most lengthy account of the former, written largely from Franco's point of view, is L. Suárez Fernández, *Franco y la Iglesia: Las relaciones con el Vaticano* (Madrid, 2011). For a brief treatment, see S. G. Payne, *Spanish Catholicism: An Historical Overview* (Madison, WI, 1984), 149–91, and, on the broader context, see J. M. Cuenca Toribio, *Nacionalismo, franquismo y nacionalcatolicismo* (Madrid, 2008).

29. Garriga, *Nicolás Franco*, 159–66.

30. It is interesting to note that Ramón's nearest Italian counterpart, Umberto Nobile, also experienced major rejection and switched political sides because of it. Ramón piloted seaplanes, Nobile airships. Achieving renown for his flight over the North Pole in 1926, a second flight ended in disaster two years later. Humiliated by the Italian government, Nobile went to work for the Soviet air industry in 1931 but returned to Italy for the last phase of his life. L. Zani, "Between two Totalitarian Regimes: Umberto Nobile and the Soviet Union (1931–1936)," *Totalitarian Movements and Political Religions* 4, no. 2 (2003): 63–112.

31. A facsimile of the letter is reproduced in Franco Salgado-Araujo, *Mis conversaciones privadas*, 441.

32. The best treatment of Ramón during the Civil War is found in Zavala, *Franco, el republicano*, 291–325. See also Garriga, *Ramón Franco*, 270–98.

33. Ramón's wife received the full pension of a widow of a lieutenant colonel in the Spanish air force, but the family concocted the story that the real father of her daughter Angeles had been a circus sword-swallower and that her parents had never been married. Years later, when Angeles herself married, she was shocked to see that her birth certificate in the Registro civil of Barcelona had been altered to include only her mother's maiden name and made no mention of a father.

34. On this minor cause célèbre, see Togores, *Yagüe*, 566–75, R. Garriga, *El general Juan Yague* (Barcelona, 1985), 147–48, and D. Ridruejo, *Casi unas memorias* (Barcelona, 1976), 150–51.

35. A. Marquina, "Primero la Victoria, luego el rey," *Historia 16* 4, no. 35 (1979): 23–36.

36. All quotations drawn from the Rodezno diary as cited in J. Tusell, *Franco en la Guerra Civil* (Barcelona, 1992), 313–14.

37. Dionisio Ridruejo, interviews with Stanley Payne in Madrid, Nov. 27 and Dec. 4, 1958; Ridruejo, *Casi unas memorias*, 195–96; Serrano Suñer, *Entre el silencio*, 262.

38. One of the principal canards about Franco's modus operandi during the war is the frequently cited anecdote, apparently invented by Sainz Rodríguez, to the effect that he signed death sentences over his morning breakfast while having *chocolate con churros* (thick chocolate and doughnuts). In fact, there is no known occasion on which Franco ever signed a death sentence, all of which were handed down and signed by military tribunals. His action was either to ratify or commute them, not infrequently choosing the latter. Second, family members insisted that he never mixed any kind of work with breakfast and never drank chocolate, always preferring "café con leche." Major judicial decisions were usually reviewed with his juridical adviser Martínez Fuset.

39. Ridruejo, *Casi unas memorias*, 96.

40. The only serious attempt to define the charismatic basis and characteristics of Franco's leadership, partly on the basis of the concepts of Max Weber, was made by Francisco Javier Conde, in 1939 head of the Institute of Political Studies (Instituto de Estudios

Políticos), the regime's think tank, in his works *Espejo del caudillaje* (1941), *Contribución a la doctrina del caudillaje* (1942), *Teoría y sistema de las formas políticas* (1944), and *Representación política y régimen español* (1945), all these reprinted in his *Escritos y fragmentos políticos*, 2 vols. (Madrid, 1974). Conde sought to argue that the *caudillaje* rested on "reason, tradition, personal example and special divine assistance," which enabled it to achieve a higher level of charismatic legitimacy than democratic systems. The pamphlet *Los combatientes y el Caudillo*, distributed to the troops in 1938, also declared that the *caudillaje* did not constitute an interim, or Cincinnatian, regime: "The responsibility of *caudillaje* is incompatible with any time limit." The first authorized biography was published by Franco's old acquaintance from Oviedo, the journalist Joaquín Arrarás, in 1938.

41. Recent accounts of Nationalist propaganda include G. Santonja, *De un ayer no tan lejano: Cultura y propaganda en la España de Franco durante la guerra y los primeros años del nuevo estado* (Madrid, 1996), F. Sevillano, *Rojos: La representación del enemigo en la Guerra Civil* (Madrid, 2007), Javier Rodrigo, ed., "Retaguardia y cultura de guerra," special issue, *Ayer* 76, no. 4 (2009), and R. R. Tranche and V. Sánchez-Biosca, *El pasado es destino: Propaganda y cine del bando nacional en la Guerra Civil* (Madrid, 2011).

42. The best treatment of the Portuguese strongman is F. Ribeiro de Meneses, *Salazar: A Political Biography* (New York, 2009).

Chapter 8. Winning the Civil War

1. By October the number of troops defending Oviedo had been built up to twenty-one thousand, about the same number as those advancing on Madrid from the southwest. Both were heavily outnumbered by Republican militia.

2. Quoted in Cerdá, "Political Ascent."

3. See the collective work *Guerra de liberación nacional* (Zaragoza, 1961), 171.

4. As Néstor Cerdá points out, Franco saw to it that the handbook, *Servicio en campaña: Reglamento para el empleo táctico de las grandes unidades*, was revised in 1938 to assert that secondary attacks merely "display a lower intensity and rhythm than the main ones and hinder the objective of forcing the enemy to employ his reserves." This also insisted that "an officer's tactical knowledge, supported by his men's morale and skill, combined with a true desire to win will make up for any inferiority in equipment and numbers." Quoted in Cerdá, "Political Ascent." Franco would largely hold to this doctrine of frontal attack throughout the war, though later he would enjoy superiority in weaponry, beginning with his northern offensive at the close of March 1937, and then, in the very long run, toward the end, superiority of numbers, as well.

5. As recorded in the memoir by his air force chief, General Alfredo Kindelán; see *Mis cuadernos de guerra*, 37.

6. Cerdá, "Political Ascent."

7. Whitaker, *We Cannot Escape History*, 103.

8. The classic study of Italy's role is Coverdale, *Italian Intervention*.

9. Faupel to Neurath, Dec. 10, 1936, *DGFP*, D:3, 159–62.

10. The best brief account is J. F. Coverdale, "The Battle of Guadalajara, 8–22 March 1937," *Journal of Contemporary History* 9, no. 1 (1974): 53–75. For the broader Italian effort, see B. R. Sullivan, "Fascist Italy's Military Involvement in the Spanish Civil War," *Journal of Military History* 59, no. 4 (1995): 697–727. There is a lengthy bibliography in Italian.

11. Franco's direct communication to the Italian command has not been located, but his stinging critique of the CTV, its commander, and the poor Italian performance is expressed in two documents in Spanish archives, published by J. Tusell, in "Franco, indignado con los italianos: Dos documentos inéditos sobre la batalla de Guadalajara," *Historia 16* 12, no. 135 (1987): 11–18.

12. The full table of recruitment for both armies is available in J. Mathews, *Reluctant Warriors: Republican Popular Army and Nationalist Army Conscripts in the Spanish Civil War, 1936–1939* (Oxford, 2012), 35–38.

13. J. Mathews, "'Our Red Soldiers': The Nationalist Army's Management of Its Left-Wing Conscripts in the Spanish Civil War," *Journal of Contemporary History* 45, no. 3 (2010): 511–31, and, more broadly, his *Reluctant Warriors*.

14. Quoted in J. Tusell, "¡Menos mal que los rojos son peores!," *La Aventura de la Historia* 2, no. 16 (2000): 22–36.

15. Roberto Cantalupo, Mussolini's first ambassador, has presented his recollection of Franco's explanation in his memoir, *Fu la Spagna: Ambasciata presso Franco, febbraio–aprile, 1937* (Milan, 1948), 231. General Emilio Faldella described much the same account by Franco in his letter of February 25, 1971, to the historian John F. Coverdale. Coverdale, *Italian Intervention*, 216.

16. In an interview with *Le Figaro* (Paris) in October 1937. Franco, *Palabras del Caudillo*, 214.

17. As mentioned in chapter 7, Franco's brother-in-law Serrano Suñer maintains that, at the time of his death, Mola "was getting ready to raise the issue of separating powers," an arrangement in which Franco would remain chief of state and military commander-in-chief but appoint someone else as prime minister to lead the government. Serrano Suñer, *Entre el silencio*, 213.

18. To the above list might be added the name of José Antonio Primo de Rivera, leader of the Falange. Primo de Rivera might have been Franco's chief political rival, but he had remained in a Republican prison and then was executed by the Republican authorities in November 1936. The most elaborate example of such commentary is F. Bravo Morata, *Franco y los muertos providenciales* (Madrid, 1979).

19. Interview with Mola's personal secretary José María Iribarren by Stanley Payne in Pamplona, Dec. 18, 1959.

20. For his full career, see J. S. Corum, *Wolfram von Richthofen, Master of the Air War* (Lawrence, KS, 2008).

21. There is a large literature on Guernica, much of it misinformed and misleading. The best brief analysis is J. S. Corum, "The Persistent Myth of Guernica," *Military History Quarterly* 22, no. 4 (2010): 16–23. The most complete and reliable account is J. Salas Larrazábal, *Guernica, el bombardeo: La historia frente al mito* (Valladolid, 2012).

22. Republican propaganda concerning Nationalist air raids is studied in R. Stradling, *Your Children Will Be Next: Bombing and Propaganda in the Spanish Civil War, 1936–1939* (Cardiff, Wales, 2008).

23. It should be pointed out that Guernica had not initially inspired the painting, which Picasso had already begun in the late winter of 1937 as a protest against the horrors of war in the tradition of Goya, adding the name only after the propaganda campaign developed.

24. Cf. U. Bialer, *The Shadow of the Bomber: The Fear of Air Attack and British Politics, 1932–1939* (London, 1980).

25. Reproduced in Salas Larrazábal, *Guernica*, 337.

26. By comparison, there had been fewer than fourteen hundred executions in Vizcaya and Santander combined, according to a report sent to Franco on October 18, 1937. FNFF, *Documentos inéditos*, 1:163.

27. Archivo de la Fundación Nacional Francisco Franco, 42:118, 119. (Hereafter cited as Franco Archive.)

28. The most recent account is S. Montero Barrado, *La batalla de Brunete* (Madrid, 2010).

29. G. Cardona, *Historia militar de una Guerra Civil: Estrategia y tácticas de la guerra de España* (Barcelona, 2006), 219. Some of Franco's top commanders—Yagüe, Varela, Aranda—preferred to abandon Teruel temporarily in order to deliver the knockout blow on Madrid. Yagüe was a very loyal old comrade but also one of Franco's most frequent critics. He had urged the caudillo to bypass Toledo in 1936 and then to avoid the most direct approach to Madrid and attack from the northwest instead. Other disagreements would follow in 1938. In almost every case, Yagüe, arguably, was right and Franco wrong.

30. Kindelán, one of the most analytically minded of Franco's generals, attributed this especially to lack of coordination and leadership, in a report prepared for Franco on January 6, 1938. FNFF, *Documentos inéditos*, 1:174–76.

31. This increasing narrow-mindedness supposedly led General Juan Vigón, his chief of staff, to observe soon afterward to one of Franco's first government ministers that "there are times when I think that what is going to be done should not be done, but since with Franco raising an objection is enough to make him insist on having his own way, I have decided to follow the tactic of saying the opposite of what I really think so that what I really propose will be done." Sainz Rodríguez, *Testimonio y recuerdos*, 342. Since inventing and recounting negative anecdotes about Franco was a specialty of the droll Sainz Rodríguez, this perhaps need not be taken literally, but it can serve to illustrate, however fancifully, the problem of his increasingly overweening providentialism, which became a kind of messianic complex.

32. Togores, *Yagüe*, 449–53. Moreover, Vigón, the chief of staff, Kindelán, who commanded the air force, and the new head of the Condor Legion all seem to have agreed on this.

33. In later years, Franco would refer alternately to each of these arguments, without ever fully clarifying the matter.

34. R. Whealey, *Hitler and Spain: The Nazi Role in the Spanish Civil War* (Lexington, KY, 1989), 60.

35. J. M. Martínez Bande, *La ofensiva sobre Valencia* (Madrid, 1977), 69–96.

36. A good brief account from the Nationalist viewpoint is given in L. Togores, "La campaña de Levante, 23 de abril–25 de julio de 1938, el penúltimo capítulo de la Guerra Civil," *Aportes* 21, no. 1 (2006): 100–129. E. Galdón Casanoves, *La batalla de Valencia, una victoria defensiva* (Valencia, 2012), offers a more detailed treatment from the opposing side. One of the war's major atrocities, normally overlooked, took place as the Nationalists reached the edge of Castellón, the last provincial capital north of Valencia, on June 13. Nationalist sympathizers began prematurely to put up banners hailing their liberators, which infuriated troops of the Republican Sixth Division, suddenly called in to defend the city. They responded with explosive violence, slaughtering several hundred civilians, in the worst atrocity of mass killing of civilians by infantry forces on either side in the war. Soon

afterward, one brigade of the division fell prisoner to the Nationalists, who summarily court-martialed all its principal officers and commissars, executing twenty-one and sentencing five more to life imprisonment. See the differing versions in Galdón Casanoves, *La batalla de Valencia*, 108–13.

37. Quoted in M. Merkes, *Die deutsche Politik gegenüber dem spanischen Bürgerkrieg, 1936–1939* (Bonn, 1969), 112–13.

38. It was nonetheless sometimes a struggle to maintain the flow of Italian supplies, as well. On November 17, 1938, Kindelán reported to Franco that parts and other supplies for the Italian planes flown by Spaniards in the Nationalist air force would soon be exhausted if new shipments were not rapidly made available. FNFF, *Documentos inéditos*, 1:223–24.

39. Togores, *Yagüe*, 458–66.

40. Ibid., 494–96.

41. There are a number of histories of the climactic encounter of the Civil War. The most recent are A. Besolí et al., *Ebro 1938* (Barcelona, 2005), and J. Reverte, *La batalla del Ebro* (Barcelona, 2012).

42. On French military policy concerning the Spanish war, see T. Vivier, *L'armée française et la Guerre d'Espagne 1936–1939* (Paris, 2007), and J. Martínez Parrilla, *Las fuerzas armadas francesas ante la Guerra Civil española (1936–1939)* (Madrid, 1987).

43. I. Montanelli, *Soltanto un giornalista* (Milan, 2002), 37.

44. G. Ciano, *Ciano's Diary, 1937–1938* (London, 1952), 46, 147.

45. In a report to Franco of August 16, 1938, Kindelán attributed this perseverance to the Republicans' occupation of advantageous and well-fortified terrain and improvement in the number and quality of planes, automatic weapons, antiaircraft guns, and also artillery, though he acknowledged that Republican artillery was not particularly numerous. Kindelán concluded that the resistance of the Republican forces did not stem from any improvement in combat ability, for, with the broad extension of the Republican draft, "the quality of most units has declined considerably." By contrast, he judged Nationalist units in general to be improving with experience and with the leadership of the *alféreces provisionales*, who showed "great spirit," though the quality of middle-rank combat leaders such as battalion commanders had declined because of heavy casualties among the professionals, which sometimes meant more sluggish performance by their units. He also noted that war weariness was getting to be a problem. FNFF, *Documentos inéditos*, 1:193–98.

46. These tensions and disagreements are variously recorded and commented on in Kindelán, *Mis cuadernos*, 184–86, 205, Franco Salgado-Araujo, *Mi vida junto*, 264, and *DGFP*, D:3, 742–43.

47. Besolí, *Ebro*, 284–85.

48. Of 721 regular naval officers on active duty at the beginning of the war, by one means or another the left executed 255, or about half of all those in the Republican zone. R. Cerezo, *Armada española siglo XX*, vol. 3 (Madrid, 1983), 119–33.

49. For a brief synopsis of the war at sea, see W. C. Franks Jr., "Naval Operations in the Spanish Civil War, 1936–1939," *Naval War College Review* 37, no. 1 (1984): 24–55. The fullest account will be found in the thirty-four hundred pages of F. and S. Moreno de Alborán y de Reyna, *La guerra silenciosa y silenciada: Historia de la campaña naval durante la guerra de 1936–1939*, 5 vols. (Madrid, 1995). See also J. Cervera Pery, *La historiografía de la guerra española en el mar (1936–1939): Aproximación bibliográfica, reflexión histórica* (Murcia, 2008). Nationalist naval policy was sometimes overly aggressive and on occasion counterproductive.

Neutral shipping supplying the Republicans was frequently targeted. Between mid-April and mid-June 1938, twenty-two British ships were attacked, resulting in the sinking or serious damage of eleven. London protested sharply, and Nationalist naval action became somewhat more circumspect.

50. The principal study of Franco's air force is J. Salas Larrazábal, *Guerra aérea, 1936–39*, 4 vols. (Madrid, 1998–2003).

51. There is an extensive literature on the Condor Legion. A brief scholarly overview may be found in J. S. Corum, "The Luftwaffe and the Coalition Air War in Spain, 1936–1939," *Journal of Strategic Studies* 18, no. 1 (1995): 68–90. See also R. Proctor, *Hitler's Luftwaffe in the Spanish Civil War* (Westport, CT, 1983), and Corum, *Wolfram von Richthofen*, 117–51.

52. Drawing attention to Franco's bombing had become so important in its propaganda that the Republican government urged the League of Nations early in 1938 to send a mission to Spain to evaluate the nature and effects of Franco's air raids. The league dispatched a commission, whose report concluded "that both the small numbers [of planes] usually involved as well as the bombing patterns pointed towards a doctrine which prioritized the destruction of specific targets like bridges or railway stations," not civilian targets per se. Quoted in K. Schneider, "German Military Tradition and the Expert Opinion on Werner Mölders," *Global War Studies* 7, no. 1 (2010): 6–29.

53. As Hugo García has written, "The terrorist tactics often blamed on the insurgents were extensively used by the government." Review of *Your Children Will Be Next*, by Robert Stradling, *Journal of Contemporary History* 44, no. 4 (2009): 782. The bombing of a town that was least justified militarily was the Republican attack on Cabra, a small town in Córdoba province, which took place near the end of the war on November 7, 1938, and killed more than a hundred civilians, almost as many as at Guernica. Cabra had no military significance whatsoever. A. M. Arrabal Maíz, *El bombardeo de Cabra: El Guernica de la Subbética* (Barcelona, 2012). For a list of Republican air attacks on cities, see Salas Larrazábal, *Guernica*, 231–34.

The most heavily bombarded city of any size was neither Madrid nor Barcelona but the Asturian capital of Oviedo, subjected to constant shelling, as well as considerable bombing, by Republican forces for more than a year. One calculation is that 120,000 cannon shells and nearly 10,000 small bombs were used. Much of the city center was destroyed—far more of it than in other larger towns—including one hospital. Altogether, approximately two thousand civilians were killed, more than in any other city.

54. General directives by Kindelán on March 28 and June 23, 1938, stipulated that only military and economic targets on the periphery of cities could be targeted and that the "urban core" must be avoided. Full text of orders can be found in Salas Larrazábal, *Guernica*, 338, and FNFF, *Documentos inéditos*, 1:190–93.

55. For a brief general analysis that compares and contrasts the two opposing forces, see M. Alpert, "The Clash of Armies: Contrasting Ways of War in Spain, 1936–1939," *War in History* 6, no. 3 (1999): 331–51.

56. The best brief treatment is A. J. Candil, "Soviet Armor in Spain," *Armor* 108, no. 2 (1999): 31–38.

57. The total number of captured Soviet tanks reached approximately 150, but many were not fully usable. "Relación de los tanques y camiones blindados recuperados en toda la campaña," June 15, 1939, Franco Archive, 124:6322.

58. W. L. S. Churchill, *The Gathering Storm* (London, 1948), 221.

59. The postwar year of greatest excess mortality was 1941, when there were approximately 124,000 deaths beyond the norm.

Chapter 9. Franco and the Nationalist Repression

1. For a brief account of the revolutionary civil wars, see Payne, *Civil War in Europe*.

2. These took quite varied form in the Republican zone and included members of all the leftist organizations, even to some extent the semimoderate left Republicans, though to a lesser degree. See J. Ruiz, *El terror rojo en Madrid* (Madrid, 2012), and Mir, *Diario de un pistolero anarquista*.

3. *Boletín Oficial de la Junta de Defensa Nacional de España*, July 29, 1936.

4. Ibid., Sept. 1 and 9, 1936.

5. See his "Instrucción reservada número uno," prepared at the close of April 1936, quoted in F. Beltrán Güell, *Preparación y desarrollo del Movimiento Nacional* (Valladolid, 1938), 123.

6. Iribarren, *Con el general Mola*, 94. With Mola dead, this book was quickly suppressed by Franco's government, though earlier Mola had personally approved the manuscript and thanked the author for rendering a faithful account. José María Iribarren, interview with Stanley Payne, Pamplona, Dec. 15, 1958.

7. *ABC* (Seville), July 22–27, 1936; I. Gibson, *Queipo de Llano: Sevilla, verano de 1936 (Con las charlas radiofónicas completas)* (Barcelona, 1986).

8. Many of the published sources frequently cited in the general literature are not reliable. The two principal eyewitness denunciations of the Nationalist repression published during the Civil War were A. Bahamonde y Sánchez de Castro, *Un año con Queipo de Llano* (Barcelona, 1938), and A. Ruiz Vilaplana, *Doy fe: Un año de actuación en la España de Franco* (Paris, 1938).

9. See Juliá, *Víctimas*, A. D. Martín Rubio, *Paz, piedad, pardon . . . y verdad: La represión en la Guerra Civil: Una síntesis definitiva* (Madrid, 1997), and Martín Rubio, *Los mitos de la represión*. There are many monographs on individual provinces and regions, some of them excellent and others misleading. For a discussion of the controversies involved, see Ruiz, "Seventy Years On."

10. It might be noted, however, that after the occupation of Vizcaya by Franco's forces in 1937, two more Basque nationalist militants among the local clergy were executed. By comparison, while they were in power, the revolutionaries had killed fourteen clergy in Guipuzcoa and forty-one in Vizcaya.

11. Mussolini's special envoy the Fascist leader Roberto Farinacci reported after his visit to the Nationalist zone in March 1937 that "to tell the truth, Red and Nationalist atrocities are equivalent here. It is a sort of contest to see who can massacre more people. . . . The population is used to it by now and pays no attention; it is only we sentimentalists who create a tragedy over people who don't deserve it." Quoted in Coverdale, *Italian Intervention*, 191.

12. Cantalupo, *Fu la Spagna*, 131.

13. For example, the Catholic Action leader Francisco Herrera Oria made several protests to Franco in 1937, which led Franco to soon stop receiving him altogether. In 1939, after

Herrera Oria criticized continuation of the dictatorship, Franco sent him into internal exile. See the account by Herrera Oria's son in J. A. Pérez Mateos, *Los confinados* (Barcelona, 1976), 81–90.

14. It should be kept in mind that martial law and military tribunals had been frequently invoked during times of emergency in modern Spain. Under the Second Republic, for example, between October 1934 and February 1936 more than two thousand revolutionaries involved in the insurrection of 1934 had been prosecuted by military tribunals. Martial law had been a standard response to violent protest, insurrection, and revolution since the nineteenth century. When opposition forces took power, they sometimes adopted the same procedures against which they had protested. See M. Ballbé, *Orden público y militarismo en la España constitucional (1812–1983)* (Madrid, 1983).

15. The official *documento nacional de identidad*, however, was only decreed in March 1944. More important in the first years after the war was the formal *salvoconducto* required for domestic travel.

16. Ministerio de Gobernación, *Dictamen de la comisión sobre la ilegitimidad de poderes actuantes en 18 de julio de 1936* (Madrid, 1939).

17. E. Fernández Asiaín, *El delito de rebelión militar* (Madrid, 1943), quoted in Ballbé, *Orden público*, 402.

18. It generated an enormous archive of data, much of it accurate but a portion fabricated, which remains the main single archival source on the Republican repression.

19. M. Cajal, ed., *La Ley de responsabilidades políticas, comentada y seguida de un apéndice de disposiciones legales y formularios más en uso* (Madrid, 1930); M. Minués de Rico, ed., *Ley de responsabilidades políticas y de depuración de funcionarios políticos* (Madrid, 1939); and L. Benítez de Lugo y Reymundo, *Responsabilidades civiles y políticas* (Barcelona, 1940).

20. On the persecution of Masons, see J. J. Morales Ruiz, *El discurso antimasónico en el franquismo (1936–1939)* (Zaragoza, 2001), X. Casinos and J. Brunet, *Franco contra los masones* (Madrid, 2007), J. Domínguez Arribas, *El enemigo judeo-masónico en la propaganda franquista (1936–1945)* (Madrid, 2009), and, most succinctly and usefully, J. Ruiz, "Fighting the International Conspiracy: The Francoist Persecution of Freemasonry, 1936-1945," *Politics, Religion, and Ideology* 12, no. 2 (2011): 179–96.

21. FNFF, *Documentos inéditos*, 1:292–94.

22. F. Franco Martínez-Bordiú (with E. Landaluce), *La naturaleza de Franco: Cuando mi abuelo era persona* (Madrid, 2012), caption to one of the illustrations facing p. 161. The author also recounted this anecdote verbally to Jesús Palacios and Stanley Payne in January 2008.

23. *Anuario estadístico de España 1944–1945.*

24. J. M. Solé i Sabaté, *La repressió franquista a Catalunya (1938–53)* (Barcelona, 1985), 268.

25. A very limited amount of information on this is available in the Franco Archive. The principal historian of the postwar repression is Julius Ruiz. See his *Franco's Justice: Repression in Madrid after the Spanish Civil War* (Oxford, 2005) and, for a brief overview, "A Spanish Genocide? Reflections on the Francoist Repression after the Spanish Civil War," *Contemporary European History* 14, no. 2 (2005): 171–91. In the former, he concludes that the total number of executions may have been higher than twenty-eight thousand.

26. J. Ruiz, "'Work and Don't Lose Hope': Republican Forced Labor Camps during the Spanish Civil War," *Contemporary European History* 18, no. 4 (2009): 419–41. For a case

study, see F. Badia, *Els camps de treball a Catalunya durant la Guerra Civil (1936–1939)* (Barcelona, 2001).

27. Report to Franco of June 7, 1943. FNFF, *Documentos inéditos*, 4:271–73.

28. Suárez Fernández, *FF*, 2:383–86.

29. According to Garriga, *Los validos*, 171–72.

30. Cf. J. P. Fusi, *Franco: Autoritarismo y poder personal* (Madrid, 1985), 79.

31. This is the estimate by J. Tomasevich, *War and Revolution in Yugoslavia: Occupation and Collaboration* (Stanford, CA, 2001), 765.

Chapter 10. From Civil War to World War

1. On concepts of nationalism in the early years of the regime, see C. Almira Picazo, *¡Viva España! El nacionalismo fundacional del regimen de Franco, 1939–1943* (Granada, 1998), and I. Saz Campos, *España contra España: Los nacionalismos franquistas* (Madrid, 2003).

2. The Franco family acquired various properties over the years, though these did not amount to the gigantic patrimony of some dictators. In November 1937 one aristocratic admirer had willed him the Canto del Pico, a property of considerable value in Torrelodones, northwest of Madrid, whose crowning mansion, the Casa del Viento, had been declared a national artistic monument in 1930. This became a favorite retreat for the family. Much later, in 1962, the banker Pedro Barrié de la Maza, who had provided much of the funding for the Pazo de Meirás, purchased and gave to Doña Carmen as a present the Palacete de Cornide, a distinguished eighteenth-century building in the city of La Coruña, where, in fact, she would spend a great deal of time in the final years of her life. Doña Carmen also possessed some inherited property, and subsequently family members would acquire quite a number of other properties. On these real estate holdings, see M. Sánchez Soler, *Los Franco, S.A.* (Madrid, 2003).

3. It has been claimed that an anarchist group made an assassination attempt on Franco during one of these trips in the first months after the war. The only version available says that they fired on the wrong car and, in turn, all the attackers were killed by police. E. Bayo, *Los atentados contra Franco* (Barcelona, 1977), 58–59. This, however, cannot be confirmed.

4. For a synopsis, see G. Di Febo, *Ritos de guerra y de victoria en la España franquista*, rev. ed. (Valencia, 2012).

5. J. Larraz, *Memorias* (Madrid, 2006), 351.

6. Carmen Franco observes that being called dictator "did not particularly bother him, because ultimately it was a dictatorship, and he had thought highly of the dictatorship of Primo de Rivera. In those days it was not so demonized as now, when someone might say 'Uff, a dictatorship! You call me a dictator?' He understood that well enough, as did my mother." Sensitivity about the term nonetheless increased markedly after 1945, following the military victory of liberal democracy in Western Europe.

7. On the relations between Franco and his generals, see G. Cardona, *Franco y sus generales: La manicura del tigre* (Madrid, 2001), and also, less helpfully, M. A. Baquer, *Franco y sus generales* (Madrid, 2005).

8. Such qualities made Varela likeable, but to this was added their common combat experiences and military professionalism, though they differed in some of their political opinions. Finally, Varela, like Franco, had taken a bullet to the abdomen in Morocco and lived to tell the tale. See Martínez Roda, *Varela*.

9. M. Jerez Mir, *Elites políticas y centros de extracción en España, 1938–1957* (Madrid, 1982), 121–30.

10. On his career until 1939, see L. E. Togores, *Muñoz Grandes: Héroe de Marruecos, general de la División Azul* (Madrid, 2007), 15–219.

11. On the political identities and background of the intermediate personnel in the new regime, see G. Sánchez Recio, *Los cuadros políticos intermedios del regimen franquista, 1936–1959: Diversidad de origen e identidad de intereses* (Alicante, 1996).

12. The greatest wit in the Falange, the writer Agustín de Foxá, liked to say that Franco's relationship with the Falange was analogous to that of a man who married a widow and then had to listen to her spend all her time praising the virtues of her first husband. That made a good joke, but in fact nearly all Falangists served Franco loyally.

13. A. Romero Cuesta, *Objetivo: Matar a Franco* (Madrid, 1976), and interviews by Stanley Payne with two of the surviving conspirators, Madrid, March–May 1959.

14. Serrano Suñer later gave his version of this affair in H. Saña, *El franquismo, sin mitos: Conversaciones con Serrano Suñer* (Barcelona, 1982), 154–57.

15. Franco Archive, 68:17.

16. L. J. Pazos, *Buques hundidos o dañados seriamente durante la Guerra Civil (1936–1939)* (Pontevedra, 2011), gives the records of approximately a thousand vessels of all nationalities sunk or seriously damaged during the war.

17. The principal, if impressionistic, recorder of the systematic pillage is F. Olaya Morales, *La gran estafa: Negrín, Prieto y el patrimonio nacional* (Barcelona, 1996), *El oro de Negrín*, rev. ed. (Barcelona, 1998), and *El expolio de la República*. Since the author is sympathetic to the anarchists, he does not treat looting by them. For that, see Mir, *Diario de un pistolero anarquista*. On restoration of goods and spending the loot abroad, see Sánchez Asiaín, *La financiación*, 1053–1113.

18. For this and other macrostatistical conclusions, see the semidefinitive new study by Sánchez Asiaín, *La financiación*, 959–87.

19. Centro de Estudios Sindicales, *Francisco Franco*, vol. 3, *Pensamiento económico* (Madrid, 1958), 626. It is curious that in the middle of Franco's regime a collection of statements would appear that included many of his economic errors and extravagances.

20. C. Velasco Murviedro, "Las pintorescas ideas económicas de Franco," *Historia 16* 8, no. 85 (1983): 19–28.

21. Franco, *Palabras del Caudillo*, 135–45.

22. "Fundamentos y directrices de un Plan de saneamiento de nuestra economía armónico con nuestra reconstrucción nacional," published with commentary by J. Tusell in *Historia 16* 10, no. 115 (1985): 41–49.

23. Larraz, *Memorias*, 181.

24. The sense of reality among his fellow ministers varied, depending on the issue. One of the more lucid was the intelligent naval minister Moreno, who seems to have understood that the grand military projects were a pipedream. On occasion, Beigbeder and Galarza also supported Larraz.

25. Larraz's own account is given in some detail in his *Memorias*, 184–350. See also N. Sesma Landrín, *En busca del bien común: Biografía política de José Larraz López (1904–1973)* (Zaragoza, 2006), 107–32.

26. Cf. Carceller's remarks in the *New York Times*, Feb. 29, 1940.

27. Even the Political Council of the FET recognized the need for foreign loans and

credits and assistance from the international market, and its National Council soon stressed the importance of obtaining foreign exchange for necessary imports, all the while promoting the general policy of autarchy. "Proyecto de Acuerdo de la Junta Política en material económica," Nov. 17, 1939, Franco Archive, 37:1369; Consejo Nacional de la FET, "Fundamentos de la Política de Creación de Trabajo y problemas de su financiación," Feb. 28, 1940, Franco Archive, 68:2737. R. Gay de Montellá, *Autarquía: Nuevas orientaciones de la economía* (Barcelona, 1940), is a general exposition of the autarchist policy.

28. A. Ballestero, *Juan Antonio Suanzes, 1891–1977: La política industrial de la posguerra* (Madrid, 1997).

29. E. San Román, *Ejército e industria: El nacimiento de INI* (Barcelona, 1999), and P. Schwartz and M. J. González, *Una historia del Instituto Nacional de Industria* (Madrid, 1978).

30. Sánchez Soler, *Los Franco*, 23–25.

31. Franco Salgado-Araujo, *Mis conversaciones privadas*, 178.

32. Franco, *Palabras del Caudillo*, 157.

33. Heiberg, *Emperadores del Mediterráneo*, 196–98.

34. Franco Archive, 15:658, 67:2659, 2673, 2675, 2681, 2698, 105:4590. The preamble to the original "Bases orgánicas del ejército del aire," presented to Franco in April 1939, proposed to make the new air force Spain's principal offensive weapon in the future. Franco's marginalia revealed some skepticism about this. Though he wanted a greatly expanded air force, he did not wish to see this limit naval expansion. Franco's staff informed Yagüe that his plan for aircraft construction had to be reduced by more than 50 percent, but the fall of France inspired the air minister to ask for even more. For a sketch of Yagüe's work as air minister, see Togores, *Yagüe*, 597–619.

35. *I documenti diplomatici italiani*, 8th series, 13 vols. (Rome, 1942), 12:458–62.

36. Reports of June 16 and June 22, 1939. FNFF, *Documentos inéditos*, 1:523–33.

37. Cited in J. Tusell, *Franco, España y la II Guerra Mundial: Entre el Eje y la neutralidad* (Madrid, 1995), 46.

38. The strategic plan drawn up for Franco by Captain Luis Carrero Blanco of the naval staff on October 30 and the report on the condition of the fleet by Admiral Moreno on November 16 sought to be positive, but in fact they revealed the strategic and maritime vulnerability of Spain. FNFF, *Documentos inéditos*, 1:613–36, 640–50.

39. M. Ros Agudo, *Guerra secreta* (Barcelona, 2002), xxiii–xxv, 44–55. On the Spanish army during the initial period after the Civil War, see G. Cardona, *El gigante descalzo: El ejército de Franco* (Madrid, 2003), 19–77.

40. The key study is C. B. Burdick, "'Moro': The Resupply of German Submarines in Spain, 1939–1942," *Central European History* 3, no. 3 (1970): 256–84. See also Ros Agudo, *Guerra secreta*, 72–117.

41. Franco Archive, 103:4489. These early months of World War II were the last period in which relations with Italy would be as important, or even more important, than those with Germany. The relations between Madrid and Rome during the European war are treated in J. Tusell and G. García Queipo de Llano, *Franco y Mussolini: La política española durante la Segunda Guerra Mundial* (Barcelona, 1985), and G. Carotenuto, *Franco e Mussolini* (Milan, 2005).

42. Quoted in Diario 16, *Historia del franquismo* (Madrid, 1982), 164.

Chapter 11. The Great Temptation

1. Quoted in M. S. Gómez de las Heras Fernández, "España y Portugal ante la Segunda Guerra Mundial desde 1939 a 1942," *Espacio, tiempo y forma*, ser. 5, Historia contemporánea, vol. 7 (1994): 153–67. This was widely reflected in the Spanish press. For the latter, see F. Vilanova, *El franquismo en guerra* (Barcelona, 2005).

2. Quoted in Tusell, *Franco, España*, 81.

3. The fullest treatment of such aims in one volume is M. Cattaruzza et al., eds., *Territorial Revisionism and the Allies of Germany in the Second World War: Goals, Expectations, Practices* (New York, 2012).

4. On this agitation by the Spanish regime, see A. Salinas, *Quand Franco réclamait Oran* (Paris, 2008).

5. N. Goda, *Tomorrow the World: Hitler, Northwest Africa, and the Path toward America* (College Station, TX, 1998), 59.

6. For this copious literature, see S. G. Payne, *Franco and Hitler: Spain, Germany, and World War II* (New Haven, CT, 2008), 292–93. A sober scholarly account of major aspects of Spanish policy in Morocco may be found in G. Jensen, "The Peculiarities of 'Spanish Morocco': Imperial Ideology and Economic Development," *Mediterranean Historical Review* 20, no. 1 (2005): 81–102.

Somewhat paradoxically, these years of would-be expansionism in which some Spanish commentators liked to stress their cultural and ethnic identity with the people of northern Morocco were also the time of a brief blossoming of a separate Spanish racist literature, which posited the existence of a distinct and superior Spanish race. On the latter, see J. L. Rodríguez Jiménez, *Franco: Historia de un conspirador* (Madrid, 2005), 248–54.

7. Denis Smyth was the first to uncover these data in the British records, which he presented in his "Les chevaliers de Saint-Georges: La Grande-Bretagne et la corruption des généraux espagnols (1940–1942)," *Guerres mondiales et conflits contemporains* 41, no. 162 (1991): 29–54. These data are repeated in a somewhat exaggerated form in D. Stafford, *Roosevelt and Churchill: Men of Secrets* (London, 1999), 78–110. An account of Hillgarth in Spain may be found in P. Day, *Franco's Friends* (London, 2011), 55–192. The bribes were usually represented as payments from wealthy Spanish businessmen and financiers who wanted to keep the country out of the war, and the middleman in many of the transfers was the multimillionaire Juan March, who had provided substantial support to the Nationalists in 1936 but during the world war played both sides. M. Cabrera, *Juan March (1880–1962)* (Madrid, 2011), 330–33.

8. R. Powell Fox's memoir, *The Grass and the Asphalt* (Cádiz, 1997), reveals little and contains quite a few errors.

9. On the role of Beigbeder, see C. R. Halstead, "Un 'africain' méconnu: Le colonel Juan Beigbeder," *Revue d'histoire de la Deuxième guerre mondiale* 21, no. 83 (1971): 31–60. Unlike much of the Spanish leadership, Beigbeder soon drew the correct conclusions from Germany's defeat in the Battle of Britain and its inability to pull off a cross-channel invasion. Toward the end of September he told the American ambassador "that Germany had already 'lost the short war' and that within a month this fact would be apparent to the world. His implication was that Germany would either eventually lose the struggle or that a peace barren alike to victor and vanquished would be the result." Ambassador Alexander Weddell

to Secretary of State Cordell Hull, Sept. 26, 1940, box 57, Alexander Weddell Papers, Franklin Delano Roosevelt Presidential Library. (Thanks to Joan María Thomàs for this document.)

10. His Fascism had not prevented Yagüe from urging more generous treatment of patriotic Republicans. He had even brought a few apolitical former Republican officers into the air force, while Varela had done the opposite in the army, cashiering a number of veteran Nationalist officers. Franco could not abide Yagüe's constant talking and criticizing and went to the unusual lengths of writing a detailed memorandum for his showdown (attended also by Varela), berating Yagüe that "wherever anyone is peeing blood, you're there, too." The text of the memo is reproduced in J. Palacios, *La España totalitaria* (Barcelona, 1999), 261–62. The original memo, as well as the reports that Franco received on Yagüe, may be found in the Franco Archive, 67:49. The fullest discussion of this affair is in Togores, *Yagüe*, 619–37.

11. Complete text in J. Palacios, ed., *Las cartas de Franco* (Madrid, 2005), 114–15.

12. *Arriba* (Madrid), official organ of the FET, July 19, 1940. This imprudent speech would be suppressed in the official edition of the *Palabras del Caudillo* in 1943.

At this point a plan was drawn up for potential conversion and expansion of industry for military production ("Apuntes sobre organización económica de la defensa nacional," July 1940, Franco Archive, 34:1279), while a new naval plan completed on July 28 proposed a more modest naval construction program than the one presented the year before, targeting construction of nine light cruisers, nine destroyers, ten submarines, and ten torpedo boats, based on recent Italian models. Franco Archive, 67:2700. This goal would not be achieved, either.

13. Palacios, *Las cartas de Franco*, 118–19.

14. Despite the ill health that was much noted when he was foreign minister (which seems to have been caused by little more than a stomach ulcer), Serrano Suñer lived to the age of 102, dying in 2003, the last surviving major European political actor of World War II. In his numerous memoirs, interviews, and public lectures, he declared that he and Franco were basically in agreement on major international issues (which seems to have been correct), but he sometimes could not resist the temptation to portray his brother-in-law as a relative simpleton, compared with his own sophistication and intellect. In fact, Franco was the more shrewd and adroit politician of the two. The only objective biographical account of Serrano is by J. M. Thomàs (especially the introduction "El personaje real y el personaje inventado") in A. Gómez Molina and J. M. Thomàs, *Ramón Serrano Suñer* (Barcelona, 2003).

15. The text is in Palacios, *Las cartas de Franco*, 136–39. Parts of these letters have been published by Serrano Suñer in his *Entre el silencio*, 342–49.

16. Larraz, the finance minister, recalls that Franco articulated such a concern to him. Larraz, *Memorias*, 339. Carmen Franco says the same: "That was something he realized could happen. . . . Then my mother decided that she must pray all she could. . . . She ordered the Sacred Host in our chapel to be uncovered, something she had never done before. The sacred form was housed in a little tabernacle there, which was normal, but for two days she ordered it to be uncovered. That impressed me a great deal."

17. According to Carmen Franco, "Papá arrived late not because he wanted to, but because of the disastrous state of our railroads, not repaired for years, and the train could only go very slowly, slower than could be admitted. As a military man, my father was very

punctual. Then they said he did it on purpose to make Hitler nervous, but not at all. My father would have wanted to arrive on time."

18. FNFF, *Documentos inéditos*, 2:1, 380–81.

19. *DGFP*, D:11, 371–76.

20. It is not known if indeed Hitler really said such a thing, although one might say "se non è vero, è ben trovato." The principal source for this is P. Schmidt, *Hitler's Interpreter: The Secret History of German Diplomacy, 1935–1945* (London, 1951), 194. Schmidt further declares that dealing with Franco made Hitler visibly nervous, irritated, and frustrated. At one point he jumped up, as though to break things off, but quickly got control of himself and resumed the discussion.

21. G. Ciano, *Ciano's Diplomatic Papers* (London, 1948), 402–3.

22. This document, titled "Los derechos de España en el Africa Ecuatorial," which Hitler never saw, proposed expanding Spanish holdings in the region from 28,000 square kilometers to no less than 1,628,900 square kilometers, an area that would have even included all the former German colony of Cameroon, which it was known that Hitler intended to regain. See G. Nerín and A. Bosch, *El imperio que nunca existió* (Barcelona, 2002), 177–79.

23. *DGFP*, D:11, 376–79, 466–67.

24. Schmidt, *Hitler's Interpreter*, 193–94.

25. Palacios, *Las cartas de Franco*, 140–42. The main German transcript of the original meeting has been lost and the Spanish papers either destroyed or sequestered. Principal sources are *DGFP*, D:11, 371–80, Serrano Suñer's two accounts, *Entre el silencio*, 283–324, and *Entre Hendaya y Gibraltar*, 199–322, and that of Schmidt, *Hitler's Interpreter*, 189–94. See also the accounts in D. Detwiler, *Hitler, Franco und Gibraltar* (Wiesbaden, 1962), 51–66, and Tusell, *Franco, España*, 158–64. The independence of Franco's position is emphasized and perhaps somewhat exaggerated in the unpublished eight-page memorandum drawn up two days later by the Barón de las Torres, Franco's translator.

26. *DGFP*, D:11, 466–67.

27. Ros Agudo, *Guerra secreta*, 58–63. J. J. Téllez, *Gibraltar en el tiempo de los espías* (Seville, 2005), treats Gibraltar during these years.

28. P. T. Pereira, *Memorias* (Lisbon, 1973), 2:213–32; C. R. Halstead, "Consistent and Total Peril from Every Side: Portugal and Its 1940 Protocol with Spain," *Iberian Studies* 3, no. 1 (1974): 15–28. The policy and politics of Portugal in World War II are treated in F. Rosas, *Portugal entre a paz e a guerra (1939–1945)* (Lisbon, n.d.), and more extensively in A. Telo, *Portugal na Segunda Guerra*, 2 vols. (Lisbon, 1987, 1991). N. Lochery, *Lisbon: War in the Shadows of the City of Light, 1939–1945* (New York, 2011), is a recent journalistic account that adds a few documentary details.

29. Franco Archive, 68:2803.

30. *DGFP*, D:11, 598–606, 619–23. Serrano Suñer has presented his version in *Entre el silencio*, 305–8.

31. *DGFP*, D:11, 705–6, 725, 739–41, 787–88.

32. Franco Archive, 27:15007. The full text is in P. Moa, *Franco para antifranquistas* (Madrid, 2009), 234–41.

33. *DGFP*, D:11, 852–58. One of the enduring myths of Spanish-German relations was that Canaris, who was politically a crypto-opponent of Hitler, warned Franco that it would not be in Spain's interest to enter the war. There is no evidence of this, though by December

1940 the point might be considered obvious. Canaris was a German patriot and, so long as Hitler was winning, he had little incentive to try to thwart his strategy.

34. Ibid., D:11, 1140–43.

35. Ibid., D:11, 1157–58.

36. Ibid., D:11, 1173–75.

37. Ibid., D:11, 1188–91, 1208–10, 1217–18, 1222–23.

38. Ibid., D:12, 36–37; Palacios, *Las cartas de Franco*, 152–58.

39. *DGFP*, D:12, 58, 78–79.

40. The best account of this meeting is in Tusell and García Queipo de Llano, *Franco y Mussolini*, 119–22. In later years, amid moments of leisure in several of his numerous *cacerías* (hunting parties), Franco liked to pretend that he had boldly spoken the truth to Mussolini, claiming that he had asked him: "Duce, Duce, if you could get out of the war, wouldn't you get out?" and after Mussolini glumly nodded his head yes, the caudillo supposedly added, "Well, for that reason I'm not getting in." Carmen Franco has offered a parallel version of this anecdote. It made an amusing story, but was probably made up whole cloth. (The original version was provided by Fabián Estapé, interview by Stanley Payne in Barcelona, June 1974.)

41. Quoted in Tusell, *Franco, España*, 200.

42. There was a great deal of speculation in Spanish publications about this sort of thing. See J. Beneyto Pérez, one of the chief ideologues of the era, *España y el problema de Europa* (Madrid, 1942), on the history of the imperial idea in Spain and a new leadership role.

Hitler himself only once used the term "new order," which was much more in vogue among allies and satellites like Mussolini and Pétain. Hitler only thought in terms of a general order of nations briefly in the autumn of 1940 as he negotiated with his quasi-allies and Stalin. Nazi propaganda invoked the "West" more and more after the invasion of the Soviet Union, but Hitler usually approached matters only in primordial terms of domination, or hegemony. See M. Mazower, "National Socialism and the Search for International Order," *Bulletin of the German Historical Institute* 50 (2012): 9–26, and L. Klinkhammer, "National Socialism and the Search for International Order: Comment," *Bulletin of the German Historical Institute* 50 (2012): 27–38.

43. See F. Piétri, *Mes années d'Espagne, 1940–1948* (Paris, 1954), 55, and the Spanish diplomatic summary of April 23, 1941, quoted in Togores, *Yagüe*, 666. The broadest study of relations between the two chiefs of state is M. Séguéla, *Franco Pétain: Los secretos de una alianza* (Barcelona, 1994).

44. The fullest account is in Ros Agudo, *Guerra secreta*. See also W. Bowen, *Spaniards and Nazi Germany: Collaboration in the New Order* (Columbia, MO, 2000).

45. The whole issue leads to the ultimate counterfactual—what effect, if any, would Spain's military entry have had on the course and eventual outcome of the war? The most serious attempt to answer this question has been made by Donald S. Detwiler, "Spain and the Axis during World War II," *Review of Politics* 33, no. 1 (1971): 36–53. His conclusion is that it would have closed off the West Mediterranean, leading to the fall of Gibraltar and Malta and the possible loss of Egypt and the Suez Canal. This would have made any Allied invasion of France much more difficult and might have led to a "Japan first" strategy, with the first atomic bomb then dropped on Berlin rather than Hiroshima. The question has frequently been debated. What is not at all in doubt is that continuation of Spanish nonbelligerence was in the Allies' interest, as Churchill acknowledged in 1944.

46. Franco Archive, 18:53.

47. For a time the most active Monarchist conspirator was the vigorous rightist intellectual Eugenio Vegas Latapie. See his *Memorias políticas*, 325–30. A broad overview, together with key quotations from the negotiations with Yagüe, perhaps the principal general involved during this phase, may be found in Togores, *Yagüe*, 673–93.

48. The opportunistic Aranda, as head of the Escuela Superior de Guerra, apparently played a role in drafting the plan for the invasion of Portugal, about which he indiscreetly boasted to others. Nicolás Franco to Franco, Nov. 20, 1940, FNFF, *Documentos inéditos*, 2:2, 397–99.

49. *DGFP*, D:12, 611–15.

50. Spanish-British relations during the war are treated in E. Moradiellos, *Franco frente a Churchill* (Barcelona, 2005), and R. Wigg, *Churchill y Franco* (Barcelona, 2005).

51. When Larraz presented his resignation as minister of finance several days later, Franco acknowledged that Larraz faced much opposition and added, "Serrano is not very likeable. My daughter, Carmencita, once asked me, 'Papá, why is Uncle Ramón so disagreeable?'" Larraz, *Memorias*, 340.

52. Franco found the very tall and handsome Miguel Primo de Rivera a winsome and pliable person, if something of a mediocrity. Carmen Franco recalls that "Miguel was a very likeable man. He knew how to get along with people and women were crazy about him. . . . My father always had very good relations with Miguel."

53. As Carmen points out, her father's cordial relations with Arrese were only strengthened after her mother became very friendly with Arrese's strongly Catholic wife. Arrese is lucidly treated in A. de Diego, *José Luis de Arrese o la Falange de Franco* (Madrid, 2001).

54. The best guide to these active but totally secondary maneuverings is K.-J. Ruhl, *Franco, Falange y III Reich* (Madrid, 1986).

55. See Cardona, *El gigante descalzo*, 95–115.

56. The earlier bibliography is listed in W. Haupt, "Die 'Blaue Division' in der Literatur," *Wehrwissenschaftliche Rundschau* 4 (1959). The massive bibliography up to 1988 is described in C. Caballero and R. Ibáñez, *Escritores en las trincheras: La División Azul en sus libros, publicaciones periódicas y filmografía (1941–1988)* (Madrid, 1989), and a good deal more has appeared since that time. G. R. Kleinfeld and L. A. Tambs, *Hitler's Spanish Legion: The Blue Division in Russia* (Carbondale, IL, 1979), remains the best one-volume narrative, while X. Moreno Juliá, *La División Azul: Sangre española en Rusia, 1941–1945* (Barcelona, 2004), provides the fullest perspective, treating political, military, and diplomatic aspects.

57. For a broad sketch of Hitler's auxiliaries, see R.-D. Müller, *The Unknown Eastern Front: The Wehrmacht and Hitler's Foreign Soldiers* (London, 2012).

58. R. Ibáñez Hernández, "Escritores en las trincheras: La División Azul," in S. G. Payne and D. Contreras, eds., *España y la Segunda Guerra Mundial* (Madrid, 1996), 55–87.

59. *Arriba*, June 24, 1941.

60. Ibid., July 18, 1941. Needless to say, this highly imprudent speech was not included in the subsequent edition of *Palabras del Caudillo*.

61. *DGFP*, D:13, 222–24.

62. Ibid., D:13, 441–43.

63. *Solidaridad Nacional* (Barcelona), July 31, 1941, quoted in F. Vilanova, "España en el nuevo orden europeo," in A. C. Moreno Cantano, ed., *El ocaso de la verdad: Propaganda y prensa exterior en la España franquista (1936–1945)* (Gijon, 2011), 241.

64. Memorandum of Conversation by Cordell Hull, Sept. 13, 1941. Thanks to J. M. Thomàs for this document. A full account of U.S.-Spanish relations in this period may be found in his *Roosevelt and Franco during the Second World War: From the Spanish Civil War to Pearl Harbor* (New York, 2008). See also M. A. López Zapico, *Las relaciones entre Estados Unidos y España durante la Guerra Civil y el primer franquismo (1936–1945)* (Gijón, 2008).

65. R. Gubern, *"Raza" (un ensueño del General Franco)* (Madrid, 1977), examines the text and film in detail.

66. On development of the new Tripartite Pact, see E. Mawdsley, *December 1941: Twelve Days That Began a World War* (New Haven, CT, 2011), 236–39, 247–53.

Chapter 12. Surviving World War II

1. The full text is in J. Tusell and G. García Queipo de Llano, *Carrero: La eminencia gris de Franco* (Madrid, 1993), 61–64.

2. C. J. H. Hayes, *Wartime Mission in Spain* (New York, 1946), 30.

3. For an evaluation, see E. Kennedy, "Ambassador Carlton J. H. Hayes's Wartime Diplomacy: Making Spain a Haven from Hitler," *Diplomatic History* 36, no. 2 (2012): 237–60, and, more broadly, J. M. Thomàs, *Roosevelt, Franco, and the End of the Second World War* (New York, 2011).

4. Monarchists talked with officials in Germany in the winter and again in the spring of 1941, and at the end of the year tried to bring the commander of the Blue Division into their confabulations. Togores, *Muñoz Grandes*, 336–44. Don Juan, the pretender, continued to move in this direction as late as March 1, 1942. Ibid., 349–50.

5. Despite his experience as a staff officer, Vigón was completely unable to perceive the importance of American entry into the war. On February 19, 1942, he wrote to Muñoz Grandes that the Allies had already lost, but if the war continued much longer the "modest participation" of Spain on the German side would be necessary. He observed that the British were treating Spain with kid gloves ("they are tolerating more than a little impertinence from us"). The Americans, he said, took a stronger line but were hopelessly naïve and inept and would soon be defeated. In another letter of April 29, he expressed confidence that the Royal Navy would soon be swept from the Mediterranean and explained that he was trying to store up enough aviation gasoline to enable Spain to fight for two decisive weeks on the side of the Axis. Ibid., 346, 351.

6. Jaráiz Franco, *Historia de una disidencia*, 59–60.

7. On the final years of Don Nicolás, see Franco Bahamonde, *Nosotros*, 29–30, and González Duro, *Franco*, 33–39.

8. On political tensions with Carlists, see M. Martorell, *Retorno a la lealtad: El desafío carlista al franquismo* (Madrid, 2010).

9. The full text of the conversation was first presented in L. López Rodó, *La larga marcha hacia la monarquía* (Barcelona, 1978), 503–7.

10. The reports of August 20 and 28 that Franco received on the accused, Juan José Domínguez Muñoz, were incomplete but did not present him in a favorable light. FNFF, *Documentos inéditos*, 3:585–86.

11. Varela's version of the crisis is in Martínez Roda, *Varela*, 339–49.

12. Carmen Franco says that at one point Serrano Suñer sought to use his wife, Zita, to influence her sister to have Franco change his policy. "Since Serrano believed that my father

should be more pro-German, Aunt Zita came one day to harangue my mother. She became extremely upset and began to cry afterward, but my father told her: 'Don't pay any attention to your sister Zita, because she is only repeating what Ramón has just told her. That's why she says these things, but she would never do it on her own, so don't be upset.' But after that, relations became colder. I still got along well with my cousins, but between my mother and Aunt Zita things were no longer the same."

13. Saña, *El franquismo sin mitos*, 267.

14. Kleinfeld and Tambs, *Hitler's Spanish Legion*, 206–8.

15. *Akten zur deutschen Auswärtigen Politik* (hereafter *ADAP*) (Göttingen, 1969), E:3, 454.

16. Tusell, *Franco, España*, 411.

17. F. Gómez-Jordana Souza, *Milicia y diplomacia: Diarios del conde de Jordana, 1936–1944* (Burgos, 2002), 130–31.

18. Hayes, *Wartime Mission*, 71.

19. Ruhl, *Franco, Falange y III Reich*, 182.

20. Tusell and García Queipo de Llano, *Carrero*, 83–87.

21. Ibid., 87–90.

22. Franco, *Palabras del Caudillo*, 523–27.

23. *Informaciones* (Madrid), Dec. 19, 1942.

24. Kleinfeld and Tambs, *Hitler's Spanish Legion*, 231–32.

25. *ADAP*, E:5.1, 29–31, 41–42, 94–95, 125–28.

26. E. Sáenz-Francés, *Entre la antorcha y la esvástica: Franco en la encrucijada de la Segunda Guerra Mundial* (Madrid, 2009), presents an exhaustive study of German-Spanish relations during 1943.

27. J. M. Doussinague, *España tenía razón (1939–1945)* (Madrid, 1950), 150–79; J. Tusell, *Franco, España*, 393–96; A. Marquina Barrio, *La diplomacia vaticana y la España de Franco* (Madrid, 1982), 341–44.

28. Church leaders in Spain generally avoided involvement with the regime's politics but at the same time followed Vatican instructions to beware of Nazism, and the denunciation of aspects of the latter in two different Spanish diocesan publications, the second in October 1942, had caused a minor "sensation," in the words of the American ambassador. See Hayes to Hull, Oct. 9, 1942, United States Department of State, *Foreign Relations of the United States, 1942*, 3 vols. (hereafter *FRUS*) (Washington, DC, 1943), 3:297–98, and A. Calvo Espiga, "Precedentes de la pastoral de 12 de marzo de 1942 de D. Fidel García Martínez, Obispo de Calahorra, sobre el régimen nazi," *Kalakorikos* 12 (2007): 9–57.

29. Tusell, *Franco, España*, 410.

30. *FRUS*, 2:613–15.

31. Togores, *Yagüe*, 723–24.

32. *Boletín Oficial del Estado*, Oct. 14, 1943.

33. Franco had first received a report on August 17 that some such initiative might be in the offing. Franco Archive, 172:21.

34. For the details and the text of the letter, see Martínez Roda, *Varela*, 358–61, 544, and de la Cierva, *Franco*, 638–40.

35. Tusell, *Franco, España*, 429.

36. *ADAP*, E:7, 250–54.

37. Franco Archive, 31:2554.

38. Ibid., 64:2568.

39. On March 6, Asensio prepared a very long and respectful letter to Franco insisting that Spain could not merely capitulate to the Allies but recommending that the only way out would be the restoration of the monarchy. Franco took nearly six weeks to reply, assuring his minister of the army that Spain would not simply capitulate and would make no political concessions. Franco Archive, 41:44.

40. Thomàs, *Roosevelt, Franco, and the End of the Second World War*, 67–128.

41. R. García Pérez, *Franquismo y Tercer Reich: Las relaciones económicas hispano-alemanas durante la Segunda Guerra Mundial* (Madrid, 1994), 476 and passim.

42. The second and most extensive of these memoranda he titled "Consideraciones sobre una futura constitución política del mundo," which concluded that the outcome of the war in Europe would be politically catastrophic, leaving the United States and the Soviet Union in hegemonic positions. Franco Archive, 1:127.

43. F. Sánchez Agustí, *Maquis y Pirineos, la gran invasión (1944–1945)* (Lleida, 2001); D. Arasa, *La invasión de los maquis: El intento armado para derribar el franquismo que consolidó el régimen y provocó depuraciones en el PCE* (Barcelona, 2004).

44. M. J. Cava Mesa, *Los diplomáticos de Franco: J. F. de Lequerica, temple y tenacidad (1890–1963)* (Bilbao, 1989), is a very antiseptic biography.

45. Carmen Franco recalls that "Lequerica was very likeable . . . , a bon vivant, very amusing. But no, he was not cynical, but a Basque and a bon vivant. He always said that the greater part of Spain was uninhabitable, but that thanks to electricity one could live with air conditioning, with power and heating. And that the only really inhabitable territory was from Burgos to Arcachon."

46. An undated directive posited the goal "that *the world assimilate our political doctrine,* as we carry out the providential historical destiny of Spain, Instructor of the Peoples and Apostle of the new Christian-Social Era that is dawning." Franco Archive, 64:2571.

47. For a critical survey, see I. Rohr, *The Spanish Right and the Jews, 1898–1945: Anti-semitism and Opportunism* (Brighton, UK, 2007).

48. On Jews in early-twentieth-century Spain, see D. Rozenberg, *La España contemporánea y la cuestión judía* (Madrid, 2010), G. Alvarez Chillida, *El antisemitismo en España: La imagen del judío (1812–2002)* (Madrid, 2002), A. Marquina and G. I. Ospina, *España y los judíos en el siglo XX: La acción exterior* (Madrid, 1987), I. González, *Los judíos y la Segunda República española, 1931–1939* (Madrid, 2004), and I. González, *Los judíos y la Guerra Civil española* (Madrid, 2009).

49. Arrests in Spain were very few, but one German Jewish refugee died in a Spanish prison. R. Sala Rosé, *La penúltima frontera: Fugitivos del nazismo en España (1940–1945)* (Barcelona, 2011).

50. For brief sketches of these brave diplomats, see E. Martín de Pozuelo, *El franquismo, cómplice del Holocausto (y otros episodios desconocidos de la dictadura)* (Barcelona, 2012), 85–111.

51. The key study is B. Rother, *Franco y el Holocausto* (Madrid, 2005), and his articles "Franco als Retter der Juden: Zur Entstehung einer Legende," *Zeitschrift für Geschichtswissenschaft* 45, no. 2 (1997): 121–46, and "Spanish Attempts to Rescue Jews from the Holocaust: Lost Opportunities," *Mediterranean Historical Review* 17, no. 2 (2002): 47–68. See also D. Carcedo, *Un español frente al Holocausto* (Madrid, 2000) and *Entre bestias y héroes: Los españoles que plantaron cara al Holocausto* (Barcelona, 2011), as well as D. Salinas, *España, los sefarditas y el Tercer Reich (1939–1945)* (Valladolid, 1997). For a brief overview, see Payne, *Franco and Hitler*, 209–35.

The contacts in Lisbon had been promoted first by Jordana, who had sent the Falangist intellectual Javier Martínez de Bedoya to the Portuguese capital as press attaché early in 1944 to develop relations with Jewish agencies. For Bedoya's version of these events, see L. Palacios Bañuelos, *El franquismo ordinario* (Astorga, 2011), 221–25. For Portugal's policy, see A. Milgram, *Portugal, Salazar, and the Jews* (Jerusalem, 2011).

52. Hayes reported that he had said to Lequerica on August 26 that "some Americans could understand why, back in 1940 and 1941, Spain might have felt obliged to pursue a policy of benevolent neutrality toward Germany, but no American could understand why, during the past six months at least, Spain should seek to pursue a policy of narrowly legalistic neutrality when it should so obviously, in the light of military developments, be pursuing a policy of benevolent neutrality towards the Allies. Spain, in many respects, was a more important country than Switzerland, Sweden, Portugal or Turkey, yet its policy lagged much behind these countries." Hayes to U.S. Dept. of State, Sept. 5, 1944. (Thanks to J. M. Thomàs for this document.)

53. Quoted in F. Diaz Plaja, *La España política del siglo XX*, vol. 4 (Barcelona, 1972), 149–52.

54. The original theorist of organic democracy in Spain had been the renowned polyglot intellectual Salvador de Madariaga, who feared that inorganic democracy might destroy Europe during the interwar period. A tepid supporter of Franco during the first months of the Civil War, he turned in 1937 to the need for mediation and then, from 1939 to the end of Franco's life, was one of his sharpest critics. See P. C. González Cuevas, "Salvador de Madariaga y la democracia orgánica," *Historia 16* II, no. 127 (1986): 27–31.

55. These were the first elections within the syndical system for *enlaces sindicales* (partly analogous to shop stewards).

56. Suárez Fernández, *FF*, 3:453.

57. Quoted in D. Reynolds, *In Command of History: Churchill Fighting and Writing the Second World War* (London, 2004), 463. See D. Smyth, *Diplomacy and Strategy of Survival: British Policy and Franco's Spain, 1940–41* (Cambridge, 1986), 247–48.

58. On relations with Japan, see the thorough study by F. Rodao, *Franco y el imperio japonés* (Barcelona, 2002). Of the nearly thirteen hundred Spanish missionaries in the Far East, at least sixty-six were killed in the war, many of these deliberately murdered by the Japanese. D. Arasa, *Los españoles y la guerra del Pacífico* (Barcelona, 2001), 373.

59. Franco Archive, 41:1447.

60. A. J. Lleonart and F. J. Castiella y Maíz et al., eds., *España y ONU (1945–1946): La "cuestión española"* (Madrid, 1978), 30–33; R. E. Sanders, *Spain and the United Nations, 1945–1950* (New York, 1966).

61. For the Soviet accusations, see S. Pozharskaya, *Tainaya diplomatiya Madrida* (Moscow, 1979), 189–241.

Chapter 13. Franco at Bay

1. The French intelligence report, dated February 27, 1946, is cited in D. W. Pike, "Franco and the Axis Stigma," *Journal of Contemporary History* 17, no. 3 (1982): 369–407.

2. Franco's government looked into the feasibility of atomic weapons, but Franco decided that these would be too complicated and difficult. In 1947, for example, the Commission for the Study of Applied Physics (Comisión de Estudios de Física Aplicada), a unit created by the Higher Council of Scientific Research (Consejo Superior de Investigaciones

Científicas), examined the problems involved in developing "the military applications of nuclear energy" and found that such a project was not feasible given Spain's resources, according to Cardona, *Franco y sus generales*, 124. Nonetheless, some Spanish military leaders did not give up, and Franco's old chief of staff, Juan Vigón, is given credit for convincing him to create an Atomic Research Council (Junta de Investigaciones Atómicas) in September 1948 to explore peaceful uses of nuclear energy. Alongside this was set up a new corporation, Studies and Projects for Special Alloys (Estudios y Proyectos de Aleaciones Especiales), secretly charged with the direction of nuclear research. Cardona, *El gigante descalzo*, 176. These efforts, however, did not go very far.

3. The Axis refugee colony included the SS commando leader Otto Skorzeny, the Belgian Fascist Léon Degrelle, various French collaborators, a group of Rumanian legionnaires (some of whom, however, had passed through Buchenwald as prisoners), and a few Croatian Ustashi. See C. Collado Seidel, *España, refugio nazi* (Madrid, 2005).

4. For a vivid account of Communist urban guerrilla activities in Madrid, see A. Trapiello, *La noche de los cuatro caminos: Una historia del maquis, Madrid, 1945* (Madrid, 2001).

5. E. Marco Nadal, *Todos contra Franco: La Alianza Nacional de Fuerzas Democráticas, 1944–1947* (Madrid, 1982).

6. D. W. Pike, "L'immigration espagnole en France (1945–1952)," *Revue d'histoire moderne et contemporaine* 24, no. 2 (1977): 286–300.

7. There is an extensive literature on opposition politics and the insurgency of the Maquis, disproportionate to its significance and effectiveness. For a brief survey, see B. de Riquer, "La dictadura de Francco," in J. Fontana and R. Villares, eds., *Historia de España*, vol. 9 (Barcelona, 2010), 192–245, and, more broadly, J. Tusell et al., eds., *La oposición al regimen de Franco*, 2 vols. (Madrid, 1990). For a brief overall account of the insurgency, see A. Nieto, *Las guerrillas antifranquistas* (Madrid, 2007).

8. *FF*, 4:8.

9. For example, among them were a number of professional officers who had been reincorporated after limited service in the Republican People's Army but who in the new purge were summarily expelled.

10. This "Linea Gutiérrez" was no Maginot Line, but consisted of a series of strong points, fortifications, and obstacles stretching from the Cantabrian coast to the Mediterranean. Cardona, *El gigante descalzo*, 116–40.

11. Information from the Ministry of Justice, dated April 18, 1944, reportedly leaked to the British embassy, gave the figure of approximately 120 executions in preceding months, according to a report of August 31 of that year received by Franco. Franco Archive, 35:1. In addition, the director of prisons was said to have admitted to a British diplomat that seventy more executions took place in the month of September. H. Heine, *La oposición política al franquismo: De 1939 a 1952* (Barcelona, 1983), 293.

12. See J. López Medel, *La milicia universitaria: Alféreces para la paz* (Madrid, 2012).

13. Kindelán, *La verdad*, 75–79.

14. This well-known text has been frequently reprinted, notably in López Rodó, *La larga marcha*, 48–50.

15. Kindelán, *La verdad*, 187.

16. All this was expounded in a memorandum from Carrero Blanco to Franco following the royal manifesto. López Rodó, *La larga marcha*, 54–55.

17. Franco explained most of this in a prolix interview on May 1 with the Catholic leader Alberto Martín Artajo, soon to be his new foreign minister. J. Tusell, *Franco y los católicos: La política interior española entre 1945 y 1957* (Madrid, 1984), 50–51.

18. *FF*, 4:43–44.

19. Tusell, *Franco y los católicos*, 50–51.

20. *Fundamental Laws of the State* (Madrid, 1967); *Leyes fundamentales del estado* (Madrid, 1967).

21. Arrese retained his seat in the Cortes and also his position in the good graces of the caudillo. Two years later he produced a new book, *Capitalismo, comunismo, cristianismo* (Madrid, 1947), which declared that "fascism is not a complete formula" because of its materialism and lack of religiosity and pointed toward Catholic syndicalism as the best solution.

22. Treated in detail in Tusell, *Franco y los católicos*, 52–79.

23. According to Serrano Suñer, *Entre el silencio*, 394–403.

24. The full text is in ibid., 394–400; Franco's annotated copy is in the Franco Archive, 206:119.

25. F. García Lahiguera, *Ramón Serrano Suñer: Un documento para la historia* (Barcelona, 1983), 260–67.

26. Allegedly, Franco made these remarks at several cabinet meetings; the notes were taken by Martín Artajo. See Tusell, *Franco y los católicos*, 103. Minutes were never kept of Franco's cabinet meetings and at the beginning of 1947 he forbade any minister to take detailed notes.

27. Quoted in López Rodó, *La larga marcha*, 57–58.

28. There were certain strings attached, involving terms of probation, to the amnesty granted to the prisoners.

29. *FF*, 4:57–58.

30. Quoted in A. de Miguel, *La herencia del franquismo* (Madrid, 1976), 29.

31. *Arriba*, Mar. 6, 1947.

32. The U. S. Department of State published a documentary booklet, *The Spanish Government and the Axis*, in March 1946. Madrid's reply may be found in Lleonart and Castiella, *España y ONU*, 67–80.

33. F. Franco, *Textos de doctrina política: Palabras y escritos de 1945 a 1950* (Madrid, 1951), 335.

34. F. Portero, *Franco aislado: La cuestión española (1945–1950)* (Madrid, 1989), provides the broadest treatment of foreign affairs during the years of ostracism.

35. U.S. Embassy, *Semanario gráfico*, Mar. 6, 1946.

36. Franco, *Textos de doctrina política*, 66.

37. M. A. Ruiz Carnicer, "La idea de Europa en la cultura franquista 1939–1962," *Hispania* 58, no. 2 (1998): 679–701, treats the regime's alternative concept of Europe.

38. Lleonart and Castiella, *España y ONU*, 69.

39. On British policy toward Spain in these years, see Q. Ahmad, *Britain, Franco, Spain, and the Cold War, 1945–1950*, rev. ed. (Kuala Lampur, 1995), and J. Edwards, *Anglo-American Relations and the Franco Question, 1945–1955* (New York, 1999).

40. On Franco's relations with leaders in Latin America and the Arab world, see M. Eiroa San Francisco, *Política internacional y comunicación en España (1939–1975): Las cumbres de Franco con jefes de estado* (Madrid, 2009).

41. The key study is R. Rein, *The Franco-Perón Alliance: Relations between Spain and Argentina, 1946–1955* (Pittsburgh, PA, 1993); see also Rein's "Another Front Line: Francoists and Anti-Francoists in Argentina, 1936–1949," *Patterns of Prejudice* 31, no. 3 (1997): 17–33. For an overview of economic relations with Latin America in these years, see V. Torrente and G. Manueco, *Las relaciones económicas de España con Hispanoamérica* (Madrid, 1953), 423–526.

42. Soriano, *La mano izquierda*, 73.

43. On the career of Segura, see F. Gil Delgado, *Pedro Segura: Un cardenal de fronteras* (Madrid, 2001), and R. Garriga, *El Cardenal Segura y el nacional-catolicismo* (Barcelona, 1977).

44. *Iglesia, estado y Movimiento Nacional* (Madrid, 1951), 75–76.

45. The literature on Catholicism and Francoism is enormous. Among the best works are G. Hermet, *Les catholiques dans l'Espagne franquiste*, 2 vols. (Paris, 1980–81), R. Gómez Pérez, *Política y religión en el régimen de Franco* (Barcelona, 1976), S. Petschen, *La Iglesia en la España de Franco* (Madrid, 1977), J. J. Ruiz Rico, *El papel político de la Iglesia católica en la España de Franco* (Madrid, 1977), and G. Sánchez Recio, *De las dos ciudades a la resurrección de España: Magisterio pastoral y pensamiento político de Enrique Pla y Deniel* (Valladolid, 1995). The political side is emphasized in G. Redondo, *Política, cultura y sociedad en la España de Franco, 1939–1975*, 3 vols. (Pamplona, 1999–2008), A. Ferrary, *El franquismo: Minorías políticas y conflictos ideológicos, 1936–1956* (Pamplona, 1993), J. Andrés-Gallego et al., *Los españoles entre la religión y la política* (Madrid, 1996), and Cuenca Toribio, *Nacionalismo, franquismo y nacionalcatolicismo*. For a brief overview of the question, see Payne, *Spanish Catholicism*, 171–91.

46. López Rodó, *La larga marcha*, 55–56.

47. Ibid., 57–60.

48. According to Martín Artajo, in Tusell, *Franco y los católicos*, 58.

49. The text can be found in J. Tusell, *La oposición democrática al franquismo* (Barcelona, 1977), 114.

50. Cf. C. Fernández, *Tensiones militares bajo el franquismo* (Barcelona, 1985), 71–72. Kindelán spent seven months in the Canaries and then was passed to the reserve list three years later (1949), unremitting in his Monarchism. It was an ironic end to the career of the military commander who had contributed more than any other single individual to making Franco generalissimo.

51. López Rodó, *La larga marcha*, 73.

52. *Fundamental Laws of the State*, 119.

53. Ibid., 112.

54. For further perspective, see A. Cañellas Mas, "Las Leyes fundamentales en la construcción del nuevo estado," in A. Ferrary and A. Cañellas, eds., *El régimen de Franco: Unas perspectivas de análisis* (Pamplona, 2012), 219–52.

55. On the mission to Estoril and its aftermath, see Tusell, *La oposición democrática*, 161–70, and López Rodó, *La larga marcha*, 76–88.

56. The full text is reproduced in F. González-Doria, *¿Franquismo sin Franco . . . ?* (Madrid, 1974), 38–40.

57. In fact, the report sent to Franco recorded somewhat lower figures: an electoral census of 16,187,992, of whom 14,054,026 voted. Affirmative votes totaled 12,628,983, with 643,501 voting no, and more than 300,000 abstentions or null votes. Franco Archive, 206:128.

According to data in D. Sueiro and B. Díaz Nosty, *Historia del franquismo*, 2 vols. (Barcelona, 1985), 2:106–7, the highest rates of abstention were in Asturias (32.48 percent), Madrid (30.08 percent), and Barcelona (29.50 percent). Vizcaya was only in seventh place at 21.59 percent and Guipuzcoa was far down the line with 15.13 percent. The fullest turnouts on behalf of the regime were registered in Valladolid and Avila.

58. "Notas sobre el balance de diez años del Movimiento Nacional," in Tusell and García Queipo de Llano, *Carrero*, 190.

59. Cardona, *Franco y sus generales*, 136. Franco had first honored Queipo six years earlier, when he personally awarded the elderly general the Gran Cruz Laureada de San Fernando in a major ceremony in Seville in 1944.

60. Franco Archive, 1:224. F. Aguado Sánchez, *El maquis en España* (Madrid, 1975), later supplied a more comprehensive account, presenting slightly higher casualty figures for all parties. J. Aróstegui and J. Marco, eds., *El último frente: La resistencia armada antifranquista en España, 1939–1952* (Madrid, 2008), is a broad survey.

61. On the military in the years following World War II, see Cardona, *El gigante descalzo*, 135–93.

62. Tusell, *Franco y los católicos*, 180.

63. Danvila to Franco, July 6, 1948, Franco Archive, 149:32.

64. J. A. Pérez Mateos, *El rey que vino del exilio* (Planeta, 1981), 24–25.

65. Carmen Franco reports that among the family Franco only "remarked upon what a good sailor Don Juan was and how he loved the sea."

66. J. M. Gil Robles, *La monarquía por la que yo luché* (Madrid, 1976), 276.

67. "Boletín de actividades monárquicas," Franco Archive, 151.

68. Pérez Mateos, *El rey*, 94–97.

69. Gil Robles, *La monarquía*, 308–10.

70. Don Jaime lost most of his capacity for speaking and hearing after a botched treatment for a mastoid infection at the age of four. He had officially renounced his rights on June 21, 1933, ten days after his older brother, the hemophiliac Don Alfonso, had done the same.

71. Heine, *La oposición política*, 401–3.

72. This regulation, known colloquially as the "Aranda law," was promulgated on July 13, 1949, providing for the permanent retirement, at the discretion of the high command, of senior officers at the rank of colonel and above who had been passed over for promotion by at least 10 percent of the holders of their rank. Aranda was given one last chance to repent, then placed in premature retirement along with a score or so other pro-Monarchist officers. In 1977, just before his death, King Juan Carlos restored Aranda's full seniority. So far as is known, he retained all the money paid in bribery by the British.

73. *FF*, 4:383–87.

74. Some of the reports that Franco received on the international activities of Masonry during the 1940s have been published in Casinos and Brunet, *Franco contra los masones*.

75. These articles were later collected and published under the name of Hakim Boor, *Masonería* (Madrid, 1952). This has sometimes been referred to as Franco's third book, after *Diario de una bandera* and *Raza*. Carrero Blanco published similar pseudonymous articles under the name Ginés de Buitrago.

76. M. D. Algora Weber, *Las relaciones hispano-árabes durante el regimen de Franco: La ruptura del aislamiento internacional (1946–1950)* (Madrid, 1995).

77. A full account appears in R. Rein, *In the Shadow of the Holocaust and the Inquisition: Israel's Relations with Francoist Spain* (London, 1997).

78. A. J. Telo, *Portugal e a NATO* (Lisbon, 1996), 71–75, 191–92.
79. Interview with H. V. Kaltenborn, March 24, 1949, Franco Archive, 130:103.
80. Numerous documents describing the trip may be found in the Franco Archive, 254.
81. See Garriga, *Los validos*, 122–24. However, Garriga mistakenly identifies Laureano López Rodó as Carrero's counselor, but in fact his counselor was Professor Amadeo de Fuenmayor.
82. Preston, *Franco*, 598. Soviet strategists were, of course, fully aware of this, and Soviet memoirs have referred to a contingency plan as part of Stalin's final grand strategy of 1951–52 that proposed to preempt any Western redoubt in the Iberian peninsula by means of a large amphibious operation that would accompany outbreak of general war in Europe. This cannot be confirmed, however, and was probably beyond Soviet capabilities.
83. According to Franco's version of this meeting in *FF*, 4:27–31.
84. In his discreet fashion, Carrero had been urging Franco to reorganize his government for more than a year, presenting him with a particularly lengthy memorandum in this regard on April 4, 1951. Franco Archive, 21:39. As usual, the caudillo would not be hurried, and there is no information as to whether or not the disfavor into which Carrero fell temporarily with Doña Carmen was a factor. At any rate, Franco rejected a number of the specific recommendations by Carrero, who wanted to see a diminished role for Falangists and greater attention to the economy and to the evolution toward monarchy.
85. The full text is in R. de la Cierva, *Don Juan de Borbón: Por fin toda la verdad* (Madrid, 1997), 594–612.
86. F. Guirao, *Spain and the Reconstruction of Western Europe, 1945–57* (Houndsmills, 1998).
87. Most of these data are taken from A. Carreras and X. Tafunell, eds., *Estadísticas históricas de España: Siglos XIX–XX*, 3 vols. (Bilbao, 2005).
88. In Palacios, *Las cartas de Franco*, 293–94.
89. On this exchange, see A. Viñas, *Los pactos secretos de Franco con Estados Unidos* (Barcelona, 1981), 144–47.
90. Report of Feb. 2, 1952, Franco Archive, 168:27.
91. A. J. Lleonart, "El ingreso de España en la ONU," *Cuadernos de historia contemporánea* 17 (1995): 111.
92. Francisco Franco, *Pensamiento político de Franco*, 2 vols. (Madrid, 1975), 1:256.
93. These arrangements are treated in detail in A. Jarque Iñiguez, *"Queremos esas bases": El acercamiento de Estados Unidos a la España de Franco* (Alcalá de Henares, 1998), and A. Viñas, *En las garras del águila: Los pactos con Estados Unidos, de Francisco Franco a Felipe González (1945–1995)* (Barcelona, 2003), 23–285. A broader perspective on American relations with rightist authoritarian regimes during the Cold War may be found in R. Escobedo, "El dictador amistoso: Estados Unidos y los regímenes no democráticos durante la Guerra Fría," in Ferrary and Cañellas, *El régimen de Franco*, 253–85.
94. J. C. Jiménez de Aberásturi, *De la derrota a la esperanza: Políticas vascas durante la Segunda Guerra Mundial (1937–1947)* (Bilbao, 1999).

Chapter 14. Franco at His Zenith

1. This speech would later be among others, mainly from the years 1940–43, suppressed in the *Antología del pensamiento de Franco* that was published in 1964. The text appears in *FF*, 5:144.

2. For years Franco had been strongly anti-American, an attitude that external circumstances had forced him to drop in the second half of 1944. Once the rapprochement had been effected, his basic attitude seems to have changed somewhat, despite continuing apprehension about the Masonic affiliation of many American leaders. Carmen Franco reports that in later years in private conversation he would praise the United States for heading the struggle against Communism, as well as its generosity in assisting other countries.

3. Carmen Franco claims that the material to which they objected did not come from Pacón himself, insinuating that the publisher added foreign material, which is doubtful. She observes: "Uncle Pacón was a person who always made his career in the shadow of my father, and I don't know why, always had a slightly critical attitude. My mother was quite upset when she read his book because she said it presented my father through certain things inserted by the publisher, which Uncle Pacón had not written. She was at odds with his widow because the latter had not protested to the publisher when they added things to give the book greater consistency and interest and had changed other things. Uncle Pacón's widow could have protested, but she did not. And then Mamá froze her relationship with that lady."

4. Franco Salgado-Araujo, *Mis conversaciones privadas*, 28.

5. Franco stipulated that the prince would not have to present himself for the formal examinations but that he must be adequately prepared in mathematics to follow technical military studies. Ibid., 9.

6. The full correspondence between Franco and Don Juan is in P. Sainz Rodríguez, *Un reinado en la sombra* (Barcelona, 1983), 378–84.

7. Ibid., 63–64.

8. Ibid., 222–35.

9. Togores, *Muñoz Grandes*, 437–52.

10. See the analysis in Cardona, *Franco y sus generales*, 152–64.

11. M. Parra Celaya, *Juventudes de vida española: El Frente de Juventudes* (Madrid, 2001), is a recent admiring account that nonetheless makes no effort to conceal the small numbers involved by the 1950s.

12. As late as December 1955, only a few months before he was forced to abandon the protectorate, Franco announced that Morocco would not be ready for independence for at least twenty-five years. *ABC*, Dec. 16, 1955.

13. R. Velasco de Castro, *Nacionalismo y colonialismo en Marruecos (1945–1951): El general Varela y los sucesos de Tetuán* (Seville, 2012).

14. For the contradictory Spanish policy during the last years of the protectorate, see Madariaga, *Marruecos*, 383–460, and V. Morales Lezcano, *El final del protectorado hispano-francés en Marruecos: El desafío del nacionalismo magrebí (1945–1962)* (Madrid, 1998).

15. Report dated July 4, 1956, Franco Archive, 166:3.

16. Palacios, *Las cartas de Franco*, 330–44.

17. There are numerous versions of this fatal incident. The preceding narration is based on the recounting given by King Juan Carlos to his long-time personal secretary, General Sabino Fernández Campo, as related by the latter to Jesús Palacios.

18. Franco, *Pensamiento político*, 1:251.

19. Franco Archive, 165:25, 26.

20. Ibid., 165:30.

21. As Carmen Franco sees it, "He rather supported Arrese's plan and the doctrines of the Movement, that is, he supported them but only to a certain point because he understood he couldn't swim against the stream."

22. In 1944, during the first phase of the regime's defascistization, Arrese, who fancied himself a major theorist and intellectual, had published a small book, *El estado totalitario en el pensamiento de José Antonio*, which claimed that the Falange had never supported a totalitarian system, a great oversimplification.

23. Franco Archive, 165:41, 42.

24. González Gallarza died soon afterward but of a major infection, not from the injury.

25. The definitive study is X. Casals Meseguer, "1957: El golpe contra Franco que sólo existió en los rumores," *Revista de historia contemporánea* 72, no. 4 (2008): 241–71.

26. The letter of resignation is in Togores, *Muñoz Grandes*, 421–22.

27. Franco had appointed Barroso head of his *casa militar* the preceding year, when his cousin Pacón had reached mandatory retirement age of sixty-six and passed to the reserve, or "B" list.

28. Despite Artajo's years of faithful service, Franco followed his customary practice of not informing him of his dismissal in a personal meeting, but by sending him an abrupt dispatch by motorcycle messenger.

29. Franco Archive, 258.

30. There is now a fairly extensive literature. See R. Casas de la Vega, *La última guerra de África (Campaña de Ifni-Sáhara)* (Madrid, 1985), J. R. Diego Aguirre, *La última guerra colonial de España: Ifni-Sáhara (1957–1958)* (Málaga, 1993), L. M. Vidal Guardiola, *Ifni, 1957–1958* (Madrid, 2006), and J. E. Alonso del Barrio, *¿Encrucijada o abandono?*, vol. 1 of *Sáhara-Ifni* (Zaragoza, 2010).

31. Moroccan occupation of the Tarfaya strip is said by some to have marked the beginning of Saharan nationalism, for the native Saharauis quickly found that the sultan's regime was much more oppressive than that of Franco. For a broader analysis, see G. Jensen, *War and Insurgency in the Western Sahara* (Carlisle, PA, 2013).

32. Franco's opinion of his neighboring dictator had risen greatly over the years. In 1939–40 his attitude had been condescending to the point of secretly threatening invasion, but he came to esteem Salazar more and more as a fully supportive ally. During these months Franco granted his most extensive interview ever to Serge Grossard of *Le Figaro* (June 12, 1958), in which he praised Salazar as "the most complete and respectable statesman of all those whom I have known. . . . His only defect perhaps is his modesty."

33. Franco Salgado-Araujo, *Mis conversaciones privadas*, 222–23; Franco Archive, 165:79.

34. Franco Salgado-Araujo, *Mis conversaciones privadas*, 166.

35. Franco Archive, 258:6.

36. The technical design is explained in detail by the principal architect Diego Méndez, in his *El Valle de los Caídos: Idea, proyecto y construcción* (Madrid, 1982). For commentary, see A. Cirici, *La estética del franquismo* (Barcelona, 1977), 112–24, and A. Bonet Correa, ed., *Arte del franquismo* (Madrid, 1981), 115–30.

37. His cousin quoted him as opining: "There were many dead on the Red side who fought because they sought to fulfill a duty to the Republic, and others who had been forcibly drafted. The monument was not constructed to continue dividing Spaniards into two irreconcilable bands. It was built, and this was always my intention, as a memorial to

the victory over Communism, which had sought to dominate Spain. That was justification for my goal of burying the fallen of both political bands." Franco Salgado-Araujo, *Mis conversaciones privadas*, 239.

38. There is uncertainty on this point. Carmen never heard her father express such a wish: "No, the only person who said that my father wanted to be buried there was the architect. We had no idea, nor did I, of where he wanted to be buried, but apparently he did tell the architect, because my father visited the Valley of the Fallen many times while it was under construction." Franco may also have mentioned it to his successor, King Juan Carlos. "I think he did. Since his final agony was so long and drawn out, people certainly had time to talk among themselves and it seemed to them it was the most appropriate spot."

39. Both Franco and his daughter enjoyed horseback riding, and she remembers accompanying him as a teenager on horseback through the rough countryside to inspect the works: "In the beginning my father was extremely interested in the great sculptures of the four evangelists and in the dimensions of the cross. . . . He talked about this a good deal with the architects, who said that the cross could not be so large, but Papá insisted that they study it more, and they could figure it out. Many people were buried there who had been in mass graves, that is, executed by one side or the other. More of those who fell on our side than from the other, but, still, to some extent a site of burial for both sides."

40. Data on the construction of the Valley of the Fallen may be found in D. Sueiro, *La construcción del Valle de los Caídos* (Madrid, 1976), and J. Blanco, *Valle de los Caídos* (Madrid, 2009).

41. Personal security arrangements for Franco were elaborate but by no means fool-proof. Carmen says that her father was "very providentialist," which was undoubtedly correct, and never discussed such things. "For example, when the Christmas lights were put up in Madrid, my mother always said, 'Paco, let's take a ride to see Madrid.' And the two went by car, with only one escort car behind them, no more." She also insists that the stories that he employed a "double" to impersonate him on certain major occasions are pure fabrications.

42. V. A. Walters, *Silent Missions* (New York, 1978), 305.

43. Ibid., 307.

44. Part of the conversation is presented in E. Martín de Pozuelo, *Los secretos del franquismo: España en los papeles desclasificados del espionaje norteamericano desde 1934 hasta la Transición* (Barcelona, 2007), 224–28. Castiella delivered the message to the White House on March 23, 1960, and reported that "he could assure the president that this matter would very soon be resolved to his satisfaction," since "General Franco had decided that this be done." He promised a full report, which was sent by Madrid on April 6. This was full of doubletalk, complaining that Protestants as a minority were "not very patriotic," compared with Jews and Arabs resident in Spain. The report admitted a problem but then proceeded to dodge it. On the one hand, it alleged that Protestants really were not persecuted, and, on the other, said measures were being taken to correct problems. All of this was an "artificial" dilemma, it was claimed, perhaps due to the misplaced zeal of certain local officials who felt pressured by anti-Protestant public opinion. There was to be established a central registry for dissenting confessions (*registro central de confesiones disidentes*) through which groups with a certain number of members could obtain official recognition, all of which sounded like the official registries in Communist countries. Protestants were slowly being shown

somewhat greater toleration, and the State Department did not press the issue. Ibid., 229–36.

45. Carmen says that her father "was extremely interested in this visit. . . . And then he found Eisenhower very likeable, for they were both military men. . . . He took a real shine to him, for Eisenhower was very nice and knew how to deal with people. Their conversation was very enjoyable, because, though some translators are very slow or twist the meaning a little, the American general Vernon Walters was an excellent translator, a man with much personality and talent." The full transcript of the principal conversation is in the Franco Archive, 98:16, and is published in Suárez, *Franco*, 566–72.

46. D. D. Eisenhower, *The White House Years: Waging Peace, 1956–1961* (New York, 1965), 509–10.

47. Walters, *Silent Missions*, 306.

48. Ibid., 307.

Chapter 15. Franco at Home

1. L. de Galinsoga (with F. Franco Salgado Araujo), *Centinela de Occidente* (Barcelona, 1956).

2. The American edition of the memoirs of the former British ambassador Sir Samuel Hoare was titled *Complacent Dictator* (New York, 1947).

3. For an anthology of such dithyrambs, see C. Fernández, *El general Franco* (Barcelona, 1983), 311–24.

4. Professor Philip Powell was at one time director of the University of California's program in Madrid and related this anecdote to Stanley Payne in Los Angeles in May 1965. Though sometimes of dubious authenticity, one of the best collections of personal anecdotes is Baón, *La cara humana*.

5. Quoted in Franco Salgado-Araujo, *Mis conversaciones privadas*, 50.

6. Ibid., 55.

7. Ibid., 50.

8. Ibid., 178.

9. A. Bayod, ed., *Franco visto por sus ministros* (Barcelona, 1981), 128.

10. Franco Salgado-Araujo, *Mis conversaciones privadas*, 159.

11. M. Fraga Iribarne, *Memoria breve de una vida pública* (Barcelona, 1981), 41.

12. According to Laureano López Rodó; see Bayod, *Franco visto*, 167.

13. José María López de Letona, quoted in ibid., 209.

14. Carlos Rein Segura, quoted in ibid., 74.

15. Franco Salgado-Araujo, *Mis conversaciones privadas*, 285.

16. Ibid., 207.

17. Ibid., 185, 317.

18. Carmen has observed that her father liked to write his own texts "in the early days certainly, always. Toward the end of his life each minister would send him an outline, so that he could grasp things better, particularly with regard to statistics . . . , but he always did a draft of his own by longhand and then had it typed. But Papá always wrote, and he very much enjoyed doing it."

19. Soriano, *La mano izquierda*, 125.

20. The full list is provided by his household staff member Cobos Arévalo, *La vida*

privada, 240–42. This is the frankest, the most objective, and one of the best-informed memoirs about Franco.

21. For the history of this relic, see G. Huesa Lope, *La mano de Santa Teresa de Jesús* (Ronda, 1996).

22. His public statements on religion were collected and published under the title *Francisco Franco: Pensamiento católico* (Madrid, 1958).

23. By the time of his death, the official count was a total of 5,023 individual commissions, made up of 68,506 persons. Pozuelo Escudero, *Los últimos*, 107–8.

24. Failure to have learned English well seems to have been a source of some frustration. As his foreign minister Martín Artajo noted, his pronunciation was poor and phoneticized in Spanish style. Tusell, *Franco y los católicos*, 113.

25. Franco Martínez-Bordiú, *La naturaleza de Franco*, 67–68. According to his daughter, Franco "read the Bible and very boring books that he said were very interesting, but that I couldn't manage. They had to do with a nun in the time of Philip II, a nun who wrote a lot and fascinated him [Santa Teresa de Avila?]. They were small, old-style books set in terrible type. . . . My father read a great deal, mainly at night. He had supper early and later read in bed—too much, according to my mother, until very late. He loved that. And he read a little of everything: novels, of course, he did not, he was only interested in serious books. He had a personal secretary, a naval officer, father of a singer who sadly died young. This naval man pointed out certain things, telling him about new books that might interest him. He liked biographies and current affairs and also history books, as well as books on religion and other faiths, which also interested him a good deal."

26. Cobos Arévalo, *La vida privada*, 106.

27. Interview with Carmen Franco Polo, *Boletín de la Fundación Nacional Francisco Franco*, 57 (1992).

28. The principal memoir of hunting parties, which is not particularly informative, is A. Martínez-Bordiú Ortega, *Franco en familia: Cacerías en Jaén* (Barcelona, 1994). The author was the brother of Franco's son-in-law.

29. Carlos Rein Segura, agriculture minister from 1945 to 1951, recalls that when Franco took up hunting regularly in the mid-1940s, "he was only an average shot, in fact, rather poor." Bayod, *Franco visto*, 78.

30. Franco Salgado-Araujo, *Mis conversaciones privadas*, 72. See L. A. Tejada, "Las cacerías de Franco," *Historia 16* 4, no. 37 (1979): 19–30.

31. Franco Salgado-Araujo, *Mis conversaciones privadas*, 270. The psychiatrist Enrique González Duro, author of the principal attempt at a psychological biography, conjectures about the potential sexual symbolism involved in this compulsive hunting by a man who led an extremely circumspect sex life, but that must remain a matter of speculation. González Duro, *Franco*, 313–18.

32. Carmen Franco also became a minor victim on February 1, 1961, when Manuel Fraga Iribarne, one of Franco's top officials (soon to become a minister), was an invited participant. Fraga had little experience in such matters and allowed his aim to stray in pursuit of a partridge after failing to make use of a *pantalla* (blind), splattering a little buckshot on Carmen Franco, who was not far away. She was not seriously injured, and Franco, though miffed, did not make a big thing of the incident. It does not seem to have interfered with Fraga's political career. Fraga Iribarne, *Memoria breve*, 59.

33. Franco Salgado-Araujo, *Mis conversaciones privadas*, 37. Vicente Gil eventually

published his own memoir of his long service as Franco's physician, *Cuarenta años junto a Franco* (Barcelona, 1981).

34. Described by Gil, *Cuarenta años junto*, 63–76.

35. Carmen Franco explains: "He always liked drawing. At one point . . . his physician, Vicente Gil, said that he had to move about more, that sitting all day in his office and then eating, and sitting down again for coffee, was bad for his health: he had to get out and walk, not just sit. . . . But since he had little free time and, when he went out, he had to call for his guards and car and a retinue to get out in the country, all that was too complicated. On the other hand, if he devoted himself to painting after eating, when the others were taking coffee, that gave him a chance to use his time, and he was standing and moving. When you are painting on an easel, you are up and moving from one side to the other. And in that way he began to paint more seriously. But he didn't paint out of doors, no, inside."

36. The best published small collection of Franco's paintings will be found in the illustrations accompanying the book by his grandson, Franco Martínez-Bordiú, *La naturaleza de Franco*. Some of the paintings were destroyed in the two fires that broke out at the Pazo in the years after Franco's death, very possibly arson.

37. Gil, *Cuarenta años junto*, 134–35.

38. That the insurance syndicate was fabrication is the conclusion of R. Garriga, *La Señora de El Pardo* (Barcelona, 1979). The best discussion of Doña Carmen's acquisitions and purchases is in Enríquez, *Carmen Polo*, 105–13.

39. Franco Salgado-Araujo, *Mis conversaciones privadas*, 180.

40. Franco Martínez-Bordiú, *La naturaleza de Franco*, 52–54.

41. Franco Bahamonde, *Nosotros*.

42. Sánchez Soler, *Los Franco*, 182.

43. Garriga, *Nicolás Franco*, 272–85.

44. Nicolás and Pilar Franco, not their brother, saw to it that she received a widow's pension.

45. The letter is quoted in full in Fernández, *El general Franco*, 310.

46. For fuller treatment of this bizarre story, see Togores, *Millán Astray*, 415–17. Though unable to legitimize fully the daughter that was born, Millán Astray proved a devoted father and visited her almost daily.

A cognate problem was that of the respected sometime captain-general of Madrid, Miguel Rodrigo. He hoped to marry his long-time housekeeper, but knew that Franco would consider this quite irregular, and so Rodrigo dared to take the step only shortly before he died.

47. *Diez Minutos*, Oct. 15, 1980.

48. The Spanish "cafetería" has no precise equivalent in the English-speaking world. It is neither a bar nor a coffeehouse in the American sense and not quite a pub in the British style, but combines features of all these.

49. There was also talk about the candidacy of Cristóbal Colón, son of the Duque de Veragua and direct descendant of the discoverer of America, though this may have had more to do with symbolism than reality.

50. Quoted in R. de la Cierva, *Historia del franquismo*, 2 vols. (Barcelona, 1978), 2:99.

51. Carmen explains, "As a grandfather, Papá really enjoyed having the grandchildren around. It has been said that his favorite granddaughter was Carmen [the oldest], but that's not true. Carmen was the favorite of my mother, but my father's favorite was Mery [Mariola], a lively and sassy little girl. Papá said that she seemed to be a *ferrolana* because the girls that

he remembered from his childhood in El Ferrol were like that, very, very outspoken. When they were little they visited all the time, or rather, didn't visit but lived regularly at El Pardo during the weekends. They stayed in a special part that was not too well kept up but was reserved for them and the Englishwoman whom I hired to care for them. They spent all of Saturdays and Sundays there and then went back to school on Monday mornings, staying at home until Fridays."

52. The clearest testimony is that of the oldest grandson, Francisco Franco Martínez-Bordiú: "She took care of us day by day, and we only noticed the presence of our parents if we got sick. Most days there was barely time to tell them about our grades and get a kiss before they went out to dinner.

"Miss Hibbs was like a cavalry sergeant and everyone at El Pardo was afraid of her. She set rules and duties and protected our interests like a lioness with her cubs. She permitted no one, not even my grandfather, to interfere with her supervision of the children. I spent much more time with my grandparents than did my siblings, but when Nanny punished me, which was not infrequently, my grandmother would try to intercede, saying 'His grandfather will be displeased when he learns that his grandson cannot accompany him. . . .' But, implacably, she would reply that she did not care 'what His Excellency might say.' And she rarely canceled the punishment." Franco Martínez-Bordiú, *La naturaleza de Franco*, 35.

53. Enríquez, *Carmen Polo*, 150–51.

54. This explains why to date he is the only descendant of Franco to write a book about him. His own account of moving back to El Pardo will be found in Franco Martínez-Bordiú, *La naturaleza de Franco*, 175–77.

55. Ibid., 33.

56. J. L. Palma Gámiz, *El paciente de El Pardo: Crónicas de una agonía imprevisible* (Madrid, 2004), 106.

57. J. Giménez Arnau, *Yo, Jimmy (Mi vida entre los Franco)* (Barcelona, 1980). All the family members and close associates who published memoirs—Franco Salgado-Araujo, Pilar Franco, her daughter Pilar Jaráiz, and Vicente Gil—refer to Villaverde in rather scathing terms. For a different, rather more balanced, portrait of Villaverde, see Palma Gámiz, *El paciente de El Pardo*, 243–46.

58. Franco Martínez-Bordiú, *La naturaleza de Franco*, 32–33.

59. Cobos Arévalo, *La vida privada*, 91–92.

60. Martínez-Bordiú Ortega, *Franco en familia*, 192.

61. Ibid.; Franco Martínez-Bordiú, *La naturaleza de Franco*, 138–40.

62. For example, his nephew Alfonso Jaráiz Franco wrote to him in October 1946: "Dear Uncle Paco: I want you to be the first to know that I have asked my sweetheart to marry me. I know that you would prefer someone else but we love each other and she is very good. Mamá [Doña Pilar] is still opposed, but once she gets to know her she will get over it. For a wedding present I would prefer a dining-room set." A month later, on November 29, Pilar Jaráiz Franco asked for help in paying the fees for her admission to the College of Lawyers: "The expense is considerable and we need help. Toñuco [her son] has been approved for admission [to the General Military Academy] and we have two girls in the Sacred Heart [Catholic school]. Since you have always been very generous with us, I want to ask a favor: to enter . . . I have to pay a fee of two thousand pesetas and would be very grateful if you could help with that." Both letters are in the Franco Archive, 74.

63. Accounts for this period are in ibid., 29 and 29bis (reverse).

64. On June 30, 1956, the total was 21,764,230.60 pesetas, and on June 30, 1961, it amounted to 23,405,098 pesetas. Ibid., 29bis:74, 95, and 99. It might be pointed out that if the very low Spanish price level of 1961 is adjusted to twenty-first-century values, this would be worth more than ten times as much.

65. Franco Martínez-Bordiú, *La naturaleza de Franco*, 168.

66. In the twenty-first century, after Madrid had expanded a great deal, the local government rezoned part of the estate for suburban development, making it possible for Franco's heirs to sell that portion for a considerable sum for construction of housing.

67. Gil, *Cuarenta años junto*, 131; Franco Salgado-Araujo, *Mis conversaciones privadas*, 395.

68. M. Sánchez Soler, *Villaverde: Fortuna y caída de la casa Franco* (Barcelona, 1990), and *Los Franco* investigate the family business dealings in detail. See also Garriga, *Nicolás Franco*, 293–320.

69. Franco Martínez-Bordiú, *La naturaleza de Franco*, 32.

70. Franco Salgado-Araujo, *Mis conversaciones privadas*, 178–79.

71. Ibid., 111.

72. Cobos Arévalo, *La vida privada*, 85–87, 101.

73. Ibid., 93, 97–98.

74. Of these, 470 were Spanish productions and 1,492 came from abroad. Ibid., 134.

75. Ibid., 133–37, 235–36.

76. Ibid., 251.

Chapter 16. Development Dictator

1. For a survey of the 1950s in Spain, see J. Soto Viñolo, *Los años 50* (Madrid, 2009).

2. Franco Archive, 156:9.

3. According to Navarro Rubio in Bayod, *Franco visto*, 89.

4. M. Navarro Rubio, *Mis memorias* (Barcelona, 1991), 124–31, and his "La batalla de la estabilización," *Anales de la Real Academia de Ciencias Morales y Políticas* 54 (1977): 174–203.

5. He listed his concerns in a memo titled "Problemas de la estabilización." Franco Archive, 258:82. Carmen says that he was surprised by the success of the stabilization plan, since he had really not expected that much. "I don't think that he believed the economy would grow so rapidly, but of course he was quite satisfied to have made the change."

6. The other decade was the 1920s. The earlier decade advanced no farther than an early-middle phase of modernization that ended in civil war, while the later decade would achieve decisive growth that could make possible political democratization, though this was not what Franco had in mind. On these decisive changes and the entire later phase of the regime, see N. Townson, ed., *Spain Transformed: The Late Franco Dictatorship, 1959–75* (Hampshire, UK, 2010).

7. The principal letters are published in Sainz Rodríguez, *Un reinado*, 397–406.

8. A memo that Franco drew up a year or so later even included a brief list of the books that he thought Juan Carlos should read. Franco Archive, 86:34.

9. According to Juan Carlos, who was repeating his father's account. J. L. de Villalonga, *El Rey* (Barcelona, 1993), 78–79.

10. Franco Salgado-Araujo, *Mis conversaciones privadas*, 300.

11. During the defascistization phase after 1945, this ceremony had virtually died. On November 20, 1958, when José Antonio's remains were still buried at the royal church of San Lorenzo de El Escorial, Stanley Payne attended the ceremony and found no one present but a small four-man honor guard from the movement and himself. After the opening of the Valley of the Fallen, however, an elaborate ceremony was revived.

12. Franco was not entirely surprised. For years he had received reports on the murmuring among activists and radicals of the Falange movement, including an account from the Directorate-General of Security (Dirección General de Seguridad) of April 7, 1960, concerning a previous incident at the Valley of the Fallen. Franco Archive, 234:1, 2.

13. Franco Salgado-Araujo, *Mis conversaciones privadas*, 290–91. For a broader account of this whole affair, see R. Ramos, *¡Que vienen los rusos! España renuncia a la Eurocopa 1960 por decisión de Franco* (Granada, 2013). Four years later, with conditions more relaxed, the Soviet soccer team was invited to Madrid, where it lost a match to the Spanish national team, with Franco in attendance. This was hailed by the press as a second victory over Communism.

14. For a discussion of Castiella's foreign policy, see J. M. Armero, *La política exterior de Franco* (Barcelona, 1978), 171–200.

15. Franco is paraphrased as having observed privately, "Although there is no alternative to entry, since we belong to Europe, I do not know if it is really in our interest or may be prejudicial, given that our farm products are sold in other countries, especially Germany. Nonetheless, our industry—particularly the small enterprises, which are the most numerous—might suffer from such competition." "Moreover, with the embargo against our regime, they create many obstacles, complaining that we are not democratic, that we are authoritarian, and so on. Then they pull other complaints out of their sleeves. The main point is to delay our entry as long as possible. There are countries like Italy or France that have no interest in our inclusion in the Common Market." Soriano, *La mano izquierda*, 82–83. Franco Salgado-Araujo cites similar comments in *Mis conversaciones privadas*, 332, 334.

16. This difficult relationship is studied in detail in W. T. Salisbury, "Spain and the Common Market, 1957–1967" (PhD diss., Johns Hopkins University, 1972).

17. Franco Archive, 100:151.

18. Franco outlined these concerns in a six-point memo that he drew up in preparation for Rusk's visit on December 16. Ibid., 93:98.

19. Soriano, *La mano izquierda*, 70–72.

20. Franco Archive, 92:78.

21. Franco also marked the occasion by granting the title of marques de Kindelán to his old air force commander, now in retirement, who had been arguably the principal leader of the initiative that had boosted Franco to the status of commander in chief.

22. F. Franco, *Discursos y mensajes del jefe del estado 1960–1963* (Madrid, 1964), 320–21.

23. Sainz Rodríguez, *Un reinado*, 403–4.

24. Franco Archive, 86:30. Don Juan did yet a third 180-degree shift before Franco died, but the perpetual opportunism of a pretender who played such a weak hand never achieved anything.

25. Soriano, *La mano izquierda*, 46–49.

26. The United States Embassy obtained a much more complete and precise report

about the surgery than was given to the Spanish public, apparently leaked to reassure Washington.

27. Carmen Franco reports that Juanito, the assistant who regularly loaded the shotguns, attended Franco that day, as usual. There was some concern that something might have fallen from the ash tree above him, interfering with the firing mechanism, but the faulty cartridge soon was clearly identified as the culprit. "We were not terribly worried, no, because it was not a vital problem, but an uncomfortable complication. . . . We went to the Hospital General del Aire . . . and the night that they operated, which was Christmas Eve, we slept in the hospital." Then they all returned to El Pardo on Christmas Day.

28. The fullest account is in Soriano, *La mano izquierda*. Franco's grandson Francisco emphasizes that his grandfather always stressed gun security and would repeat the warning "Don't shoot in the air." Franco Martínez-Bordiú, *La naturaleza de Franco*, 40, 93–94.

29. P. Urbano, *El precio del Trono* (Barcelona, 2011), 271–75.

30. Years later, as reigning king, Juan Carlos would virtually destroy the marriage with his numerous infidelities, his own recklessness and self-indulgence being to blame. Queen Sofía, technically the only non-Spanish member of the new royal family, would always be its most exemplary representative.

31. According to Carmen, he declared that Juan Carlos "has enjoyed good fortune, has chosen very well," and that was certainly the case. Later Doña Carmen is said to have remarked to her best friend, "The princess has stolen Paco's heart," according to what the friend told José María Pemán, recounted in María Pemán's *Mis encuentros con Franco* (Barcelona, 1976), 218–19.

32. As she recounted it years later to the journalist Pilar Urbano, in Urbano's *La reina muy de cerca* (Barcelona, 2008), 148.

33. Ibid.

34. Urbano, *El precio*, 288.

35. Franco Archive, 61:7. Franco, of course, received a lengthy series of detailed reports, most of them found in the Franco Archive, 73.

36. Ibid., 270:88.

37. Ibid., 98:65. The claim that it was planned at the wedding may well have been a deliberate fabrication to discredit the Monarchists.

38. At least, this is what Pacón records Franco as saying on July 21, 1962. Franco Salgado-Araujo, *Mis conversaciones privadas*, 346.

39. Carmen recalls hearing Franco talk about these problems with the family's chaplain, P. Bulart, saying such things as "many priests support those people" and "it seems unbelievable." The best study of the changing relationship between the Catholic Church and state for these years is F. Montero, *La Iglesia: De la colaboración a la disidencia (1956–1975)* (Madrid, 2009).

In the winter of 1962 Franco observed privately that "the great sin of the Church is simony," and criticized the fees charged in Catholic schools, declaring that he would complete the development of a system of free state schools. Soriano, *La mano izquierda*, 103.

40. A year later, on July 5, 1963, Muñoz Grandes would hold the powers of chief of state for one day when Franco had the flu. Togores, *Muñoz Grandes*, 455.

41. A. Cañellas Mas, *Laureano López Rodó: Biografía política de un ministro de Franco (1920–2000)* (Madrid, 2011), treats his extensive role in public affairs.

42. Concerning her father's attitude, Carmen Franco has observed: "Carrero Blanco

Notes to pages 403–408

was, in fact, the champion of all those technocrats, many of them members of Opus Dei, and my father accepted that government because they seemed to him the most qualified people for that phase. And he was very friendly with some of them. López Bravo was a friend of his, and he liked him quite well. My father received visits from José María Escrivá Balaguer [the subsequently canonized founder of Opus Dei]. Relations with him were very good, very good, though toward the end perhaps a bit less, but he received him every two or three months, and they talked. He had written a little book called *Camino* [*The Way*], a book of meditations, that my mother had on her nightstand. It was a little like a Catholic Masonry, because they had the habit of helping the other members. . . . Many people didn't like them. Cristóbal, my husband, detested Opus, but my father liked them. My father was acquainted well enough with the religious organization and, as I say, saw a good deal of Monsignor Escrivá Balaguer. He did say that he did not like the way they resembled Masonry in always favoring each other. It seemed to him unfair, especially when they were selecting members for special positions. . . . But he found them very able . . . and he thought that every era has its own religious orders. . . . He liked Opus."

43. Franco Archive, 30:35. The full text is in J. Palacios, *Los papeles secretos de Franco* (Madrid, 1996), 360–61.

44. Ibid.

45. Franco Salgado-Araujo, *Mis conversaciones privadas*, 369.

46. Urbano, *El precio*, 292–95. An alternate version has Sofía's father, the king of Greece, intervening with Don Juan.

47. It might be inferred that he had a tendency to identify her, as a loyal wife and mother, with his own mother, similarly married to an unfaithful husband. Carmen explains his attitude more objectively: "My father always had a great deal of sympathy for her, because he said that she had had a very difficult life in Spain, that she came here very young and had to face a lot of serious problems, while her husband was very young and did not help her all that much."

After the Civil War Franco had restored the royal patrimony confiscated by the Republic, and also sent personal pensions to Victoria Eugenia and to Doña Eulalia, the sister of Alfonso XIII. Doña Eulalia lived in Irún (very near the French border) and wittily observed, according to Carmen, that "every month General Franco sends me 25,000 pesetas for flowers that I convert into potatoes."

48. Franco Archive, 98:68.

49. Franco Salgado-Araujo, *Mis conversaciones privadas*, 378–81.

50. Historians of the Spanish Communist Party have had the same question as Franco, that is, why someone with Grimau's past had been sent back into Spain, but the Party leaders are said to have been unaware of his role in the Civil War. For the best brief summary of this whole affair, see C. Rojas, *Diez crisis del franquismo* (Madrid, 2003), 133–54.

51. Memorandum of July 16, 1963, Franco Archive, 241:27.

52. Ibid., 241:6.

53. Ibid., 30:99.

54. Ibid., 104:14. Carmen agrees that Mussolini's IRI was to some extent the inspiration for the INI and insists on Franco's high regard for his old friend. He had intervened on various occasions to smooth relations between Suanzes and the technocrat ministers, but "every time that my father made peace between them all, Suanzes soon presented his resignation again . . . I don't know how many times," and so Franco finally gave up.

55. *FF*, 7:127–29. See P. Hispán Iglesias de Ussel, *La política en el régimen de Franco entre 1957 y 1969* (Madrid, 2006), 332–40.

56. Franco Archive, 99:66.

57. Pacón quoted him as saying, "For me the problem with the traditionalists is not their doctrine, which is good, but their insistence on bringing a foreign prince to our country whom no one knows, who has always lived in France and for whom the Spanish people feel nothing." Franco Salgado-Araujo, *Mis conversaciones privadas*, 311.

58. For further details, see Palacios, *Los papeles secretos*, 380–81.

59. Carmen observes: "He always said of the Common Market, 'Bah, that's just something for merchants.' He did not lend it the importance it now has. He never did, because for himself, who was basically nationalist, the union of all Europe seemed very difficult."

60. More than three years earlier, on March 31, 1962, the Catholic president of South Vietnam, Ngo Dinh Diem, had written a friendly letter to Franco stressing the common goals of their two regimes in opposition to Communist aggression. Franco Archive, 208:12.

61. Ibid., 180:230; full texts of the two letters are reproduced in Palacios, *Las cartas de Franco*, 452–59.

62. On these first steps, see Cardona, *Franco y sus generales*, 178, 199, and *El gigante descalzo*, 296.

63. According to Urbano, *El precio*, 878, the essence of the project, as a plan for inertial nuclear fusion, was later presented by Velarde in *Inertial Confinement Nuclear Fusion: An Historical Approach by Its Pioneers* (London, 2007), 188–89. Velarde was both a university professor and an army officer, eventually promoted to major general (*general de división*), as Otero eventually reached the rank of counteradmiral.

64. It has been alleged that France was willing to provide 25 percent of the capital for the project, since De Gaulle sought to have another atomic power in western continental Europe, friendly to France. Urbano, *El precio*, 319–21, 877–79.

65. Ibid.; interview with Guillermo Velarde Pinacho by Jesús Palacios in Madrid, May 2012.

66. Franco Archive, 191:69.

67. J. C. Jiménez Redondo, *El ocaso de la amistad entre las dictaduras ibéricas 1955–1968* (Mérida, 1996).

Though it received no publicity in the controlled press of the two dictatorships, a unique atrocity occurred in Spain near Badajoz in April 1965, when Portuguese police agents murdered the leading figure in the Portuguese opposition, General Humberto Delgado, when he resisted their efforts to abduct him to bring him back to Portugal. Ibid., 108–15.

68. F. M. Castiella, *España y la Guinea Ecuatorial* (Madrid, 1968); D. Ndongo-Bidyogo, *Historia y tragedia de Guinea Ecuatorial* (Madrid, 1977); *International Herald Tribune*, Jan. 28, 1980; *New York Times*, Sept. 12, 1982. For the history of the long relationship with Equatorial Guinea, see M. de Castro and D. Ndongo, *España en Guinea: Construcción del desencuentro, 1778–1968* (Madrid, 1998), and G. Nerín, *Guinea Ecuatorial, historia en blanco y negro* (Barcelona, 2003).

69. Franco Archive, 114:268.

70. See the remarks attributed to Franco by his finance minister of the late 1960s, Juan José Espinosa San Martín, in Bayod, *Franco visto*, 156–58. Spain's first elected Socialist government reopened the frontier in 1984. For a history of the long controversy, see G. Hills, *Rock*

of Contention: A History of Gibraltar (London, 1974). The most recent account of the Spanish battle in the United Nations, updated to the twenty-first century, is J. M. Carrascal, *La batalla de Gibraltar: Cómo se ganó, cómo se perdió* (Madrid, 2012).

Chapter 17. Facing the Future

1. For a more detailed account, see Hispán Iglesias de Ussel, *La política en el regimen de Franco*, 281–618.
2. *ABC*, April 1, 1964.
3. Carrero Blanco summarized the early discussions for Franco in a lengthy memorandum of March 7, 1959. Franco Archive, 167:1.
4. Fraga Iribarne, *Memoria breve*, 115.
5. López Rodó, *La larga marcha*, 225.
6. Ibid., 229–30.
7. Franco followed the decisions of the council in detail, commenting extensively on the conclusions. Franco Archive, 47:19, 268:64, 66, 67.
8. Franco explained his unwillingness in detail in his draft notes and subsequent letter to Pope Paul VI of June 12, 1968. Ibid., 17:2. Franco did not blame the growing tension with the papacy on the pope himself but on the efforts by "various monsignors" (unnamed) who supported "enemies of the state." Ibid., 230:54.
9. Franco's ambassador to the Vatican reported to Franco on at least two different occasions that the Vatican had concerns about Opus Dei. Ibid., 19:27 and 229:4.
10. Ibid., 157:1.
11. Fraga Iribarne, *Memoria breve*, 145. Carmen explains her father's perspective: "Nowadays television is more important than newspapers, but newspapers were very influential among people who lived in the years before our war, that is, in the 1930s. . . . When those who had committed major crimes were executed, my father used to say to our domestic chaplain, José María Bulart, 'Go to those who want confession . . . and ask them what motivated such hatred and killing in the way that they killed so many people.' And there was a common response among such people. They used to say that what had influenced them was *Mundo Obrero*, the Communist newspaper. And there were some who said, 'I don't want my children to read *Mundo Obrero*.' This convinced my father that freedom of the press had done a great deal of harm. But he understood when Fraga's reform came up, and they enacted a very qualified freedom of the press. He saw that all the young people wanted that, that everyone could say what he thought or what he wanted. He always used to say that there was no true freedom of press in other countries, because the press was in the hands of pressure groups who could change the way people thought. . . . But I heard him say that times had changed a great deal, which he could tell even from his ministers, who were so much younger than he was. That the old press law could no longer be put up with, let's say."
12. F. Cendán Pazos, *Edición y comercio del libro español (1900–1972)* (Madrid, 1972).
13. Franco Archive, 176:46. This led Fraga to open a study center in his ministry on the Civil War and recent Spanish history, under the direction of Ricardo de la Cierva.
14. López Rodó, *La larga marcha*, 238.
15. For the ministerial infighting during its gestation, see Hispán Iglesias de Ussel, *La política en el régimen de Franco*, 432–40.

16. *Fundamental Laws of the State.*

17. Franco, *Discursos y mensajes*, 317–19.

18. R. Fernández-Carvajal, *La constitución española* (Madrid, 1969), the same title used for the government's subsequent publication of the Fundamental Laws, *La constitución española: Leyes Fundamentales del Estado* (Madrid, 1971).

19. In a speech to the Cortes of November 17, 1967. Franco, *Pensamiento político*, 2:370.

20. Franco even alleged that the government failed to advance certain kinds of legislation to the Cortes "due to the lack of a receptive atmosphere there." Franco Salgado-Araujo, *Mis conversaciones privadas*, 390.

21. Carmen comments on their relationship: "Carrero Blanco was absolutely the person who solved many problems for him. He was the one who, when it was necessary to appoint new ministers, proposed and introduced them. In his first governments my father knew the people whom he named to his cabinet, at least to a certain degree. But in his later years the person who knew people and pointed them out or described their abilities for a certain ministry was Carrero Blanco. . . . Carrero . . . conferred with my father almost every working day. . . . He didn't have lunch with him or take tea with my mother and me, or spend weekends together. Only on certain occasions, since Carrero also hunted, he would participate in a *cacería*, and then they would eat together, but there would be lots of other people there, too. But he normally didn't participate, just at El Pardo, where there were very limited hunts, but not in the big partridge hunts, no. I never knew of a real disagreement between Carrero and my father. I don't think there was one ever."

22. Franco, *Discursos y mensajes*, 324.

23. Quoted in Fernández, *El general Franco*, 214.

24. Franco Salgado-Araujo, *Mis conversaciones privadas*, 344.

25. According to the finance minister Juan José Espinosa San Martín, in Bayod, *Franco*, 154.

26. López Rodó, *La larga marcha*, 263.

27. Eventually a sizable literature about dissident Falangism would develop, its volume in inverse proportion to the significance of the phenomenon. One of the latest publications is F. Blanco Moral and J. L. García Fernández, *FES: La cara rebelde de la Falange (1963–1977)* (Molins del Rei, 2008).

28. Franco Salgado-Araujo, *Mis conversaciones privadas*, 525.

29. The most notable example of a Spanish version of Bell's hypothesis is G. Fernández de la Mora, *El crepúsculo de las ideologías* (Madrid, 1965).

30. G. Jackson, "The Falange Revised: Fascism for the Future," *Nation*, October 7, 1968, 328.

31. According to Pemán, *Mis encuentros*, 82.

32. As quoted by one of his major interlocutors at the Fundación Ortega y Gasset Symposium on the transition (Toledo), May 11, 1984.

33. Ambassador Alfonso Merry del Val provided a detailed report of his press conference with the American journalists, dated Jan. 27, 1967. Franco Archive, 153:64.

34. Directorate-General of Security report of May 30, 1966. Ibid., 109:86.

35. Franco Salgado-Araujo, *Mis conversaciones privadas*, 388–89.

36. Queen Sofía later recounted: "I was very near Franco and I saw how his eyes glistened in the presence of Queen Victoria Eugenia. He was a sentimental man." Quoted in Urbano,

La reina, 196. Carmen agrees: "I think the atmosphere was very cordial because she was very nice and my father kissed her hand. He was moved to see her again after so many years. . . . My father and mother drew her off to one side, and my mother said she was charming, an enchanting lady." The former queen would die at her residence in Lausanne scarcely more than a year later.

37. There are several different versions of these two messages, both delivered only verbally, the first by a third party, but all sources agree on the substance and on the response. See Palacios, *Los papeles secretos*, 436–39.

38. Franco Archive, 208:55; the full text of Calvo Serer's letter can be found in Palacios, *Cartas de Franco*, 483–87.

39. *New York Times*, July 10, 1968.

40. The approximate text of the letter reached Franco. Franco Archive, 205:7.

41. L. López Rodó, *Años decisivos*, vol. 2 of *Memorias* (Barcelona, 1991), 314.

42. Both documents are in the Franco Archive, 243:50, 51.

43. A more complete account appears in Palacios, *Los papeles secretos*, 453–56.

44. Press clippings can be found in the Franco Archive, 205:5.

45. López Rodó, *La larga marcha*, 301.

46. According to J. Bardavío, *Los silencios del rey* (Madrid, 1979), 49–50, Fernández-Miranda visited the prince on July 18, 1969, three days before Franco officially presented his name as successor. He explained that swearing the oath to uphold Franco's fundamental laws would not prevent him from reforming them in the future. Miranda pointed out that no system of laws is eternal and that all legal systems provide means for their amendment. Franco had instituted the referendum law for political ratification of significant changes, and the crucial requirement was that any reform be carried out through strictly legal channels.

In his memoirs, Miranda paraphrased his discussion with Juan Carlos as follows:

On swearing the Fundamental Laws you swore them in their totality and, therefore, you also swore Article 10 of the Law of Succession, which says that laws can be canceled or reformed. Thus these laws themselves admit the possibility of reform.

[Juan Carlos:] But the Principles declare themselves permanent and immutable.

An article in the laws establishes that, but that article is itself reformable, since the reform clause makes no exceptions.

[Juan Carlos:] Are you certain of that?

I am. The Law of Principles consists of two parts: the statement of the principles and the law with three articles which establishes them and puts them into effect. All that law is one of the seven laws, and therefore the reform clause refers to it as well.

[Juan Carlos:] Then why does it say they can't be changed?

That is something not in the laws themselves. The character of the principles is defined in an article of a fundamental law that establishes it, and the reform clause does not admit exceptions. All that is very clear. That Article 1 of the Law of Principles says these are a synthesis of the Fundamental Laws, so that if the text can be modified, it's obvious that also modifies the synthesis. (T. Fernández-Miranda, *Lo que el rey me ha pedido* [Barcelona, 1995], 62–63)

Fernández-Miranda would be key to the reform process after the death of Franco. As Adolfo Suárez later put it, "Torcuato Fernández-Miranda had a great deal of influence over Juan Carlos, because he could explain to him many things." Fundación Ortega y Gasset Symposium on the transition, May 13, 1984.

47. López Rodó, *La larga marcha*, 321–22. Five months later, in October, Franco promoted Alonso Vega to captain-general on the reserve list, the third commander, after Franco and Muñoz Grandes, to hold that rank.

48. Ibid., 419–31.

49. The text is in Sainz Rodríguez, *Un reinado*, 414–15.

50. For a full reconstruction of these events, see Palacios, *Los papeles secretos*, 471–505. Alfonso Armada, the secretary and key advisor of Juan Carlos, has stated that he accompanied the prince on a trip to Estoril at the beginning of May 1969 to discuss the likelihood of Franco's imminent decision. The Conde de Barcelona, he reports, remained unconvinced, though Armada quotes him as saying, "Juanito, if he names you, you can accept, but you can be certain that will never happen." Armada, *Al servicio de la corona* (Barcelona, 1983), 120. Yet Don Juan had begun to worry, writing to Franco on May 8 to request a personal meeting. Franco ignored his letter. Sáinz Rodríguez, *Un reinado*, 414.

51. There are numerous political biographies of Don Juan, which vary considerably in length and quality, but, on the final phase, see R. Borràs Betriu, *El rey de los rojos: Don Juan de Borbón, una figura tergiversada* (Barcelona, 2005).

52. López Rodó, *La larga marcha*, 494–495.

53. Cf. R. A. H. Robinson, "Genealogy and Function of the Monarchist Myth of the Franco Regime," *Iberian Studies* 2, no. 1 (1973): 18–26.

Chapter 18. Franco and the Modernization of Spain

1. W. Bernecker, "Modernisierung und Wandel eines autoritären Regimes: Spanien während des Franquismus," in K. H. Ruffmann and H. Altrichter, eds., *"Modernisierung" versus "Sozialismus": Formen und Strategien sozialen Wandels im 20. Jahrhundert* (Nürnberg, 1983), 113–66. An extended debate has been carried on by Ricardo de la Cierva and Sergio Vilar; see *Pro y contra Franco* (Barcelona, 1985).

2. These may not have impressed professional economists, but Franco's self-confidence in such matters impressed some of his military colleagues. Navarro Rubio recounts that Muñoz Grandes once remarked to him: "The Chief knows a lot about economics, right?" Navarro Rubio, *Mis memorias*, 243.

3. J. Catalán, *La economía española y la Segunda Guerra Mundial* (Barcelona, 1995).

4. J. Harrison, "Early Francoism and Economic Paralysis in Catalonia, 1939–1951," *European History Quarterly* 39, no. 2 (2009): 197–216.

5. T. Christiansen, *The Reason Why: The Post Civil-War Agrarian Crisis in Spain* (Zaragoza, 2012).

6. J. Simpson, *Spanish Agriculture: The Long Siesta, 1765–1965* (Cambridge, 1995), presents a broad perspective and, to some extent, agrees with Christiansen's conclusions.

7. The economist Juan Velarde Fuertes observes that from 1949 to Franco's death in 1975, the GDP, measured in pesetas of 1995, grew 389.4 percent. By comparison, from 1850 (arguably the first year of consistent data) to 1935, a period three times as long, the economy grew 299.3 percent. Or, taking the 115 years from 1820 to 1935, using the data of Angus Maddison adjusted by Leandro Prados de la Escosura, growth was 416.2 percent. Quoted in L. Palacios Bañuelos, *El franquismo ordinario* (Astorga, 2011), 275. For broad accounts of modern Spanish economic development, see G. Tortella, *El desarrollo de la España contemporánea: Historia económica de los siglos XIX y XX* (Madrid, 1994), L. Prados de la

Escosura, *El progreso económico de España (1850–2000)* (Madrid, 2003), and, more briefly, A. Carreras, *Industrialización española: Estudios de historia cuantitativa* (Madrid, 1990).

8. L. del Moral, "La política hidráulica española de 1936 a11996," in R. Garrabou and J. M. Naredo, eds., *El agua en los sistemas agrarios: Una perspectiva histórica* (Madrid, 1999), 184.

9. The criticism of the influence of big banks was one to which Franco was sensitive, since he himself remained suspicious of large banks and in 1965 apparently vetoed the merger of two of the largest. Franco Salgado-Araujo, *Mis conversaciones privadas*, 428, 458–59.

10. A. de Pablo Masa, "Estratificación y clases sociales en la España de hoy," in FOESSA, *Informe 1975* (Madrid, 1975), 758.

11. On the regime's tourist policy and its unintended consequences, see S. D. Pack, *Tourism and Dictatorship: Europe's Peaceful Invasion of Franco's Spain* (New York, 2006).

Chapter 19. Twilight Years

1. Franco received detailed reports. Franco Archive, 99:93–98 and 261:4.

2. Carrero's lengthy memorandum has been published in López Rodó, *La larga marcha*, 864–71.

3. The two ministers, against whom charges were never proven, had already resigned, while protesting their innocence.

4. Franco, *Discursos y mensajes*, 107–21.

5. The program for the new government that Carrero drew up on March 17, 1970, was, at ninety-eight pages, perhaps the longest document that he had ever prepared for Franco. It emphasized continuity but made minor concessions in the direction of *apertura*. Nearly a year later it was updated by a shorter ten-point program in a report of January 14, 1971. Franco Archive, 197:9 and 153:1.

6. Carrero Blanco's shorter works are collected in his posthumous *Discursos y escritos 1943–1973* (Madrid, 1974), though this volume does not include his pseudonymous newspaper articles.

7. *New York Times*, June 9, 1973.

8. The text of the letter later appeared in *Cambio 16*, Dec. 5, 1983.

9. Vilá Reyes's sentence, however, was not downgraded to house arrest until the following year. The three principal government figures involved protested the pardon because it deprived them of the possibility of proving their innocence. Franco Archive, 149:98.

10. E. Alvarez Puga, *Matesa, más allá del escándalo* (Barcelona, 1974), is a work of investigative journalism. See also M. Navarro Rubio, *El caso Matesa* (Madrid, 1979), and Fraga Iribarne, *Memoria breve*, 251–73.

11. Franco, *Pensamiento político*, 2:760.

12. G. Fernández de la Mora, *El estado de obras* (Madrid, 1976).

13. Franco Archive, 212:12. Among the dissenters was García Valiño, who sent a letter to the captain-general of Burgos on December 1 protesting the use of military tribunals for such matters.

14. All this according to Gil's memoir, *Cuarenta años junto*, 100–101.

15. Franco was quoted as saying privately in 1962 that "a military man is prudent, despite what you might think, and fears war," pointing out that Hitler and Mussolini were civilian politicians. Soriano, *La mano izquierda*, 159.

16. On the military in Franco's later years, see J. A. Olmeda Gómez, *Las fuerzas armadas en el estado franquista* (Madrid, 1980), Cardona, *El gigante descalzo*, J. Busquets, *El militar de carrera en España* (Barcelona, 1971), C. Ruiz-Ocaña, *Los ejércitos españoles: Las fuerzas armadas en la defense nacional* (Madrid, 1980), J. M. Comas and L. Mandeville, *Les militaires et le pouvoir dans l'Espagne contemporaine de Franco à Felipe González* (Toulouse, 1986), and J. Ynfante (pseud.), *El ejército de Franco y de Juan Carlos* (Paris, 1976).

17. See L. Gámir, *Las preferencias efectivas del Mercado Común en España* (Madrid, 1972).

18. According to the version De Gaulle gave to his favorite journalist, Michel Droit, recounted in J. Lacouture, *Le souverain, 1959–1970*, vol. 3 of *De Gaulle* (Paris, 1986), 776–79.

19. Walters, *Silent Missions*, 551.

20. Urbano, *El precio*, 384.

21. Walters, *Silent Missions*, 554–56. A kind of myth has developed in Spain that Franco stressed Spain's future would be peaceful because he had succeeded in building a large middle class, but there is no reference to this in Walters's memoir.

22. R. Graham, *Spain: A Nation Comes of Age* (New York, 1984), 147.

23. Bardavío, *Los silencios*, 51.

24. Cobos Arévalo, *La vida privada*, 265.

25. Bardavío, *Los silencios*, 51–52. Bardavío adds that "on a certain occasion I had opportunity to explain these observations personally to Juan Carlos and he endorsed them completely."

26. P. Urbano, *La reina, muy de cerca* (Barcelona, 2008), 165–66.

27. Franco received full reports on the declarations in Washington, during one of which Juan Carlos said, "I think that the people want greater freedom. It's all a matter of determining with what speed." In an interview published by the *Chicago Tribune* on January 27, 1971, he categorically defended Franco but also affirmed the need for reform, for which he would be willing to use "all the means within the constitution" (that is, the fundamental laws of the regime), a discreet forecast of his future policy as king. Franco Archive, 149:87.

28. Bardavío, *Los silencios*, 53–54.

29. López Rodó, *La larga marcha*, 401. J. M. de Areilza published his own memoir concerning his political activities in these years, *Crónica de libertad* (Barcelona, 1985).

30. López Rodó, *La larga marcha*, 404.

31. Franco Archive, 153:1. This program outlined the course that Carrero would follow when named president of government two years later.

32. See B. Díaz Nosty, *Las Cortes de Franco* (Barcelona, 1972), 141–83. "Búnker" is the derisive term coined by a Madrid journalist and later popularized by Santiago Carrillo, head of the Spanish Communist Party, to designate die-hard supporters of the regime. For a brief survey, see the special section "El búnker," *Historia 16* 119 (March 1986): 43–68.

33. On the new shadow political culture, see J. Reig Cruañes, *Identificación y alienación: La cultura política en el tardofranquismo* (Valencia, 2007).

34. J. R. Torregosa, *La juventud española* (Barcelona, 1972), 131–48.

35. Gil, *Cuarenta años junto*, 42–43.

36. On a more serious level, three books that appeared in Madrid in 1972 about the prince and the monarchy were Juan Luis Calleja, *¿Don Juan Carlos, por qué?*, an Editora Nacional publication on the theory and logic of the succession; Miguel Hererro de Miñón, *El principio monárquico*, a discussion of the new monarchy's legal structure and powers that

stressed its theoretically broad authority; and José Luis Nava, *La generación del príncipe*, which treated some of the younger politicians and public figures who had associated themselves with the prince. Two collections of the speeches of Juan Carlos were published, one containing remarks on ceremonial occasions, *Palabras de su alteza real el príncipe de España Don Juan Carlos de Borbón* (Madrid, 1972), and a second containing more substantial remarks, *Por España, con los españoles* (Madrid, 1973).

37. The wedding publicity was lavishly chronicled in the society glamor book by J. M. Bayona, *Alfonso de Borbón-María del Carmen Martínez Bordiu* (Barcelona, 1971).

38. Franco Archive, 40:1.

39. Carmen Franco insists that she was not involved in such maneuvers but was more worried about the marriage itself, which she saw as potentially shaky, since her daughter was barely twenty-one and Alfonso thirty-five: "It worried me, because my daughter Carmen was very young and seemed to me immature beside him, for he was a quite a bit older. I had considered Alfonso de Borbón a friend of my brother-in-law José María. Don Alfonso was a very sad fellow, a good person and very able, but too serious for my daughter, who was a little immature and in my opinion not prepared for this. . . . Some girls at twenty-one are more mature and others at that age not ready for marriage. . . . What worried me was his tendency toward sadness, while she was gay and lively. I did not see their two characters very well matched and I was concerned about how they would get along together. Yet it was true that my father felt somewhat flattered that his granddaughter was marrying a grandson of Alfonso XIII."

Though two sons were soon born to the couple, the marriage did not last very long. Don Alfonso's remaining years were few and tragic. First he ran a stop sign in Navarre on returning from a ski trip and his car was hit by a truck, resulting in the death of his older son. Later, in 1989, Alfonso ignored warning signs while skiing downhill in the western United States and was caught in the neck by a low-hanging wire, which virtually decapitated him. His surviving son, Franco's oldest great-grandson, the strapping Luis Alfonso de Borbón, is, as a result of a complex pattern of inheritance, recognized by many French legitimists as the heir to the throne of France.

40. According to what the prince told López Rodó; see *El principio del fin*, vol. 3 of *Memorias* (Barcelona, 1992), 506. The memorandum is in the Franco Archive, 40:15, reprinted in J. Palacios, *Franco y Juan Carlos: Del franquismo a la monarquía* (Barcelona, 2005), 569–70.

41. As recounted by the authors of the report to Pilar Urbano, in her *Yo entré en el Cesid* (Barcelona, 1997), 138–44.

42. F. Franco, *Tres discursos de Franco* (Madrid, 1973), 28.

43. A. Diz, *La sombra del FRAP: Génesis y mito de un partido* (Barcelona, 1977).

44. R. Carr and J. P. Fusi, *Spain: Dictatorship to Democracy* (London, 1979), 194.

45. Secretariado Nacional del Clero, *Asamblea conjunta obispos-sacerdotes* (Madrid, 1971), 160–61. Franco received detailed reports on such developments. Franco Archive, 85:6, 7, 96:7, 108:9.

46. Franco Archive, 72:2, 6–21.

47. Ibid., 95:22; the text is reproduced in Palacios, *Las cartas de Franco*, 533–39.

48. According to an extract from "Diario de Fernández Miranda," *ABC*, Dec. 20, 1983.

49. Tomás Garicano Goñi, quoted in Bayod, *Franco visto*, 203; the letter is in the Franco Archive, 108:6, and reprinted in López Rodó, *La larga marcha*, 440–42.

50. At the beginning of 1973, Carrero Blanco had prepared for Franco a seven-page outline for what he considered should be the future course of policy: continuity with the past leading to a limited evolution but fully consistent with the former. Franco Archive, 95:16.

51. Ibid., 96:63.

52. "Julen Agirre" (Genoveva Forest), *Operación Ogro* (New York, 1975). Whether Carrero Blanco genuinely constituted the continuation of the regime is, however, not so clear. Juan Carlos has said that he was sure that, had the Carrero government survived the death of Franco, Carrero Blanco would have been willing to resign the presidency in order for the new king to appoint a new leader of the government. J. L. de Vilallonga, *El rey: Conversaciones con Don Juan Carlos I de España* (Barcelona, 1993), 210. Beyond that, however, it is not clear that, as has been alleged, Juan Carlos had a "pact" with Carrero, one that a supposedly repentant Carrero Blanco then confessed to Franco.

53. Lieutenant Colonel Francisco Aguado Sánchez, head of the 111th command of the Civil Guard that was to have conducted the raid, so informed Pilar Urbano in 2001. Urbano, *El precio*, 504–6, 910. See also C. Estévez and F. Mármol, *Carrero: Las razones ocultas de un asesinato* (Madrid, 1998), 103–11.

54. The assassins' own account is presented in the book previously cited by Forest, herself an activist of the Madrid section of the Communist Party and a major accomplice. On the collaboration of Madrid Communists, who provided the principal collateral support for the Basque assassination team, see I. Falcón, *Viernes y trece en la calle del Correo* (Barcelona, 1981). Further details are available in M. Campo Vidal, *Información y servicios secretos en el atentado al Presidente Carrero Blanco* (Barcelona, 1983). "Argala," the ETA leader who actually triggered the explosion, was himself blown up exactly five years and a day later by a bomb device in his car in France, evidently set by agents of the Spanish security forces, who exacted their revenge. *Cambio 16*, May 20, 1985, 26–36.

55. According to what Fernández-Miranda subsequently told his wife. V. Prego, *Así se hizo la Transición* (Barcelona, 1996), 26–27.

56. Iniesta Cano has given his version of this incident in his *Memorias y recuerdos* (Barcelona, 1984), 218–22. He claims that Fernández-Miranda had nothing to do with rescinding the order, though this seems doubtful.

57. Detailed accounts of the events of that day may be found in R. Borrás Betriu, *El día en que mataron a Carrero Blanco* (Barcelona, 1974), and I. Fuente et al., *Golpe mortal* (Madrid, 1983). This was the first significant initiative of ETA outside the Basque country, and the authorities initially believed that it must have been the work of "Maoists," such as the recently organized FRAP, while Franco himself saw the fell hand of Masonry.

58. As reported by Utrera Molina in a television interview some years later. Prego, *Así se hizo*, 51–52.

59. Carrero Blanco's greatest virtues were austerity and incorruptibility, combined with his commitment to hard work and his devotion to duty. After more than three decades as Franco's right hand, he left an estate amounting to no more than an admiral's pension, a less than luxurious though good apartment still not fully paid for, a savings account of less than five hundred thousand pesetas (about eight thousand dollars), and a fully paid-for tomb in the cemetery, according to C. Fernández, *El almirante Carrero Blanco* (Barcelona, 1985), 258.

60. Vicente Gil did everything he could to prejudice Franco against Fernández-Miranda, telling the caudillo that "in every new post he has named people who are either from the

socialist youth or, at least, politically amorphous. Just look at the example he has set with the new delegates of the Frente de Juventudes. And the Guardia de Franco." Gil, *Cuarenta años junto*, 140.

61. From the diary of Fernández-Miranda in an article titled "Diez años de Carrero," *ABC*, Dec. 20, 1983.

62. According to what Urcelay told José Utrera Molina, recounted in Molina's memoir *Sin cambiar de bandera* (Barcelona, 1989), 77–78.

63. According to the account that Valcárcel gave a close friend, in J. Figuero and L. Herrero, *La muerte de Franco jamás contada* (Barcelona, 1985), 30.

64. A great deal of controversy arose over this selection. The most detailed reconstruction is J. Bardavío, *La crisis: Historia de quince días* (Madrid, 1974), but a later, more accurate account has been provided by L. Herrero, *El ocaso del régimen: Del asesinato de Carrero a la muerte de Franco* (Madrid, 1995), 28–52. A partially parallel explanation may be found in J. Fernández Coppel, *General Gavilán: Memorias* (Madrid, 2005), 185–94, and also in Gil, *Cuarenta años junto*, 139–60.

65. His background is treated in J. Tusell and G. G. Queipo de Llano, *Tiempo de incertidumbre: Carlos Arias Navarro entre el franquismo y la Transición (1973–1976)* (Barcelona, 2003), 1–52.

66. Carmen Franco concludes, no doubt accurately, that her mother may have made comments or suggestions but says that she herself found the selection of Arias surprising, concluding that her father had few alternatives: "Nearly all his friends were dead. . . . None of my father's contemporaries were left, except for Admiral Nieto Antúnez, who was as old as he was. He didn't have Parkinson's but he was a little old man. . . . I don't know why he chose Arias. In fact, it was strange to select him, because he had been in charge of security. . . . That shocked me, but I didn't say anything. And my father never explained anything about it. . . . My mother thought very highly . . . of Carlos Arias. But I don't think that she influenced his designation. She may have said something about him in comparison with two or three he was considering and so led him toward Arias. But no more than that. And certainly no campaign. No, nothing, she was tranquil and in poor health."

67. Quoted in J. de las Heras and J. Villarín, *El año Arias: Diario político español 1974* (Madrid, 1975), 52–53.

68. The full text is in ibid., 104–32.

69. Utrera Molina, *Sin cambiar*, 103.

70. J. Oneto, *Arias, entre dos crisis* (Madrid, 1975), 68–76, and Herrero, *El ocaso*, 77–81. Tarancón's version of this affair may be found in J. L. Martín Descalzo, *Tarancón, el cardenal del cambio* (Barcelona, 1982), 203–17. For a broader perspective on such conflict, see M. Ortiz Heras and D. A. González, eds., *La Iglesia española entre el franquismo y la Transición* (Madrid, 2012).

71. Herrero, *El ocaso*, 81.

72. López Rodó, *La larga marcha*, 469.

73. According to his last personal physician; see Pozuelo Escudero, *Los últimos*, 136–37.

74. C. J. Cela Conde, ed., *El reto de los halcones: Antología de la prensa apocalíptica española en la apertura (febrero de 1974–junio de 1975)* (Madrid, 1975), offers a collection from the ultra press.

75. After the death of Franco, Díez Alegría provided his own version of this affair in his "Primicias de una confesión," *Anales de la Real Academia de Ciencias Morales y Políticas* 61 (1984): 143–76.

Chapter 20. The Death of Franco

1. Herrero, *El ocaso*, 109. Sometime after Franco's death the hospital was renamed Hospital General Universitario Gregorio de Marañón.

2. L. López Rodó, *Claves de la transición*, vol. 4 of *Memorias* (Barcelona, 1993), 57–58.

3. See Gil, *Cuarenta años junto*, 251, and Villaverde's account given to Herrero, *El ocaso*, 115.

4. Utrera Molina, *Sin cambiar*, 139.

5. Cobos Arévalo, *La vida privada*, 309–10.

6. Vicentón, "tough Vince," was the common nickname for Gil.

7. Cobos Arévalo, *La vida privada*, 312.

8. Gil, *Cuarenta años junto*, 189–90.

9. Gil claims that Villaverde ducked behind members of Franco's retinue and that he waited for a minute or two to see if he could catch Villaverde alone in order to punch him up. Ibid., 192.

10. Ibid., 193.

11. Cobos testifies that he had earlier heard Doña Carmen say things such as "Dr. Martínez Bordiú. . . . If you didn't have the father-in-law that you have! Doctor of what?" Cobos Arévalo, *La vida privada*, 313.

12. Carmen Franco presents a somewhat different version: "My father had known his personal physician all of the latter's life. He was very Falangist, one of the first Falangists. His own father had been a village doctor, in the same district where my mother's *finca* was located in Asturias, where we went every summer, and he had known Vicente since he was a boy. He served in the war and then became a doctor. But my husband did not consider him a really good doctor, deeming him an adequate physician only as long as my father was in reasonably good health. For that he was all right, and he always passed on news about what was happening in Madrid. He was a fount of information and showered my father with affection, because he was completely devoted to him. But when the phlebitis appeared, Cristóbal said that he needed to be treated by specialists and Vicente did not accept that, so they became antagonists. Then my mother said to Vicente: 'Look, he is my son-in-law, what can I do? You will have to leave.' So Vicente left, and we turned to Pozuelo, because Pozuelo was very calm and orderly. Vicente was always getting my father worked up, because he said that everyone else was causing trouble for him, he wore him out, and this couldn't go on. . . . Yes, the decision was taken by Mamá because she realized that she could not have Cristóbal and Vicente always at odds." Of Gil's total devotion to Franco there was never the slightest question. As Franco's oldest grandson testifies, "If you were to ask me who was the person who most loved Franco, I would reply Vicente Gil." Franco Martínez-Bordiú, *La naturaleza de Franco*, 200.

13. Pozuelo Escudero, *Los últimos*, 51.

14. Utrera Molina, *Sin cambiar*, 155–60.

15. Ironically, one of the chief go-betweens whom Juan Carlos used in contacting the opposition was his good friend Nicolás Franco Pascual de Pobil, Franco's nephew, the only son of his brother Nicolás.

16. Utrera Molina, *Sin cambiar*, 163.

17. On political developments during Franco's illness and the role of Juan Carlos, see Bardavío, *Los silencios*, 95–102, Diario 16, *Historia de la Transición* (Madrid, 1984), 50–59, and de la Cierva, *Historia del franquismo*, 2:412–16.

18. Pozuelo Escudero, *Los últimos*, 75–125.

19. Ibid., 206, 147.

20. Ibid., 126–46.

21. Ibid., 112.

22. Quoted in Herrero, *El ocaso*, 152.

23. This, at least, was the perception of Antonio Carro Martínez, minister of the presidency; see Bayod, *Franco visto*, 355.

24. The director general of popular culture appointed by Cabanillas, the historian Ricardo de la Cierva, had encouraged the publication of Stanley Payne's study of early Basque nationalism, *Historia del nacionalismo vasco*, brought out in Barcelona a month before Cabanillas was fired. The planned presentation of the book in Bilbao was then canceled by Cabanillas's successor. De la Cierva was one of those who resigned in sympathy with Cabanillas.

25. Utrera Molina, *Sin cambiar*, 209.

26. These polls mostly used small samples, but the most extensive was conducted by FOESSA in 1969. This study was suppressed by the government but later appeared in abridged form as Amando de Miguel, "Spanish Political Attitudes, 1970," in S. G. Payne, ed., *Politics and Society in Twentieth-Century Spain* (New York, 1976), 208–31. The full text was only published many years later as an appendix to the memoir by its director; see Amando de Miguel, *El final del franquismo: Testimonio personal* (Madrid, 2003), 223–361. See also A. Hernández Sánchez, *La opinión pública en el tardofranquismo* (Valladolid, 2011).

27. Pozuelo Escudero, *Los últimos*, 122.

28. The source for this description of Franco's thought process is Pozuelo's recorded explanation to Luis Herrero, which went well beyond what the former had chosen to reveal in his own memoir. Herrero, *El ocaso*, 171–73.

29. Utrera Molina, *Sin cambiar*, 266–73.

30. F. Herrero Tejedor, *Memorial elevada al Gobierno nacional* (Reus, 1974).

31. Pozuelo quoted Franco in such terms to Luis Herrero. See Herrero, *El ocaso*, 195–96.

32. Herrero Tejedor is said to have personally vetoed a proposal by Girón to form a new political association called Falange Española de las JONS on the grounds that such a name was anachronistic and provocative.

33. The text of these proceedings is in S. Chavkin et al., eds., *Spain: Implications for United States Foreign Policy* (Stamford, CT, 1976).

34. Enríquez, *Carmen Polo*, 233–34.

35. Quoted in Urbano, *El precio*, 743, 947.

36. Ibid., 740–44; L. G. Perinat, *Recuerdos de una vida itinerante* (Madrid, 1996), 157–61; C. Powell, *El amigo americano: España y Estados Unidos, de la dictadura a la democracia* (Madrid, 2011), 221–25.

37. In fact, during the four years that Valcárcel served as president, the Cortes dealt with only 98 legislative proposals from the executive, the great majority of which passed unanimously, while 101 decree-laws were promulgated by the government. During those four years there had been just six interpellations of ministers, only one of them taking place during the current session. Though individual *procuradores* did sometimes voice mild criticism, record a few individual no votes, and manage to add an occasional minor amendment, no law originating in the Cortes was ever accepted by the government. A total of 120 *procuradores*,

21.4 percent of the deputies, were still directly appointed by the chief of state or the government, and the rate of turnover became very high. Between 1971 and 1975, 180 deputies resigned or were dismissed and were replaced by 172 new appointees, for a "coefficient of
fluidity" of 32 percent. M. A. Aguilar, *Las últimas Cortes de Franco* (Madrid, 1976), 11–15.
The irony would be that this specially prorogued Cortes of Franco was the one that
eventually under King Juan Carlos voted in October 1976 for the legislation that began the
political dismantling of the regime. That took place after the king had replaced Valcárcel
with Torcuato Fernández-Miranda, who would masterfully manipulate the political
hara-kiri of the last Francoist parliament. See A. de Diego González, *El franquismo se suicidó*
(Málaga, 2010).

    38. According to the memoir of his military aide, General Juan Ramón Gavilán, who
coordinated Franco's intelligence reports. Fernández-Coppel, *General Gavilán*, 210.

    39. Figuero and Herrero, *La muerte*, 20.

    40. Pozuelo Escudero, *Los últimos*, 193.

    41. As reported in Fernández-Coppel, *General Gavilán*, 211.

    42. This was the impression, for example, of Rodríguez Valcárcel. López Rodó, *Claves
de la Transición*, 119.

    43. His delight in the royal children is reported in Pozuelo Escudero, *Los últimos*,
187–89.

    44. This was mentioned in various CIA reports from Madrid, cited in Urbano, *El pre-
cio*, 734–35, 945. After Franco died, King Juan Carlos had legislation steered through parliament granting Doña Carmen multiple pensions as Franco's widow, stemming from the
various positions and honors that Franco had held. In toto these were said to amount to
about 50 percent more than the salary of the prime minister and were paid regularly until
her death in 1988.

    45. As reported by Juan Carlos to Welles Stabler, the new American ambassador, cited
in ibid., 736–37, 946.

    46. In 1994 the historian Geoffrey Parker, who then taught at Yale, wrote to Stanley
Payne that during the preceding year Yale University Press had been approached by an
American journalist, Thomas H. Lipscomb of Infosafe Systems in New York. "He had
formerly been a feature writer on the *New York Times* and, with a group of colleagues, was
interested in securing publication of the Franco material he claimed existed in Zurich
(naturally in a bank vault!). He had seen the Marquis of Villaverde, who claimed he had
two 'steamer trunks' full of material evacuated from the Pardo Palace in the days immediately
before and immediately after the General's death. This included, Lipscomb assured us, a
journal kept by the General as well as the correspondence received by him directly from
ambassadors abroad. However, when we said we wanted to send in an expert to view the
material before becoming involved, the line went dead." Geoffrey Parker to Stanley Payne,
May 11, 1994.

    47. Pozuelo Escudero, *Los últimos*, 125–29.

    48. Fernández-Coppel, *General Gavilán*, 212.

    49. Though the Basque terrorists made clear the fact that their goal was the partition of
Spain, not overthrowing Franco, the leftist opposition persisted in the romantic notion
that somehow they were democratic freedom fighters. Only after the *etarras* turned even
more viciously on the post-Franco democratic regime were the leftist parties cured to an
extent of their illusion.

50. Nicolás wrote to his brother, "Dear Paco: Don't sign that sentence. It is not desirable and I tell you this because I love you. You are a good Christian, and afterward you would repent of it. Now we are old, so listen to my advice, for you know how much I love you." Quoted in Diario 16, *Historia de la transición*, 144. Nicolás, however, had suffered several strokes in recent years from which he would never fully recover. The letter may have been written by his son, Nicolás Franco Pascual de Pobil, a friend of Juan Carlos and a proponent of a democratic transition.

51. According to what Cobos Arévalo reports that he overheard at El Pardo. Cobos Arévalo, *La vida privada*, 320–21.

52. One of the few voices abroad to speak up on behalf of Franco was that of the painter Salvador Dalí, quoted in *Le Monde* in unstinting support.

53. The two intensive care nurses who had been stationed regularly at El Pardo since the summer of 1974 referred especially to the effects of the papal messages, after which Franco exhibited symptoms of agitation he had not shown before, according to Dr. Palma Gámiz, quoted in Prego, *Así se hizo*, 272.

54. López Rodó, *Claves de la Transición*, 419–21.

55. Diario 16, *Historia de la Transición*, 144.

56. Palma Gámiz, *El paciente de El Pardo*, 111.

57. Many Spanish officials and commentators were convinced that this tactic was thought up in Washington as a means of permitting the American ally Hassan to grab most of the Sahara without fighting. J. R. Diego Aguirre, *Sáhara: La verdad de una traición* (Madrid, 1988).

Franco had dispatched his military aide Gavilán on a one-day mission to Rabat on October 6 to learn Hassan's intentions. The Gavilán report can be found in the Franco Archive, 157:18, and a later account is available in Fernández-Coppel, *General Gavilán*, 212–16.

58. According to the cardiologist Dr. Isidoro Mínguez, quoted in Prego, *Así se hizo*, 271.

59. Figuero and Herrero, *La muerte*, 24–26; Cobos Arévalo, *La vida privada*, 329–33.

60. Vilallonga, *El rey*, 228.

61. Palma Gámiz, *El paciente de El Pardo*, 256–58. Carmen says, "I don't know exactly when he wrote [the statement], because he didn't say. But he must have done so about that time, because those were the last days he entered his private office, which was very small but sacrosanct to him. He had the big office, where he received visitors, square and very attractively furnished, a salon. And then he had his little private office, full of papers and clutter, where he found refuge. He would always go there and wrote there. At the beginning of his illness, when he had a moment he went there to look at papers and organize things. It was on one of those occasions that he wrote it, because later he was bedridden and didn't get up. And when he called for me he was in bed. He told me to go look for some notes he had prepared. . . . I corrected them, because reading them to him in bed, for example, where it said 'your loyalty to the Prince' and not Juan Carlos, I suggested: 'Say Juan Carlos, because he is already Prince, so that there is no uncertainty at all.' And he replied: 'Yes, yes, say Juan Carlos' and so I wrote in Juan Carlos. And then, possibly, added some other detail. . . . He was totally conscious and at ease in bed, propped up on pillows. To get into his office I had to ask his aide to open the door, because it was always locked. The only people who had keys were my father's aides." She provided a more detailed account in an interview with *El Alcázar* (Madrid), Mar. 26, 1976.

62. This has been the subject of much speculation, and there are no conclusive data as to exactly what Franco was thinking during his last week or so as head of state, since, as usual, he said very little. The conclusion offered here is based on weighing all the indirect evidence available. On the final meeting with Arias, see López Rodó, *Claves de la Transición*, 153, and Herrero, *El ocaso*, 240–41.

63. Vilallonga, *El rey*, 221–22.

64. Relevant State Department cables are cited in Urbano, *El precio*, 775–76, 951.

65. According to the surgeon Dr. Alonso Castrillo, quoted in Prego, *Así se hizo*, 287.

66. Ibid., 287; Pozuelo Escudero, *Los últimos*, 156.

67. Palma Gámiz, *El paciente de El Pardo*, 145.

68. These atrocities are well documented. The best account of the fate of the Saharans is Jensen, *War and Insurgency in the Western Sahara*, but see also T. Bárbulo, *La historia prohibida del Sahara español* (Barcelona, 2002). A considerable bibliography has developed.

69. The frankest of these was the cardiologist José Luis Palma Gámiz, who later wrote of his patient that "that man was very strange and managed to surprise us all. I don't think that in any time in my professional life I ever encountered an equivalent patient: slippery in his symptomology, delayed in his vital crises, discreet in his requests, exaggerated in his clinical signs, and opulent in his hemorrhages. He outflanked you when you least expected it. With him nothing was foreseeable. If he had passed away the night of November 3, he would have ended his days drowned in his blood and opinion, you may be sure, would have condemned us for it." Palma Gámiz, *El paciente de El Pardo*, 162–63.

70. Pozuelo Escudero, *Los últimos*, 238. Palma Gámiz, *El paciente de El Pardo*, 175, confirms that one of the things from which Franco suffered most in the last weeks was the sheer physical indignity of his situation, though, in his typical style, he complained very little.

71. The first physician to publish his brief narrative was M. Hidalgo Huerta, chief surgeon in the three major operations, in his *Cómo y por qué operé a Franco* (Madrid, 1976).

72. On December 2, King Juan Carlos would appoint his reformist former tutor Torcuato Fernández-Miranda to be president of the Cortes, and hence also head of the National Council. In 1976, Miranda designed and led the initial phase of democratization, during which Franco's parliament was replaced with a system based on direct universal suffrage.

73. Palma Gámiz, *El paciente de El Pardo*, 136. Dr. Pozuelo Escudero has been categorical on this point (Herrero, *El ocaso*, 270), which is further corroborated by Dr. Mínguez, quoted in Prego, *Así se hizo*, 317–18.

74. Palma Gámiz was present at this macabre scene; see *El paciente de El Pardo*, 190–91. Some of the photos suddenly appeared in a popular magazine in 1984. Villaverde then claimed that they had been stolen when he had been forced to close his medical office. In the lawsuit that followed, the publisher refused to name the source of the photos but said that they were not provided by any member of the Franco family. Franco Martínez-Bordiú, *La naturaleza de Franco*, 30–31.

75. It was quickly noted that by an irony of history this was also the anniversary of the death of his potential rival for the leadership of Nationalist Spain José Antonio Primo de Rivera, founder of the Falange, executed by the Republicans in Alicante on November 20, 1936.

76. The final illness has been chronicled by "Yale," *Los últimos cien días* (Madrid, 1975), G. Lopezarias, *Franco, la ultima batalla* (Madrid, 1975), and J. Oneto, *Cien días en la muerte de Franco* (Madrid, 1976).

77. Quoted in Cobos Arévalo, *La vida privada*, 348–49.
78. Soriano, *La mano izquierda*, 177.
79. J. L. Granados, *1975: El año de la instauración* (Madrid, 1977), 541–49.
80. Urbano, *El precio*, 811.
81. Carmen states that the family did not know where Franco was to be buried but that the original architect of the Valley of the Fallen, Diego Méndez, testified that Franco had declared that he wanted to be buried there, and the government agreed. Fray Anselmo, prior of the Benedictine monastery to the rear of the monument, testified in 2012 that no preparations had been made for a site of interment, which had hurriedly to be excavated between the twentieth and the twenty-second. Enríquez, *Carmen Polo*, 252.

"Soon the abbey of the Valley began to receive . . . many letters, from Spain and from abroad, declaring the person buried there to be a saint and asking for objects that came into contact with his tomb, to keep as relics." Sueiro, *La verdadera historia del Valle de los Caídos* (Madrid, 1976), 272. Though some visitors during the next few years would deposit petitions on Franco's grave as though it were a holy shrine, it never became the major religious center that the family might have wanted. It would remain a special focus for Franco's keenest admirers, but in general it mainly attracted tourists, domestic and foreign. The Socialist Zapatero government of 2004–12 eventually restricted access to the basilica. Though as a religious site it pertained to the Roman Catholic Church, the structure was officially part of Spain's national patrimony.

King Juan Carlos almost immediately awarded Carmen Franco Polo de Martínez-Bordiú the hereditary title of Duquesa de Franco, with the category of *grandeza de España*, and a lesser title was later awarded to her mother. Doña Carmen did not vacate El Pardo until January 31, 1976. It was then declared a national historical site, and she herself would be buried there following her own death in 1988. The greatest sorrow of her last years was that she and her husband were not to be buried together. The simplest and most fitting epitaph was penned by her estranged brother-in-law Serrano Suñer: "She was the wife most absolutely and unconditionally devoted to her husband." Enríquez, *Carmen Polo*, 267.

Some of Franco's papers were burned, and others taken away by the family, their future disposition still uncertain at the time of writing. The main set of many boxes of documents in Franco's office was saved from destruction by the historian Luis Suárez Fernández, who arranged that they constitute the archive of the newly founded Fundación Nacional Francisco Franco. This archive, however, contains few personal papers; it consists primarily of reports and documents that Franco received over the years but little that he originated.

In the years following Franco's death, the family suffered only a limited amount of harassment. The worst was inflicted on the person who was by far its most unpopular member, the Marqués de Villaverde, who was suspended from the practice of surgery for five years by the Ministry of Health in 1984, a decision eventually reversed by the courts two decades later, after his death.

Two mysterious fires, probably arson, broke out at El Pazo de Meirás, but no one was injured. The only deadly incident involving the family was a major blaze that enveloped the Hotel Corona de Aragón, Zaragoza's finest, early on the morning of July 12, 1979. Doña Carmen, her daughter and son-in-law, and one granddaughter were staying in the hotel to attend the forthcoming graduation at the military academy, where José Cristóbal, the only one of Franco's grandsons to follow in his professional footsteps (though just for a few years), was about to be commissioned. All the family members were rescued safely, the women by ladder from the balcony, though the athletic Villaverde leaped out a window from a different part of the hotel to escape smoke inhalation, suffering no more than an injured ankle and foot. Many others were not so fortunate, for the death toll was horrendous; according to reports, possibly as many as eighty-three people died. At that time the Spanish government refused to call the fire an act of arson, though the Aznar government in 2000 recognized all those killed as victims of terrorism, and a lengthy judicial investigation completed in 2009 finally recognized the blaze as deliberate arson, though without identifying the arsonist or any political motive. Many have seen this tragedy as a terrorist deed carried out by ETA, which was near the height of its activity in 1979. See Palacios and Payne, *Franco, mi padre*, 702–6, and Martínez-Bordiú, *La naturaleza de Franco*, 221–22.

Conclusion

1. Larraz, *Memorias*, 351.

2. Julián Marías, arguably the wisest and most balanced Spanish intellectual of the later twentieth century and a former Republican, remarks that "the Spanish were deprived of many liberties, which I always found intolerable, but not too many people really missed them, for they still had others, particularly those affecting private life, which they feared to lose. Such deprivation came from the outcome of the Civil War, but the majority were persuaded that if the result had been the reverse, the sphere of liberty would not have been greater because both belligerents had promised the destruction of the other, and they had both carried it out during the war itself. Thus it was not easy to mobilize Spaniards toward an *inversion* of the outcome of the war, and since that basically was what the most politicized fragments of the country were proposing, the majority remained relatively indifferent. It can be said that a large number of Spaniards *waited without haste* for the end of the regime." J. Marías, *España inteligible* (Madrid, 1985), 379.

3. There was surprising symmetry between the political thinking of Franco and that of Juan Negrín, the principal wartime leader of the Republic. Negrín agreed that a competitive parliamentary electoral system could not be allowed to return to Spain, no matter how much the Popular Front exploited such a concept for international consumption, because it left open the danger that the right could come to power peacefully, as had happened in 1933–34. He emphasized this point in 1938 to Anatoly Marchenko, the Soviet chargé, whose report is published in R. Radosh, M. Habeck, and G. Sevostianov, eds., *Spain Betrayed: The Soviet Union in the Spanish Civil War* (New Haven, CT, 2001), 499–500.

4. Saz has debated this issue more than anyone other than Juan Linz and has called Franco's system "the least fascist of the fascist regimes or the one nearest fascism among the non-fascist regimes." By the same token, in its first phase it was "the most totalitarian of the authoritarian regimes or the least totalitarian of the totalitarian regimes." I. Saz Campos, "El franquismo: ¿Régimen autoritario o dictadura fascista?," in J. Tusell et al., eds., *El régimen de Franco (1936–1975): Política y relaciones exteriores*, 2 vols. (Madrid, 1993), 1:192. See also Saz, *Fascismo y franquismo* (Valencia, 2004), L. Casali, ed., *Per una definizione della dittatura franchista* (Milan, 1990), and F. Sevillano Calero, "Totalitarismo, fascismo y franquismo: El pasado y el fin de las certidumbres después del comunismo," in R. Moreno Fonseret and F. Sevillano Calero, eds., *El franquismo: Visiones y balances* (Alicante, 1999), 12–26. Broad comparisons between the Spanish and Italian regimes may be found in J. Tusell et al., eds., *Fascismo y franquismo cara a cara: Una perspectiva histórica* (Madrid, 2004), J. M. Thomàs,

ed., *Franquismo/fascismo* (Reus, 2001), and G. Di Febo and R. Moro, eds., *Fascismo e franchismo: Relazioni, immagini e rappresentazioni* (Catanzaro, 2005).

5. S. G. Payne, "The Defascistization of the Franco Regime (1942–1975)," in S. G. Larsen, ed., *Modern Europe after Fascism, 1943–1980s*, 2 vols. (Boulder, CO, 1998), 2:1580–1606.

6. Tusell, *Franco, España*, 647–48.

7. The brief Ifni conflict of 1958, in which several hundred Spanish troops died, qualifies as a military incident, not a war.

8. J. Beneyto, *La identidad del franquismo* (Madrid, 1979), 10–11.

9. H. L. Matthews, *The Yoke and the Arrows* (New York, 1957).

10. This seminal study has been reprinted several times: an English version, "An Authoritarian Regime: Spain," appears in S. G. Payne, ed., *Politics and Society in Twentieth-Century Spain* (New York, 1976), 160–207; the Spanish version, "Una teoría del régimen autoritario: España," appears, inter alia, in J. J. Linz, *Obras escogidas*, 7 vols. (Madrid, 2008–11), ed. J. R. Montero and T. J. Miley, 3:23–64. The extensive debate about Linz's interpretation is well summarized and analyzed in T. J. Miley, "Franquism as Authoritarianism: Juan Linz and his Critics," *Politics, Religion, and Ideology* 12, no. 1 (2011): 27–50.

11. W. Pfaff, "Splendid Little Wars," *New Yorker*, Mar. 24, 1986, 62–64.

12. The differences, however, are at least as important as the similarities, for the Chinese regime remains more statist and also more militaristic, having reached the rank of superpower.

13. S. L. Brandes, *Migration, Kinship, and Community* (New York, 1975), 76.

14. M. Vázquez Montalbán, "Adios, de la Cierva, Adios," *Triunfo*, Nov. 1974. The democratization of Turkey after 1945 might be adduced as an earlier example, but the Kemalist regime in Turkey had been the first Third World "guided democracy" rather than an institutionalized new authoritarian regime of the European fascist area.

15. It may be objected that the process was begun by the Portuguese revolution and the overthrow of the regime of the Greek colonels, both of which took place during the preceding year. Both those cases, however, merely replicated the common experience of regimes toppled by direct overthrow due to external influences; they were not instances of nonviolent democratization from the inside out.

16. He attributed this failing to the prevalence of envy in Spain—a common moralistic observation by Spaniards—and told Dr. Pozuelo that he had sought to overcome it through the tutelage of the movement and the broad expansion of basic education. However, he confessed his failure: "But I have achieved very little. Bureaucracy has triumphed instead." Pozuelo Escudero, *Los últimos*, 160–61.

17. The abortive *pronunciamiento* of February 23, 1981, scenes of which were televised around the world, might seem partially to contradict this conclusion. Though the most dramatic action took the form of an armed occupation of parliament, simulating a kind of coup, this abortive initiative was not designed to overthrow the constitutional regime but to install a multiparty national government to carry out new reforms that would repress terrorism and achieve greater unity. Contrary to common representation of the event, it did not represent an attempt to impose a military dictatorship, though this was the subsequent impression. The clearest account is J. Palacios, *23-F: El Rey y su secreto, 30 años después se desvela la llamada "Operación De Gaulle"* (Madrid, 2010).

18. One professor, lamenting the moderation and tepidity of post-Franco society, has suggested that "these three phases of the same extreme dictatorship will probably be seen as

a continuum of capitalist development in our land, during which Francoism *permitted* the passage from a Third Word condition to postmodernity and in which Franco transfused his own frozen blood into the contemporary sang-froid of the Spanish, who are no longer susceptible to fanatization either by Tejero or ETA and who will never again be disposed to die for any ideal but only to live modestly, indeed as well as possible." J. A. González Casanova, "El franquismo a diez años vista," *Historia 16* 10, no. 115 (1985): 35–40. There is some truth to this observation.

19. See the discussion of polling results in E. González Duro, *La sombra del general: Qué queda del franquismo en España* (Barcelona, 2005), 223–24.

Index

Index

Index

Index

Index

Index

Index

Index

Index

Printed in the United States
By Bookmasters